THROUGH ADVERSITY

Britain and the Commonwealth's War in the Air 1939–45

Volume 1

Ben Kite

Helion & Company

Dedicated to the memory of Lieutenant Paul Rollo Eastlake Woods
Fleet Air Arm, 809 Naval Air Squadron
Killed in Action, 23 July 1941

Helion & Company Limited
Unit 8 Amherst Business Centre
Budbrooke Road
Warwick
CV34 5WE
England
Tel. 01926 499 619
Email: info@helion.co.uk
Website: www.helion.co.uk
Twitter: @helionbooks
Visit our blog http://blog.helion.co.uk/

Published by Helion & Company 2019
Designed and typeset by Mach 3 Solutions Ltd (www.mach3solutions.co.uk)
Cover designed by Paul Hewitt, Battlefield Design (www.battlefield-design.co.uk)
Printed by Gutenberg Press, Tarxien, Malta (www.gutenberg.com.mt/)

Text © Ben Kite 2019
Images © as individually credited
Maps drawn by George Anderson © Helion & Company 2019

ISBN 978-1-912866-23-6

British Library Cataloguing-in-Publication Data.
A catalogue record for this book is available from the British Library.

For details of other military history titles published by Helion & Company Limited contact the above address or visit our website: http://www.helion.co.uk.

We always welcome receipt of book proposals from prospective authors.

But each one, man for man, has won imperishable praise … Take these men for your example. Like them remember that prosperity can only be for the free; that freedom is the sure possession of those alone who have the courage to defend it.

Funeral Oration of Pericles (429 BC)

Contents

List of Maps   vii

List of Figures   viii

List of Annexes   ix

Acknowledgements   x

Foreword   xii

Introduction   xiii

Part I Antecedents   15

1   Foundations   17

2   Learning to Fly   26

Part II Air Superiority   39

3   'Guardians of the Heart' Fighter Command's Air Defence of Britain   41

4   'Seek and Destroy' A Battle of Britain Fighter Command Mission   59

5   'Firmness of Purpose' Offensive Air Operations over Fortress Europe   87

6   'Always Ready' Countering German Night Raiders and V-Weapons   101

7   'With Fists and Heels' Malta's Battle for Air Superiority in the Mediterranean   130

8   'In the Middle of Things' The British Loss of Air Superiority and Collapse in the Far East   156

9   'Boldness to Endure Anything' Turning the Japanese Tide   174

10   Concluding Thoughts on Air Superiority   193

Part III Strike   195

11   'Strike Hard, Strike Sure' Bomber Command's Offensive   197

12   'We act with one Accord' A Bomber Command mission – the Route Out   211

13   'The King's Thunderbolts are Righteous' A Bomber Command Mission – the Strike and Return Leg   233

14   'Through to The End' The Development of a Precision Bombing Capability   257

Part IV The Air War at Sea   277

15   'They Shall Not Pass Unseen' Coastal Command's Hunt for U-Boats   279

16   'We Ambush the Ambusher' Coastal Command's Battles to Sink the U-boats   303

17   'Woe to the Unwary' The RAF's Early Anti-Shipping Operations   322

18   'Strike and Strike Again' Anti-Shipping Operations Mature   342
19   'I Seek Higher Things' The Fleet Air Arm's War – Ships and Aircraft   372
20   'Safeguard and Avenger' The Operational Roles of the Fleet Air Arm   392
Concluding Thoughts   424

Annexes   425
Bibliography & Sources   469
Index   481

List of Maps

1   Radar Chain and Observer Corps Network and Coverage 1940.   ii

2   Disposition of British Fighter Forces 9 July 1940.   iii

3   Taking the Offensive – England, France and the Low Countries.   iv

4   Distribution of Major Night Attacks on British cities 1940-41 and RAF night-fighter Bases.   v

5   Malta: The Mediterranean Air Base.   vi

6   The Mediterranean Theatre.   vii

7   South East Asia and the Pacific Theatre.   viii

8   The Invasion of Burma January to May 1942.   ix

9   Bomber Command Stations and Airfields, 25 September 1944.   x

10   Bomber Command Range and Major German Cities Attacked.   xi

11   The North Atlantic Including Coastal Command Areas of Operation and the Routes of *Prinz Eugen* and *Bismarck*.   xii

12a Main Atlantic Convoy Routes and Aircraft Coverage, June to August 1943.   xiii

12b Main Atlantic Convoy Routes and Aircraft Coverage, September 1943 to April 1944.   xiv

13   Maritime Operations.   xv

14   The Pacific Theatre.   xvi

List of Figures

Figures

1   (left) Pathway to Pilot 1941.   27
2   (right) Pathway to Pilot 1944.   27
3   The Fighter Command System.   47
4   Aircraft Production Figures February to August 1940.   51
5   Mk IV Air Intercept Radar.   109
6   'Cut-away of V1 Fiesler Fi 103 flying bomb (also known as FZG 76 or V1 weapon'.
    (Crown Copyright – Air Historical Branch).   119

Annexes

A	Personnel Strength of Royal Air Force 3 September 1939 to 1 September 1945	427
B	First Line Aircraft Strength of the RAF and German and Italian Air Forces, 30 September 1938 to 1 January 1945	428
C	Flying Training Schools in Operation on 3 September 1943	429
D	Analysis, by Air Forces, of the Total Output of Qualified Aircrew 1939-45	430
E	Organisational Diagrams	432
F	Order of Battle Fighter Command, 8 August 1940	436
G	Order of Battle Middle East Command, 11 November, 1941	438
H	Order of Battle, Coastal Command, 15 February, 1943	440
I	Order of Battle, Bomber Command, 4 March 1943	442
J	Operational Aircraft of the Royal Air Force and Fleet Air Arm, 1939-1945	443
K	Operational Aircraft of the German Air Force, 1939-45	450
L	Operational Aircraft of the Italian Air Force, 1939-45	453
M	Operational Aircraft of the Japanese Air Forces, 1942-45	454
N	Spitfire MK II Cockpit Check	456
O	Common RAF Codenames	458
P	Civilian Casualties Caused in the United Kingdom by various Forms of Long-Range Bombardment 1939-45	459
Q	Analysis of British Night-Fighter Effort January to May 1941	460
R	Flying Bomb Offensive	461
S	Yearly Tonnage Dropped by Bomber Command and the United States Eighth Air Force	462
T	Comparison of Actual Output of Particular Classes of Armaments in Germany and the United Kingdom	463
U	Bomber Command Casualties 3 September 1939 to 8 May 1945	464
V	Bomber Command Aircraft Destroyed and Damaged	465
W	Analysis of Submarines Destroyed by Aircraft	466
X	Enemy Surface Vessels Destroyed in the Atlantic and NW European Waters by RAF Aircraft 1939-45	467
Y	British Carriers in Service with the Royal Navy	468

Acknowledgements

This book has taken several years to complete and benefited from the assistance of many people and organisations. First and foremost is the RAF's Air Historical Branch. Though many members of staff have helped me pore over their collection at RAF Northolt, I would single out two people in particular. Seb Cox, the branch head who has served within it for well over 30 years and has become an institution within the RAF in his own right. Seb was kind enough to critique the manuscript and offer wise advice as well as deep historical insights on how to improve it. Furthermore, Lee Barton collated the marvellous Air Historical Branch pictures, which form the vast majority of those contained within this book. They are an undoubted strength of the book and bring the atmosphere and events of the time to life. Further afield Air Commodore John Meier and his team at the Royal Australian Air Force Air Historical Branch have guided me on Australian and RAAF perspectives. He has also put me in touch with the RAAF museum, where Emily Constantine sourced some valuable photographs that capture the RAAF in action at Port Moresby and Darwin.

Michael Bowyer – author of so many first-class aviation books, including *2 Group* and *Mosquito,* gave his advice and vast knowledge of the RAF in the Second World War freely and unstintingly. Graham Mottram, Chairman of the Society of Friends of the Fleet Air Arm Museum, also brought deep knowledge of the Fleet Air Arm and helped me craft the relevant maritime chapters. John Clifford, a close associate of the Pathfinder Heritage Centre at RAF Wyton added insights on Bomber Command too and particularly Pathfinder operations.

Three individuals read the earliest drafts when they were at the most rough and ready. My father, Peter Kite, who was a professional airline pilot all his life. Sam Biles a close family friend, whose attention to detail prevented many errors from being baked in and Major Andrew Shepherd, a fellow Army officer. I first met Andy when he was a young Royal Irish officer in Helmand, Afghanistan. I was bowled over by his interest and knowledge of the Second World War then and he has helped me get the wider historical context right and prevent the book from becoming incoherent. Lieutenant Colonels Nathan Smith and Tim Ventham also did the final checking of the draft for which I am again very grateful – particularly given the compressed timings.

This book's greatest strengths are the veteran's own stories. The majority are extracted from autobiographies and I am therefore very grateful for either the author's permission, or those of his family, or publishing house, to reproduce them within this work. I have done my utmost to find the original author or their descendants, on the few occasions I have been unsuccessful I ask the copyright holder's forgiveness and hope they will feel I have done the author's work justice. Many of the other quotes in the book come from the sound archives of the Imperial War Museum and Australian Memorial. These are two fantastic resources, which I cannot praise highly enough. They each contain a treasure of important historical detail and are a delight to listen to, the two institutions have done a marvellous job in making them available to the public online.

Thanks too go to Helion the publishers. Duncan Rogers and his team have been brilliant as ever in providing guidance and supporting the book's growth into a two-volume publication. I am especially grateful to George Anderson who has produced brilliant maps. They play a huge role in helping the reader keep track of what is going on. I am also most grateful to the Chief of the Air Staff, Air Chief Marshal Mike Wigston for his generous foreword and placing a modern perspective on the book.

My final and greatest thanks go to my wife Elsa and my two daughters, Jemima and Lucy. They have had to put up with a father and husband who has undoubtedly been over-occupied on this project. Their tolerance, patience and support has meant that this book was completed and not abandoned halfway through.

Ben Kite

Foreword

We are fortunate to have a rich recorded history of the RAF, with a number of great works covering the Second World War. Ben Kite's book takes a different approach to many because, rather than a chronology of events or analysis of operational outcomes, he has focused his analysis on how the British Commonwealth fought the Second World War in the air domain. What tactics, techniques and equipment did we employ? How did we defeat our enemies? What was the experience for those involved? This is clearly an ambitious task, not only because of the global scale of the conflict, but also because air power was involved, to greater or lesser degrees, in almost every significant action the Allies undertook. The two volumes take you to all major theatres of operation, from the jungles of Papua New Guinea to the lethal skies over Berlin. Ben has brought new material to a wider audience and, perhaps most importantly, he reminds us of the very human aspects of warfare through his use of first-person accounts and quotes.

Ben's book highlights many points of great relevance to the RAF today. His analysis brings to life the incontrovertible link between operational success and the character and training of the people who demonstrated such courage, selflessness and sense of service. The material also makes clear the decisive importance of teamwork and leadership. You will be struck by how international the RAF was in the Second World War, with people serving from across the United Kingdom, Commonwealth and occupied countries. From a diverse group of people, they formed unified and cohesive teams, motivated by shared values and goals as well as inspiring leaders. You will also observe the importance of strong collaboration enabling the employment of air power to maximum effect; the relationship between Coastal Command and the Royal Navy explored in this volume offers a striking illustration of the enduring importance of an effective joint operational framework. Finally, perhaps what strikes me most is the RAF's eagerness to embrace technology, to innovate, invest and operationalise the cutting-edge developments of the day, including radar or sophisticated weapons such as the 'Tallboy' bomb. In stark contrast, the experience of the Brewster Buffalo squadrons fighting superior Japanese aircraft is a salutary lesson from history of the consequences of fighting an air campaign with obsolete equipment.

I welcome this book for its important contribution to the rich historical record of the RAF and wider British Commonwealth air forces. Ben Kite reminds us of the sacrifice and great service of our predecessors, their courage, determination and spirit in the dark days of 1939-45. But just as important, his book also brings to life the themes of enduring relevance to the RAF of today, delivering Air and Space power to protect our nation.

Air Chief Marshal Mike Wigston CBE ADC
Chief of the Air Staff, Royal Air Force

Introduction

Before 1939 we really knew nothing about air warfare.
Marshal of the Royal Air Force, Sir John Slessor

Through Adversity is the first volume of an ambitious and complex book yet, at its heart, lie three simple aims. First, to capture the main themes and strands of the war in the air as fought by the British Commonwealth. To do this justice has meant covering the major campaigns the RAF and Commonwealth air forces were involved in. To achieve this, even in a two-volume book, is hard and it has meant not giving the larger, traditionally dominant air campaigns, such as the Combined Bomber offensive over Germany, a disproportionate emphasis. In addition, the book could also be challenged for not covering smaller operations in greater detail, such as the anti-U-Boat campaign in the Indian Ocean, the Norwegian campaign or the RAAF and RNZAF operations in the South Pacific. Despite these limitations, the scope of the book is still greater than any others I have encountered in my research. Even John Terraine in his magisterial history of the Commonwealth air forces, the *Right of the Line,* apologises for only including the RAF's European and Mediterranean war and omitting the Far East campaigns entirely. This two-volume book allows one to go into much more detail and introduce some strange locations and unfamiliar campaigns to the reader. The Desert Air Force's support for Eighth Army at Tebaga, Tunisia, the Fleet Air Arm raid on Palembang, Sumatra and the Mosquito strike on the Schott and Zeiss factories at Jena, Germany are all included as good examples of air involvement in a truly global conflict.

The second aim of the book is to explain the tactics and operational techniques used by the RAF, certainly in more detail than most histories have had time to cover. I am always interested in how missions are planned and executed, how the technology and tactics of the Allies and the enemy interact. The book therefore explains everything from how an anti-shipping mission off the Dutch coast was put together, to the ways in which a close air support sortie against German armour in the desert was executed. The book pays far more attention to these details than it does to either the grand strategic discussions in Whitehall, the decisions and ambitions of the most senior commanders, or in offering a strict chronology of events. As a result, I believe it fills an important gap in the existing literature.

Finally, the two volumes focus on the people involved in the war in the air, concentrating mainly on the aircrew themselves, for it was predominantly that group who put themselves in greatest danger and ran the highest risks. Using their own powerful words, *Through Adversity* (Volume 1) and *Undaunted* (Volume 2) give honest and compelling insights into the aircrews' experience in undertaking some of the most hazardous operations of the Second World War. I hope the reader will feel as humbled as I did when reading their modest accounts, which routinely contain impressive displays of valour and devotion to duty.

The air contribution to Allied operations in the Second World War was clearly vast and a reader could easily get lost within the many overlapping strands of activity. For the sake of clarity, the book is broken down into two volumes and seven parts. Volume 1 contains four parts, the first of which describes how the RAF and the Commonwealth air forces approached the Second World War and how they trained their pilots and aircrew. Part Two, entitled *War In The Air,* examines Britain's efforts to win air superiority, probably the most important function of air power. It covers this in a number of campaigns, starting with the Battle of Britain and moving towards decisive clashes in Malta and the Far East. Part Two also includes broader aspects of air superiority too, such as the 'fighter sweeps' over Europe from 1941, night-fighter operations and efforts to defeat the V-Weapons. Part Three focuses on the RAF's strike operations and includes Britain's major attempt to knock Germany out of the war through the strategic bomber offensive, a massive campaign that lasted throughout the Second World War. Part Three also covers the development of precision bombing operations by the RAF's aircraft, particularly those of 2 Group.

Part Four focuses upon the *Air War at Sea*, which includes not just the RAF's decisive contribution to the anti-U-boat campaign, but also how the Battle of the Atlantic was almost lost because of short-sightedness at the Air Ministry. It continues by looking at the RAF's anti-shipping strikes, whether for strategic purposes such as those off the Dutch coast or in support of an operational campaign, such as those in the Mediterranean. Part Four concludes with a study of the Fleet Air Arm's carrier operations, and how they were used to support Fleet actions, protect convoys and enable amphibious operations across the globe.

The Second Volume – *Undaunted* – continues the study of the RAF's war in the air. Volume 2 looks at air intelligence, reconnaissance and support to special duties. It includes a study of air photographic reconnaissance, bringing to wider attention the role the RAF played in developing one of the major strands of intelligence: an intelligence discipline whose widespread impact must surely make it as important as Enigma. It includes the accounts of the Special Duties Flights which connected resistance forces in occupied territories with the Allies. The major element of Volume 2 is its coverage of air support to the Army: a fascinating story of how Britain, informed by the debacle in France, developed a sophisticated air-land operational technique in the Western Desert and adapted it further in the campaigns in Europe and the Far East. The provision of close air support and air interdiction by the British Commonwealth became a new, game-changing 'way of war' for the Allies and a fundamental tenet of post-war doctrine. Volume 2 also covers the British role in developing airborne forces, as well as the decisive use of air transport in providing both operational and tactical mobility to the British Army's campaign in Burma.

The series concludes appropriately enough by covering the experiences of those aircrew who became casualties, or simply failed to return. Their accounts either in the Prisoner of War (POW) camps, escaping and evading, adrift in the sea, or as a burns victim undergoing treatment, are arguably the most poignant of the book and offer examples of heroism that easily match those demonstrated in the air.

This is a wide spread of activity touching almost every aspect of this global war. I expect the reader will be struck by the decisive contribution airpower was able to make to all Allied campaigns, the extent to which the RAF was a profoundly international and cosmopolitan organisation, and the innovation and flexibility with which it met its foes. Above all, I expect the reader will be awed by the highest examples of courage and determination contained within this volume.

Part I
Antecedents

1

Foundations

The RAF's impressive performance in the Second World War was not inevitable. It was built on solid foundations established by the RAF from 1918, when it became the world's first officially recognised independent air force. Led initially by Marshal of the Royal Air Force Hugh Trenchard, its first Chief of the Air Staff from 1918 to 1929, the RAF not only survived but, by the end of Trenchard's tenure, had established its squadron structures, its officer academy at Cranwell, a Staff College at Andover and an apprentice school for skilled tradesmen at Halton. It had also created a five-year short service commission system, a clever initiative which provided it with a steady supply of young aircrew, but without committing either the service or the individuals to long careers. The RAF was also actively marketed as a potential career amongst the Commonwealth countries, consequently many young men from Canada, Australia and New Zealand journeyed to Britain to join up, lending a cosmopolitan feel to the service, well before war broke out. To bolster its numbers in times of war, the RAF deliberately copied the Army by creating within its structure a part-time reserve element, known as the Royal Auxiliary Air Force (RAuxAF).[1] The Auxiliaries were initially created around a few University Air Squadrons, or a readily identifiable set of the wealthy and privileged class. No.601 (City of London) Squadron, for example, was formed by Lord Grosvenor in 1926, largely from the members of White's Club.[2]

However, it was apparent that the Auxiliaries alone would not provide sufficient numbers in time of war. Therefore, in 1937, a more egalitarian system of reserve units, in the form of the Royal Air Force Volunteer Reserve (RAFVR), was established, this drew its members on a local basis, from more modest elements of society. When war broke out in September 1939, the RAFVR comprised 6,646 pilots, 1,625 observers and 1,946 wireless operators.[3] The different backgrounds and cultures within the regular RAF, the RAuxAF and RAFVR led some to joke that the RAF regular officer was a pilot trying to be a gentleman, the Auxiliary officer was a gentleman trying to be a pilot, and the Volunteer Reserve officer was 'some poor sod trying to be both'.

The final element of the jigsaw came on 9 September 1938 when the government set up the Auxiliary Territorial Service (ATS). This offered women the chance to enlist on a voluntary and part-time basis as non-combatant personnel, to assist the regular and reserve components of all three services. The RAF had been the most insistent of the three services to advocate for such an organisation, arguing that in case of war it would have to face almost immediate attack and an already trained woman's organisation would be of great benefit.[4] By 1939 the air force branch of the ATS was moving steadily under the orbit of the RAF and in June 1939 a Royal Warrant was signed which reconstituted these elements into the Women's Auxiliary Air Force (WAAF). Before the war the WAAF totalled just 1,734 women; three short years later it peaked at 181,835. Though

---

1   John Terraine, *The Right of The Line: The Royal Air Force in the European War 1939-1945* (London: Hodder and Stoughton, 1985), p. 3.
2   Patrick Bishop, *Air Force Blue* (London: William Collins), p. 70.
3   John Terraine, *Right of the Line*, 1985, p. 44.
4   Beryl Escott, *Women in Air Force Blue* (Yeovil: Patrick Stephens, 1989), p. 87.

Marshal of the RAF, Lord Trenchard visiting Royal Canadian Air Force Fighter squadrons at their airfields in the UK 1943. They are left to right – Group captain D.M. Smith BC Squadron Leader R.A. Dick Ellis DFC, Wing Commander E.H. Moncrieff AFC, Lord Trenchard, Air Vice-Marshal W.F. Dickson CB, OBE DSO AFC, Squadron Leader H.P. 'Herbie' Peters DFC. (Crown Copyright – Air Historical Branch)

barred from carrying weapons, women replaced men in as many ground duties as possible and excelled in positions that involved delicacy of touch, speed of reaction, patience, tact and intuition. Women joined the WAAF from across the Commonwealth, as well as from some occupied countries. The WAAF brought the total numbers of personnel in the RAF to a wartime peak of 1,171,421 on 1 October 1944. Further details are included at Annex A.

The female contribution to the war in the air was not just limited to ground duties. Women also served in the Air Transport Auxiliary (ATA) which helped ferry aircraft from one place to another. The ATA also recruited pilots who were deemed unsuitable for operational duties by the RAF and Fleet Air Arm through either age, fitness, gender or because they came from neutral countries. The criteria allowed those with physical handicaps to join as long as they could fly – earning the ATA the nickname 'Ancient and Tattered Airmen'. A total of 166 women served in the ATA and in July 1943 the government agreed that they should receive identical rates of pay to men, a groundbreaking initiative at the time.

RAF development between the wars was naturally influenced by the politics of the era. The 1920s post war parsimony hit all three services hard and Trenchard did well to simply preserve his force, utilizing numerous arguments including highlighting the RAF's relative economy. For example, the idea of using the RAF to police areas of the Empire from the air, including the British Mandate of Mesopotamia, Somaliland and the North-West Frontier, appealed to the treasury as an alternative to expensive ground troops, though the degree to which this practice was actually effective is debatable.

Post-war financial constraints also coincided with a period defined by a strong political desire for peace and disarmament. This period could be said to have started from the 27 August 1928 'Kellogg-Briand Pact', where 45 nations pledged themselves to renounce war as an instrument of national policy. It ended only in November 1934, when the final disarmament conference at Geneva collapsed amidst the realities of worrying world events. Frustratingly for the RAF, it was during this same period that they sought to modernise their fleet of machines from the open-cockpit, slow, canvas and wood biplanes with which they still operated, to modern, fast, heavily-armed, monoplanes. This stagnant period has sometimes been described as the 'years the locusts ate'[5] where not only was the RAF unable to modernise its equipment, but its very existence also came under threat.

By 1934, the rise of the dictatorships in Italy and Germany and the Japanese invasion of Manchuria had shattered wishful thinking. The international danger to Britain was not just manifesting itself as hostile intentions and heated words, but also, in the case of Germany's *Luftwaffe*, as a credible military capability and threat. Adolf Hitler publicly announced the existence of the *Luftwaffe* in March 1935, in direct breach of the Versailles Treaty which had specifically banned Germany from having either submarines or an air force. Even before this date its growing strength had been observed by the Air Ministry and the statistics leaked to Winston Churchill. In July 1934, Churchill predicted the growth of this increasing peril to the House of Commons, challenging the Government to contradict him. He asserted, first, that Germany already possessed a military air force nearly two-thirds as strong as Britain's existing home defence air force and secondly, that the German Air Force would nearly equal Britain's home defence force numbers by the end of 1935. By 1936 he predicted it would be substantially stronger and argued that once the Germans had established a lead, the RAF might never overtake them. He challenged Stanley Baldwin, the Prime Minister at the time, to refute his view:

> Nothing, would give me greater pleasure than to learn that I have discovered another mare's nest … … but unless these facts can be contradicted, precisely and categorically, it seems to me that our position is a very serious one.[6]

Fuelled by facts and statistics covertly supplied by Ralph Wigram, a like-minded Foreign Office official, Churchill kept referring the matter to the House throughout 1934, forcing the government to confront the consequences of a German build-up of the *Luftwaffe*. Baldwin stated that his Government was determined not to accept any position of inferiority to German air power.[7] Yet a visit by a British Government delegation to Berlin in March 1935 discovered, through a direct conversation with Hitler, that Germany's air strength was already equal to the Royal Air Force. Hitler was probably exaggerating, but his bold ambition was sufficient to shock the British into implementing a series of RAF expansion schemes in an to attempt to catch up.

The growing threat from Germany meant that the RAF's thoughts on its operational approach took on increasing importance. The dominant view within the service was that bombers were the most important element of the force and capable of delivering a war-winning 'knock out blow', a strike which the enemy could neither stop, nor recover from. Partly fuelled by the RAF's instinctive preference to conduct their own independent air operations, rather than support land and maritime campaigns, it was also an argument that was supported by influential military thinkers such as Basil Liddell-Hart. He caricatured it as a typically British way of warfare, one that removed

---

5   John Terraine, *Right of the Line*, p. 8.
6   Denis Richards, *Royal Air Force 1939-45 Volume 1* (London: HMSO, 1953), p. 5.
7   Denis Richards, *Royal Air Force 1939-45 Volume 1*, p. 12.

the need for any enduring, bloody and costly land campaigns, similar to those fought on the western front during the First World War. The bomber doctrine was to dominate RAF and wider defence expenditure at this critical moment and for years to come. However, it ignored two important facts: first, the state of the RAF's bomber fleet, which would need a massive transformation to come anywhere close to inflicting a meaningful degradation of Germany's war making capacity, let alone a 'knock-out blow'. Secondly, that Germany was a continental land power and the major element of her power rested in its large Army. It would be primarily through the actions of a rejuvenated *Wehrmacht*, supported by the *Luftwaffe*, that Germany would conquer Europe, a combination we now know as *Blitzkrieg* – or 'lightning war'. By summer 1940 these misperceptions had come home to roost and Britain faced the threat of both a seaborne invasion and an air blitz – both of which required defensive air superiority fighters as the highest air priority. This was not the only area where pre-war air power theories were found to be incorrect. Indeed, the pre-war conceptual and financial focus on bombers and fighter defence was at the expense of air support to the Army and Royal Navy. This was particularly inexcusable given the role aircraft played in defeating German U-boats in the First World War, as well as the RAF's admirable delivery of close air support to the British Army at the climactic Battle of Amiens in 1918.

Britain's rearmament programme came just in the nick of time, it also allowed the RAF to take a considered approach and focus on the quality of the new equipment, rather than just quantity. This approach contrasted to that of the French who rushed to bolster their numbers with aircraft that, by 1940, were hopelessly outmatched by the Germans. Fortunately, the RAF's new investments coincided with a number of important technological developments that were being achieved in the mid 1930s. These included 'radio direction finding', an invention which would become an important element in all air operations, as well as a 'Typex' – a new secure cipher system (somewhat ironically an adaptation of the German Enigma machine), that would be used by RAF headquarters throughout the war.[8]

A further crucial development in 1933 was Rolls-Royce's new Merlin aircraft engine. Powerful and reliable, it would be fitted into many British and Allied aircraft throughout the future war. The late 1930s also saw the advent of fast, stressed metal-skinned, eight-gun monoplane fighters: most noticeably the Supermarine Spitfire (introduced into service in 1938) and Hawker Hurricane (introduced into service in 1937). These fighter aircraft coincided with the arrival of larger (but still twin-engined) bombers such as the Vickers Wellington and Handley-Page Hampden (both in 1936) and the Armstrong Whitworth Whitley and Bristol Blenheim bombers (both in 1937). These were the bomber aircraft with which the RAF would fight the first years of the war. The designs of heavier four-engined bombers were also submitted in 1936, from which the Short Stirling, Handley Page Halifax and Avro Lancaster would all be developed. Plans were also laid down in 1938 for fast, twin-engined light bombers and fighters, that would lead to the Bristol Beaufighter and de Havilland Mosquito. The latter was particularly revolutionary and illustrates how the RAF was prepared to challenge orthodoxy in using wood, rather than steel and aluminium, as well as placing a reliance on speed rather than defensive armaments as the best protection against fighters. Other aircraft ordered included: The Short Sunderland flying boat, which originated from a 1933 specification and was the mainstay of Coastal Command throughout the war.

The quick introduction into service of many British aircraft was made possible by the RAF ordering 'off the board'. This was a change in its previous procurement strategy that carried more financial risk but speeded up the whole process. In addition, the RAF were granted permission (despite protests from British manufacturers) to purchase aircraft in the United States, the

---

8   John Terraine, *Right of the Line*, p. 42.

Pilots of 306 Polish Fighter Squadron being taught the English language between flights by a schoolmaster. RAF Church Stanton, 26-28 January 1942. (Crown Copyright – Air Historical Branch)

Lockheed Hudson being the first of a long line of American aircraft that would enter British service during the war.

Once war was declared the RAF's rate of expansion increased as the economy was mobilised and American supplies, including the life-saving Lend Lease arrangements, also began to manifest themselves. However, there was often little margin in the early war years and progress often seemed slow. Churchill captured the challenges of munitions production in an address to the House of Commons on 2 December 1941 (just five days before Pearl Harbor):

> The House will remember how I have several times described to them in the last five or six years the time-table of munitions production. First year, nothing at all; second year, very little; third year, quite a lot; fourth year, all you want. We are at the beginning of the third year. The United States is getting through the second year. Germany started the war already well into the fourth year. If one does not prepare before a war, one has to prepare after, and be very thankful if time is given.[9]

The details of British aircraft available throughout the war years is included at Annex B. The figures are compared to Germany's and Italy's and illustrate how those powers failed to mobilise their war effort as quickly, or comprehensively, as the British.

---

9   Winston Churchill, *House of Commons Debate on Maximum National Effort*, Hansard, Volume 376, 2 December 1941.

To accommodate the growing RAF service, an ambitious programme of airfield construction, orientated towards Germany, began in 1934. This increased the number of RAF airfields from 52 to 89 by 1938, with a further 389 being built during the period 1939-43. The airfields were primarily sited in eastern England, including Norfolk, Yorkshire, Lincolnshire and Cambridgeshire and typically contained new facilities, such as concrete runways for the anticipated heavier aircraft and three large 'C' type hangers. Many of the new 'expansion' era airfields, as well as the existing ones brought up to scratch, are still in use today (e.g. RAF Wyton, Waddington and Scampton) and the hangers, as well as the distinctive brick station headquarters, messes, dining halls and accommodation are easily recognisable. The quality is apparent not least because the architect, Sir Archibald Bulloch, was advised by the Royal Fine Arts Commission (which included Sir Edwin Lutyens), as well as the Council for the Preservation of Rural England. As war approached, the need for dispersal would cause airfields to expand further into the countryside, with field fortifications and pill boxes constructed to defend the bases against ground attack. The expediencies of wartime also meant that many of the airfields built during the war were cheaper, more utilitarian in design and lacked the comfort of their earlier inter-war counterparts.

Since the First World War the basic unit within the RAF had been the squadron. These varied in size depending on the roles they performed, but would typically number anywhere between 12 and 24 aircraft, usually divided into flights of three or four aircraft. Three or more squadrons would comprise a wing and a group would consist of two or more wings. The wing's role was an important one, often providing the squadrons with shared facilities or services, such as maintenance and intelligence, as well as performing an operational command and control function. Depending on where the squadron was based some of these functions might be performed by 'station' facilities too and the station commander (either a Wing Commander or Group Captain) was usually regarded as an important command appointment. At a more strategic level the RAF had divided their force into a series of commands that ran along functional lines (e.g Fighter, Bomber, Coastal, Training) as well as overseas commands where mixed squadrons or wings of aircraft (i.e fighter, bomber, maritime, transport) would operate together. Details of these organisations are included at Annexes E through to I.

One of the biggest challenges for the RAF was in training its personnel. Particularly as numbers would have to grow substantially in time of war and there was an obvious concern that Britain would become an aerial battleground, where it would be too dangerous to conduct training. Furthermore, Britain's weather and the expected operational pressure on its airfields, lent additional weight to the argument that air training would be better conducted overseas. Consequently, Britain, Australia, Canada and New Zealand agreed in December 1939 to establish the Empire Air Training Scheme (EATS), often also referred to as the British Commonwealth Air Training Plan (BCATP). This was a massive aircrew training programme which involved setting up shared training centres in the dominions to which the pilots of the four nations would travel and undergo training. The plan directed that elementary training would normally be conducted in a home nation, whilst the majority of advanced training would take place in Canada. This country was selected because it was closer to the aircraft factories and the main theatre of war (as it was understood in 1939, at least). As the war progressed flying schools in the United States were also established. The training costs were to be divided by the four nations and each nation also committed to generate aircrew on an annual basis in the following numbers: Britain, 22,000; Canada, 13,000; Australia, 11,000 and New Zealand, 3,300. Canada's weather and wide-open spaces made it an ideal training environment and 92 training centres would be established there. Annexes C and D show the total number of schools in operation across the Empire and the United States, together with their output in trained aircrew.

Britain and the Dominions also agreed that when Commonwealth aircrew were assigned to service with the RAF, they should be placed in specific 'Article XV units' and identified as belonging to that particular nation. As an example, there were 17 Article XV Royal Australian Air Force (RAAF) Squadrons serving alongside the RAF in the UK, numbered from 450 to 467 (465 was not formed) and a further five Article XV squadrons were also formed in the Middle East. Australia also provided a few of her pre-war regular RAAF squadrons, including 10 Squadron, which flew Sunderlands as part of Coastal Command throughout the war. Similar Article XV units were set up by the RAF for other Commonwealth countries, though in spite of these arrangements many Commonwealth pilots served in normal RAF squadrons for much of the war, enjoying, it seems, the international mix of the RAF units. Furthermore, even a squadron designated as RCAF, RAAF, or RNZAF would still have many other nationalities within it, including British. As the oldest dominion Canada argued more vociferously for exclusively Canadian units and was generous in sending her squadrons overseas throughout the war. Canada provided, amongst many other units, an entire Canadian group in Bomber Command (6 Group), a highly respected Canadian Fighter Wing in Britain (127 Wing), as well as transport squadrons for operations in Burma. Whether fighter, bomber, reconnaissance or coastal command, there was not a single aspect of British air operations in which the Canadians were not involved, and Canada ended the war with the fourth largest air force in the world. With the friendly and powerful United States to the south, as well as two oceans separating her from any potential enemies, Canada had the luxury of feeling secure from external threats. Australia and New Zealand were much more wary.

Japanese aggression in Manchuria in 1931 and China in 1937 highlighted the threat to these countries from the north. Additionally, as part of the League of Nations South Pacific Mandate, Japan had gained control of the German Pacific Islands (including the Carolines, Marshall Islands, Marianas and Palau Group) in 1919. This meant that the Japanese military presence was now significantly closer to Australia and New Zealand: it was also well known that Japan harboured expansionist ideas to secure and control the resources she needed for her economic prosperity. Australia and New Zealand put their faith in Britain to come to her aid if they were threatened, an intention that was given substance by the construction by Britain of a base for her fleet at Singapore. Australia and New Zealand in turn generously sent significant Army and Air Force units to help Britain combat the Germans and Italians and it was thought that success in those theatres would help deter any Japanese aggression. Controversially, there was little concurrent preparation in Australia, or New Zealand, for the air defence of their own territories and only the most modest efforts to set up their own aircraft industries. This took the form of the Commonwealth Aircraft Corporation which would make Wirraway trainer aircraft at Melbourne, an initiative strongly objected to by the British government and aircraft industry at the time. Australian security was rudely shattered by a series of calamitous events in early 1942, when in quick succession Singapore fell, Java and Sumatra were conquered, a Japanese carrier group struck Darwin and the Japanese advanced as far as Timor and Papua New Guinea. This was effectively the last stepping stone before reaching Australia itself. It then became apparent that Britain's priorities were focussed on Europe and Australia and New Zealand's best bets for security lay in American support and their own efforts.[10]

South Africa declared war against Germany on 6 September 1939. This followed a furious debate in the South African parliament, when the existing Prime Minister of the anti-British National Party, J.B.M. Hertzog, was deposed in favour of the United Party's General Jan Smuts. The South African Air Force (SAAF) was poorly prepared for war and when faced with the immediate task of securing its maritime waters, had to resort to hastily commandeered civilian aircraft. The SAAF's offensive debut occurred during the highly successful 1940-41 campaign in East Africa against the

---

10   Paul Kelly, *100 years: The Australian Story* (Crow's Nest: Allen and Unwin, 2001), pp. 218-224.

Italians. Increasing numbers of South African bomber and fighter squadrons would also go on to play an important role in the North African and Mediterranean campaigns throughout the war.

The population of India had little choice in their entry into the war. The British Viceroy, Lord Linlithgow, declared war on behalf of India, without even consulting India's increasingly assertive nationalist politicians. A grave mistake as some, including Jawaharlal Nehru, might well have supported a war against fascism, but instead found themselves opposing the British. In contrast Mohammed Ali Jinnah supported the British and took advantage of the absence of Nehru and Gandhi from the political scene. He turned himself from a minor politician into the almost sole spokesmen for India's Muslims, advocating for a separate Indian Muslim state which would eventually lead to partition and the creation of Pakistan. Despite these political machinations Indians volunteered in huge numbers; of the five million citizens of the British Empire who joined the military services between 1939-45 a staggering two million were Indian. Though mainly Army personnel, a significant element also joined the embryonic Indian Air Force, which had been created in 1933 and included a mixture of British and Indian aircrew. Many Indians were attracted by the technical training and the opportunities it might offer them in civilian life after the war. Some Indian airmen rose to relatively senior rank and the force was granted its Royal title in 1945: a just reward for hard service, most notably in the Burma Campaign. Individual Indians also served with RAF squadrons in the UK, albeit in relatively small numbers. The most famous was probably Mohinder Singh Puji, a Sikh who arrived with the initial batch of 24 Indian pilots in 1940 and served throughout the Battle of Britain, Middle East and Burma Campaigns – there is a statue of him in Gravesend, Kent. There were also individuals from other colonies, such as the West Indies, that also served in the RAF in a similar manner.

Some nationalities serving with the RAF were not from Commonwealth countries and had no formal ties to the Empire. Many of these had fled from occupied Europe when their countries were defeated. The largest contingent were the members of the Polish Air Force (*Polskie Siły Powietrzne*) who, following the German invasion in 1939, had made their way via Hungary and Rumania to France. This exodus, which included technicians and ground staff as well as pilots, stemmed from the Franco-Polish Military Accord of 1921, which meant that small Polish air units would be formed by the French if Poland collapsed. These Polish pilots took part in the 1940 Battle of France before they were evacuated to Britain, though the Poles had not been impressed by the French, who had billeted them in poor accommodation and provided them with obsolescent aircraft. Most of all, the Poles felt frustrated that the French did not appear to mirror their own levels of resolve and general fighting spirit. As one Polish pilot recalled, 'For them a German in the sky was something you needed to close your eyes to, in order not to have to gaze at him too long.' Another Polish pilot observed that the French Air Force was 'thick with resignation and defeat', noting that whilst the news of France's surrender caused the Polish airmen to break out in tears of sorrow, in the French Officers' mess 'the Champagne was flowing freely, because the war was over.'[11]

After France's defeat the Poles arrived on British soil, where the RAF were initially lukewarm towards these new, yet highly experienced, allies. They declared that the Polish airmen would only be allowed to join RAFVR squadrons as individuals, would have to begin as Pilot Officers, wear British uniforms and take an oath to the King. The British Government followed this ungrateful attitude up by informing their Polish leader, General Sikorski, that Poland would be charged for all costs involved in maintaining Polish forces in Britain. One has to admire the consistency of the Treasury's single-minded focus on financial probity, if not their inability to see the wider strategic picture. Common sense fortunately prevailed and Polish squadrons, with British officers attached,

---

11   Lynne Olson and Stanley Cloud, *For Your Freedom and Ours* (London: Arrow Books, 2004), p. 90.

A Vickers Wellington X of 99 Squadron lands at Jessore, India, on returning from a bombing sortie over Burma in August 1944. The Wellington was one of the few aircraft that remained in service right through the war.
(Crown Copyright – Air Historical Branch)

were eventually formed. A total of 145 Polish pilots fought during the Battle of Britain, the largest non-British contribution within the RAF during the battle. By the end of the war, an impressive total of 19,400 Poles were serving in the Polish Air Force and the wider RAF.

Czech pilots had also made their way to France and then to Britain after the fall of their country. They, too, were commissioned as pilots in the RAFVR and eventually formed squadrons in both Fighter Command and Bomber Command. Although part of the RAF, they were, like the members from other occupied countries, fiercely proud of the Czech badge displayed on their aircraft, their national flag at their airbases and having the word 'Czechoslovakia' emblazoned on the shoulders of their RAF uniforms. At the end of the war, there were a total of 1,500 Czechs still serving with the RAF. There will be numerous mentions within this book of airmen from other occupied countries fighting with the RAF: Belgium, Norway, Holland and France all contributed personnel who formed distinct national squadrons or served as individuals in RAF units. Citizens of neutral countries, but often with British connections, also served with the RAF, including those from as close as Ireland or as far away as Argentina. Prior to their own nation's entry into the war, a number of Americans also elected to serve with the RAF. This was a brave decision for a number of reasons, not least because they would be prosecuted by the FBI if caught. Some Americans served in the famous 'Eagle Squadrons' whilst others fought as individuals in RAF squadrons. Following the entry of America into the war in December 1941, the majority transferred to the United States Army Air Force (USAAF) – yet a few remained as part of the RAF, preferring to stay with their comrades and a familiar organisation. This, one has to suppose, was a difficult decision – not least because of the disparity in pay.

2

Learning to Fly

When war broke out it was expected that a large cohort of new recruits from across the Empire would join the RAF. Full-scale conscription began on the day hostilities commenced and all males between the ages of 18 and 41, bar a few exempt categories, were liable for call up. On registering at the local labour exchange they would be asked a simple question, 'Which service did they wish to join?' Of those registering for the first proclamation on 21 October 1939, 30 percent stated they wished to serve with the RAF, by February 1941 it had risen to 50 percent. These new recruits included many who would serve as ground crew, training for which could last several years depending on the technicality of the trade. Those who wished to serve as aircrew would also begin a long process, taking them through various schools or holding centres, before they eventually joined an operational unit. The first stop on the journey was at an aircrew selection centre where the recruits (all aircrew were volunteers), would be judged suitable. The process changed throughout the war and the two charts below at Figures 1 and 2 show how the system evolved.

Let us suppose that the individual is successful and is sent to the Initial Training Wing (ITW) where he would be inducted into the service. ITW consisted solely of ground training and included mathematics, navigation, weapon training on aircraft machine guns, Morse code, meteorology and the principles of flying, all of which served as a foundation for subsequent training. Harry Yates attended No.10 Initial Training Wing at Scarborough and describes the experience as well as his subsequent graduation to Elementary Flying School:

> The syllabus initiated us into the mysteries of airmanship; theory of flight: armaments; aero-engines; navigation; astronomy, meteorology; instruments; map reading; photography; RAF law and aircraft recognition – all in just six weeks. This demanded a Herculean effort, even from the more academic among us. Looking again at my notebooks after all these years I am astonished at the technical content and variety of facts which we absorbed. To do so we studied all day and late into the evening. There was barely a moment for relaxation, and Scarborough's publicans certainly weren't on first name terms with many of us. For all that, much of the syllabus was of little practical benefit. Parts of it had no connection to flying whatever. For example, in the dusty corners of RAF Law we studied the abstruse restrictions placed upon civilians trading with airmen. Any such trade was at the civvies' risk. No airman could be arrested or compelled to appear before the courts for any debt below £30.
>
> Some of the boys thought it was safe to ignore such pedantry. No examiner, they argued, could seriously expect to determine our suitability as pilots with questions about trade or debt. Others suspected that the more eccentric the subject, the more inevitable was its appearance on the exam paper. Bereft of such subtle reasoning I just learned all I could, and fortunately so because the second opinion proved the more accurate. Having scraped together a bare minimum of exam passes I was entitled to display the white flash of a Leading Aircraftsman on my forage cap. The pay increased modestly, too. But to me these were trifles. All along I had been driven by a single and once seemingly impossible ambition. But now I knew. I would sit at the controls of an aircraft in a matter of only days.

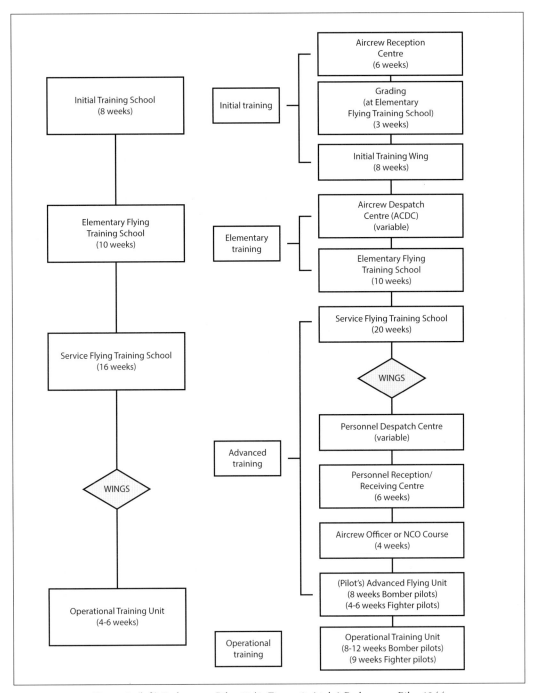

Figure 1 (left) Pathway to Pilot 1941. Figure 2 (right) Pathway to Pilot 1944.

At the beginning of July I reported to the de Havilland School of Flying at Hatfield, officially titled No. I Elementary Flying Training School. In those days the airfield was simply a large, green expanse. There were no runways. On the perimeter were the brick-built administration quarters. The office of the Chief Flying Instructor, Squadron Leader Pedley, was located in the centre to afford him an uninterrupted view across the field. Each new intake was mustered before this somewhat formidable man and treated to a pithy address, much mimicked afterwards by the barrack's wags but never disregarded. 'Gentlemen,' he bristled, 'I hope you appreciate how privileged you are to be here. We are going to give you the opportunity to bend one of His Majesty's aeroplanes.' And off he went.[1]

Elementary Flying Training School (EFTS) was essentially a filter, through which those who successfully passed were accepted onto further flying training and those who failed were diverted onto other aircrew duties (including navigator, bomb aimer, engineer, gunner or wireless operator). Achieving a successful grading involved about 12 hours flying on simple aircraft, like the de Havilland Tiger Moth, much of which was dual instruction with two important flying aptitude tests. It was widely understood that if a pilot was to be able to progress, he needed to be able to fly solo in less than 10 hours. This initial instruction was usually the most memorable period for the budding pilot and not without its difficulties. Ken Robinson was one of the trainees who went to an American EFTS. He would go on to fly four-engine Sunderlands, one of the largest RAF aircraft as well as a flying boat, but he was not impressed with his initial attempts at Grosse Isle:

As we gathered speed across the bumpy field, the tail began to lift, and I could now look out over the nose and see exactly where we were going. Suddenly, the bumping ceased, and the ground receded. We were airborne. The pilot throttled back, and we were able to continue climbing with less power. I felt discomfort in my ears due to the changing pressure as we gained height. We'd been told that the air pressure decreased as you climbed, and you needed to swallow to equalize the pressure on both sides of the eardrums. Coming down, as pressure increased, it was more effective to yawn, which was something I had great difficulty in doing to order.

As the airfield disappeared behind us, the port wing dropped, and we began to turn to make a circuit of the base. Feeling insecure as we banked, I clung on to the side of the cockpit for fear of falling out. In spite of being safely strapped in, I found myself worrying about what would happen if the seat belt failed and I was pitched out before we'd gained enough height for me to use my parachute.

These thoughts were interrupted by Clabaugh [the instructor] who looked very relaxed and certainly didn't share my alarm. 'I'm going to climb up to 2,000 feet and then you can take the controls.' He obviously thought that with that amount of height in hand he would have time to take the necessary action should I do anything stupid. Completing this manoeuvre, he said, 'OK, Robinson. We're flying at 2,000 feet and we're on a heading of 250 degrees. Look at the nose of the airplane and see where it comes in relation to the horizon. That's where it always needs to be when you're flying straight and level, right? Now take over the controls and see if you can maintain height, airspeed and course. You've got it.'

I made a determined effort to do what Clabaugh had said. The nose went up and the airspeed started to fall off. Stick forward, push the nose down … whoops, too far … The airspeed picked up again as the nose dropped. Each time I took corrective action I found I overshot and had to reverse the procedure. It occurred to me that my path in the air must

---

1   Harry Yates, *Luck and a Lancaster* (Shrewsbury: Airlife, 1999), p. 17.

De Havilland Tiger Moth II, R4922, of 7 Elementary Flying School based at Desford, Leicestershire, in flight, March 1941. (Crown Copyright – Air Historical Branch).

have resembled that of a roller coaster at the fair. After a while I began to get the feel of the controls and my corrections became more subtle. I found that I was having greater success in maintaining the required altitude. While concentrating on that, I'd forgotten our heading. I glanced at the gyro compass … 230 degrees and spinning. Bank to the right, rudder and aileron … oh no! 254 degrees … straighten out … that's better. What's our height? 1,980 feet. Oh hell!

Clabaugh, seeing my obvious discomfort, came to the rescue. 'OK, I've got it! don't worry about it, you're doing just fine. It takes time to get used to the controls' …

I was glad to be relieved of the controls. I didn't think much of my first attempt at flying an aeroplane.[2]

The instruction at EFTS consisted of a series of lessons in the sky covering subjects such as 'Effect of Controls', 'Straight and Level Flying'. 'Climbing, Gliding and Stalling'. 'Medium Turns', 'Taking off into Wind', 'Powered Approach and Landing'. All of these would be neatly recorded in the pilot's log book. The pilots were taught how to recover from stalls, which is a simple process when as a result of losing flying speed in the climb, both of the wings on the aeroplane stall simultaneously. The nose then drops, flying speed is regained and the aircraft comes back under positive control. A stall that led to the aircraft 'spinning' was much more challenging and probably one of the most important and nerve-wracking problems for the novice pilots to master. The lesson normally required a climb to 3,000 feet, stalling the aircraft once more, but on this occasion the stick would be pulled hard back, the rudder pushed hard left and the nose would jerk up. The left wing would then stall and flick down, putting the pilot and his aircraft in a dizzying spin, the earth swinging over in a terrifying arc as the aircraft rapidly rotated around its own axis and dived steeply to the ground. As the needle on the altimeter steadily unwound, the pilot had to recover his wits and push the stick hard forward whilst applying hard opposite rudder – on a well-mannered aircraft like the Tiger Moth the plane swiftly recovered.[3]

2   Ken Robinson, *Dice on Regardless: The Story of an RAF Sunderland Pilot* (London: R.J. Leach and Co., 1993), p. 15.
3   Hugh Popham, *Sea Flight* (London: Futura, 1974), p. 16.

As in any other form of training the pilot's progress was often determined by the quality of the instructors. Many were civilians, or older RAF pilots taking a 'rest' between operational sorties. Others were pilots who had only recently gone through training themselves but had been held back to train a new batch of pilots. Inevitably each instructor was different, some were calm and genuinely inspirational, others were tyrants, annoyed at being posted as instructors whilst the war was on, or resented having their lives risked by novice pilots. Anthony Leicester became a pilot on Wellington bombers, but he had a difficult start and remembered Flight Lieutenant Liversidge as a particularly difficult tutor:

> After the first few short flights, however, I became disillusioned. Liversidge wasn't the perfect instructor I had believed him to be. On each training flight, before we climbed into the Tiger Moth, Flt Lt Liversidge explained, in detail, the exercise we were going to fly. 'This morning we're going to do powered approach landings, precautionary landings and some instrument flying.' Using his hands he illustrated how the plane would turn, dive or climb.
>
> Later, in the air, flying from the front seat, he demonstrated the manoeuvres while giving me the instructor's 'standard patter' of what he was doing and why. Then, with his voice coaching me through the Gosport tube – a thin pipe connected to the headphones in the pilot's helmet – he made me follow the manoeuvres with my hands and feet on the controls. Finally he had me fly the aircraft and go through the exercise again. But while I was flying he constantly berated me, using foul language and telling me that everything I did was wrong. 'You clot. Watch your airspeed.' … 'Silly bugger, I didn't tell you to do that.'
>
> One morning, while going through the seemingly endless 'circuits and bumps' and battered with constant criticisms, I did a bouncy landing and he yelled at me, 'I've got it!'
>
> He shoved the throttle forward and with a roar from the four-cylinder Gypsy engine we lurched back into the air and went around again. With my hands on the controls, on the circuit's downwind leg, I felt a movement in the control-stick move and I knew that his hand was on the dual-controls. I banked and turned across wind and I again felt his hand on the controls. I turned into the wind, closed the throttle and started my glide approach. The wind whistled by the open cockpit. I watched my throttle lever inch forward, then back. 'Keep the wings level,' he shouted at me. I eased the stick over.
>
> 'Level, you silly bugger!' Liversidge shrieked through the Gosport tube. I let go of the stick. The wings levelled and the aircraft continued its approach. Then, the 'plane rounded out over the grass landing area, but too late. The wheels hit the ground hard and we bounced into the air.
>
> 'You bloody little fool! I have control,' Liversidge screamed adding a string of foul oaths as he shoved the throttle forward. At that point I almost lost what little confidence I had in my flying ability. On the next circuit he constantly nagged me over the intercom. I was supposed to fly the aeroplane and make my own mistakes, but he was flying it for me!
>
> I didn't get angry very often but now I was furious, no livid, at the attitude of the foul-mouthed man in the front cockpit. The next time he shouted at me over the intercom, I lost control of my anger. I took hold of my Gosport and bent it around the side of the windscreen, so it faced forward into the slipstream. A strong gale shot into Liversidge's ears ballooning his leather helmet like a football. In the little rear-view mirror I could see part of his enraged face. That's done it, I thought. I've had it now. I'll probably be court martialled.[4]

---

4   Anthony Leicester, *Flights into the Night* (Manchester: Crecy Publishing, 2010), p. 26.

Leicester had the moral courage to demand a new instructor and to his credit Flight Lieutenant Liversidge granted the request. Under the tutelage of a calm SNCO pilot, Leicester soon went solo and successfully passed Elementary Flying Training.

One area that students often had difficulties with was in landing. Some struggled in 'rounding out', the first step in landing from a gliding approach when the aircraft is flown level to the ground. Some students had problems telling how far they were from the ground and would round out too high. The aircraft would then drop with a bump and bounce into the air once more. The ideal landing was a perfect 'three-pointer' where both the main wheels and tail wheel would hit the ground at the same time. Trainee Bert Horden went through EFTS at Bulawayo in Rhodesia and struggled with this particular aspect, trying to land in his own words '30 ft under ground or 30 ft above ground.' His first instructor despaired and Horden was transferred to 'X' Flight where pilots with problems were specially coached.

There his new instructor, Flying Officer Cousins, tried a different method, taxiing the aircraft to the far edge of the field, where he got out. He then leaned into the cockpit and spoke bluntly: 'Horden, you will —— well sit there till you get it into your ——, —— thick skull that the aircraft lands in the exact position you are in now. Look at the horizon and the attitude of the aircraft to it and —— well sit there till I come back.' With that Cousins left the aircraft and walked to the crew room, leaving Horden to stew in the cockpit for an hour or so. When Cousins returned he gave Horden one last chance to do a good landing, which he successfully accomplished, going solo shortly thereafter.[5]

The solo flight was a memorable milestone for all pilots. Lord Kilbracken would eventually fly a Fairey Swordfish with the Fleet Air Arm (FAA), in some of the harshest flying conditions any pilot could expect to encounter. Like many FAA pilots he was trained by RAF instructors, in his instance on a Miles Magister at No. 24 Elementary Flying Training School. He subsequently observed:

> I never heard of a death on a first solo. You are concentrating for every second and you know that every second your grounded instructor is watching. Taxiing circumspectly round the perimeter to the chosen downwind position – of course no runways [like most EFTS airfields RAF Luton had just a simple expanse of grass]. Checking controls, looking to leeward for other aircraft, lowering goggles. Throttle and rudder to turn into wind, pick up a point to aim at. Right, this is it, open her up to full throttle. Gathering speed, bumpity-bump over the grass, keep her straight, now ease the stick very gently forward, up comes the tail-wheel. Hold her a few more seconds, keep her straight for Christ's sake. You can't yet tell when she's ready just by the feel of the stick, without checking on the airspeed, though that will come quite soon, so just a quick glance. Now, **now**: ease back imperceptibly, the nose rises, the last little bump. Jesus we're airborne, airborne. Keep full throttle, keep straight, keep the correct climbing speed. I'm on my own, totally detached, unattainable, on my own in the sky. The airfield perimeter flashing under my wing tip, the whole world stretched before me.
>
> Laughing and cheering aloud. Inarticulate cries with no one to hear them, bouncing up and down, the need to express somehow the exhilaration and joy, the release of tension, the relief. Off goggles, whole face into the slipstream, still cheering and singing, feel the clear air rushing on my face till tears in my eyes, run a tenth of an inch and arc swept away astern of me. Reaching 500 feet. Throttle back, level out, medium turn to port through 90 degrees, open up again, continue climbing. Luton a toy-town below. Stay on this crosswind course to 1,000 feet, throttle back to cruising revs. Now look around. Relax. Check everything. I'm

5   Bert Horden, *Shark Squadron Pilot* (Bromley: Independent Books, 2002), p. 24.

allowed 10 minutes of soaring and climbing. Then back into the circuit. Downwind, cross-wind, then upwind for the landing. Parr [Kilbracken's instructor] will be watching closely, now's the time to show him. There goes the perimeter 50 feet below me. Level out, close throttle, now back with the stick, come on back, come on back, we've done it. Bumpity-bump as we run across the field, keep her straight, brake her ever so slightly, come to a joyous standstill. Taxi back to dispersal. Grin and wave to waving grinning comrades. OK now let's start flying, you reckless birdman.[6]

Not all students successfully passed. Trainee Eric Cropper found that though he could recover from spins and his landings were competently executed, his circuits were just a bit too 'ragged' for his instructor's liking. After 12 hours flying training, he had still not 'gone solo' and failed the Chief Instructor's flying test. Like many others, he was sent to an aircrew holding unit and after several weeks there was re-mustered as a Navigator and sent to No.1 Elementary Air Navigation School at Bridgnorth, Shropshire. There they were taught the basic methods of navigation, with an emphasis on Dead Reckoning (DR) navigation. This is the estimation of position by the use of the known compass course and airspeed, adjusted to allow for the best-known wind velocity. The subject had been taught at Initial Training but now, at Bridgnorth, they were taught how to use more advanced equipment such as the Dalton navigational computer.

The budding navigators were also taught how to maintain and operate a navigation log, (RAF Form 441), including the use of prescribed abbreviations and codewords. Initially DR plots and instruction took place in the classroom, but as the students' training progressed, they would conduct exercises in the DR Trainer. This was a hut in which they received instructions through headphones and worked against the clock trying to keep up with their navigational duties, all the while a loudspeaker piped aircraft engine noise in to the hut in a feeble attempt to simulate flying conditions.

Navigational instruction also included astro-navigation, meteorological studies and wireless direction finding where the aircraft's 'loop aerial' was used to take a bearing on a ground station. After passing a series of written examinations the navigators would then progress to an Air Observers' School where they would undergo practical navigational training in aircraft such as Ansons. Other students who had failed to pass pilot training would also be filtered off, to become air gunners, wireless operators, flight engineers or bomb aimers, with a raft of other special schools for these disciplines.

For the pilots who had successfully passed EFTS, further training at the Service Flying Training School (SFTS) beckoned. Here the emphasis lay on cross-country navigational flights, instrument flying, formation flying, radio exercises and reconnaissance missions. Night training was also given greater prominence, with two or three cross country exercises. Many pilots commented that at SFTS the flying curriculum had a more serious and professional aspect and greater maturity and responsibility was expected from them. The aircraft were also more advanced, including North American T-6 'Harvard' trainers, with retractable under-carriage, powerful engines and variable pitch propellers. By this stage pilots were becoming more relaxed and confident, which might mean they were too cocky and took risks beyond their competence. Canadian Murray Peden attended SFTS in Canada before becoming a bomber pilot on Stirlings and recalled one Leading Aircraftsman, whose name he changed to Strutter, trying to impress his new girlfriend and her family with his flying skills:

---

6   Lord Kilbracken, *Bring Back My Stringbag* (London: Peter Davies, 1979), p. 13.

September 1940 – Air Observers under training – they had to be proficient in navigation, bomb-aiming, photography, ship recognition and meteorology. These air observers are playing 'Sieg Heil!', a card game in which silhouettes of enemy and allied aircraft are on the card faces. The game tested aircraft recognition skills. (Crown Copyright – Air Historical Branch).

So loud was the engine [on a Harvard] that, to announce one's arrival to everyone in an area of 10 square miles, all one had to do was ease back on the throttle momentarily then rev up again: The snarling, swelling roar that emanated while the prop was caught in the fully fine position would rattle window panes and china for miles around.

Strutter swirled ostentatiously onto the scene at a 1,000 feet, revving his engine dementedly, and shortly drew his audience into their back yard to watch admiringly while he passed in review. He executed two or three runs at roof top level in fine style, leaving the watchers breathless with delight and excitement, then climbed briefly so that he could build up a good head of steam for the piece de resistance and grand finale.

Whistling in with 150 m.p.h. showing on the clock and absolute zero on the altimeter – this crude instrument was simply not up to Strutter's exacting flying standards, for later measurement proved conclusively that he was fully five feet ten inches clear of the ground – Strutter made a minor miscalculation, and with his right wing tip and an ear splitting crash tore the top off the family outhouse. Not to be outdone, the outhouse tore three feet off Strutter's wing tip, and the asymmetrical Harvard staggered leadenly away like a badly hit bird.

Finding that he could climb, albeit with difficulty Strutter did lots of that, while he anxiously checked to ensure that the main parts of the aeroplane were with him … Everything else appeared normal, and it began to appear encouragingly probable that he would survive to face the carload of charges the air force would undoubtedly bring against him as soon as he put his two feet on the ground … He patiently climbed still further and found by repeated

Three Harvard Is – N7125/L, N7095/N and N7061 – of 20 Flying Training School based at Cranborne in Southern Rhodesia, practicing formation flying over the Mazoe river valley during a training flight in 1941. (Crown Copyright – Air Historical Branch)

experiments (with an apprehensive eye on the ragged wing tip) that the Harvard now stalled around 90 m.p.h. instead of around 60. That meant landing at over 100 to preserve a margin of safety and wheeling her on in a precariously unstable condition. Nothing daunted, Strutter decided to chance it, flew her back, and set her down safely at base, intact except for the three foot calling card beside his girl friend's open and airy outhouse. Strutter's flagrant violation of the low flying prohibition could quite justifiably have been punished in the manner he had feared; but in an uncharacteristic display of common sense and magnanimity the Air Force took into account the coolness and sound airmanship he had displayed after the outhouse affair, and, instead of washing him out, they tossed him into the guardhouse and transferred him back to a later course. Eventually, despite the outhouse and the guardhouse, he won his wings.[7]

SFTS in Canada must have seemed a glamorous location for many Britons, some of whom had never left their own country. One can therefore only imagine the delight of students such as Ron Pottinger, who escaped a rationed and blacked-out Britain, to undertake EFTS and SFTS in Florida. Despite this exotic location his training was still undertaken in a serious and diligent manner and his account below showed how he had learnt to handle emergencies:

7   Murray Peden, *A Thousand Shall Fall: The True Story of A Canadian Bomber Pilot in World War Two* (Toronto: Stoddart, 1979), p. 64.

The flying training went as before, only more so. We flew formation, culminating in a flight of nine aircraft led by Gunner Brink. This was not looked forward to by many. Gunner was apt to spend most of the time yelling at one or another to get in closer, and the boys, especially those in the centre of the formation, had visions of the inexperienced pilot behind chewing his way through the tail with his prop.

We did more cross-countries, longer ones. It was on one of these that I ran into trouble. On the way out to the lines of planes, I saw Laurie Coupland taxiing out. I yelled to him to wait and I would meet up and take pictures. He said, 'Okay, but hurry!' I suppose my cockpit drill was a bit cursory, and any-way, by the time I got out to the takeoff point, he had already been sent off by the control tower. I never did meet up with him that day.

I took off and flew the first leg up to the north. Turning south west I was half way down the second leg well over the swamplands when the engine spat a few times and stopped running. A quick look around the cockpit showed that the main tanks were dry. A switch to reserve and a quick mental calculation showed I had about 15 minutes of flying time. On the map I saw a club flying field marked at Wauchula just about within reach. A new course was set, and in due course, to my relief, I saw the windsock and building at Wauchula. I also saw cows grazing all over the field.

I made an approach the long way of the field, this being into wind, but as I got nearer the ground I could see that I was never going to miss all the cows, so I opened up and took off again. As I pulled up the engine spat a couple of times and I quickly looked for a likely flat area ahead. However, it kept going and I got around to land in a comparatively clear area, but cross wind and with not much length of runway. I got it down and taxied to the upwind end of the field and stopped the engine. All four petrol gauges were showing zero.

All the way across I had been trying to raise the field on the radio without success. The radios we had were very limited in range. One of the others on the cross country who had got petrol flew high over Wauchula and relayed my message. The airfield at Wauchula was obviously no longer in regular use, thus the cows. The grass was also somewhere near two feet high in places. After about an hour another AT6A turned up and landed. In it was the Chief Flying Instructor and another 'advanced' instructor. The instructor was left to await a tanker to refuel the plane, and I returned to the field with the C.F.I. As soon as we were airborne, he had me under the hood flying on instruments, even for the landing. I realised that I was on trial and was keyed up to do the best I could. Though I say it myself, I performed well, prob-ably the most precise flying I had ever done, and the landing barely bumped as we touched and stayed down.[8]

Pottinger was criticised by the American instructors who blamed him for not ensuring his aircraft's fuel tanks were full. However, a new British station commander, fresh from a light bomber squadron and the Middle East, was on his side and backed him up when it was found that the ground crew were late starting the refuelling and the bowser had somehow missed his aircraft. Sadly, there were some mistakes pilots could not walk away from. SFTS accidents were not uncommon and could shock their surviving classmates. Murray Peden recalled one fatal accident:

On 12 August, I did a three-hour cross-country solo and landed to find that Plate and I, along with other members of 'E' Flight, were scheduled for our first twin-engined night flying. We checked the schedule and went off to supper together discussing it. Plate was on the first shift, but because of the time of year, even the first shift couldn't get started until about 10 o'clock.

8   Ron Pottinger, *Soldier in the Cockpit* (Mechanicsburg, Pennsylvania: Stackpole, 2007), p. 66.

I was on the second shift and was supposed to report to the flight room at midnight. There was a movie being shown in the drill hall at nine o'clock that night, a movie which I thought held some promise. I tramped off to see it just before nine, telling Plate, who was lying on his bunk reading, that I would likely see him at the flights sometime after midnight.

I left the drill hall before 11 and came back to my bunk to see if I could catch 40 winks before going night flying. I dropped off briefly and woke up about a quarter to 12 when someone came into the hut. It was Mullins; I caught a glimpse of his face as he passed under the small bulb in the vestibule and headed for my bunk. I swung my feet to the door and rubbed the sleep out of my eyes as he came up to me. It was quite dark.

'Plate's dead, Murray,' he said, speaking rather softly.

'That's a pretty poor kind of a joke' I responded; but as I looked at him I suddenly knew he wasn't joking, and I stammered: 'What do you mean … what happened?'

'He crashed on his first solo; I heard he just dove into the ground.'

He stood there a few moments longer, saying nothing, and then moved down to his own bunk. For the next five minutes I sat staring vacantly at the next bunk trying to absorb the news. The shock began to make me shaky. I pulled on my tunic and walked in the darkness over to the flights, almost unconscious of what I was doing. The lights in the flight room were harsh and I screwed my face up and blinked as I entered.

'Hey, Peden, Pilot Officer Orr's looking for you,' someone called.

I stuck my head into the instructors' room; Orr saw me and came over. 'We're in 7824,' he said, 'be ready in five minutes.'

As we walked out to the aircraft he told me that Plate had taken off on his first night solo, climbed to 500 feet, began his climbing turn to the left, and then somehow slipped into a spiral dive and failed to recover. He had gone in with full climbing power on and must have been doing 200 miles an hour when he hit the ground. The impact threw his body through the upper and forward portions of the cabin, well clear of the wreckage, which burned. We took off and flew right over the smouldering wreckage on three circuits. Then a rain squall moved in and the balance of the night flying programme was cancelled. I walked back to the hut alone and lay awake on my bunk until dawn.[9]

Graduation from the SFTS meant the pilot was now permitted to wear RAF wings on his uniform as a qualified pilot. This training could have been achieved in as little as six months, but it was more common for it to be spread over an 18 month to two-year period, with the pilot completing anything from 200-320 flying hours. As most SFTS were abroad the pilot would usually travel back across the Atlantic to the UK, where he would embark on the final stage of his flying training, initially at an Advanced Flying Unit (for either bombers and fighters) followed by an Operational Training Unit (OTU). These two units would prepare him for frontline duties on modern operational types of aircraft. For the fighter pilots this instruction included gunnery, night-flying, air tactics and low-level flying. Pilot Officer David Ince was posted to 41 OTU in Cheshire which was responsible for generating fighter reconnaissance pilots. Low-level flying was therefore a critical skill for these pilots as David Ince recalled:

Low level Tac-R was something else again. Down on the deck, you hugged the contours, watching for powerlines, checking your track. In a Tiger Moth the countryside had flooded past like a river in spate. With a Hurricane it became a raging torrent. Slowing as you lifted briefly over some obstruction, accelerating violently as you dropped close to the ground on the other side. A familiar illusion which never failed to excite. Low flying was and always will be an addiction, an exhilarating pastime, requiring skill and absolute concentration.

The lethal temptation, to fly lower still, was always present. There was an issue of 'Tee Emm'[10] with a picture displaying the remains of a Hurricane, just to remind us! A trail of wreckage littered the length of an open field and, where it ended, a larger collection of debris surrounded a battered Merlin engine and a bucket seat. That the pilot, incredibly, had survived almost unscathed was, beside the point. The total disintegration of his aircraft was enough.[11]

The OTUs were where the crews of the larger aircraft would be brought together. Many of the aircraft at the OTUs had been retired from operational frontline service and were at the end of their service life. They were frequently described as 'clapped out'. Accidents were not uncommon, sometimes because of pilot or crew error, but frequently because of mechanical issues on these tired machines. Pilot Officer Phil Darby was introduced to the Wellington at his Bomber Command OTU at RAF Harwell:

The training programme soon settled into a fixed routine. We were each sent off with an experienced pilot to gain air experience with the aircraft and find out exactly what its idiosyncrasies were. It seemed heavy and big and it could not be flung around in the sky like the lighter aircraft I had been flying before. But it was a friendly beast and very rapidly I began to like it. After a few circuits and bumps, two trainee pilots were put together and from then on, they operated as a duo. One of them was first pilot and the other was second pilot/navigator. On the next trip the position was reversed.

It was on one of these trips, when I was skipper, that I discovered a problem which cropped up from time to time. Certain of the flying controls were operated by hydraulics and these were relatively easily damaged or subject to natural failure. On the occasion in question, when returning from a cross-country exercise, I did a routine circuit of the airfield and on the cross-wind leg prior to turning in I selected 30 degrees of flap, turned and lined up the runway for the final approach, and selected the rest of the flap down. I then trimmed the aircraft to hold the nose down so that it would make a normal approach to the airfield.

Suddenly it fell out of the sky. The air-speed indicator showed I had adequate speed but when I glanced at the flap indicator I realised that the flaps were coming up. I put on full power to get rid of the stall before I hit the ground. But the aircraft was trimmed nose heavy and I could not pull it out of the shallow dive. We hit the ground in the middle of the runway, bounced into the air, staggered on a little bit across a couple of fields, and then hit ground again and skidded over yet another field before coming to rest across a road. In the process we had gone between two elm trees and both wings had been taken off, but the fuselage was almost intact. We dived out through the cockpit lid, ran, found a ditch and lay there expecting an explosion. Nothing happened, and in a few moments the fire-tender and blood-wagon appeared, and we were whisked off to the sick quarters. The MO checked us over and pronounced us fit and well and ready for service. So we were issued with another aircraft and told to go and do a few circuits and bumps but not to repeat the last stage.

There were no further problems and when we re-appeared the accident report had already been completed. It seemed that the whole incident had been observed from the ground and instead of getting black marks, as we expected, we were told we hadn't done badly. Apparently

---

10 *Tee Emm* was an official RAF magazine that offered tips to aircrew on aspects of flying. Avoiding common mistakes through negligence or stupidity was a common theme.

11 David Ince, *Brotherhood of the Skies* (London: Grub Street, 2010), p. 54.

there had been a hydraulic failure before the flaps were locked down and they had folded up causing the aircraft to stall, and as it was trimmed nose down it could not be adequately controlled. We begged a lift back to the crash to collect the clock from the dashboard, as a souvenir, but it had already been taken, much to my annoyance.[12]

From the OTUs the aircrew would disperse to whatever squadrons and duties awaited them. Between the 3 September 1939 and 2 September 1945, the various training schools around the globe produced 326,552 qualified aircrew, 117,669 of whom were pilots.[13] The exact numbers for other aircrew roles are also included at Annex D. These large numbers bring to life the scale of the training endeavour needed to man the RAF and its sister commonwealth air forces. Nonetheless, it took time for this pipeline to generate a sizable flow of aircrew, initially it would seem similar to how Churchill described the production of munitions, *'First year, nothing at all; second year, very little; third year, quite a lot; fourth year, all you want.'* Therefore in that desperate first part of the war, before the training schools had got into their stride, the line was held by just a small number of regular and reserve pilots – often there were just a few of them.

---

12   Phil Darby, *Press on Regardless* (Privately Published, 1997), pp. 45-6.
13   Air Historical Branch, Air Publication 3233, *Flying Training, Volume 1, Policy and Planning*, 1952, Appendix No. 3.

Part II
Air Superiority

3

'Guardians of the Heart'[1]
Fighter Command's Air Defence
of Britain

Air superiority is generally accepted as the primary role for any Air Force, but it can come in many forms and achieving it is rarely a simple proposition. It can be localised air superiority, generated in a specific geographical area – perhaps over a battlefield for a limited period of time, or it can be offensive in nature and projected long distances over enemy territory in order to allow an air strike to take place or support a maritime or ground operation. Arguably the most important type is strategic air superiority over a combatant's own home territory, its factories, population, centre of government and key naval, air and military facilities. Without such air superiority a nation's ability to wage war is diminished both physically and in terms of morale.

We now understand that enemy air attacks can be confronted and challenged in many ways. However, between the two World Wars the prevailing view of air power theorists was that attempts to prevent enemy bomber fleets from reaching their targets were simply impractical. The RAF took this theory one step further, arguing that Britain's best approach to defeating an enemy air attack, was to develop a powerful bomber force of its own. A force that would serve not only as a deterrent but could also administer a 'knockout blow' against any potential enemy. This philosophy was actively promoted by Trenchard, who was probably influenced by his desire that the RAF remained independent and became Britain's dominant military service. Trenchard and his disciples were consistent in their approach, spending the 1920s and 1930s actively promoting the idea of a militarily decisive bomber fleet, often at the expense of fighter defence.

It was the much-maligned government of Neville Chamberlain who sensibly challenged this view, primarily for financial reasons, arguing that greater time and effort should be allocated to the fighter defence of the United Kingdom. Sir Thomas Inskip (Minister for the Coordination of Defence (1936-39)) was an unlikely champion of the fighter. A lawyer by background, he remains most famous for challenging the adoption of a new version of the Church of England's Book of Common Prayer. Yet it was Inskip who persuasively argued in his 1937 'Aide Memoire on Air Policy',[2] that a defensive fighter capability against German bombers should be the primary requirement of the RAF:

> What we want to do in the first weeks of a war is to knock out as many German aeroplanes as we can, with a view to upsetting the morale of their Air Force … They must come to this country to damage us. They are likely to concentrate on the great centres, such as London, which provide an irresistible target. In fact, it would seem in accordance with strategic

---

1   Motto of No.11 Group, Fighter Command.
2   Leo McKinstry, *Spitfire – Portrait of a Legend* (London: Murray, 2007), p. 11.

principle that the decisive place and the decisive time for the concentration of our own forces would be somewhere over our own country.[3]

The Air Staff were appalled at this shift from an offensive to a defensive doctrine. Yet Inskip had the weight of the Cabinet behind him and correctly identified that even a dramatic increase in the already significant investment in bombers, would neither deter any potential adversary, nor cause them to capitulate. He argued that the nation had to be prepared to wage a long war and that this must include the ability to combat enemy bombers over Britain. Inskip's advocacy of a defensive fighter capability was underpinned by emerging technologies, such as radar, that created new opportunities to prevent an enemy bomber force from always being able to reach its target unhindered. Instead, these new technologies lent weight to the idea that, with strong fighter defences, Britain could realistically counter *Luftwaffe* bomber attacks. One should not credit Inskip too much, because his arguments had more to do with Treasury desires to curb expensive bomber procurement and there was no actual promise of an increase in fighter squadrons in his policy. Yet his words did serve as an important conceptual catalyst.

To provide an effective air defence the RAF required a number of distinct operational capabilities. First, an early warning and command and control system that could effectively scramble aircraft held at readiness. This minimised the use of standing patrols which caused excessive machine wear and aircrew fatigue, quickly eroding an air force's effectiveness. Secondly, it would need modern fighter aircraft, operating from a network of well-sited airfields. These machines would have to be able to climb rapidly to reach an advantageous height and attacking position, where they could engage the enemy with effective firepower.

Until the late 1930s the first part of this air defence system, the ability to give early warning, had always been the most challenging. The RAF had no means with which to detect fast, high-flying German aircraft, in sufficient time for an interception to be made and before they reached important targets, such as London. Initial and unsuccessful attempts to develop early warning systems had been tried, including huge concrete acoustic sensors (such as the one at Hythe in Kent – 200 feet in length), as well as attempts to detect the aircraft's heat or magnetic signature, all to no avail. It was the advent of 'radio direction finding' in 1935, led by Robert Watson-Watt, which was to provide the breakthrough (the term RDF was commonly used until 1943, when the American nomenclature 'radio detection and ranging' or 'radar' was adopted). In his 1935 experiment Watson-Watt successfully detected a Handley-Page Heyford bomber in flight with radar. Though it would take a further four years of tireless work before the system could be deemed accurate enough to be operationally useful, radar nonetheless showed the potential to form the central element of Britain's early warning system.

The RAF still needed an effective command and control system that could direct the right number of fighter aircraft, to the right place and at the right time. This operational problem began to be solved by the newly formed Fighter Command. Created in 1936, its mission was to defend the UK from air attack using a combination of radar, Anti-Aircraft (AA) guns, searchlights and tightly controlled fighter forces from well dispersed and protected airfields. Headquarters Fighter Command was located in Stanmore, Middlesex and was led from the outset by Air Chief Marshal Sir Hugh Dowding. It was Dowding who not only developed Britain's ground-breaking air-defence system, but also successfully led it throughout the Battle of Britain. Dowding had been a fighter pilot on the western front throughout much of the First World War and had held the post of Air Member for Supply and Research at the Air Ministry in the 1930s, where he became familiar with both radar as well as the new Spitfire and Hurricane aircraft. Often considered

---

3   TNA AIR 8/226: Aide Memoire on Air Policy by Sir Thomas Inskip, 9 December 1937.

1 AMES Type 1 CH East Coast radar installation at Poling, West Sussex. On the left are three (originally four) in-line 360 ft steel transmitter towers, between which the transmitter aerials were slung, with the heavily protected transmitter building in front. On the right are four 240 ft wooden receiver towers placed in rhombic formation, with the receiver building in the middle. (Crown Copyright – Air Historical Branch)

aloof and commonly known by the nickname 'Stuffy', he was nevertheless seen as a fatherly figure amongst the pilots who respected his wise, firm and steady hand on the tiller.

Dowding was due to retire at the outbreak of war, but was instead extended in post, reflecting the RAF's appreciation of his unique expertise and importance. Perhaps Dowding's greatest contribution was in ensuring that there were sufficient RAF squadrons retained in the United Kingdom to defend it. From the beginning of the war Dowding argued that 'the Home Defence Organization must not be regarded as a co-equal with other Commands, but that it should receive priority to all other claims until it is firmly secured, since the continued existence of the nation and its services, depends on the Royal Navy and Fighter Command.' Dowding would have to argue that point with regular frequency, most especially during the crisis in May 1940 when Fighter Command's squadrons were very nearly offered up as a sacrifice to Anglo-French solidarity.[4]

Under Dowding radar was steadily integrated into an effective operational system. Exercises were held throughout 1938-39 and successfully resolved many issues, including how to determine the numbers of approaching enemy aircraft and how to automatically convert the range and bearing of the aircraft onto the standard grid map used by the RAF. The radar research staff also developed a small transmitter which, when switched on, gave British aircraft a distinctive blip on

4   Denis Richards, *Royal Air Force 1939-45 – Volume 1*, pp. 63, 124.

radar screens and allowed operators to quickly discriminate between enemy and friendly aircraft. Known as Identification Friend or Foe (IFF), this vital technology is still in widespread use today.[5]

The first radar stations to be constructed were known as Chain Home (CH) stations and by the summer of 1940 there were a total of 21 operational sites, deployed around Britain. These CH stations had a range of 120 miles but were only able to detect aircraft flying at significant heights. Fortunately, a series of maritime coastal defence radars had also been developed by the British. These were originally designed to detect enemy ships so that they could be engaged by coastal artillery, but it was also found that they could pick up low flying aircraft at ranges of up to 50 miles. By 1940 these 30 Chain Home Low (CHL) sites had been incorporated into Fighter Command's maturing radar network. Finally, a series of mobile radar stations were also developed, which were used to cover gaps or replace any radar stations that had been damaged or destroyed.[6] For an illustration of the coverage obtained see Map 1.

These were important steps, but the radar system was still in its technical infancy and there remained four major weaknesses. First, although easy to plot incoming raids by range, it was much harder to accurately identify an approaching aircraft's course. Even an aircraft flying in a straight line to a target would still resemble a zig-zag when plotted by radar, making it very hard for the operator to discern the actual bearing. Secondly, radar's ability to determine height was still crude at this stage and for aircraft flying over 25,000 feet often unreliable. Thirdly, the radar system was sited so that it could observe out to sea, but once an aircraft crossed the coast the radar was very poor at tracking its subsequent movements. Finally, perhaps most importantly, the early RAF radar was unable to accurately portray the numbers of enemy aircraft, so that any assessment produced was the result of the operator judging the size and flicker of the echo on the screen. Consequently, the actual German formations encountered by the RAF fighters could be anywhere from half to double the strength first reported by the radar operators.[7]

Despite these limitations, radar offered a distinct advantage to the defending fighter forces, particularly as the secrecy of Britain's radar system had been preserved, though not in the way that is widely believed. Germany was not ignorant of radar technology per se, indeed they had begun developing their own radar in the VHF range as long ago as 1929. What the Germans had not appreciated was that the British system had been developed along cruder lines operating on the HF range. The large British radar masts on the south coast had been easily spotted by German intelligence, who dispatched the *Graf Zeppelin II* airship on a series of electronic reconnaissance missions in the summer of 1939, to try to understand the new British system. The airship was ideally suited to the task because it had great endurance and travelling slowly could loiter in interesting areas. Although festooned with a variety of antennae and electronic listening equipment, the Germans did not pick up any relevant signals on the missions flown and were unable to understand the manner in which the British radar system was being used as part of an integrated air defence system. It was fortunate for the British that the German monitoring equipment was both unreliable and that they were focussing on the wrong part of the electro-magnetic radio spectrum. Had the *Graf Zeppelin II* successfully picked up its transmissions, then the Germans would almost certainly have undertaken a more serious study of Britain's air defence system. This might have resulted in sustained and punishing attacks on the Chain Home radar stations during the Battle of Britain, or even attempts at electronic jamming.[8]

---

5   Derek Wood and Derek Dempster, *The Narrow Margin* (Washington DC: Smithsonian, 1990), p. 92.
6   Derek Wood and Derek Dempster, *The Narrow Margin*, p. 92.
7   Alfred Price, *Battle of Britain 18 August 1940: The Hardest Day* (London: Granada, 1980), p. 53.
8   Vincent Orange, *Dowding of Fighter Command* (London: Grub Street, 2008), p. 134.

Chain Home receiver room at an East Coast station showing one of the two RF7 Receivers (left) and the Mark 3 Console (right) in use. (Crown Copyright – Air Historical Branch)

The function of radar as Fighter Command's long-range early warning system was complemented by the Observer Corps, who visually tracked the aircraft once they had crossed the coast. On mobilisation, in August 1939, the Observer Corps numbered 30,000 personnel, the vast majority of whom were civilian volunteers. These observers were deployed in over 1,000 12- to 14-man posts that were typically primitive constructions of sandbags or railway sleepers. At the centre of an observer post was an instrument with a height bar and geared sighting arm, which assisted the volunteers in estimating the enemy aircraft's height and bearing. The instrument was mounted in the centre of a gridded circular map of 10 miles radius and when an aircraft was sighted the observer would place the aircraft in a ring sight, judge its height and the plotter would automatically move it to a particular square of the gridded map. His companion would then pass the plot on by telephone to an Observer Corps control centre in a standard format, for example 'B2 calling, three planes seen 6153 flying north, height 8,000 feet.' These control centres would have between 30-34 posts reporting to them and their role was to collate the reports adding details, such as the type of aircraft, whenever it became available. The information would be passed to up to six separate Fighter Command Sectors; for instance the Observer Corps Control Centre at Bromley in Kent supported Sectors at Biggin Hill, Hornchurch, North Weald, Kenley, Northolt and Tangmere. Plots would also be passed to Group Headquarters and direct to Fighter Command.

The weakness of the Observer Corps visual system was often poor recognition of aircraft types, misidentifying Allied for German aircraft and poor height estimation. Judging height accurately was vital, but it took great skill and if incorrect, would cause the post instrument to identify the wrong grid square and location of the aircraft. Disappointingly, mistakes were common and the Observer Corps posts were persistently responsible for unidentified tracks. These would inevitably cause confusion amongst controllers, as they tried to determine if the plot was any one of a number

Two members of the Observer Corps man post no. 17/K1 situated on top of the Senate House, London University, in September 1940. The No 1 Observer operates the recording instrument (complete with telescope) while the No 2 reports the information to centre using a head and breast telephone set. Centre then passes the information on to Fighter Command. The post is surrounded with sandbags and the numbers hung round the walls indicate the 2km squares on the British Grid System. (Crown Copyright – Air Historical Branch)

of scenarios: a new raid freshly plotted, a raid missed by radar, or a friendly aircraft misidentified. Despite these weaknesses the Observer Corps played an important role as a supplement to radar and in providing essential visual contact with the aircraft once over the coast. Its responsiveness was such that a plot obtained by even the most remote post could be with Fighter Command in less than 40 seconds.[9] The Corps' contribution and importance in the Battle was recognised by the award of the title 'Royal Observer Corps' in April 1941. All this early warning information was a vital part of Fighter Command's command and control system, which was not replicated anywhere else in the world at the time and whose sophistication was poorly understood by the Germans. Figure 3 below gives a good illustration of the system.

By the time the Battle of Britain commenced in the summer of 1940, Fighter Command consisted of a Headquarters at Stanmore and a number of subordinate Groups. Number 10 Group covered the South West, 11 Group defended London and the South East, 12 Group – Eastern England, 13 Group – Scotland and finally 15 Group was in Northern Ireland. (Map 2 shows these dispositions together with fighter stations and radar sites.) Unsurprisingly, given their responsibility for London and close proximity to France, it was 11 Group, under Air Vice-Marshal Sir Keith Park, who

---

9   Derek Wood and Derek Dempster, *The Narrow Margin*, p. 92.

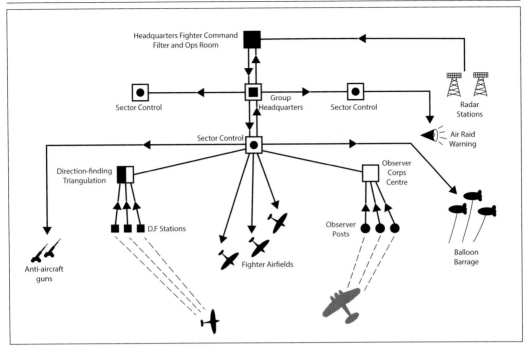

Figure 3 The Fighter Command System.

would bear the brunt of the Battle of Britain. Park was a New Zealander, who had fought as an artillery officer at Gallipoli and the Somme, before transferring to the Royal Flying Corps in 1916, becoming an ace by downing 20 German aircraft. By 1938, Park was Dowding's Senior Air Staff Officer and helped him develop and refine the Fighter Command Air Defence System. He took over command of 11 Group on 10 April 1940. Regarded as a distinctive 'hands on' commander, he was revered by those he led and his visits to frontline stations, in his personalised Hurricane, meant that he kept a firm grip on his pilots and had a sensitive feel for squadron operations. Park was a shrewd tactician and emphasised the requirement for the support and cooperation of both Air Vice-Marshal Brand's 10 Group and 12 Group under Air Vice-Marshal Sir Trafford Leigh-Mallory. The relationship with 10 Group worked well, but that with 12 Group was fractious and would cause Park and Dowding frustration throughout the battle, as well as afterwards.

The Fighter Command system effectively exploited radar's ability to act as a set of long-range eyes and alert Fighter Command's 'Filter Room,' at its HQ in Stanmore. The radar plots would be compared to the known positions of RAF aircraft and, if it was new, the plot was marked as either 'hostile' or 'un-identified'. IFF was a useful aid, but a double-check was always instituted as a fail-safe mechanism. These radar plots would then be passed by telephone to Fighter Command's Group and Sector operations rooms. Eileen Younghusband's first post in the RAF was in the filter room as a plotter, she described the training for this role:

> Reporting next morning to the training room for Filter Plotters I found there would be 10 of us undergoing training there, all young women between 19 and 24 years of age. The room was large, almost completely taken over by an oddly shaped table. Looking at it more closely I could see that it followed the shape of the coastline from the north of Norfolk to the Isle of Wight. As well as part of the inland area behind the coast it extended over the English Channel and part of the North Sea and continued over the coast of Holland, Belgium and France. The table was divided into large squares, each bearing two capital letters.

Together with her fellow students, Younghusband was reminded by their instructor, Squadron Leader Mann, that the work they would be doing was of critical importance for the defence of Britain, so they had to be quick and accurate at all times:

> He [Mann] told us that the whole of Britain, the sea and countries surrounding it were mapped in this same way, in squares identified with two letters, starting with AA to AB and moving through the alphabet. Each place where we were seated was connected to a different Chain Home RDF station. All positions plotted on the table would be referred to by two letters and four figures, for example Victor Willie 5-3.7-4. To find the position we would measure each square as in decimals, east to west and north to south, so the number would signify 5.3 across and 7.4 down. He gave us a list to learn of the RAF code names for each letter Apple, Beer, Charlie, Dog and so on. These designations were used in the RAF throughout the war. We were told we had to learn these names at once as we would use them all the time. It was the Americans who introduced the code names now used such as Alpha, Foxtrot, Tango. But I use the original names to this day since they had become part of me from that first day of training.
>
> We were given a box of counters. Each station was allocated a different colour. Painted on the map table, there were a series of arcs radiating from each station. These were in the station's colour and were 10 miles apart. I found that my position was connected to Rye on the south coast, and green was my colour. I noticed that there were several different shapes amongst the counters. This was our next lesson. Circles were used to show the position, triangles the estimated number of aircraft, and squares the estimated height. In addition, there were rectangles marked IFF short for Identification Friend or Foe; a friendly aircraft: and others BIF, a Mayday code giving warning that the aircraft was in distress.
>
> Putting on our headsets and plugging in the lead, we made contact with our mock station. For a while we were told just to listen. A man's voice announced: 'New track, Victor Willie 9-1 4-3, 15 plus at 20, showing IFF.' At first it made no sense, but after listening for a few minutes I was able to understand the instructions. Squadron Leader Mann emphasised that we must be accurate and fast. There was no time for misunderstandings. For this reason, all those chosen as either plotters or tellers had to speak clearly with no regional accent.
>
> A WAAF sergeant sitting at one of the stations demonstrated how to display the plots but first she pointed out they each bore a number from one to five. This number would indicate the time the plot was put down. The counter used had to relate to the period indicated by the Sector Clock on the wall. After a certain period out-of-time plots had to be removed to avoid confusion. It was explained that the Filterer Officer, when correcting the position of a raid, needed to collate information from several stations and the information from all sources must be equally up-to-date. It was getting more and more complicated. Would I ever learn all these procedures?[10]

All Fighter Command Group's areas were divided into a series of Sectors. No. 11 Group for instance, had Sectors at Middle Wallop, Northolt, Tangmere, Kenley, Biggin Hill, Hornchurch and North Weald with the Group Headquarters at Uxbridge. This included an operations room, housed in a bunker nearly 100 feet below ground. In contrast, most Sector operations rooms were not even hardened, a dangerous oversight given that they were frequently sited in the middle of RAF airfields and therefore highly vulnerable to enemy air attack. Fighter Command operations rooms were co-located with the Filter Room whch received all the relevant information

---

10   Eileen Younghusband, *One Woman's War* (Cardiff: Candy-Jar Books, 2011), p. 89.

WAAF plotters at work in the underground bunker at HQ 11 Group, Uxbridge (Crown Copyright – Air Historical Branch)

and intelligence. The operations rooms all resembled small theatres, with seats raised in a gallery looking down upon a modest stage. At the centre of the stage was a large table furnished with a gridded map of the area of operations, in 11 Group's case this was part of northern France, the English Channel and Southern England. A dozen airmen and WAAFs, equipped with telephone headsets, would use croupier's rakes to push around the wooden blocks to reported aircraft locations. On each block coloured counters were placed that denoted the number of aircraft in the formation, its altitude and an identifying track number, the latter being preceded by an 'X' to denote it as unidentified and an 'H' to denote it as hostile.[11] The Operations room also contained a weather board with the latest meteorological information. This would be used to guide Fighter Command's operations of the day and give some prediction as to the likelihood of German attack, though of course a German interpretation of the weather might be different to that of the British.

The WAAFs and airmen updated the 'tote' board, which showed the current state of the fighter squadrons within the Group. On the tote board each squadron was given its own panel and underneath, a statement of its availability for action. Terms included 'released' (not available for action), 'available' (airborne in 20 minutes), 'standby' (pilots in cockpits – airborne in 2 minutes), 'airborne and moving to ordered position', 'in ordered position', 'enemy sighted', 'ordered to land', or 'landed and refuelling'. The four sections of a squadron each had their own coloured bulb (red, yellow, green and blue) and this allowed the controllers to change the state of sections within a squadron as required. Only when the enemy was sighted were all four red bulbs turned on.[12]

11   Alfred Price, *The Hardest Day*, p. 53.
12   James Holland, *The Battle of Britain* (London: Bantam Press, 2010), p. 350.

Above the stage, in a sound-proofed gallery, sat the duty fighter controller, his assistant controller and two deputy controllers. On either side of these controllers were two further officers: Ops A – who was in touch with Fighter Command and Ops B who was in touch with the squadrons directly and would call on the squadrons to scramble as and when required.

The fighter controller's role at Group HQ was to scramble the fighter squadrons and change the readiness state of other squadrons – as his assessment of the German raid developed. In a sense he was positioning the chess pieces on the board in anticipation of the enemy's future moves, this required sound judgement as well as decisiveness for he had little time in which to consider the issue. To illustrate the pressure, a well-drilled radar station in Kent could give 20 minutes of warning that an attack was likely, sites further west slightly less, there would also need to be four minutes for the filtering process to work and get the information into the controller's hands. In that period, a German formation could have covered three-quarters of the distance from Calais to Dover. It took about 13 minutes for a Spitfire squadron to climb to 20,000 feet and 16 minutes for a Hurricane squadron, the Group controller therefore had to make up his mind quickly. If he was too slow the aircraft would not have the advantage of height, or be in a good position to attack the German formation, but if he scrambled his aircraft to an emerging but ill-defined threat, then there was a risk that his aircraft could be drawn off by an enemy feint and they would be low on fuel when an actual attack materialised. Unsurprisingly, most controllers erred on the side of caution, choosing to commit aircraft in small numbers to emerging threats, though this resulted in British aircraft being outnumbered on many occasions. The controller's problems were also often exacerbated by inaccurate height estimation, this might mean that the intercepting fighters would be too low and forced to attack from a disadvantageous position. If the controller erred on the side of caution, by adding an extra 1,000 feet to the patrol position for instance, they could miss the German formation altogether as it might be hidden by an intervening layer of cloud.[13]

Once airborne the control of the fighters would pass from the Group fighter controller to Sector Control. The Sector Control operations rooms were smaller, but otherwise laid out in exactly the same way as at Group. It was Sector Control's responsibility to communicate with the aircraft once airborne and vector them into a good position, typically attacking out of the sun and with the advantage of height.

As well as an effective early warning and command and control system, Fighter Command also depended upon good squadrons equipped with modern, high quality fighters. Fortunately, there had been exciting developments in the design of a new generation of high-performance fighters immediately prior to the war. In 1935, the same year as Watson-Watt's radar experiments were proving successful, the first flight of Sidney Camm's new Hurricane fighter took place. This was followed, in March 1936, by that of the Spitfire. Both aircraft marked a step change in speed, climbing ability and firepower and were probably two of the world's most effective fighters at the time. The feasibility of intercepting and destroying German bombers was beginning to look more likely and the views expressed by Inskip in 1937, made much more sense.

Fighter Command primarily fought the Battle of Britain with its Spitfires and Hurricanes and the two months grace, granted between Dunkirk (26 May to 4 June 1940) and the opening of the Battle in mid August, was critical in building up the numbers of these aircraft. On 4 June 1940 Dowding had just 446 operationally serviceable aircraft, of which 331 were Hurricanes and Spitfires. On 11 August, that number had risen to 704 operationally serviceable aircraft, of which 620 were either Hurricanes or Spitfires. Behind this there was an even stronger backing of reserves. On 4 June, there had been 36 Hurricane and Spitfires immediately available for issue to

---

13   Basil Collier, *Defence of The United Kingdom* (London: HMSO, 1957), p. 171.

A flight of Hurricane I fighters flown by pilots of 85 Squadron, RAF Church Fenton. Leading the formation is Squadron Leader Peter Townsend. Image taken 5 October 1940. (Crown Copyright – Air Historical Branch)

the squadrons from the Aircraft Storage Units, by 11 August that number had risen to 289.[14] A list of the Fighter Command squadrons and their locations on 8 August 1940 is enclosed at Annex F.

Dowding could also take comfort in the expanding industrial production that would ensure his fighter reserves kept growing, this was partly as a result of setting up the Ministry of Aircraft Production, under Lord Beaverbrook in May 1940. Beaverbrook was a controversial figure, but he nevertheless successfully galvanized British fighter production, particularly at the Castle Bromwich plant run by Lord Nuffield. The table below shows a steady improvement in both overall numbers of aircraft, as well as fighters produced, this was to prove a critical factor in both the Battle and the overall war.

Month	Planned Production of all types by the Harrogate programme of January 1940	Actual Production of all types	Planned Production of fighters by the Harrogate Programme	Actual fighter production
February 1940	1,001	719	171	141
March 1940	1,137	860	203	177
April 1940	1,256	1,081	231	256
May 1940	1,244	1,279	261	325
June 1940	1,320	1,591	292	446
July 1940	1,481	1,665	329	496
August 1940	1,310	1,601	282	476

Figure 4 Aircraft Production Figures February to August 1940.[15]

14   Denis Richards, *Royal Air Force 1939-45 – Volume I*, p. 156.
15   Denis Richards, *Royal Air Force 1939-45 – Volume I*, p. 152.

Two Spitfires of 19 Squadron at Fowlmere, Cambridgeshire, in September 1940.
(Crown Copyright – Air Historical Branch)

Of the fighters being produced, the Hurricane was neither as modern or revolutionary as the Spitfire; the lines of the older Hawker Fury biplane from which it had been developed were easily visible. However, its more traditional design of tubular metal and fabric had led to an easier production and introduction to service, which partly accounts for its greater numbers within Fighter Command. The Hurricane's simplicity of design is best reflected in the 170,000 man-hours of design, development and construction it took to get the Hurricane ready for operational service, significantly less than the 300,000 man-hours for the Spitfire.[16]

Although the Hurricane had a slower speed and climb rate, it was regarded as an easier aircraft to fly. This was a particular virtue given the number of novice pilots arriving at RAF squadrons in the summer of 1940. Its crude design also made it more robust and resilient, for instance if a Hurricane was damaged by German cannon fire often all that was required for repair was to stick on a new bit of fabric and seal it up with some 'dope'. In contrast, repairing any damaged metal panel on a Spitfire was much more complicated and usually required a new sheet to be beaten and riveted in. The Hurricane's other great virtue was as a gun platform, its long sloping nose gave the pilot a superb view and its eight guns were set in a compact block of four in each of its thick wings, nice and close to the fuselage and easier to harmonise. This meant that when it fired its machine guns, the solid Hurricane remained steady. In contrast the Spitfire's guns were spread along its thin wings, making the recoil effect and wing bending more pronounced.[17] Despite these strong points, even the most fervent defenders of the Hurricane would probably admit that by the summer of

---

16   Leo McKinstry, *Hurricane* (London: Murray, 2010), p. 152.
17   Leo McKinstry, *Hurricane*, p. 153.

1940 it had reached the peak of its operational development. This did not mean it would disappear completely after the Battle of Britain. Indeed, it would continue to serve in many operational theatres throughout the war, particularly the Mediterranean and Far East.

The Spitfire had many virtues compared to the Hurricane, including a better rate of climb, greater responsive agility in the air and above all speed – undoubtedly one of the most important comparative factors between any fighter aircraft. The Spitfire and Hurricane were both fitted with the same Rolls-Royce Merlin engine, but the design of the Spitfire's wings and stressed metal skin gave it a top speed of 353 mph at 18,500 feet, an extra 30-40 mph when compared to the Hurricane.[18] For those who piloted it, the Spitfire was initially a difficult aircraft to fly, land and even taxi, but its performance in the air swiftly captivated all who flew it. Hugh Dundas, nick-named 'Cocky' because of his bright red hair, served throughout the war, becoming the youngest Group Captain in 1944 at the age of just 24. He made his first flight in a Spitfire on 13 March 1940:

> It is certainly true that there never was a plane so loved by pilots, combining as it did sensitive yet docile handling characteristics with deadly qualities as a fighting machine. Lovely to look at, delightful to fly, the Spitfire became the pride and joy of thousands of young men from practically every country in what, then, constituted the free world. Americans raved about her and wanted to have her; Poles were seduced by her; men from the old Dominions crossed the world and the oceans to be with her; the Free French undoubtedly wrote love songs about her. And the Germans were envious of her.
>
> Little did I know as I taxied in from that first Spitfire flight that I would not taxi in from my last until late in 1949. We went through the war together, with only a year's separation when, in 1942, I temporarily – and not very happily flirted with the Typhoon … In all those years no misfortune which came our way was ever the fault of the Spitfire … I do not know exactly how many hundreds of hours I spent in the Spitfire's cockpit, over sea, desert and mountains, in storm and sunshine, in conditions of great heat and great cold, by day and by night, on the deadly business of war and in the pursuit of pleasure. I do know that the Spitfire never let me down and that on the occasions when we got into trouble together the fault was invariably mine.[19]

A pilot's first flight in the Spitfire was always a memorable occasion, the Spitfire offering a marked change in performance to the previous types of aircraft a trainee might have flown. There were no two-seat dual instruction Spitfires at that early stage of the war and student pilots, like Sergeant Jimmy Corbin, were simply left to take the aircraft up alone after the controls had been explained to them by an instructor:

> I fastened the Sutton harness, shut the side flap to the cockpit and plugged in my radio transmitter (R/T) lead. The petrol cocks were already in the 'on' position, but it needed a few strokes on the primer knob to prime the Merlin engine. One of the ground staff then opened the flap on the side of the Spit's nose and plugged in the end of the mobile starter cable. He pressed the button on the battery top and held up his thumb. I switched on and pressed the starter button, and the airscrew began to turn the propeller slowly. There was a slight cough, a cloud of blue smoke and the Merlin engine roared into life …

---

18   Annex J provides full details of the major operational Aircraft of the Royal Air Force and Fleet Air Arm 1939-45.

19   Hugh Dundas, *Flying Start* (New York: St Martin's Press, 1989), p. 19.

The fitter unplugged the battery, closed the flap on the side of the engine and gave me another 'thumbs up', signalling that I was ready for the off. He then removed the chocks wedged in front of my wheels. The propeller began to turn. This was it, my first flight in a Spitfire Mk 1.

I moved off along the airfield. I kicked the rudder bar from side to side so I could zig-zag down the field and get a better view of what was ahead of me. The craft trundled the 200 yards or so to takeoff point. There I paused and went through the cockpit drill – RAFTS, as it was known.

The 'R' referred to the retractable undercarriage. Yes, the green light was on and the wing pegs were showing. I noticed that part of one of them had been broken off where someone had used it as a convenient hand hold for getting on the wing. Next was 'A' which meant that I had to make sure the airscrew was in fine pitch for take-off. Those pilots who left it in coarse pitch paid dearly with their lives, because in coarse pitch, the aircraft could not gather enough speed for take-off. 'F' meant I had to make sure the flaps were up, and wing indicators were flush. 'T' was trim. That was just a little behind the mid-point on the cockpit wheel and 'S' was the 'Sperry gyro' in the instrument panel which was caged or locked so that it did not spin unnecessarily.

I scanned the skyways in all directions to make sure there was no other aircraft in sight. No, it was all clear. I turned the Spit into the wind and opened the throttle as far as it would go. A great roar followed. The aircraft churned across the ground, bumping along its uneven surface, and gathering speed all the time. I pushed the stick forward, taking care not to let it go too far forward otherwise the propeller could just dig into the ground. I checked my speed and as the needle glanced 65 mph the aircraft lifted from the ground and began to climb with ease.[20]

A full description of the Spitfire cockpit check for take-off and landing is enclosed at Annex N. The Spitfire may have been an ungainly machine taxiing on the ground, but once in the air it was in its true element. The only awkwardness for the novice pilot was the requirement to pump the undercarriage up with his right hand, whilst trying to hold the control column steady with the left. The coordination and effort required to do this was tricky and inexperienced pilots were usually easy to identify as their Spitfire's 'porpoised' through the air immediately after take-off. Wilfred Duncan Smith[21] remembered the superb handling of the Spitfire in the air:

Climbing into the blue I sensed the tremendous power, the lightness of control. At 19,000 ft I levelled out and practised medium and steep turns, the Spitfire responding to the lightest touch. The forward visibility now excellent, the blind spot behind the tail helped by a rear-view mirror mounted on top of the windscreen. Later, I dived to 5,000 ft, noticing how quickly the speed built up while the ailerons became progressively stiffer the faster I dived.

I chanced some aerobatics and found the aircraft's response sweet and positive. One of the features of the Spitfire I discovered was how beautifully she behaved at low speeds and at high 'g' close to the stall. With full power in a steep turn and at slow speeds she would judder and shake, rocking to and fro, but so long as she was handled correctly she would not let go and spin – surely a unique feature for a high performance aeroplane. I had to find this out for myself: no one particularly pointed it out but with continuous practise dog-fighting I came to explore every part of her handling characteristics, till eventually flying her became second

---

20   Jimmy Corbin, *Last of the Ten Fighter Boys* (Stroud: History Press, 2010), pp. 71-2.
21   Father of the British Conservative politician Ian Duncan-Smith.

 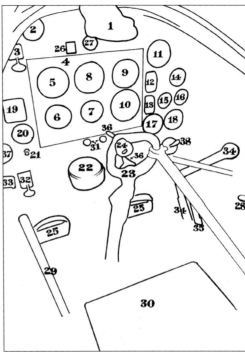

SPITFIRE INSTRUMENT PANEL KEY AND ANNOTATION

1   Platform for gun-sight
2   Flap position indicator
3   Flap Lever
4   Instrument Flying Panel
5   Air-speed indicator
6   Altimeter
7   Direction indicator
8   Artificial Horizon
9   Rate of climb indicator
10 Turning indicator
11 Revolution counter
12 Oil and fuel pressure gauge
13 As above
14 Engine boost gauge
15 Oil and radiator temperature gauges
16 As above
17 Fuel gauges
18 As above
19 Chassis position indicator
20 Flying position indicator

21 Lights switch
22 Compass
23 Control Column
24 Gun Button
25 Foot stirrups on rudder bar
26 Reflector sight light switch
27 Dimming switch for reflector sight
28 Key for downward recognition lamp
29 Radiator flap control
30 Pilots seat
31 Floodlight switches
32 Lever for lowering and raising the landing light
33 Throttle
34 Pump for operating undercarriage
35 Selector lever for undercarriage (to be placed in raise or lower position before 34 is operated
36 Pneumatic brake lever
37 Air pressure control for pneumatic system (guns and brake)
38 Fuel cock

Cockpit and layout of Spitfire Mk 1.

nature. I was to bless these qualities when it came to the real thing: they got me out of trouble more times than I care to remember.

Returning to land I pushed the airscrew into fine pitch, slid back the hood, lowered wheels, turned cross-wind and selected 'flaps down' straightening out for the final approach and landing. I came in rather fast, the Spitfire 'floated' on for a bit before touching down on the main wheels. Holding the stick right back brought the tail down and as I lost speed turning towards dispersal, selected 'flaps up'. The Spitfire had a natural tendency to 'float' because of her clean lines with minimum drag.[22]

Apart from Hurricanes and Spitfires, there were a few other aircraft employed by Fighter Command in 1940, though these were small in number and played only a minor role in the Battle. Perhaps most notorious was the Boulton Paul Defiant, this aircraft had no forward-facing guns at all, and was instead armed with a mid-upper rearward facing turret of four .303 machine guns. The design was based on the flawed premise that because the enemy bombers would be flying from Germany, they could not be escorted by short-range single engine fighters, therefore all the Defiants would have to do was simply fly through the massed German bomber formations firing at the aircraft as they passed. However, the German occupation of Belgium, France and the Netherlands in 1940 altered the battlefield geography and meant the *Luftwaffe* short-range fighters were now able to escort bombers. Once the German fighter pilots learnt not to approach the Defiant from its dangerous rear, the aircraft became a lethal liability. The Defiants were withdrawn from the Battle on 19 July, after the Biggin Hill based 141 Squadron lost six out of nine aircraft in a single engagement with Me 109s. The surviving Defiants briefly converted to night-fighter duties, before being used in 515 Squadron as an early Electronic Counter Measure (ECM) aircraft to jam German radar. They were then phased out altogether from operational service.

Dowding also had a small number of twin-engined Bristol Blenheim fighter squadrons. However, The Blenheim Mk 1 was really designed for use as a ground attack aircraft and Dowding recognised that these aircraft lacked the agility or speed to combat German fighter aircraft. For that reason, they too did not play a significant role in the battle. Dowding relied instead on the Hurricane and Spitfire, so how did these two aircraft compare to the German aircraft, particularly the *Luftwaffe*'s short-range fighters that from June 1940 would appear over the United Kingdom?

At the outset of the war the twin-engined Messerschmitt Me 110 was the most feared of the German fighters. Known as the *Zerstorer* or Destroyer, it was one of Reichsmarschall Hermann Goering's favoured machines and certainly looked impressive on paper, where its maximum speed of 350 mph at 21,500 feet equalled the Spitfire's performance and surpassed that of the Hurricane. The Me 110 was also armed with four 20mm cannon in its nose, an impressive amount of firepower in comparison to the eight .303-inch machine guns which the British fighters possessed at the time. However, the Me 110's reputation was illusory. This became evident on 29 March 1940 when three Hurricanes of No. 1 Squadron brought down three Me 110s over Metz without loss. The pilots subsequent report highlighted that: 'As a result of the combat it may be stated that the Me 110, although very fast and manoeuvrable for a twin-engined aircraft can easily be outmanoeuvred by a Hurricane.' It was also reported by the pilots that 'it appeared that the rear gunner was incapable of returning fire while [the] Me 110 was in combat because of steep turns 'blacking him out' or making him too uncomfortable to take proper aim'. These liabilities were to be highlighted even more dramatically during the Battle of Britain and the Me 110 would play an increasingly marginal part in the battle.[23]

---

22   Wilfred Duncan Smith, *Spitfire into Battle* (London: John Murray, 2002), pp. 22-3.
23   Patrick Bishop, *Fighter Boys* (London: Harper, 2004), p. 138.

German Messerschmitt Me 109 in France 1940. (Bundesarchiv, Germany)

It was the Messerschmitt Me 109 which was the main threat and adversary for the RAF fighters. This was a superbly-designed machine, adopting a simple technical approach that attempted to wrap the lightest airframe imaginable around one of the world's most powerful engines. The design incorporated exceptionally thin wings to achieve a superior performance when flying fast, though as these were inefficient at slower speeds a system of slots in the leading edges were installed to obtain the required lift for take-offs and landings. The fragility of the Me 109's thin wings necessitated the undercarriage being supported by the fuselage which led to a narrow and unstable wheelbase. This was a notorious hazard for inexperienced pilots when landing on rough ground and caused frequent accidents. The aircraft's top speed of 357 mph meant it was slightly faster than the Spitfire and 30 mph faster than the Hurricane. For firepower the Me 109 E carried two machine guns in its nose and two 20mm cannon, one in each wing.[24] The advantage of cannon as opposed to machine guns was to be a hotly debated subject in RAF messes over the summer of 1940, though most would agree that the destructive power of exploding cannon shells was worth the extra weight of both the larger guns and heavier rounds. The major disadvantage of the Me 109 that would be revealed in the Battle was its range, designed as a short-range intercept fighter the aircraft struggled to escort the bombers across the Channel to London and still have sufficient time to engage in prolonged combat. Finally, the Me 109 had a superior rearward view when compared to the Hurricane.[25]

Impressive though the Me 109 was, the Spitfire and Hurricane were both more manoeuvrable than the Me 109 and able to out-turn it. The RAF had also done their best to increase their aircraft's performance, seizing whatever advantages presented themselves. This included aviation fuel, the British having managed to obtain 100-octane fuel from the Dutch East Indies, a

---

24   Annex K gives details of the major operational Aircraft of the German Air Force 1939-45. Annex L details major Italian aircraft.

25   Patrick Bishop, *Fighter Boys* (London: Harper, 2004), p. 143.

significantly higher grade to the 87-Octane fuel they had used previously, and the Germans were still stuck with. The 100-octane fuel gave British engines added performance, both in climbing to altitude, as well as overall speed.[26] In addition, immediately prior to the Battle, both the Spitfires and Hurricanes were fitted with Variable Pitch propellers which would make them more effective at altitude. The RAF contract for this work was given to de Havilland on 22 June 1940, with the instructions to convert all Merlin-powered fighters as soon as possible. Even today de Havilland's response strikes one as astonishingly fast and effective. Starting on 25 July de Havilland engineers were simultaneously sent to 12 stations. At each location they were given a picked team of RAF fitters, who observed the de Havilland engineer convert the first aircraft, the RAF fitters then converted the second aircraft with his help and the third one under his supervision. If all was working well the engineer would then leave for the next squadron, or station, leaving the trained team of RAF fitters to finish converting the remaining aircraft in the squadron. A total of 1,051 Spitfires and Hurricanes were converted by 15 August, just three weeks later. A remarkable achievement given that each conversion added an estimated 7,000 ft to a fighter's service ceiling, increased its manoeuvrability at height and improved its takeoff and landing performance.[27]

Other changes were also afoot. As a result of combat experience in France the Hurricanes and Spitfires had the underside of their wings painted a duck-egg blue, making it harder to detect than the previous practice of having one wing black and the other white. Early lessons in France had also demonstrated the necessity of armour plate immediately behind the pilot. Whilst front line fighter pilots unsurprisingly saw the value of such an installation, convincing the Air Ministry was a little more difficult. It took an unorthodox approach by the CO of 1 Squadron, Squadron Leader Bull Halahan, to grab the Air Staff's attention, as Paul Richey, one of his pilots, relates:

> At this time the only armour our fighter aircraft carried was in the form of a thickish cowling over the front petrol tank and a bullet-proof windscreen. The Battles however, [Fairey Battle – a light bomber], had thick armour-plating behind the pilot ... we decided that we should have back armour, too, and we asked for it. The Hawker Aircraft Company, makers of the Hurricane, was eventually consulted, and our request was refused by higher authority because it was decided that back-armour would disturb the Hurricane's centre of gravity and lead to flying troubles.
>
> The Bull [Squadron Leader Halahan] decided to take action on his own. He found a 'written-off' Battle on one of our local bomber airfields and asked for the back armour out of it. We then fitted the back-armour into a Hurricane and carried out our own flying tests with it. They were very satisfactory. The Bull then told the Air Ministry what he had done and sent Hilly Brown over to the Royal Aircraft Establishment at Farnborough to demonstrate the armoured Hurricane to the experts. Hilly put up a show of aerobatics and manoeuvres that included everything in the book and a bit more, the experts were convinced, and back armour was henceforth fitted as standard equipment to RAF fighter aircraft.[28]

The British victory in the Battle of Britain must rank as a pivotal turning point in the course of the war. It is not however the purpose of this book to give either a chronology or analysis of this battle, but instead show how it was fought by Fighter Command and how a defensive air superiority campaign was won by the RAF over its own country. The next chapter will describe Fighter Command operations around the framework of a sortie.

---

26   Leo McKinstry, *Hurricane*, p. 87.
27   Derek Wood, and Derek Dempster, *The Narrow Margin*, p. 149.
28   Paul Richey, *Fighter Pilot* (London: Arrow, 1955), p. 39.

4
'Seek and Destroy'[1]
A Battle of Britain Fighter Command Mission

A typical day at a southern RAF airfield during the Battle of Britain would begin with the aircrew being woken before dawn and washing and shaving in their mess accommodation. This included the sergeants' mess as well as the officers' mess, as one third of the pilots at the Battle of Britain were SNCOs. A few pilots might not have had to shave at all given that the average age of an RAF pilot in 1940 was only 20, with many as young as 18. The pilots were then driven out to a small hut normally at the edge of the airfield known as 'dispersal', so-called because it was around this building that the aircraft were parked, usually well apart from each other and in some cases in revetments, thus mitigating the damage of an enemy air attack. At dispersal they might eat a rudimentary breakfast, before checking the flight board to determine the order of battle for the day, this would show which section they would be flying in and who they were paired with as either 'No.2', or as a leader. Picking up their parachute and flying helmet, there would then be a quick walk to their individual aircraft to check the ground crew were preparing the aircraft for readiness. Geoffrey Wellum was a Spitfire pilot on 92 Squadron and describes the actions at dispersal early in the morning:

> One after the other, Spitfires are starting up. The fitters warm up their engines. Twelve Merlins all 1,200 revs or thereabouts. The power of the moment is awe inspiring. The still morning air reverberates with the sound of harnessed energy. Slipstreams flatten the grass behind the quivering aircraft. In its way it is exciting, wonderful and not without a certain beauty. It is also tragic; which of us is going to be killed this day?
>
> … Dispersal pen and my Spitfire. I pause and look at her. A long shapely nose, not exactly arrogant but, nevertheless daring anyone to take a swing at it. Lines beautifully proportioned, the aircraft sitting there, engine turning easily and smoothly with subdued power. The slipstream blows the moisture over the top of the wings in thin streamlets. Flashes of blue flame from the exhausts are easily seen in the half-light, an occasional backfire and the whole aeroplane trembling like a thoroughbred at the start of the Derby.
>
> The engine note increases as my fitter opens up the Merlin to zero boost while the rigger stands with his hand on the wingtip, watching expectantly. I think to myself, 'Don't open her up any more, you twit, or the tail will lift and the whole shooting match will end up on its nose.' The engine note changes fractionally as the magnetos are tested. The fitter, intent on his instruments, red cockpit lights reflecting on his face. Sounds OK, no problem there

---

1 41 Squadron was a Spitfire-equipped squadron that provided covering operations over Dunkirk, before alternating between Yorkshire and the South East of England during the Battle of Britain. On 8 August 1940 it was based at RAF Hornchurch.

Pilots and groundcrew of 601 (County of London) Squadron pictured at Exeter in November 1940. A spitfire is prepared for its next sortie (Crown Copyright – Air Historical Branch)

at all. Throttle back, mag check again at 1,500 revs by the sound of it and then throttle right closed, engine idling, smoke from exhausts, cutout pulled and the engine splutters to a stop. Peace again.

Bevington, the fitter, looks from the cockpit and gives me the thumbs up. He levers himself out on the wing and jumps to the ground. I walk forward and hang my parachute on the port wing for a quick getaway; you can easily put it on while the engine is being started, saves a lot of time.

Now to the cockpit. Up on the wing and step in. I hang my helmet on the stick and plug in the R/T lead and oxygen tube. At the same time, I check the bottle contents: full. Fuel? Press the fuel gauge button, reads full also. Now brake pressure. OK, that's fine. Trim? Let's adjust it now and then it's done with. Full rudder bias to help with the swing on take-off, elevators one degree nose heavy, that's good. Airscrew, full fine pitch. That's about it, then, ready to scramble when the time comes. Bound to come sometime. It'll be a miracle if we get through to midday without one.[2]

As well as exchanging pleasantries with the ground crew, the pilot might also help them wipe the dew from his canopy, to ensure un-restricted visibility, before returning to the dispersal hut to join the other waiting aircrew. John Bisdee was a junior officer flying Spitfires in 609 Squadron and described the three states of standby:

---

2   Geoffrey Wellum, *First Light* (London: Penguin, 2003), pp. 137-9.

You might be on readiness in which case it was a matter of pride that you were in the air in about two and a half minutes at the most from the call. The next stage was 15 minutes down from readiness, and thirdly there would be '30 minutes available', which gave you a chance probably to dash up to the mess and have lunch or something like that. But then the tannoy in the mess would say '609 Squadron to immediate readiness' and one would have to drop one's knife and fork and dash down to dispersal. There was a constant tension; one never knew when the tannoy was going to go.[3]

Hubert Raymond Allen (known to all as 'Dizzy Allen') flew Spitfires on 66 Squadron and described the set up at Gravesend, a satellite airfield in Biggin Hill's sector:

Gravesend was immensely to our liking. It was a pre-war airport, not a regular fighter station, and it lacked all the pretence that goes with the latter. Our pilots' dispersal room was the old clubhouse, furnished with not uncomfortable chairs and integral to its design was a bar (we didn't need Dutch courage, but it was useful to have Brandy available if one landed with a bullet hole in a limb). Behind the room were the kitchens and so on, and in the room was a microphone intended to relay the scramble order around the airfield. We immediately got hold of a gramophone and our favourite records and installed them within easy reach of the microphone. From dawn to dusk our kind of music sighed round the airport, breaking our neighbour's eardrums – assuming they hadn't been already broken by the roar of the Merlins being run up, or on take-off; but we also used the microphone for the scramble order, to allow the mechanics time to get the engines started ahead of our sprint to the Spitfires.

The 'hot-line' was merely a field-telephone. To contact the controller our telephone orderly would turn a handle, and a bell would ring at the Sector Operations Room at Biggin Hill, under whose aegis we lay. How he in return made our telephone ring, I don't know, and I don't care. I hated controllers; they were the people who gave us the scramble order. They gave such orders all too frequently for my liking. Our ground crews had their offices and rest rooms in wooden sheds nearby. We all had our billets not far from the Spitfires, and the airmen's dining rooms etc., were all nice and handy. It was a cosy set up and we liked being there.[4]

Pilots recalled that waiting around for the order to scramble was often the most nerve-wracking period. For long, summer days half an ear was permanently cocked towards the telephone and nerves set on edge whenever it rang, sometimes irritatingly for just a minor administrative matter, on other occasions to scramble the aircraft into the sky. More than one former-pilot claimed they detested the sound of a ringing telephone for the rest of their lives. New Zealander Bob Spurdle was a young Spitfire pilot, who joined 74 Squadron in the summer of 1940. Based at Biggin Hill, he fought in the latter stages of the Battle of Britain and recalled the frequent scrambles:

October 22nd, Sortie 37. 1.00 hour duration:

Sure enough, the warning wailed as we tore back to dispersal after a hasty lunch. George put his foot down and the brake (station-wagon) howled round the perimeter track. We could see the white fog-trailers weaving fantastic clouds far above us. I felt dead inside; it was our third scramble of the day. How long would this keep up? How long could it?

3   Matthew Parker, *The Battle of Britain* (London: Headline, 2000), p. 145.
4   Dizzy Allen, *Fighter Squadron* (London: Granada, 1982), p. 82.

19 Squadron Spitfire Ia X4474/QV-I departing Fowlmere, Cambridgeshire, for a sortie on 21 September 1940. The pilot is Sergeant B.J. Jennings. (Crown Copyright – Air Historical Branch)

We clattered out before the Humber had rolled to a stop and ran to our lockers. Yellow Mae Wests on; the tapes were difficult to tie with nervous fumbling hands. Helmets and gloves snatched up. No one spoke we knew we'd be on the next patrol.

The board was being filled in. Good show; I was No 2 to the CO and Wally Churches was No 2 to Mungo in Blue Section. The telephone rang; the operator repeated aloud: 'Maidstone 20,000.' We didn't wait for more, but shot out of the door, the scramble buzzer hideous in its haste and urgency. The brake was rolling slowly down the track and we flung ourselves aboard. One of the new sergeants gave an excited laugh, but heaven only knows what there was to laugh about. Wally dropped off and ran to his kite – then Bill Armstrong, Roger and I. The car kept rolling, the pilots leaping for their machines. I was feeling dreadful; each scramble seemed that it would be my last and I was honestly afraid. Sergeant Soars' parachute was loose, the straps fell off my shoulders, but the Sutton harness was good and tight and held them up.

I was using his 'R', too, a plane harsh but fast. Soon it was – 'Chocks away, crew away.' The green turf rolled under smoothly and I taxied for the runway. I switched on the radio and its slow warming-up drone covered the engine's rumble.

Sailor was in position and I rolled up to his starboard. The runway stretched before us. Steve and his No 2 slid to Malan's port and we roared off down the field. 'R' swung a bit, lifted, bounced once and slid into the warm air. Behind and below, 20 feet away, I could see Steve sliding into line astern. I half-laughed; as if a flyer like Steve would chop off my tail … but Sailor was haring along and climbing like a rocket.

Up, up, oxygen on, air-scuttle open-slowly the blue sky turned a deeper shade and at 23,000 feet faint trails of mist formed, thickened, and streamed behind like comet's tails.[5]

---

5   Bob Spurdle, *The Blue Arena* (Manchester: Crecy, 1986), p. 38.

As the controller scrambled the aircraft into the air, he would give pilots the area to be patrolled and the operating height. When hostile aircraft came into that area, he would vector the fighters to a position from which to attack, by giving them a bearing to intercept. The controller would alter that vector to match any enemy change of direction. This process had been devised in 1936 through a series of trials at Biggin Hill, which solved the interception problem with basic trigonometry. The process treated the anticipated path of the enemy formation and the RAF fighter's interception course as two sides of an isosceles triangle, whose base was a straight line drawn between their respective positions at any given moment. If the fighters flew a course whose angle to this base matched that of the enemy's track, then an interception would follow at the triangle's apex. If the fighters went too fast, the controller could instruct them to circle and if the enemy altered course he could produce another isosceles triangle from which to give the fighters a new intercept course.[6] The system was simple and practical and at least one answer to the familiar schoolboy's question: 'What possible use is trigonometry?' One of the most famous Sector Controllers during the Battle of Britain was Group Captain Alfred 'Woody' Woodhall, who describes his role in a little more detail:

> As I saw it, my job as Sector Controller was to vector the Fighter Leader on a course and to a height which would place him above and up sun of the enemy and then to keep him informed of the enemy's positions, course, speed as accurately as possible from the information we had on the operations table. As soon as our Fighter Leader sighted the enemy it was over to him.
>
> In those early days, the radar information was not very accurate, particularly as regards height and numbers of aircraft. There was also a time lag of several minutes before the information reached the Sector Operations room.
>
> The Sector Controller therefore had to use intelligent guesswork in order to direct his fighters on an intercepting course and to position them up sun and above the enemy.[7]

Woodhall was much respected as a controller, both during the Battle of Britain and later on in Malta. It was perhaps the manner in which he discharged his duties that made him so revered, Spitfire pilot James 'Johnnie' Johnson recalled Woodhall fondly:

> Over the radio Woodhall's deep resonant voice seemed to fill our earphones with confidence and assurance … it was as if the man was in the air with you, not issuing orders but giving encouragement and advice and always watching the precious minutes, and the headwind which would delay our withdrawal. And the low cloud creeping up from the West which might cover Tangmere when we returned, tired and short of petrol. Then he was always on the ground to meet us after the big shows, to compare notes with Bader and other leaders. Always he had time for a cheerful word with the novices.[8]

Not all controllers inspired such respect and Johnson reserved some more damning judgements for poorer examples:

> We were often irritated by one pompous individual (not at Tangmere) who directed our activities with flamboyant showmanship. They were his interceptions. He had shot down three enemy aircraft during his watch and when we shouted 'tallyho' he dropped back into

---

6   Graham Wallace, *Biggin Hill* (London: Putnam, 1957), p. 93.
7   A.B. Woodhall, *Soldier, Sailor and Airman Too* (London: Grub Street, 2008), p. 137.
8   Johnnie Johnson, *Wing Leader* (London: Chatto and Windus, 1956), pp. 81-2.

Squadron Leader Peter Townsend leads his Squadron – No 85 – in formation on 5 October 1940. After intensive action with 11 Group at the height of the Battle of Britain, the squadron and its Hurricanes were moved to Church Fenton, Yorkshire. (Crown Copyright – Air Historical Branch)

his chair with an exaggerated gesture. All that remained was for the pilot to press the firing button! Over the radio his voice portrayed his personality, and you felt that had the size of cockpit permitted you should be stood to attention to acknowledge his commands.

As the fighters climbed to intercept, they would have formed into squadrons each of which would have generated v-shaped formations of three aircraft, known as 'vics', the centre aircraft being the leader. This might look 'neat', but it was in fact a poor combat formation. The two 'following' aircraft would spend most of their time concentrating on making sure they tucked in neatly with their leader, rather than the more important task of looking out for enemy aircraft. Many aircraft were caught unawares when squadrons flew in this type of formation. By the time the Battle of Britain commenced, it was beginning to dawn on RAF fighter pilots that this manner of pre-war flying was unsuitable for the type of combat they were now engaged in, as Jimmy Corbin relates:

> It is quite ludicrous to think that as we went into battle, uppermost in our minds wasn't the enemy but holding our correct position in the formation so we didn't crash into one of our own. Even then it had begun to dawn on me and others that tight formation flying had no place in the battlefield and should be consigned to air shows.[9]

One method of mitigating the chance of a surprise attack was to have a 'weaver', a single aircraft that flew behind the squadron, slightly higher. Whilst this might give improved warning of an

---

9   Jimmy Corbin, *Last of the Ten Fighter Boys* (Stroud: History Press, 2010), p. 92.

attack to the remainder of the squadron, it left the individual himself in a very vulnerable position. Hugh Dundas hated it:

> The 12 aircraft of a squadron were divided into four sections of three aircraft each. Normally these flew in 'Vic' formation – that is to say one plane on each side of the leader and a little behind him. When going into action this formation would be changed to line astern. The last man in the last section was responsible for 'weaving', swerving from side to side in order to keep a good look out to the rear.
> Having frequently flown in that tail-end position, I knew well the difficulties and hazards involved. If you weaved too much, you got left behind. If you did not weave enough you got picked off. I said that I thought it was a lousy formation and that no variation of it would be any good. For instance, we had been experimenting with the idea of flying in three sections of four aircraft line astern. The last man in each section was still excessively vulnerable. We needed to find something quite different, some way of flying which would cut out all that weaving around and enable everyone to cover everyone else's tail.[10]

The use of 'Vic' formations was linked to another pre-war tactic that was equally unsound: Fighter Area Attacks. These had been developed at a time when the RAF believed that its fighters would be encountering massed formations of unescorted German bombers, therefore attacking in a tightly controlled squadron formation was believed to be the most effective method. A number of variations were developed, all of which were given numbers to differentiate them. For example, Fighter Area Attack No.2 involved an attack towards the rear of the bomber with all squadron aircraft in line astern. New Zealander Alan Deere recalls 54 Squadron learning the futility of these attacks whilst patrolling over Dunkirk:

> The squadron had not been on patrol very long before Max Pearson's voice screeched over the R/T, 'Tallyho, tallyho, enemy aircraft above and ahead.'
> About 3,000 ft above us and clearly silhouetted against a blue sky a large formation of German bombers ploughed westwards towards Dunkirk unmolested and apparently unprotected. 'Sitting Ducks,' I thought.
> 'Hornet squadron, full throttle, climbing to attack,' came the order from 'Prof' who was leading the squadron.
> It seemed an age before we made the extra 3,000 ft in height and even longer before we closed the gap in firing range.
> 'Hornet squadron, No.5 attack, No.5 attack, GO.'
> Simultaneously the sections fanned out into the various echelons necessary for this type of attack and as they did so individual pilots selected a particular bomber target. So far, all very nice and exactly according to the book. But we had reckoned without interference from fighter escort; after all no consideration had been given to it in designing this type of attack and our peacetime training had not envisaged interference from escort fighters. Experience is dearly bought.
> 'Christ, Messerschmitts – BREAK, BREAK.'
> There was no need for a second warning. At the word 'break' and with one accord, the squadron split in all directions, all thoughts of blazing enemy bombers momentarily ousted by the desire to survive. Messerschmitts hurtled through the formation. As I pulled back

10 Hugh Dundas, *Flying Start* (New York: St Martin's Press, 1989), p. 63.

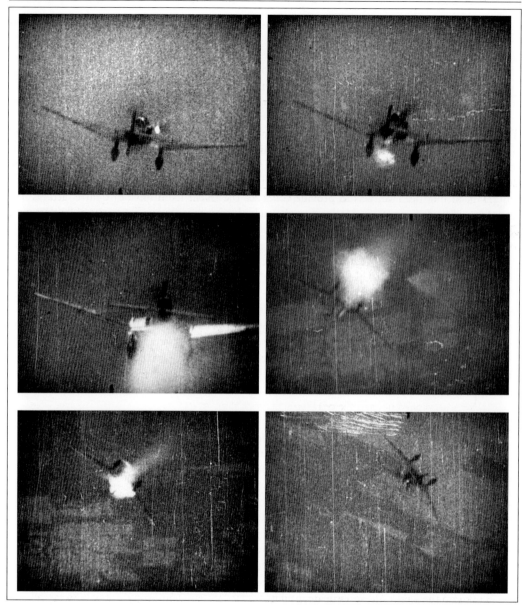

Gun camera footage of a Ju 87 Stuka being shot down by an RAF fighter, 1940. (Crown Copyright – Air Historical Branch)

violently on the stick into a steep turn, one fairly singed my eyebrows as it screamed past my port wing, the pilot endeavouring unsuccessfully to haul his aircraft around to attack me.'

The RAF's early encounters with the *Luftwaffe* demonstrated the inadequacies of both Fighter Area Attacks and Vic Formations. Back on the ground at their base at Hornchurch, Alan Deere and the pilots of 54 Squadron expressed their contempt for Fighter Area Attacks and they were not the only ones.

George Gribble, who had destroyed a Me 109 was, strangely enough, not babbling about how he did it but was cursing the fact that we had been jumped by fighters.

'Begging your pardon, 'Prof',' he said, 'but No.5 attack, I ask you! Didn't we agree that those stupid set piece attacks were all right in peace but unlikely to prove any bloody good in war. Everybody was so damn busy making certain he got into the right position in the formation that we were very nearly all shot down for our pains.[11]

This British inexperience contrasted sharply with that of the *Luftwaffe*, many of whose pilots had previously served in Poland and during the Spanish Civil War. This had led the *Luftwaffe* fighters to develop a much looser formation, based on a two aircraft element known as a *rotte*. About 200 yards separated these aircraft from their neighbouring pair and the main responsibility of a wingman, or number two, was to provide cover for the leader from stern or quarter attack. The leader would in turn cover his wingman and also look after navigation. Two pairs of fighters were called a *schwarme* by the Germans and the British began to imitate it throughout the summer of 1940, christening it the 'finger four' (based on the idea that the formation resembled the fingers on a hand).[12] Wilfred Duncan Smith describes how, as the squadron commander of 64 Squadron, he used these new tactics successfully:

Our tactics consisted of flying in a loose 'finger four' squadron formation almost line abreast, keeping up a high cruising speed with the sections slightly stepped. Depending on the sun, the stepping and formation pattern would be changed to suit the conditions. If my reader looks at his right hand with the fingers outstretched, he will see what I mean. If the sun was, say, on the port beam or quarter, the section looked like fingers with the palm of the hand upwards and the leading and starboard sections like the back of the hand. The starboard section was stepped up, and the port stepped down slightly. In this way four pairs of eyes were continually watching an arc round the sun, and a total of six pairs of eyes was able to cover the sky above, behind and below. It was impossible to suffer a blind spot provided everyone kept well-disciplined station. Another advantage was that in the event of a surprise attack we could turn and manoeuvre rapidly either way without the risk of colliding with each other and were also able to slip into line astern without juggling. We cut out weaving and maintained a high cruising speed. This enabled us to accelerate quickly to maximum speed for attacks on any enemy formations sighted below, or zoom climb into any attack from above.

The real worth of these ideas lay in the fact that we took much pleasure in luring Germans into attacks with us. Having sighted them, we would hold our positions steady waiting for them to get into range. The enemy fighters would think we hadn't seen them and commit themselves to an attack; then just as they were about to open fire, I would give the order to break into the attack; the top section, usually led by Don Kingaby, would break in the opposite direction climbing hard. To do any good the Germans would be forced to stay and turn with us, which suited us as our Spitfires could out-turn them. In the meantime, Don Kingaby and his merry men would get above and behind the Germans, taking them by surprise and swooping down like eagles on a chicken run.[13]

Advantageous though the finger four formation was, it still required a pilot to have sharp eyes and keep a keen look out, constantly moving his head around to check his tail. As a result, many pilots

11   Alan Deere, *Nine Lives* (Manchester: Crecy, 2005), pp. 57-8.
12   Derek Wood and Derek Dempster, *The Narrow Margin*, p. 172.
13   W.G.G. Duncan Smith, *Spitfire into Battle* (London: John Murray, 2002), p. 92.

wore a silk scarf to stop the back of the neck from chafing, undid the top button of their collar and loosened their tie, something that was to become an unofficial badge of the fighter pilot, on and off duty. When the enemy aircraft was sighted, good clear communication between aircraft was important. Johnnie Johnson was to finish the war as the RAF pilot with the highest number of kills (38 confirmed, though his tally was probably higher) and he successfully commanded a series of fighter wings throughout some of the toughest fighting in the European campaign. He can therefore be easily forgiven for the mistake he made early in his career at 616 Squadron. A mistake for which his squadron commander, the legendary Wing Commander Douglas Bader, laid into him as Johnson recalled.

> Suddenly I spotted three lean 109s only a few hundred feet higher than our formation and travelling in the same direction. Obviously they hadn't seen us and would make an ideal target for a section of 145 squadron who were still higher than the 109s. I should have calmly reported the number, type and position of the 109s to our leader, but I was excited and shouted, 'Look out, Dogsbody.'[14]
>
> But the other pilots weren't waiting for further advice from me. To them 'look out' was a warning of the utmost danger – of the dreaded bounce by a strong force of 109s. Now they took swift evasive action and half-rolled, dived, aileron-turned and swung out in all directions, like a wedge of fast-moving teal avoiding a wild-fowler on the coast. In far less time than it takes to tell, a highly organized wing was reduced to a shambles and the scattered sections could never be re-formed in time to continue the planned flight. I was the last to land, for I had realized the error and knew the consequences would be unpleasant. They were all waiting in the dispersal hut.
>
> 'Close the door, Billy,' ordered Bader. And then: 'Now who's the clot who shouted, "look out"?'
>
> I admitted that I was the guilty party.
>
> 'Very well. Now tell us what we had to 'look out' for?' demanded the angry wing commander.
>
> 'Well, sir, there were three 109s a few hundred feet above … '
>
> 'Three 109s!' interrupted Bader. 'We could have clobbered the lot. But your girlish scream made us think there were 50 of the brutes behind.'[15]

In calmer moments communication between aircraft could be given by hand signals. These dated back to Royal Flying Corps days but were still useful. A pilot for instance would clench his fist and pretend to beat the back of his helmet to indicate he wanted his Section to form line astern. By pointing his hand to the right, he indicated that he meant aircraft to echelon starboard and by pointing at his number two and screwing his hand around he would show he wanted the number two to takeover. In some cases, the aircraft would be used as a sign, a waggle of the wings and pointing downwards would show to others that the aircraft had become unserviceable and the pilot was going to land.[16]

Alternatively, R/T could be used, not just between fighters but also with the sector controller, who as we have seen could advise the aircraft whilst in flight. To aid this communication a series of codewords were devised, 'angels' meaning altitude, 'bandits' – enemy aircraft, 'pancake' – an instruction to land, 'vector' – the course to steer to intercept and 'buster' meaning to go flat out. (A list of common RAF codenames is included at Annex O.)

---

14   The call sign of the wing leader derived from his initials; in this sortie the leader was Douglas Bader.
15   Johnnie Johnson, *Wing Leader* (London: Reprint Society, 1958), p. 76.
16   Dizzy Allen, *Fighter Squadron* (London: Granada, 1982), p. 148.

Detecting and identifying enemy aircraft was very hard, eyes often struggled to focus in clear blue skies and into the sun. One natural phenomenon that could help was condensation, so called con-trails, which occur when moisture in an aircraft's exhaust gases condenses and turns into a highly visible, cloud-like vapour along the machine's path. These conditions normally existed between 20,000 and 30,000 ft, in bands of around 5,000 ft depth. They were used by fighter pilots in a number of tactical ways, first having identified the band, a pilot could fly just below it, which reduced the likelihood of him being jumped from above. Alternatively, he could fly above it and not only spot aircraft approaching him from below, but also dive down rapidly on to his prey in the hope that his trails would not be spotted quickly.[17]

As the RAF fighter formation's track neared the point of interception the fighter leader would do all he could to obtain a height advantage, sometimes even flying away from the enemy and inland for a period. Height was always the surest way to maintain the initiative. Tim Vigors was an Irishman who flew with the Irish Tricolour on his 222 Squadron Spitfire during the Battle and describes an intercept:

> Passing through 10,000 feet Johnny gave the command to switch on oxygen. Despite the fact that it was a warm summer's day it soon started to get cold. We were all dressed in fur-lined leather jackets and wore flying boots and fleece-lined gloves but by 20,000 feet extremities were starting to hurt. 'Your bandits are now about 15 miles to the southeast,' the controllers advised over the radio. 'Look out, because some of them are still above you.'
>
> 'Tally ho!' yelled one of the weavers behind us.
>
> 'Hundreds of bandits at three o'clock!' I looked to my right and there they were. The sky was full of what looked like black specks, stretching from way above us to thousands of feet below us.
>
> 'OK, I've got 'em', called the wing leader, 'we'll keep on climbing and then swing in over their tails.'
>
> It was obvious that we weren't going to get above them all before they had passed us. I could now distinguish the twin engines of the bombers below us and the sharp noses of the masses of 109s protecting them from above. 'Bandits attacking from above nine o' clock!' came a yell in the headphones. The next moment the sky was full of tracer and about 12 Messerschmitt 109s dived straight through our formation from our left quarter.
>
> 'Turn starboard and attack the main formation!' yelled the wing leader. 'Take the fighters first if you can and then go for the bombers.' Clawing for height our squadron swung towards the enemy. I could see two Spitfires dropping away from our formation, one enveloped in white steam and another with black smoke pouring from its engine casing.[18]

During the battle RAF pilots encountered German formations composed of either just fighters, or bombers escorted by fighters. Typically, the German bombers would be either Junkers Ju 87 dive bombers or medium twin-engine bombers such as the Heinkel He 111, Dornier Do 17 or the Junkers Ju 88. All German bombers were much slower than the fighters and usually flew at lower altitudes too, typically somewhere between 10,000 and 15,000 ft. The *Luftwaffe* understood that the ideal way to protect the bombers was by clearing a wide arc around the aircraft and that this was best achieved by the use of free-ranging fighters. These would fly well out of sight of the bombers, taking full advantage of local tactical conditions as well as their fighter's speed and manoeuvrability.

---

17   Brian Kingcome, *Willingness to Die* (Stroud: History Press, 2010), p. 201.
18   Tim Vigors, *Life's Too Short to Cry* (London: Grub Street, 2008), p. 196.

This had been the specific instructions to the *Luftwaffe* early on in the battle and Reichsmarschall Goering himself specifically warned 'Putting the majority of fighters and *Zerstorer* close to the bomber formations will prevent them from being used as effectively as they might. They would be unable to achieve their full fighting capability and would inevitably have high losses'.[19] However as Hurricanes and Spitfires managed to find a way through this fighter screen and inflict casualties, the *Luftwaffe* bomber crews' demands became more insistent, particularly for close escort *Luftwaffe* fighters that they could *actually see*. Instead of reinforcing the fighter sweeps and focussing them on British airfields or trying to intercept Spitfire and Hurricane formations as they climbed up to engage, the *Luftwaffe* made the mistake of succumbing to the bomber crews' demands and reinforced the close escort. This would eventually result in almost the entire German fighter force being tied to the bombers, flying in formation in front, above, behind and on the flanks of the

Dramatic picture of a Hurricane being engaged by an Me 109 during the Battle of Britain. (Bundesarchiv)

bombers, as well as below and occasionally even in between bomber formations.[20] These tactics reduced the offensive capabilities of the German fighter aircraft dramatically.

The *Luftwaffe*'s problems were further complicated by the growing realisation that the Me 110s could not meet the Hurricanes and Spitfires on equal terms. In addition, the Me 109's lack of fuel endurance over England was proving to be a significant limiting factor. If the *Luftwaffe*'s objective was to be London the fighters could protect the bombers for just 5-10 minutes over the target. Furthermore, on their return journey to France, the Me 109s would be particularly vulnerable and frequently took evasive action rather than turning to fight the RAF and risk running out of fuel. On occasions additional fighters were sent out from German airfields to protect withdrawing fighters on the return leg – in effect fighters escorting other fighters.[21]

During his actual attack, the RAF fighter pilot would drop his seat a little to obtain maximum protection from both his back armour and engine block. He would also switch his gun button to fire and if he had not already done so, turn up the illumination in his reflector sight. This sight was an ingenious design, consisting of a system of lenses which projected an image of a gunsight onto a small glass plate inside the cockpit, just behind the windshield. The intensity of the image

19   James Holland, *Battle of Britain*, p. 413.
20   Johnnie Johnson, *Wing Leader* (London: Reprint Society, 1957), p. 55.
21   Karl Bartz, *Swastika in the Air* (London: William Kimber, 1956), p. 70.

could be adjusted for various combat conditions and projected a faint red circle with a dot in the centre. Two lines ran across the circle, which could be adjusted inwards and outwards for various wing-spans, when the enemy's wings filled the gap between the lines, the pilot knew the aircraft was in range. The beauty of the reflector sight was that the pilot could engage targets easily whilst concentrating on flying.[22] Geoffrey Wellum recalls what a huge bonus this was when his squadron was scrambled to meet a bomber formation over the Thames Estuary:

> A couple of Junkers 88s flying very tight together about half a mile distant and a fraction below. I've got my eye on you, you buggers. Just you hold on a bit mateys and I'll have your guts for garters. Even as I watch they drop their bombs and start a slow turn away. Below is fairly open country, only a smallish village and a few scattered houses or cottages. Pray God that the bombs miss them but, at least, it's not a built-up area such as the East End of London. Presumably they chucked their loads off in a bit of a panic. A pair of 109s sail above and behind them but they have not seen me. Where on earth do all these bloody 109s come from? They must have hundreds of the blighters. They still haven't seen me. Perhaps I can get a burst at the bombers and get out of it before they do. Astern of the four of them I have a little height in hand.
>
> Throttle open, dive under the fighters, a quick burst and away. Come on then, let's get it over with. Ease the stick forward, feed on more power and down we go. A quick look around. Clear behind, but there is so much going on who can tell?
>
> OK, now watch the target. Speed building up too quickly. Ease the throttle back slightly. The 109s still haven't seen me. I begin to swallow hard and my left knee begins to tremble for some stupid bloody reason. I'm getting excited again, although tensed up. Wish I was the cold calculating type with steely blue eyes.
>
> There's no time to consider anything but those 88s. Astern of the bombers. They come towards me at astonishing speed; too fast. Shit! Sight on. Oh damn, I'm still miles too fast. Bloody hell! Overtaking like a rocket, open fire. The guns going, trembling Spitfire, smell of compressed air or cordite or something. Hold it a fraction longer; hits on the left hand one, lots of them. Christ, Geoff, you're going to ram him. Stick forward, a thump. Either you've hit him or it's slipstream. Hope it's slipstream. Blimey, we're going vertically towards the ground. This is rather off-putting, but I think it's alright. You didn't hit him; you broke away a bit late and hit the slipstream. Strewth that all happened quickly; bloody close as well. Pull up and start to climb to have another go.[23]

Good British pilots understood that to be successful in air-to-air combat, they needed to pay attention to two important factors. The first of which was the requirement to get in close enough to do real damage. Initially, RAF fighters had their guns harmonized to converge at 400 yards, producing concentrated fire at that distance. However, experience in France and over Dunkirk had led RAF squadrons to conclude that was too far away and they needed to get in much closer, without waiting for authorisation they harmonised their guns to 250 yards. An armaments officer from Whitehall came to one particular squadron and enquired why they were not complying with the original direction – he was unsurprisingly given very short shrift by the pilots.[24] The other technique good RAF pilots adopted was to fire only short and accurate bursts. The ammunition drums for the eight .303 Browning machine guns on Spitfires held only 300 rounds each, this

22   Leo McKinstry, *Spitfire*, p. 173.
23   Geoffrey Wellum, *First Light* (Penguin: London, 2003), pp. 166-8.
24   Derek Wood and Derek Dempster *The Narrow Margin* (Washington, DC: Smithsonian, 2000), p. 148.

equated to just 15 seconds worth of firing time. In addition, the small calibre of the gun meant that it took many rounds to inflict the sort of damage that could bring down an aircraft. No. 74 Squadron recorded that on one occasion they had collectively fired a total 7,000 rounds of .303 into a Do 17 and yet still failed to destroy it.

In contrast the Me 109 was much better equipped in terms of firepower. It had two 20mm cannon, which could inflict great damage, especially with the new and more powerful explosive shells being issued to the *Luftwaffe*. This was in addition to two nose mounted MG 17 machine guns, which required no convergence or harmonisation and were fed by 1,000 round ammunition drums. This meant that the Me 109 could fire its machine guns for around 55 seconds though the concentration of rounds was obviously less.[25] All of this meant that for British pilots short and precise shots were more effective than long squirts, as Bob Stanford-Tuck a Flight Commander with 92 Squadron recalled:

> Quite contrary to what the average person in the street would think, actual shooting was quite a precision business. I always looked upon it as that. Never fire very long bursts, spraying away. Wait until you are very close up to him and you know your built-in compensator says that is the position to shoot ahead of him as he is turning that way. When you have got every-thing dead right, and you are close and you know you are going to hit him hard, a two-second burst was all you required, certainly you never had to continue. I am quite sure some of the pilots when they started, the youngsters who perhaps had little experience of combat, were guilty of locking their thumb on the firing button and squirting away as hard as they could go. But it really was a precision business.[26]

The process of deflection shooting, or giving 'lead', alluded to by Bob Stanford-Tuck, was one of the hardest elements of marksmanship a pilot had to master. The problem was that if you aim directly at a flying target passing in front of you, then you will invariably miss, because the aircraft will have gone past the point you aimed at by the time the machine gun rounds arrive. The pilot therefore needed to aim ahead of the aircraft, which was a question of judging the distance and crossing speed accurately. Game shots were found to be particularly adept and often achieved impressive numbers of kills as a result (top fighter pilots like Bob Stanford Tuck, Johnnie Johnson and Hugh Dundas were all accomplished with shotguns). Average shots could still rely on aids such as the recently issued .303 de Wilde ammunition. This should not be confused with the better known tracer ammunition that burns during flight, de Wilde rounds did not do that, instead they sparked and flashed when they struck the target thus indicating to the pilot that he was engaging and hitting his target. For the novice shot sometimes the best method was simply to try and over-haul the fighter from astern, hose-piping it with his machine guns.[27] Though this was still not an easy process as 'Mac' Mackenzie, a Hurricane pilot in 501 Squadron recalled:

> Climbing to gain more height we 'bustered' with the sun behind us and spotted the forma-tions. With the tit pulled for absolute power we broke formation to attack. Gyro sights 'on', guns to 'fire', harness tight, attacking individually. They had not seen us and we had a superb advantage, they broke wildly on seeing us and being shot at, I took a Bf 110 very fast, too fast from astern and below with a four second burst from 250 yards, broke away to avoid another 110 but saw no apparent damage to the one attacked.

25   James Holland, *The Battle of Britain*, pp. 506-7.
26   Leo McKinstry, *Spitfire*, p. 174.
27   Johnnie Johnson, *Wing Leader* (London: Reprint Society, 1957), p. 125.

As I pulled away and up to attack a Bf 109 above me, another Bf 109 flew across my flight path, so I reefed hard round, nearly blacking out to get a full deflection shot at him from over 100 yards. Ah, that was better! ... Strikes visible all over him but our crossing speed too fast. He slowed visibly as I pulled up and above him as he dived. With my height and speed advantage, he did not draw away as the 109s usually did initially and took no evasive action as I followed him at about 1,200 yards and closing, no other aircraft about – we had lost them, though I kept a wary eye on my rear-view mirror. Puffs of smoke and then white smoke came from his exhaust as we neared Margate, going south-east. When just off Margate I followed him at 600 yards down over the sea, closing fast, as he levelled off at about 20 feet – still no evasive action. I closed to 100 yards and gave him a long burst from dead astern, watched the strikes, but no immediate result. Throttling back, I waited and then suddenly he just dived into the sea in a cloud of spray so that I had to pull up sharply to avoid his tail as it came up.

I zoomed up to 2,000 feet, had a good look round and orbited the spot, but there was nothing to be seen but oil and disturbed water.[28]

The other method of attacking the German aircraft was head-on, this was a popular tactic against German bombers in particular as it stood a good chance of killing the aircrew, including the pilot. Head on attacks were not without risk as Alan Deere discovered when using the tactic against a fighter:

I soon found another target. About 3,000 yards directly ahead of me, and at about the same level, a Hun was just completing a turn preparatory to re-entering the fray. He saw me almost immediately and rolled out of his turn towards me so that a head-on attack became inevitable. Using both hands on the control column to steady the aircraft and thus keep my aim steady, I peered through the reflector sight at the rapidly closing enemy aircraft. We opened fire together, and immediately a hail of lead thudded into my Spitfire. One moment the Messerschmitt was a clearly defined shape, its wingspan nicely enclosed within the circle of my reflector sight, and the next it was on top of me, a terrifying blur which blotted out the sky ahead. Then we hit.

The force of the impact pitched me violently forward on to my cockpit harness, the straps of which bit viciously into my shoulders. At the same moment, the control column was snatched abruptly from my gripping fingers by a momentary, but powerful, reversal of elevator load. In a flash it was over; there was clear sky ahead of me, and I was still alive. But smoke and flame were pouring from the engine which began to vibrate, slowly at first but with increasing momentum causing the now regained control column to jump back and forwards in my hand. Hastily I closed the throttle and reached forward to flick off the ignition switches, but before I could do so the engine seized, and the airscrew stopped abruptly. I saw with amazement that the the blades had been bent almost double with the impact of the collision.[29]

Amazingly, despite the extensive damage to his aircraft, Deere managed to crash-land his Spitfire only five miles from his airfield at Manston and he was able to rejoin his squadron later that night.

Whether the RAF fighters were surprised from above, or were able to seize the initiative and pounce themselves, the air combat would often degenerate into a chaotic dog fight. Here the skill of the pilot and the technical characteristics of his aircraft would become crucial. We have already observed the Me 109's advantages over the Spitfire and Hurricane, including its faster speed which

---

28   K.W. Mackenzie, *Hurricane Combat* (London: Grenville Publishing, 1990), p .50.
29   Alan Deere, *Nine Lives* (Manchester: Crecy, 2005), p. 101.

was especially evident in the early stages of a dive. This benefit was derived from the Me 109's Daimler Benz fuel injected engine. Messerschmitt had wanted to fit a supercharger to the engine but the requirement to place some armaments in the nose precluded this, so the Germans used a Bosch multi-point injection system that sprayed fuel directly into the cylinders. The great advantage of this was that when the Me 109 was aggressively pushed into a dive, the effect of negative 'G' was eliminated. In contrast, the Merlin engine of the Spitfire and Hurricane had fuel fed to the cylinders through a float carburettor and if it was made to dive quickly the negative 'G' would act on the float, causing the fuel valve to close, temporarily interrupting the fuel supply and losing vital speed. This meant that the British fighters were unable to dive sharply away from a pursuer or, if chasing a diving Me 109, would often fail to keep up, even after their engine had recovered.[30] These technical differences were learnt and exploited by the better *Luftwaffe* pilots.

The theoretical minimum turning circle of an Me 109 was 885 feet and a Spitfire 696 feet, in theory this meant that a Spitfire and Hurricane could out-turn a Me 109. However, this oversimplifies the matter as tests conducted at the RAE in Farnborough, on captured German aircraft, showed that a Me 109 could stay on the tail of a Spitfire. The Farnborough tests also revealed that some RAF pilots would not tighten their turns up sufficiently for fear of stalling and going into a spin, this was particularly the case amongst Hurricane pilots, who knew that their plane would always drop a wing in such circumstances. In addition, the Me 109 suffered less sideslip when banking than the British fighters, meaning it lost less altitude and could therefore keep an enemy aircraft in its sights more easily.[31] Despite these technical considerations many RAF pilots did successfully out-turn their German counterparts, certainly on the Spitfire, where the aircraft would give a warning shudder prior to stalling, which helped guide the pilot to make the turn as tight as possible. In addition, pilots would often use the effect of 'G' to their advantage. Most pilots would begin greying out at four 'G' and lose their vision, something that was a common experience in a dog fighting situation particularly when a pilot was making a tight turn. A greyout is distinctly different to a blackout, in that it is not an actual loss of consciousness but a precursor to it. Johnnie Johnson recalls the onset of a greyout and blackout during a dog fight and how it helped him escape:

> The wicked tracer sparkles and flashes over the top of your own cockpit and you break into a tight turn. Now you have two enemies. The 109 on your tail and your remorseless, ever-present opponent 'g', the force of gravity. Over your shoulder you can still see the ugly, questing snout of the 109. You tighten the turn. The Spit protests and shudders, and when the blood drains from your eyes you 'grey-out'. But you keep turning, for life itself is at stake. And now your blood feels like molten lead and runs from head to legs. You black-out! And you ease the turn to recover in a grey-unreal world of spinning horizons. Cautiously you climb into the sun. You have lost too much height and your opponent has gone – disappeared. You are completely alone in your own bit of sky, bounded by the blue vault above and the coloured drapery of earth below.[32]

Whatever the tactics used, the experience of a dog fight was a relentless, confusing and draining experience for the fighter pilot as Jimmy Corbin relates.

30   Derek Wood and Derek Dempster *Narrow Margin*, p. 148.
31   James Holland, *Battle of Britain*, p. 504.
32   Johnnie Johnson, *Wing Leader* (London: Reprint Society, 1957), p. 46.

At one point, a Me 109 shot past overhead, closely followed by one of ours, I think. Another 109 dived down past my starboard wing. Was it being chased or was he chasing someone? I couldn't see. Overhead several planes swooped and then climbed. I couldn't even tell which side they were on. What the hell was going on? And what the hell was I meant to be doing? It was like taking part in a complicated dance routine when I didn't even know the basic steps.

The R/T provided a clipped commentary to the scene being played out around me, but it didn't appear to tally with the action, and I was no nearer understanding what was happening. The controlled voice of the CO was now replaced by random and disconnected shouts of 'He's on you Blue Two' and 'I've got him', which were then followed by long eerie silences.

My training such as it was, kicked in. I knew that my main priority was to get above the enemy and behind them. Only when I had the height advantage could I have any hope of hitting one of them or indeed of not getting hit myself. Whatever happened, I couldn't let one of them get on to my tail. If they did it would probably be a case of 'good night nurse' for me.

I checked my rear mirror. It was all clear. I searched for a potential target but couldn't make any out as they were either too far away or in the wrong position to get into my sights.

I checked my mirror again and froze with fear. Was it? Yes, by Christ, it was. I had a Messerschmitt 109 locked onto my tail and I was now almost certainly in his sights. Silver bullets streamed from his wing. My God, the bastard is firing at me.

I pulled the Spitfire into a tight evasive turn and rolled it into a dive to avoid the burst of gunfire coming from the 109. The Spitfire had a carburettor and relied on positive G for the petrol to flow, so if you pushed the stick or control column forward quickly the engine would cut out and the aircraft would go into a half roll and automatically dive downwards. But the positive G had other effects which I was now about to experience. As the aircraft plummeted, I felt a huge pressure on my backside and the blood seemed to drain from my head. Before I knew what was happening I had blacked out. When I came to I had dropped several thousand feet and was close to the coast of Calais.

I checked my mirror it was all clear. I looked all around me and there wasn't a soul, enemy or otherwise, about. The skies were empty. The battle might be continuing elsewhere, but for me it was over. For now.[33]

Many fighter pilots would experience the same situation at the conclusion of a dog fight, or their part in it. One moment a mass of swirling fighters and then in an instant, an almost empty sky. Those who survived would learn from their experience and improve as fighter pilots. The highly skilled and respected South African pilot Group Captain Adolph 'Sailor' Malan[34] made the following points about what a fighter pilot needed to do to survive:

He has to be cold when he is fighting. He fights with his head, not his heart. There are three things a first-class fighter pilot must have. First, he must have an aggressive nature. He must think in terms of offence rather than defence. He must at all times be an attacker. It is against the nature of a Spitfire to run away. Second, both his mind and body must be alert, and both must react instinctively to any tactical situation. When you are fighting you have no time to think. Third, he must have good eyes and clean hands and feet. His hands and feet control

33   Jimmy Corbin, *Last of the Ten Fighter Boys* (Stroud: History Press, 2010), p. 108.

34   Malan was known as 'Sailor' as a result of his prior service as a Seaman and Naval cadet, perhaps also because his Christian name of Adolph must have been an uncomfortable one during the war. He achieved 27 confirmed kills before retiring from the RAF to his native South Africa, where he played an important part in the anti-apartheid movement before his death in 1963.

this plane and they must be sensitive. He can't be ham handed. When your Spitfire is ambling along at 390 miles an hour a too-heavy hand on the rudder will send you in an inadvertent and very embarrassing spin. Your hands, your feet, your mind, your instinct must function as well, whether you're right side up or upside down.[35]

Malan also provided 10 rules for air-fighting. Although written in 1943, whilst Station Commander at Biggin Hill, they reflect his operational experience and were just as relevant in 1940:

1.   Wait until you see the white of his eyes. Fire short bursts of one to two seconds, and only when your sights are definitely 'on'.
2.   Whilst shooting think of nothing else. Brace the whole of the body, have both hands on the stick, concentrate on your ring sight.
3.   Always keep a sharp look-out. 'Keep your finger out'.
4.   Height gives you the initiative.
5.   Always turn and face the attack.
6.   Make your decisions promptly. It is better to act quickly, even though your tactics are not of the best.
7.   Never fly straight and level for more than 30 seconds in the combat area.
8.   When diving to attack, always leave a proportion of your formation above you as top guard.
9.   INITIATIVE, AGGRESSION, AIR DISCIPLINE, and TEAM WORK are words that MEAN something in air fighting.
10. Go in quickly – Punch Hard – Get Out![36]

Even those skilled pilots who instinctively followed the rules outlined above could still be shot down by German fighters. German bullets and cannon shells could easily make a mess of a Spitfire or Hurricane, the control surfaces could be damaged and a hit on the Merlin engine could easily result in a significant oil or glycol leak, which would swiftly cause it to overheat, fail, or even catch fire. The most common way to be shot down was to be hit by the aircraft you just did not see, which is exactly what happened to 'Cocky' Dundas. He recalled that the first inclination he had that he was being attacked, was the sound of cannon fire from a Me 109 ripping into his aircraft:

The explosions were so unexpected, so shattering, their effect on my Spitfire so devastating, that I thought I had been hit by our own heavy ack-ack.

White smoke filled the cockpit, thick and hot, and I could see neither the sky above nor the Channel coast 12,000 feet below. Centrifugal force pressed me against the side of the cockpit, and I knew my aircraft was spinning. Panic and terror consumed me, and I thought 'Christ, this is the end.' Then I thought, 'Get out, you bloody fool; open the hood and get out.'

With both hands I tugged the handle where the hood locked onto the top of the windscreen. It moved back an inch, then jammed. Smoke poured out through the gap and I could see again. I could see the earth and the sea and the sky spinning round in tumbled confusion as I cursed and blasphemed and pulled with all my strength to open the imprisoning hood.

If I could not get out I had at all costs to stop the spin. I pushed the stick hard forward, kicked on full rudder, opened the throttle. Nothing happened. The earth went spinning on,

35   Oliver Walker, *Sailor Malan* (Cassell: London, 1953), p. 101.
36   Graham Wallace, *Biggin Hill* (London: Putnam, 1957), p. 268.

came spinning up to meet me. Grabbing the hood toggle again, I pulled with all my might, pulled for my life, pulled at last, with success. I stood up on my seat and pushed the top half of my body out of the cockpit. Pressed hard against the fuselage, half in, half out, I struggled in a nightmare of fear and confusion to drop clear but could not do so.

I managed to get back into the cockpit, aware now that the ground was very close. Try again; try the other side. Up, over – and out. I slithered along the fuselage and felt myself falling free. Seconds after my parachute opened I saw the Spitfire hit and explode in a field below. A flock of sheep scattered outwards from the cloud of dust and flame.

For a few moments there was silence and peace. Then the ground swung up fast and I remembered to bend my knees and roll over and bang the quick release catch of my parachute harness. I lay under a hedge by the side of a wood. Two or three hundred yards away my Spitfire burned. My left leg was sticky with blood and my left shoulder, badly dislocated, hurt abominably.

A farmer with an old-fashioned hammer gun stood over me and I thought his attitude none too friendly. Probably he did not much like having aeroplanes making holes in his field and frightening his sheep.[37]

Those that survived the dog fight would make their way home. Disorientated, they would need to find a landmark to navigate their own way back or ask to be vectored back to the airfields by the sector controller. Some pilots would have had to land on other airfields, because of either damage, a lack of fuel, or sometimes just simply because they were lost. As they cruised in to land, their ground crew would try to determine if they had been successful, by seeing if the fabric over the gun ports had been blown away. The pilots might also let those on the airfield know they had been in action by side-slipping the aircraft as it approached, an action that caused the wind passing over the open gun ports to make a distinctive noise.

The pilots would all be de-briefed by the squadron Intelligence Officer after every sortie, he would wish to know about any aircraft encountered and the tactics employed by the Germans. He would also ascertain what aircraft each pilot may have shot down – their so-called 'claims', this was a particularly difficult job as this Intelligence Officer's account of a 609 Squadron sortie relates.

First comes P/O de Spirlet with a faulty oil gauge. He has nothing to relate. Then other pilots arrive in driblets which pre-suppose action. The CO taxies up with gun canvasses shot away and emerges from his plane sweating. He has fought for at least 10 minutes, he says, and is obviously very tired. He thinks he has got one, he saw a splash, but before that he saw a Spitfire go in. Then Sgt Rigler appears, all cock-a-hoop, he has got one – 'no doubt about that' – and probably another (all very difficult, for of the three, one says the CO's returned to France). Next comes Ortmans. 'Yes, I fire' he laughs, 'but the Jerry, he go on' (thank goodness HE doesn't claim one, thinks the IO). Suddenly pilots stop arriving, and there are still five more missing. Everyone seems to be certain that one 109 and one Spitfire have gone into the drink. We speculate – the latter must be either Sgt Boyd or P/O Van Lierde, both No.4s. Four aircraft are reported at Hawkinge and West Malling. Momentarily there is a rumour of another one at Manston. Momentarily the CO smiles, for it seems that after all we have lost no one, and the Spitfire was another 109. Boyd and Van Lierde both come in. Then it suddenly dawns upon us, the almost unbelievable – the missing pilot is Johnnie – Johnnie Curchin.

37   Hugh Dundas, *Flying Start* (New York: St Martin's Press, 1989), p. 40.

Three Spitfire pilots with 19 Squadron based at Fowlmere, Cambridgeshire, gather to confer after a mission in September 1940. L-R: Flight Lieutenant W.J. 'Farmer' Lawson, Squadron Leader B.J.E. 'Sandy' Lane (officer commanding) and Flight Sergeant G.C. 'Grumpy' Unwin. (Crown Copyright – Air Historical Branch)

As reconstructed afterwards, after much checking and cross-checking of times and observations made by Dover guns, balloon barrage, Air/Sea Rescue officer etc, it appeared that the first plane to dive into the sea was not after all a Spitfire, but the 109 which broke away and dived. It attacked not Boyd or Van Lierde, but Ortmans who had been kept back by oil pressure and high temperatures. He took such effective evasive action that the enemy aircraft broke up and plunged into the sea. S/L Robinson's arduous battle was with the second 109 flown by a very experienced pilot who remained out of reach until the CO tried flying straight and level. Just as it was about to open fire, S/L Robinson turned sharply and throttled back, and was able to fire a long burst from astern. The 109 smoked heavily, turned on its side and dived to sea level. But the splash he saw, it was decided, was not the 109, but Curchin's Spitfire. P/O Mackenzie had seen an enemy aircraft dart between Curchin and himself and was unable to attack it through getting into a spin. Sgt Rigler meanwhile had ascended up to 1,000 feet after a third 109 and brought it down with a full deflection shot from below. In a head on combat with another, probably the CO's, he claimed to have shot pieces off its wing.'[38]

Most claims were made in good faith, but in any air battle where aircraft are moving at high speeds in many different directions, it was virtually impossible for the pilot to know the actual

---

38   Peter Caygill, *The Biggin Hill Wing 1941* (Barnsley: Pen and Sword, 2008), pp. 65-6.

results of his attack. Unless the aircraft blew up, lost a wing, or was seen to crash there was little certainty and it was a foolhardy pilot who would try and follow a machine down, or even keep his eyes on it as it fell. Often pilots would fire at a machine, lose it, then see an aircraft (but perhaps not the one they had engaged) hit the sea or ground and claim that as a definite kill. The problem was that other pilots would also claim that crashing plane as a kill too.[39] Inflation of claims was not unusual, perhaps because it was known that five claims usually resulted in a Distinguished Flying Cross (DFC), though DFCs could be awarded for other reasons too. Many pilots deplored any sense of personal ambition and felt the squadron score was much more important than any one individual's tally. Dowding judged that the majority of his pilots were sincere in their claims, but he was realistic enough to know that total claims were probably an overestimation of German losses. Consequently, he was much more interested in calculating his own losses and understanding how well Fighter Command was standing up to the German onslaught. He was also well aware that in certain quarters over-inflation was particularly rampant. Bader's wing in 12 Group was notorious for such behaviour, claiming twice as many as other squadrons (which were also probably inflated). A frustrated Dowding felt compelled to write to 12 Group's commander, Leigh-Mallory: 'I read a great many combat reports and I think I am beginning to pick out those which can be relied on and those which throw in claims at the end for good measure.'[40] However despite Fighter Command's wariness the press and the BBC loved a good tally and were keen to identify the RAF aces and publicise them as heroes. Most squadrons were hostile to such press interest, recognising that it could be divisive within a unit and often put undue pressure on an individual approaching 'ace' status.

During the Battle of Britain RAF Squadrons could fly three to four sorties a day, an exhausting amount for the pilots. In this intense period a squadron could lose 50 percent of its pilots as casualties in just one week. As one example 616 Squadron and its 18 pilots moved down from Leconfield in Yorkshire to RAF Kenley, near Croydon on 19 August 1940, from which they operated until they were withdrawn on 4 September. During that two-week period, 616 Squadron lost five pilots killed or missing and had six pilots wounded including their squadron commander. To set against its own losses the squadron claimed 16 enemy aircraft definitely destroyed, six probables and 15 damaged.[41] These were punishing casualty levels.

Many Fighter Command sorties could best be judged as partially successful. Though German aircraft may have been destroyed and all the RAF pilots safely returned, the German bombs might have still succeeded in reaching their targets. The German tactical focus shifted throughout the battle, but their enduring and overarching objective was to achieve air superiority. The dominant thinking was that air superiority was to allow the invasion of the United Kingdom to take place, but there were certainly some elements in the German government who proposed alternative ways of defeating Britain, including striking the ports and starving the country into submission, or bombing the cities until the government caved. Regardless of the strategic confusion, neutralising Fighter Command remained key and the Germans believed that they could accomplish it in four ways. First, they could attack militarily or economically important targets to force the RAF into the air, where they could be destroyed by fighters or the defensive armament of German bombers. Secondly, they could attack the RAF's fighter airfields and put aircraft, as well as their essential ground support out of action. Thirdly, they could attack Fighter Command's Early Warning System, including radar stations and the sector, group and command Headquarters, or stations and finally they could

39   Norman Franks, *The Greatest Air Battle* (London: Grub Street, 1997), p. 190.
40   Vincent Orange, *Dowding of Fighter Command* (London: Grub Street, 2008), p. 200.
41   Hugh Dundas, *Flying Start* (New York: St Martin's, 1989), p. 43.

Pilots and groundcrew of 601 (County of London) Squadron pictured at Exeter in November 1940. Hurricane P3886/UF-K is being prepared for its next sortie. (Crown Copyright – Air Historical Branch)

attack the factories which were producing the fighters.[42] These options are typical for any air force attempting to gain air superiority and on other occasions they have proved successful. However, the Germans made the major mistake during the Battle of Britain in not focussing on any one of them with sufficient persistence and determination. The case of German attacks on British radar is a case in point. At Goering's direction heavy attacks were made on 12 August on six CH stations in the south-east, with considerable damage done. Ventnor was knocked out for 11 days, but the British deployed an ordinary radio transmitter to the area which was soon broadcasting pulses on the same frequency. Though this equipment could not receive any returning echo, the enemy could only assume that the radar site had been repaired. Goering consequently cancelled further attacks on CH targets arguing 'It is doubtful whether there is any point in continuing the attacks on radar sites, in view of the fact that not one of those attacked has so far been put out of action.'[43]

The attack on Fighter Command's airfields has usually been considered a pivotal moment in the battle and the point when the Germans came closest to achieving air superiority. Their failure was partly because of their lack of persistence as well as the poor German intelligence which did not understand British dispositions. For example, although there were 53 main attacks on airfields between the 12 August and 6 September, only 32 of these were directed against Fighter Command airfields. The remaining raids struck Coastal Command bases, or other airfields that were not playing a critical role in the battle.[44] The Germans did not know which were the Sector airfields and interestingly failed to attack either Bentley Priory or Uxbridge at any point in the battle. The numbers of RAF machines destroyed on the ground was also surprisingly small, partly because

42   Alfred Price, *The Hardest Day*, p. 27.
43   Brereton Greenhous, *The Crucible of War 1939-1945: The Official History of the Royal Canadian Air Force* (Toronto: University of Toronto, 1994), p. 182.
44   Richard Overy, *The Battle of Britain* (Penguin: London, 2000), p. 69.

of the efforts to disperse aircraft and camouflage them after the attacks began. A total of only 56 aircraft were destroyed on the ground during this period.

The defence of RAF airfields was undertaken in a number of ways. For instance, RAF Kenley was protected first by Light Anti-Aircraft (LAA) guns, including the 40mm Bofors gun. These modern automatic weapons could fire a 2lb high explosive shell at the rate of 120 rounds per minute. If one of these shells struck the metal surface of an aircraft it would make a hole large enough for a man to climb through. At this stage of the war the Bofors guns that defended airfields were manned by members of the Royal Artillery rather than the RAF Regiment, but the problem was that there were simply not enough of these weapons. Kenley had only four Bofors in place when it was attacked on 18 August 1940, but it needed twice as many as that to give the base an adequate defence.[45] LAA guns were supplemented by antique 3-inch guns fired over open sights, as well as Lewis .303 machine guns. These were sited not just to counter air attacks, but also as a potential ground defence against an attack by enemy airborne forces. Like some other airfields, Kenley also had a novel Parachute and Cable (PAC) system deployed near the airfield. This rather Heath Robinson, but occasionally successful, device fired salvoes of 480-foot long steel hawsers 600 feet into the air, where they would hopefully snag on an aircraft wing, deploying a parachute at the end of each cable and dragging the aircraft into the ground.

Air-raid shelters had been constructed as part of Kenley's defences and key buildings were hardened with sandbags, but like many other sector airfields the all-important control centre at Kenley was not hardened, despite being located within the airfield perimeter. Fortunately, German intelligence had not identified what the building was, or even developed an accurate view of how the Fighter Command system worked. Nevertheless, this lack of protection is surprising and was an important vulnerability. During the battle, Flying Officer Jack Hill worked within the Kenley Sector Operations Room, which was simply a bungalow shaped building protected with nothing more than a 6-foot blast wall and a camouflage net. He recalls being shown round his new place of work on arrival and remembers asking his guide. 'Yes, but where's the proper underground one, the one we will use when things start happening?' He was incredulous when told that he was looking at it.[46]

The impact of the German attacks on airfields was dramatic. The attack on Kenley, on 18 August, for example, consisted of two raids of bombers, one at high-altitude and one at low altitude. The AA guns and PAC system succeeded in downing two aircraft and the Kenley sector controller dispatched two squadrons to deal with the high-altitude attack and one squadron for the low-level attack. The Germans dropped over 100 bombs on Kenley during this raid and were able to destroy eight aircraft, three hangers and a number of other buildings. The operations room's communications were cut and the operations staff had to temporarily move in to a local shop until the lines were restored two and a half days later.

Alan Deere recalls being 'at readiness' in Hornchurch when the *Luftwaffe* were focussing their attacks on the sector airfields. It had been a quiet day up to that point, when his squadron was suddenly scrambled from dispersal. As they were taxiing, they were informed by an almost hysterical controller to get airborne as quickly as possible, as bandits had been reported in the immediate vicinity.

> Hurriedly, desperately, for I had no wish to be caught taking off, I swung my aircraft into wind only to find my take-off run blocked by a Spitfire, the pilot of which was looking vaguely around for his position in the formation.

45 Alfred Price, *The Hardest Day* p. 65.
46 Alfred Price, *The Hardest Day*, p. 63.

'Get to hell out of the way, Red two,' I bellowed, recognizing my number two from the letters on his aircraft. It was a second or two before he made up his mind to move; immediately he did so I opened the throttle and careered across the airfield in pursuit of the squadron which had by now cleared the far hedge, and with wheels retracting was turning and climbing away from the airfield.

I was not quite airborne when a bomb burst on the airfield, ahead of me and to my left. 'Good, I've made it,' I thought. To this day I am not clear exactly what happened next; all I can remember is that a tremendous blast of air, carrying showers of earth, struck me in the face and the next moment thinking vaguely that I was upside down. What I do remember is the impact with the ground and a terrifying period of ploughing along the airfield upside down, still firmly strapped into the cockpit. Stones and dirt were thrown into my face and my helmet was torn by the stony ground against which my head was firmly pressed.

Finally the aircraft stopped its mad upside-down dash leaving me trapped in the cockpit, in almost total darkness, and breathing petrol fumes, the smell of which was overpowering.[47]

It would take the assistance of another pilot, who had also been downed, to extract Deere from the wreckage.

Although Dowding had pressed for concrete runways before the war many airfields had remained as simple grass fields. The advantage of this was the ease with which they could be repaired, particularly as quantities of earth and hardcore had been stockpiled at airfields before the battle began.[48] Whilst the craters were being filled in, yellow markers would be placed to show aircraft the safe route in. At some airfields repair work took longer and at others there were examples of labour shortages delaying repairs, this in turn was exacerbated by some workers refusing to operate under such dangerous conditions. It prompted Park to take matters in to his own hands and elicit the help of Army battalions to act as labourers.[49] The attacks on the airfields was also the first period when large numbers of WAAFs came under sustained enemy fire. Any doubts as to their fortitude were quickly dispelled. During a major attack on Biggin Hill on 18 September, Sergeant Joan Mortimer, a telephone operator, who was also responsible for replenishing the ammunition of the nearby gun positions, remained at her very dangerous and exposed post throughout the raid. As soon as the bombs stopped falling and long before the 'All Clear' was sounded, she began planting red flags around the craters in which there were unexploded bombs. Later on in the Battle, Sergeant Helen Turner and Corporal Elspeth Henderson were also singled out for the calm manner in which they continued to maintain communications, after their operations block received a direct hit.[50]

The RAF responded to the attacks on its airfields by seeking to preserve its diminishing force. It accomplished this by restricting its engagements with the *Luftwaffe* to just those over the British mainland and refusing to get drawn into battles out at sea. It sought to attack the bombers first and tried to avoid direct combat with enemy fighters. Additionally, at the first warning of a major raid stations were ordered to send up a squadron to patrol below cloud cover over the airfield and minimize the risk of a surprise attack. Fighter Command also adapted to the German attacks by dispersing aircraft further inland and utilising prepared satellite airfields. Finally, whilst 11 Group were engaging the German raiders their inland circle of airfields was supposed to be protected by 10 Group and 12 Group fighters.[51]

---

47   Alan Deere, *Nine Lives* (Manchester: Crecy, 2005), p. 158.
48   James Holland, *Battle of Britain*, p. 452.
49   James Holland, *Battle of Britain*, p. 520.
50   Denis Richards, *Royal Air Force 1939-45, Volume I*, p. 180.
51   Richard Overy, *The Battle of Britain* (London: Penguin Books, 2004), p. 70.

The controlled detonation of a German bomb, which fell on the parade ground at RAF Hemswell, Lincolnshire, on 27 August 1940. The bomb did not explode but buried itself deep in the ground where it was subsequently destroyed by the Station Armament Officer. (Crown Copyright – Air Historical Branch)

The execution of this last tactic was less than perfect. Whilst Park praised Brand and 10 Group for their assistance, he criticised Leigh-Mallory's 12 Group for failing to protect his airfields when his fighters were engaged. This feud developed into criticism by Leigh-Mallory of the way Park was engaging fighters with single squadrons. Leigh-Mallory advocated an approach that emphasised one large mass of fighters attacking German formations simultaneously, at least three squadrons operating in one 'Big Wing' was his suggested method, though this would grow to five squadrons by September. However such a formation took a long time to assemble its aircraft, 45 minutes in some cases, leading to criticism that it usually failed to intercept the enemy and if it did, it was often after the bombers had attacked their target.[52] The debate between Park and Leigh-Mallory about their preferred tactics did not affect the outcome of the Battle, but it did lead to some shameless back-stabbing by Leigh-Mallory of both Park and Dowding once it was over. Dowding and Park were both removed from post after the Battle, which caused bitterness amongst many veterans, particularly as it was Park and Dowding, who had made the most significant contribution to the British Victory.

The German attacks on the airfields were a testing time for the RAF, but like the previous *Luftwaffe* attacks on the radar sites they were not persistent and once the Germans switched to attacking London the RAF were able to recuperate. The German bombing attacks on London had been partly in retaliation for a British attack on Berlin, though there were also some in Germany who felt that attacks on London might push a tottering Britain on to its knees. Frontline *Luftwaffe*

---

52   Patrick Bishop, *Fighter Boys* (London: Harper, 2003), p. 295 and Vincent Orange, *Dowding the Fighter Years* (London: Grub Street, 2011), p. 201.

commanders were more realistic and understood that it would take much more than that, particularly given the small bomb loads German aircraft could carry.

Dowding recognised that if Fighter Command could survive until November, then long winter nights and more marginal weather would negate any serious chance of the *Luftwaffe* achieving air superiority and successfully launching an invasion of Britain. As August turned into September the conflict increasingly became one of attrition and though the pipeline of new RAF aircraft was sufficient to replace losses, the shortage of combat ready pilots became more acute. There were already many Commonwealth pilots already serving in RAF Squadrons in the battle, including 32 Australians, 112 Canadians, 127 New Zealanders, 25 South Africans and 3 Rhodesians. There were also nine Americans serving too, yet Dowding was initially reluctant to use Polish and Czech pilots and squadrons in the Battle. This was an oversight and proved highly effective once introduced. The Polish *Kosciuszko* Squadron (known to the RAF as 303 Squadron) based at RAF Northolt, in west London, was the first into battle. Led by a combined command team of RAF and Polish officers, the Squadron's Hurricanes inflicted disproportionately high losses on the Germans whilst receiving fewer casualties themselves. This was partly because the Poles had experienced combat over Poland and France and understood the need to get in very close to achieve a kill. Some argued that the lack of an effective command and control and radar system in Poland had also meant the Poles were better at visual sightings and were more diligent at searching the sky than their British counterparts, often being the first to spot adversaries.

Initially RAF commanders did not believe the Poles successes or claims and thought they were inflated. The Station Commander of RAF Northolt, Wing Commander Stanley Vincent, was one of the doubters and flew with the Poles of 303 Squadron on 11 September with the specific intention of observing their abilities in combat. Once the Poles found the German bomber formation, he noted they dived almost vertically at the German aircraft with 'suicidal impetus', causing the German formation to break up and the Poles to attack the bombers one by one, closing almost to collision point before engaging their targets. Vincent was shocked at the ferocity: 'Suddenly the air was full of burning aircraft, parachutes, and pieces of disintegrating wings. It was all so rapid that it was staggering.' When Vincent himself tried to engage he kept finding a 'diving Pole would cut in between, and I had to pull away to avoid being hit myself'. A convinced Vincent returned to Northolt and told his Intelligence Officer 'My God, they *are* doing it!',[53] he subsequently became one of the Pole's fiercest supporters.

Polish effectiveness was to make them heroes within Britain and aces such as Pilot Officer Jan Zumbach would become well known in RAF circles, though names were not publicised for fear of German reprisals against their families in Poland. By the end of September admiration of Polish effectiveness had reached the most senior levels. John 'Jock' Colville, Churchill's Assistant Private Secretary and himself an RAF pilot, recorded a September dinner party discussion on the Poles one evening. Winston Churchill argued that one Pole was easily worth three Frenchmen. Lord Gort, the former commander of the British Expeditionary Force and Dowding both disagreed and suggested the ratio was more like 10 Frenchmen per Pole.[54] Their effectiveness and old-fashioned gentlemanly charm also made the Poles popular across the nation. Following the battle, it became fashionable for Polish pilots to be invited to society parties and some Polish squadrons were adopted by famous society hostesses, (though one pilot observed that one particular hostess was careful to only ever invite girls uglier than herself to country parties). The Polish pilot's romantic habits, such as kissing girl's hands and bestowing large bouquets of flowers on them, allegedly meant they were

---

53   Lynne Olson and Stanley Cloud, *For Your Freedom and Ours* (London: Arrow Books, 2004), p. 142.
54   Lynne Olson and Stanley Cloud, *For Your Freedom and Ours*, p. 144.

Pilots of 303 (Polish) Squadron at Leconfield, Yorkshire on 24 October 1940. From left to right they are: Pilot Officer Witold Lukociewski, Pilot Officer Miroslaw Feric, Flight Lieutenant J.A. Kent (Flight Commander), Flying Officer Bogdan Grzeszczak, Pilot Officer Jan Zumbach, Pilot Officer Jerzy Radomski and Flying Officer Zdzislaw Henneberg. (Crown Copyright – Air Historical Branch)

as successful with the girls as they were as fighter pilots. One cannot help but feel sorry for the RAF pilots, eclipsed in war and love by the Poles.[55]

The role of the Poles, as well as the Czechs, is well-known. The cutting of RAF OTU courses from a month to just a fortnight, in order to generate front line pilots quickly is probably less familiar.[56] Although providing more pilots, it caused an immediate drop in quality and one of the saddest British aspects of the Battle was the arrival of hugely inexperienced pilots at front line squadrons, sometimes with as little as 20 hours on Spitfires, no gunnery practice, and no understanding of a reflector sight. This poor standard of basic combat airmanship was matched by similar ignorance of squadron tactics, that were of course evolving all the time. The casualties were predictably high amongst these inexperienced aircrew. Two new novice fliers arrived at Croydon airfield and were told by the leader of the Squadron 'I'm sorry, but I'm afraid you'll have to go in today.' One hour later one of them was seriously wounded and the other dead – their kit was still unpacked in their room. Many years after the battle a RAF pilot was scrolling through a book listing the names of the pilots who had been in the squadron he had fought with during the battle. 'Some I couldn't remember,' he said. 'They passed through and had been shot down before I could get to know them.' Christopher Foxley-Norris was a pilot with No.3 Squadron and recalled 'You just took an ignorant young man, stuck him an aeroplane, and told him, 'Go and fight the

55   Olson and Cloud, *For Your Freedom and Ours*, p. 181.
56   James Holland, *Battle of Britain*, p. 531.

Germans ... Most people who went into 11 Group didn't last. They couldn't last. They had no chance at all. But there was no means of stopping it. You had to fill the cockpits.'[57]

These drastic measures were just enough for Dowding to preserve Fighter Command as a fighting force and compel the *Luftwaffe* to admit that they had failed to gain air superiority for the planned for invasion of Britain. Hitler accepted this verdict and temporarily postponed the invasion on 17 September 1940, subsequently accepting the impossibility of launching it in 1940 on 12 October and then finally giving up all hope in February of 1942.

The Battle of Britain remains the RAF's most cherished battle honour, celebrated on 15 September as Battle of Britain day each year. This is justly so – it was Britain's first significant victory in the war and established the RAF's reputation. It was a decisive defensive battle that prevented the Germans from achieving air superiority, launching an invasion and arguably winning the war in the west. It should also be celebrated for the longer-term impact too – *Feld Marschal* Gerd von Rundstedt was asked by Soviet interrogators after the war what he considered to be the most decisive battle of the Second World War. They expected him to reply with Stalingrad but instead the old general commented that it was the Battle of Britain, for if the RAF and Britain had been crushed, then the Germans would have had a free hand in their war against the Soviets and would have been victorious. The Soviet interrogators apparently closed their notebooks and left in a huff.

The RAF's success in the battle rested on a number of important factors. They had a well-established early warning and command and control system, well-sited and constructed airfields and modern aircraft that were able to match the enemy's opposing fighters. Importantly the RAF had just enough pilots and aircraft to maintain the defence despite inevitable losses and attrition. Understanding these essential factors is an important step in comprehending how strategic air superiority is achieved over home territory. However, air superiority is not exclusively about the defence of one's home base. Fighter Command's next operations were attempts to project air superiority into western Europe, in order to gain the initiative against the Germans.

---

57   Lynne Olson and Stanley Cloud, *For Your Freedom and Ours* (London: Arrow Books, 2004), p. 123.

5

'Firmness of Purpose'[1]
Offensive Air Operations over
Fortress Europe

The end of the Battle of Britain was followed by the onset of bad autumn weather and a growing German night bombing campaign. Fighter Command was a tired force at this point and many of the most experienced leaders were posted from their squadrons, either to the growing training organisation, or to emerging theatres of war overseas. As 1941 began there was also a new command team at the helm of Fighter Command. Air Marshal Sir William Sholto Douglas had become the Commander-in-Chief in November 1940 and Leigh-Mallory had replaced Park at 11 Group in December of the same year. Though in a poor position to take the offensive against the Germans in France, the Fighter Command leaders nevertheless placed a high value on regaining the initiative and developed the operational concept of fighter and mixed fighter/bomber sweeps over France.

Enthusiasm for such activity had been in existence for some time, the Air Ministry directing that all commands should 'take every opportunity of destroying enemy aircraft wherever met'.[2] Indeed during 1940 there had been regular night intruder raids over German airfields in France and Park had also proposed sweeps by wings of three squadrons to surprise the weak German patrols still being maintained over the straits of Dover. However, about the time Douglas took over at Fighter Command the Air Staff went further stating that the fighter force should, if conditions allowed, 'lean into France'. Douglas directed his commanders to 'get away from the purely defensive outlook' and recommended sweeps encompassing French coastal towns such as Calais, as well as encouraging Park to explore the potential of combining these sweeps with daylight bomber activity (see Map 3 for a sense of this new area of operations). When Park was replaced by Leigh-Mallory the planned sweeps became more ambitious in nature and included both pure fighter-sweeps, as well as those where they escorted bombers. The aim for both was to write down German fighter strength and force the enemy on the defensive.

The degree of penetration into France was initially modest, though the RAF maintained that there were many important military targets along the Channel coast including ports, bases, supply dumps and airfields. These were thought sufficiently important from the German perspective for the *Luftwaffe* to be enticed to tackle the bombers – though unsurprisingly many within the British bomber force were unenthusiastic about their role as bait.[3]

These new operations quickly attained their own codenames and became a strong feature of RAF operations over the coming years. 'Circus' operations were those where bombers were escorted by

---

1   Motto of 64 Squadron – a Spitfire-equipped squadron that operated on offensive fighter sweeps over Europe from 1941 to 1944.
2   Basil Collier, *The Defence of the United Kingdom* (London: HMSO, 1957), p. 290.
3   Basil Collier, *The Defence of the United Kingdom* (London: HMSO, 1957), p. 291.

Armourers of 306 (Polish) Squadron reloading a Spitfire's 20mm cannon with ammunition at RAF Church Stanton. (Crown Copyright – Air Historical Branch)

A flight of Supermarine Spitfire Mark VBs of 122 Squadron takes off from Hornchurch, Essex, for a fighter sweep over France. (Crown Copyright – Air Historical Branch)

fighter escorts against short range targets, a 1941 Circus typically consisted of a small number of bombers, usually Blenheims, with a fighter escort.

The fighter escort wing of Spitfires or Hurricanes would usually meet the Blenheims at 15,000 ft over North Weald, Biggin Hill or Northolt, from there the combined force would then fly at the bomber's speed of 180 mph across the Channel to France. By the time they crossed the French coast they would have climbed to about 17,000 feet. The 'close escort squadron' would fly 1,000 feet above and slightly behind the highest box of bombers with strict instructions not to leave the bomber aircraft except to repel attacks. It was the least popular role for the fighter pilots. Two further escort squadrons would be behind and to the flanks of the bomber force cruising from 3,000 to 5,000 feet higher. Their role was to engage any fighters that threatened the bombers. They were to remain in their positions during the withdrawal, but once the force had returned half-way across the Channel, they were allowed to turn and carry out their own sweep to seek and destroy any enemy aircraft.

The bomber force and escort wing were in turn protected by the high cover wing which consisted of two or three squadrons. These aircraft provided top cover for the bombers and their escorts and flew both above and behind them at altitudes up to 30,000 feet, with squadrons normally stacked up at different heights 2,000 to 3,000 feet apart. The commander of this force had the greatest latitude to dive down on any enemy fighters, though it was still mandatory to leave the highest squadron as cover for the rest of the wing, only in exceptional circumstances would they be deployed to fight. The high cover wing would support the escort wing once it was freed from its bomber burden and was conducting its own sweep. Finally, there was the mopping-up wing. This comprised two or three squadrons, who would independently fly at 25-30,000 feet and meet the returning force as it crossed the French coast heading back to England. By careful planning the mopping up wing would be in an advantageous position up-sun and escort the bombers and its close escort home, this in turn would free both the escort wing and its protecting high cover wing to conduct its sweeps.[4] As can be seen the complexity of this operation was high, as was the intensity of the fighting. Duncan Smith describes a 'Circus' in June 1941:

> Our task was to act as high cover to bombers whose targets were the marshalling yards at Hazebrouck. We crossed the coast at 28,000 ft, the sun glinting on the perspex of our cockpit hoods and long vapour trails streaming behind us. Below, I could see the stepped formations of the lower escort squadrons stretching down to the neatly packed group of Blenheims with their close escort of Hurricanes at about 12,000 ft. We called it the 'beehive' because with individual aircraft weaving and jinking about the whole affair looked like a swarm of bees.
>
> As we approached Hazebrouck a formation of 10 ME 109s, slightly below, came towards us. Eric Stapleton turned into them and started to dive; immediately the enemy formation rolled onto their backs and disappeared past the tail of the 'Beehive'. Almost on top of the target another formation of 15 Me 109s appeared below and we promptly dived for them. They saw us coming and broke into our attack. I stuck close to 'Polly' as we waltzed around trying to get on to their tails. One group of 109s then broke right with two sections after them, while 'Polly' called me: 'Take the right 109 Charlie Two I'll get the other'.
>
> We were now well placed and the 109s stayed with us in a tight circle. They were staggered, the one on the right slightly above and behind the left-hand one with ourselves in a commanding position behind and a couple of hundred feet above.
>
> I swung my nose across closing fast and as the 109 filled the width of my windscreen I blasted into the side of his cockpit and engine. Bits flew off and thick smoke gushed; the 109

---

4   Peter Caygill, *The Biggin Hill Wing* (Barnsley: Pen and Sword, 2008), p. 12.

rolled slowly over and plunged vertically down. As I prepared to follow, tracers streaked past my cockpit and over the top of my propeller. I broke sharply in a right-hand climbing turn. Polly's voice hit my earphones: 'Good boy, Charlie Two. Climb I'm above.'

Wildly I looked round for 'Polly'. Turning, I saw two Me 109s flash past behind me, then above them the unmistakable wing pattern of a Spitfire. Giving my aircraft every pound of boost I had I rocketed upwards in a tight spiral. 'Polly' saw me coming and nosed towards me.

'Did you get one Charlie Leader?' I called him.

'Think so, can't tell – had to break – attacked by six bastards.' His reply snapped and crackled as other voices cut in.

We searched for the rest of the Squadron but could not see them. Below and above Spitfires wheeled. We were somewhere near the tail-end of the 'Beehive'. I glanced at my altimeter and saw we had lost a lot of height. Smoke and dust clouds were rising from the target below, and away to our right the bombers were flying homewards, angry black puffs of AA Shell bursts following them.

'Let's get right into the 'Beehive' and climb up.' 'Polly's voice was flat.[5]

Experience had taught Duncan Smith never to fly straight and level and to search the sky continually, his heart leapt into his mouth as he saw streaking straight towards him a gaggle of nine Me 109s:

Close together we swung into a tight climbing turn to face the enemy. It was no good. Three more 109s came at us from ahead. I saw the guns of the leading 109 wink at me and tracers flew past – there was a loud bang somewhere along my fuselage. The next second I was fighting for my life.

Again, I heard 'Polly's voice as I turned my Spitfire in a tight circle, wings shuddering, vision clouded in a grey mist as the blood drained from my head.

'Look out behind – dive for the deck.' My radio was terribly noisy.

I slewed round in my harness and looked behind. I saw a Me 109 slightly above with 'Polly' on his tail firing. I heaved my Spitfire round trying desperately to get behind 'Polly's machine. Suddenly the 109 which 'Polly' was firing at broke into a red glow; black smoke gushed, and it hurtled down. More tracer whizzed past and once again I was corkscrewing out of the way. I caught a glimpse of 'Polly' as he rolled on his back and dived for the ground in a tight spiral, and immediately lost sight of him in the dark pattern of fields and woodland below. Just then the 109 that had fired at me shot past my port wing tip terribly close and I got a glimpse of a black-helmeted head peering out as the enemy dived below me.

I rocketed down after the 109. He was out of range, losing height in a gentle dive. I glanced round behind, above, below – the sky was clear. Fairly close now and over on my left I could see the French coast. Slowly I gained on the enemy still diving and keeping just below his slipstream. Then at last the 109 began to loom large in my windscreen. I held my fire; a quick look behind; I had no intention of fouling it up. I was determined not to open fire until I was sure I could not miss. Now, I was ready to make the kill: I eased the stick forward a little and at close range pulled the nose of my Spitfire up sharply, lined up my sight and opened fire, pouring cannon shells into the enemy's belly. There was a sheet of flame, the 109 flicked over onto its back and dived straight into the ground. It crashed close to a corner of a wood, near a white-washed and neat looking farmhouse. I circled once clipping the tops of the trees with

---

5   W.G.G. Duncan Smith, *Spitfire into Battle* (London: John Murray, 2004), pp. 63-66.

Hurricane fighters of 312 (Czechoslovakian) Squadron escort Stirling from 15 Squadron based at Wyton in Huntingdonshire during a daylight Circus raid on Lille on 5 July 1941. The Stirlings, however, suffered a large numbers of losses to anti-aircraft fire and were soon withdrawn from this type of mission. (Crown Copyright – Air Historical Branch)

my wing-tip, watching the column of black smoke belching into the air from the wreck. I felt elated and terribly pleased with myself.

I scrambled somehow back to Manston, hugging first the grey-green fields of France at treetop height, then the uninviting and hostile waters of the Channel. I didn't have much fuel to spare; I got down with about two sherry glasses left, and by now in a thoroughly filthy frame of mind, upset and frightened.[6]

The number of Circuses increased throughout 1941, though there were many who doubted the operational wisdom of the sweeps and pointed out that all the advantages now lay on the German side. Just like the British in 1940, the *Luftwaffe* had developed an efficient radar-based air defence system, in addition, any damaged *Luftwaffe* aircraft could reach nearby bases and be swiftly repaired and *Luftwaffe* pilots who baled out could be returned into action almost immediately. In contrast any RAF machine damaged over France had to face a risky journey back across the Channel and pilots who baled out over France, with a few rare exceptions, were almost immediately captured and out of the war for good. Whilst leading the Tangmere Wing Douglas Bader was captured in just such a manner, when his Spitfire was downed on 9 August 1941 in the Pas De Calais area. Bader was only able to exit his spinning Spitfire by detaching his artificial legs. The Germans who captured Bader requested the British drop a spare leg over the airfield – the RAF obliged as part of a bombing run. One area where the RAF's experience did differ from the German defensive operation over Europe was that the British in the summer of 1940 had been compelled to intercept each raid, this was because of the threat they collectively posed to the nation's survival. In contrast each Circus would usually only have a dozen or so Blenheims operating within it, each carrying only 4 x 250lb bombs that would be dropped from 17,000 feet on what was essentially occupied territory. This did not constitute a severe threat and the Germans could afford to simply ignore the Circus, avoiding battle if they felt the advantage did not lie with them.[7]

The dangers and disadvantages of Circus operations were widely understood by British aircrew, particularly as in May 1941 the Me 109F appeared which gave the enemy a renewed technological advantage. The Me 109F had a better ceiling than any RAF fighter and better overall performance including speed of climb. The Spitfire might be able to out-turn a Me 109F, which was a definite defensive asset, but of little value when attacking. Whenever they chose to fight, the new German fighters would simply dive through the stacked British squadrons, then zoom off to regain the height advantage, diving again if the situation warranted.[8] Veteran fighter pilot Paul Richey had one lucky escape as his subsequent report to Fighter Command makes clear:

> I was Yellow 1 of 609 Squadron taking part in Circus 62, 7 August 1941. Having failed to rendezvous with the main formation of the Biggin Hill Wing, I proceeded to carry out a 'Sphere' entry at Dunkirk and flying over St Omer with the intention of leaving France at Cap Gris Nez. 609 Squadron was top squadron, 92 middle and 72 bottom, and heights were originally from 25-28,000 ft.
>
> Over St Omer many 109s were sighted far below against the cloud and 72, led by Wing Commander Robinson, attacked. 92 lost height by diving and then circled for some time followed by 609 Squadron. If I may suggest it, I think 92's tactics were mistaken, for both height and speed were lost, and nothing gained. In addition the stepped-up formation of 92

6   W.G.G. Duncan Smith, *Spitfire into Battle*, pp. 63-66.
7   Peter Caygill, *Biggin Hill Wing* (Barnsley: Pen and Sword, 2008), p. 155.
8   Brereton Greenhous, *The Crucible of War*, p. 202.

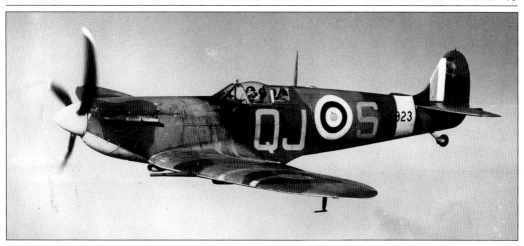

Spitfire Vb, R6923/QJ-S, of 92 Squadron based at Biggin Hill, Kent, in flight. R6923 was originally a Mark I, converted to a Mark V after serving with 19 Squadron and 7 Operational Training Unit in 1940. It was shot down over the sea by a Messerschmitt Bf 109 on 22 June 1941. (Crown Copyright – Air Historical Branch)

and 609 were messed up and generally confused, while the Huns were able to gain height and time and get up-sun with a good view of what was going on.

I was troubled with ice on my hood and windscreen, I was also very bored and cold and was flying sloppily. While my attention was concentrated on a formation above me, I was shot-up in no uncertain manner by a gaily coloured Me 109 diving from behind. My glycol tank was pierced, and all my glycol lost. I throttled back and went into an involuntary spin. I could see nothing but smoke, glycol etc. and could not recover from the spin which became very flat. I opened the hood to bale out but had great difficulty in removing my harness pin, I think because a) I did not look what I was doing and b) I was experiencing a lot of 'g'. When I got the pin out I was slowly deciding to stay in and try to recover, by winding the tail wheel fully forward and using considerable strength on the stick, I did so (the tail was damaged). I dived for cloud and the French coast, weaving, and was attacked by another 109 which I evaded by turning violently and entering cloud. My 'Maiz-dez' [*sic*] was answered immediately over the sea on Button 'D' and I was given a vector.

I was unable to use the vector because of having to weave and control the aircraft. Half way across the straits at 1,000 ft I tried my engine and was able to use it to the English coast by cutting down boost and revs to a minimum. I had great difficulty in doing up the straps again because of instability of the aircraft which necessitated strong forward pressure on the stick but succeeded after five minutes. I was confronted by the sight of many rescue launches and buoys and by the Hurricane low cover off the Goodwins. On a fast belly landing at Manston and with a still smoking aircraft I found the Fire tender very prompt. I would like to stress the following points for the benefit of young pilots:

1. Slackness in the vicinity of the Huns is easy but usually fatal.
2. A Spitfire will last long enough without glycol and even practically without oil, if revs and boost are reduced to an absolute minimum.
3. The sea is much more hospitable than German occupied territory. It is well worth risking attempting reaching it. The chances of rescue are excellent.

Squadron Leader NG Pedley, the Commanding Officer of 131 Squadron assisted by his ground crew, prepares to set out on a sweep in his Supermarine Spitfire Mark Vb, BM420/NX-A 'Spirit of Kent/Lord Cornwallis', from Merston, a satellite airfield of Tangmere, Sussex, June 1942. (Crown Copyright – Air Historical Branch)

    4.   Do not try a slow forced landing, with damaged control surfaces.[9]

The large and complicated Circuses were complemented by smaller bombing operations ('Ramrods'), pure fighter sweeps, ('Rodeos') and small low-level fighter operations involving just a few aircraft (called 'Rhubarbs'). These latter Rhubarb operations took place during periods of low cloud and poor visibility, when sections of Spitfires would slip across the Channel. Once over France, they would let-down below cloud to search for opportunity targets, such as locomotives, rolling-stock, staff cars, enemy troops and occasionally airfields. At some stations they were arranged on a voluntary basis and though there were a few eager pilots who preferred this sort of individual low-level work, many were un-enthusiastic and thought that the dividends yielded by Rhubarbs fell far short of the cost in valuable pilots and aircraft.

Airfields were widely considered to be the most dangerous targets. 'Mac' Mackenzie, a Hurricane pilot, found out the risks for himself during an attack on Lannion airfield in Brittany on 29 September 1941. This Rhubarb was undertaken by four Hurricane IIcs of 247 Squadron who set off from Predannack, Cornwall at 1850 hours:

> As we dipped down onto the sea from Predannack to cross the Channel at about 200 feet in order to get under the German radar, we spread out into two flights of two aircraft on a course of 152 degrees, throttling back to a cruising speed of 230 knots with Red 1 and myself (Blue 1) slightly ahead of our No. 2s.

---

9   An 11 Group Tactical Memorandum quoted in Caygill, *Biggin Hill Wing*, p. 106.

The weather was hazy with some high stratus cloud and the sea looked dark and, as usual cold and uninviting, but calm. Keeping radio silence we skimmed over the water, settling ourselves into our seats with a tight harness and well positioned, relative to the gun sights: the Merlin engines were droning steadily at high boost and low revs for best cruising speed and economy before re-adjusting for the final attack … After some 25 minutes we made out the French coast with lower cloud inland drifting towards the target area. Passing Les Triege Islands to our east we selected full power, checked all instruments, switched on the Gyro gunsights and guns to 'Fire' and pulled up 600 feet for the diving attack on Lannion.

Flying in line abreast and 200 yards apart, we dived to attack at 100 feet; Red 1 and 2 [Red 1: Flight Lieutenant D Smallwood and Red 2: Pilot Officer Hordern] attacked the western perimeter and I, with my No.2 [Sergeant Deuntzer] took the east side. As we dived to attack the flak defences opened up immediately with intense and accurate fire from all sides of the airfield and outside it. Visibility was poor, even with our canopies open, in the hazy fading light, so that the tracer bullets of the flak showed up like a stream of fireworks, only more deadly. Red 1 and Red 2 fired long bursts into what looked like dispersal pens without any visible result.

With my No.2 we weaved and fired at buildings and dispersals; I silenced a gun post about half a mile from the north of the aerodrome. The flak was a constant stream by now and getting more accurate, missing me a few feet only as I jinked and could only get short bursts of fire at the guns. Red 1 and 2 and Blue 2 had pulled away, but I was determined to have a last quick attack on my way out towards the coast.

By now the sky was alive with flak and I was sweating like a pig and very angry about the whole mission. I silenced one more gun position but was coned by the rest as I passed to the south of the airfield down to about 50 feet to upset their aiming, but too late and I felt the thud of bullets hitting the aircraft, all – thank God – in front of me, in the engine, radiator and oil with one across the top of the windscreen and a crack on the top of my head. I pulled straight up, nursing the engine. Height, I must get height as a means of escaping towards the sea and base. Visibility was now very poor with long dark shadows and haze. With a failing engine and a sore head, I continued weaving as the flak fell away out of range though still following me in vain.[10]

Mackenzie came down in the Channel and after a difficult night in his dinghy, was captured by the Germans and spent the rest of the war in a POW camp.

In June 1941 RAF senior leaders concluded that these operations were not successful in placing RAF fighters in tactically favourable positions. Douglas commented that this was because the aircraft were operating too low, he would have preferred the lowest fighters to be at 18,000 ft with the highest at 30,000 ft, sadly this was not a practical proposition as it took a long time for the Blenheims to climb to even 17,000 ft.[11]

The Circus operations were stepped up, in June 1941, in a bid to assist Britain's new Russian allies and prevent the Germans from reinforcing the eastern front. The RAF believed that the Germans had reacted strongly to attacks on Bethune, Lille and Lens and so these were made a focus of new attacks. On occasions Stirling bombers were used instead of Blenheim bombers, these could carry a greater weight of bombs and were preferred by the fighter pilots as they had proportionally less charges to look after. Forty-six Circuses were carried out from 14 June to 31 July, involving 374 bomber and 8,000 fighter sorties, this was supplemented by 1,000 fighter sorties

---

10   K.W. Mackenzie, *Hurricane Combat* (London: Grenville Publishing, 1987), pp. 13-15.

11   Peter Caygill, *Biggin Hill Wing* (Barnsley: Pen and Sword, 2008), p. 148.

Spitfire pilots of 234 Squadron at rest in the pilots' room at Warmwell, 26 July 1941. (Crown Copyright – Air Historical Branch)

supporting attacks on shipping (known as 'Roadsteads') and a further 800 purely fighter sweeps (the Rodeos). A further 26 Circuses were undertaken in the month of August and though German opposition was noted to be much more effective, instructions were still issued in September for the Circuses to attack new targets beyond the Nord and Pas de Calais area including Amiens, Le Havre and Ostend.[12] From October onwards the sweeps reduced in numbers, a combination of the deteriorating weather and concern that an American entry into the war would stifle the supply of aircraft and equipment. There was of course also a growing demand for aircraft and resources from other theatres, particularly from the woefully equppied RAF in the Far East. In summing up the Circus offensive Douglas reminded others what his objectives had been:

1.   To wrest the initiative from the enemy for the sake of the great moral and tactical advantages bestowed by its possession.
2.   In co-operation with Bomber and Coastal Commands to prevent the enemy from withdrawing any more flying units from the Western Front after the middle of June.
3.   To induce the enemy to return some of the units already withdrawn by that time thus weakening his offensive capacity on the Eastern Front.

The official Fighter Command conclusion was that the Circuses had seized the initiative and inflicted substantial damage to the German air force. Though it was also acknowledged that result had only been achieved at considerable cost to the RAF themselves and it could not be determined what the *Luftwaffe*'s capacity to recuperate was like. These losses caused many to question the

12   Caygill, *Biggin Hill Wing*, p. 150.

effectiveness of Rhubarbs and Circuses. For the period from 14 June to 31 December 1941, Fighter Command claimed 731 German aircraft shot down for a loss of 411. The actual German losses were in fact only 154 aircraft, including 51 not attributed to British action and 11 more lost over the UK itself in other operations. The balance sheet would appear to be four-to-one in Germany's favour[13] – many of the British losses were amongst the veteran senior fighter pilot leaders that the RAF could ill afford to lose. In addition, a total of 75 day fighter squadrons were retained in the UK to conduct these operations, as well as guard against a German disengagement from the Eastern Front. If one considers the difference these aircraft and experienced personnel could have made to Malta, the Middle East and Far East, in one of the most crucial years of the war, you begin to understand why they have been criticised as wasteful. Douglas disagreed and later justified these efforts by outlining the main benefits as he saw them:

> It was said at the time and after that the sweeps carried out by Fighter Command in 1941 were a waste of effort. I cannot agree with this view, even though Peirse, who was then command-ing Bomber Command, and subsequently Bert Harris, were against them. First the question of morale. I hold that no air force can achieve air superiority by remaining continuously on the defensive and confining their efforts to the defence of their own country. The sweeps, therefore, were an essential preliminary to a switchover to the offensive, and in this sense they were the forerunners of the invasion of the Continent.
>
> Secondly, such sweeps produced many tactical lessons which the pilots of Fighter Command were able to learn and adjust in the best possible circumstances. Thirdly, from a purely tacti-cal point of view, the sweeps kept a high proportion of the German fighter force confined to Europe, and if they had not been carried out much of this force would have been sent to the Eastern Front to operate against Russia. While I do not claim that the sweeps caused the Germans to withdraw fighter squadrons from the newly created Eastern Front, I do think, in fact I am sure, that they did discourage them from reinforcing those fighter squadrons at the expense of the west. Therefore, as what I may call a retaining action, those sweeps were well worthwhile.[14]

Given the scale of the RAF's global commitments in 1941-1942 Douglas' view seems very narrow, though his arguments seem to have been accepted by the Air Staff in London, who failed to rein-force the Middle East and Far East sufficiently. It highlights how sometimes those geographically closest to the corridors of power can have a disproportionate influence in their demands, certainly in comparison to those lobbying from many thousands of miles away by telegram.

The RAF's bomber and fighter sweeps did not end in 1941 but continued at various levels of intensity throughout the succeeding years. Yet Fighter Command recognised that the short range of its fighter aircraft limited its ability to project air superiority over the continent. Initially it was felt this would not change until the Allied armies were able to set foot on the continent once more and provide them with advanced landing grounds from which to operate. This was impossible prior to the American entry into the war and would still require significantly more preparation and resources than were available in 1942 and 1943. The difficulty of invading Europe was made abundantly clear during Operation JUBILEE, the invasion 'dress rehearsal' at Dieppe in August 1942. There the Germans had inflicted a punishing defeat not just on the assaulting Canadian Division but also on the air support to the raid, the RAF losing 108 aircraft during the operation, the *Luftwaffe* admitting only to losing 14. On a more positive note there were two other events in

---

13   John Terraine, *Right of The Line* (London: Hodder and Stoughton), 1985, p. 285.
14   Peter Caygill, *Biggin Hill Wing* (Barnsley: Pen and Sword, 2008), p. 147.

1942 that offered an indication of how air superiority over Europe would be achieved in advance of an invasion.

Two days prior to Dieppe, United States Army Air Force (USAAF) heavy bombers undertook their first mission in Europe: a limited penetration raid to Rouen-Sotteville rail yards. This growing American bomber fleet would eventually present the *Luftwaffe* with a day-bomber threat over their own country, one that they simply could not ignore. Initially the German fighters were able to successfully combat this new menace when the American bomber force strayed beyond the protection of the short-range fighters. However, fortuitously the British had fitted the North American Aviation P-51 Mustang with a Rolls-Royce Merlin engine and created one of the war's most outstanding machines. This was subsequently operated by the American Air Force and when fitted with long range tanks could escort bombers all the way to Berlin and battle in the skies over that city against the very best German aircraft. The long-range Mustang's arrival over German skies marked the beginning of the end of German day-fighter superiority in Western Europe. This was especially so as from January 1944 General James H. Doolittle, Commander of the American Eighth Air Force, changed the tactics of the American fighters from one where their main role was to 'bring the bombers back alive' to one which was to 'destroy German fighters'. As the Mustangs were released from guarding bombers they engaged *Luftwaffe* fighters wherever they could be found. As one German commander recounted: 'Wherever our fighters appeared, the Americans hurled themselves at them. They went over to low-level attacks on our airfields. Nowhere were we safe from them; we had to skulk on our own bases. During takeoff, assembling, climbing, approaching the bombers, once in contact with the bombers, on our way back, during landing, and ever after that the American fighters attacked with an overwhelming superiority.[15]

Additionally, on 27 May 1942, the Mosquito conducted its first mission with 105 Squadron of 2 Group. This aircraft surpassed the wildest expectations and presented the RAF with a light bomber aircraft fast enough to penetrate German airspace and evade enemy fighters, yet still retaining a 4,000lb bomb carrying capacity that was able to inflict significant damage.

In the 18 months prior to D-Day the *Luftwaffe* day-fighters began to face British and American modern medium bombers at 12,000 to 14,000ft level, American Boeing B-17s and B-24s at 32,000 to 38,000 feet and Mosquito raids at any height up to 25,000 ft. These would all be escorted by short-range fighter aircraft such as Spitfires as well as the long-range Mustangs when required. At night they would have to put up with Bomber Command's raids and night-fighter intruder operations over their airfields, designed to disturb their sleep and sap their strength. Unsurprisingly by the time the Normandy invasion commenced in June 1944, the *Luftwaffe* in the west was a shadow of its former self.[16] This made the Allied entry into Europe and subsequent land battles much more successful.

Yet throughout this period the Rhubarbs, Circuses, Ramrods and Rodeos continued, despite the debatable operational benefits they bestowed. The increasingly experienced Johnnie Johnson was certainly not a fan of Rhubarbs:

> First of all we had to contend with the weather. Usually the cloud base was less than 1000 feet when we slipped our two Spitfires into its concealing vapour. During the next few minutes all our thoughts were concentrated on the likely height of the cloud base over France. Our let-downs from the cloud were usually made over reasonably flat country-side, but here and there small hills rose and presented serious hazards, If we weren't in the clear when the altimeter recorded 500 feet, then we climbed back into the cloud and called the show off.

---

15   Brereton Greenhous, *Crucible Of War*, p. 292.
16   Jerry Scutts, *Fighter Operations: The Tactics and Techniques of Air Combat from World War 1 to the Gulf War* (Yeovil: Patrick Stephens, 1992), p. 66.

Low-level oblique photograph taken during a 'Circus' operation, showing an attack on the docks at Cherbourg, France, by 12 Bristol Blenheim Mark IVs, drawn from Nos. 21 and 107 Squadrons RAF. A dockside store on the west quay of the Darse Transatlantique explodes from a direct hit (left), while another bomb bursts close to a moored tanker. (Crown Copyright – Air Historical Branch)

So it was difficult to be cool and calculating when making our let-downs in Rhubarb flights. Perhaps two of us had flown in cloud, in tight formation, for a distance of 50 miles at 2000 feet. Time to descend, for we are over the target area – or should be if we have steered an accurate course and the wind hasn't changed. We ease the throttle back and put the Spitfires into a gentle dive. The engine note changes, but it seems strangely loud in the cloud and the stick trembles in your hand. You flash a grin of encouragement at your wingman who is only a few feet away, his eyes and hands attuned to every movement of your Spitfire, for if he loses you in this bumpy, swirling greyness there is not enough height for him to make the difficult transition to instrument flight. You ease her down slowly. Are we slightly off course? Will the ground be higher than where we planned to break out? And the flak? 600 feet on the altimeter and you catch a glimpse of a wet sombre landscape of hedged fields and copses. Then you are at the bottom of a sort of inverted bowl, whose translucent sides of falling rain seem dangerously confining.

Then there was the light flak. Gibbs told us that once beyond the heavily defended coastal belt we should be lightly opposed from the ground, but it always seemed as if the enemy gunners were ready and waiting. Airfields were always extremely well defended, and it was a dangerous business to try and make more than one fast, low-level attack. Straight in and straight out was the only method on these occasions.

The Germans prepared unpleasant counter-measures against these low-level attacks. Here and there decoy targets were established, and these sometimes took the form of stationary locomotives heavily armoured and surrounded by numerous well-camouflaged light flak guns, arranged to provide a deadly concentration of fire against air attack. Many pilots received the shock of their lives when they streaked down upon what they imagined to be a sitting duck.

Usually our Rhubarb efforts yielded little more than a staff car (or was it a French civilian vehicle?) or some target ineffectively sprayed with the puny bullets of our machine guns. Whenever we went after bigger game on the airfields we took some bad knocks, and our first losses were from such operations … I loathed those Rhubarbs with a deep, dark hatred. Apart from the flak, the hazards of making a let-down over unknown territory and with no accurate knowledge of the cloud base seemed far too great a risk for the damage we inflicted.

During the following three summers hundreds of fighter pilots were lost on either small or mass Rhubarb operations. Towards the end of 1943, when I finished this tour of ops and held an appointment of some authority in 11 Group, my strong views on this subject were given a sympathetic hearing and Rhubarbs were discontinued over France, except on very special occasions.[17]

As the RAF were beginning these offensive daylight sweeps into France, the *Luftwaffe* kept Britain under attack by night, with a series of 'blitz' campaigns that targeted British cities. They had also been simultaneously generating an entirely new genre of weaponry that was launched after D-day and would keep British cities in a state of alert until the last weeks of the war.

---

17   Johnnie Johnson, *Wing Leader* (London: Chatto and Windus, 1956), p. 79.

6

'Always Ready'[1]
Countering German Night Raiders and V-Weapons

7 September 1940 saw the first, large daylight raid on London, the Germans dropping 300 tons of high explosive and many thousands of incendiaries in just an hour and a half. As the bombers withdrew, they left large fires burning in the dockland areas East of Tower Bridge and among the factories and oil installations further downstream. Len Jones was a young 18-year-old boy, who lived in the east London district of Poplar and remembered this first raid:

> It was very exciting because the first formations were coming over without any bombs drop-ping, but very, very, majestic, terrific. And I had no thought that they were actual bombers. Then … the bombs began to fall, and shrapnel was going along King Street, dancing off the cobbles. Then the real impetus came … the suction and the compression from the high-explo-sive bombs just pushed you and pulled you, and the whole of the atmosphere was turbulating so hard that, after an explosion of a nearby bomb, you could actually feel your eyeballs being [almost] sucked out … and the suction was so vast, it ripped my shirt away, and ripped my trousers. Then I couldn't get my breath, the smoke was like acid and everything round me was black and yellow. And these bombers kept on and on, the whole road was moving, rising and falling.[2]

The 7 September also witnessed the first major night raid on the city. A total of 250 bombers were despatched that night, who dropped 330 tons of high explosive and 440 incendiary canisters. The German bombers from *Luftflotte 2* and *3* found it was easy to identify the city by both the raging fires and the sweeping curves of the River Thames. Consequently nine-tenths of the German aircraft were able to successfully drop their munitions within 10 miles of Charing Cross. The riverside areas east of the City of London suffered the most, with approximately 1,000 Londoners killed during the course of this 24-hour period.[3] Bernard Kops was just a young schoolboy at the time but he remembers the experience of sheltering from this first raid:

> Imagine a ground floor flat [in Stepney Green Buildings], crowded with hysterical women, crying babies and great crashes in the sky and the whole earth shaking. Someone rushed in, 'The docks are alight. All the docks are alight.' I could smell burning … The men started to

---

1   The 68 Squadron Motto. The unit was formed on 7 January 1941 as a night-fighter squadron. It was equipped with Blenheims initially before converting to Beaufighters in March 1942. The squadron had a strong Czechoslovakian element within it, including the flying ace Miloslav Mansfeld.

2   Juliet Gardiner, *The Blitz – The British Under Attack* (London: Harper Press, 2010), p. 13.

3   Basil Collier, *Defence of the United Kingdom* (London: HMSO, 1957), pp. 239-240.

Two Dorner Do 17s of the *Luftwaffe* pictured over West Ham, London, during a raid on the capital on 7 September 1940. (Crown Copyright – Air Historical Branch)

play cards and the women tried a little sing song, singing 'I saw the old homestead and faces I loved' or 'Don't go down the mine, Daddy, dreams very often come true' or 'Yiddle mit his fiddle'. But every so often 20 women's fists shook at the ceiling cursing the explosions, Germany, Hitler … Yet cursing got my mother and my aunts through those early days. I sat under the table where above the men were playing cards, screwing my eyes up and covering my ears, counting explosions.

'We're all gonna get killed, we're finished,' one of my aunts became hysterical.

'Churchill will get us through, he's a friend of the Yiddisher people.' With these words she was soothed.

When the All Clear eventually sounded the atmosphere in the shelter changed at once:

Everyone relaxed, the men arguing politics and the women talking about food, but the younger people wandered out to see the fires and I went with them along the Commercial Road. The closer I got, the more black and red it became with flames shooting higher than the cranes along the dockside. Sparks were spitting everywhere, and tongues of flames consumed the great warehouses along the black and orange waters of the Thames. Everything was chaos except the fire which was like a living monster with an insatiable appetite. And I was afraid of being devoured ... so I left and wandered back towards Stepney Green where black smoke covered the sky. Yet, with all this, there was a feeling of unreality. I couldn't believe it, it was like a film being shown before our eyes, Men were rushing around selling newspapers, screaming about the amount of German planes that were brought down, and there had been a family wiped out where I had been standing.[4]

Sometimes the casualties from the German raids were very large. After a raid on Sunday 8 September 1940 which destroyed significant amounts of local housing in Canning Town, a rest centre was established at Hallsville School. A total of 600 people congregated there awaiting evacuation before the next night raid. Ritchie Calder, a journalist with the *Daily Herald*, recalls the survivors waiting evacuation, including the Reverend Paton, a popular local clergyman, known to all by his nickname: 'The Guv'nor'.

His pulpit still stood, but the roof and front wall had gone. I found 'The Guv'nor' at last, he was ashen grey with the anguish of the night. He had been out in the raids, helping his people throughout the night. His lips trembled and his eyes filled with tears when he spoke of his friends who were dead, injured or missing. But his main concern was for the living. He was dashing round the streets seeking out the survivors whose homes had been wrecked.

I went with him. We found many thousands sheltering in a school in the heart of the bombed area. I took a good look at the school. From the first glance it seemed to me ominous of disaster. In the passages and classrooms were mothers nursing their babies. There were blind, crippled and aged people ... Whole families were sitting in queues perched on pitiful baggage waiting desperately for coaches to take them away from the terror of the bombs which had been raining down on them ... these unfortunate people had been told to be ready for the coaches at three o'clock. Hours later the coaches had not arrived. 'The Guvnor' and I heard women, the mothers of young children, protesting with violence and with tears about the delay. Men were cursing the officials who only knew that coaches were expected. 'Where are we going?' 'Can't we walk there?', 'We'll take a bus!', 'There's a lorry we can borrow!' The crowds clamoured for help, for information, for reassurance. But the officials knew no answer other than to offer a cup of tea.

One mother complained that her children had been forbidden to play in the playground ... [the official showed me why]. In the playground behind the school was a crater. The school was, in fact, a bulging dangerous ruin. The bombs which had rendered these people homeless had also struck the building selected by the authorities as a 'Rest Centre' ... the school had already been bombed at the same time as 'the Guv'nor's' church had been bombed. So had the parish church ... So had other buildings and streets within a direct line with it. And then I knew that Sunday afternoon, that as sure as night would follow day, the bombers would come again with the darkness, and that the school would be bombed.[5]

For reasons that have never been fully explained, the buses that were to evacuate those in the Canning Town rest centre never turned up. As Calder predicted the overcrowded school received a direct hit. Despite the best efforts of rescue teams, who were still digging for survivors 12 days after the raid, as many as 450 people are thought to have died in the centre. A number sufficiently large, and in circumstances that reflected so poorly on the government administration, that any publication of the story was banned. Many were never identified and are buried in a large communal

---

4   Juliet Gardiner, *The Blitz – The British Under Attack* (London: Harper Press, 2010), pp. 12, 22.
5   Gardiner, *The Blitz – The British under Attack*, pp. 31-32.

grave in the East London Cemetery at Plaistow.[6] Horrors, such as the Hallsville School bombing, understandably resulted in increased pressure on Fighter Command to defend the capital.[7]

The British had just 264 anti-aircraft guns in the London area at the time (92 in the Inner Artillery Zone, 120 in the Kent and Essex marshes and 52 in the western outskirts of the city). This was a shockingly low number – even the pre-war defences had consisted of 480 guns, but sadly many of these had been diverted to reinforce other areas. In addition, the two night-fighter Blenheim squadrons in the London area had not been very effective during the night-raid of 7/8 September. One squadron could not take off because of thick smoke billowing across its Hornchurch base and the second patrolled a line north and east of London but did not encounter any German aircraft. Thus, for a seven hour period the German bombers were able to fly unimpeded by fighters, the only threat posed to them was by balloons and anti-aircraft fire, which at least forced them to bomb from a greater altitude.[8]

As the German bombers were driven from the daylight skies over Britain the *Luftwaffe* increased the frequency of their night-time raids, which would become a familiar experience for many British cities over the winter of 1940/41. German bombers were relatively light compared to the RAF heavy bombers used later in the war, but when used en masse they could still inflict a punishing blow. In addition, *Luftwaffe* bomber accuracy was assisted by the *Knickebein* or 'crooked leg' navigation system, which provided electronic beams for the target marking aircraft of *Kampf Gruppe 100* (KGr 100) to navigate. This allowed them to release their bombs accurately over the cities, despite not being able to see the ground below them (so-called blind bombing). These first aircraft would drop incendiaries to start fires that would act as a guide to the following aircraft, which were not equipped with *Knickebein*. This new enemy system had been uncovered by Dr Reginald V. Jones of Air Intelligence and the RAF swiftly developed counter measures to jam and disrupt *Knickebein*, this included adapting British beam approach beacons to receive and re-transmit enemy *Knickebein* signals, thus widening the beam to the point it was no longer accurate.[9] In addition, Bletchley Park were able to intercept and decode KGr 100's Enigma traffic, so that the Air Intelligence staff could warn Fighter Command where and when the attacks could take place. Dr Jones describes these breakthroughs:

> It was a day, late in October, when they [Bletchley Park] achieved this fantastic feat for the first time. Thereafter, they were able to repeat it on about one night in three. I was then able (having first worked out the position of the cross-beam stations near Calais) to tell the Duty Air Commodore at Fighter Command the exact place of attack, the time of the first bomb to within 10 minutes or so, the expected ground speed of the bombers, their line of approach to within 100 yards, and their height to within 200 or 300 metres. Could any air defence system ask for more? Despite this detailed information – and much to our disappointment – our night-fighters repeatedly failed to locate KGr 100 aircraft and I almost began to wonder whether the only use the Duty Air Commodore made of my telephone calls was to make a bet with the rest of the Command as to where the target would be for that night.[10]

---

6   Gardiner, *The Blitz – The British Under Attack*, p. 32.
7   Annex P contains the details of civilian casualties in the United Kingdom caused by long range bombardment including aerial bombing.
8   Basil Collier, *Defence of the United Kingdom* (London: HMSO, 1957), p. 239.
9   Denis Richards, *Royal Air Force – Volume 1*, p. 200.
10   R.V. Jones, *Most Secret War* (London: Hamish Hamilton, 1978), pp. 139-140.

Frustrating though this may have been for Air Intelligence, the problems of successfully night fighting in the air were severe. Trials had been undertaken by both the French and British before the war, with some concluding that the best way to detect, identify and attack enemy aircraft at night would be for night-fighters to operate using purely visual means in conjunction with search-lights. One pre-war trial report had concluded:

> It is likely even under good conditions that searchlights will only help the fighters by 'flick overs', to close with and attack a bomber in the dark. If however, the lights continue to hold the bomber or make a series of flickovers without dropping behind it while the fighter closes until he can see the bomber itself, it is practically certain that the fighter will be able to deliver an attack. The approach to and attack on both a lit and unlit target should be made behind and below, fire probably being opened at a maximum of 200 yards. Fighter patrols should be placed at least 10 miles behind the front line of searchlights in order to avoid confusion and allow the fighter to go forward to intercept when a pick-up has been made. Use of the aircraft landing light as a searchlight did not prove successful.[11]

This report turned out to be overly optimistic and night-fighter operations against German bombers using purely visual means proved to be very difficult in actual practise. Even on moonlit nights, when the ambient light was high, enemy aircraft could only be visually detected by the flames from poorly shrouded exhausts or the inadvertent use of cockpit lights. Additionally, it was very hard for RAF night-fighter crews to preserve their night vision, which could be easily destroyed by searchlights, their own aircraft's exhausts or careless use of lights pre-take-off. In a paper published on 28 May 1941, the RAF's Air Fighting Committee gave advice to night flyers on how a trained eye could improve the chances of spotting an enemy aircraft:

> A study of the night search and the factors which aid successful night search are of vital importance for the night-fighter. The night-fighter pilot's task calls for precision and care for detail both in preparation for a sortie and when engaged in search for the enemy. Be night adapted – don't let a dirty windscreen spoil your efforts, look to the detail – study the weather and think how you intend to apply it to your tactics before each sortie. Remember, once you have picked up your Hun it is easier to hold him in view than to start your search afresh – therefore, hold him! A moving target is much easier to see than a still one, make relative movement, therefore, by gently rocking your aircraft when searching. Don't search vaguely into space. Try to visualise your target at the range at which you expect to find it and search accordingly.[12]

Squadron Leader J. Simpson, OC 245 Squadron, illustrates the challenge of such missions, whilst he was conducting a patrol in his Hurricane near Belfast on 8 April 1941:

> I was in the Mess when news came that the Germans were dropping bombs on a town nearby. It seemed rather strange. The war had not come so close to Ulster before. Incendiaries had been dropped and high explosive bombs were on the way. I was next to patrol. It was about 1:15 in the morning, dark with a sickly moon shining through a mist. I took off and climbed to about 9,000 ft, passing above the clouds into another world, where the moon, in its second quarter, shone out of a blue-black sky.

11   Ken Delve, *Nightfighter* (London: Cassell, 1995), p. 49.
12   Delve, *Nightfighter*, p. 52.

Hurricane IIc, BD867/'QO-Y' of 3 Squadron on the ground at Hunsdon, Hertfordshire, on 6 September 1941. Note the exhaust shields above the exhaust outlets, which were fitted to the squadron's aircraft during night fighter operations. (Crown Copyright – Air Historical Branch)

I was told that there were aircraft near me. My eyes searched the blackness. There was no horizon: no object upon which to fix one's eyes. And one had the illusion, travelling at 200 miles per hour, that every one of those brilliant stars was the tail light of an aircraft. I searched among that moving pattern of lights and my eyes rested upon two black objects. I could see them because, as they moved, they obliterated the stars. They were quite near when I recognised them as aircraft ... whether enemy or not, I was unable to tell. So I flew nearer and learned soon enough. The rear gunners of both aircraft fired a shower of bullets at me, some with whitish-green light of tracer bullets, some glowing red. They missed me and for a minute I lost them.

Then I saw them again, farther apart, moving against the white floor of the clouds below me. They were black and quite clear. The advantage was now mine for they were perfectly placed as targets. I crept down to attack the rearmost of them. They were flying slowly. It was difficult for me to withhold my speed so that I could not overtake him. At a distance of about 200 yards I opened fire from slightly below. Then came my next surprise ... the blinding flash of my guns, in the darkness. In day time one does not see it. At night it is terrific, and I was so blinded that I lost sight of my enemy. I broke away and lost him for a few seconds I next saw him going into a gentle dive towards the clouds.

The increase in speed made it easier for me to attack and I closed to 80 yards. I opened fire once more. This time I was prepared for the flash and kept my eyes on the enemy. His rear gunner returned my fire, but only for a second. I had apparently got him for he was silent after that. I continued my fire closing in to about 50 yards. Then I saw a comforting red glow in his belly. I was still firing when the Heinkel blew up, with a terrific explosion which blew me upwards and sideways. When I righted myself, I was delighted to see showers of flaming pieces ... like confetti on fire ... falling towards the sea. I was able to enjoy the satisfaction of knowing that I had brought him down before he had released his bombs. The second Heinkel had disappeared, and I asked for homing instructions over the wireless.[13]

---

13   Delve, *Nightfighter*, p. 87.

The RAF night-fighters operating purely on visual means were known as 'cat's-eye' fighters. They were used to operate near the major targets and cities and would work in concert with searchlights (See Map 4 which shows the RAF night fighter bases and British cities attacked). The close proximity to anti-aircraft artillery meant that close coordination with the guns was required, something that was sometimes not always achieved. 'Mac' Mackenzie was a pilot on Hurricanes in 247 Squadron, a night-fighter squadron based at Predannack, Cornwall and part of 10 Group. Like all RAF night-fighters, the Squadron's Hurricanes had been painted a matt black and exhaust shields fitted over the stub exhausts. These were essential to both eliminate the glare from the stubs when flying, as well as reducing the flame and sparks that would be emitted from the exhausts when throttling back for landing. On the night of 8 July 1941, Mackenzie was scrambled to intercept a raid of German bombers over Plymouth:

> Scrambled at 9.30pm to patrol the Plymouth baseline, the inland line, I watched a rather sporadic raid on the city and harbour area with considerable searchlight and anti-aircraft activity. After about half an hour, with the moon well up, but no visual sightings so far, I spotted an He 111 quite clearly illuminated, and then another, crossing from west to east. I turned in, called the guns and signalled my downward identification light, as I crossed the AA zone the searchlight lost the bandit and the firing ceased.
>
> I locked onto the second raider which was about 1,500 yards away but had difficulty in seeing it clearly. Height was around 8,000 feet and closing rapidly on him, I settled down to dive and get him from astern and below. When at 800 yards or so and slightly below, I had a very clear silhouette and, closing to 400 yards, was just about to go in for the kill when there were two shattering explosions on either side of me.
>
> My aircraft was tossed about like a toy; I lost sight of the He 111 and control of the aircraft and went into a dive, being momentarily stunned and disorientated. Immediately regaining control and getting back to level flight, I cursed the gunners who obviously had opened fire when they should not have and then suddenly remembered the Plymouth balloon barrage. Were they up or down? I was by then down to 5,000 feet, over the harbour. I pulled up into a steep climb and got back to 8,000 feet as quickly as possible, while calling Control and reporting the loss of a pretty certain kill owing to the blasted gunners, I was in a cold sweat and furious.
>
> The aircraft felt OK and I went back on to the patrol line but by then the raid was over, raiders gone, and the stupid gunners had nearly got me instead. More than just frustrating – inefficient gunnery control. We had a right royal verbal battle the next morning and they finally apologised – not much help – and promised to tighten up their coordination instructions.[14]

In the autumn of 1940, as the German night blitz got into its stride, there had been considerable debate about what the approach to night-fighters should be. Some, such as Douglas, argued that increasing numbers of day fighter squadrons should be converted to night-fighter duties. Others, including Dowding, saw the future in fighters equipped with Airborne Interception (AI) radar who could hunt down the enemy aircraft themselves. That same autumn, AI radar, though still temperamental, was reaching an advanced stage of development. In addition the Bristol Beaufighter, though it had been beset by numerous teething problems, was just coming into service to replace the Blenheim which was found to be too slow for night-fighter operations.[15] The debate between

14   K.W. Mackenzie, *Hurricane Combat* (London: Grenville Publishing, 1990), p. 106.
15   Basil Collier, *Defence of the United Kingdom* (London: HMSO, 1957), p. 252.

Bristol Beaufighter IF, R2198/PN-B, of 252 Squadron based at Chivenor, Devon, in flight over the snow-covered West Country. (Crown Copyright – Air Historical Branch)

the two approaches should not be seen as a mutually exclusive one, the converted day fighters still shot down reasonable numbers of German bombers and AI-equipped night-fighters would take a while to arrive in front-line units, even when they did they were not a miracle cure.

The AI-equipped night-fighter would typically have to get within three miles of the enemy aircraft to establish contact with its radar. This was hard to achieve because fighters patrolling fixed lines were seldom lucky and though coastal radars could be used, the RAF were understandably reluctant to let the AI night-fighters travel considerable distances across the Channel in case the secret radar equipment fell into enemy hands. Patrolling the *Knickebein* beams seemed a profitable tactic; but German crews understood the danger and were very wary. Searchlights it seemed offered the best chance, pointing towards enemy aircraft to guide nightfighters, but at this stage of the war they too lacked radar and often struggled to detect the bombers.

Fortunately, the War Office had begun to issue Gun Laying (GL) radar sets to some of its anti-aircraft batteries at this time, these were capable of accurately tracking the bombers at vertical, or slant, ranges of up to 40,000 ft. Although the GL sets were scarce Dowding persuaded the Army to lend him a few and installed them experimentally with a number of searchlight posts in the Kenley sector. Direct communication between the GL radar-equipped searchlight post and the sector operations room allowed the controller to vector an individual night-fighter onto an acquired target. The final stages of acquisition being achieved by a mixture of the night-fighter's AI radar, radio and the radar-directed master searchlight pointing directly at the tracked bomber. The system worked and was further improved by the establishment of Ground Control Intercept (GCI) radars. GCI radars shifted the burden of the intercept from the sector controllers, who were now only required to order the night-fighters to a patrol line, from where they would be handed over to the GCI station's control. At the end of the mission the sector controller would then take

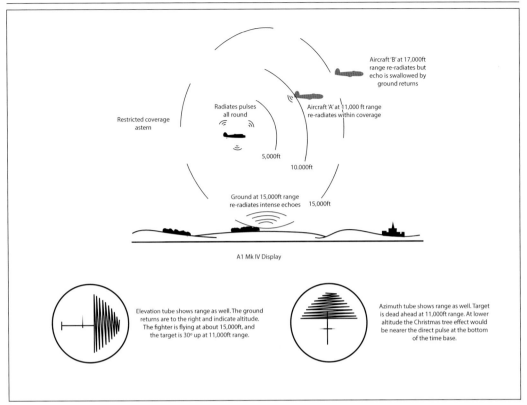

Aircraft 'B' at 17,000ft range re-radiates but echo is swallowed by ground returns

Aircraft 'A' at 11,000 ft range re-radiates within coverage

Radiates pulses all round

Restricted coverage astern

5,000ft

10.000ft

Ground at 15,000ft range re-radiates intense echoes   15,000ft

A1 Mk IV Display

Elevation tube shows range as well. The ground returns are to the right and indicate altitude. The fighter is flying at about 15,000ft, and the target is 30° up at 11,000ft range.

Azimuth tube shows range as well. Target is dead ahead at 11,000ft range. At lower altitude the Christmas tree effect would be nearer the direct pulse at the bottom of the time base.

Figure 5 Mk IV Air Intercept Radar.

back control of the night-fighter and direct it to another patrol line or back to their home base, where newly established Aerodrome Control Officers would be responsible for their safe night-time landings.[16]

By the close of 1940, GCI sets were becoming more numerous as were AI sets in the new Beaufighter aircraft. The Beaufighter was an aggressive looking machine, powered by two Hercules engines that jutted out in front of the pilot's cockpit and gave the aircraft the appearance of a squat boxer with two massive fists. The Beaufighter was one of the war's most successful aircraft, performing a wide variety of roles in many theatres, including ground attack and anti-shipping as well as a night-fighter. It carried a crew of two, the pilot who sat at the front and was separated by a set of armoured doors from the navigator who sat behind him just above the wings. The Beaufighter was armed with 4 x 20mm cannons, a fiercesome set of weapons and was loved by its crews for its rugged simplicity, reliability and toughness. In night-fighters, the navigator worked as a radar operator and the Beaufighter, when equipped with the AI Mk IV radar set, can claim a leading role in neutralising the German night Blitz of 1941.

The AI Mk IV radar transmitted pulses at a frequency of about 93 Mhz with a wavelength of 1.5 metres. This necessitated large antennas including a transmitting dipole mounted on the nose of the Beaufighter and sets of receiving antenna positioned above and below the aircraft's wing. These receivers would measure the differences in time between the broadcasting signal and the returning echo from any large object covered by the Mk IV's radiating pulse. The measurements would be displayed on two separate Cathode Ray Tubes, one showing the angle and range in azimuth and the other the angle and range in elevation. From these two readings the radar operator would have to determine the location and behaviour of the enemy aircraft. This was very hard as the displays gave no indication of whether the aircraft was turning, accelerating, slowing down, or even which heading it was flying on. The radar operator would have to judge all of these from changes to the angles and ranges of elevation and azimuth in the two screens in front of him.

As the radar transmitter floodlit the sky, it meant that the ground beneath the fighter received as many pulses as did the sky in front. Figure 5 demonstrates this meant that a massive return echo was received from the ground, at a range equal to the fighter aircraft's height, which effectively drowned out any smaller target such as another aircraft, if it were beyond that range. This ground radar return was shown on both the Azimuth and Elevation tubes as large spiky green triangles, the radar operators calling them the 'christmas trees.' Thus, a fighter equipped with AI Mk IV which was flying at just over 5,000ft altitude had a maximum radar range of one mile, while at 21,000ft this went up to four miles.[17] There was also a minimum range of about 400 feet at which the contact would be lost to the radar operator, if the pilot had not visually acquired the target at that point then the final stages of the intercept would be almost impossible.

The speed with which the enemy and AI night-fighter aircraft moved in relation to each other, meant that clear and descriptive instructions between the radar operator and pilot were vital. These would be communicated as the order first, how quickly or severe the manoeuvre should be taken and then what the enemy aircraft was doing. Thus, a control might sound like this: *'Right, hard right. Tighten the turn, he's crossing port to starboard range about two miles. Ease the turn. Steady. He's 10 degrees starboard and 10 degrees up. Range still two miles. Starboard again gently. Steady. Dead ahead now, still slightly up, throttle back a bit, range coming down rather fast.'* Not for nothing did some pilots jokingly consider themselves to be little more than glorified taxi-drivers to the radar operator. One of the most successful night-fighter teams of the war was pilot John Cunningham and his radar operator Jimmy Rawnsley. Both had started the war as part of the Royal Auxiliary Air Force in 604 (County of Middlesex) Squadron, Rawnsley initially as an Air Gunner. Cunningham attained 20 aerial kills, three probable and six damaged, all but three of these he achieved with Rawnsley. As one of the first night-time fighter aces John Cunningham's exploits were published in the press and in order to mask the secrecy of radar the public were told his success was attributable to his exceptional eyesight and the Vitamin A in the carrots he ate. He was given the nickname 'Cat's-Eyes', which he hated and as will be seen below his ability to acquire targets was down to the skill of both the radar operator and the GCI team. The narrative below by Rawnsley concerns one of the first patrols in which they were supported by GCI in late 1940. At the time 604 Squadron were based at RAF Middle Wallop in Hampshire, from which this sortie was flown.

> We climbed away to the eastward and at 3,000 ft we broke through the cloud into a clear, moonlit sky. John called up the Tangmere GCI – which bore the apt name 'Boffin' – and the controller turned us south, sending us out into the Channel. When we got to the coast we found that the cloud stopped short, hanging like a sharply trimmed ice-cap over the gleaming chalk cliffs of the Seven Sisters. I sat watching the cliffs as they receded into the moon haze on the horizon.
>
> 'Hallo, Blazer Two Four,' Boffin called. 'Orbit … orbit. There is a bandit coming in. Angels eleven.'
>
> 'OK, Boffin,' John acknowledged. 'Orbiting.'

---

17   J.H. Williams, *Night Intruder* (Newton Abbott: David and Charles, 1976), p. 22.

The engines took on a deeper, sterner note as John opened up the throttles. Over the intercom he said to me.

'I'm going up to 15. We'd better have a bit of height in hand.'

The vectors began to flow in from Boffin. One five zero … turn starboard on to two one zero … turn port on to zero six zero …

Although I was keeping my eyes fixed on the tubes of the AI set I had in my mind a picture of what this all meant. We had been turned aside so as to allow the bandit to pass. Now we were swinging around in pursuit and heading back towards the coast.

'Flash your weapon' came the instruction from Boffin.

For about the twentieth time I adjusted the tuning control.

'No joy yet,' I reported to John.

We were fairly humming along. The chase was on and we could not be far behind. Was that a bulge just beginning to form at extreme range, at the foot of the Christmas tree? I held my breath and hoped that I would not make a hash of this one. It was definitely a blip, just appearing. I gave it a few more seconds to get clearly out of the ground returns, and then I moistened my lips and found my voice.

'Contact at 15,000 ft,' I told John. 'Slightly port and well below.'

I had stuck my neck out and admitted liability for what was about to happen; now I should have to do something about it. Well first of all to get dead astern of the target.

'Check port' I said.

The blip swung across the trace as John turned to the left and then centred again as he straightened out on the same course, having executed a neat side-step.

'Dead ahead … range 10,000.' I reported 'We'd better lose some height before we get any closer.'

In a manoeuvre such as this it was no good just diving. That would only have meant gathering more speed and finally shooting over the top of the bomber. But John had already worked out a plan for this. He throttled back the engine, dropped the wheels to act as an air brake, and gently started to sink. The range went on decreasing but at a rate that was well under control.

The blip was slowly drifting out to the left again, so we went through another side-step. While I was concentrating on this I forgot to keep an eye on the height. A timely reminder came from John as he said:

'On course. I'm still losing height by the way.'

'OK. Level out now,' I replied. I hoped that it sounded as if I had thought of it myself. 'Range, 8,000 dead ahead and level … increase speed again.'

The two Hercules engines stopped their sulky spitting and the aircraft surged forward to their happier purring as John opened up the throttles. But that blip would keep drifting to the left. We must be on a slightly diverging heading. I gave a correction:

'Turn port 10 degrees', that ought to take care of it. We were in to 5,000 ft now, and the blip was sharp and clear. But now it was drifting to the right. I had over-corrected in the last turn.

'Turn starboard 5 degrees.'

'Starboard 5,' John acknowledged.

That was better. We seemed to have made a lucky guess at the height too. But it was time to slow up. I increased my commentary, giving John as complete a picture as possible of what was happening.

'Range 3,000. Throttle back a bit. It's dead ahead and slightly above.'

Squarely astride the trace, the blip was coming down quite well as the range decreased. But I was becoming rather excited, and with that there came a fear that we might be coming in too fast.

'Range 2,000 … still ahead … 15 degrees above. Throttle right back. Range 1,500 … '

The blip was moving steadily down towards the minimum range, and I became really scared that we were going to overshoot.

'1,200 … 1,000 … still ahead and 30 degrees above. 900'.

The aircraft was swinging uneasily. John had cut the throttles right back, and the engines were coughing and popping. And there, at the bottom of the trace, sat the blip, fat and squat. There was a horrible moment of crisis as it hovered at minimum range. Then slowly it started to climb the trace again as our own speed dropped off.

'Increase speed again,' I told John. 'It's still there, 30 degrees above.'

At these close ranges quick thinking was essential. John, I knew, would be keyed up to the limit, quick to react to every call I made. His eyes would be searching where I directed, his hands and feet and brain flying the aircraft by instinct born of long experience.

As the engines picked up again I felt the aircraft settle into her normal easy stride. And then there was a sudden unexpected movement, followed by a short exclamation from John. The blip started moving again but with a new certainty of movement.

'OK. I can see it!' John said.

My heart leapt … covering over the visor I swung my seat sideways. There, just where the AI had indicated was a dark shadow, its outline blurred by the moonlight, silhouetted against the soft velvet of the night sky.[18]

With the aircraft in visual sight, the pilot would alter the light on his reflector sight a little. This was the same gunsight used in the day fighters and it was very hard to adjust this to an optimum setting. If it was too bright the pilot could not see through the ring to the target, if he set it too dim then the spot within the ring disappeared altogether.[19] The pilot of the Beaufighter sat well forward with a large glass windshield all around him giving him an excellent view of his target. During these final stages, with the enemy aircraft visually acquired, the radar operator would still man the AI set in case the pilot lost sight of it and he would be needed to re-acquire the target. If he had time the radar operator might re-check the safety catches and air pressures of the 20mm cannon located in the aircraft's belly once more. During the combat he would also be ready to dash down to the catwalk between the cannon and change the drum magazines or clear any stoppages. This was a cumbersome business, which involved undoing fiddly clips before the four empty drums could be removed, it was particularly difficult to do if the aircraft was moving violently. The radar operator would then have to clip the empty drums back in as they could not afford to have them flying around the cockpit. All of this he would need to do on a portable oxygen tank and off the intercom so if the pilot wished him to go back to the AI set, or plug into the intercom, he would simply waggle his wings. In later models of Beaufighters the ammunition was kept in one large tank and this duty was no longer required. Rawnsley describes the final stages of a kill.

A violent thunderstorm was raging in the depths of that heaving turmoil of cloud, and every few seconds the lightning flashed across, lighting the whole scene with a horrible, steel blue clarity. We could see clear-cut every detail of the Heinkel.

Surely, I thought their gunners would be able to see us just as plainly as we could see them. We were barely 100 yards away. As we crept in, each flash of lightning was a stab at the nerves, and as the darkness leapt back over us I sighed with relief. The Heinkel rode on, beautiful, serene and unheeding. Finally we were right below it ready to attack.

---

18   R.F. Rawnsley and Robert Wright, *Nightfighter* (Manchester: Crecy Publishing, 1998), pp. 55-7.

19   Rawnsley and Wright, *Nightfighter*, pp. 55-7.

'OK?' John asked.

'Yes,' I replied. 'Hold your hat on.'

'Right. In we go!'

Slowly, very slowly, the Heinkel sank towards our sights. This was their gunner's chance, just before we could bring our cannon to bear. We were a sitting duck, only 80 yards away, and in moonlight. Pale-blue exhaust flames licked along the engine cowlings of the bomber, and John, in his cool detached way, noticed that the outboard flames were on a lower level than those inboard.

Our aircraft wriggled nervously as John brought the gunsight on to his target. Then he opened fire, and almost at once the whole sky ahead of us seemed to dissolve in flame. My knees caved in as the floor heaved underfoot. Every slot and chink in the hull was lit by the lurid glow of the sea of fire from the exploding Heinkel as we ploughed on through it. Things bumped and scraped along outside. And then we were through it all and out into the darkness. My eardrums and breathing relaxed, and I became conscious again of the reassuring roar of our own engines. We still seemed to be flying.

'Are we all in one piece?' I asked.

'Yes … I think so,' John replied. His voice was still quite calm as he took stock, methodically checking his instruments. 'Let's see now. Oil pressures … temperatures … yes … everything seems all right.'

There had come back into our Beaufighter the typical smell of a burning German aircraft, a smell that was to make a deep and most unpleasant impression on me. It was sweet and sickly, and came, I understood from the light alloy used in the airframe as it burned. Others had remarked on that smell and we all found it rather nauseating.

I looked out quickly over our starboard quarter, and there I saw a terrible sight. The shattered Heinkel, with only one wing left, was spinning down vertically spewing out as it went a helix of burning petrol. It looked like a gigantic Catherine Wheel, and I watched until it plunged into the floor of the cloud below. The snows flurried and glowed from within for a few seconds, and then it was all swallowed up by the cloud. The severed wing fluttered slowly down, a falling leaf spilling out drops of flame. Then that, too, disappeared into the cloud, and we sailed on alone. Two miles below us the icy black water of the Channel would be quenching that dreadful fire.[20]

By March 1941, half of the 22 German aircraft destroyed by British fighters were claimed by the AI-equipped Beaufighters and their performance only got better. During a single raid on London on the night of 19/20 May 1941, a total of 24 aircraft were shot down by night-fighters, in contrast only two German aircraft were downed by anti-aircraft ground fire.[21] The punishment being inflicted on the bombers was becoming unsustainable for the *Luftwaffe* as RAF night-fighters destroyed nearly one tenth of the bombers which set out for Chatham on 13 June and between June and December 1941, the *Luftwaffe* lost 114 bombers mainly in night operations. This was a heavy blow for the small force of 200 bombers kept in the West after the Eastern Front had opened in Russia. As the official history observed, there is a reasonable claim that the main German offensive ended at the very moment when Fighter Command's night-fighter force had developed a sharp edge to their operations.[22] Annex Q contains details of the British night-fighter effort from

---

20   Rawnsley and Wright, *Night Fighter*, pp. 67-8.

21   Phillip J.R. Moyes, *The Bristol Beaufighter I & II (Aircraft in Profile Number 137)* (Leatherhead: Profile Publications, 1966), pp. 10, 197.

22   Basil Collier, *Defence of the United Kingdom* (London: HMSO, 1957), p. 301.

A view of the cockpit of a Bristol Beaufighter. (Crown Copyright – Air Historical Branch)

The navigator of a 125 Squadron Bristol Beaufighter MK. VIF settles into his position, ready for another night patrol from Exeter, 14 September 1943. (Crown Copyright – Air Historical Branch)

January to May 1941. The reader will notice the significant contribution 'cat's-eye' night fighters were still making.

The British night-fighter successes, did not mean the *Luftwaffe* bombers were an entirely spent force and there were repeated German attempts to renew their bomber offensive against Britain. Between April and August 1942, the Germans massed 430 bombers in the west and embarked upon the so-called Baedeker Blitz. This targeted British cultural centres featured in the Baedeker guide, as a response to the Bomber Command strikes on Cologne, Essen, Rostock and Lübeck that spring. Cities such as Exeter and Bath were struck and the British night-fighters were busy once more, though this time their capability included an increased number of Mosquitoes. Once more, the vast majority of *Luftwaffe* aircraft were destroyed by AI-radar equipped aircraft rather than 'cat's-eye' fighters. This was not the last conventional German bomber offensive against Britain. From January to May 1944, the Germans launched Operation STEINBOCK, more usually known as the 'Baby Blitz', though this was less intensive than previous German bomber campaigns, it still required considerable effort to combat and significant damage was inflicted on both London and southern English towns. Nevertheless these German efforts were the exception and there is no denying that German bomber capability was on a steep, downward trajectory from 1942.

To meet these continuous offensives the British continued to develop their night-fighter capability and AI sets in particular. This work was undertaken by the Telecommunications Research Establishment (TRE) in Malvern, whose new inventions were tested by the Telecommunications Flying Unit (TFU) at nearby RAF Defford. TFU's trials on airborne radar were ground breaking and included Anti-Surface Vessel (ASV) radar for maritime use, as well as AI. Successful equipment would then be further tested in a frontline setting by the Fighter Interception Unit at Ford in Sussex. By November 1941, the 10cm wavelength radar was coming into service and this allowed the development of the Mk VIII AI radar. The advantage of the new wavelengths was that smaller dipole aerials could be used, which could be mounted in the front of the fighter with a reflecting mirror or scanner behind. This allowed the radar pulse to be directed and focused in a narrower beam, minimising the ground return echo. It meant that a low-flying night-fighter could pick up German aircraft, even if it was at a greater range than his own altitude, a timely development as the *Luftwaffe* were beginning to alter their tactics to single low-flying intruders. The development of the AI Mk VIII radar also introduced a host of electronic upgrades, including Cathode Ray Tubes that were easier to read for the radar operator. The new radar was often fitted to the latest twin-engined fighter being brought into service, the Mosquito.

In time the Mosquitoes would undertake offensive night missions across the Channel in support of the RAFs bomber offensive. These included flying across Germany on the flanks of the bomber stream as well as intruder missions against German night-fighter airfields, attacking the *Luftwaffe*'s own night-fighters taking off, or coming in to land at their home base when they were at their most vulnerable. The year 1942 saw a great expansion of the German night-fighter force and as a consequence a significant proportion of the Mosquito squadrons (an average of 10 for most of 1942) were directed against these airfields. By October 1942, Mosquito intruder operations were being controlled from a special operations room at Fighter Command Headquarters, favourite targets being the *Luftwaffe* night-time airfields at Leeuwarden, Deelen, Twenthe and Venlo in Holland and Germany.[23]

The Mosquito was a truly marvellous twin-engine aircraft, it first flew in November 1940 and by late 1941 was arriving in operational frontline units. Powered by Merlin engines and constructed entirely out of wood, partly to offset the predicted scarcity of strategic materials such as steel, the Mk II could fly at 370 mph and the Mk XVI could reach 415 mph, making it one of the fastest

---

23   Ken Delve, *Night fighter* (London: Cassell, 1995), p. 121.

operational aircraft in the world at the time. It had originally been conceived as a fast bomber, but it was found to be a suitable aircraft for many roles including fighter bomber, photo reconnaissance aircraft, maritime strike aircraft and of course, as a night-fighter. It was also used by the British Overseas Aircraft Corporation as a fast transport to ferry small and valuable cargoes to neutral countries like Sweden. This included carrying passengers who would ride in the bomb bay when necessary. The range of the Mk II Mosquito was impressive: a 900-mile range was normally achievable with its 410-gallon fuel load, which was extended even further to 1,500 miles, in the Mk XVI.

One feature the Mosquito did not have was a roomy cockpit, the crew of two sitting snugly side by side. Dave Mcintosh was a navigator with 418 (City of Edmonton) Squadron RCAF and flew throughout the war with American-born Sid Theid. He describes getting into the notoriously cramped cockpit of a Mosquito night-fighter.

I went up one step on the ladder and handed my maps to Sid. Then I put my chute on the floor and tossed the dinghy into my seat. I climbed up the other two steps and struggled through the door. My Mae West caught on the hinge and I couldn't free it right away.

'You coming or not?'

'I'll be there in time for takeoff,' I said.

I ripped the Mae West only slightly getting clear of the door. I plunked myself down on the dinghy, the little rubber lifeboat all done up in a neat square package. The rubber sucked out your piles if fear didn't. I felt for the hooks on my harness and snapped the dinghy clamps into them. If I jumped the dinghy came with me. If I didn't, I unhooked it at the end of the trip.

'Can you help with these damn straps?' Sid asked.

I reached over and found Sid's straps, which locked him in his seat, and passed them over his shoulders. Two went over his shoulders, two came up from the sides of his seat. Sid gathered the four together and locked them together with the brass pin, I did the same, twisting in my narrow seat. My parachute was on the floor between my feet. There we were, as snug as two peas in a pod. There was no place for claustrophobia. I had room enough to twirl a pencil between my fingers and that was about it.

I felt in my small, upended box at my right knee to make sure all the maps were in place. First the map of southern England, then the Gee grid chart of the English Channel, then France, Belgium, Holland, western Germany and southern Germany, central Germany and eastern Germany and so on, just in case.

Hal took the ladder away and then came close, his chin just below the edge of the doorway. 'OK, Sid?'

'OK.' The door slammed shut and Hal turned the latch from the outside.[24]

Intruder operations over Europe were difficult and lonely missions. A great deal was expected of the navigator who had to identify an enemy airfield deep in occupied territory, this was not an easy task and the enemy often had a few tricks up his sleeve. McIntosh and Theid were assigned a 'flower' mission in the Munich and Ingolstadt area. During these missions the Mosquitoes were tasked to patrol over German airfields or night-fighter radio beacons, whilst a bomber mission was being conducted:

I watched the ground unfold picking out the pinpoints easily, a bend on the Moselle, the big bend on the Rhine, a bend on the Neckar, another on the Danube and Ammer Lake. A piece

24   David McIntosh, *Mosquito Intruder* (London: John Murray, 1980), p. 49.

Crews from 605 Squadron, based at Ford in Sussex, relax before a night intruder operation in early March 1942. (Crown Copyright – Air Historical Branch)

of cake. It was great not to worry about the height because of the moonlight. We figured we lost a lot of guys on black nights when they simply ran into the deck.

We were on our final leg to Munich when Sid said, 'That looks like a field ahead lit up.'

… The field was probably Argelsried. Sid did a circuit to port at a fairly respectable distance from the field, though it was still too close for me. Then he did another, closer this time. The flarepath remained lit but we couldn't see any signs of activity in the air. We didn't carry interceptor radar like the standard night-fighters and a Jerry had to be showing some light before we could see him.

This time around, I peered at the perimeter, trying to make out any planes parked on the ground. Not only did I fail to spot any planes; I couldn't see any hangars or a control tower or damn all. Just woods and a few roads. If we were going to see anything on the ground, this was the night for it. Suddenly lights showed on the flarepath, moving slowly. It looked like a plane taxiing to the east end for take-off.

'Here we go' said Sid. He pulled farther away so that he could turn and line up on the flarepath, went into a shallow dive and got his firing finger on the tit.

The moment he fired, all the crap in the world came up at us. My guts dropped right through my ring. I could feel my pants flapping against my legs. This was because my legs were shaking.

Flak as orange, yellow and red tennis balls, coming up in a steady awesome stream. Every ball seems to come right through the nose of the aircraft.

Sid shoved the speed up and we were through it in a couple of seconds, untouched, apparently. We'd been suckered.

'Dummy,' said Sid, speaking of the field, not me. 'The dirty bastards,' he added.

We hadn't even been thinking of the possibility this far into Germany. And this dummy field was pretty rudimentary. There were none of the fake strips, hangars, and perimeter lights some of our guys had run across. Dummy fields were as old as the war.

'We'd better look for the real one,' Sid said. After a few more seconds, he said, 'What's the course?'

I still couldn't speak. My mouth was opening and closing but the voice box wouldn't work. 'Just a second,' I finally squeaked.

The map I had been reading was wadded up in a tight ball in my right fist. I smoothed it out as best I could, still holding my flashlight in my left hand. I couldn't concentrate properly, and my flashlight searched about wildly for the track I had drawn on the map in the ops room. At last the light hit it accidentally. I figured we were considerably north of our course and guessed at a new course.

'One-zero-zero,' I said.

'A nice round figure,' Sid said

For a guess it was pretty good, though. We flew smack over Argelsried, one of the fields we were supposed to patrol. There was a village with a stream running through it, then a wood, then a bloody runway, a real one. We weren't supposed to start a patrol by doing a run right over the field. We were supposed to approach surreptitiously, though how you could be surreptitious between two roaring Merlin engines was more than I could figure.

'Best navigation you've ever done,' Sid said, knowing damn well that flying directly over the field had been the farthest from my intentions.

We pulled away a mile or two and began circling the area. We fiddled around for half an hour; my nerve ends slowly ceasing their twanging. If Jerry had gone to the trouble of dragging a dummy plane across a dummy field, we figured there would be some activity with real planes here.

We were about to leave when the lights came on and we got into his circuit, hoping we'd see a Jerry and be able to crawl up his chuff for a shot. But we didn't see anything. After a little while, one burst of flak went straight up from the end of the runway, a warning that there was an interceptor (us) lurking about. We thought Jerry might still have tried to get in, but after a while the lights went out. It was possible, of course, Jerry had sneaked in without us seeing him.[25]

By 1943, RAF night-fighter tactics and technology were preventing the *Luftwaffe* from achieving any significantly damaging bombing attacks against Britain. As a result, both the *Luftwaffe* and German Army (*Wehrmacht*), had been developing weapons that might be able to circumvent conventional British day and night-fighter defences. The *Wehrmacht* had pursued the idea of a large rocket, which would eventually become the V2, the *Luftwaffe* in contrast had been focussing on a 22-foot long pilotless aircraft with a pulse-jet engine that could carry a warhead of about 1,870lb, this became known as the V1. The cost of producing the V1 was low – only 500-man hours were required to construct one and the aircraft used thin steel plate rather than scarce aluminium. It even ran on low grade petrol, rather than aviation fuel, carrying 130 gallons to drive its simple jet engine.[26]

---

25   McIntosh, *Mosquito Intruder,* pp. 73-4.
26   Hilary Saunders, *Royal Air Force 1939-45 – Volume 3* (London: HMSO, 1954), p. 147.

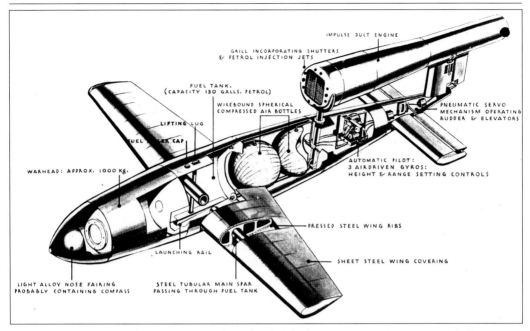

Figure 6 'Cut-away of V1 Fiesler Fi 103 flying bomb, (also known as FZG 76 or V1 weapon'. (Crown Copyright – Air Historical Branch).

The progressively destructive nature of Bomber Command's assaults on German cities prompted the Germans to increasingly prioritise these aircraft's development as revenge weapons.[27] In 1943 German efforts to launch the V1 pilotless aircraft intensified, under the command of Colonel Max Wachtel's Flak Regiment 155(W). Wachtel's Regiment was composed of 4,000 men organised into 48 platoons and 13 batteries and he had established, in an arc from the Cherbourg peninsula to Holland, a series of ramps and bunkers for launching V1s en masse at south-east England. The German hope was that they would be ready by the end of 1943.

Air intelligence had made the Allies aware of the forthcoming V1 offensive. Through a combination of French resistance reports and aerial photo reconnaissance, they were able to observe the construction of both the launch ramps, as well as the concrete buildings in which the flying bombs were stored prior to launch. In late 1943, a programme of strikes against the sites involving Fighter Command, 2nd Tactical Air Force, as well as RAF and American heavy bombers was established and codenamed 'NO-BALL'. The NO-BALL strikes disrupted German preparations and delayed the introduction of the V1 into service. They also forced the Germans to construct smaller, less elaborate and more discrete launch sites as well as adopting a more mobile approach to its operations. The new launch sites involved a minimum of construction, including a simpler ramp, concrete roads and just a few essential buildings. It was believed that the sites took about six days to erect and were simply abandoned when detected and attacked by Allied bombers.[28] The novelist H.E. Bates was working in the public relations department at the Air Ministry and noted the challenges with these new targets:

27   Bob Ogley, *Doodlebugs and Rockets* (Westerham: Froglet Publications, 1992), p. 12.
28   Bob Ogley, *Doodlebugs and Rockets* (Westerham: Froglet Publications, 1992), p. 25.

Such small targets demanded a far greater degree of accuracy than was needed to knock out a factory. The Germans favourite site then was a small wood of five to 10 acres close to a hard road, where trees in both summer and winter gave them perfect cover. In such woodland sites the Germans built hundreds of sites and supply depots. But they also chose more domestic sites. Orchards of apples and pears were favourite places nor had they any compunction whatsoever about putting them in the back gardens of French peasants in remote villages. And on at least one occasion they built an entire launching site in a village street.[29]

The much anticipated German V1 offensive actually began on 13 June 1944, seven days after D-Day. The Observer Corps had been briefed on pilotless aircraft and were waiting for just such an assault – the first observers to clearly identify a V1 were Mr E. Woodland (a greengrocer) and Mr A.M. Wraight (a builder), who were manning Mike 2, an observation post in an old Martello tower at Dymchurch on the Kent coast. They recalled that shortly after 0400 they spotted an approaching object with red flames spurting from its rear end, making a noise like 'a Model T-Ford going up a hill'. They immediately reported the sighting to their operations centre at Maidstone, using the new codename of 'Diver, Diver, Diver' to indicate it was a Flying Bomb. The message was relayed to both Fighter Command and Whitehall and the air raid sirens sounded over London and south-east England once more. The V1 sited by Mike 2, flew its eerily straight course north-west over Kent. Mike 2 handing it over to Fox 3 at Pluckley near Ashford, who in turn handed it to Easy 3 near Maidstone, the missile rattling on towards Gravesend when its engine cut out and it hurtled into open farmland at Swanscombe.

The Germans had hoped the first V1 attack on 13 June would inspire mass terror and fear, but the scale was too small. The continued 'NO-BALL strikes, as well as the Allied pre-D-Day bombing of the French railways, had meant that Colonel Wachtel had only been able to establish 18 out of 64 modified sites in the Pas de Calais. Essential equipment was also missing and on 13 June the Germans had only been able to launch 10 V1s, of which five immediately crashed on take-off. This slow start was mis-leading as the Germans swiftly picked up the pace and in a 24-hour period, that began at midday on 15 June, a total of 200 missiles were fired. The British defensive plan to counter them began to swung into action.

The V1 could be knocked down in a number of ways. First by aircraft, though the 400 mph speed of the V1 meant that the only aircraft fast enough were Tempests, boosted Mustangs and Spitfire Mk XIVs. Even these found it hard to engage the aircraft in a tail chase, unless the pursuer started well above it and increased his speed in a dive. Over time, efforts were made to increase the speed of even these aircraft, by removing all armour and external fittings, polishing the paint and the surface of the wings and adapting the engines to use 150 Octane fuel.[30] The RAF fighters found they were more successful at intercepting the V1 by flying roughly the same course and allowing it to overtake them on its way to London.[31]

The size of the V1 meant that harmonization of guns to 200 yards was essential, but there was a considerable hazard if the V1's 1,870lb warhead detonated, as flying through the fireball could scorch the fabric covered elevators and rudders and burn the arms of the pilot.[32] It was subsequently found that the flames were entering the Tempest cockpit through the air ventilator, which because of the hot summer weather was left in the open position just above the pilot's throttle hand. The burns problem was quickly solved by keeping the ventilator closed for V1 operations.

29   Ogley, *Doodlebugs and Rockets*, p. 21.
30   Hilary Saunders, *Royal Air Force 1939-45 – Volume 3*, p. 165.
31   Basil Collier, *Defence of The United Kingdom* (London: HMSO, 1957), p. 374.
32   Roland Beamont, *My Part of the Sky* (Wellingborough: Patrick Stephens, 1989), p. 180.

A German Fiesler Fi 103 flying-bomb (V1) in flight, as seen by the gun camera of an intercepting RAF fighter aircraft, moments before the fighter destroyed the V1 by cannon fire. (Crown Copyright – Air Historical Branch)

Wing Commander Roland Beamont commanded 150 Wing at the time of the V1 onslaught and was largely responsible for the aircraft tactics that were used in anti-Diver operations. It was he who suggested that the slower Thunderbolts, as well as the earlier marks of Mustangs and Spitfires should be withdrawn from the battle. He also suggested that the Observer Corps could usefully help the pilots identify the V1s by firing a distress flare at the pilotless-jets, this would enable the pilot, who had been guided to the area by radar, to see the point of convergence and identify the flying bomb. Roland Beamont recalls the first missions against these aircraft:

In the evening of 15 June the Newchurch Tempest squadrons of 150 Wing were warned to come to 'Readiness' before dawn on the following day, after the arrival of a small number of V1s during the previous night. Still no detailed intelligence was available as to what to expect beyond the fact that these were small, pilotless aircraft of unspecified shape, travelling it was thought, at about 400 mph and at heights up to about 5,000 ft.

Soon after dawn on 16 June, a drizzling wet morning, the expected alert warnings came and with Sergeant Bob Cole as my No 2, we led the Wing into an action which was to continue at maximum intensity for the next six weeks, and to destroy over 600 V1s in the process. But now it was all conjecture – what were these pilotless aircraft, and how to destroy them?

Immediately after takeoff we were given a heading south-east to a point off Folkestone. There was broken cloud at 2,000 ft and rather poor visibility in showers, and when radar control indicated that our target was closing rapidly ahead and then passing down the port side we had still not seen it, so I pulled around in a tight turn to port and at that moment saw a small dark shape go through a break in the clouds.

Still at full power we dived to increase to absolute maximum (level) speed, about 410 mph indicated at that height, and then suddenly out of the murk to starboard saw what appeared to be a small monoplane with a bulky, glowing jet engine at that back. We crossed in just over Folkestone in heavy rain and rapidly overtook the V1 which was flying at about 370 mph, but

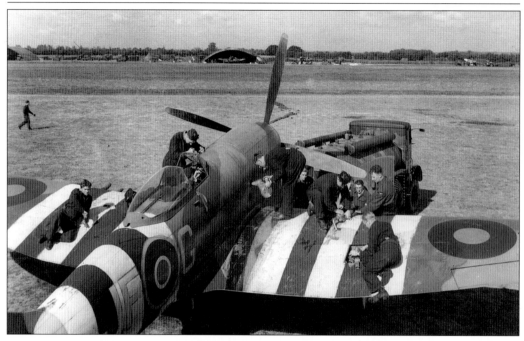

Groundcrew refuel and re-arm a Hawker Tempest V of 3 Squadron by the grass north-south runway at Newchurch, Kent, on 12 June 1944. On the far side of the runway is the dispersal of 56 Squadron. (Crown Copyright – Air Historical Branch)

it was a very small target and, opening fire from about 400 yards astern, I missed completely with the first burst.

Steadying up at about 300 yards, another short burst hit its port outer wing; and then with all the remaining ammunition a long burst hit it first on the fuselage without immediate effect, and finally on the engine which stopped and it began to go down. The V1 slowed rapidly but remained on an even keel, and as I overtook it on the port side I was able to get a quick look at its slim, pointed fuselage, high mounted ram-jet engine at the back and short stubby wings. It was painted dull grey overall and the jet pipe at the back was smoke blackened.

I called in Bob Cole to finish it off, which he did with a well-aimed burst and it rolled over on its back and dived into a field south of Maidstone, exploding with a lot of flame and black smoke and a clear goldfish bowl of blossoming shock-wave which was to become a familiar feature of these activities in the weeks ahead.[33]

Not all V1s downed by aircraft would be as a result of the fighter's guns, some pilots, to avoid detonating the warhead, simply toppled them over. This technique was first tried by Australian Flying Officer Ken Collier on 23 June, who intercepted a V1 in his Mk XIV Spitfire at 2,500 feet over the Channel. Collier's initial attempts to hit the V1 with his guns had proved fruitless, as he was now out of ammunition, he manoeuvred his Spitfire next to the V1 and tried to topple it on to its back by flipping it with the tip of his wing. His first attempt failed, but on his second the V1 spun and crashed in a field to the rear of an old people's home in Kent. Collier was delighted with the result, however his account was greeted with scepticism by the debriefing intelligence officer, until the ground crew were able to verify his story by pointing to the V1's paint on the Spitfire's wing tip.

---

33   Beamont, *My Part of the Sky*, pp. 178-9.

Collier's technique was widely adopted, though sadly he did not survive the war and was shot down and killed in December 1944.[34] Other pilots also learnt that when flying in front of the bomb their slipstream would throw it off balance and that technique was used too. The British had to reorganise their night-fighter defences to counter the V1s. Mosquitoes were initially used and had some success, though given the Tempest's strong performance during the day the decision was made to place a number of Mosquito night-fighter pilots in Tempest squadrons and fly those aircraft at night too. To assist them the TRE produced a small spectroscope with a re-fracting system, this clever device displayed the exhaust glow of the V1 as two images until, at a range of 200 yards, it merged into one single picture. Despite these initiatives shooting V1s at night still remained a very difficult proposition.[35]

The V1s had been programmed to fly on a straight bearing to London, without deviation, between 2,000 and 3,000 ft. This was a comparatively low altitude which meant that they could be brought down by some of the ground defences within Fighter Command, including the barrage balloons of the RAF's Balloon Command. Team's from the Balloon squadrons had visited Biggin Hill four months before the first V1 fell, to identify the areas from which they could operate their balloons and to establish Biggin Hill as their Balloon Centre. The concentration of these additional balloons began on 16 June, with squadrons coming from as far away as Glasgow, Manchester, Liverpool and South Wales. When an aircraft struck the balloon cable, the middle portion of the wire would break away and wrap itself round the enemy's wing, deploying parachutes at either end – the so-called 'double parachute link'. This equipment was not designed to cope with anything faster than an ordinary bomber and it was not known just how well it would perform against fast moving missiles.

The balloon barrage succeeded in downing its first V1 on 20 June and by the middle of July a large barrier of 1,750 balloons was floating over the North Downs, the line having been broadened and thickened since the first deployments. There were also some changes made to the original layout, so that bombs brought down by balloons would not fall near buildings on the southern outskirts of London in Kent and Surrey.[36] Many regarded the sight of the balloon barrage and the wind whistling through the cables as one of the the more beautiful sights in the war. But they were not just for show, a total of 231 bombs were downed by balloons,[37] though this was not without hazard to the crews. At Brasted, Kent, one airman and three WAAFs were killed when a V1 'ran down the cable' a rare, but not unheard-of occurrence.[38]

The gunners of the Army's Anti-Aircraft (AA) Command, under the highly experienced General Pile, had also planned for anti-Diver operations. In just 24 hours they moved 192 heavy anti-aircraft guns, and a similar number of light anti-aircraft guns to new dispositions. This was a remarkably quick feat when one considers that this entailed moving 40 batteries of gunners with all their stores and equipment. By the end of June there were 376 heavy guns and 576 40mm LAA guns deployed in a belt stretching from Maidstone to East Grinstead, with a further 560 LAA weapons of the RAF Regiment along the south coast.[39] The numbers of guns was impressive, but in the early stages of the campaign the AA gun's performance was lacklustre for a number of reasons. First, the V1s flew between 2,000 and 3,000 feet which was too far from the ground to

34   Bob Ogley, *Doodlebugs and Rockets* (Westerham: Froglet Publications, 1992), p. 50.

35   Ken Delve, *Nightfighter* (London: Cassell, 1995), p. 169.

36   Basil Collier, *Defence of the United Kingdom* (London: HMSO, 1957), p. 373.

37   Basil Collier, *Defence of the United Kingdom* (London: HMSO, 1957), p. 522.

38   Bob Ogley, *Doodlebugs and Rockets* (Westerham: Froglet Publications, 1992), p. 42.

39   Frederick Pile, *Ack-Ack – Britain's Defence against Air Attack during the Second World War* (London: George Harrap, 1949), p. 288.

suit the light guns, yet too close for the heavy guns to engage easily. Secondly, though the missile flew in a neat straight line, it was fast enough to make it an awkward target, particularly for the heavy guns who needed time to use their instruments and traverse the 3.7-inch mobile guns with which they were equipped. There were new devices on the way that would help, notably the No.10 Predictor and the S.C.R. 584 radar set from the United States, but these were not immediately available. In contrast to its mobile counterpart the 3.7-inch static gun could traverse and respond more quickly, but it needed emplacing on concrete which would take a long time.

An ingenious alternative to concrete bases was developed by the Chief Royal Electrical and Mechanical Engineer (REME) officer in AA Command, Brigadier Burls. It consisted of a portable platform of steel rails and sleepers, arranged in a latticework arrangement and filled with ballast. Christened the 'Pile Mattress', this provided the stable base and anchor points needed for the static AA guns and Pile correspondingly uprooted 3.7-inch static guns from other parts of Britain to replace his mobile ones. More than 700 Pile Mattresses were eventually constructed requiring 35 miles of railway lines and 22,500 sleepers.[40] Despite these arrangements, Pile was still acutely aware that his own AA guns were having less success in shooting down V1s than the RAF fighters. This was partly because his London-based guns were restricted from firing, for the obvious reason that 50 percent of the bombs the AA gunners hit would not explode in the air but detonate as they fell on London – precisely the result the Germans were after. Pile pressed for changes to the system, as he recalls.

> It was during this first stage of the battle that the ground and air defences were overlapping to such a degree that complicated rules of engagement of targets had to be laid down, giving priority now to one arm of the defences and now to the other according, mainly to that state of the weather. Under certain conditions both fighters and guns operated together. These rules and the constant changing from one state to another, as well as overlapping of spheres of influence, led to many opportunities being missed by one side or the other. The average fighter in those days had a slight command of speed over the flying bomb and required a large area in which to make its kill. As things were, the fighter often had to break off the attack just as it was closing in, for no better reason than it had reached the entrance to the gun zone. And as it was the fighters who were having the greater success (our percentage of kills had fallen to a figure as low as nine percent of the targets engaged), it was we who were almost invariably restrained. Never before had the rules of defence been so complicated.

By this stage the V1 bombs had become a significant political issue and Churchill had taken over direct control of the anti-Diver operations, holding a conference every second night to examine the measures being taken. By mid-July 1944, Pile's frustration at the restrictions was beginning to boil over:

> Once more I spoke as strongly as I could. I insisted that eventually the guns must be the answer, but that under present circumstances the guns never got a chance to improve. I further pointed out that the RAF, comparatively well as they had been doing, were still not really on terms with the menace and were not increasing their bag. As they had had a completely free run, it appeared as if other steps should be taken. The Prime Minister listened to what I had to say, and then said, 'All right, from next Monday for a week General Pile is to have a free hand.'[41]

---

40   Basil Collier, *Defence of The United Kingdom* (London: HMSO, 1957), p. 373 and Bob Ogley, *Doodlebugs and Rockets* (Westerham: Froglet Publications, 1992), p. 47.

41   Frederick Pile, *Ack-Ack – Britain's Defence against Air Attack during the Second World War* (London: George Harrap, 1949), p. 288.

The DIVER Plan. An RAF Regiment light anti-aircraft gun team man their Bofors 40mm LAA gun in a rain-sodden emplacement in south-east England, as part of the 'Diver' gun belt established in Surrey and Kent to defend London from flying bombs. (Crown Copyright – Air Historical Branch)

This change of emphasis from fighters to guns was combined with a move of the AA guns from the North Downs right down to the south coast, where a compact gun-belt was established from Beachy Head to Dover, that was 5,000 yards deep and could fire 10,000 yards out to sea. This would allow the fighters to intercept V1s out to sea, but also act as 'wicket keepers', picking up any V1s that had been missed by the anti-aircraft guns. The balloons just south of London acted as a final line of defence.[42] The gun belt now consisted of Heavy AA gun sites, each with at least eight guns. These were spaced evenly along the whole length of the new gun belt and were supplemented by LAA gun sites, located either close to the heavy guns, or to cover gaps. The new American radars were now coming into service, as well as twin rocket anti-aircraft batteries and proximity fuses. The American's lent support providing a total of 20 batteries of 90mm guns, General Eisenhower taking the view that London was as much a base for American troops as it was for British. All of which was helpful, as was the whole-hearted support of Air Marshal Hill, the AOC Fighter Command under whose command Pile's gunners rested. However, the Air Council took a different view and kicked up a row believing that Hill had been unduly influenced by Pile at the RAF's expense. This did not reflect well on them as Pile recollected:

---

42   Pile, *Ack-Ack – Britain's Defence against Air Attack during the Second World War*, p. 294.

The fact was that Hill, regarding the matter less parochially against the background of civilian death and destruction, realised, as we all did, that the Air Defence of Great Britain was a combined operation, that the combined efficiency of the defences was of greater importance than the individual glory of one or other Service, that what mattered was that, somehow, the flying bombs should be mastered, and it did not matter by whom. Anyway, the Air Council were very displeased. They left Hill in absolutely no doubt that he must take the full consequences of the failure – for failure was forecast in their every word attending upon this decision. Much to everybody's surprise but our own, the move was the most enormous success, and Hill ended up on the Air Council.[43]

The pressure on the guns was immense – troops had to be at constant readiness, spotters alert and sleep was difficult with the loud noises from both guns and bombs. But the gunners were at last having success, in the first week of the new deployment on the coast the guns shot down 17 percent of all targets entering the gun-belt. In the second week that figure rose to 24 percent, and by the fifth week the guns were shooting down 55 percent of flying bombs passing overhead. By the time the German launch sites in the Pas De Calais were being overrun by the invading Allied armies in early September, the total had risen to 74 percent, making a grand total of 1,550 flying bombs shot down by the gunners at the time, an impressive achievement. Further details on the Flying Bomb Offensive, including the proportion of V1s destroyed by guns and aircraft are contained at Annex R.

The Germans were forced to adapt their tactics as a result of the gun belt, the 'NO-BALL' strikes and the advance of the Allied armies into the Pas de Calais area. One method was the use of modified He 111s which would fly from Belgium and Holland at night, with a V1 strapped under its belly, which would be launched once airborne. It allowed the Germans to not only increase the range of the V1, but also attack London from the east and north-east, forcing Pile to re-position his entire gun belt to meet V1s coming up the Thames Estuary. British night-fighters were used to attack the He 111s, aided by a radar picket ship, HMS *Caicos*, acting as a maritime GCS, as well as radar equipped Wellington bombers, who could also pick up the low-flying HE 111. Dick Leggett flew a 125 Squadron Mosquito on missions to down these aircraft and describes such operations:

> Once the ram-jet of the flying bomb had ignited, the pilot [of the He 111] would quickly descend to his original height and head for home, using low stratus or sea fog to cover his retreat. During the few minutes taken to launch the missile the enemy aircraft was vulnerable to attack from the numerous nightfighters which would always be in the area due to the prior warning given to us from intelligence sources. However, as winter set in, the German pilots became more adept at cutting their exposure time to a minimum, thereby avoiding interception during the launching period.
>
> It was under these circumstances that Operation Vapour was evolved, in early 1945, so that Heinkels could be intercepted and destroyed whilst at low altitude. Prior to this tactic, life had been more difficult as the Heinkel could happily cruise at a speed well below the stalling speed of a Mosquito XVII. On one particular intercept, each time visual contact was attempted the severe turbulence from the slipstream of the Heinkel destabilised my aircraft and created an incipient stall.
>
> Throughout the interception my nav/rad, Egbert Midlane, miraculously held radar contact with the target and repeatedly guided me into his minimum AI range of 100 yards, but cloud and darkness prevented a visual sighting. We decided to wait for the greyness of dawn and

---

43   Pile, *Ack-Ack – Britain's Defence against Air Attack during the Second World War*, p. 294.

A section of the barrage-balloon defence put up against the flying bomb over the South Downs.
(Crown Copyright – Air Historical Branch)

were eventually rewarded by the destruction of the Heinkel as it approached Den Helder. Some 55 min had elapsed from first radar contact to firing the four 20mm cannon.[44]

Clearly the greatest chance the V1 had of causing casualties was to reach the centre of London itself, striking the most populated areas and the heart of government. On Friday 30 June 1944 a V1 struck the Strand, at Aldwych, 40 yards in front of the Air Ministry's building at Adastral House. It was a beautiful mid-summer's day and many office girls were sunbathing on the roof during their lunchtime break. Miss Cecille Day was working nearby at the BBC's Bush House:

> I like fresh air and, as it was a sunny day, I opened my office window, when suddenly there was a terrible explosion. The bomb impacted on a row of buses and, when the dust lifted, there was a scene of terrible slaughter – pavements were littered with the dead and wounded and, on the road were the twisted, unrecognisable frames of a line of buses. The sunbathing girls had been blown to eternity. My secret papers had been scattered far and wide and I was lucky to be suffering only cuts and bruises. The blast damaged the face of Bush House and the two statues above the door had their arms blown off. I was taken to hospital in one of the many ambulances which arrived, and, on the way, the ambulance crew asked me to help give injections to the badly wounded.[45]

Sometimes the V1s would hit a particularly densely occupied building and cause great devastation. One such occasion was on 18 June 1944 when a V1 struck the Guard's Chapel on Birdcage

44   Ken Delve, *Nightfighter* (London: Cassell, 1995), p. 169.
45   Bob Ogley, *Doodlebugs and Rockets* (Westerham: Froglet Publications, 1992), p. 56.

Walk, during the Sunday morning service, killing 58 civilians and 63 service personnel. Many were buried alive under 10 feet of rubble, Elizabeth Sheppard-Jones later wrote of the incident and her rescue:

> I was suddenly aware that somewhere far above me, above the black emptiness, there were people, living helpful people whose voices reached me, dim and disembodied, as if in a dream … Someone frantically scraped rubble from round my head … My eyes rested with horror on a blood stained body, that had my hands been free I could have touched … the body of a young soldier whose eyes stared unseeingly at the sky … I turned towards a Guardsman who was helping with the rescue work … 'How do I look?' 'Madam,' he said, 'You look wonderful to me!'[46]

Elizabeth Sheppard-Jones later learnt she had suffered a fractured spine and was paralysed from the waist down. She never walked again.

An opportunity to reduce the numbers of flying bombs landing on London was identified when the Germans, in an effort to correct their aim, sent requests to their agents in London to report the times and places of flying bomb strikes. Air Intelligence noted that, as at the V1 test-range in Peenemunde, the V1s were falling short of their intended central London target, the mean point of impact being Dulwich in South East London. As many German agents had been turned by the British, R.V. Jones in consultation with MI5, devised a plan where these double agents would report only those flying bombs that had struck north of London, this it was hoped would cause the Germans to shorten the flight times of all their weapons and cause the bombs to drop into less populated areas. The deception plan was opposed by some Labour politicians in the War Cabinet including Herbert Morrison, the Home Secretary, who felt it was an 'interference with providence'. The British deception plan nevertheless worked. In fact when Wachtel's planning maps were eventually captured they showed that they had been using Tower Bridge as the aim point and the radio-direction transmitters fitted to a small proportion of V1 flying bombs had shown the V1s were falling short. This contradicted the (false) agents reports which stated they were flying too far, however German intelligence commented that Wachtel should accept the agents' reports as they had proved reliable in the past.[47] During the V1 Campaign a total of 2,419 V1s dropped in London boroughs killing 5,126 people, a further 2,789 flying bombs struck outside London but these caused just 350 deaths – vindicating Air Intelligence's approach.[48]

The threat to Londoners had not passed though, for by September the second of Hitler's vengeance weapons, the V2, was operationally ready. This 46-foot long monster dwarfed the V1 and carried a 1 tonne warhead. It flew at around 3,600 miles an hour, climbing into the stratosphere and arriving without warning. It took just five minutes to travel from launch to impact and was impossible for the British to track. From September 1944 to March 1945 1,115 V2 rockets were launched at Britain, killing 2,754 people and seriously injuring 6,523. The V2s were never defeated until the sites in Holland and Germany were overrun in March 1945. The era of the ballistic missile had now arrived, and warfare would never be the same again.[49]

The combination of German bombers, V1s and V2s caused a total of 146,374 British civilian casualties of whom 60,447 were killed. In the London area alone there were 80,397 casualties. This is a soberingly large figure, though one that would have been much larger had the British

---

46   Ogley, *Doodlebugs and Rockets*, p. 44.
47   R.V. Jones, *Most Secret War* (London: Hamish Hamilton, 1978), p. 423.
48   Bob Ogley, *Doodlebugs and Rockets* (Westerham: Froglet Publications, 1992), p. 5.
49   Ogley, *Doodlebugs and Rockets*, p. 42.

not adapted and evolved their night-fighter and other AA defences. The damage the Blitz and V-weapon campaigns inflicted are still physically visible in many of our cities today, particularly London. More immediately, the German attacks created considerable popular support for Britain's own bomber offensive. The new head of Bomber Command, Air Chief Marshal Sir Arthur Harris captured this national sentiment in a speech he made, shortly after he took over command in early 1942:

> The Nazis entered this war under the rather childish delusion that they were going to bomb everybody else, and nobody was going to bomb them. At Rotterdam, London, Warsaw, and half a hundred other places, they put that rather naïve theory into operation. They sowed the wind, and now, they are going to reap the whirlwind.[50]

---

50   Robin Cross, *Fallen Eagle* (London, John Wiley and Sons 1995), p. 78.

7

'With Fists and Heels'[1]
Malta's Battle for Air Superiority in the Mediterranean

The RAF's air defence commitments were not limited to the British mainland. The nation was, of course, fighting a global war in many theatres, which required it to defend a multitude of bases and territory as well as provide air cover for its armies and the Royal Navy. We shall pick up these latter two themes later in the book, but it is worth contrasting now the difference between providing air defence over the United Kingdom, as opposed to that of Malta and the Far East. This will highlight the difficulties faced by the less well-resourced overseas commands, raising questions about the RAF's relative priorities and in the case of the Far East, a salutary lesson on the consequences of failure.

Few places in the Second World War can claim to have been on the front line for as long as Malta. At the beginning of the war Malta had not been a priority for defence because the initial focus for overseas reinforcement had been France and for a brief period Norway. That all changed with the fall of France and Italy's entry into the war in the summer of 1940. Suddenly Britain's positions in Egypt and Gibraltar became essential in order to safe guard Middle East oil supplies, the route to the Far East and to assist the Royal Navy in their Mediterranean operations against the Italian fleet. Malta's position, though uncomfortably close to Italy, was strategically advantageous both as a Royal Navy base and as the only place to refuel aircraft transiting between Gibraltar and Egypt. This was particularly important whilst the trans-African (or Takoradi) air-ferry route was still under construction. Britain also aimed to use Malta in an offensive manner and the island eventually became a crucial base from which to attack German and Italian supply lines to North Africa. Later still, once the pendulum had swung firmly to the Allied cause, the island would also play a major role in the invasion of Sicily in July 1943.

The story of Malta provides a fascinating illustration of the way air, maritime and land environments interact with each other (see Maps 5 and 6 for detail on Malta and its strategic position in the Mediterranean). The fight for air superiority over the island and central Mediterranean allowed the Royal Navy greater command of the sea and together with the RAF, the opportunity to strike Axis supply lines. Starving the German and Italian forces in Africa of supplies was of great assistance to the British Army's North African campaign, whose territorial gains in Egypt and Libya provided forward airfields that enabled air cover to be provided for convoys re-supplying and reinforcing Malta. It sounds such a simple and virtuous cycle, but to get it to work in the face of determined German and Italian opposition took great effort and sacrifice from

---

1   'With Fists and Heels' – Motto of 249 Squadron RAF, after serving in the Battle of Britain the squadron was moved by aircraft carrier to Malta in May 1941 and fought throughout the battle, converting from Hurricanes to Spitfires in 1942. They finally moved from Malta to support the Italian campaign in October 1943.

all services, including the RAF's Middle East Command (The Order of Battle for RAF Middle East Command is included at Annex G).

The French surrender, together with the Italian entry into the war meant the dilemma now facing the British was to both reinforce Malta with extra aircraft and begin to build a strategic airbase from scratch. The neglect of the island's air defences is perhaps most starkly illustrated in that the first defending aircraft, consisted of just three Sea Gladiator biplane fighters that had been assembled from crates. Nicknamed 'Faith', 'Hope' and 'Charity' they would become the initial line of defence against the Italian Air Force fleet of 140 SM 79 bombers and 76 fighters.[2] Despite the direct threat of invasion to Britain at the time, the requirement to reinforce Malta was felt to be so acute that Churchill dispatched a small number of Hurricanes to bolster the island's defences. This brave, though limited reinforcement, was all that could be spared at the time and much more needed to be done to ensure Malta's security.

When Air Commodore Hugh Lloyd took up his post as AOC Malta, on 1 June 1941, he still found the facilities on Malta were rudimentary to say the least, particularly in comparison to those the United Kingdom-based RAF enjoyed.

> Motoring up a hill for barely a mile I came to the first of the three aerodromes – namely Hal Far – which was a few hundred yards from the sea and overlooking it. The landing area was a triangle with the base next to the sea, whilst the two sides were hemmed in on one side by rising ground studded with big chunks of rocky outcrop and on the other by ground falling to a nullah. The aerodrome had been in use for many years before the war, and the buildings had an air of dignity about them. Fighters were based there, also a squadron of Fleet Air Arm Swordfish commanded by Lieutenant Commander Howie, which was operating under my command. The aerodrome looked extremely small and, whatever the wind, there was only one direction for take-offs and landings, while on the perimeter there were a few pens of solid stone to shelter the aeroplanes from bomb blast and splinters. The other aerodromes were identical in this same respect, so much so indeed, that I expected a few well aimed bombs to result in serious damage. In Britain, on the other hand, there was a craze for dispersal; the aerodromes had overflowed into the surrounding countryside, hedges had been torn down and trees felled to build miles of concrete taxiways and dispersal points on which to stand the aircraft. In Britain the work was being done by contractors utilising civilian labour under peaceful conditions, but similar work on Malta was liable to interference by one or two or more raids a day with the aerodromes as the targets.[3]

In his tour of Malta's three other major airfields, Luqa, Safi and Takali, Lloyd found that Luqa was the only one that had a tarmac runway, though just one look at the 1,200-yard strip had been enough to 'give him a fright'. Apart from its pronounced slope, which would have ruled it out in Britain, it had a deep ravine on one end and a 'nasty, rocky, steep-sided obstacle, and a quarry at the other.' Safi was worse; with two roughly made landing strips in the shape of a V, it was so unsuitable that even experienced Hurricane and Blenheim pilots hated using it. Finally Takali, the old civil aerodrome, had a simple grass airfield with the massive ramparts of M'dina lining one side like a football stadium. Tom Neil, although an experienced Hurricane pilot and Battle of Britain veteran, noted with trepidation the surrounding countryside near Takali, as well as around Malta generally.

2   Brian Cull and Frederick Gallea, *Hurricanes over Malta* (London: Grub Street, 2001), p. 7.

3   Hugh Lloyd, *Briefed to Attack* (London, Hodder and Stoughton, 1949), p. 26.

Hawker Hurricane IIa Z2961/K being refuelled and rearmed at Takali, Malta, September 1941. (Crown Copyright – Air Historical Branch)

As our dispersal was at the southern end of Takali, we mostly took off south to north, which reduced taxying – and the filth – to a minimum. In this direction, we were faced with rising ground at the end of the airfield and a mass of ridges and stone walls. Every time my wheels left the ground, I prayed; prayed that my engine would keep going and that I would not end up ploughing into the hill or crashing through a score of obstructions. There were very few places to force land in Malta and to bale out was considered to be the only sensible course of action. But below 1,000 feet even baling out was a hazard.[4]

The tour of his bases left Lloyd in a sober mood, not only were the airfields in a parlous state but the ancillary services and maintenance were also equally neglected:

The small size of the three aerodromes was sufficiently depressing a spectacle, but the air raid shelters for the men were woefully inadequate, while underground operations rooms, in which there might be telephones, existed only in name. The valuable stores and equipment were also above ground, and they were priceless, if only because of their complete inadequacy! How the technical personnel maintained and operated the aircraft baffled my imagination. The humble, spanner, hammer and screwdriver were as scarce as hens' teeth; and the motor transport had it been in Britain, would have been used for road blocks. Even the offices and workshops were also above ground. All manner of other things which we had taken for granted in Bomber Command were missing too, such as petrol pipe lines laid deep underground from some central bulk storage organization to the aircraft refuelling points. There was not one single petrol pump even such as could be seen in any British village. Our stock was kept in bulk storage of very limited capacity away from the aerodromes but by far the greater proportion of it was distributed in five-gallon tins in small dumps spread over the island – most of them open to the sky …

4   T.F. Neil, *Onward to Malta* (Shrewsbury: Airlife Publishing, 1992), p. 152.

The 'Grand Finale' to this day's work was to hear that there were 59 serviceable aircraft. Twenty-nine were Hurricanes, the rest being Blenheims, Swordfish and Marylands. I was then told that the total of airmen was only 1,910. As I had reason to remember that when commanding a station in Bomber Command during the war I had 1,400 men to operate 36 aeroplanes I was sceptical of this information; but it was correct.

These figures of personnel were depressingly small when one considers that Lloyd's team were responsible for managing so much. This included a command and control organisation to rival Fighter Command, their own base and repair workshops and auxiliary services, such as medical support or Air-Sea rescue. Malta was a mini-version of Bomber, Coastal and Fighter Command Headquarters with Maintenance Command and an element of the the Ministry of Aircraft Production all rolled into one.[5]

One other important disadvantage Malta had was its proximity to the German and Italian airfields at Sicily. Malta did have radar, which was a vital part of its early warning system, but the posts were easily identifiable on the small bare island. Pilot Officer Dick Sugden, a Hurricane pilot, remembered this well:

> One of the main weapons was radar, giving us early warning approach of enemy aircraft. Sometimes it didn't give you quite enough time, though, with the Italians only 60 miles away. By the time they had appeared on the radar and we got our aircraft into the air, they were waiting above, and by the time you got up to their height they were watching and could time their attacks accordingly.[6]

This meant that the defenders would often adapt their tactics and fly south, or away from the approaching enemy to gain a height advantage. Peter Davies was a fighter pilot on Spitfires and describes this unorthodox process:

> The experience of last month when Mike and I had tried to climb south of the island and ran our heads into a mass of 109s; made me think that the old hands were right when they said it would not work. Since then we'd tried to gain height over or near the island and had still run into trouble, so we'd talked it all over again and decided to give the original plan another trial. We'd asked Fighter Control to scramble us in good time (they could see the plot building up over Sicily long before it reached the island and therefore had plenty of warning) and had determined to gain height as much as 20 miles south of the island. To-day this plan worked splendidly and we'd reached 15,000 feet without molestation … feel convinced now that the important points are (1) to climb to 15-20,000 feet without being attacked or shadowed (2) to arrive over the target at the same time as the bandits (3) to conserve plenty of height or speed so that the attack on the bombers can be delivered and completed before they reach the protective cordon. The only mistake today was in losing too much height in looking for the first wave, otherwise it was encouraging.[7]

5   Hugh Lloyd, *Briefed to Attack* (London: Hodder and Stoughton, 1949), pp. 27-9.
6   Brian Cull and Frederick Galea, *Hurricanes over Malta, June 1940- April 1942* (London: Grub Street, 2001), p. 15.
7   Peter Davies, *Tattered Battlements* (London: Windmill Press, 1943), p. 97.

One of the biggest risks such poor radar coverage meant, was that the RAF pilots and their aircraft could be more easily caught on the ground. Tom Neil again gives an account on how enemy low-flying aircraft would sometimes sneak in under Malta's radar:

> For more than half an hour, nothing; no excitement, no tension even. We sat around, fanning ourselves and trying to keep cool. Waiting. Outside the chore-horses [generators] chattered on monotonously and the sun continued to bake the acres of glaring white sandstone beyond our canvas cover so that the heat rose in shimmering eddies, making Rabat on the distant hill wobble and shake. And all around was that subtle smell – of Malta.
>
> I had already spoken to control some 15 minutes earlier and had been assured that nothing unusual was happening, so that when a distant air raid siren began its whooping dirge, it came as a surprise and unpleasant shock. Air raid siren! What were we doing sitting here if the Huns were within even 50 miles of us? I jumped to my feet, as did everyone else, and went outside to waken myself up and to observe. Nothing though, or nothing that I could see. Even so, I didn't like it – some sixth sense. We wouldn't be hanging about like this at North Weald, by George!
>
> Anxious to be in the best possible state of preparedness, I ordered everyone to 'Standby', which meant that they sat, strapped up, in their cockpits, after which I spoke again to control.
>
> We could hear air-raid sirens, I observed tersely. What was going on?
>
> Hearing voices in the background and discussion, I sensed uncertainty. Then their reply: nothing as far as they knew. As soon as anything developed they would let us know. OK?
>
> Still suspicious, I went out into the sun again, and walking back to my aircraft, climbed in and strapped up, leaving off my helmet.
>
> Minutes passed. Nothing. Then another air-raid siren, this time very much closer.
>
> Hell's bells! What was going on? I flung off my straps, and jumping down, ran the 50 yards back to the tent. By God, I'd give them what for!
>
> Jogging into the tent, I had barely ordered the airman-of-the watch to: 'Get me control!' when it all started.
>
> First, the shrill, deafening scream of racing engines and the ripping tearing bedlam of machine-guns and cannons. All hell let loose!
>
> I dropped the telephone like a hot plate and threw myself to the ground, only to find the airman-of-the-watch had beaten me to it and, knees to chin, was clutching his head like a hear-no-evil monkey. Lying on my left side, with my face to one open end of the tent, I had the briefest glimpse of a small aircraft, which I immediately recognised as a German 109, about 50 feet up and pointing, it seemed, straight at me. Firing! Shocked absolutely into a numbed paralysis, I closed my eyes and cringed, waiting for the impact of bullets and shells, wondering quite stupidly meanwhile whether they were likely to go right through my body or only partly so, and if they would penetrate that of the airman as well. For all of four seconds.
>
> Then with a final explosion of sound and fury, they were gone, their lightning departure marked by the rapid 'clump-clump-clump' of the several Bofors guns around the airfield and the chatter of defending machine-guns.
>
> Scrambling to my feet, I ran outside to see the rapidly diminishing silhouettes of at least three aircraft, their wings glinting in the sun as they sped away to safety in the direction of the area later known to me as St Paul's Bay. In their wake streamed several clutches of red balls as the Bofors gunners strive to catch them before they finally disappeared.[8]

---

8   T.F. Neil, *Onward to Malta* (Shrewsbury: Airlife Publishing, 1992), p. 118.

From 1940 to early 1942, the Hurricane was the aircraft primarily used to defend the island and during this time no Spitfires were sent at all. The majority of Hurricanes were shipped to Malta by aircraft carriers that would sail from Gibraltar and fly off the machines when within range of the island. At some periods of the desert war, the British Army was successful in capturing airfields close enough to fly Hurricane's direct to Malta, though for the majority of the time the British line was too far to the east. Pilot Officer John Pain had helped ferry Hurricanes to Egypt on the newly established Takoradi route and with five other Hurricane pilots and a Wellington bomber was to fly to Malta as reinforcements from a Libyan airfield:

> In order to lighten the aircraft we were instructed to take out the wireless and all ammo, so what could we have done if the damned Wimpy [Wellington] was attacked? In return for our protection it was to drop a dinghy if we dropped into the drink. What a help! With serious misgivings about our survival on this trip we took off and formed a vic on either side of the Wimpy. One of the types turned windy at the last moment so we had to clobber one of the 33 Squadron pilots for the trip. Unfortunately, the bloke that turned windy came on as a passenger in the Wimpy, a thing that we were to regret later on.
>
> We flew along the coast as long as possible. Then we altered course slightly out to sea, and the coast of Cyrenaica faded away. There was nothing to be seen but the water, the Wimpy and the cloud. About half way across we sighted a destroyer. A welcome sight. Our course would have taken us right over the top of him, but we did a wide circle round him as the navy blokes are notoriously trigger-happy. Not that I blame them. Anything with wings is enemy, to hell with markings and silhouettes. The next moment this speck erupted and the barrage burst about 2,000 feet below us. The Wimpy made a dignified concession and altered course starboard by at least five degrees. The next burst was about 500 feet below us and slightly behind. It was quite astonishing how much muck came out of that little ship. We never did find out if it was Royal Navy or Italian. The weather started to get a bit thick soon after we passed the ship, and the closer we came to Malta the worse it got, until we were at sea level. Very damaging to our fuel consumption. Heavy rain started. We were close to the Wimpy by this time. It was very bumpy, and the aircraft were approaching dangerously close to each other. Almost as suddenly as we ran into it, we came out of the rain into low, broken cloud with an occasional rain squall …
>
> We climbed a little, zig-zagging through cloud until we came about 50 miles south of Malta, where we went right down to the sea. This was the area any attack was expected. Pantelleria was 70 miles to our left, and Sicily 60 miles beyond Malta. Low down and far ahead appeared the smudge that indicated the cliffs of Malta. Rapidly they rose up so that we could see the houses at Hal Far. Almost immediately white puffs appeared above, and through gaps in the clouds we saw the Stukas come down in line astern. Through another gap dropped another flight of them. We counted 40 but where was the fighter escort? We saw them soon enough. We were circling south of Filfla at sea level when they appeared through a gap in the clouds above us. Thirty of the bastards, six of us with no ammo. There was only one thing to do – and that was to go for them. I waggled the others into a vic and one in the box. The Wimpy stayed below.
>
> As the fighters swung down at us, we turned up at them in a head-on attack and straight through the middle of them. We steep-turned to the left onto where they should have been, but instead of going for the Wimpy they had turned and were going south away from the island. I thought we had got the biggest fright, but apparently they had. Turning once more for Hal Far, the drome at which we were to land, the recipient of quite a lot of recent hate, we circled above the battered white houses with their broken walls, the runway with its white craters and aircraft burning on the boundary. Only two as they were well dispersed. We saw

the Wimpy land at Luqa and then we came in between the craters to the surprising sight of a Wing Commander in full blue, waving us into our various dispersal points. Having landed safely we were met by AVM [Air Vice-Marshal] Maynard[9] – the first and only time I saw the man – who was intrigued by our un-RAF appearance. This included some six day's growth of beard and six day's accumulation of sand where the grit would be most irritating. Water in the desert was reserved for tea, not washing![10]

The British ability to reinforce Malta with greater numbers of fighters, from either carriers or bases in Libya, meant that the RAF were able to keep the larger numbers of Italian aircraft at bay over the island. Such protection allowed Malta to achieve an offensive edge, in air terms this included growing numbers of Wellington medium bombers, Fairey Swordfish torpedo aircraft and Martin Maryland reconnaissance aircraft. The air defence of Malta also allowed the Royal Navy to build up the 10th Submarine Flotilla's boats, based at Manoel Island, which, though never numbering more than 12 submarines, was able to sink 412,575 tons of Axis shipping between January 1941 and December 1942.[11] Similarly, Royal Navy vessels in the central Mediterranean achieved a startling carrier strike success against the Italian fleet at Taranto, which compelled the Italian Navy to withdraw its vessels to Naples. These British air and maritime sucesses in the central Mediterranean were partly a result of Italian Air Force units being dispatched to North Africa, in a bid to stem the disastrous retreat of the Italian Army in Libya. Sadly, this period was not to last.

German concern over the Italian defeats in North Africa prompted the dispatch to Libya of General Rommel's Afrika Korps from February 1941. Furthermore, the Germans understood that if they wished to have secure transport and supply lines across the Mediterranean, then Malta would have to be neutralised as an operating base and the naval forces operating around the island defeated. Consequently, the Germans dispatched *Fliegerkorps X* to Sicily in January 1941 and on 10 January, Ju 87 dive bombers successfully struck HMS *Illustrious* when it came within range of Sicily. The damaged carrier was brought to Malta for temporary repairs and became the focus of what was known as the 'Illustrious Blitz'. Joe Micallef, a local Maltese, recalled the attacks on HMS *Illustrious*:

Thursday was a bright, sunny January day … It was 1.55 pm when the alarm sounded. The Stukas came in waves. More and more flew into sight. And as they drew into range the Malta barrage was heard in all its strength for the first time in history. The heavies from the forts opened up with a reverberating roar. The guns round the Harbour area joined in with tremendous emphasis. The Navy's guns transformed the uproar into a stunning crescendo of sound. Through the symphony of gunfire could be heard the menacing drone of the Junkers as they raced towards their objective. The crash and clamour of the barrage was sharpened by a new note as the leading Stukas dipped their noses towards Parlatorio Wharf and dived into the maelstrom of steel, flame and smoke. With the whine of the dive … came the accompanying rush of the bombs as the Germans released them from their racks in the direction of the HMS *Illustrious*, now hardly visible behind a pall of smoke and spouting columns of water.

The entire island rocked to the shock of the battle. The thud of the heavy stuff which the Junkers were dropping, the roar of the bombs as they exploded, and the rumbling crash of falling masonry as Senglea and Vittoriosa caught the weight of the enemy's attack, completed an unforgettable sound-picture. The Stukas followed their squadron leaders in the screaming

---

9   Hugh Lloyd's predecessor as AOC Malta.
10   Brian Cull and Frederick Galea, *Hurricanes over Malta, June 1940- April 1942*, p. 15.
11   TNA ADM 234/381: Submarines Vol. II – Operations in the Mediterranean.

plunge into the inferno that was raging over the Creek. Some of them did not emerge. Hardly one came out unscathed, the defenders were just as tough as the attackers. It required nerve to stick to your guns with those thousand-pounders thudding and bursting around you, with those screaming furies diving over you. In spite of this danger, people looked on fascinated, watching the suicide tactics of the Germans. Others in their shelters, rocked and swayed and wondered if this was the end of it all …

The British fighters joined in the battle and put a magnificent show against tremendous odds. In the heat of the fight they seemed to chase the planes right into our murderous barrage, bent on destroying their prey. After what seemed an eternity, but was in reality some 15 minutes, the noise stopped and a strange silence reigned as the smoke of battle wafted out to sea, and the clouds of dust gradually settled thickly on the ground.[12]

HMS *Illustrious* was lucky, she survived this Blitz and and was able to slip out of Malta's Grand Harbour for Alexandria initially and then to the United States for more lengthy repairs. Malta was less fortunate, and the *Luftwaffe* and *Regia Aeronautica* launched a combined total of 3,000 bombing raids over the next two years. It would surpass the London Blitz and make Malta one of the most intensively bombed places on earth. The *Luftwaffe* intervention tipped the scales against the RAF, for though the Hurricane could take on German bombers, including the highly vulnerable Stuka, it was simply no match for the Me 109. Pilot Officer Pain illustrates this in an encounter he and six Hurricanes of B Flight, led by Flight Lieutenant Watson, had with Me 109s.

He led us out to sea after four Ju 88s in a long stern chase – always deadly, particularly over Malta and when I saw we were actually overtaking the 88s, I realised they were acting as decoys. I pulled out to starboard and went through the gate [boosted the engine to maximum]. Watson, Thacker and Bradbury maintained their position and speed. As I banked to port to make a full beam attack on the nearest 88, I sighted the 109s coming down on the other three. I shouted a warning over the R/T and raked my 88 from nose to tail. One 109 closed with Watson who made no effort to evade, despite further calls from me. Thacker and Bradbury broke away and into the attackers. Watson rolled straight over onto his back and went straight in. I got the 109 which got Watson and he crashed into the drink about 200 yards away from Watty. I got two more bursts into two other 109s before running out of ammunition and, thank God, targets. I have no idea what happened to the 88.

Thacker, who was the sort of swimmer who needed a Mae West to stay afloat in his bath, battled his burning Hurricane back over the Maltese coast at about 6,000 feet; he then pulled his hood back, rolled her and baled out. I was in company, but not formation. I followed him down. Unfortunately for Thacker the wind was offshore and instead of drifting over the island he went in the opposite direction out to sea. By now I was low on petrol and flew back to Takali after Thacker hit the water. I refuelled and re-armed and went back to keep an eye on Thacker, who was about three miles out in the Channel. To my surprise this man who could not swim a stroke had covered a quarter of a mile towards Malta, judging by the fluorescine trail.[13]

Pilot Officer Thacker was successfully retrieved by an RAF rescue launch after 30 to 45 minutes in the sea. B Flight's patrol highlights the difficulties Hurricane pilots had in combatting the Me 109s, this was partly because of the Messerschmitt's superiority as an aircraft, but also because

---

12 Joseph Micallef, *When Malta Stood Alone* (Privately Published, 1981).
13 Brian Cull and Frederick Galea, *Hurricanes over Malta, June 1940- April 1942*, p. 66.

of the relative inexperience of some of the RAF pilots and leaders. In the account above Flight Lieutenant Watson is one such example, although senior in rank to the other pilots his flying experience had been on Wellington bombers rather than fighters and his understanding of aerial combat was immature. Pain justifiably criticised the local RAF direction that senior officers should always lead patrols, even if they had little operational experience. The RAF would progressively relax this direction as the war went on, but the experience of B Flight and Flight Lieutenant Watson was not uncommon at the time. It is also worth highlighting that the speed of the Ju 88 (317 mph for the Ju 88A) was comparatively fast for a bomber and made it a hard aircraft to catch. The Hurricanes did however find the Ju 87 a much easier proposition and as long as Me 109s were occupied elsewhere, the pattern of Stuka vulnerability established during the Battle of Britain, was also continued over Maltese skies.

The arrival of the Me 109s in the winter of 1940-41 led to a rise in RAF losses. The *Luftwaffe* fighter pilots were experienced, tactically astute, better equipped, well led and unsurprisingly – confident. The British Hurricanes brought in during the Autumn were being progressively worn down, combat losses being made worse by a lack of maintenance and servicing and Hurricanes often only kept flying through cannibalising other aircraft. Few replacement aircraft were being sent in and the *Luftwaffe* began to neutralise Malta's offensive capability by destroying all the Wellington bomber aircraft, as well as targeting the Royal Navy warships based at the island. The Hurricanes were outnumbered and outmatched and the future looked very gloomy. The British recognised that something must be done, and efforts were made in May 1941 to fly 48 Hurricanes off *Ark Royal* and *Furious*, this allowed the defenders to create further Hurricane squadrons which could assist the hard-pressed British units. Nevertheless the strain on the fighter pilots was immense, though this was sometimes not always appreciated by even those on Malta. One pilot wrote in his diary on 14 April that a Pukka English 'mem-sahib' had asked him at a party on the island how long he had been in Malta, '3½ months' he stated, 'Oh, quite a short time' she replied. 'I hope,' the appalled pilot wrote, 'that when this old cow has a baby, she looks forward to the few hours of labour in the same spirit.'[14]

The Hurricanes from *Ark Royal* and *Eagle* were an undoubted tonic to the island defenders, who would undoubtedly have been aware of the sobering events taking place in the eastern Mediterranean at the time. It did not require a huge leap of imagination to see how the German airborne invasion of Crete in particular, could be similarly launched against Malta.

The Battle for Crete (20-30 May 1941) marked the end of the Greek campaign, a campaign where the British had initially assisted Greece in its fight against Italy, but were not strong enough to halt the German invasion of the country in April 1941. The British intervention in Greece was controversial at the time as it was a major distraction from the North African theatre, at a point when the British had the upper-hand and might have been able to clear the North African shore. However, Churchill, always conscious of American public opinion, judged it to be a political mistake not to come to Greece's aid in her hour of need. When the British position in Greece collapsed, most of the British forces were evacuated directly to Egypt, but a total of 28,500 servicemen were taken to the island of Crete. Many arrived without their equipment and were in a poor state to continue fighting, after what had been a difficult campaign on the Greek mainland. To defend the island, Air Marshal Arthur Tedder, who had taken over from Air Marshal Arthur Longmore as the AOC-in-C Middle East on 1 June 1941, could only provide four squadrons of aircraft, including Hurricanes, Gladiators and some Fleet Air Arm Fairey Fulmars, which would operate from just two airfields (Retimo and Maleme). With poor radar coverage on the island they were quickly overwhelmed as Squadron Leader Howell describes:

---

14   Denis Richards, *Royal Air Force 1939-45, Volume 1*, p. 307.

Hawker Hurricane IIs of 185 Squadron lined up at readiness at Hal Far, Malta, September 1941. Hurricane IIb, Z5265/T (centre), was the aircraft flown by the squadron's commanding officer, Squadron Leader PWO Mould, when he was shot down and killed after the squadron had scrambled to intercept Italian fighters north-east of the island on 1 October 1941. (Crown Copyright – Air Historical Branch)

Vickers Wellington B.Ic, DV513, refuelling at North Front, Gibraltar, while staging through on a ferry flight to the Middle East in March 1942. DV513 formerly belonged to 99 Squadron and was retained in the UK when the Squadron moved to Far East in February 1942. It eventually joined 70 Squadron at LG104 in Egypt only to be lost on 13 August 1942 when it force-landed in a lake near Fayum after running out of fuel. (Crown Copyright – Air Historical Branch)

I called over one of my newly joined sergeant pilots and he went over the cockpit with me showing me the position of the various controls. I could not make the radio work … In the grey dawn, I noticed that the other two pilots were in their places, sitting quietly in the aircraft, waiting …

Suddenly there was the roar of engines starting up. I saw the other two Hurricanes take-off in a cloud of dust. I waved the sergeant away and prepared to start the engine. As soon as it kicked, I noticed the fitter pull the starter battery to one side and run; I thought 'this is efficiency – the boys run about their business!' Then I looked up. Through the subsiding dust, I saw the others twisting and turning among a cloud of Me 109s. Even as I watched, an enemy aircraft dived into the ground in flames.

I opened the throttle and saw a string of five Messerschmitts coming in over the hill firing at me. It seemed an age before my wheels came off the strip, I went straight into a turn towards the approaching 109s, my wing tip within inches of the ground. The faithful old 'Hurrybus' took it without a murmur, the enemy flashed past and I went over instinctively into a steep turn the other way.

My mind was set on practical things. How to get my undercarriage up, the hood closed, the gunsight switched on, the prop into coarse pitch, the firing button on, the engine temperature down. All the time I kept the nose up, straining to gain height to manoeuvre. I found many difficulties. My rear-view mirror was not adjusted so that I could see over my tail. This meant that I had to do continuous steep turns with my head back to see what was coming after me. Every time I put my head back, my helmet, which I had borrowed and was much too big for me, slipped over my eyes. Then I could not find the switch to turn on my gunsight. I had to look about inside the cockpit for it. Eventually I found it and saw the familiar red graticule glow ready to aim.

Enemy aircraft kept diving in on me in threes or fives. They were travelling fast and did not stay to fight. They just had a squirt at me and climbed away out of range again. It kept me fully occupied with evasive action. Out of the corner of my eye I saw two aircraft diving earthwards in flames. One was a Hurricane. There was no sign of the other. I was alone in a skyful of Jerries.

All of a sudden, the sky seemed to empty of aircraft … Five miles to the south was the airfield. Streams of tracers and red Bofors shells were coming up focused on small black specks which were enemy fighters still strafing it fiercely. Four pillars of black smoke indicated the position of burning wrecks on the ground.

Just level with me and about a mile away two 109s were turning in wide line astern formation. I headed in their direction … I drew in closer and closer with an eye on my own tail to make sure that I was not jumped. I restrained myself with difficulty. It is only the novice who opens at long range …

Howell shot down the first Me 109 and damaged the second. With his ammunition exhausted he headed back for Maleme but found himself among Bofors fire and turned east for Retimo, where he landed, refuelled and returned to Maleme.

A crowd gathered round me as I taxied in … Everyone had assumed that I had been shot down. They had seen my 109 come down and they were delighted that I had opened my score. We had accounted for six Me109s and had lost the other two Hurricanes, shot down in flames. Sergeant Ripsher had been shot down near the airfield and was credited with two enemy aircraft destroyed. We buried him the next day in a little cemetery by Galatos a few miles down the road. Sergeant Reynish had also accounted for a couple and had bailed out of his flaming Hurricane over the sea. We had given him up when he walked in late that evening.

He had been two hours in the water and had been picked up by a small Greek fishing-boat. We had also lost one Hurricane on the ground. It had been unserviceable but could have been flying again within a few hours. Now it was a mass of charred wreckage. We had only one aircraft left. The Fleet Air Arm squadron had lost their Fulmars, burnt out on the ground, as well as a couple of Gladiators. The prelude to invasion had entered upon its last phase.[15]

The pressure on the few surviving RAF aircraft was intense and their piecemeal destruction inevitable, consequently Tedder withdrew the few remaining aircraft off the island just a few days before the invasion. Major General Freyberg, the New Zealand commander of the British garrison at Crete, was aware that the German intention was to launch an airborne assault on the three key airfields, Heraklion, Retimo and Maleme. To that end open ground around the landing ground was obstructed with trenches and mounds of earth. All spare ground at Heraklion and Retimo was blocked by barrels filled with earth and at Maleme by barrels filled with petrol waiting to be ignited by machine gun fire. Freyberg knew that he could not defend the whole of the island, so made the three airfields his key defensive positions, protected by infantry, field guns, anti-aircraft guns and two or three tanks. These, together with the area around Canea and Suda bay, became his four defended areas. It was all he could do with the forces available, including just eight 3.7-inch AA guns and 20 Bofors 40mm LAA guns on the island. The German airborne invasion was launched on 20 May 1941, at which time Pilot Officer R.K. Crowther was in charge of the rear party of 30 Squadron and recalled what happened:

At 0700 the alarm was sounded and within a few minutes very severe and prolonged bombing of the defence positions started. The Bofors crews as the result of sustained bombing and machine-gunning attacks during the past seven days were by this time almost completely unnerved, and on this particular morning soon gave up firing. One Bofors gun was seen to go into action again but the shooting was rather inaccurate. While the Camp was being bombed, enemy fighters made prolonged machine-gun attacks on the Bofors positions and inflicted heavy casualties. At the same time there was intensive ground strafing of troops over a wide area in the locality. These attacks lasted for two hours, with the result that the nerves of our men became ragged, and that intended reinforcements moving towards the aerodrome were unable to do so.

A fuller effect of the bombing was that the men kept their heads down and failed to notice the first parachutists dropping. This particularly applied to those which landed South West of the aerodrome sheltered by hilly country. Gliders were already seen crashed in the river bed on the west side of the aerodrome and had apparently been dropped at the same time. There was no opposition to them except from the two R.A.F. Lewis guns which kept firing throughout the landing. The remnants of R.A.F. personnel and New Zealand infantry on the hill-side were being subjected to persistent ground strafing from a very low height. The Germans were able to profit by the spare time allowed them to assemble trench mortars and field guns which later in the morning were instrumental in driving our men back.

Meanwhile, troop-carrying aircraft were landing along the beach at intervals of 100 yards. They appeared to land successfully in the most limited space, and the enemy did not seem to mind whether they could take-off again or not. At least 8 aircraft were seen crashed in this way. None of these aircraft did take-off again to my knowledge. At the beginning of the attack I reached the pre-arranged position [on a hill near the airfield] at the rear of the New Zealand troops and remained there during the morning.

---

15   Denis Richards, *The Royal Air Force, 1939-1945, Volume 1*, p. 329.

It was here that I gathered a handful of men and obtained a hold; the men on the deep dug-outs on that side had not been warned of the approach of parachute troops. After mopping up the parachute troops here, we discovered that the enemy had obtained a foothold on the eastern side of the aerodrome, actually above the camp. We gathered 30 New Zealand troops who appeared to be without any leader and with my handful of R.A.F. three counter attacks were made and we suceeded in re-taking the summit. Throughout this period we were subjected to severe ground straffing by Me 109s. The enemy's armament at this stage was very superior to ours, namely, trench mortars, hand grenades, tommy guns and small field guns. One particularly objectionable form of aggression was by petrol bombs. These burst in the undergrowth and encircled us with a ring of flames.

At this time, we tried to obtain contact with the remainder of No. 30 Squadron personnel, cut off at the bottom of the valley by the side of the camp, in order to withdraw them to more secure positions on the slopes overlooking the aerodrome. The time was now about 1400 hours. The enemy drove our men who had been taken prisoners in front of them, using them as a protective screen. Any sign of faltering on their part was rewarded with a shot in the back. Our men were very reluctant to open fire and gradually gave ground. A small party of R.A.F. succeeded in outflanking them on one side, and I and a handful of New Zealand troops on the other were able to snipe the Germans in the rear and succeeded thereby in releasing at least 14 prisoners. Towards the close of the day we discovered that our communications with our forces in the rear had been cut, and after an unsuccessful advance made by our two 'I' tanks we decided to withdraw under cover of darkness in order to take up positions with the 23rd Battalion of the New Zealand forces. During the next morning we were un-successful in locating them and had to withdraw from our cover under heavy aerial attack for another three miles, where we at last made contact.[16]

The Battle of Crete was effectively lost with the German capture of Maleme airfield. Despite counter attacks to restore the situation and recover the airfield, the Germans were able to bring in between 20-30,000 troops over the following days. The evacuation from southern beaches on Crete began on 28 May 1941 and 14,500 of the 28,000 Commonwealth troops were successfully evacuated, though this was at the cost of three cruisers and six destroyers sunk, as well as eight destroyers and an aircraft carrier damaged. Such was the *Luftwaffe*'s daylight ascendancy over the Eastern Mediterranean that two Ju 88s were able to sink the anti-aircraft cruiser *Calcutta*, just 100 miles from Alexandria.

The recriminations against the RAF from the other services began, echoing similar complaints made in France in 1940. Churchill weighed in as well and urged the Secretary of State for Air to make every airfield 'a stronghold of fighting air-groundmen, and not the abode of uniformed civilians in the prime of life protected by detachments of soldiers'. It was an unfair accusation of RAF ground crew who had fought determinedly at Maleme, Heraklion and Retimo, but the Prime Minister's directive prompted the formation of the RAF Regiment, which would put airfield defence on a more serious and less ad hoc footing.[17]

The campaign in Greece and Crete took 4-6 weeks for the Germans to accomplish. This extra time needed to secure his Balkan flank meant a delay to Hitler's impending Russian invasion until 22 June 1941 and the German army now faced a shortened campaigning season. The consequences of this would result in their offensive coming to a freezing halt in December 1941, just 12 miles outside the gates of Moscow. For Malta there were two positive consequences to events in the

16   Denis Richards, *The Royal Air Force, 1939-1945, Volume 1*, p. 333.
17   Denis Richards, *The Royal Air Force, 1939-1945, Volume 1*, p. 335.

Soldiers construct aircraft revetments at Takali airfield, Malta, using locally quarried limestone blocks, 13 August 1942. (Crown Copyright – Air Historical Branch)

summer of 1941. First, the Russian invasion would result in the transfer of *Fliegerkorps X* to the Russian front – a blessed relief. Secondly the determined resistance by the British in Crete had generated very high levels of casualties amongst German airborne troops. Hitler was so shocked by the losses that he decreed that they should not be used in an airborne role again – potentially reprieving Malta.

At the time Tedder could take little comfort from these circumstances. Instead the early summer of 1941 saw him attempt to balance numerous competing air commitments in the Mediterranean from very modest resources. These included: continued support to the British Army in the Western Desert, the final efforts to subdue the Italians in East Africa, assisting the isolated British garrison in Iraq as they put down a German inspired rebellion and supporting an invasion of Syria to topple the Vichy French government there. Given the demands on Tedder as well as the limited resources at his disposal, the 48 Hurricanes brought to Malta in May 1941 on *Ark Royal* and *Hermes* seem positively generous. They highlight Tedder's understanding of Malta's position as a keystone of Mediterranean air power.

The Hurricanes coincided with the arrival of Lloyd and saw a renaissance of British strength on the island. Lloyd rectified a number of issues. These included drafting thousands of Maltese and British Army soldiers to repair and maintain the airfields, as well as constructing proper dispersals to provide better resilience against German and Italian attacks. Lloyd explains how this major engineering programme was delivered:

> The work began early in June 1941. In one month not one aircraft was left within the perimeters of the aerodromes. In two months the total number of aircraft had been doubled; and in four months we were operating over 200 aircraft. But the real significance of the work is that in a period of six months the area in which the aircraft were dispersed had been increased nine-fold. The three compact Axis targets had been replaced by something resembling a sprawling octopus with three nodal points, where aeroplanes were to be seen only when taking off and landing. The Axis in Sicily appeared to take almost as much interest in the progress of the work as we did, and they would send over photographic aeroplanes complete with escorts two

or three times a week. Doubtless they learnt a good deal from us in more ways than one, and in October we noted the beginning of similar work in their aerodromes ...

On the ground we were hemmed in by physical geography and villages. I did not like overflowing into cultivated land as the maximum amount of food had to be extracted from the soil. Every ounce of food which could not be grown in Maltese soil had to travel by sea, and we were in a state of siege ... The full force of our wretched state then became apparent. Making dispersal points was just one item; these had to be connected by taxi-ways to the aerodromes and these taxi-ways had to be as firm and as hard and as level as a main trunk road.

But there was no equipment or material. There was no concrete, nor any means of making it, so it was not surprising that there was not a single concrete mixer anywhere. Although there was a little bitumen and tar it was infinitesimal for our needs and had to be reserved for the roads and the tarmac strip at Luqa; moreover, unless the tracks were sealed off in some way, the rain would go through them like a hot knife into butter; as indeed it did. Rain in England is but a trickle to what it can be in Malta. Then the steam rollers. What historic pieces of equipment – and all of them far too light! Only one was the equivalent weight of a Blenheim. It did not matter how much some dispersal points were rolled: if a Wellington had been left standing in one place for seven days it would never have got out again under its own power; so it had to be moved from day to day, if possible. Even a foot would do, but this was another task for the airmen as there was not a single tractor available.[18]

Another benefit for the British during the summer of 1941 was the arrival of the cannon armed Hurricane IICs. Although still not as fast as the Me 109, it was at least beginning to approach the German aircraft's performance in firepower. The *Luftwaffe*'s absence in the second half of 1941 also allowed the Hurricanes to regain air superiority over the island once more. Lloyd took advantage of this new freedom and adopted a more offensive operational approach, increasing the number of anti-shipping strikes. This was frequently done in conjunction with Force K of the Royal Navy, who were once more able to utilise Malta as an operational base. Another positive impact on air superiority were the operations encouraged by Lloyd over Sicilian airfields, including strikes by his small force of bombers as well as fighter aircraft.

As these daylight operations became more dangerous, aircraft began to be dispatched at night, to loiter over the airfields on intruder operations. Pilot Officer Douglas Robertson recalls one such sortie:

The most thrilling tasks given to us were flights over enemy territory in eastern Sicily. These trips were nuisance raids, carried out on moonlight nights, to keep the enemy night bombers on the ground. The procedure was to fly near an enemy bomber airfield, at 500 feet, to avoid being picked up by radar. The assignment over Sicily was to stay there for one hour, then be relieved by another pilot from our Flight. Aircraft taking off were guided by a totem pole with lights. All these lights were shaded so that they could not be seen above a few hundred feet. The night landing at Takali was assisted by runway lights. Malta, of course, was otherwise blacked out.

[On one occasion] I flew towards an airfield near Catania, south of Mount Etna. Before reaching the airfield perimeter I turned sharply away. This tactic would be repeated by an approach to another side of the airfield. Each time I turned away; my rear-view mirror gave me a sight of the sky lit up with anti-aircraft fire. The operation proved to be successful as the enemy bombers did not attempt to take-off while my presence kept them under air raid

---

18   Hugh Lloyd, *Briefed to Attack* (London: Hodder and Stoughton, 1949), pp. 62-4.

A line of Macchi MC200 fighters on Reggio di Calabria airfield in southern Italy, under attack by cannon fire from two Bristol Beaufighter ICs of 272 Squadron detached to Luqa, Malta, in 1941. (Crown Copyright – Air Historical Branch)

alert. Once I flew north of Catania and found myself uncomfortably close to Etna, so I moved away from the mountain. In the bright moonlight, when I was flying over what looked like a park. I could see enemy soldiers moving about amongst the trees. Small light flashes made me presume that they were shooting at me with their rifles. They must have been bad marksmen as I was never hit.[19]

Malta's reprieve was only temporary and by December of 1941 the Germans were so alarmed by the losses inflicted on Axis shipping across the Mediterranean, that they moved *Fliegerkorps II* from the Eastern Front to Sicily. The German force, quickly neutralised Malta's striking forces and once more put the defenders of the island under pressure. There were 169 raids launched against Malta in December 1941 increasing dramatically in January 1942 to 263 raids, about one-third of which were directed against airfields. The usual tactic would be a fighter sweep to clear the skies in advance of the German bombers and allow the Ju 88s to bomb with only slight losses. This new threat to his airbases increased the importance of protecting his dispersed aircraft in some form of revetment, or protective pen, but Lloyd had too many construction tasks for his limited force to manage:

Mere dispersal of aeroplanes on the ground was never intended as an adequate security – not with the Axis forces only 60 miles away. Dispersal was the first phase. The second was to erect

---

19   Brian Cull and Frederick Galea, *Hurricanes over Malta, June 1940- April 1942*, p. 146.

blast walls or pens on each dispersal point to protect each aeroplane from blast and splinters. I do not suggest that we should have been ready for Kesselring's real onslaught on 1 December had it not been for the rain; but such progress as had been made was painfully affected by it. By the end of October the building of pens had come to a halt. All available labour – and it was civilian only – had to be diverted to the maintenance of taxi tracks and dispersals; indeed without it the aircraft would never have been able to reach the aerodromes and fly off.

Then, on 1 December, the bombs began to fall out of the sky in real earnest and the incredible mess which they made had to be cleared up by someone. Thus the vicious circle began. With the labour available it was a full-time task to mend the taxi-tracks and the dispersal points from the ravages of the weather and when the bombs came it was impossible to attempt both tasks – it was either one or the other. But it was useless moving aircraft up to the aerodrome if they could not be flown or mending the aerodrome if the aeroplanes could not be moved there. These conflicting requirements were further complicated by a third factor – the building of pens. If none were made it would have been useless repairing the aerodrome or anything else because there would have been practically no aircraft left to fly.

In mid-December it was evident that unless more pens were built at once the damage rate to aircraft would become greater than our ability to repair them. To have big aeroplanes like the Wellingtons standing out on a dispersal point without any protection from bomb splinters was an intolerable situation at a time when there was every chance of profiting from Rommel's dilemma.

These protective pens could not be constructed overnight and took significant labour. As an example: a pen for a Wellington covered three sides of an area 90 feet by 90. To build one of empty petrol tins filled with soil took 200 men, working nine hours a day, over 21 days. If the pen was constructed in stone it would take 28 days. This already sounds like a long time, but of course first

Ground crew service a Martin Baltimore IIIa bomber, FA353/X, of 69 Squadron in a revetment at Luqa airfield, Malta. (Crown Copyright – Air Historical Branch)

the ground had to be levelled off for a foundation and the wall built up with tins (with one end torn off and filled with earth or stone), to a height of 14 feet. The base layer of the dispersal pen would be 12 tins deep, tapering off to two tins at the very top of the wall. Each pen required 3,500 tons of earth and stone and lifting each tin to the top of the pen was tough work, particularly when all on the island were on severe rations as a result of the siege. Once all stacked up the tins were then wired into position – 60,000 tins for each pen. A pen for a Hurricane required a quarter of the effort to that of a Wellington, and a Blenheim, one-half. Pens would also be required for critical items of equipment, including the petrol bowsers and even the precious steamroller Lloyd alluded to earlier. Lloyd felt he was heading for disaster, but at his request the British Army garrisoning the island provided extra manpower and started to play an increasingly important role in the construction and operation of the airfields, its dispersals and pens.

Important though this defensive work undoubtedly was, it was clear to many, that the only way to combat the *Luftwaffe* successfully would be with a fighter that could meet the Me 109 in an equal contest. This had been a recurring theme throughout autumn 1941, though bizarrely Lloyd does not seem to have pressed for Spitfires as hard as he should have, despite his own RAF fighter pilots advocating for them strongly. Even the Naval commander on the island, Vice-Admiral Wilbraham Ford, was concerned about the Hurricane's relative weakness against the Me 109s and the consequent loss of air superiority. Ford made his feelings clear in a letter to his superior, written on 3 January 1942, where he highlighted both the impact a loss of air superiority was having on his command, as well as a demand for modern fighters:

> I've given up counting the number of air raids we are getting. At the time of writing, 4 p.m., we have had exactly seven bombing raids since 9 a.m., quite apart from over a month of all-night efforts. The enemy is definitely trying to neutralize Malta's efforts, and, I hate to say, is gradually doing so. They've bust a sad number of our bombers and fighters etc … Now we have Libya, and soon I trust Tripoli, I consider Malta must be made stiff with modern fighters – Mosquitoes which can fly out from the U.K on their own and Spitfires from Takoradi if a carrier cannot buzz them off. Guns and stores must come in a submarine beforehand. Just a bit of co-operation between Air and Admiralty and quite simple …
>
> The powers at home must give us safety first and send us out the latest if they want to hold Malta and use it as a base … Minesweeping is now difficult, and they appear to be laying them everywhere. Poor *Abingdon*, the only sweeper, and in daylight she got machine gunned, eight casualties in *Abingdon* alone. I am trying to sweep during the dark hours … Work in the yard is naturally very much slowed up at present as the result of constant raids … Until we get net defence I shall continue to be worried, especially Marsamuscetto and the submarines. Nothing really to stop 'em. Why, why did not [name deleted] press for my scheme of underground shelters. They would have been finished by now. As I write another bombing raid is just over and at least two more of ours burnt out – damnable to be quite useless. Something must be done at once. How I can unload convoys I cannot think … [20]

This pressure for modern fighters had been picked up by the Air Staff, who dispatched Group Captain Basil Embry, a highly experienced bomber pilot who had also served in Fighter Command, to make a first-hand report on the air situation at the end of January. Embry visited all of the airfields and spoke to the pilots personally; he came away utterly convinced that the Hurricane was not holding its own against Me 109s and needed replacement immediately.

20   Viscount Cunningham, *A Sailor's Odyssey* (London: Hutchinson, 1951), p. 439.

A Hawker Hurricane II of 261 Squadron taxiing at Takali, Malta, following a sortie in September 1941. (Crown Copyright – Air Historical Branch)

I am informed that the German fighter pilots often fly in front of our Hurricanes in order to show off the superiority of the 109fs … This is bound to have an increasingly adverse effect on the morale of the pilots. I therefore consider that every possible step should be taken to make Spitfire Vs and Kittyhawks available without the least delay.[21]

Embry also commented on the way fighter operations were being managed.

Lloyd had asked me to observe the raid from the central fighter operations building, which had been excavated out of solid rock and was therefore well protected against bombing. The layout of the operations room and the adjoining signal cabins was approximately similar to that of Fighter Command, so I was quickly familiar with my surroundings. The raid lasted about 10 minutes, the enemy's objective being the dockyard. After the 'all clear' sounded, Lloyd asked me if I had any comments to make about the handling of the fighter force and the control of the air defence battle. I replied that I would study the problem in detail and have discussions with the fighter pilots and fighter controllers before making any recommendations, although I would straightaway like to bring to his notice the question of allowing persons with no specific duties into the operations room. I had noticed that it was overcrowded with spectators who in my opinion distracted the attention of those on duty and taxed the ventilation system beyond its capacity. In consequence, the air quickly became fouled and affected the efficiency of personnel. Lloyd appreciated my point and gave orders at once that the operations room was out of bounds except to those on duty.

During the next few days I visited the squadrons and talked to the pilots about tactics. I also spent long hours in the central operations room studying the problem of raid reporting and the methods used to control our fighters.

---

21   TNA AIR 23/1200: Letters and ciphers relating to the number of aircraft flown to Malta and copies of Parks' 'Forward Interception Plan'.

It seemed that enemy bombers usually approached Malta flying at a high or medium altitude, then released their bombs either in a shallow dive across the target or by using a full dive-bombing technique.

Intercepting them was difficult because they were always escorted by fighters, and in the Me 109F which flew as top cover the enemy had an aeroplane which always had the advantage of height over our Hurricanes. Even if our pilots sat in their cockpits ready for an immediate take-off as soon as the first warning came over the enemy's approach, they could not gain sufficient height over the 109Fs before they were committed to battle. Indeed, the Hurricanes had to climb away from the approaching enemy in order to gain enough height to engage the bombers, and this imposed a difficult problem of control.

It was the job of the fighter controller on the ground to tell our fighters when to turn back towards the enemy, and this demanded nice judgement and a fair share of luck as there was no ground control interception radar in Malta.

In addition, it followed that interception took place too near Malta, with the result that as often as not the bombs had been released before the enemy formations were broken up, and our anti-aircraft guns were forbidden to fire in case they shot down our own fighters. The ideal to aim at was for the fighters to intercept the enemy as far out to sea as possible, thus giving freedom of action to the guns over the target.

The only fighter in RAF service at the time which had the performance to deal with the tactical situation was the Spitfire. Unfortunately there were none in the Middle East, and moreover someone had stated that the Malta airfields were too small for their operation. A quick inspection convinced me that they were perfectly suitable.

I next went into the question of why there was no ground control interception radar equipment in Malta, and it was the same old story. I was told that someone had said it would not function effectively on the island and carrying out a reconnaissance on the ground, I was certain that a mistake had been made. I suggested to Lloyd that he should signal Air Ministry and ask for a scientific team, expert in siting ground control radar, to be flown out from the United Kingdom as a matter of urgency to examine the possibility of installing a set. This he did. Within a few days two scientists arrived and after a thorough look round the whole island, selected a site near the place I myself had thought suitable.

I also proposed to Lloyd that he should ask Air Ministry to establish a Group Captain who was up-to-date in current fighter operations as a member of his staff, to take charge of the central fighter operations room and coordinate the work of his fighter forces on the lines of a sector commander in Fighter Command. I made this proposal because there was no senior officer in Malta with up-to-date experience or knowledge of fighter operations, and this made itself manifestly clear in the handling of the fighter force and in the procedures employed in the operations room![22]

Lloyd accepted Embry's report which was sent back to the Air Ministry with Embry himself. This, together with the pressure from other commanders, had the desired result and on 7 March 1942 17 Spitfires were launched off the carrier HMS *Eagle* and escorted to Malta. Squadron Leader Grant describes the preparations being undertaken:

We were well clear of land. Hughes [Sqn Ldr Hughes, the senior engineer officer] brought the aircraft up to deck to run the engines and, above all, to test the functioning of the long range tanks without which the operation was not on. These first 90-gallon tanks had evidently been

---

22   Basil Embry, *Mission Completed* (London: Quality Book Club, 1956), p. 229.

Pilots of 'B' Flight, 126 Squadron, snatch some refreshment between sorties, in their flight tent at Luqa, Malta. On the left is Pilot Officer F.D. Thomas of Harrow, Middlesex, and on the right, Flight Sergeant C.F. Bush of Gravesend, Kent. (Crown Copyright – Air Historical Branch)

produced in a great hurry and were a bit of a lash-up. The fuel was drawn up into the main tanks by suction and if there was the slightest air leak in the seal between the tank and the fuselage, there was no transfer. Hughes soon found that the seals were not satisfactory and although he and his team strove hard all that day and well into the night he could not make them work properly. Accordingly, around midnight with our take-off due the next morning, Hughes sent a message to the Admiral via Wg Cdr John McLean, saying that the aircraft could not be allowed to take-off without further extensive tests. And since his men had been working for over 20 hours without rest, they could not continue without some sleep.

We heard later that the Admiral nearly exploded and sent back the message that under no circumstances could his ships hang around in daylight in the middle of the Mediterranean within easy range of enemy bombers. The Spitfires had to take-off the next morning – at all costs. But Hughes was adamant. The aircraft were, in his view, not serviceable and he would not agree to their take-off until he was certain that the tanks would work. So the Admiral had to give in, and the whole fleet turned around and steamed back to Gibraltar.[23]

After repairing the tanks, the carrier sailed once more from Gibraltar and by 7 March was in a position to launch. It was not normal for Spitfires to operate from a carrier, so there was naturally some nervousness about whether Spitfires could take-off on such a short deck. One measure to assist the Spitfires was to create 'partial flaps down' for additional lift on take-off. This was done by using blocks of wood cut into wedges. Before the pilots took-off they dropped their flaps and

---

23   Brian Cull and Frederick Galea, *Spitfires over Malta*, p. 11.

the mechanics held the blocks of wood in place, two on each flap, as the pilot closed the flaps once more these were wedged between the flaps and the wing. After take-off, the pilots raised their undercarriage, climbed to a couple of thousand feet, then dropped their flaps to allow the blocks of wood to drop out, before quickly raising them once more for the rest of the journey. Sergeant Yarra was one of the pilots due to take-off from *Eagle*. Two Spitfires had been declared unserviceable so only 15 could fly:

> When the time came – 7am – on the second day out everyone was keyed up and expectant and most of us wondering if the Spitfires would really get off the deck quite OK. … All the aircraft were lined up waiting and everyone was in their cockpits half an hour before the first Blenheim, which was to lead us there, arrived. The Blenheim was sighted, and the ship turned into wind. The first motor started and was run up. Suddenly the naval controller gave 'Chocks Away' and Sqn Ldr Grant opened his throttle and went roaring down the deck. He lifted off the end, sank slightly below the level of the deck, and sailed away, gaining altitude, proving that a Spitfire can take-off an aircraft carrier. All the aeroplanes got off within the hour.[24]

The arrival of Spitfires on Malta made an immediate qualitative impact. However the quantities of reinforcing aircraft delivered were too few to alter the air superiority advantage Britain's way. *Eagle* and other British carriers could only carry small numbers of aircraft and therefore Churchill directly appealed to Roosevelt for the loan of the USS *Wasp*. She flew her first cargo of 48 Spitfires out to Malta on 20 April 1942 during Operation CALENDER, however the aircraft were dispatched only partially operational and the ground elements were not prepared to receive them correctly. Within a few days the *Luftwaffe* had successfully destroyed most of the fighters on the ground. *Eagle* continued to ferry aircraft throughout this period, but it was Operation BOWERY that decisively tipped the balance in the Allies' favour. On 9 May a total of 64 Spitfires were flown off using *Wasp* for a second time (47 aircraft) and *Eagle* (17) once more. This time the lessons from Operation CALENDER had been digested and the ground preparations on Malta were much more adequate, as Lloyd described:

> The first point was that every effort should be made to fly off the Spitfires [from the carriers] earlier in the day, preferably before midday, so that they could be flown before they were grounded by bomb holes at dusk. As the risk to aircraft carriers in the Western Mediterranean was always a serious factor this was a matter which had to be left to the commander at the time … The second point was the paramount importance of ensuring that the aeroplanes were serviceable in every respect before they were flown off the carriers and would be ready to go into action immediately they had landed on Malta and had been re-fuelled; those which arrived on 20 April were in so bad a state that even after being worked on all night many were not serviceable for the battle on the following morning. The guns were dirty, and they had not been synchronised; most of them had not been fired since they had been installed in the aeroplanes and the radio was often not working and could not be made to work for a day or so. In fact, there was a good deal wrong and we could not afford to keep them on the ground for two or three days while they were being re-furbished and put right.
>
> Our organisation was capable of improvement, too. Provided the Spitfires arrived in a moderately serviceable condition and in good daylight we thought they could be back in the air again within 10 minutes after landing. The organization to achieve this was to place five men in each pen with a pilot experienced in flying over Malta whose duty was first to ensure

---

24   Brian Cull and Frederick Galea, *Spitfires over Malta*, p. 11.

RAF groundcrew, assisted by a soldier and sailor, refuel and rearm a Supermarine Vc of 603 Squadron in a revetment constructed from empty fuel tins filled with sand at Takali airfield, Malta, in April 1942. (Crown Copyright – Air Historical Branch)

that each man knew exactly what he had to do and then to climb into the cockpit when it had been done and remain at immediate readiness for take-off. The petrol was kept in five-gallon tins especially protected by sandbags outside each pen, because there was no time to use petrol bowsers, even if we had enough of them. In fact each pen contained all that was necessary to re-arm, re-fuel and service the Spitfires. The long distance tanks fitted under the belly had to be removed and all the various parts had to be tested. If any were unserviceable it was the task of the three specialist tradesmen who were allocated to each group of five pens to replace them.

It was equally essential to ensure the minimum of delay between the landing of a Spitfire and its arrival in its allotted pen; consequently the aerodrome control officer had a representative from each pen under his orders. When he shouted, 'number 36', for example, the representative of that pen would run, jump up on the wing of the aeroplane beside the pilot and direct him. As soon as the engine had been stopped the men would seize the aeroplane, push it into the pen until its tail rested against the rear wall and then work as fast as they could.[25]

The aircraft were successfully flown off the carriers and on their arrival in Malta were quickly turned-round and ready for operations within seven minutes. Operation BOWERY was sufficient to turn the tide in the Allies' favour. The British were now able to maintain five full Spitfire Squadrons on the island (126, 185, 249, 601, and 603 squadrons) and could at last begin to dominate the skies over Malta. This force fought a major action on 10 May, sometimes described as a turning point for the island, where the defenders at last met their attackers on even terms. The *Luftwaffe* were attracted on this day by the approach of the fast minelayer HMS *Welshman*,

---

25   Hugh Lloyd, *Briefed to Attack* (London: Hodder and Stoughton, 1949), pp. 183-4.

carrying a precious cargo of ammunition for unloading in Valetta. Flight Sergeant Brennan describes a Spitfire sortie against a large *Luftwaffe* formation sent to destroy the ship:

We managed to reach 14,000 feet when 109s attacked us over Filfla. As they came in we could see more 109s above, waiting the opportunity to jump us. All five of us started turning with the 109s attacking us. Woody called up and told us the 87s were diving the harbour. While Buck and his pair held off the hun fighters, Johnny and I beetled over the harbour. The barrage was the heaviest I had seen so far in Malta. The smoke puffs were so numerous that they formed a great wall of cloud, contrasting oddly with the Bofors shells shooting up like huge, glowing match heads. We dived through the barrage to get at the 87s on the other side. I looked down as we went through the flak, and the ground seemed to be on fire with the blaze of guns. My aircraft was not hit, but it rolled and yawed, and almost got out of control. We came out of the barrage suddenly. The whole sky seemed to be filled with aircraft. The first thought that struck me, was that so numerous were the aircraft that there was great risk of collision, and that I would have to watch out carefully. Spitfires were coming in from all points of the compass, and there were plenty of 109s about as well …

Tracers started to whip past my port wing. I turned to starboard. An 87 was right in front of me. It was in the act of pulling out of its dive. I gave it a quick squirt, but overshot it, and found a 109 dead ahead of me. I had a quick squirt at him, but again overshot. Buck was yelling: 'Spits over the harbour, for Christs sake climb! They're up here'. I pulled up my nose to gain height, giving the motor all she had. As I shot up, climbing 5,000 feet in a few seconds, I had another quick squirt – this time into the belly of an 87. I saw cannon shells go into his motor but had no time to see what effect they had on him. Then I was above the 87s, and went into a steep climbing turn, waiting to pick one out. Spits seemed to be everywhere, weaving beside the barrage, to pounce on the 87s as they pulled out of their dive. It was not long before the Spits were getting on the tails of the 87s. Wherever I looked I could see only 87s with Spits already on their tails.

It was several seconds before I saw one which I reckoned was my meat. Diving on his tail, I opened fire, noticing an 87 crash into the sea and start to burn as I did so. My fellow went into a hell of a steep turn, and, I followed him round, firing all the time. I had given him three seconds when the thought flashed through my mind, 'this damn 87 should blow up.' But to my surprise, he didn't, so I kept firing. There came no return fire; either the barrage or my fire had got the rear gunner. The 87 continued in his steep turn, climbing all the time. I hung to him grimly and kept on firing. I could see all my stuff going into his cockpit and motor. Suddenly he went to pieces. He literally flew apart – an awesome but satisfying sight for a fighter pilot. His radiator fell off, the air scoop broke away, the pilots hood whirled off in one piece, and bits of fuselage scattered in every direction. Black smoke poured from him.[26]

The arrival of increased numbers of Spitfires was capitalised upon by the posting, in mid-July 1942, of Air Vice-Marshal Keith Park to Malta to replace Lloyd. Park's experience as a fighter commander in the Battle of Britain contrasted with that of Lloyd, who was a bomber commander at heart. The additional fighters and improved radar allowed Park, together with Woodhall his experienced fighter controller, to alter the tactics previously used under Lloyd. The RAF fighters, by virtue of their diminutive numbers and quality of aircraft, had habitually flown away from Malta to obtain height and when they turned around, met the German aircraft over the island itself. Park considered this to be to defensively minded, and instead directed that the RAF fighters

---

26   Brian Cull and Frederick Galea, *Spitfires over Malta*, p. 108.

Air and groundcrew from 249 Squadron take a break from readying their Supermarine Spitfire Vc fighters to oberve some activity on the airfield at Takali, Malta in the early summer of 1942. (Crown Copyright – Air Historical Branch)

should be held at 2-3 minutes' readiness and once scrambled, one squadron should climb into the sun and then turn with it behind them to attack the high Me 109s flying as top cover. The second squadron should intercept the bombers and any close fighter escort they possessed and the third would fly directly to the bombers, to make a head on attack. This caused the bombers to break formation and in some cases jettison bomb loads. The tactics made an immediate impact and the Germans responded by flying fighter sweeps at increasingly higher altitudes in a bid to regain the initiative and air superiority, Park responded by restricting his Spitfire Mark Vs to flying no higher than 20,000 feet, where they out performed the 109s.[27] Park was helped by the fact that the *Luftwaffe* had also been re-focussed on to direct support of Rommel's land campaigns in the Western Desert, which had now reached a critical stage.

Malta was therefore able to build up its strength once more, this included the arrival of elements of the critical 'PEDESTAL' convoy in August 1942. The air superiority, painfully won during the summer of 1942, allowed Malta to reinforce the island with Beaufort torpedo bombers and submarines, turning it once more into an offensive base that hampered Rommel's supply efforts. By the time the Germans refocussed their attention on Malta, they were too late and simply could not subdue the massed numbers of Spitfires that were now operating off the island. The German *Luftwaffe* commander called the operation off on 17 October 1942, having failed to achieve his aim of neutralising Malta. Malta's security was finally assured on 5 November, when the British Eighth Army won the battle of El Alamein and began to advance west, making the ability for convoys to sail under North African-based air cover much easier to achieve. The importance of this success in the North African land campaign was demonstrated when the STONEAGE convoy succeeded in reaching Malta, from Alexandria, on 20 November 1942. It is widely regarded as

27   James Holland, *Fortress Malta – An Island Under Siege* (London: Phoenix, 2003), p. 339.

marking the end of the siege of Malta. By June 1943 Malta had been transformed from a besieged and isolated post, to an offensive base from which to launch the invasion of Sicily. American engineers had built a new landing strip on the neighbouring island of Gozo, new radar equipment had been installed on Malta itself and a spacious operations and filter room hewn out of the rock. On the eve of the invasion of Sicily, 40 squadrons of fighters were poised to support the operation from Malta, Gozo and Pantelleria.[28]

The margins had been close at Malta, but by reinforcing the island with sufficient numbers of high-quality fighters, improving the defensive structures and radar on the island as well as adjusting tactics where necessary, the British were successful in holding on and regaining air superiority, even when it had been temporarily lost. One might question whether some of the RAF fighters conducting Rhubarbs and Circuses over France could not have been diverted earlier to Malta? The presence of RAF Spitfires on the island in 1941 could have made a decisive difference. In other parts of the Mediterranean the RAF were not as fortunate, the campaigns in Greece and Crete highlight the thin margins the British were working on in these early years of the war. The British narrowly succeeded in Malta and the Mediterranean. In contrast the campaign in the Far East demonstrated the consequences of failing to prepare adequately for an air campaign, or resourcing it with the men and machines necessary.

---

28   Denis Richards and Hilary Saunders, *Royal Air Force 1939-45, Volume II* (London: HMSO, 1954), p. 303.

8

'In the Middle of Things'[1]
The British Loss of Air Superiority
and Collapse in the Far East

Britain's worst strategic nightmare was to wage a European conflict simultaneously with one in the Far East. In Asia there were important British strategic interests that had to be protected, including access to raw materials such as rubber and oil, the defence of India and maintaining contact with elements of her empire including Australia and New Zealand. The cornerstone of her position in the Far East was the naval base at Singapore, to which Britain could dispatch a fleet in time of war, or heightened periods of danger. Singapore too was part of a wider Allied barrier against Japanese expansion that included Java, Sumatra and Celebes, in the Dutch East Indies, as well as the American-garrisoned Philippines and further east still: New Guinea, New Britain and New Ireland. The degree to which some of these more isolated areas could realistically be defended was debatable, though for the Allies to have abandoned them without any form of resistance was also politically untenable.

The war in Europe meant that from 1939 onwards British forces in the Far East, including those at Singapore, found themselves to be at the very bottom of British priorities. Australia and New Zealand had also generously deployed forces to Europe and the Middle East, leaving their own defences dangerously weak. The loss of France and Italy's entry into the war only exacerbated that problem, presenting Britain with a difficult campaign to win in the Mediterranean and turning French Vichy possessions in Indochina into potential bases for Japanese offensive operations. The only cause for optimism was that any Japanese aggression in the Far East would probably increase the chances of American entry into the war, potentially against Germany and Italy too.

The distances in the Far East (see Map 7) are enormous and often hard for those more familiar with the European conflict to appreciate. Land lines of communication were often rudimentary, though the Japanese were to demonstrate how the jungle was not an impenetrable barrier and could be used for tactical manoeuvre. Perhaps more impressive was the Japanese ability to project military power in a series of long-range offensive operations, through a remarkably skilled combination of both maritime and air power. The ability of the Allies to defend their critical bases in this area and prevent Japanese naval assaults would depend significantly on its air defence capability. The problem was that British and Allied preparations and resources were inadequate.

As we have already witnessed in Europe, an air defence system needed efficient early warning and command and control mechanisms. This was vital in avoiding unnecessary air patrols that wear down machines and increase aircrew fatigue.[2] The distances in the Far East also meant that such air patrols would be highly unlikely to detect, meet or defeat any enemy offensive air action.

---

1   Motto of 258 Squadron RAF, 258 Squadron was a Hurricane squadron deployed to the Far East in 1942. After a few days in Singapore they were evacuated to Java and Sumatra, suffering many losses.
2   Peter Preston-Hough, *Commanding Far Eastern Skies* (Solihull: Helion, 2015), p. xxvii.

Vickers Vildebeest IIs of 100 Squadron being refuelled at Kuala Lumpur, Malaya, 18 May 1938. (Crown Copyright – Air Historical Branch)

Radar, the obvious choice for such an early warning system, was not widely available in the Far East and its coverage patchy and inconsistent. Despite consistent pleas for radar from as early as 1939, the Air Ministry showed reluctance to pay for either equipment or staff. The original hope was to have 20 radar stations operational in Malaya by 1 December 1941, but pressures in providing both equipment, as well as the technical personnel to man, service and repair them, meant that only six had been established by that date. Burma too was to receive sets to protect the oil fields at Siriam as well as the docks at Rangoon.

This paucity of radar could not hope to generate comprehensive coverage, particularly given the numerous blind spots the central mountains in Malaya and Burma generated against any aircraft approaching inland. Once the Japanese struck on 8 December 1941, there were some belated attempts to provide mobile sets, but it was all too little and too late. Tim Vigors commanded a squadron of Brewster Buffalo fighters that were deployed to Butterworth, one of the northern airfields in Malaya, on 12 December. Although only 20, he was an experienced Battle of Britain fighter pilot by the time he was sent to the Far East.

> On landing [at Butterworth] I could see a hut and some petrol tankers. As I climbed down from my Buffalo, I was met by the officer commanding the airfield.
>
> 'Mighty glad to see you Tim! The japs are very active, and we have been strafed several times in the last 24 hours. They normally dive in from the north but there's very little warning. The only radar we have is that man there.' He pointed to an airman standing on the roof of the hut. 'When he starts waving his red flag it means he's spotted them and you'd better get off the ground, quick!'

Brewster Buffalo Is of 21 Squadron RAAF, lined up at Sembawang, Singapore, on the occasion of an inspection by Air Vice Marshal CWH Pulford, Air Officer Commanding Royal Air Force Far East. (Crown Copyright – Air Historical Branch)

I cast an eye towards the hut and sure enough there was the man. I was about to look away when I saw him raise the flag he had been holding by his side and began to brandish it wildly from side to side above his head. It took a couple of seconds for the penny to drop but then I was yelling at my boys, scramble. As I started my engine I saw three Japanese aircraft diving on the field from the north. That sharp stab of fear with which I had grown so familiar over the past 12 months, shot through me. 'Here we go again,' I thought.

With my No.2 taxiing beside me, I swung my aircraft northwards and pushed open the throttle. As we left the ground a stream of tracer streaked over us as we passed beneath the oncoming enemy. Turning sharply, I saw behind me one of the Buffaloes explode in a ball of flame, But the other three were off the ground safely and were climbing towards me.[3]

3   Tim Vigors, *Life's Too Short to Cry* (London: Grub Street), 2006, p. 7.

Not only were the radar sets too few in number, but unlike either Britain or Malta the connecting communication links were also very primitive. Landlines were often absent and where they existed, had to be patched through telephone exchanges. Communications cable was in short supply and deteriorated quickly in the wet, tropical environment. Radio could have been used, but sets were rare.

In addition to an effective early warning and command and control system, those charged with air defence would also need good, modern fighters capable of climbing to advantageous heights quickly and then successfully engaging the enemy with effective combat tactics. Those serving in the Far East were once more at the back of the queue and were provided, in 1941, with the American-designed Brewster Buffalo. This short, squat, mid-winged machine was a truly dreadful aircraft. First produced for the United States Navy in 1938, it was bought by the British Purchasing Commission in 1939 ostensibly as a land-based fighter. On its arrival in the UK in September 1940, it was very quickly established that it would be hopelessly outclassed against modern German fighters and the suggestion was made that all 170 aircraft could be deployed to the Far East, where it might be usefully employed, even if only as a short-term measure. This was a judgement that reflected the widespread assumption that Japanese aircraft were inferior to European designs. By the time the Far East war started there were four Buffalo Squadrons in Malaya (243 Squadron RAF, 21 and 453 Squadrons RAAF and 488 Squadron RNZAF) a fifth Buffalo squadron, 67 Squadron RAF, had also been deployed to Burma. This generated a total frontline strength in Malaya of just 67 aircraft to meet the Japanese onslaught, not exactly a large quantity, but numbers were not the only problem.

The Buffalo was simply no match for modern Japanese fighters such as the Nakajima (also manufactured by Mitsubishi) Navy-0 or Zeke 52, nicknamed the 'Zero' by Japanese pilots after the final numeral in the Japanese imperial year (2600) in which it was manufactured. The Allies also called it the 'Zero' and many pilots may have used the same term for the Army variant, known as the Nakajima Army-1, or 'Oscar 3', which was very similar in performance and looked almost identical. Although the Buffalo was reasonably armed with two .5-inch machine guns in the wings and two .5-inch guns that fired through the propeller arc, the aircraft took 6.1 minutes to reach 13,000 feet as against the Zero's 4.3 minutes. At 10,000 feet it could fly little more than 270 miles, much slower than the Zero's 315 at that altitude and its fighting efficiency was reduced further, by obsolete and unreliable radio instruments.[4] Moreover the main Japanese fighters were incredibly agile and could easily out-turn a Buffalo. The refusal of the British to recognise the quality of Japanese fighters is one of the most glaring oversights of Air Intelligence in the war, owing far more to wishful thinking than sober intelligence analysis (Annex M gives details of the major operational aircraft of the Japanese Air Force from 1942-45). In August 1940 Air Intelligence believed that the Japanese failure to win a contract to supply a South American country, was because of their inability to produce a modern design. A ludicrous intelligence assessment on Japanese comparative strength was drawn up in February 1941, it arrogantly asserted:

> Recent information tends to confirm the belief, hitherto held, that the operational value of the Japanese Air Forces is less than that implied by their numerical strength … estimates must be approximate, but it can be safely assumed the correct figure lies between 2,000 and 2,500 (538 shipborne) … the performance of Japanese aircraft are much below those of equivalent RAF types. There are good grounds for believing that, allowing for the probable superiority of Italian pilots over their Japanese allies, the operational value of the Japanese air arm is less than that of the Italians.[5]

---

4   Denis Richards and Hilary Saunders, *Royal Air Force 1939-45, Volume II*, p. 10.
5   TNA AM/WIS 75, 5 February 1941.

Although the intelligence report above was balanced by subsequent assessments, that suggested the Japanese would use modern types as the leading edge of any offensive, there was nonetheless an alarming complacency in British thinking and a dangerous underestimation of the Japanese capability. The development of the Zero, should have attracted more attention. Its maximum speed was 358 mph (60 mph faster than the Buffalo), its ceiling 34,000ft and it possessed 2 x 13.2mm cannon and 2 x 7.7mm machine guns. Perhaps most astonishingly, it had a huge fuel load which gave it an impressively long seven hours endurance and if the wing tanks were supplemented by a drop tank then the Zero had a maximum range of 1,900 miles. In contrast, it was not until 1944 that the acclaimed long range P-51 Mustang came into service and helped achieve air superiority over Europe, even then, the Mustang still only had a range of 1,710 miles.[6] The Zero's long range would be particularly advantageous given the great distances the aircraft would need to operate over, in both the Pacific and Far East campaigns. It was a significant factor in allowing the Japanese to conduct sweeping maritime assaults under air cover. The only weakness in the Zero, was that its speed and agility had been achieved by sacrificing armour and other forms of protection, such as self-sealing tanks. Any hits on the Zero that the British fighters did succeed in achieving could be satisfyingly catastrophic, though even that Japanese weakness was offset by the Zero's Nakajima Sakae air-cooled radial engine, which unlike the Hurricane, Spitfire or Tomahawk's in-line engines did not have a complex, vulnerable cooling system that could be easily damaged and cause the engine to seize up.

The Zero had first been used over China, performing well against Russian-made fighter aircraft encountered there, but British minds were blinkered and conditioned to an assessment of Japanese inferiority, refusing to accept a growing body of contradictory information. One senior officer at the Far East Combined Bureau of Intelligence apparently refused to pass on the performance data on the Zero to the fighter stations, because he simply did not believe that the Japanese could possess such an aircraft.[7] The result was that some Buffalo pilots were so misled over their enemies true capabilities, that they were surprised to encounter monoplane aircraft.[8] Sergeant Kinninmont was serving with 21 Squadron RAAF at Sungei Patani airfield and had taken off to conduct a reconnaissance over Singora. He describes his first combat with the potent Zero fighter, as well as the equally manoeuvrable Mitsubishi Type-97 fighter bomber:

> Then the sky seemed full of red circles (the red roundels on their aircraft) and the Japs all tried to shoot us down at once. I pulled up to meet one as he dived down … I was in such a hurry to shoot something that I didn't use my gun sight. I simply sprayed bullets in his general direction. Somebody was on my tail and tracers were whipping past my wings … Chapman was turning and shooting with four Japs. I decided to get out. I yelled to Chapman (over the radio telephone) 'Return to base. Return to base.' And went into a vertical dive. As I went down I glimpsed the Sergeant diving straight for the ground with three Japs on his tail, shooting; then I lost sight of him. At 3,000 feet I had a quick shot at a four-engined Kawanishi Jap flying-boat and missed … Of the three Japs that followed me down in that dive one stuck and he stuck like a leech … As I watched him, my neck screwed around, I saw his guns smoke and whipped into a tight turn to the left. It was too late, and a burst of bullets spattered into the Buffalo … I opened the throttle and the motor took it without a murmur.
>
> It was then that I felt the first real fear in my life … . It struck me in a flash. This Jap was out to kill me. I broke into a cold sweat and it ran down into my eyes. A noise throbbed in my

---

6   Henry Probert, *The Forgotten Air Force – The RAF in the War Against Japan* (London: Brasseys, 1995), p. 27.

7   Air Historical Branch Lulow-Hewitt Papers, Memorandum of Pilot Officer Cox, folder 14, p. 8.

8   Air Historical Branch Narrative, *The Campaigns in The Far East*, Vol. 1, p. 63.

RAF personnel inspect six Australian-built Bristol Beaufort Vs, shortly after their arrival at Kallang, Singapore, in early December 1941. The aircraft were intended for the re-equipment of 100 Squadron but, as they were unarmed and their crews possessed no operational training, five were returned to Australia, while the sixth was employed on photographic-reconnaissance duties. (Crown Copyright – Air Historical Branch)

head and I suddenly felt loose and weak. My feet kept jumping on the pedals. My mouth was stone dry, and I couldn't swallow. My mouth was open, and I was panting as though I'd just finished a 100 yard dash and I felt cold. Then I was jibbering … 'watch those trees. That was close. He'll get you next burst. You'll flame into the trees. No, he can't get you. He mustn't get you. You're too smart. He'll get you next time. Watch him, watch his guns. Watch those trees.' My feet were still jumping on the pedals. I couldn't control them. Then I saw his attacks were missing me. I was watching his guns. Each time they smoked I slammed into a tight turn. And then my whole body tightened, and I could think. I flew low and straight, only turning in when he attacked. The Jap couldn't hit me again. We raced down a valley to the Thai border and the Jap quit.[9]

The Commander-in-Chief Far East Command, Air Marshal Brooke-Popham, later wrote that the 'strength of the Japanese Air Force came as a complete surprise – in the quality, performance,

---

9   Douglas Gillison, *Royal Australian Air Force 1939-42* (Canberra: Australian War Memorial, 1962), p. 222.

mobility and experiences of its personnel'.[10] Even experienced pilots, such as Tim Vigors, were surprised when they encountered the Japanese Air Force for the first time. Having taken off under a strafing attack, Vigors flew to 10,000 feet to attack what looked like 20 aircraft:

> I yelled over the intercom to my three pilots, telling them to go after the Japs who had attacked the airfield while my No.2 followed me. We two climbed at full throttle to intercept the enemy formation heading for Penang. Broken fluffy clouds gave plenty of cover as we clawed for height, making for the classic attacking position, up sun and above the opponents. To my surprise I identified the Japanese aircraft as Army 97 fighters, old-fashioned and slow compared with the Messerschmitt 109s with which I had been tangling so often over the previous year over England. I could not believe my luck. Here was Tim Vigors, the hardened Battle of Britain fighter ace, about to show these bloody little Japs in their antique fixed undercarriage toy planes how the *Luftwaffe* had been brought to its knees. I called my No.2 'OK, let's attack these little bastards and knock them all out of the sky!'
>
> Did somebody say that pride comes before a fall? Well, I was certainly full of pride, but I was about to learn in the next few minutes that there was indeed a long way to fall. Four guns blazing I tore into the attack only to experience a rude shock; it was obvious that the Army 97 was not only the most manoeuvrable fighter with which I had fought but was also being flown by pilots who knew how to fight and fly. Black smoke billowed from the aircraft in front of me and I knew I'd got the first one. But I had another one on my tail. Out of the corner of my eye I saw my No.2 in dire trouble as he tangled with two of the enemy and I hauled even harder on the stick to try to come to his assistance. I could sense by the closeness of the tracer whistling past my wing tip that my opponent was turning inside me. I wrenched the nose of the Buffalo downwards and for a moment managed to escape his attention. At the same moment I got another of his friends in my sights. More black smoke and I yelled with glee out loud, 'That's two of the bastards!'
>
> My joy was shortlived. In the Brewster Buffalo the petrol tank was located almost exactly beneath the pilot's seat. The shock of having even a half tank of petrol explode underneath one is, to say the least, traumatic. It causes one hell of a big bang! A bang in fact so big that it stuns. Something had gone wrong and it took me a couple of seconds to realise that I was sitting in the middle of a bonfire. I thought, 'Well old fellow, it's happened at last!' It just seemed too much of an effort to do anything about it. I even thought quickly of all the many good friends who had gone the same way over the last two years. Then suddenly, the will to survive rose in me.
>
> A long-held habit of mine had been always to slide open the cockpit hood of any aircraft I flew in action. This habit had become ingrained, though sometimes it could be a less than pleasurable experience, such as when flying at extreme heights. On this morning with fire all around me it wasn't the cold I was worrying about though. Pulling the pin to release my shoulder harness I placed my right foot on the stick and kicked it. Although an un-orthodox way of leaving an aircraft, it is certainly a quick way. Kicking the control column of an aircraft flying at some 250 mph creates a catapult effect which throws a human body about 200 feet into space. This was to ensure the fast exit I was looking for that morning.[11]

The badly burnt Vigors was picked up by two native Malays, who carried him off a mountain where he was picked up by jeep and taken to Penang hospital. He was eventually moved to hospitals in

---

10   Air Historical Branch Narrative, *The Campaigns in The Far East*, Vol 1, p. 50.
11   Tim Vigors, *Life's Too Short to Cry* (London: Grub Street, 2006), p. 11.

Johore and then Singapore, where he was subsequently evacuated by flying boat just as the city was falling.

The capabilities of the Japanese Air Force also came as a surprise to the Army and Royal Navy, who had to operate under constant highly skilled and determined air attacks. The fact that the Navy headquarters was 35 miles from the air headquarters exacerbated confusion and misunderstandings about air operations over the region, as well as the enemy air threat. The Royal Navy's 'Force Z' was commanded by Admiral Sir Tom Phillips and consisted of the Battleship *Prince of Wales,* the Battlecruiser *Repulse* and a handful of destroyer escorts. It was the most powerful maritime force the British had in the region, though it was also supposed to have been accompanied by a British carrier, HMS *Indomitable,* but this had run aground at Jamaica and needed repair. Phillips was made aware by the RAF that the short-range Buffaloes would not be able to provide adequate fighter cover as the ships moved north to strike the Japanese invasion fleet. However, Phillips ignored these warnings, probably underestimating the power of the Japanese aircraft and putting too much faith in his own ship's anti-aircraft defences. On 10 December he was caught off the east coast of Malaya, by a powerful force of Japanese bombers and torpedo aircraft and the two capital ships were swiftly put out of action by torpedoes and bombing attacks, reinforcing the lesson that maritime forces were not invulnerable. Captain William Tennant RN recounted the attack by Japanese aircraft in his official report:

6. The **first attack** developed shortly after 1100 when nine aircraft in close single line abreast formation were seen approaching REPULSE from about Green 50 (50° on the starboard bow) and at a height of about 10,000 feet. Fire was at once opened on them with the Long Range H.A. by PRINCE OF WALES and REPULSE. It was very soon obvious that the attack was about to be entirely concentrated on REPULSE. The formation was very well kept and bombs were dropped with great accuracy, one near miss on the starboard side abreast B turret and one hit on the port hangar burst on the armour below the Marines' mess deck and caused damage. The remainder of the salvo (it was thought seven bombs were dropped altogether), fell very close to the port side and this concluded this attack. There was now a short lull of about 20 minutes during which the damage control parties carried out their duties in a most efficient manner and fires which had been started by this bomb had all been got under control before the next attack; and the bomb having burst on the armour no damage was suffered below in the engine or boiler rooms. It is thought that the bombs dropped were about 250 pounds.

7. The **second attack** was shared by PRINCE OF WALES and REPULSE and was made by torpedo bomber aircraft. They appeared to be the same type of machine, believed to be Mitsubishi 86 or 88. I am not prepared to say how many machines took part in this attack but on its conclusion I had the impression that we had succeeded in combing the tracks of a large number of torpedoes, possibly as many as 12. We were steaming at 25 knots at the time I maintained a steady course until the aircraft appeared to be committed to the attack, when the wheel was put over and the attacks providentially combed. I would like to record here the valuable work done by all Bridge personnel at this time in calmly pointing out approaching torpedo bombing aircraft, which largely contributed to our good fortune in dodging all these torpedoes. PRINCE OF WALES was hit on the port side right aft during this attack and a large column of water appeared to be thrown up, larger than subsequent columns of water which were thrown up when REPULSE was hit later on.

The third attack was a high-level bombing attack, concentrated on the *Repulse,* as she tried to provide some protection to the *Prince of Wales* who had signalled that they were 'no longer under control'. The fourth attack was a torpedo bombing attack by eight aircraft. Captain Tennant continued:

> When about three miles away they split into two formations and I estimated that those on the right hand would launch their torpedoes first and I started to swing the ship to starboard. The torpedoes were dropped at a distance of 2500 yards and it seemed obvious that we should be once more successful in combing their tracks. The left hand formation appeared to be making straight for PRINCE OF WALES who was at this time abaft my port beam. When these aircraft were a little before the port beam at a distance of approximately 2000 yards they turned straight at me and fired their torpedoes. It now became obvious that, if these torpedoes were aimed straight, REPULSE would be most certainly hit as any other altera-tion of course would have caused me to be hit by the tracks of those torpedoes I was in the process of combing. One torpedo fired from my port side was obviously going to hit the ship and it was possible to watch its track for about a minute and a half before this actually took place. The ship was hit amidships port side. The ship stood this torpedo well and continued to manoeuvre and steamed at about 25 knots. There was now only a very short respite before the final and last attack …
>
> The bomber aircraft seemed to appear from several directions and the second torpedo hit the ship in the vicinity of the Gunroom and apparently jammed the rudder, and although the ship was still steaming at well over 20 knots she was not under control. Shortly after this at least three torpedoes hit the ship, two being on the port side and one on the starboard side. I knew now that she could not survive and at once gave the order for everyone to come on deck and to cast loose Carley floats.[12]

Repulse sank at 1233 hours. Captain Tennant was rescued by the destroyer *Vampire* though 436 men were lost. Admiral Sir Tom Phillips went down with the *Prince of Wales*, along with 327 other men. The loss of *Repulse* and the *Prince of Wales* gave the Japanese undisputed command of Far Eastern waters just two days after the outbreak of war. It also marked the end of traditional surface-orientated views of sea power as preached by Mahan and practised by Nelson.[13]

As it dawned on the RAF that the Buffalo was inadequate, the Air Ministry diverted a number of Hurricanes to Malaya and Burma. These had been intended to reinforce Russia's fight against Germany on the eastern front, but the need in the Far East was seen as too pressing and these crated Hurricanes, as well as their crews and maintenance staff, were all diverted to Singapore. They arrived in late January, by which time the four Buffalo squadrons, having been totally outmatched by the Japanese fighters, were on their last legs. The arrival of the Hurricanes prompted great anticipation as Air Vice-Marshal Paul Maltby the assistant AOC Singapore recounts:

> It is difficult to adequately convey the sense of tension which prevailed as these convoys approached Singapore, and the sense of exultation at their safe arrival. The feeling spread that at least the Japanese were going to be held on the ground if not driven back, whilst many confidently expected that the Hurricanes would sweep the Japanese from the sky. On their arrival they were immediately unloaded, and the majority dispersed to previously selected concealed positions, where they were erected and wheeled to a nearby airfield for testing; the

---

12   Initial Report from Captain W.G. Tennant RN to Commander-In-Chief Eastern Fleet, 11 December 1941, *London Gazette*, 1948.

13   Denis Richards and Hilary Saunders, *Royal Air Force 1939-45, Volume II*, p. 24.

Brewster Buffalos in flight. (Royal Australian Air Force Museum)

remainder proceeded direct to 151 MU for erection at other dispersal points. The speed with which these aircraft were erected was a remarkable achievement.

Twenty-four pilots arrived. When AHQ first heard of their diversion to the Far East, it had been planned to give the aircrew a [rest] spell before employing them in operations. This spell was obviously desirable, not only because of their time at sea, but also because of the need for acclimatising pilots to local conditions. However, events moved too fast and the stake was too high for delay to be acceptable. The Hurricanes had to be used immediately.[14]

Although there was considerable hope that these Hurricanes would be able to match the Japanese, the pilots themselves were becoming less confident of their aircraft, particularly after conversations with the Buffalo pilots. Pilot Officer Jerry Parker of 232 Squadron voiced his concerns:

The Hurricanes were IIBs with the more powerful engine than we'd had at RAF Ouston, but the radios were the old, almost useless TR9Ds. Also, they were equipped with heavy filters on the air intakes [originally it was thought the Hurricanes would be operating in dusty, sandy conditions and would require these to protect the engine]. It was a pity they could not apparently be removed, except in one case of a plywood panel being fitted locally to replace that which in the main carried the filter. We never got a good performance from our Hurricanes over Singapore.

Another disability of our aircraft in terms of manoeuvrability was that they were equipped with 12 machine guns instead of eight. Although for marksmen of our calibre a congregation of machine guns was desirable, the extra four guns and their ammunition must have weighed half a ton. The Hurricanes became not only slow, particularly in the climb, but also very heavy and unwieldy in manoeuvre. However, we were most anxious to get amongst the formations of bombers which daily flew over Singapore. This did not prevent me – and the others, I suppose – from growing nervousness about the approaching series of battles, which must be fought in the air.[15]

They did not have to wait long. Parker recalled an operation on 26 January, when his squadron gave air cover to a group of Swordfish and Vildebeest torpedo bombers attacking the Japanese amphibious landing at Endau. This was an important operation, for if the Japanese could consolidate at Endau, then a final offensive towards Singapore would follow quickly.

Brooker [The Squadron Leader] issued us with maps of Malaya and told us we'd be doing a couple of special patrols that afternoon, following an early lunch. We were to go up the east coast at about 10,000 feet to Mersing and patrol west and east between the middle of the peninsula and the coast. Other aircraft would be carrying out operations near the coast and our job was to attract enemy fighters, which were not expected, away from them … We spent some minutes forming up and then climbed off up to the north. I was not looking at the map at all since we had Malaya on our left and the sea on our right and I knew I'd have no difficulty in getting home as long as there was no cloud. I was constantly searching the skies ahead, behind and above and checking my position in relation to Brooker and Ken Holmes, my No.2.

We'd reached our operational height when I saw a fair amount of smoke above the coast a few miles ahead and a couple of steamers lying just offshore. As we came nearer – and we flew no faster – I could see several aeroplanes starting to burn in the air at a low height and go crashing in flames into the greenness of the trees below, there to look like enormous bonfires at the end of a trail of black smoke which spread and grew again from each. Brooker looked around and pointed to the fracas and went down in a fast shallow dive. I felt ill as I saw several Vildebeest and Swordfish biplanes being harried by Jap fighters and the now familiar sensations of suspense and anticipation took charge of me as I checked my cockpit for readiness and the sky for more of the enemy in the last few seconds. Apart from the aircraft already burning, I could see two other British biplanes with smoke spiralling back from their slipstreams whilst they were closely followed by the little silvery fighters with the big red discs on their wings.

Brooker took the nearest Jap and I took on one chasing a biplane on his right, but I found that owing to my high speed and the offset of the tailfin to counteract torque, the plane skidded wildly as I pulled out of my dive and I didn't have time to line up the Zero properly. I pulled up to come round again and found a fixed undercart monoplane going straight into the air and on the point of stalling. My speed had dropped considerably, and I had the plane under control so that I was able to hit the Jap with several seconds of fire during which it remained in the same attitude before falling off under my nose. I pulled round in a sharp turn but could not see it where I anticipated and instead I found it or another similar coming at me from behind when I'd straightened out. I panicked madly, pushed the stick forward, was saved by my straps from going through the roof of the cockpit and broke down to the ground before pulling up towards the cloud several thousand feet away. However, I found I'd left the Jap behind and so I came down again in another shallow dive to take on a Zero chasing a Vildebeest almost towards me. They both turned further towards me and I turned inside

15   Brian Cull and Paul Sortehaug, *Hurricanes over Singapore*, p. 25.

Australian Lockheed Hudson. This aircraft was used as both a bomber and reconnaissance aircraft during the early part of the Far East Campaign. (Royal Australian Air Force Museum)

them so that I was able to rake the Zero at close range with a short burst and he was unable to bring his guns to bear either on the biplane or myself. I didn't hope to have destroyed him in such a fraction of a second, but we had met only just above the trees, and when I looked back, he was burning there and the Vildebeest pilot, who had been shot, confirmed this very lucky kill.

I swept up again towards the clouds but did not let my speed drop below 300 mph. Of course I didn't glance at the air speed indicator but could tell by the engine note at what rate the speed was falling off. There were still 10/10ths of stratus clouds above so I could easily check that there were no fighters waiting to come down on me and I looked for further targets. I reckoned that I still had several seconds of unused ammunition left but apart from the Vildebeest now moving off south, no other aircraft were in the sky. I cruised over towards the steamers lying offshore but could see no unusual activity nor did there seem to be any shooting going on and finally I turned towards Singapore and fell in behind a Lockheed Hudson until I reached Seletar.[16]

That the Hurricanes were also struggling with the agile Japanese fighters was something the Buffalo pilots also noticed, this included Sergeant Kinninmont who wrote about the Hurricanes' first appearance over the city:

At the sight of those planes, morale skyrocketed 100 percent, and the sun shone again, and the birds sang … That evening at all the night spots the gay topic of conversation was 'Hurricanes'. The miracle had happened. The Hurricanes were here, and the world was saved. 'Boy! More

16   Brian Cull and Paul Sortehaug, *Hurricanes over Singapore*, p. 43.

stengahs[17] – long with ice!' … The RAF boys flying them began to mix it with the Zeros which we knew was practically impossible. The Zero was just about the nippiest, most highly manoeuvrable fighter in the world. They buzzed around the Hurricanes like vicious bees. The RAF Hurricane pilots fought gallantly and courageously against overwhelming odds and during their brief period of operation in Malaya they scored several brilliant victories and shot down many Japs. But they too 'took the knock'.[18]

Hurricane and Buffalo pilots, not only flew inferior aircraft, but also faced overwhelming numerical odds that were established early on in the campaign.

The original superiority in numbers the Japanese possessed had been lengthened by strikes against Allied aircraft on the ground, as well as in the air. These raids had started on the first day of the Far East war, when the Japanese struck out of the blue in a seven-point assault across a vast region, including attacks on Malaya, Hawaii, Thailand, the Philippines, Guam Island, Wake Island and Hong Kong. These coordinated pre-emptive strikes had all taken place within a 14-hour period, capitalising on surprise to achieve as much destruction on the ground as possible. On 8 December, from about 0700, around 150 fighters, many of them long range, launched a series of attacks from their bases in Indo-China against seven airfields in northern Malaya. The attacks were directed against aircraft on the ground, as well as airfield installations and usually consisted of strafing attacks, so that the airfields would not be excessively damaged and the Japanese could use them later.

Whilst some airfields were empty of aircraft, at other bases the impact was severe. At Sungei Patani, only four aircraft were left serviceable from 21 and 27 Squadrons after two raids. Butterworth was only a care and maintenance airfield but found itself under attack when 34 Squadron's Blenheims were diverted there. Only two Blenheims were serviceable after the attack. At Alor Star, a fuel dump and much of the accommodation was destroyed as well as four of 62 Squadron's Blenheims. Finally, Kota Bharu was attacked no less than seven times and the decision to evacuate the airfield at 1600 given. The consequences of both air combat and ground attacks on the Malayan airfields on 8 December meant, that on the first day of the Malayan campaign, 40 aircraft were destroyed and 20 seriously damaged out of 110 operational aircraft – a reduction of 55 percent.[19] The scale of destruction was exacerbated by poor dispersal, a lack of protective pens and anti-aircraft guns, all of which were symptomatic of continued complacency, as well as the poor original design of the airfields.[20]

These attacks on British airfields, which were continued throughout the campaign in Malaya and the Far East, were an important aspect in achieving air superiority. As well as causing physical damage, they eroded the morale of the ground crew and other staff at the airfield, sometimes to the extent that rash decisions were made to prematurely and hastily evacuate airfields. On occasions, this meant that a destruction plan was not properly executed and vital stores and fuel, as well as the runway itself, were all left intact for the Japanese. Certainly, the Japanese considered it an important element in their overall success, the Chief of 25th Japanese Army's Operations and Planning Staff commenting:

17   Stengah: A Whisky and Soda. The term stems from the Malay word *Stengah* meaning 'half'.
18   Douglas Gillison, *Royal Australian Air Force 1939-42*, p. 340.
19   Henry Probert, *The Forgotten Air Force*, pp. 43-4.
20   Douglas Gillison, *Royal Australian Air Force 1939-42*, p. 166.

Possession of two fold numerical air strength was one reason for our air superiority over the Malayan theatre of operations, but the decisive factor was that we were able to take immediate advantage of the captured 'Churchill aerodromes'.[21]

There is a sad irony in that the Army had never wished to defend Malaya from a line so far north, it had only agreed to do so in order to defend the airfields which the RAF insisted needed to be sited there, now that these had been swiftly evacuated the Army, not unreasonably, felt some bitterness towards the RAF for bestowing upon them unwanted and now unwarranted dispositions. It was to be a common complaint in other theatres in the Far East. What was the point of the Army undertaking commitments to defend, or construct, airfields if the Air Force disappeared the moment they were attacked? The Japanese bombing of airfields continued throughout the Malayan campaign, by the time the Hurricanes arrived in mid-January the attacks were causing poor morale, as well as a notable loss of efficiency. Hurricane pilot Sergeant Kelly, records one example at Seletar airfield:

The ground crews were busy and working under difficulties. They had never worked on Hurricanes before, their spanners didn't fit, and the removal of long-range tanks was proving to be a stubborn mystery. They possessed no spares and they had no supplies of Glycol which was the coolant fluid for the Rolls Royce Merlin engines. Above all the guns, the twelve .303 Brownings, six in either wing, were presenting them with an unconsidered problem. Presumably to protect them from salt at sea they were thickly caked with sticky grease of which incidentally we had known nothing – had we met Japanese, or even tried trial bursts we would probably have blown the wings off! Or so they said.

Anyway there was nothing to do but strip them down to each tiny part and clean these in hot thin oil and reassemble … and there were a lot of parts and a lot of guns.

We hung around Bruce and me – not because there was anything we could do but because there was not much else to do anyway, and I suppose we felt that hanging around was the right thing to do. We chatted, smoked, remembered the odd bits and pieces, including our revolvers stowed away in the cine gun camera mountings and retrieved them.

At about half past nine the attention of the ground crews began to wander, and their eyes turn with growing frequency to the sky. Not that there was any sound of aircraft – there was only the sound of birds and the gentle shift of the morning breeze in the nearby rubber trees. The sun had begun to gather heat, the damp ground begun to shimmer – voices drifted, insects hummed. And the war seemed very far away. And then quite suddenly, one man called something to his mates and the man working on my guns dropped the sear pin or whatever it was he happened to be wiping at the time back into the bath of amber oil and set off with the rest with one accord toward the rubber.

I never knew till then that Bruce McAlister could be angry. 'What the hell,' he shouted in his twangy nasal voice, 'do you think you're doing? Where the hell do you think you're going?' They stopped, momentarily, and one man pointed to the sky. I looked up and there in an otherwise unmarked blue sky was drawn a white circle, a vapour trail which even as I looked at it was thickening lazily and leaving behind the white sparkling diamond of the reconnaissance aircraft which had made it. 'So?' said Bruce, puzzled. 'Means it's us this morning, sir'. That made no sense – that circle must have encompassed the whole of Singapore. So I asked him what he meant. 'It's what they do, Sarge. They send a kite ahead and draw a circle where they're going to bomb. They'll be here in half an hour.' And he set off towards the rubber,

---

21   Masanobu Tsuji, *Singapore: The Japanese Version* (New York: St Martin's Press, 1960), p. 130.

with no more ado, with the rest of them after a momentary hesitation straggling after him ... Get your gun out.' I heard Bruce say and to my surprise I saw that he already had his revolver in his hand. I fumbled for my own with a feeling that the situation was extra unreal. 'Stop!' shouted Bruce to the back of the departing men. They stopped, turning their heads. 'Come back,' he ordered them. They came slowly back. When they were near enough, Bruce said: 'Anyone who heads back that way again until I've said he can is going to be shot.' There was a pause. I think we both felt the same as we stood there pointing our revolvers at that knot of unhappy men – uncomfortable and embarrassed. 'It may not be very pleasant,' he said, 'but there does happen to be a war on and we've got to be able to get these Hurricanes into the sky and you're going to stay and clean our guns until we say you can go and that's all there is to it. Now get on with it.' We didn't have any more trouble.[22]

Seletar was not bombed that morning, though that was becoming an increasingly rare event towards the end of the campaign (and the circle was formed through a photo-reconnaissance aircraft's vapour and was not a method of target marking). As the Japanese advanced down the peninsula the British radar positions were progressively dismantled and withdrawn, as a result, the early warning of raids was reduced from 30-20 minutes and then, just before the end of the siege, to almost nothing. This gave little time for British aircraft to respond and had particularly severe consequences for the depleted Buffalo squadrons, who took more than half an hour to reach 25,000 feet, the usual height at which the Japanese bomber formations and their escorts operated. This meant that the Buffaloes were almost always beneath the enemy and at a grave disadvantage.

Singapore finally capitulated on 15 February 1942 – it was the worst defeat the British suffered in the Second World War. The Japanese of course did not stop there, and their assaults continued, as part of their wider Far East offensive. Imagine a heel of a hand based on a line stretching from Indo-China to Formosa with the fingers splayed in different directions. These fingers represent the separate Japanese offensives. One goes West to strike the British in Burma, another South through the Malayan peninsula to Singapore and beyond that to attack the Dutch colonies on Sumatra and eastern Java. A third goes to Borneo and a fourth to attack the American-defended Philippines, then south around Celebes to southern Borneo and western Java/Timor. Finally, an extended finger goes all the way into the Pacific to capture Rabaul in New Britain, strike at New Guinea and threaten the Australian-held garrison at Port Moresby. It is hard to imagine the psychological impact these extraordinarily successful series of Japanese operations must have had on the Allies. They demonstrated not only the stunning results that could be achieved by powerful air and maritime forces working in close concert, but also that it was impossible for the Allies to maintain or preserve small and weak air force units in close proximity to a large and powerful enemy air force. The long range of the Zero in particular allowed great projections of air power, including the initial strike from Formosa to Southern Luzon in the Philippines – over a distance of 550 nautical miles.[23]

It meant that the Japanese were to establish air superiority very quickly in the campaign, conversely the Allied power to strike back was much less effective. One sympathises with General Brereton, the US Air Force Commander in the Philippines who, having lost a considerable portion of his aircraft on the ground, was then berated by his superior, General Arnold, in Washington.

He was excited and apparently under great strain. 'How in the hell could an experienced airman like you get caught with your planes on the ground?' General Arnold asked. 'That's what we sent you there for, to avoid just what happened.' I tried to explain what had happened,

---

22   Terence Kelly, *Hurricane over the Jungle* (London: Arrow, 1990), pp. 50-3.
23   Douglas Gillison, *Royal Australian Air Force 1939-42*, p. 223.

Two Consolidated Catalina Is of 205 Squadron based at Seletar, Singapore, in flight along the Malayan coastline. The nearest aircraft, Z2144/FV-R, was shot down by Japanese naval fighters in the Bay of Bengal on 5 April 1942. (Crown Copyright – Air Historical Branch)

but halfway through the conversation the Japs came over strafing the field. 'What in the hell is going on there?' General Arnold shouted. 'We are having visitors.' I replied. I asked General Arnold to withhold his judgement until he got a complete report on what had happened at Clark Field and said that we had done everything in our power to get authority to attack Formosa on 8 December but had been relegated to a 'strictly defensive attitude' by higher authority.[24]

Some of the saddest tales during this period come from the isolated garrisons, such as Rabaul in New Britain. To have left these islands undefended was not apparently politically acceptable. Therefore there was a small garrison of Australian Infantry on the island, supported by a tiny RAAF component, with eight obsolescent Commonwealth Aircraft Corporation (CAC) Wirraway advanced trainer aircraft (that were sent there to operate as fighters – a hopeless task) and the odd Hudson. The commander of the RAAF, Wing Commander John Lerew, was well aware of the impossible situation his team was in and pleaded regularly and repeatedly for reinforcements, to no avail, as there were none to give. When the Japanese onslaught began on 20 January, the Wirraways were wiped from the skies by the overwhelming Japanese force. Lerew signalled 'Waves of enemy fighters shot down Wirraways. Waves of bombers attacking aerodromes. Over 100 aircraft seen so far.' He followed this signal later with a further one 'Sending A16-38 [a Hudson aircraft that had been under repair] to Moresby with casualties. Two Wirraways useless defence. Will you now please send some fighters?' The blunt reply from the Australian North East Area Headquarters was simply: 'Regret inability to supply fighters. If we had them you would get them'. Lerew replied 'Wirraways and Hudsons cannot be operated in this area without great loss and sacrifice of skilled personnel and aircraft. Pilots and aircraft as good as equivalent types of Japanese aircraft doing

24   Lewis Brereton, *The Brereton Diaries: The War in the Pacific, Middle East and Europe (3 October 1941 to 8 May 1945)* (Plano, Texas: Tannenberg Publishing reprint of 1946 edition), p. 50.

most damage. One squadron Type 0 fighters enables others to operate. As fighters cannot be obtained only one course if services of trained personnel valued.'[25]

As the situation on Rabaul became more severe, Lerew followed this up with further signals: 'My orders were to take action if necessary in the event of attack. In consultation with Army and Navy [have] holed all fuel drums and destroyed publications. This necessary as Army cannot protect and you have given no indication any possible chance to defend Rabaul. In meantime air force personnel stand every chance of being cut off. RAAF willing fight with Army but Army cannot handle untrained personnel. These men will be required by RAAF before long – Lerew'. The reply was swift – 'From AOC to Wing Commander Lerew. Begins. Rabaul not yet fallen. Assist Army in keeping aerodrome open. Maintain communications as long as possible.' This signal written in a heroic 'the Empire expects' vein contradicted previous direction that Lerew should use his discretion to withdraw his forces (who now had no aircraft to service or fly). Lerew matched such heroism with impish humour sending a phrase in Latin *Nos morituri te salutamus*. At first the cipher clerks were confused and thought they had decoded the message incorrectly; it took someone with a knowledge of Latin to translate the old gladiator slogan – 'We who are about to die salute you!' North East Area Headquarters instructed Lerew to come home.

Though the Australian Army ground forces under Colonel Scanlan were unable to escape, the Air Force personnel were able to trek across the jungle to the south coast of Rabaul.[26] The majority were picked up by RAAF flying boats over a series of nights from 23-25 January. A total of 1,000 Australians were captured at Rabaul of whom only a fraction survived, many being killed in July 1942 when the Japanese transported them from Rabaul in the merchant ship *Montivideo Maru*, which was unfortunately torpedoed by an American submarine causing a large loss of life. The heroic tragedy at Rabaul was sadly not unique and there were similar stories of allied air units being overwhelmed at many of the Allied Indonesian, Pacific and Far East island garrisons.

For the Hurricanes and the other surviving aircraft at Singapore, there began a weary session of retreats, first to Sumatra where they were joined by Hurricane reinforcements that had been flown off HMS *Indomitable*. These aircraft undertook operations from two airfields around Palembang (P1 and P2), including some successful attacks on Japanese maritime assault forces. Despite this, Sumatra was evacuated after a Japanese parachute assault on the two airfields and the surviving RAF and Army units withdrew to Java. Despite valiant efforts Japanese air superiority was assured and again some of the last aircraft were destroyed on the ground. Pat O'Brien was a Hudson pilot and recalled the Japanese strafing one of the last few operational airfields.

> They manoeuvred into position at cruising speed, patiently careful as if in practice on the range – and probably smiling as they passed over the wooden guns, pointing up in ridiculous attempt at threat. I think there were nine machines in that first group but it was difficult to tell because each one made more than one steady gun-shattering run down the strip. Looking up from the trench near the end of the strip I could see them turn in slowly for each run as if coming in to land, they would straighten out at about 50 feet just in front of us, so low I could see a pilot clearly in helmet and goggles sitting upright in the cockpit, hood back to enjoy the breeze perhaps … down the length of the strip … thunder of gunfire … pull up into a gentle left-hand circuit … back down for another run. I saw one pilot turn his head on the run-in and he seemed to look straight down at us in that enormously wide shelter, which began to feel more and more like a gentle declivity in the surface rather than a manufactured trench.

---

25   Douglas Gillison, *Royal Australian Air Force 1939-42*, p. 364.
26   Lerew and his team were lucky; he survived the war and later settled in Vancouver.

Peter kept popping his head up to give a running commentary about aircraft that were being hit, but as our own aircraft was out of sight I had no interest in watching the destruction. I wished he would keep his head down; I could have cheerfully shot him myself he seemed so unconcerned. A column of black smoke spiralled up from the field and there were explosions as fire reached the aircraft fuel tanks. Then there was a lull for a minute, the first group had had enough, they climbed away to let the top lot down for their turn. Even Peter grew quiet then, staying low like the rest of us as the second group started on their orderly runs of destruction. They went on and on and on, and the smoke from fires began to drift across the trenches. They could see us every time they turned, banking at the end of the strip to get into line, but still they concentrated on their prime target, the machines. Had we had just a single machine gun, even a repeater rifle, they must have suffered, but we were as defenceless as the aerodrome itself – even our revolvers had been handed in to be checked that morning.

Suddenly the next one did not come, there was just the thrumming of many aircraft and I looked up to see them circling into formation, and a moment later they set off northwards, their vibrating sound fading into the airfield clamour – the crackling of fire and the staccato chatter of exploding ammunition from burning aircraft. It was the end. I could have wept at the sight of V9129; it had not burned like our other remaining Hudson, but it would never fly again. It was riddled with cannon shell and bullets to such an extent that large chunks of fuselage and wings had ripped away. Cockpit and turret were smashed into a tangle of metal and perspex and cables. I cannot understand why it had not burned, both tanks had been hit repeatedly and petrol was pouring on to the ground. There was still a strong risk of fire, however, for the nearby aircraft was ejecting great woofs of flame through its twisting smoke coils. Suddenly realizing there were bombs aboard at least one of the burning aircraft, we all withdrew to the top hangar. No buildings had been touched. The Japanese had come to destroy aircraft and had done so with deadly effect.[27]

Java itself fell on 8 March 1942 and those who could not escape went off into a long spell of brutal captivity. Only large aircraft like Sunderlands or Catalinas could make the long journey across the sea to Australia, however three enterprising Hudson pilots managed to refuel their aircraft in flight by knocking out a side window, opening the fuel cap on the wing and pouring in fuel from 25 petrol cans and a rubber hose brought into the aircraft itself. For others, including substantial numbers of RAF and RAAF ground personnel, evacuation by sea was the only recourse. Though in this instance the Battle of the Java Sea in which the Japanese had destroyed five Allied cruisers and now dominated the seas around the Dutch East Indies meant that many of these were intercepted and sunk. O'Brien was lucky the master of his ship, the *Kota Gede,* one of three, took a gamble and sailed independently west into the vast Indian Ocean rather than south to Australia. They evaded the Japanese Navy and in due course reached Ceylon with 2,152 RAF officers and men aboard.[28] The other two ships elected to sail south to Australia, but both were sunk by the Japanese. Perhaps most astonishing is the escape of Wing Commander J.R. Jeudwine, who had commanded 84 Squadron, equipped with Blenheims. Together with three other British officers and seven Australian Sergeants, they set off from Tjilitjap on 7 March in a ship's lifeboat capable of holding only 12 people. After a 47-day voyage, marked by blazing sun, torrential rain and an over-inquisitive whale, they were eventually picked up by a US Navy Catalina near Frazer Islet and taken to Perth.[29]

27   Terence O'Brien, *Chasing After Danger* (London: Collins, 1990), p. 238.
28   O'Brien, *Chasing After Danger*, p. 239.
29   Denis Richards and Hilary Saunders, *Royal Air Force 1939-45, Volume II*, p. 54.

9

'Boldness to Endure Anything'[1]
Turning the Japanese Tide

The fall of Singapore on 15 February had sharply exposed the gravity of the Japanese threat, shattering the confidence of Australian politicians and air force leaders. Their fears were further underlined four days later by an attack on Darwin, from the same Japanese carrier group that had struck Pearl Harbor and included the aircraft carriers *Akagi* (Admiral Nagumo's flagship), *Kaga*, *Hiryu* and *Soryu*. The raid on Darwin involved 188 Japanese aircraft, which made it larger than the strike on Pearl Harbor and it struck at both shipping, the harbour and the recently arrived P-40 Kittyhawks from 33rd Pursuit Squadron USAAF. The latter were parked in neat lines on the ground at Darwin airfield and those few machines that were able to get in to the air were quickly shot down by the Japanese. If that was not alarming enough for the Australian government, the arrival of Japanese forces in early March 1942 at Lae and Salamua, on the North Coast of Papua New Guinea, certainly was. It put the Japanese within reach of Port Moresby, just across the Owen Stanley Mountain Range. Port Moresby was a vital strategic objective for the Japanese, not only would it secure their southern defences, it also meant that Australia, just a few hundred miles across the Torres Straits, was within striking distance. As Australia's ground forces, mostly composed of half-trained militia thrown together at the last moment, fought a gallant defence on the Kokoda Trail, the RAAF also began to make a desperate attempt to contest Japanese air superiority over Port Moresby and Northern Australia.

This was no easy task for the RAAF for such was the lack of preparedness of the Australians own defences that they had no fighters to defend their own territory and had to rely on American support, initially in the form of the USAAF 49th Pursuit Group. This American unit, led by Lieutenant Colonel Paul Wurtsmith, quickly began to contest the Japanese strikes over Darwin. Wurtsmith and his unit forced the bombers to fly at 25,000 feet or even higher and at this height the Japanese bombers were almost ineffective. This neutralisation of the Japanese bomber force meant that the Darwin network of airfields could be safely built up without interference and was able to receive General MacArthur's expanded and offensively configured air force. The 49th Pursuit Group had been sent to Darwin, not as an act of charity by the Americans, but because they recognised it as an essential base from which they could launch their counter-offensive in the South West Pacific – up through New Guinea to Rabaul. The build-up of the Darwin area included the construction of a network of airfields built by RAAF Airfield construction squadrons, the US Army's 808th Engineering Battalion and civilian road crews provided by the Australian state government. Each airfield was given a circuit of taxiways that led from the runway to camouflaged and revetted dispersal sites under cover of the trees. Engineering and logistic units had also moved

---

1   The 54 Squadron RAF motto, this squadron was engaged heavily in the Battle of Britain and conducted fighter sweeps over France in 1941. It was deployed to Darwin in June 1942 and defended North Western Australia from Japanese aircraft based in the Dutch East Indies.

RAAF Kittyhawk pilots walking back from a Squadron sortie. (Royal Australian Air Force Museum)

in and newly built roads linked the whole system together. By April 1942 the Japanese would not be able to simply destroy neat lines of aircraft on the ground at Darwin anymore.[2]

While Wurtsmith and the 49th Pursuit Group began to defend Darwin, Australia became the unexpected beneficiary of 75 Curtiss P-40D Kittyhawks,[3] these had originally been destined for Java, but were now found to be surplus to American requirements and were given to Australia. The Kittyhawks were used to equip three new Australian Squadrons, 77 Squadron who were formed in western Australia for the defence of Perth, together with 75 and 76 Squadron who would be based in Queensland. In time the 49th Pursuit Group would hand the air defence of northern Australia to 76 and 77 Squadron in August 1942 – who would in turn be replaced by the Spitfire-equipped No. 1 Fighter Wing in 1943. More immediately 75 Squadron, under Squadron Leader John Jackson would deploy to Port Moresby on 21 March 1942, to contest the Japanese advance. Jackson was one of a number of pilots who had served in the western desert or Europe and he brought an element of much needed experience to the otherwise novice squadron.

The Squadron was lucky that their arrival at Seven-Mile strip[4] near Port Moresby was not detected by the Japanese, this was despite the attention of a Japanese reconnaissance aircraft that appeared a few hours after their arrival but was immediately shot down by the newly arrived squadron. The Japanese aircraft had tried to transmit a signal, but fortunately, a quick-witted Australian signals officer had picked up the Japanese aircraft's radio signal and by ordering his radio operator to hold down his morse key, he had successfully jammed its transmission. With security still maintained 75 Squadron was well set to deliver a pre-emptive strike on the Japanese aircraft at Lae, a dramatic reversal of the trend so far encountered where the allies were usually

2   Anthony Cooper, *Darwin Spitfires* (Barnsley: Pen and Sword), 2013, pp. 6-8.

3   The British Commonwealth used the term Tomahawk for models equivalent to the P-40 B and C and Kittyhawk for models equivalent to the P-40 D and all later variants.

4   The airfield was known as 'Seven-Mile Strip', because that was the distance it was from Port Moresby.

RAAF Kittyhawk taxiing in New Guinea. (Royal Australian Air Force Museum)

the victims of Japanese strikes on their own airfields. On this occasion it would be 75 Squadron who were to find the enemy's aircraft lined up in neat rows, just as the reconnaissance photographs from a Hudson sortie the day before had shown. 75 Squadron split into two groups, one to target the line of Japanes fighters and the second to strike the line of bombers. Flight Lieutenant John Piper was one of the strafing pilots, on what was be his first operational sortie:

> I set a few aeroplanes on fire, you know, on the ground ... When you're strafing you're supposed to come in [low] like that, keeping down as you're shooting you see, and you tend to get lower and lower and more and more horizontal and finally I hit a prop and it tore the gun out and it severed the spar. It was, you know, an aircraft parked on the ground. Well, that was where a P-40 was excellent because with that it just didn't show any trouble at all with it. I remember at Lae I got chased out with the others and it was the first time I had seen cannon shells and they're really interesting because if you're looking out the back you can see them. They're about the size of cricket balls; they look sort of on fire. And all of a sudden they're there and 'zoot', they go past you. Anyway, theoretically, you just skid slightly, and you go through them but then you're terrified of skidding a little bit too much in case you pull a [mile an hour] off it ... No, I thought it was all very stimulating.[5]

Whilst an element of the squadron were strafing, others were providing top cover. John Pettet was also in action for the first time and recalls his initial encounter with the dreaded Zero. Prior to this Pettet had only had a single hour-long shooting practise on the Kittyhawk against a drogue. He

---

5   AWM Sound Archives S00577: Interview with Flight Lieutenant John Piper, 75th Squadron.

watched his wingman make a beam and quarter attack on a Zero, which then executed a Split-S stall turn, Pettet observed the Zero performing this manoeuvre on his wingman, but the Japanese pilot had not observed him:

> This aeroplane had apparently been attacking the ground strafers and had pulled up into a climbing turn that the Zero did very well – a very steep climb and a sort of flick turn to turn in the opposite direction … suddenly this character pulled up right in front of me and all I instinctively did was pull back on the stick and pull the trigger and allowing what I thought was enough deflection and that aircraft went down and I got one confirmed.[6]

The operations of 75 Squadron began to include regular strikes on the Japanese airfields, often accompanying American Douglas SBD Dauntless dive bombers that had also arrived at Port Moresby. The Japanese, now thoroughly alerted to the Australian squadron's presence, would fly over to Port Moresby and attempt to bomb it, the bombers being escorted by Zeros. To tackle these raids the Australians had set up a rudimentary warning system, in the form of No.4 Fighter Sector under Wing Commander G.E. Sampson, who had served as a fighter controller in the Battle of Britain. However, the hasty set up in Port Moresby was a far cry from the Dowding system. The control room was simply a cave overlooking the bay in which alerts were passed to the anti-aircraft positions, the air-strip on which 75 Squadron was based and the headquarters in Port Moresby. Furthermore, the radio sets in the Kittyhawks were so unreliable that once airborne the Australian pilots were effectively out of contact.[7] No.4 Fighter Sector were supported by 29 Radar Station; however these radars could not detect Japanese aircraft beyond the high Owen Stanley range and were therefore practically blind to the north. The Australians therefore relied on their network of observers, known as the 'Coastwatchers'.

The Coastwatchers were individuals who were selected for their maturity and knowledge of the country to penetrate behind the lines and set up observation posts, from which they would radio reports of weather, shipping movements and Japanese aircraft. Pilot Officer Leigh Grant Vial was one of the most successful ones on New Guinea, acquiring the nickname 'Golden Voice' for his calm, accurate and authoritative reports. Vial positioned himself so that he could observe Lae and Salamua airfields and spot the Zero fighter escorts climbing to meet the Japanese bombers that had flown from Rabaul. Before being commissioned into the RAAF, Vial had worked for the colonial administration in New Guinea as a patrol officer and knew the north coast of the island and its people well. He was therefore adept a living off the land and surviving on a diet of yams, taro, okari tree nuts and occasionally the odd animal he had successfully snared. The Japanese were clearly aware of his presence, but he evaded both their radio direction finders and the frequent patrols searching for him. Japanese attempts to bribe the locals into giving him away were also unsuccessful. Vial manned his post from the end of February until August 1942 reporting up to nine times a day, providing critical intelligence to both the Australians and the Americans at Port Moresby. He was sadly killed later in the war, when the B-24 Liberator bomber he was a passenger in crashed into the New Guinea jungle killing all on board.[8]

The No.4 Fighter Sector controller would scramble the Kittyhawks of 75 Squadron, to meet the Zeros and bombers as they approached Port Moresby. The Australians' Kittyhawks were well armed with 6 x .5inch machine guns and had a powerful Allinson in-line engine. This made it heavy but relatively fast, especially in a dive, though it was still not very manoeuvrable when

---

6   Michael Veitch, *44 Days* (Sydney: Hachette, 2016), p. 89.
7   Michael Veitch, *44 Days*, p. 146.
8   Michael Veitch, *44 Days*, pp. 147-9.

compared to the Japanese Zero. John Piper describes some of the Kittyhawk's strengths when compared to the Japanese bomber aircraft it was sent to intercept:

> Well, of course, the main thing was that it was faster than the Japanese – we found that out later – we could always get away ... I belonged to the school of thought that I could never see much point in battling round if you're going to be shot; it seemed to be much better to shoot somebody else down and come back another day. Dead heroes never appealed to me. Well its strength was it was very strong; very robust and well amour-plated, and it was quite fast. But other than that it didn't have anything much.
>
> It had a poor ceiling, you know, its best operating ceiling was from about 12-15,000 feet so when we were trying to operate it, you know, from 22 to 25 [thousand feet] we were just sort of wallowing around the place.
>
> In New Guinea, you would find if you did a head-on attack on a series of Japanese bombers by the time you'd got around and caught up again, you know, the day was nearly over. The fact was that we had trained ourselves – and had been trained – to make these quarter attacks and attacks from underneath and we didn't realise if we'd just sailed right up behind them and just shot them to pieces – they had nothing to shoot us with very much – we could have just demolished them just by being in formation with them. We didn't really realise that until it was sort of virtually all over. We were still doing the textbook attacks really.[9]

No. 75 Squadron's commander was well aware of the relative performance of the Kittyhawk and Zero in a dogfight. Jackson instructed his squadron that they were to climb to height as quickly as their aircraft would allow in the hot tropical air, get into a position above and up sun of the Japanese formation and then dive down on them, using their aircraft's speed and heavy armament against the lightly armed and armoured Zeros and bombers. If they got into trouble the Kittyhawk pilots would 'bunt' effectively pushing the stick to the far left or far right corner, with the rudder hard over. The following Japanese Zero would effectively see the Kittyhawk dive away from it as its speed, weight, direct-injection engine and gravity all worked in helping the aircraft pull away from its pursuer. Arthur Tucker describes the process:

> You climbed up, you tried to stay together, you had a squirt at something, and if you looked as though they got on your tail you bunted – that was, you put everything in one corner – dived away to get up speed, and then come back and have another go, but on no account were you to try to dogfight the Zero because that was not on.[10]

The tactics above were not appreciated by some in the RAAF, who felt the 75 Squadron approach in refusing to engage in a dog fight with the Japanese Zeros was cowardly, the pilots being caricatured as 'Dingoes'. There is some speculation that to prove a point Squadron Leader John Jackson attempted to dog fight the Zeros, only to be shot down and killed for his pains.

The loss of their leader was clearly a blow to 75 Squadron, but it came towards the end of the Squadron's 44-day-long tour, at the end of which they were reduced to just four planes. At that stage it looked like despite the valiant efforts of 75 Squadron Port Moresby would fall, succumbing to another Japanese amphibious invasion onto Milne Bay – known as Operation MO. Fortunately, through signals intelligence, the Americans had picked up these Japanese objectives and rushed a Carrier Group to intercept the Japanese force. As 75 Squadron was being withdrawn, the two

---

9   AWM Sound Archives S00577: Interview with John Piper, 75th Squadron.
10   AWM Sound Archives S00701: Interview with Arthur Tucker, 75th Squadron.

75 Squadron personnel at New Guinea. (Royal Australian Air Force Museum)

fleets clashed in the Battle of the Coral Sea (4-8 May), this was a historic battle not just because it effectively checked the Japanese amphibious advance on Port Moresby, but also because it marked the first time two opposing fleets had struck each other using entirely carrier-borne airpower, the surface ships never coming within sight of each other. With the Japanese now unable to use their maritime forces to conduct an amphibious assault, they were forced to undertake a costly, slow and ultimately unsuccessful land offensive across the Kokoda Trail. The successful defence of this attack is rightly commemorated as one of Australia's most important battle honours.

The Japanese were now at a strategic disadvantage and the initiative passed from them to the Allies, who launched their own offensives in the Solomon Islands, as well as New Guinea. All that lay in the future, but as they left Seven-Mile airstrip in early May 1942, the survivors of 75 Squadron could take comfort in that they had not only survived, but by their actions had offered a credible defence against the Japanese air onslaught and bought the defenders the precious time needed.

As 75 Squadron were deploying to New Guinea the Japanese were also striking West towards Burma (see Map 8 for detail of the Burma theatre). The campaign in Burma would offer a chance to improve tactics and begin to meet the Japanese on an even footing. At first glance the situation resembled much of the Far East – overwhelming enemy numbers, patchy British radar coverage, a poor command and control situation and inexperienced pilots. Air Vice-Marshal Stevenson, the AOC in Burma, also considered the airfield siting tactically unsound, noting they were placed to counter potential attacks through China and northern Siam, rather than through Malaya. These airfields included Lashio, Namsang, Heho and Toungoo, all of which were in the Sittang Valley and relatively close to the eastern border. When combined with an inefficient warning system, they were very vulnerable and would probably have been much better placed in the Chindwin and Irrawaddy valleys, with radar units deployed further east.[11] The city of Rangoon was an obvious

11   Henry Probert, *Forgotten Air Force*, p. 83.

target and objective for the Japanese, it was important as a capital, centre of population and a port and logistic hub, with routes stretching into China. Whilst Burma was blessed by an efficient observer corps system, the provision of radar was weak with just one Chain Overseas Low set (517 Air Ministry Experimental Station) which moved from Moulmein to Rangoon.

In aircraft the situation was equally parlous. When Stevenson arrived in Burma on 1 January 1942, he estimated he required 224 aircraft (a mix of Hurricanes, Tomahawks and Beaufighters) to defend Burma, yet he had just one squadron of 16 Buffaloes available. He was given a further three squadrons of Hurricanes in late January (most of which came from the Middle East), but many of them were clapped out Hurricane Is and a test on arrival showed their radius of action was little more than 135 miles. There was one cause for optimism and that was the presence of a Squadron of the American Volunteer Group's (AVG) Tomahawks. These were the famous 'Flying Tigers', formed by Major Chennault, an ex-US Army Air Corps Officer and air adviser to the Chinese. He had formed three squadron of fighters, equipped with Tomahawks and flown by volunteer ex-military American pilots. The AVG were to help defend the Burma Road supply line into China from Japanese air attack and were using RAF facilities at Toungoo when war broke out. Chennault immediately and generously placed one squadron under RAF command, where they became an indispensable element in the air defence of Rangoon.[12]

The Flying Tiger pilots knew their Tomahawks could not match the Japanese fighter aircraft's agility and manoeuvrability, and Chennault, who had first-hand experience of how the Japanese fighter pilots operated, had trained them accordingly. He had observed Zeros operating in China and noted their aggressive approach and greater manoeuvrability, which gave them an advantage in any dog fight. Though it would be Japanese Oscar-3 fighters that were more typically encountered in Burma, Chennault's observations were still sound, and he used to lecture his pilots on tactics:[13]

> You can count on a higher top speed, faster dive, and superior firepower. The Jap fighters have a faster rate of climb, higher ceiling, and better maneuverability. They can turn on a dime and climb almost straight up. If they can get you into a turning combat they are deadly. Use your speed and diving power to make a pass, shoot and break away.[14]

Flight Leader George Paxton also recalled Chennault's instructions that were delivered in a blunt and uncompromising manner:

> Chennault told us that we had a sorry airplane, as fighters go. That it had two things; diving speed and gunfire. If we used those, we could get by with it. If not, we were going to get shot up, cold Turkey. He told us: never stay in and fight, never try and turn; never try to mix it with them. All we could do was to get altitude and dive on them and keep going – hit and run tactics.[15]

The Flying Tigers worked in close concert with the RAF in Burma and their observations were combined with the RAF's own conclusions from fighting the Japanese, namely that dog-fighting simply did not work. The AVG and Hurricane squadrons fought well together, a Wing Leader

12 Henry Probert, *Forgotten Air Force*, pp. 84-5.
13 Peter Preston-Hough, *Commanding Far Eastern Skies*, p. 128.
14 Claire Chennault, *Way of a Fighter* (New York: Putnam, 1949), p. 113.
15 Daniel Ford, *Flying Tigers: Chennault and the American Volunteer Group* (Washington DC: Smithsonian Institute Press, 1991), p. 78.

Fighter pilots of the American Volunteer Group – the 'Flying Tigers' – pose with one of their P-40 Tomahawk aircraft at Kunming airfield in March 1942, after a series of victories against the Japanese during the previous month. From left to right: Robert H. Neale (Squadron Commander), George T. Burgard (Flight Leader), Robert L. Little (Flight Leader), Charles R. Bond Jr (Vice-Squadron Commander), John E. Blackburn (Wingman) and William D. McGarry (Wingman). (Crown Copyright – Air Historical Branch)

system was introduced, together with a shared operations room with two R/T sets for each force. A further advantage in Burma, particularly around Rangoon, was that the Early Warning system was sufficiently good to allow the British and American aircraft to climb to sufficient altitude, before the enemy raiders arrived. They could also then employ 'dive and zoom' tactics against the Japanese. If the Japanese fighters tried to tempt them by coming in high, the fighters would simply 'lean back' on Rangoon and hold their attack until the enemy aircraft either descended to engage them, or turned for home. The Allies had also learnt that the heavy types of enemy bombers should not be attacked from either above or astern, as the Japanese had mounted heavy machine guns in the fin. In contrast these aircraft had little armament underneath and were highly vulnerable to an attack from below.

The success of these efforts quickly became apparent, from the 23-29 January 1942 a force of some 200 Japanese aircraft attempted to overwhelm the Rangoon air defences, the 40 defending Tomahawks and Hurricanes claimed some 50 Japanese aircraft destroyed. Between the 24-25 February the Japanese returned with 170 aircraft and were again rebuffed, with some 37 aircraft claimed destroyed.[16] The Japanese could not sustain such losses and Rangoon was left alone, until

---

16   Peter Preston-Hough, *Commanding Far Eastern Skies*, p. 87.

the deteriorating Allied land campaign forced its evacuation. Pilot Officer G.W. Underwood describes an attack on the RAF base at Mingaladoon that took place on 6 February 1942, it illustrates the effectiveness of the newly acquired dive and zoom tactics:

> We were at about 15,000 feet and climbing as hard as possible, when on looking up I saw two very large vic. formations of Japanese fighters about 2,000 feet above us – these turned out to be about 60 aircraft! … most were of the Army 97, fixed undercarriage type, but some appeared in the subsequent fight to be Zeros (or 01s). Almost before one could properly appreciate the situation the leading Japanese fighters rolled over to dive on us and one became very much aware of one's vulnerability due to the enemy's advantage in height.
>
> We also turned our aircraft on their backs and dived down to gain speed before pulling up outside the area of main engagement. A free-for-all developed in which I (and no doubt others) put into practise what we had been warned to do, i.e. repeatedly dive through the combat area shooting when a target presented itself but not dog-fighting by trying to out-turn and fly in a continuous engagement with the highly manoeuvrable Japanese aircraft.
>
> I hit one Japanese aircraft as he was climbing up – a quarter frontal attack – his aircraft bursting into flames. (This was later confirmed by one of the Squadron pilots.) A second dive gave me another chance and I saw bullets from my aircraft strike another fighter in a quarter attack from astern, but, in this case, the pilot was either killed or took very rapid evasive action – this was claimed as a probable. On a further dive, however, I saw a fighter almost head-on and as I passed him in the opposite direction I could see his aircraft pulling round in a hard turn and very close to me. Almost immediately afterwards bullets hit the rear of my Hurricane, presumably from that particular Jap, and my cockpit canopy disappeared – presumably shot off! I received what seemed to be a kick in the back of my left leg. With all ideas of being a hero from my initial victory earlier in the fight having disappeared in an instant, I pulled out of the fight, but that would seem to have been the end anyway, as the sky, which a moment before was full of aircraft, was suddenly and strangely empty of both our own aircraft and Japanese.[17]

As well as developing more effective tactics, the RAF in Burma had also instituted a much better dispersal system, consisting of so-called 'Kutcha' strips around a main operating base. Mingaladoon had four named after various whiskies: Highland Queen, Johnnie Walker, Haig, and Dewar (the engineer who had built them had been Scottish). Kutcha strips were primitive affairs, constructed on the dried-out rice paddy fields, with the dividing berms flattened by native labour and the occasional steam roller. The drying earth would often crack and give a cobblestone effect, which damaged many tail wheels, to the extent that ground crews would fit bamboo tail skids as a temporary measure. A typical day for a pilot would be to rise at 0400 from his quarters, drive 20-35 miles to his Kutcha strip, fly his aircraft to Mingaladoon in time for dawn 'readiness'. He would then have breakfast and spend the remainder of his day on a variety of tasks including 'being scrambled', conducting fighter sweeps, reconnaissance, low level attacks in support of the Army, or bomber escort. At the end of his day he would fly his aircraft back to its Kutcha strip and then drive back to his quarters. The nightly dispersal of these aircraft, from their main operating bases, certainly helped reduce the risk of damage from Japanese night-time raids.[18]

Though the air defence operations over Rangoon offered a signpost to the ways the Japanese might be defeated in the air, the means were still not available and by 27 February the combined

17   Norman Franks, *Hurricanes Over the Arakan* (Wellingborough: Patrick Stephens, 1989), p. 30.
18   Douglas Gillison, *Royal Australian Air Force 1939-42*, p. 407.

Flight Lieutenant Prithvipal Singh in his Westland Lysander, commander of 'A' Flight, No. 1 Squadron IAF, at Magwe, Burma, during operations in support of Allied forces retreating from Burma in March 1942. (Crown Copyright – Air Historical Branch)

fighter strength of the RAF and AVG had been reduced to only 10 aircraft. That was still sufficient to provide air cover for the seaborne evacuation of Rangoon, of which not one ship was lost. Nonetheless the deteriorating ground situation necessitated a split in the Allied air force, between an element that would depart directly for India and begin to prepare and plan for the defence of northern Burma, with a second mixed force of aircraft (a Hurricane squadron, a Blenheim squadron, the AVG and an Army co-operation squadron of Westland Lysander aircraft) that would accompany the Army during its withdrawal. This latter force would utilise the old civilian airfield at Magwe, which lay along the Army's withdrawal route down the Prome Valley. Akyab, further to the West, would also take a mixed wing and both formations would be supported by Stevenson's new base organisation, in India. Magwe was heavily attacked by the Japanese over a 48-hour period from 20 March and after a number of aircraft were destroyed on the ground the decision to withdraw was taken. Again, there was justifiable criticism from the Army, including its commander, General Slim, that this had been done prematurely.[19]

RAF commitments were also increasing in India itself. The fall of Singapore, Sumatra and now Rangoon, had left the way clear for a Japanese fleet to enter the Indian Ocean. A small force of Hurricanes was sent to reinforce the Royal Navy's important naval base on the island of Ceylon and defend the British facilities at Trincomalee and China Bay from Japanese carrier strikes. The Japanese attack was launched by the same carrier group that had struck at Pearl Harbor and

19   Henry Probert, *The Forgotten Air Force*, pp. 92-3.

Darwin. It included the Zero amongst its air component, which once more proved challenging for the British, as Sergeant Mann of 261 Squadron recollected:

We were scrambled soon after 7 a.m. – just before breakfast. I was later to regret missing that meal. At about 5,000 feet, Control called, announcing a plot of 100 plus at 12,000 feet, subsequently confirmed as 120 Navy Zeros and dive bombers. We were ordered to climb to 20,000 feet – 'Buster'! Our flight was in two vics of three in a close-packed climb. Pilots looked at each other with a grim smile and, without a word separated into a wide battle formation, about 100 yards apart. We turned oxygen on and climbed like hell!

As soon as we arrived over Trincomalee I saw bombs exploding in the harbour. Probably 6,000 feet below us was a mass of Zero fighters, beautiful in their very pale blue colour and their red roundels. We should have ignored them and attacked the bombers, but instead carried out an impetuous and poorly planned attack, which saw us in a high speed, vertical dive.

I fired a burst with 90-degree deflection from vertically above and with no hope of hitting anything. We must have passed through their formation with close to 500 mph TAS. I placed my feet on the 'G' pedals and hauled back, on the edge of blacking out, then climbed about 60 degrees and finished up about 4,000 feet above 25 Zeros. I searched for my companions, but I was a lone Hurricane, offering the only target to my enemies, who were all now climbing flat out after me!

I carried out about three dive and zoom attacks. These Japanese Navy pilots were highly trained and skilful and the Zero so manoeuvrable that, with my high-speed dives, I could not get my guns to bear on them. Meanwhile we climbed higher and higher. I was scared, inexperienced and my total flying time was only 275 hours. I knew the Zero could easily turn inside a Hurricane and we had been warned not to dog-fight them.

However, in sheer desperation and frustration, I dived amongst them and started dog-fighting. They formed a complete circle around me, and I was shot at with tracer, cannon and machine guns, from all directions. Meanwhile I had my canopy open and was watching my tail where there was a long queue. Luckily the mass of attackers were getting in each other's way. I found by looking down the barrels I had a split second, from the instant that I saw the flash of guns firing, in which to apply full rudder and skid out of the way of the long rows of smoky tracers. The whole time I was jinking and skidding to put them off their aim. The Zeros were so close around me that I had time to dive and turn at individuals. I hit one Zero in both wing tanks and he took off, heading out to sea with fuel streaming from both wings. I also damaged another Zero with hits observed in fin and rudder.

Then the inevitable happened. I received a cannon shell on my right aileron, which it blew to pieces so that I could not turn right without stalling. I had noticed that most attacks initiated from the right so finally I was forced into a steep right-hand evasive turn. My Hurricane rolled smartly into a right-hand spin, probably at about 15,000 feet or more. It never looked like coming out so at about 5,000 I fought my way out of the cockpit on the inside of the spin. I carried out a delayed drop to avoid being shot in my 'chute – a favourite sport of Japanese pilots. At first I was tumbling and completely disorientated but pulled the ripcord at about 500 feet, and severely cracked my neck in a whiplash, which still affects me to this day. Suddenly there was water and I was 20 feet under. Surfacing in the Bay of Trincomalee, I had two Zeros, relentlessly looking for me. I kicked off my boots, helmet, parachute and Mae West (too much of a target) and distanced myself from them as quickly as possible.

Then began a 10 minute game of hide and seek as the Zeros hunted me. As each Zero turned towards me I ducked under until I heard the peculiar noise of the radial engine pass over. I then had to repeat the performance as the other Zero turned in, but finally they flew off and I struck out for the shore.

At about this time the ammunition on the aerodrome – five miles away – blew up and I was treated to a most impressive display, with smoke rising thousands of feet. I was also pestered with falling shrapnel from AA fire, continually falling in the water near me. Then, just a few hundred yards from the shore, I found a large shark circling me. I fired two shots from my Browning automatic, which scared him off.

Eventually I dragged myself into a mangrove swamp and collapsed with complete exhaustion. Soldier crabs walked all over me and all I could do was say, 'Help yourselves, fellows!'[20]

Although the RAF may have withdrawn their fighter and bomber units from Burma, the final withdrawal of the British Army from Burma was still supported by the RAF, through the use of air transport, particularly the Dakotas of 31 Squadron RAF and 2nd Troop Carrier Squadron, United States Army Air Force. These not only dropped 109,562 pounds of supplies, but also evacuated 8,616 men, women and children from Magwe, Shwebo and Myitkyina. The small British garrison at Fort Hertz, together with their wives and children, were also evacuated by air transport and replaced with a force more suitable for conducting guerrilla warfare against the Japanese from that advanced post. The advantage that this RAF air transport delivered made a strong impression on the British Army, in time it would become a core element of how they would launch their own offensive against the Japanese.[21]

As the British Army retreated from Burma into northern India, the RAF's air defence efforts turned to the defence of Calcutta. This city was vital to the defence of northern India and for building up forces that would eventually take the offensive into Burma, the Japanese advance having finally been halted at the Indian border with Burma in mid-1942. There were five Hurricane squadrons based around the city (79, 135, 136, 607 and 615), all of whom had come out from England to India and had some experience of fighting the Japanese in the Arakan. Japanese air raids on Calcutta were fairly irregular. They would appear quite suddenly in force conduct a strike or two and then disappear. Whenever they appeared, scrambles would result in brief skirmishes, occasionally a bomber or fighter would be shot down and an RAF aircraft would not return. In March 1942 there was still not a single radar station in the whole of India, but by December of the same year, 52 had been established and operational centres and filter rooms built, in among other places, Calcutta, Imphal and Comilla. The radar network covered the Assam/Burma border and was supplemented by observers, who operated in the same manner as the Observer Corps but used wireless to communicate and employed only RAF personnel rather than civilians. Far from civilisation, these observers led a lonely and monotonous existence in isolated posts, positioned at 20-mile intervals along the Arakan Yomas and Chin Hills.[22]

As in other theatres, there was pressure for the Spitfire to be sent to India, not just for its performance against fighters, but its ability to quickly climb to altitude and intercept high flying bomber formations. The Japanese high-altitude reconnaissance aircraft, the Dinah, would normally presage any air attack. This could fly at 360 mph at 34,000 feet and had a range of 2,000 miles. There was not a hope in Hell that a Hurricane could catch it and the Dinahs were almost immune as they overflew Calcutta, spotting for likely targets in advance of any Japanese raid. The Spitfires promptly altered that practise, the first deployment being on 4 October 1943, by Flight Sergeant F.W.T. 'Chunky' Davis and Sergeant R.B. Henderson: Davis later recalled the interception:

---

20 Norman Franks, *Hurricanes over the Arakan* (Wellingborough: Patrick Stephen, 1989), p. 68.
21 Denis Richards and Hilary Saunders, *Royal Air Force 1939-45, Volume II*, p. 67.
22 Hilary Saunders, *Royal Air Force 1939-45, Volume III*, p. 308.

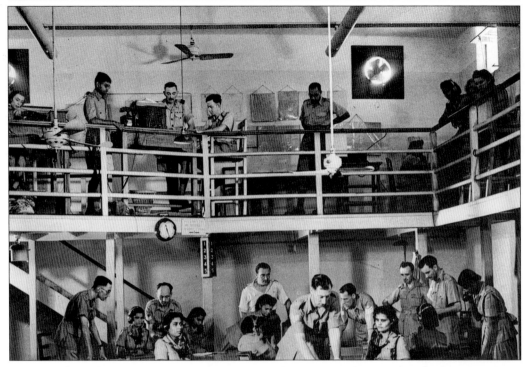

Personnel of the RAF, Indian Air Force and Womens' Auxiliary Corps (India) at work in the Operations Room at a Group Headquarters in North-eastern India. (Crown Copyright – Air Historical Branch)

We were at Baigachi at the time and as far as I can recall it was a straightforward intercep-tion, with the target heading south-east, returning from reconnaissance. It finished as a stern chase. I was concerned that the Dinah crew would see us (Brown 2 was in line astern behind me) and accelerate away. So I fired at extreme range with the gun sight over the target's tail. I saw three flashes of DeWilde ammunition striking, some pieces fly off and what appeared to be brown smoke (oil) from the starboard engine. The Dinah then went into a shallow dive and pulled away rapidly. I was told later that the target slowed down and was losing altitude when it faded on the radar.

We thought at the time that the Dinah crew must have grown overconfident and was not cruising fast enough or being vigilant enough. Sergeant Henderson was still in visual contact, although some way behind, but saw me firing at the Dinah.[23]

The novice Spitfire pilots also had the advantage of being put through the new Air Fighting Training Unit at Armarda Road, Calcutta. This organisation had been created in April 1943 by Wing Commander Frank Carey, who was not only an ex-Battle of Britain pilot, but also had extensive experience leading a Hurricane squadron against the Japanese over Burma in 1942. By 10 July 1943, Air Headquarters, India was reporting that Carey's unit was training a wide array of aircrew.[24]

23   Norman Franks, *Spitfires Over the Arakan* (London: William Kimber, 1988), p. 24.
24   TNA AIR 2/8229: Establishment of AFTU and AFDU, Air HQ India to Air Ministry, Whitehall, 10 July 1943.

A Supermarine Spitfire VII taxies to the end of the Red Road airstrip (marked by the lamp post) in Calcutta, India. (Crown Copyright – Air Historical Branch)

This tactical professionalisation of aircrew was vital, whether the fighter pilots were novices who needed to be brought up to operational efficiency, or experienced veterans from European and Middle Eastern theatres who needed to be recalibrated for fighting the Japanese. Pilots were instructed in many aspects of air-fighting including gunnery, deflection shooting and the essential 'dive and zoom' tactic. American pilots were also instructed by Carey's team of high-quality instructors, who brought clarity and positive air-fighting rules to aircrew. The new Spitfire pilots were amongst the first to benefit from the school and Carey's instruction, as he told them himself:

> The average tour is 300 operational hours or one year whichever is the shorter. In this time you may be in contact with the enemy for 30 hours. Approach and Attack probably occupy three minutes of this time. Consequently, as it takes one year's tour to do three minutes firing, you must do your best to make that three minutes as effective as possible ...

Carey added that the pilots already possessed all the necessary enthusiasm and ability required. He explained:

> I was merely put into a position of being able to pass the results of my own experience to a very capable and willing audience. Much of what was passed on had already been pushed into me during a course at the Central Gunnery School, Sutton Bridge (England). It was there that I first encountered the technique of flying not on the horizon or instruments, but solely on the gun sight and the rear of one's pants, which is the ultimate achievement of a front-gun fighter aircraft in action. Of course, I was only one of a number of instructors at Amarda Road, all of whom had been through recent combat experience against the Japanese ... [25]

---

25   Norman Franks, *Sptfires Over the Arakan*, p. 38.

At Armarda Road, Frank Carey taught the 'rolling attack' as an essential adjunct of the 'dive and zoom' tactic. In this manoeuvre the attacking aircraft passes over the target from the beam position approximately 1,500 feet above. As the enemy aircraft disappears under the wing, the attacking fighter swings the nose back in the opposite direction to that of the target and goes over into a controlled barrel roll so as to bring the guns to bear as soon as the manoeuvre is completed. The value of this manoeuvre lay in the possibility of achieving a fast overtaking speed and a quick breakaway, this in turn allowed a series of attacks to be delivered. Carey encouraged this form of attack because:

> You have a good plan view of your target
> It is easy to assess the line of flight as the ground helps you
> Your aircraft is a comfortable platform for shooting
> You always come out of the sun round mid-day and achieve surprise
> To get away, let your stick go forward and duck under. You are a difficult deflection shot for anyone else.

The combination of well-trained aircrew, in a highly capable aircraft such as the Spitfire, began to make a stark difference to the success of squadrons over Calcutta and the Arakan. Pilot Officer 'Nappy' Carroll of 615 Squadron recalls encountering a formation of Japanese bombers, heading for the RAF airfield at Agartala, on 29 November 1943:

> The height was all wrong. Our Controller had got us in position and then we found the Japs were well below us; they were just specks in the distance. We dived like crazy and everybody got split up. In a headlong dive the Spitfire tended to move to the right a bit and if not careful everyone opened out.
>
> I was really travelling, and they rapidly got larger. I realised these were the boys we were after. As I remember it there were about eight fighters on each side and about 12 bombers – Army 99s – which had bombed Agartala.
>
> I shot at two of the fighters. One from astern and I hit it but I was travelling at such a speed that I just saw strikes, then it was gone. Then another fighter came right across me which I had a go at, but chances were pretty nil.
>
> Then I pulled up and round with my speed, to get at the bombers, which was a piece of cake because I must have been going twice as fast as they were. But I couldn't pull the Spitfire round in a tight sweep to get into the nearest bombers and I came out right on the far side of the formation. I got behind one of them and by that time I was beginning to slow up so was able to give a much better and longer burst of cannon and machine gun. There were little sparkles on it from where I was hitting it and a plume of smoke or fuel came from one engine as the aircraft started to drop out of formation. By that time I was past it and had now lost all speed. I thought then that I'd had a go, fired my guns, and as there's me and about 20 of them, now's the time to leave. So I half rolled and made for home.[26]

The Japanese were quick to adapt to the 'dive and zoom' tactics. Defensive tactics included the defensive circle, as well as the use of separate formations, stacked at different altitudes, with the idea of enticing Spitfires to 'mix it' at medium and low-levels. On occasions a decoy aircraft, usually brightly coloured silver, would fly at low level as bait to draw Spitfires into low level combat where other Japanese fighters could pounce. The Japanese also developed 'beehives' or 'caged squirrels'

---

26 Norman Franks, *Sptfires over the Arakan*, p. 38.

where aircraft would fly in one formless conglomeration from anywhere between 17,000 feet and ground level. The impression was given that the formation was disorganised – in fact the Japanese fighters were moving in a prescribed fashion and ready to pounce on unsuspecting Allied fighters lured in. The options to the RAF fighter pilots, if they chose to engage, were to manoeuvre in three boxes of four aircraft, 700 feet apart in height. The Middle box would engage the enemy fighters and the other two boxes wait to pounce from height on any Japanese fighters that climbed or dived to meet the attack. Again the advice was simple, do not get drawn into a dog fight. Flight Lieutenant AG Conway, of 136 Squadron, gives a good description of just how difficult, confusing and potentially costly, it was to engage with these multi-stacked fighters. He recalls encountering a large group on 10 January 1944:

> Eric Brown was leading the squadron and we were scrambled against a whole bunch of fighters which were escorting dive-bombers and ground attack aircraft attacking our front-line troops. There were over 40 Jap fighters and they were at all heights, giving cover to those below. Until 607 were scrambled to come to our help, we were badly outnumbered, and it was a hairy affair of fast snap shooting at wildly turning fighters before breaking hard into the sun and repositioning for another attack. There was little time to observe results. I was quite certain I'd hit several, but none fell so I made no claims, but the rest of the squadron claimed five destroyed, four probables and six damaged. Dennis Garvan was again hit, this time with shell splinters in the arm and leg which led to him swinging off the strip at the end of his landing run and tipping up on his prop.
>
> My number two, the popular Irishman, Pete Kennedy, who'd bailed out just a few miles to the south a year earlier, was caught again and bailed out again. But this time a strafing Jap killed him in his parachute.
>
> Paddy Stephenson, the CO of 607, was hit by a couple of shells that came head-on through his cockpit, wounding him in the arm. He force landed at his own strip and soon let it be known that he thought he'd been hit by another Spitfire. That evening all the wing pilots who'd fired their guns, were ordered to Wing HQ where our camera gun film and combat reports had already been gathered together. In the confusion by odd coincidence, our films had not been correctly titled. So the films had to be wound over very slowly by hand, by the Intelligence Officer, until one pilot or another identified the film as his. Eric Brown was found to have shot Paddy Stephenson and left immediately for the hospital to own up and apologise.[27]

At the other end of the Far Eastern theatre, Australian homeland defences were being taken into Australian hands. Having defended Australia valiantly, the American 49th Fighter Group were transferred from Darwin, in August 1942, to New Guinea. They were backfilled by the Australian 77 and 76 Squadrons, though this proved to be a quiet period as the Japanese had transferred their aircraft from the nearby bases in Timor and Sumatra to Rabaul, in order to support their operations over Guadalcanal.

Nonetheless, the Australian government had been spurred into action by the Japanese threat to the homeland, including the raids on Darwin in February 1942. The Australian minister for External Affairs, Dr Herbert 'Doc' Evatt, travelled to London and secured the dispatch of three Spitfire Squadrons to Australia. These were to include two Australian Article XV squadrons (numbers 452 and 457 Squadrons), but also the British 54 Squadron RAF. The latter was included as a symbolic political gesture by Churchill, to showcase the fraternal ties between Australia and

---

27   Norman Franks, *Spitfires Over the Arakan*, p. 135.

Britain, as well as RAF and RAAF. However, like every other RAF fighter unit, 54 Squadron's British aircrew had been supplemented by pilots from the Commonwealth as well as an assortment of Belgians, Czechs and even American volunteers. To turn it into a 'British Squadron' required the posting out of all the 'foreigners' as well as the 'Colonials' and posting in purely British pilots – effectively creating the only all-British unit in the RAF. Dr Evatt's mission was not altogether popular in Britain, the Chief of Britain's Imperial General Staff describing the Australian's threat to withdraw 9th Australian Division from the Middle East, if the Spitfire squadrons were not forthcoming, as 'strong blackmail'. Though given the generous manner in which Australia had supported Britain in her darkest hours, this seems churlish to say the least. Nonetheless, the Spitfire squadrons were dispatched and arrived in the Northern Territory airfields in time for the mid-January 1943 raiding season to begin.[28]

The set up around Darwin, that the three squadrons of 1 Fighter Wing would operate from, was an increasingly mature one. The intensive building programme had built a network of airfields, furnished with good taxiways that led to well camouflaged and protected dispersals. The air defence system also included a new RAAF air defence radar network, under the control of the RAAF North Western Area (NWA) HQ, which had been bolstered by new officers and men, to coordinate both the air defence and offensive air campaign. Central to their operations was the new Australian radar, based on a design by the University of Sydney's Council for Scientific and Industrial Research. This began to come into operation by April 1942, with new sites being added to thicken coverage or, as at the post on Bathhurst Island, extend it further out to sea. This was a remarkable achievement given the distance between Australia and the other radar development centres in the UK and USA. To put Australia's technical achievement into further perspective, at this time there was not a single radar deployed on America's west coast.[29]

No.1 Fighter Wing's squadrons were equipped with the latest Spitfire: the Mark VC. The Spitfire VC (tropical) was the best aircraft available at the time and a large improvement on the Bell P-39 Airacobras and Kittyhawks that had equipped Australian and American forces in the South West Pacific theatre so far. It had the important advantage that its Merlin 46 engine had a supercharger that boosted power above 20,000 feet. This was an important capability as the Japanese bombers would fly in at heights a full 10,000 feet higher than their German and Italian bomber counterparts had done in the Battle of Britain, or at Malta. Less impressive was the temperamental propeller governor which in the worst case led to engine fires and in the simplest instances reduced performance. Most importantly the Spitfire's range was a grave handicap. Designed as an intercept fighter for the European theatre, the vast distances operated over in the Pacific meant that even when carrying its belly tank, which held an extra 30 gallons of fuel, its range was comparatively short. By March 1943, early operations were showing that the Spitfires could fly up to 160 km from base, fight, and just get back with fuel in their tanks. In contrast the Zeros were flying 600 kilometres from their bases in Timor, fighting and were able to return to base without any problem.[30]

The Spitfires also suffered in their armament. The Mark VC had been fitted with Hispano 20mm cannon and .303 Browning machine guns. Many pilots found the 20mm cannon was a delicate weapon and needed a constant supply of warm air to prevent it jamming. This was supposed to be provided by the Spitfire's warm air ducting system, yet in the Mark VC it seems to have been unreliable. With a cannon frequently jamming, the pilots then had to cope with the

28   Anthony Cooper, *Darwin Spitfires*, pp. 8-9.
29   Anthony Cooper, *Darwin Spitfires*, pp. 8-9.
30   Anthony Cooper, *Darwin Spitfires*, p. 116.

Flight Lieutenant Norwood of 54 Squadron RAF, warms up his Spitfire before taking off from an airfield near Darwin. (Australian War Memorial, Canberra)

asymmetric recoil of just one cannon firing by applying opposite rudder. This was hardly conducive to good gunnery.[31]

The tactics adopted by 1 Fighter Wing were also open to criticism. The squadrons had still not adopted the pairs or 'finger four' loose combat formations used by more experienced RAF units, preferring instead the formal 'Vics', with all the disadvantages to all-round observation this entailed. It is surprising that these obsolete formations were still being used in 1943, one historian attributing it to the unprogressive attitude of the Kenley Wing, where both 452 and 457 RAAF Sqns had served in 1941 and 1942. Here 'Vics' and 'line astern' formations were still being used well after other Fighter Command elements had abandoned them.[32]

The final mistaken tactical approach was the 'big wing' concept that 1 Fighter Wing's commander, Wing Commander Clive Caldwell instigated. No. 1 Fighter Wing operated under the control of No. 5 Fighter Sector Control, who were able to give the defending fighters adequate warning of approaching Japanese aircraft, typically bomber formations between 26,000 and 28,000 feet, with an escort of 30 or so fighters at 30,000 feet, an altitude at which the Zero performed well.

The Zeros were split into groups of six to nine fighters, which flew a considerable distance apart, making it hard for the defenders to visually acquire all of the groups. Moreover, Caldwell's 'big wing' took time to assemble and meant that he had to moderate the climbing speed of the

31   Anthony Cooper, *Darwin Spitfires*, p. 116.
32   Anthony Cooper, *Darwin Spitfires*, p. 114.

Spitfires to maintain the integrity of his large formation, it also meant that the fighter pilots were more focussed on maintaining station, than looking out for the enemy. Caldwell would have been better off if he had adopted the tactics of 49th Fighter Group, who had fed in sections and squadrons from different directions and times which caused confusion and created great difficulties for the escorting Zeros. In contrast Caldwell's big wing presented a predictable defensive problem for the Japanese. All the escorting Zeros had to do was counter one, easily detectable and visible mass attack, which they found quite easy to pre-position against. Had Caldwell divided his usual strength of 36 Spitfires into nine flights of four, the escorting Zeros would have struggled to anticipate and meet multiple attacks, from varying directions, at different times.[33]

Though 1 Fighter Wing could have been more effective in its operations, it was nevertheless able to contest Japanese air operations over Australia and by September 1943, the pressures on the Japanese had caused them to adopt a defensive posture in that sector of the Pacific. In time, the Japanese garrison at Timor would effectively be bypassed by the Allied 1944 offensive in the Philippines and Indonesia.

Achieving air superiority against the Japanese would continue to be a severe challenge for the Allies. Yet they had at last managed to obtain that successful blend of well-sited airfields furnished with dispersals and protected pens, an efficient early warning and command and control system and finally highly trained aircrew, utilising relevant tactics and flying large numbers of modern aircraft that could climb to altitude quickly and effectively engage enemy fighters and bombers. Successfully establishing air superiority in the Far East would allow the allies to incorporate all aspects of air power into a joint campaign, one that fully exploited the air component's reconnaissance, strike and air transport capabilities and used them in a highly imaginative way.

---

33   Brian Weston, *A Coming of Age for Australia and its Air Force – The Air Campaign over Northern Australia 1943* (Canberra: Air Power Development Centre, 2013), p. 25.

10

Concluding Thoughts on Air Superiority

The primary purpose of any air force is to achieve air superiority, for without it the other elements of air power: reconnaissance, strike and transportation cannot be brought to bear and the maritime and land forces operate at a severe disadvantage. The first few years of the war showed how air superiority can be won or lost by a number of factors. Good intelligence is critical – if you are on the offensive you must understand how the enemy air defence system works, what are its vulnerabilities and weak points. When you attack them you must do so with sufficient persistence to neutralise them and remember that like Fighter Command in 1940 and Malta between 1941-42 your adversary may be able to re-generate their capability. Your intelligence must also understand the operational capabilities of the enemy's aircraft and their relative performance to your own. The British experience of under-estimating the Japanese air force and aircraft in the Far East demonstrates the pitfalls of prejudice and wishful thinking in the intelligence world.

Good aircraft, that can meet their opposite numbers on at least an equal footing, is an absolute necessity. It is hard not to pity those who met the *Luftwaffe*'s modern Me 109Fs in Hurricanes at Malta, or the Japanese Zeros in Buffaloes over Singapore. The RAF must take some criticism for allowing such a state of affairs to occur, when from 1941 onwards so many Spitfires, our best aircraft, were languishing at Fighter Command engaged on Circuses and Rhubarbs of dubious operational or strategic benefit. A good fighter aircraft needs an effective combination of speed, agility, firepower and range. The latter may not seem immediately advantageous, but it proved a critical weakness in the Me 109 during the Battle of Britain, as well as a huge virtue in the Zero, whose long range and endurance allowed the Japanese to project power across the Far East through a daring series of amphibious offensives under that fighter's air cover.

Providing aircraft is as much about quantity as well as quality. The Allies repeatedly found that trying to maintain small quantities of aircraft, in isolated positions such as Crete or Rabaul, in the face of a large and powerful enemy was usually a forlorn hope. Concentration of force is a powerful argument in such circumstances.

A good early warning capability and an efficient command and control system was a critical factor in the RAF's success during the Battle of Britain. Radar when employed correctly is one of the obvious advantages, but one has to also admire the institutional imagination of the Australians in their coastwatcher network of observers, as well as the personal bravery of those individuals employed in such dangerous and arduous duties across the Pacific.

Good, well-sited airfields are a natural pre-requisite and if the land and maritime forces are sufficiently strong, can be captured under the air support provided, dynamically altering the battlefield geometry. The Japanese demonstrated this very well in 1941-42, hopping from one airfield to another against weak Allied ground and naval strength. Conversely, the British struggled in the Mediterranean which was often been described as 'a battle for airfields'. There the synergies between success on land in the western desert and improved air cover over the central Mediterranean were obvious, yet the British Army was simply too weak in the western desert to be able to capture these airfields until late 1942. The value of good dispersal in well camouflaged and protected pens near the airfield is also apparent and often overlooked in importance. Lloyd's efforts in Malta, the *Kutcha* strips in Burma and the efforts taken at Darwin all highlight the advantage of such work and how it helps a force's survivability when under attack.

Finally – tactics. The onset of a conflict, particularly after a long period of peace, is normally marked by the shattering of pre-existing tactical theories of the right way to combat the enemy. What is apparent from the previous chapters is how some elements learnt very quickly and others more slowly. Squadron Leader Jackson and his 75 Squadron team at Milne Bay offer an example of good practise, as do the RAF in Burma, who were wise enough to listen to the American Volunteer Group's experience and learn from it. Formalising such a process is always advantageous – the establishment of the Air Fighting Training Unit at Amarda Road certainly seems to have paid dividends. In contrast it is surprising to read of how squadrons of Spitfires at Darwin, including those that had served in Fighter Command, were still using 'Vic' formations in early 1943. It does not paint the RAF's wartime institutional operational lessons learnt processes in a universally good light.

The chapters above covered many aspects of air superiority, but in general they bring us to a point where the British and Commonwealth were gaining a degree of air superiority against their adversaries. Air Superiority is of course not an end in itself; we will see in due course how the Allies combined air power with ground and maritime manoeuvre to defeat the enemy in both Europe and Asia. This joint approach would become a hallmark of Allied operations and could be described as a 'new way of winning'. Nonetheless, it was only the American and Soviet entry into the war, that meant the British could even consider the practicalities of a land campaign against Germany in Europe. Britain would never have been able to undertake it alone. That inability lent some substance to the established pre-war ideas, that Germany could be brought to her knees by the use of massed heavy bombers on a constant and direct assault on her cities and people. As the war progressed German air defences were put to the test and the British would hope to mitigate their lack of air superiority over Germany, by using the cloak of darkness.

Part III
Strike

11

'Strike Hard, Strike Sure'[1]
Bomber Command's Offensive

Between the wars the RAF cherished its bombers above all other aircraft, setting great store by bomber operations in the event of a second European War. It was, after all, bomber attacks against London in 1917 that spurred Britain to commission the South African statesman and soldier General Jan Smuts to make recommendations on the future of air power. His conclusions, in two separate reports, were an airman's dream. Smuts not only proposed a doubling of the size of the air services, but also strongly endorsed the creation of an Independent Air Force.

Immediately after the First World War, contemporary philosophers of air power would continually highlight that the strategic bomber would transform the character of conflict.[2] No more would armies and fleets have to directly oppose each other on the field of battle they argued, the bomber would instead fly on an independent mission to disrupt and destroy not only the enemy's warfighting production capacity, but the morale of the entire country itself, rendering it incapable of resisting. Although many still foresaw a need for the new RAF to conduct operations in support of land and maritime operations, it was the independent bomber role that captured the most imaginative of air power theorists, including the Italian Giulio Douhet as well as America's Billy Mitchell. Even wider military thinkers were captivated by the bomber's potential, Basil Liddell-Hart commenting in 1925:

> A modern state is such a complex and interdependent fabric that it offers a target highly sensitive to a sudden and overwhelming blow from the air ... Imagine for a moment London, Manchester, Birmingham and half a dozen other great centres simultaneously attacked, the business localities and Fleet Street wrecked, Whitehall a heap of ruins, the slum districts maddened into the impulse to break loose and maraud, the railways cut, factories destroyed. Would not the general will to resist vanish, without organisation and central direction?[3]

It was around this general idea that the emerging RAF theology would become increasingly confident and assertive between the wars. Fostered by the experience of air policing in Iraq and on the North-West Frontier, where both air opposition and AA defences were absent, a series of misleading views began to form over the ease with which targets could be found and hit, without any apparent threat to the pilot or his aircraft.[4] The RAF also became complacent about the standard of navigation required to find targets, the technical skill to hit them accurately, as well as the bomber's survivability against enemy fighters in daylight operations (the only operations the

---

1   Motto of RAF Bomber Command.
2   N. Frankland and C. Webster, *The Strategic Air Offensive Against Germany, Volume I* (London: HMSO, 1961), p. 3.
3   Basil Liddell-Hart, *Paris or the Future War* (London: Kegan Paul, 1925), p. 4.
4   N. Frankland and C. Webster, *The Strategic Air Offensive Against Germany, Volume I*, p. 6.

RAF considered relevant at that time). The same over-optimistic view of the bomber's capability was shared by British politicians. Stanley Baldwin, the Prime Minister at the time, addressed the House of Commons in November 1932:

> I think it is well for the man in the street to realise that there is no power on earth that can protect him from being bombed. Whatever people may tell him, the bomber will always get through. The only defence is in offence, which means that you have to kill more women and children more quickly than the enemy if you want to save yourselves. I just mention that … so that people may realise what is waiting for them when war comes.[5]

As technology developed in the 1930s, the prospects of bombers being able to evade modern fighters and radar became more doubtful. Increasingly politicians and defence chiefs could not accept that the only means of defence was in maintaining parity in strategic bombers. To the chagrin of the bomber advocates, the British re-armament programme began to devote more finances towards the increase of metropolitan air defence fighter squadrons and radar, often at the expense of the bombers.

As war approached the plans for heavy bombers were laid down, they included two-engine aircraft such as the Vickers Wellington, Armstrong Whitworth Whitley, Handley Page Hampden and Avro Manchester, to be followed in due course by the larger, four-engine Short Stirling, Handley Page Halifax and Avro Lancaster. In 1936, Bomber Command was established as a separate command and a sister to Fighter Command, moving into its new headquarters in High Wycombe in 1940. This was a purpose-built facility furnished with modern telecommunications to its bases around East Anglia, Lincolnshire and Yorkshire. The split of Fighter Command and Bomber Command was one of the most significant British decisions to affect the air war in Europe. At a stroke it divided the RAF into two commands, one focussed on taking the offensive in to Germany and a second, defensive command concentrating on the air defence of Great Britain, at least initially. It is apparent that the actual and potential benefits of close co-operation between fighters and bombers was missed by the RAF, who relied upon the air staff to oversee that coordination, but who in reality were far too busy to do so. This command and control split is in stark contrast to both the RAF command structures in the Middle East, but especially the UK-based American Eighth Air Force who had responsibility for both fighters and bombers. It might help explain how it was the Americans who first met the requirement for long range fighters to escort strategic bomber forces, whereas RAF operations in North West Europe tended towards the separate employment of each.[6]

At the outbreak of war, Bomber Command found itself equipped with a modest fleet of twin-engined medium and light bombers, yet no heavy bombers at all. It was quickly established that the character of operations was very different to what had been expected prior to the war. First, fearing reciprocity from Germany the British bombers were initially restricted from bombing military as well as industrial targets, or cities, in Germany. Instead, they were only able to attack German naval shipping in the North Sea in daylight. So concerned were the politicians that the RAF was even restricted from bombing the warships when within the confines of the port itself. The losses on these first raids were fearful and though there was initially some debate over whether better formation flying might mitigate these, most realistic observers realised that daylight bomber attacks were not a practical proposition without fighter escort. This was especially the case given the weak calibre of protective machine guns the bombers carried, with few exceptions the RAF

5   'Mr Baldwin on Aerial Warfare – A Fear for the Future', *The Times*, 11 November 1932.
6   N. Frankland and C. Webster, *The Strategic Air Offensive Against Germany, Volume I*, p. 8.

Armstrong Whitworth Whitley V, N1463/GE-L, of 58 Squadron, takes off on a night sortie from Linton-on-Ouse, Yorkshire. This aircraft later went missing during a bombing sortie to Gelsenkirchen, Germany, on 17/18 June 1940. (Crown Copyright – Air Historical Branch)

Aircrews of 149 Squadron approach a line of Vickers Wellington IAs at Mildenhall, Suffolk for an early morning training sortie. The Squadron's operations at this time were directed mostly against German naval installations and shipping. (Crown Copyright – Air Historical Branch)

bombers were only ever equipped with a handful of .303inch calibre machine guns. Though these were reliable weapons with a high rate of fire, they were consistently out-ranged and out-gunned by the destructive 20mm cannons in the attacking German fighters.[7]

Once daylight operations had proved to be prohibitively costly, the RAF transitioned into a night bombing force. Continued British and French government fears of reprisals meant that these initially consisted of leaflet raids, but when the Phoney War came to an end with the invasion of France in May 1940, the RAF's Whitley, Wellington and Hampden bombers began to drop actual bombs. These were initially focussed on German troop concentrations, railway choke points and then oil facilities, the latter because the Air Staff believed at the time that oil production was at the heart of the German war potential. Oil was one of the first of many so-called 'panaceas', or target categories, that would be identified as a quick and efficient way of having a disproportionately severe effect on German military power. From September 1940, as the effects of the German Blitz on British towns were felt, the British Government became more aggressive in retaliating against German cities. This was not only as a means of popular revenge, but also a reflection that from 1940 onwards the only practical manner in which Britain could directly attack and damage Germany, was through the long-range night bomber offensive.[8]

These early bomber missions were lonely affairs, each aircraft flying separately to its target and having identified it, dropping its bombs independently. At this early point in the war, there were few navigational aids and the aircrew relied upon moonlight and clear skies to identify the target accurately. Group Captain Leonard Cheshire VC was to achieve deserved fame as one of the bravest and skilled bomber pilots of the war, but in 1940 he was learning his profession in highly difficult circumstances:

> In order to get results you have first to reach the target area; in other words, navigate. There is a navigator, of course, whose sole job it is to take you to the target area, but that is not the end of the story. With the aid of some maps and charts and rulers and other varied instruments he is able to tell you your air position – that is to say, where you would be if there were no wind. He can tell you where you actually are only if he knows, and has known ever since take-off, the strength and direction of the wind, or if he has some extraneous means of finding out his position.
>
> These means, however, are limited and not entirely reliable. He can discover the wind by taking a series of drift readings on various headings, but this requires good conditions of visibility and exceptionally accurate flying and reading off from the drift indicator. As for fixing his position, the only infallible method is visual pin-point – by map-reading – and this again, quite naturally, demands good visibility. If he cannot map read he has to fall back on W/T [Wireless Telegraphy] or Astro, but neither of these is universally accurate, and into the bargain W/T gives the position of the aircraft away, while Astro requires a high degree of training from both the pilot and the navigator. And from all this the residue is D.R. [Dead Reckoning] Given the wind velocity, and the aircraft's course and airspeed, the navigator can discover by D.R. his position at any time, but a forecast wind can hardly hope to be accurate

---

7   Despite the early RAF experience the US Air Force persisted with the concept of the self-defending bomber formation into late 1943, arguing that their greater number of larger calibre (0.50 inch) machine guns, as well as armour and self-sealing tanks would see them through to their targets. Despite advice from RAF chiefs the Americans persisted with this operational approach, until it was seen to founder with high losses on 14 October 1943 when, during their daylight raid on the Schweinfurt ball bearing factory, 198 of the 291 B-17s dispatched were either destroyed or damaged.

8   N. Frankland and C. Webster, *The Strategic Air Offensive Against Germany, Volume I*, p. 15.

The air observer of a Wellington bomber of 75 (New Zealand) Squadron 'shooting the sun' during a flight to check the aircraft's position. (Crown Copyright – Air Historical Branch)

enough under war conditions, so he has to be able to check it by some means or other, and in addition the pilot's course must be perfect, or the D.R. position will not be correct. Every deviation from course, every variation in airspeed or alteration in height, adds another mile to the final error. A difference of one degree gives an error of one mile in 60, and on the compass one degree is almost indistinguishable. On a flight of 600 miles, then it will be a good crew that has less than a 10-mile error.'[9]

If navigating to the target area was difficult enough, then actually identifying the target to be hit, a factory or marshalling yard for instance, was even harder. Conditions of good visibility were essential but so too were flares, as Leonard Cheshire continues:

A flare illuminates only a small area, perhaps three or four miles and not for very long, about three minutes. Someone has to put it in the flare-chute, and it is heavy – set the fuse-setting for the correct height and then launch it. When eventually it lights up it has fallen way back behind the aircraft, so you have to turn about and come back over the top. The flare is powerful; it will dazzle you unless you shield your eyes or look away from it, and if you want to compare what you see on the ground with the map you have to switch a light on or you will not be able to read the map. That takes time and defocuses your eyes. But there is even more to it than that. Map-reading is a navigational aid only when it produces a recognizable

9   Leonard Cheshire, *Bomber Pilot* (St Albans: Mayflower Books, 1975), p. 3.

pin-point, and recognizable pin-points are not so frequent. Roads or rivers or woods are not pin-points unless they are distinctive or unless you have been following your track all the way and know what to look for. After 400 – 500 miles without any pin-point you may well be unlucky and not find any recognizable landmark from the light of a few dozen flares, even though you are actually within a few miles of the target.

Then the actual dropping of the bombs. Once more the same problem. A bomb from 10,000 feet, takes about 25 seconds to fall. In that time the aeroplane has moved a mile or so, depending on its speed. To aim the bomb you need a bomb-sight, and a bomb-sight is a complicated instrument, in that it must incorporate the triangle of velocities, the aircraft's height, and the angle of fall of the bomb. These five readings have to be set, and the aircraft steered in such a way that its track, not its course, passes over the target, before there is any hope of success. In short, the run up must be started at least three miles from the aiming point, to allow sufficient time for all this, and if it is necessary to use a flare, you will have to drop the flare over the target, fly away far enough, turn round, pick up the target again, adjust the bomb-sight, and make good the right track all before the flare goes out. Crew co-operation must be good or there will not be any results. But every night is different from the last: clouds, visibility, strength of the defences – they all vary. And so it is the captain's decision. Come down or stay up? The lower you are the faster everything happens, and the better the co-operation has to be. The lower down, too, the more effective the defences; they may blind you altogether, or anyway preclude an accurate run-up. The higher up, the more time to act, and the more immune you are from disturbance, but on the other hand the less you can see.[10]

The challenge in accurately bombing relatively precise targets, like factories or oil refineries, is self-evident. However, in these very early days of the bombing campaign there was a conspiracy of optimism about the results being achieved. At debriefs aircrews would give very precise records of what had been accomplished – regularly distinguishing individual targets within a large German city, these misleadingly positive reports were on occasions backed up by dubious intelligence reports from Germany. Many of the RAF's senior officers understood the difficulties in night-time bombing and were sceptical of the accuracy with which their crews were finding and hitting targets.[11] This sorry state of affairs may have been set to continue, but the RAF had begun equipping their bombers with photo flashes, which showed the area the bomber had dropped its weapons on. In addition, the photographic reconnaissance branch was now in a position to accurately record the results achieved the following day, this was usually assessed by the intelligence staff in Bomber Command's own stations and units. However, at the instigation of Churchill's Scientific Adviser, Lord Cherwell,[12] who had picked up reports from the Central Interpretation Unit at Medmenham that the German cities were largely un-struck, a more comprehensive review was undertaken by Mr David Butt, a member of the War Cabinet's Secretariat.

Butt studied over 600 crew photographs, operational summaries as well as other documents. In August 1941 he published his results, coming to the depressing conclusion that only one in three aircraft succeeded in getting their bombs to within five miles of the target. These statistics varied with geography and moon states, but they also only accounted for the aircraft that had claimed to have successfully attacked the target. It was a disappointing statistic and if the total was taken from the overall aircraft dispatched, the numbers would fall by a third again.

---

10   Leonard Cheshire, *Bomber Pilot*, pp. 38-3.
11   N. Frankland and C. Webster, *The Strategic Air Offensive Against Germany, Volume I, Preparation*, pp. 217-2.
12   Formerly known as Frederick Lindemann.

A crew member on board a Vickers Wellington of 75 (New Zealand) Squadron places night flares in position in the cramped rear fuselage of the aircraft during a sortie in June 1940. Note the Elsan chemical lavatory to the right. (Crown Copyright – Air Historical Branch)

Like all unwelcome news the report was attacked, RAF chiefs highlighting the poor weather, (in June and July!) as well as how photographic equipment was normally given to the crews considered least reliable by the chain of command. Nonetheless the report was believed by Churchill and the Defence Chiefs.[13] As a result, the Air Staff were to focus significant scientific and technical effort to provide an assortment of aids for navigation at night, as well as establish a Target Finding Force, subsequently renamed Pathfinder Force (PFF), who would lead the main bomber force to its targets and mark them visually. It also led Bomber Command to consider the merits of area bombing, far more than they had hitherto. The Butt report might have been expected to have sounded the death knell of British strategic bombing, instead the Air Staff pushed for a bomber force of 4,000 aircraft, claiming yet again that it could independently win the war against Germany. The Chiefs of Staff's reaction to this new Air Staff demand was hesitant, but when the Air Staff moderated their claim to one that stated the bomber offensive would produce the conditions under which other offensive forces could be successful, they relented. Building up the heavy bomber force would become Britain's highest strategic priority and would be increasingly directed towards the area bombing of German towns and cities. Lord Cherwell was clear on what the aim and consequences of area bombing entailed, addressing the issue in a minute to the Prime Minister on 30 March 1942:

13   N. Frankland and C. Webster, *The Strategic Air Offensive Against Germany, Volume I*, pp. 178-80.

The following seems a simple method of estimating what we could do by bombing Germany:

Careful analysis of the effects of raids on Birmingham, Hull and elsewhere have shown that, on the average, 1 ton of bombs dropped on a built-up area demolishes 20-40 dwellings and turns 100-200 people out of house and home.

We know from our experience that we can count on nearly 14 operational sorties per bomber produced. The average lift of the bombers we are producing over the next 15 months will be about 3 tons. It follows that each of these bombers will in its lifetime drop about 40 tons of bombs. If these are dropped on the built-up areas they will make 4,000 to 8,000 people homeless.

In 1938 over 22 million Germans lived in 58 towns of over 100,000 inhabitants, which, with modern equipment, should be easy to find and hit. Our forecast output of heavy bombers (including Wellingtons) between now and the middle of 1943 is about 10,000, If even half the total load of 10,000 bombers were dropped on the built-up areas of these 58 German towns the great majority of their inhabitants (about one-third of the German population) would be turned out of house and home.

Investigation seems to show that having one's house demolished is most damaging to morale. People seem to mind it more than having their friends or even relatives killed. At Hull signs of strain were evident, though only one-tenth of the houses were demolished. On the above figures we should be able to do 10 times as much harm to each of the 58 principal German towns. There seems little doubt that this would break the spirit of the people.

Our calculation assumes, of course, that we really get one-half of our bombs into built-up areas. On the other hand, no account is taken of the large promised American production (6,000 heavy bombers in the period in question). Nor has regard been paid to the inevitable damage to factories, communications etc. in these towns and the damage by fire, probably accentuated by breakdown of public services.'[14]

It would take time to build up a large bomber force composed of modern aircraft. The twin-engined Hampdens, Whitleys and Wellingtons would give way in 1942, to increasing numbers of four-engined Stirlings, Halifaxes and above all Lancasters. Production and design problems hampered this transformation, the Stirling for instance was found to be fatally flawed and had a reduced operational ceiling, which made the RAF's first four-engine bomber an easy target for German night-fighters.[15] After consistently suffering the highest casualty levels in bomber operations in 1943, it was withdrawn from the main bomber offensive and spent the remainder of the war as a trainer within Heavy Bomber Conversion Units, or as an airborne tug for glider operations. The Halifax was a far better aircraft than any of its predecessors, including the Stirling, whilst it was loved by its loyal crews it did not compare with the Lancaster, widely regarded as the best British bomber of the war, which appeared for the first time in March 1942. The Lancaster was reliable, powerful, as well as easy and responsive to fly. Harry Yates was a pilot on one and admired it greatly:

I soon discovered that everything that had been said and written about the Avro Lancaster was true. Some products of the hand of man have that uncanny capacity to pull at the heart-strings, and the Lancaster was one such. Everything about it was just right. Its muscular, swept lines were beautiful to look at. It flew with effortless grace and had a precise weighted feel. It made the pilot's job easy. You could throw it all over the skies if you had the inclination

14   N. Frankland and C. Webster, *The Strategic Air Offensive Against Germany, Volume I,* pp. 331-3.
15   Murray Peden, *A Thousand Shall Fall*, p. 22.

Oblique aerial photograph showing Short Stirling B.Is of 7 Squadron lined up on the perimeter track on the north-eastern side of the airfield at Oakington, Cambridge, for a night raid on Dortmund, Germany. (Crown Copyright – Air Historical Branch)

and some physical strength. It had tremendous power from those four Rolls-Royce Merlins. At 25,000 ft, its ceiling was vastly superior to the Stirling's. And it was fast, only a whisker short of 300 mph. In every department it outstripped all other four-engined aircraft of the time. At 20,000 feet the standard bombload of 14,000lb was equivalent to that of two Flying Fortress B-17s.[16]

The Lancaster had a difficult start, its origins lay in the Manchester, also designed by Avro and equipped with two 24-cylinder Rolls-Royce Vulture engines. These engines were dreadful and the Manchester was found to be both under-powered and unreliable. Faced with such difficulties the

16   Harry Yates, *Luck and a Lancaster*, p. 75.

Avro designer, Roy Chadwick, suggested lengthening the wings and fitting a further two engines. This coincided with a recent agreement between the British government and the American firm Packard in 1940, which meant that Merlin engines were being manufactured in the United States in much larger numbers than expected and it was these which would be incorporated into the production of the Lancaster. The decision saved the Lancaster and produced one of the most outstanding aircraft of the war.[17]

The arrival of the Lancaster, in March 1942, occurred one month after Air Chief Marshal Sir Arthur Harris replaced Air Marshal Sir Richard Peirse as C-in-C Bomber Command. Peirse had been sacked for failing to conserve Bomber Command as a force for the future, particular note being taken of the raids against Berlin, Mannheim and the Ruhr on 7 November 1941, when 37 out of 400 bombers failed to return. Whilst he was swift to shift blame on to meteorologists for failing to predict the weather accurately, the Chief of the Air Staff, Sir Charles Portal was unconvinced and dismissed Peirse.[18] One can sympathise with Peirse to a degree, the problem of conserving the force was a difficult one, on the one hand it was felt important to build up the force to sufficient strength to be able to deliver a decisive concentration. On the other hand, it was widely recognised that both morale and operational effectiveness would deteriorate if the force was left dormant, or there was any hint of irresolution. As Peirse put it himself 'It is darned hard to fight a force like Bomber Command at a subdued tempo.'[19] Though Peirse was in a difficult position, the elevation of Harris to become C-in-C of Bomber Command brought renewed vitality, leadership and conviction to the main bomber offensive.[20]

Harris was fortunate in inheriting an improving command. The force was transforming itself from an organisation where lone bombers navigated individually to distant targets, to one where navigational aids, such as Gee, were being introduced and the benefits of concentrating force onto a target was becoming better understood. The attack on Lübeck was an illustration of how British concepts had evolved, as a result of the German Blitz on British cities. Guided by information from British firemen, Bomber Command came to understand that greater destruction came not from high explosives, but from incendiaries. The British had learnt that a concentrated drop (within 20 minutes) of a very large number of incendiary bombs, would overwhelm the fire-watchers and the fire-fighters. The role of the high explosive bombs, in addition to spreading the fear of death, would be to sever water mains and force the fire-fighters off the street. It was therefore understood that a concentrated attack in space and time would generate the conflagration required. Lübeck was selected on 28 March 1942, not because it possessed any particular strategic or operational advantage, but because its position on the coast would make it easy to find and the Hanseatic port's *Altstadt* contained a concentration of highly combustible wooden buildings that would burn well.[21] Harris, indicating a cold and ruthless approach that would characterise his approach to the bombing campaign, described it as 'More like a fire-lighter than a human habitation.'[22] Two hundred acres of the city were destroyed by fire, though this was largely domestic housing rather than industrial buildings which had remained surprisingly resilient.

---

17   Leo McKinstry, *Lancaster – The Second World War's Greatest Bomber* (London: John Murray, 2009), pp. 9, 29.

18   N. Frankland and C. Webster, *The Strategic Air Offensive Against Germany, Volume I*, p. 255.

19   N. Frankland and C. Webster, *The Strategic Air Offensive Against Germany, Volume I*, p. 186.

20   Peirse was dispatched to India to command the Allied Air Forces in South-East Asia. He did valuable work there in developing the air forces in support of the Burma campaign, but blotted his copybook further by embarking upon an affair with Field Marshal Auchinleck's wife in 1944.

21   N. Frankland and C. Webster, *The Strategic Air Offensive Against Germany, Volume I*, pp. 252, 392.

22   Max Hastings, *Bomber Command* (London: Michael Joseph, 1980), p. 14.

Harris capitalised on the Lübeck raid with the idea of a larger concentration over Cologne, in the form of the first 'Thousand Bomber Raid' in May 1942. Assembling the force required support from Coastal Command and temporarily stripping Operational Training Units and Heavy Conversion Units of their instructors and aircraft. This was a risk as severe losses would have had a detrimental impact on Bomber Command's growth. The Thousand Bomber Raid brought into being the idea of a large 'bomber stream', which would cross the target aiming point in a concentrated period of time. It was felt that concentration would not only produce more destruction on the ground for the reasons explained already, but that the sheer numbers of aircraft streaming over the target would overwhelm the flak and night-fighters and reduce the overall number of casualties. This theory had to be reconciled with the greater risk of collision, as Dr Basil Dickins head of the Bomber Command Operational Research Section later explained:

> There was a tremendous argument as to whether we should concentrate and accept the resultant risks. The interesting point here is that when a crew failed to return from an operation, that was just too bad, but if the crew returned with a hole in the wing caused by an incendiary bomb from above or if there was a jolly near miss, they would tell everyone about their close shave. This highlighted the collision risk. We had to reduce it all to mathematics and work out the actual chance of a collision. And it became quite obvious to us at ORS that while a collision was 0.5 percent risk, the chance of being shot down by Flak or fighters was three or four percent. So we could allow the collision risk to mount quite a bit, provided that in doing so we would bring down the losses from other causes.[23]

The bomber stream was to become one of the distinctive features of the RAF bomber offensive. The size of the stream at over five miles in length and three miles wide required strict discipline amongst aircrews in maintaining height, course and speed accurately. Even so it came as a shock to the crews to see how close they were to other aircraft, when Bomber Command temporarily transitioned to a day bomber force to support the Allied armies in Normandy in 1944. The raid however was a success, with only 3.8 percent losses amongst the aircraft and an estimated 600 acres of Cologne, including 300 in the centre of the city destroyed. It was a significant propaganda victory at a time of few Allied successes and it also confirmed the increasingly important concept of concentrating large numbers of aircraft on a target.

The exception to this general trend of area bombing in 1942 was the low-level, daylight, precision raid on the Maschinenfabrik Augsburg Nurnberg (MAN) AG factory, which manufactured U-boat diesel engines, in Augsburg, southern German. The Augsburg raid was one of the few occasions when Harris pursued a selective, rather than general, bombing tactic. Selective bombing was based upon the principle that it was 'better to cause a high degree of destruction in a few really essential industries, than to cause a small degree of destruction in many industries.'[24] Such a tactic could be pursued by precision bombing against particular factories, plants and industries, or by area bombing on specially selected towns associated with those industries. Harris was not a fan of such an approach, dismissing them as 'panaceas' and favoured a general bombing tactic, on the basis that the German industrial war machine was sufficiently resilient to be able to withstand selective bombing attacks through dispersal, redundancy and stockpiling. Harris maintained that the way to defeat Germany was by general attacks on towns and cities, the cumulative result of which would impact on all industrial activity as well as morale.

---

23   Alfred Price, *Battle Over the Reich, Volume 1* (Englewood Cliffs, New Jersey: Classic Publications, 2005).

24   'Report of the committee of Operations Analysts', 8 March 1943 quoted in: N. Frankland and C. Webster, *The Strategic Air Offensive Against Germany*, Volume I, p. 252.

Avro Lancaster B.I, R5626/OL-E, of 83 Squadron taking off for Bremen, Germany, on the third 'Thousand-Bomber' raid, from Scampton, Lincolnshire. (Crown Copyright – Air Historical Branch)

This philosophy characterised the execution of the main bomber offensive. Though Bomber Command was given specific industries to target by the Allied Joint Chiefs of Staff, such as aircraft or submarines, Harris would simply choose a town or city and subsequently justify the attack by listing the various industries contained within it. Efforts in 1943 to reconcile the American US selective bombing approach, with the British general bombing method failed and it would be wrong to describe the American and British efforts as a combined bomber offensive. They were instead two separate operations, pursuing two different courses of action.[25]

By the beginning of 1943, Harris' force had grown into six Groups (The Order of Battle, for Bomber Command is included at Annex I). Of these Groups, No. 1, 3, 4 and 5 Group were conventional bomber groups based in Lincolnshire, Cambridgeshire and Yorkshire (see Map 9). Arguably the most favoured of the bomber formations was 5 Group, led by Air Vice Marshal Cochrane, who had been a Flight Commander with Harris in Iraq and many argued could do no wrong in Harris' eyes. It was 5 Group that were specially chosen to form 617 Squadron and given the important task of the Dams raid in 1943. The privileged status of 5 Group was widely known, during one mess conversation in another bomber group, the conversation turned to speculation of who the young Princess Elizabeth might marry. 'I don't know' came the response, 'but I bet he will be in 5 Group'.

At the beginning of 1943 the Canadian 6th Bomber Group, was created from the RCAF squadrons under Harris' command. This stemmed from a 1942 policy, agreed between Canada and the RAF, to consolidate and expand the existing Canadian bomber squadrons within a new Canadian Group. Although intended to create a highly visible Canadian contribution to the war, it had three unintended disadvantages. First, lack of experience amongst RCAF personnel meant that those placed in leadership positions were often ill-qualified for their posts. Second, as latecomers to the burgeoning bomber offensive, the Canadians were based in the Vale of York, one of the

---

25 N. Frankland and C. Webster, *The Strategic Air Offensive Against Germany, Volume II* (London: HMSO, 1961), pp. 4-6.

worst geographical locations from which to bomb Germany. The Canadian airfields there, were often covered with urban smog, surrounded by hills and the furthest away from German targets. Canadian aircraft would often be the last to join the bomber stream, usually over the Dutch coast, which made them particularly vulnerable to German night-fighters.[26] Finally, RAF Bomber Command also furnished the best aircraft to the most experienced wings. As newcomers, the Canadian wings automatically received the less capable Halifax bomber, which had a lower operating ceiling, worse manoeuvrability and more visible exhaust flames.

The combination of these factors led to a weaker operational performance by the Canadians that included poor bombing accuracy, higher early returns from operations, fewer sorties per aircraft and greater loss rates. Though the 'Canadianisation' of their bomber effort may have raised the overall profile of the RCAF role and their personal bravery and commitment was never in doubt, it could be argued that had these crews or squadrons been integrated within experienced RAF formations, as others were, their effectiveness and survival rates would have been better.

The final bomber group in Harris' force were the Pathfinders of 8 Group. These had been created on the premise that a highly skilled set of crews were required to navigate to the target and then accurately mark it for the main bomber force. The Pathfinders were supposed to be more experienced than standard bomber crews and a focus for the increasing array of navigational equipment, such as Oboe and H2S. Harris had resisted the idea of an elite element within Bomber Command vehemently and it was only through persistent pressure from his organizational nemesis throughout the war, the Air Staff's Directorate of Bombing Operations, that he was eventually forced to accept such a force. No. 8 Group was established under the command of Australian Air Commodore Donald Bennett in July of 1942, its HQ being based at RAF Wyton, Huntingdonshire. Pathfinder crews would undertake a tour of 45 missions, rather than the usual 30[27] and though it was supposed to be an elite and highly-experienced force, it also included a large number of relatively novice crews. These were often used in the less complicated functions, until they had obtained sufficient experience. The Group would eventually include a force of Mosquitoes as well as Lancasters, the Mosquitoes being used not just for marking, but also for diversionary raids. 8 Group would play a significant role in the evolution of Bomber Command tactics, though they did not have the monopoly on innovation. To Bennett's obvious displeasure, Cochrane's 5 Group incorporated 617 Squadron's precision bombing techniques into Main Force operations, often with dramatic success. It is also worth mentioning 2 Group, this was a light bomber group that used Blenheims earlier on in the war before subsequently equipping with the more modern Bostons and Mosquitoes later on. No. 2 Group was not part of the main bomber force and in time would be transferred to the Second Tactical Air Force, but as we shall see later its role in precision strike was an important one.

From the beginning of 1943 the bomber offensive worked to a particular pattern and operational design. At just after 0900 each morning, Harris would be briefed in his underground bunker at High Wycombe on the success of the previous night's raids and operations, this would then be followed by the weather forecast. A number of target options would be presented to Harris, many of which would have originated from the Ministry of Economic Warfare and been passed down by the Directorate of Bomber Operations in the Air Ministry (DBOps), though the choice of target unequivocally belonged to Harris. It was the Bomber Command chief who would decide which city would be struck, aided by the Ministry of Economic Warfare's *Guide To The Economic*

26   Brereton Greenhous, *The Crucible of War, Volume III*, pp. 116-20.
27   Donald Bennett, *Pathfinder* (Manchester: Crecy, 1998), pp. 155-7.

Importance of German Towns and Cities' or *'Bomber's Baedeker'*.[28] (See Map 10 for detail of the principle German cities attacked, together with ranges from British bomber bases.)

Bomber Command understood that saturation bombing of cities, through repeating raids in quick sucession, would allow the Germans little respite to recover from previous raids. Weather would often determine if this was possible, or indeed what alternative target could be struck, and growing night-fighter concentrations might also sway the choice of city. Once Harris had decided the target, his deputy, Air Vice Marshal Sir Robert Saundby, would plan the details, usually in conjunction with the Pathfinder staff at 8 Group. Details would include bombloads, routes, take-off times and aiming points. The latter, in a concession to the Joint Chiefs of Staff POINTBLANK targeting directive, might contain a superfluous reference to an aircraft or submarine plant located within the targeted city.[29] Annex S gives the yearly tonnage dropped by Bomber Command and the United States Eighth Air Force. Two hours after Harris had made his decisions, these details would be sent out to the RAF bomber stations in the East of England, where the preparations for the operations that night would begin. The next chapter will describe what a Bomber Command mission entailed.

---

28   TNA WO 252/125: 'Bombers Baedeker'.
29   Max Hastings, *Bomber Command*, p. 24.

12

'We act with one Accord'[1]
A Bomber Command Mission –
The Route Out

Usually the first to spring into action when a mission was planned would be the armourers, who would start to remove the weapons from the bomb dump, a partially buried bunker some distance from the main facilities of the station. Walter Thompson was a Canadian pilot with 83 Squadron at RAF Wyton and describes the process of loading a Lancaster bomber.

> Depending upon the target and the role the squadron was to play, the bomb load might vary from fourteen 250 pound or 500 pound bombs to a single 8,000 pounder. The Lancasters were all fitted to carry the 4,000 pound bomb and most of them could carry the 8,000 pounder. Later on they were fitted to carry special [Tallboy] bombs of 12,000 and [Grand Slam] 22,000 pounds. The purpose of all these bombs was to smash and burn buildings even if their inhabitants were all in air raid shelters.
>
> The smaller bombs were of various types, armour piercing, semi-armour piercing and general purpose and they were of low, medium or high capacity. Low capacity bombs had a small charge to weight ratio and consequently penetrated before exploding. High Capacity bombs had a high charge to weight ratio and a light casing; these would explode on impact. A typical load was one 4,000 pound (HC) called a 'Cookie', four 500 pound General Purpose bombs and 12 Small Bomb Containers. The latter each contained eight 30 pound or ninety 4 pound incendiaries.

It was considered that blast from high explosives, when combined with fire from many incendiaries, was most effective. The 4,000lb Cookie was not just meant to demolish buildings in the immediate vicinity, but also to blow in windows and doors and knock tiles off the roofs of neighbouring houses. This allowed greater opportunities for the fire from incendiary bombs to take hold. It also further illustrates how repeating raids on the same town, one after another in quick succession, could have a disproportionately high impact together with the importance of concentrating the bombs on the target. The armourers placed the bombs un-fused on low slung, flat top 'Eagle' carriers pulled by David Brown tractors and took them to the fusing hut, where armourers would fit the bombs with a variety of fuses including those that exploded on impact, as well as those that delayed detonation from a few seconds to several days. At the hut, the Cookie would have its transit plugs removed and two detonators and a firing pistol inserted. The firing

---

1   The 35th Squadron motto. On 5 November it became the first Halifax bomber squadron flying its first night raid on 10 March 1941. After taking part in raids on Germany and Italy the squadron was transferred to the Pathfinder Force in August 1942. In March 1944 it converted to Lancasters which it flew throughout the remainder of the war.

Trolleys loaded with 500lb GP and MC bombs, and their attendant armourers, are towed by tractors from the Bomb Store at Snaith, Yorkshire, towards aircraft dispersals on the northern side of the airfield, and the awaiting Handley Page Halifaxes of 51 Squadron. (Crown Copyright – Air Historical Branch)

pistol had a small windmill device which would arm the bomb as it dropped from 20,000 feet. It was temporarily wired up to prevent the windmill inadvertently spinning in the wind, or in the slipstream of an engine, during its journey from the dump to the aircraft parked at their various dispersal points. Walter Thompson describes the process once more:

> The bomb doors of the aircraft were opened, and the bombs wheeled underneath; they were fitted to bomb-carriers which were lowered from the bomb cells of the aircraft and when securely fitted the fuse setting control was adjusted and the bombs were winched up into the bomb cells. The armourers were careful that a correct sequence of loading was maintained for a correct centre of gravity of the aircraft. Rigorous checks were made to ensure that each bomb was held securely and locked into position. The jaws of the bomb carriers for the 4,000 pound or larger bombs were locked by a lever on the side of the bomb release. During the loading operation this got released once in a while and the bomb would drop on the ground or an electrical fault might cause a premature release. Fortunately when dropped straight down from a short distance the fuse was not activated and the impact was not sufficient to cause an explosion.[2]

Bombing-up was a painstaking business, usually with little time available. If an operation was scrubbed the entire process would need to be undone and the bombs replaced back in the dump. In just over three years of war, Lancaster armourers were to load 51 million incendiaries and 608,612 tons of high explosive. To put this into perspective, this total tonnage of high explosives would

---

2   Walter Thompson, *Lancaster to Berlin* (Manchester: Crecy, 1997), p. 6.

The bomb load most commonly used for area bombing raids (Bomber Command executive codeword 'Usual') in the bomb bay of an Avro Lancaster of No. 57 Squadron RAF at Scampton Lincolnshire. 'Usual' consisted of a 4,000 impact-fused HC bomb ('cookie'), and 12 Small Bomb Containers (SBCs) each loaded with incendiaries, in this case, 236 x 4-lb incendiary sticks. (Crown Copyright – Air Historical Branch)

require a goods train 345 miles long to carry it.[3] The bombs used were perhaps not quite as stable as Walter Thompson indicates above, the Cookie in particular had a comparatively thin shell and any aircraft crashing with them on board risked detonating the bomb with catastrophic consequences.

Armourers would also service and load the Lancaster's defensive armament of .303 Browning machine guns. These consisted of a pair of guns in the nose, a pair in the mid-upper turret and four in the tail. All were in Fraser Nash hydraulically powered turrets, which moved swiftly and precisely wherever the gunners wished, each taking its power from a different engine on the Lancaster. The guns were elevated, depressed and rotated through their 180-degree arc by twisting two handles, as you might do on a motorbike. As Australian gunner Robert Chester-Master describes 'they could go from maximum depression on the starboard side to maximum elevation on the port side very quickly with no jerky movements – they needed to'.[4] The Perspex in the turrets would be polished thoroughly to ensure maximum visibility, but it was believed that no matter how well-polished the Perspex the critical rear gunner's view would still be degraded and so a portion of Perspex, directly in front of the gunner, was cut away to where it curved into the dome

---

3   Leo McKinstry, *Lancaster*, p. 13.
4   AWM S01664: Sound recording interview with Robert Chester-Master.

Avro Lancaster B.I R5868 'S-Sugar' being refuelled at RAF Hunsdon after completing its 100th operation
the previous evening, against Bourg Leopold in Belgium on 12 May 1944.
(Crown Copyright – Air Historical Branch)

at the top. The slipstream would take care of rain and snow but it was still perishingly cold for the rear gunner and must have increased his sense of exposure even further.[5]

The armourers would load the ammunition in to a series of tanks for the front and mid-upper turret guns, each holding 1,000 rounds per gun. The rear turret was supplied by a series of channels, that ran along the fuselage, motors would then pull the ammunition to the four rear turret guns when they were being fired. These channels held a total of 2,500 rounds per gun. The Lancaster had no ventral turret (i.e. underneath the fuselage). It had been part of the early design, but in February 1942, largely at the instigation of Air Vice-Marshal John Slessor (then AOC 5 Group) and with Harris' blessing, it was removed from the design as unnecessary. This decision meant the Lancaster was unprotected from any attack immediately below the aircraft.[6]

For security reasons the ground crew would only install some of the more sensitive equipment on the day of the raid, this would include H2S, Oboe and Gee. The photographic section would also install the photographic flash, which was synchronised with a camera that would automatically take a shot of the bomb release point. The fuelling process would also begin at this point. The Lancaster could hold 2,154 gallons of 100 octane petrol, which was contained in six fuel tanks in the wings. The number 1 tanks (580 gallons) were between the inner engine and fuselage on each wing, the number 2 tanks (383 gallons) between inner and outer engines and smallest of all the number 3 tanks in the outer wing (114 gallons). Fuelling was done by an AEC Matador bowser, which could hold 2,500 gallons. The Lancaster could therefore consume almost the entire contents of this tanker if it was a long trip to Berlin, or another city deep in German-occupied territory.

---

5   Ron Smith, *Rear Gunner Pathfinders* (Manchester: Crecy, 1997), p. 83.
6   Leo McKinstry, *Lancaster*, p. 13.

By late morning, the bomber crew would be warned that they were on operations by a simple battle order pinned on a notice board outside the squadron offices and messes. It would detail which crews were required and the timing of the briefing. The target would not be mentioned in the battle order, but some aircrew would try and work out if it was a distant target, normally by finding out the amount of fuel being put into the aircraft.[7]

In the early afternoon some crews might be required to conduct equipment tests, others would simply stew in their own nervous anticipation. To preserve security, most stations would prevent individuals leaving the base during the day, or making outgoing calls, they would then finally brief the crews for the operation in the late afternoon. Although there were some variations, this usually began with individual crew members being briefed by the senior specialists within the squadron (e.g. navigation leader, gunnery officer etc). The wireless operators, for instance, would be briefed by the senior signals leader on the Bomber Code for that day, R/T (voice) and W/T (Morse) call signs, frequencies for the RAF station and the Very Light flare colours for the time periods covered. Some of this information had to be written on rice paper, which was to be eaten by the wireless operator if an emergency arose over enemy territory.[8] After the specialist briefings, all the members of the crew would come together and sit as a team on benches in the large briefing hall. This would often be the first time the target was formally revealed, usually by the squadron's commanding officer who would use a long red tape to indicate the route towards the target from their base, as well as the return leg. Bomber aircrew were a cynical bunch, so if the trip was to one of the more notorious heavily defended targets, such as the Ruhr valley – known as 'Happy Valley', a large collective groan would emanate from the audience. A deep penetration raid to Berlin, 'the Big City', would also elicit a negative response, conversely a short and easy trip to France would be greeted by cheering. Arthur Doubleday was an experienced Squadron Leader, who did his best to ensure that his crews were well-motivated and that the novice members of his squadron were not overwhelmed by the dangerous reputation of some targets.

> I felt the briefing was the opportunity to give them the sort of support they needed, particularly the young chaps. I can remember briefing them on my second tour on Essen, and we hadn't been to Essen for a good while and Essen on my first tour was a shocker of a place because you had no Pathfinder Force to tell you where to go. It was a great swamp and on this occasion I said to them, 'Look, don't let the old hands frighten you about Essen. Essen with Window and Essen with Oboe and Essen with all these things we've got now is different. In addition, tonight, you've got a tail wind from round about Osnabruck, straight through to target. You've got cloud cover as soon as you come out, 320 miles an hour through to target, turn into the cloud cover, you're alright.' And that sort of thing had a good effect on them. They set off on the right foot. Now I'm not saying that saved anybody or that you could do that very often but if there were things that you could say ... I always felt it was well worth while telling the chaps about these sort of things.[9]

The squadron commander would then be followed by the Meteorological Officer, who would predict the likely weather, including winds to and from the target. Cloud was always covered in great detail, particularly what type was expected over the target, if there was a likelihood of icing

7   Leo McKinstry, *Lancaster*, p. 134.
8   Derek Brammer, *Thundering through the Clear Air – No. 61 (Lincoln Imp.) Squadron at War* (Lincoln: Tucann Books, 1997), p. 91.
9   AWM S00546: Sound recording interview with Arthur Doubleday.

Squadron Leader Peter Hill briefs crews of 51 Squadron on the forthcoming raid to Nuremberg, Germany in the Operations Room at Snaith, Yorkshire, 30 March 1944. The Station Commander, Group Captain NH Fresson, sits third from the left in the front row. No. 51 Squadron lost six Handley Page Halifaxes that night (30/31 March 1944), suffering 35 men killed (including Sqn Ldr Hill) and seven made prisoners of war. (Crown Copyright – Air Historical Branch)

in cloud, as well as forecasting what height that was likely to occur. Finally, the met officer would brief the risk of fog or mist covering or 'clamping in' their English airbases. The Flying Control Officer would come next, he would brief the plan for take-off, which was conducted on radio silence and controlled solely through the use of Aldis lamps and would also explain the returning and landing procedures. The next part of the brief was by the Intelligence Officer, who would not only explain the importance of the target, trying to place it in the context of the wider bombing campaign or war effort, but more importantly he would highlight the various flak zones and the expected concentrations of night-fighters. These were usually very carefully and dutifully noted on the navigator's charts.

The squadron commander would then explain the precise aiming points for the bombers and the type of marking being employed by the Pathfinders that night. He would normally remind the crews of the dangers of getting off track and inadvertently crossing a flak zone protecting a major city, as well as the importance of keeping to time and maintaining a concentrated bomber stream over the target.

When the briefing was finished the crews would disperse, they might then have their pre-flight meal, consisting of eggs and bacon, in the mess. This was a considerable luxury in wartime Britain, though many aircrews would sensibly guard against eating and drinking too much before a long flight to Berlin, for obvious reasons. Sandwiches, chocolate, a flask of coffee and can of orange juice, were also provided for the crew's trip. They would then move to the crew room and pick up their escape kits, consisting of foreign currency, emergency rations and silk escape maps. Aircrew would also have in their possession a number of spare photographs of themselves, if it was necessary

Following their briefing, Handley Page Halifax crews of 76 Squadron board vehicles at Holme-on-Spalding-Moor, Yorkshire, to be driven to dispersals in preparation for a raid on Kassel, Germany. This raid, on 22/23 October 1943, was the most devastating delivered on a German city since the 'firestorm' raid on Hamburg in the previous July. Of the 569 aircraft used in this attack, 43 were lost, of which 25 were Halifaxes. (Crown Copyright – Air Historical Branch)

these could be given to the resistance for the fabrication of false identity papers. Parachutes would be picked up, these were normally clipped on to the chest, with the exception of the pilot who sat on his. Finally, about 90 minutes before take-off, the crews would head to the crew room and pick up their flying suits. After changing they would leave the keys in the doors of the lockers, the station staff having quickly realised that too much damage was being done breaking into the lockers of crews that had failed to return.

The kit the aircrew wore varied considerably, depending on where one sat in the Lancaster. The wireless operator and navigator benefitted from hot air discharged from the engines and would happily fly in just their battledress, other members of the crew were less lucky, the rear gunners in particular needed to pay particular attention to what they wore. Robert Chester-Master describes what he wore on operations, as a rear gunner on 514 Squadron:

> Starting from the feet up there would be silk socks, then there would be electrically heated socks, then there would be heavy flying boots. Our flying gear would be an inner flying suit, a heated flying suit and a heavy outer flying suit. On our hands there would be silk gloves, heated gloves and flying gloves and of course our helmet. So as far as I was concerned I had on much more gear than anyone else, because the front of the aircraft was warmed by motors as opposed to the tail. So it made manoeuvring very, very limited … The one thing we were never ever to do, and certainly I never did even though it happened on one occasion [was clear stoppages gloveless]. If your guns jammed, your guns jammed. If you could not free the jam with all your gloves on you just left it. If you took your gloves off to try

and free the jam and touched the metal, your hand would just stick to the metal, the cold was that intense.[10]

Most of the crew would dress for the sortie there and then in the crew room. The rear gunners would only do so immediately before entering the aircraft, or sometimes once the aircraft was at 6,000 feet when the air cooled. If the gunner sweated too much in his suit on the ground, it would only cause him to freeze in the air. Once dressed, the crew would be driven on a crew bus to their aircraft at its dispersal site. Novice crews would be given any aircraft that was available, but once a crew had notched up a number of missions, they would ask the squadron engineering officer for a particular aircraft that would then become 'theirs'. This selection might be based on an aircraft perceived to be lucky, or alternatively the crew might just choose a new aircraft straight off the production line, with a powerful performance and no snags. The aircraft were all identified by letters of the alphabet, so the driver of the crew bus would simply call 'S-Sugar', or 'K-King' and the relevant crew would get out.

Ron Mayhill was a bomb aimer with 75 Squadron (RNZAF) at Mepal, near Ely and describes the pre-flight checks a crew would do before taking off:

> By the time we reached the oil-stained dispersal the ground crew were well into their routine jobs on W-William and a corporal electrician was working on the fuse box. Taffy and Jake joined me under the nose, pointing to the landing gear, the tyres hidden by covers to protect them from oil, had a good look at the Oleo struts and retraction jacks, and gazed up into the wheel wells. I walked back under the huge bomb lugs, crouching down to touch the smooth ventral fairing of the H2S [airborne radar] blister … We climbed up the short, steep ladder in front of the starboard tail plane, ducking our heads as we went through the door to our interior checks. Petrol, hydraulics and that indefinable smell of a Lanc pervaded the interior. Willy crawled back past the First Aid pack, Elsan toilet on his right, to check his parachute stowage and fire extinguisher outside the rear turret doors. There was no room for a parachute inside the turrets and both gunners would have to climb out and grab them in an emergency. There were stories of careless clots tossing their parachute packs onto the floor and fouling the rudder controls or not being able to find them in a hurry. For bailing out, Willy had the option of revolving the turret and flipping out backwards through the open doors or opting for the main crew door, unless of course he had time to join the rest of us through the nose hatch.
>
> Henry led us forward, treading carefully on the smooth, metal plates, shoulder and head bent to avoid obstacles, touching both sides of the narrow confines to steady himself. He checked his parachute stowage, then pulled down his step and heaved himself up into his mid-upper turret. Both gunners had plenty of time to check their Browning .303-inch machine guns, safety switches, sight illumination, the long lines of colour-coded ammunition, incendiary and armour-piercing rounds and practise clearing jams. The gunners had manual rotation only until the engines started and the hydraulics worked the turrets. Without parachutes and mae wests and all the gear we carried on flights, it was a piece of cake crawling through the gap between the mid upper turret and the ammo tracks. We had also learned how to step onto the roof of the bomb bay and over the main spar to avoid banging our heads on the escape hatch. We had no illusions how difficult it would be if the plane was falling out of control, especially for the mid-upper.

---

10   AWM S01664: Sound recording interview with Robert Chester-Master.

The radio operator would check the rescue gear, including flame floats and sea markers just forward of the mid-upper, before moving back over the ammunition tracks and storage boxes that fed the rear turret. At the rear spar step near the trailing edge of the wing he would pause to check the signal pistol, the row of coloured flares and chute stowage. Once that was completed, he would return to his wireless operator's seat. Ron Mayhill continued:

> Like all his trade, his hand automatically found the morse key fixed to his table and he tapped happily away to nobody as he viewed the edge of the wing through his small window, and the transmitters and receivers in front of him with their imposing array of bright red, green, blue and yellow knobs. The W/T (Wireless Transmission-Morse) and R/T (Radio Telephone-voice) and crew intercom systems were his domain.
>
> Dunc and I stepped past him into the navigation compartment. Dunc had his own parachute stowage and a slit window, seat, and table that covered the radio compass receiver. Before him he had duplicate altimeter, repeater compass and A/S (airspeed) indicator and dim, working light. I left him fiddling with the Gee set, the receiver which fixed our position by converting radio signals from three ground transmitters into green pulses that appeared on a screen. I would check the H2S later. It was so easy to scramble down into the nose when the engineer's seat was folded away.
>
> I noticed immediately that the nose blister and its downward facing flat surface, free of distortion, had been cleaned and polished, as had the two small side windows, giving me a magnificent all round view. The rear window into the empty bomb bay was grubby but this didn't really matter. Behind me on my left was my parachute rack and F24 camera and below me the jettison handle of the main escape hatch. Although very small, this was the safest exit in flight, head first in case we were swept against the non-retractable tail-wheel, or worse, the edge of the tailplane and fin. Back on the right was the chute for dropping the the strips of metal coated paper we called window.
>
> All switches had to be off while on the ground, so there was little we could do until we had engine power as the bombsight worked by air pressure, 'it all depending upon the shape of the blades across the jets' as we used to say in training, I wriggled up into the nose turret, to do my guns and ammunition checks.
>
> Meanwhile, Jake and Taffy had worked their way slowly forward. Jake with overall responsibility for the aircraft had by far the longest list of checks, hence he had an engineer to assist. They had stayed some time with the corporal electrician who was still testing the circuits to the blackened fuse box and had then clambered forward, stopping near the mid upper turret to examine the fire extinguisher, oxygen cylinders, dinghy release in case the automatic ditching mechanism in the starboard wing root didn't work, and roof light. Over the ammunition tracks and rear spar, they checked the oxygen stowage under the crew rest bunk, not that we ever had a rest but it could be useful if anyone was injured, and made sure the crash axe and ditching exits were secure. Jake and Taffy settled themselves into their seats and began their long cockpit checks. These were just routine DIs [Daily Inspections] and we did them whether we were detailed for air operations or on stand-down, thus becoming well acquainted with our aircraft. From the outside the Lancaster was sleek and well-proportioned, pleasing to the eye, but inside the cluttered fuselage had not been designed for crew comfort, or safety, but it was fully functional, our existence Spartan.[11]

---

11   Ron Mayhill, *Bombs on Target*, pp. 35-37.

The crews were to be at their aircraft one hour before takeoff. Once ready to start up the trolley accumulator was wheeled to the aircraft, covers and control locks were then removed from the aircraft and the pilot would give a signal to the ground crew to start the engines. The starboard inner engine was always started first since this controlled an electrical generator on board the aircraft. As they fired up one by one, a long list of instrument and control checks would be undertaken. The gunners would also load their weapons and the pilot would check the oxygen was working, with one final intercom call to all members of the crew. He would then sign Form 700, accepting responsibility that the aircraft was properly serviceable and fuelled, before handing it to a member of the ground crew who would then exit the aircraft. With a signal to remove the chocks, the aircraft would take its place in the line of aircraft taxiing to the end of the runway. There was always pressure to meet the takeoff time, but that did not stop last minute emergencies occurring. Arthur Doubleday recalls one of the last of his aircraft in 467 Squadron having troubles at its dispersal:

> I said, 'What's the matter?' He said, 'Oh we won't be able to go, the captain's got cramps in his stomach'. I said, 'Well just hop in your aeroplane and sit there and wait'. I said to the captain 'You come with me'. I picked him up, went up to the takeoff point where the medical officer was, and said, 'Doc, it's 10 minutes till last take-off, you've got five of them to either tell me this bloke is not fit to go, or fix him up. Whichever you like.'
>
> He said, 'Right, hop in, down to the surgery.' They went into the surgery and in three minutes flat, out came the kid. He was only about 20. Smiles all over his face and I said, 'Everything right?' 'Yes, that's right,' he said. So the Doc gave me a wave. He said, 'He'll be right now, I fixed him up.' So I put him in the aeroplane and pointed him off. I think it was Magdeburg, and three in the morning he's back again. If he hadn't come back I don't know what I'd have done. Jumped off the gasometer or something I suppose, but he came back and he said, 'Best trip I ever had in my life'. I said, 'Well that's wonderful … Now go have your bacon and eggs and get off back, it might be on tomorrow night.' Okay away they went in great spirit. Then I saw the medical officer and I said, 'Oh Doc, thank you very much indeed for fixing that young fellow up'. He said, 'Oh that's great,' turned away. I said, 'Doc, what did you give him.' He said, 'I gave him an aspro.' There you go, the psychological effect of the fact the doctor says this will fix you and it fixed him. It never recurred. A true placebo, he believed the effect and therefore it happened.[12]

Slowly, the aircraft would move onto the perimeter track and head for the end of the runway. They would be careful not to put a tire off the track as, with its full fuel and bomb load, the Lancaster weighed 30 tonnes and could easily sink in the mud. Taxiing was not easy, as the pilot could only manoeuvre the aircraft by alternately gunning the outer engines, on the side away from the turn. Additionally, if the engines were run on the ground for too long, they could overheat, consequently the flight engineer would be carefully watching the temperature gauges. Some Lancasters would have up to a mile of taxiing from their dispersal positions to reach the take-off point, usually marked by a chequer board hut. This was the last safe moment at which an operation could be scrubbed, usually by means of a flare – that was often followed by a cheer from the aircrew. If all was still on, there would be a simple green light from the airfield controller's Aldis lamp and that would be the signal for the aircraft to join the runway and take-off.

The pilot would run up his engines to full power and keep his brakes firmly on, releasing them once all engines were at full throttle, at 3,000 rpm and 14 inches boost. As the aircraft accelerated,

12   AWM S00546: Sound recording interview with Arthur Doubleday.

Personnel from RAF North Killinghome wave off Flight Lieutenant D.A. Shaw and crew of 550 Squadron as they take off for a bombing raid on Bochum, Germany on the 4 November 1944. This was the 100th operational sortie for Avro Lancaster B.III, ED905/BQ-F 'Press on Regardless'. ED905, having already served with Nos. 103 and 661 Squadrons survived operations, only to be written off in a landing accident at Lindholme on 20 August 1945, while being flown by 1656 Conversion Unit. (Crown Copyright – Air Historical Branch)

the flight engineer watched the temperature of the engines, as well as their pressures; an engine failure at this point would be a major emergency. The engineer would hold the throttles wide open, as the pilot applied a little pressure to the control wheel to lift the tail off the ground, by doing so the rudders entered the slipstream and it was easier to keep the aircraft straight. The flight engineer would call out the speed and the aircraft would normally take-off at about 100 mph. There would be a slow, agonising climb as the Lancaster raised its undercarriage and slowly, very slowly gained altitude – at 1,000 feet it could consider itself comparatively safe. The Lancasters would then assemble and climb to their cruising height, which could be anywhere between 15,000 to 20,000 feet. When they passed 10,000 feet they would put their oxygen masks on and from this point on if any duties required them to move around the aircraft, they would have to uncouple themselves from the main oxygen supply and use a bottle. As the aircraft began its journey to the target the members of the crew would attend to their particular duties. The wireless operator would keep a listening watch on his own station for the first 20 minutes of the flight, then switch to the Group transmitter frequency, it was this frequency which would contain messages such as upper air wind-speed information for the navigator, or if there was a recall of aircraft. To make sure all wireless operators were fully alert for the duration of the mission a series of half hour time checks were transmitted from the Group, these were all preceded by a random number and the operator would have to show a full set on his de-briefing in Britain, or incur the wrath of the squadron signals leader. Flight Sergeant Bill Perry describes the duties further:

When the English coast was reached the trailing radio aerial was reeled out. All emergency calls, SOS etc were made on a low frequency channel (long wave) and the trailing aerial was much better suited than the fixed aerial on top of the fuselage. Once the enemy coast was reached the trailing aerial was reeled back inside.

In between the half hour 9SY [5 Group's call sign] broadcasts I would spend most of my time in the astrodome helping the gunners search the sky for German night-fighters or perhaps obtaining a radio bearing for the navigator to check our position. Most navigators regarded radio fixes with suspicion, but they could be reasonably accurate if care was taken.

Just before reaching the target area the very high frequency (VHF) receiver was tuned to the channel being used by the raid's Master Bomber whose job it was to circle the target area instructing and encouraging the following main bomber force. Meanwhile his wireless operator duplicated the R/T messages in case of any communication equipment malfunction.

After delivering our bombs we would clear the target area and head for home still listening out on the controller's frequency. As soon as I received the general message 'Operation over – go home' from the Master Bomber, I reverted to a listening watch on No. 5 Group transmissions.

On the return trip, Group would send messages giving details of the general weather conditions covering cloud base, barometric pressure etc. If any airfield became clamped with fog and a diversion to another airfield was necessary, they used the W/T call signs unique to the squadron concerned.

About half an hour away from base I re-tuned to RAF Skellingthorpe's transmitter frequency to listen out for local weather reports and landing instructions. It was permitted during the return trip to break silence if absolutely necessary.[13]

Whilst this was going on the flight engineer would be busy monitoring the engines and fuel tanks, ensuring that the fuel was taken evenly from each tank, so the aircraft was trimmed properly and there was an uninterrupted supply of fuel to each engine. Fuel gauges were notoriously unreliable and the engineer would be constantly making calculations on consumption, so if the aircraft were to lose a fuel tank he could advise the pilot if there was sufficient to return to base. The engineer would monitor the temperatures of each engine, adjusting the radiator flaps to improve airflow if required. He would also synchronise the Merlin engines, through adjusting the pitch of the propellers, as well as the throttle. This was to ensure they were working in harmony together, rather than generating noisy vibrations throughout the aircraft, a machine with synchronised engines had a satisfying, singlular, throbbing pulse. Finally, the engineer was there to deal with any engine emergencies, if one caught fire he would switch on the Graviner extinguisher, which would hopefully put out the flames with a blast of methyl-bromide gas. He would then press the feathering button and lock the airscrew in position minimising the drag of the damaged engine on the aircraft.

There was no second pilot or dual controls on a Lancaster, or any of the other heavy bombers. This decision had been taken earlier in the war in order to generate more capacity amongst pilots. There were disadvantages with this approach, some argued that it meant that pilots never generated sufficient experience under the watchful eye of a more senior captain. However, to assist the pilot a properly trained navigator was provided, the experiences in the early years of the war had satisfied the Bomber Command hierarchy that a pilot could not both fly the aircraft, as well as pay sufficient attention to navigation.[14] One might expect that space, light and mental quiet were prerequisites for the navigator's role, one of the most important tasks in the bomber. Robert Murphy, an Australian with 97 Squadron, describes how that was not the case and the actual facilities and work the navigator had to tackle:

13   Derek Brammer, *Thundering Through the Clear Air*, p. 93.
14   Donald Bennett, *Pathfinder*, p. 10.

Flight Engineer Flying Officer J.B. Burnside at work in the cockpit of a 619 Squadron Lancaster on 14 February 1944. (Crown Copyright – Air Historical Branch)

I had a table or desk on the port side of the aircraft about four feet long and two feet wide and I was sitting on a chair which would move around on a swivel. Above the table was a light with a rheostat [dimmer] on it which I could could turn down as low as possible and there was a black curtain between me and the pilot. I was sitting just behind the pilot and I had to keep the light down as low as possible. There was the Gee box which gave us positions and the astrograph [star-chart], and there was the usual air speed indicator, altimeter and compass and I used to work out the plot and course and relay them to the pilot.

From the navigator's point of view we would keep track of the course and try to get as many fixes as you can either from the stars or any other way you could to keep your air plot going.

We kept an air position plot on the chart because we were flying in a media of air which itself is moving around the earth, and that media of air is changing in direction and speed constantly. Our job as navigators was to determine that change of wind speed and direction all the time and apply it to the compass course which the plane was flying and convert it from the magnetic course to the true course the plane was flying on a chart. And if we were going off track set a new course and give that to the pilot so as to bring him back on track, and this was in complete darkness except a very, very tiny light over the navigator's table …

It took great discipline and constant work, the whole time, with an oxygen mask on your face. I remember once I was giving a wrong course and the pilot realised it because it was so ridiculous and he said to the wireless operator 'Have a look at Murph and see what's wrong with him.' And sure enough my chair had slipped and the leg was sitting on top of the oxygen tube and we were at 25,000 feet and I hadn't any oxygen and had just about passed out.[15]

From 1942 onwards, a series of new navigational aids began to make themselves available to the navigator. The first of these to arrive was Gee. This was a special receiver in the aircraft, which measured the time difference between the receipt of two ground-station signals and displayed the aircraft's distance from each station on a Cathode Ray Tube. These could then be plotted on a specially prepared Gee lattice chart. The Gee system began to be used operationally in 1942, by which time there were several Gee stations operating in the United Kingdom, giving a range of about 350-400 miles, or sufficient distance to reach the Ruhr. The Germans responded by developing jamming transmitters, which cut down the operating range of Gee. Nonetheless many crews still found the system was invaluable, both for general navigation around the UK as well as finding their air bases in poor weather. Equally importantly Gee kept the bomber force more concentrated and therefore less vulnerable.[16]

The second system available to navigators was H2S, a rotating radar scanner that fitted beneath the Lancaster and transmitted a radar beam every second, at centimetric radar wavelengths. When this radar energy hit the surface of the earth below, it was reflected back into a receiver on the aircraft and the signal was shown on a circular Cathode Ray Tube display, known as a Plan Position Indicator. The radar would have few returns from the sea or any large body of water, varying signals from land and a very strong return from the large collection of buildings to be found in a town or city. When taken together, these produced a crude picture of the landscape below. The display certainly took some interpretation, but with experience could be used effectively and as it was able to operate in all weathers and was not dependent on any ground stations it proved very useful. H2S had various scales of view, longer ranges that were useful for navigation and shorter ranges for the bombing run itself. The equipment was often operated by the bomb aimer in the early part of the flight, in order to ease the navigator's workload. H2S was first used in January 1943, initially just by the Pathfinders before subsequent issue to the main bomber force. The name H2S is alleged to originate from Lord Cherwell's comments on first viewing the equipment at the Telecommunications and Research Establishment (TRE) at Swanage. By all accounts he was unimpressed and left with the disparaging remark 'It stinks.' Undeterred the scientists called the equipment H2S, the chemical symbol for hydrogen sulphide, which every chemical student will know stinks of rotten eggs.[17] Bomb aimer Thomas Tredwell served with 77 and 10 Squadrons and explained that though H2S was difficult to operate, it could be mastered:

---

15   AWM S00523: Sound recording interview with Robert Basil Gray Murphy.

16   Eric Cropper, *Back Bearings – A Navigator's Tale 1942 to 1974* (Barnsley: Pen and Sword, 2010), p. 30.

17   Donald Bennett, *Pathfinder*, p. 159.

Maps

Map 1 Radar Chain and Observer Corps Network and Coverage 1940.

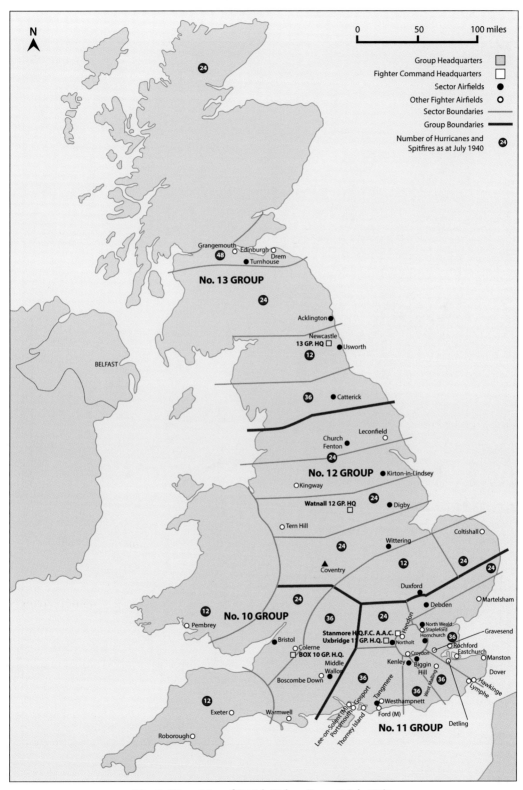

N

| 0 | 50 | 100 miles |

Group Headquarters
Fighter Command Headquarters
Sector Airfields ●
Other Fighter Airfields ○
Sector Boundaries
Group Boundaries
Number of Hurricanes and
Spitfires as at July 1940 ㉔

㉔

Grangemouth
㊽ ○ Edinburgh
Drem
● Turnhouse

No. 13 GROUP

㉔

Acklington ●

Newcastle
13 GP. HQ □ ● Usworth
⑫

㉟ ● Catterick

Church
Fenton ● Leconfield ○

㉔

No. 12 GROUP ● Kirton-in-Lindsey

○ Kingway

Watnall 12 GP. HQ
□ ㉔ ● Digby

○ Tern Hill

BELFAST

● Wittering

Coltishall ○

㉔

⑫ ㉔ ㉔

▲ Coventry

Duxford ●

㉔

No. 10 GROUP
㉔ ㊱ ㉔ ● Debden ○ Martelsham

⑫ ○ Pembrey

Bristol ● ○ Colerne
Stanmore H.Q.F.C. A.A.C. □
Uxbridge 11 GP. H.Q. □ ○ Northolt
Hendon
North Weald ●
Stapleford
Hornchurch ● ㊱ — Gravesend
Rochford ○
□ **BOX 10 GP. H.Q.**
Middle ○ Croydon Eastchurch
Wallop ● Kenley ○ ● ○ Manston
Biggin ○
Boscombe Down ● Hill ● West Malling ○ Dover

㊱ ㊱ ○ Hawkinge
○ Lympne

㉟

⑫ ● Westhampnett
Exeter ○ Warmwell ○ Ford (M)
Lee-on-Solent (M) ○ Portsmouth
Thorney Island ○ **No. 11 GROUP** ○ Detling
Gosport
Tangmere

Roborough ○

Map 2 Disposition of British Fighter Forces 9 July 1940.

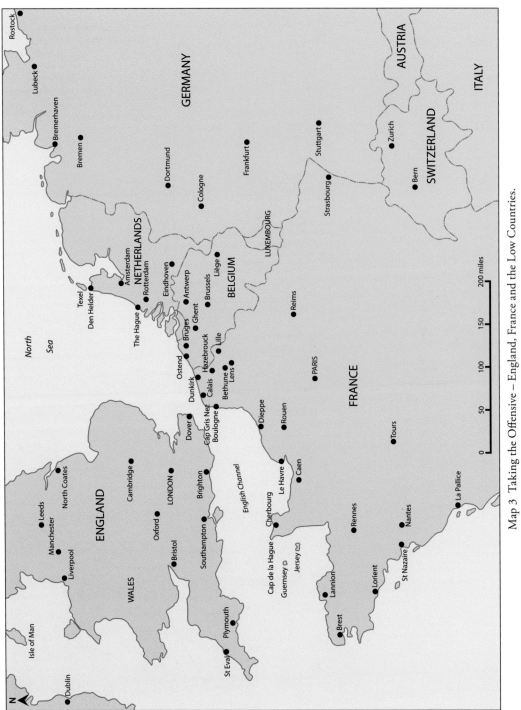

Map 3 Taking the Offensive – England, France and the Low Countries.

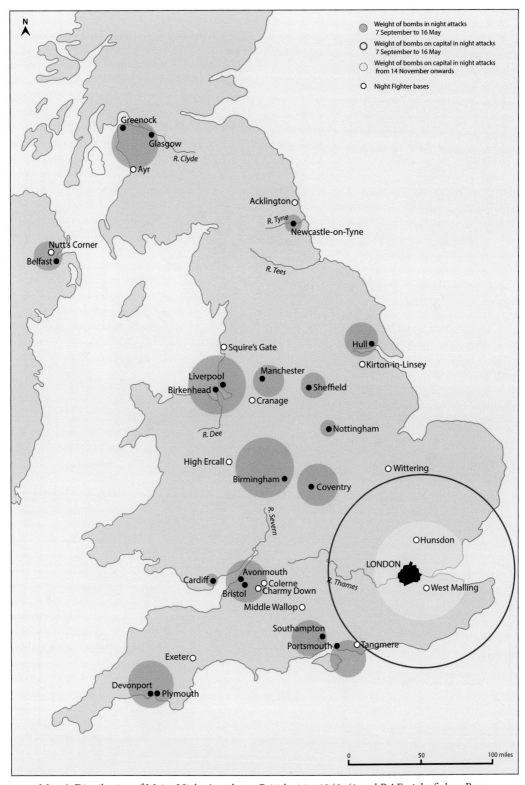

Map 4 Distribution of Major Night Attacks on British cities 1940-41 and RAF night-fighter Bases.

v

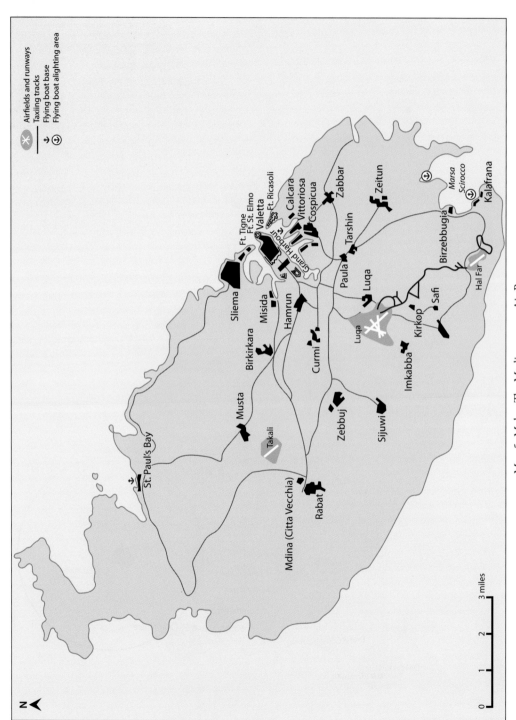

Map 5 Malta: The Mediterranean Air Base.

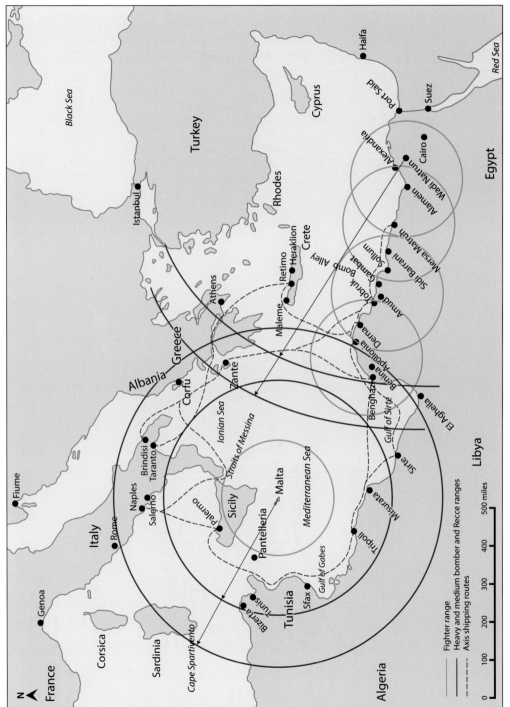

Map 6 The Mediterranean Theatre.

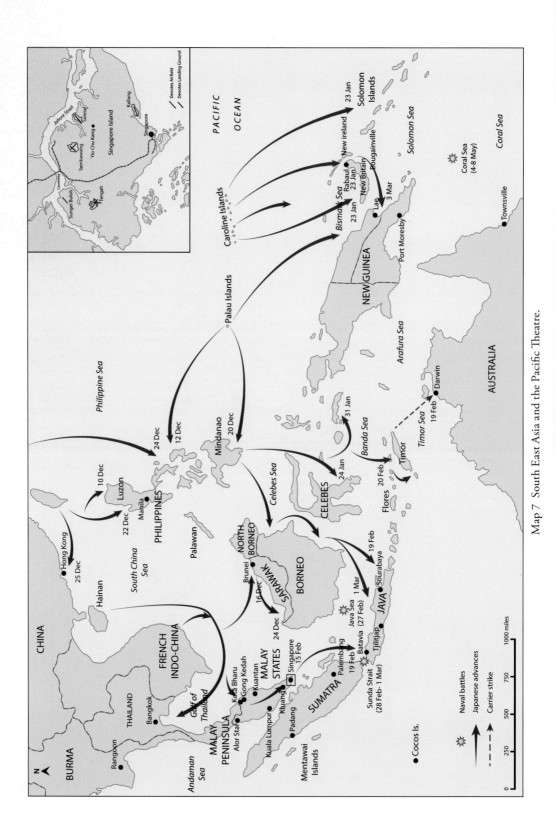

Map 7 South East Asia and the Pacific Theatre.

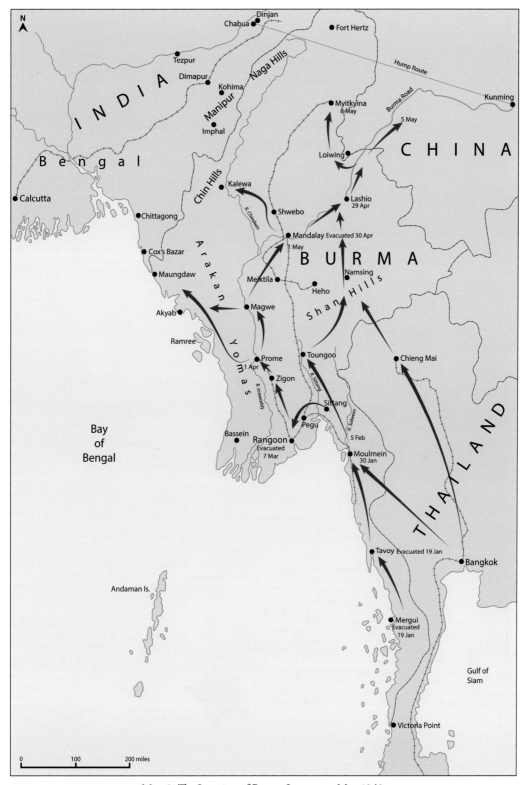

Map 8 The Invasion of Burma January to May 1942.

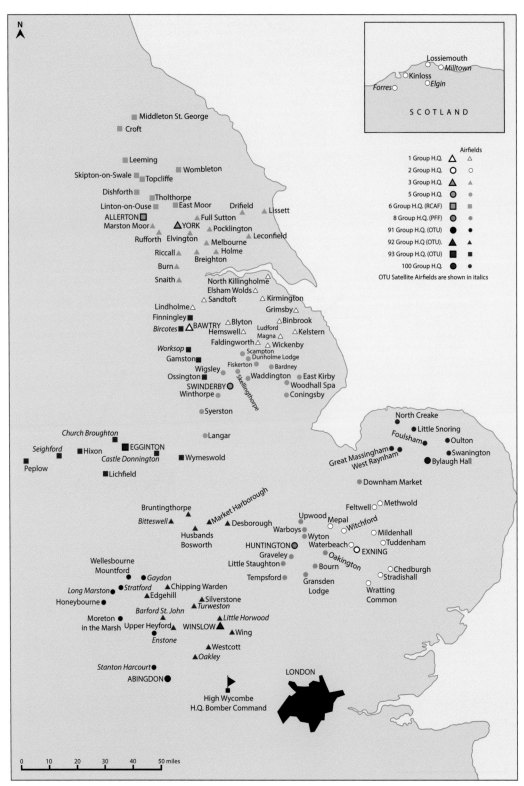

Map 9 Bomber Command Stations and Airfields, 25 September 1944.

x

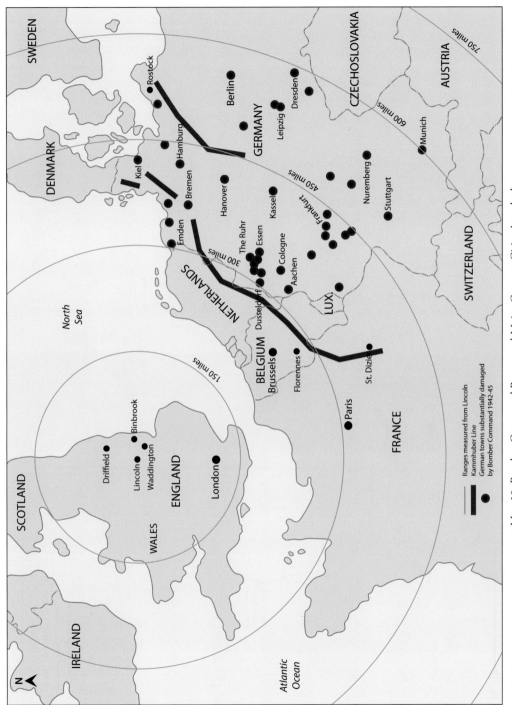

Map 10 Bomber Command Range and Major German Cities Attacked.

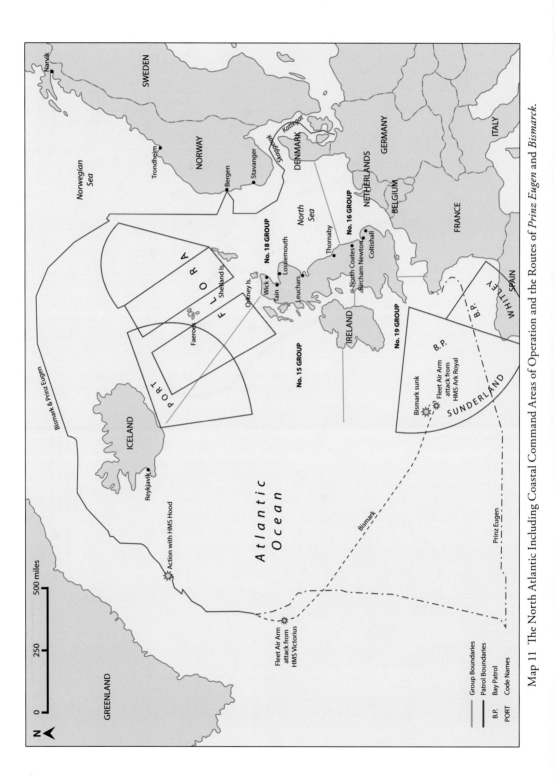

Map 11 The North Atlantic Including Coastal Command Areas of Operation and the Routes of *Prinz Eugen* and *Bismarck*.

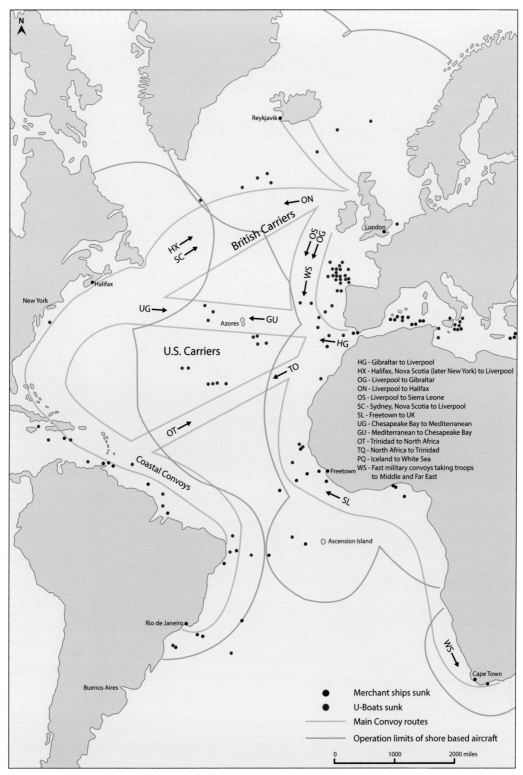

N

Reykjavik

British Carriers

ON

OS
OG

WS

London

HX
SC

Halifax

New York

UG

Azores

GU

U.S. Carriers

HG

TO

OT

Coastal Convoys

Freetown

SL

Ascension Island

HG - Gibraltar to Liverpool
HX - Halifax, Nova Scotia (later New York) to Liverpool
OG - Liverpool to Gibraltar
ON - Liverpool to Halifax
OS - Liverpool to Sierra Leone
SC - Sydney, Nova Scotia to Liverpool
SL - Freetown to UK
UG - Chesapeake Bay to Mediterranean
GU - Mediterranean to Chesapeake Bay
OT - Trinidad to North Africa
TQ - North Africa to Trinidad
PQ - Iceland to White Sea
WS - Fast military convoys taking troops
      to Middle and Far East

Rio de Janeiro

WS

Cape Town

Buenos Aires

● Merchant ships sunk
● U-Boats sunk
── Main Convoy routes
── Operation limits of shore based aircraft

0   1000   2000 miles

Map 12a Main Atlantic Convoy Routes and Aircraft Coverage, June to August 1943.

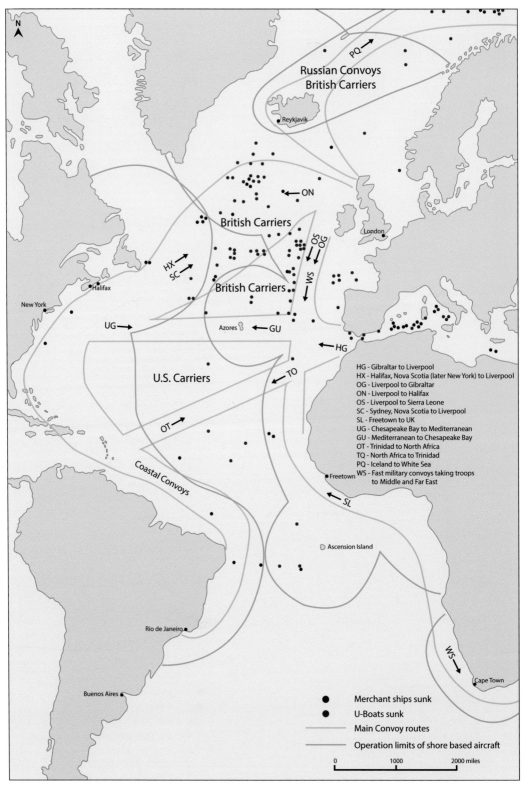

N

PQ

Russian Convoys
British Carriers

Reykjavik

ON

British Carriers

OS
OG

London

HX
SC

Halifax

British Carriers

WS

New York

UG

Azores
GU

HG

U.S. Carriers

TO

HG - Gibraltar to Liverpool
HX - Halifax, Nova Scotia (later New York) to Liverpool
OG - Liverpool to Gibraltar
ON - Liverpool to Halifax
OS - Liverpool to Sierra Leone
SC - Sydney, Nova Scotia to Liverpool
SL - Freetown to UK
UG - Chesapeake Bay to Mediterranean
GU - Mediterranean to Chesapeake Bay
OT - Trinidad to North Africa
TQ - North Africa to Trinidad
PQ - Iceland to White Sea
WS - Fast military convoys taking troops
      to Middle and Far East

OT

Coastal Convoys

Freetown

SL

Ascension Island

Rio de Janeiro

WS

Cape Town

Buenos Aires

● Merchant ships sunk
● U-Boats sunk
── Main Convoy routes
── Operation limits of shore based aircraft

0   1000   2000 miles

Map 12b Main Atlantic Convoy Routes and Aircraft Coverage, September 1943 to April 1944.

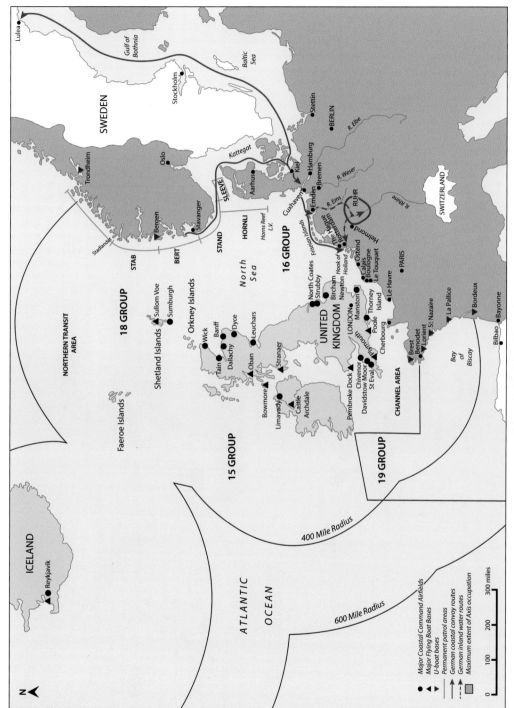

Map 13 Maritime Operations.

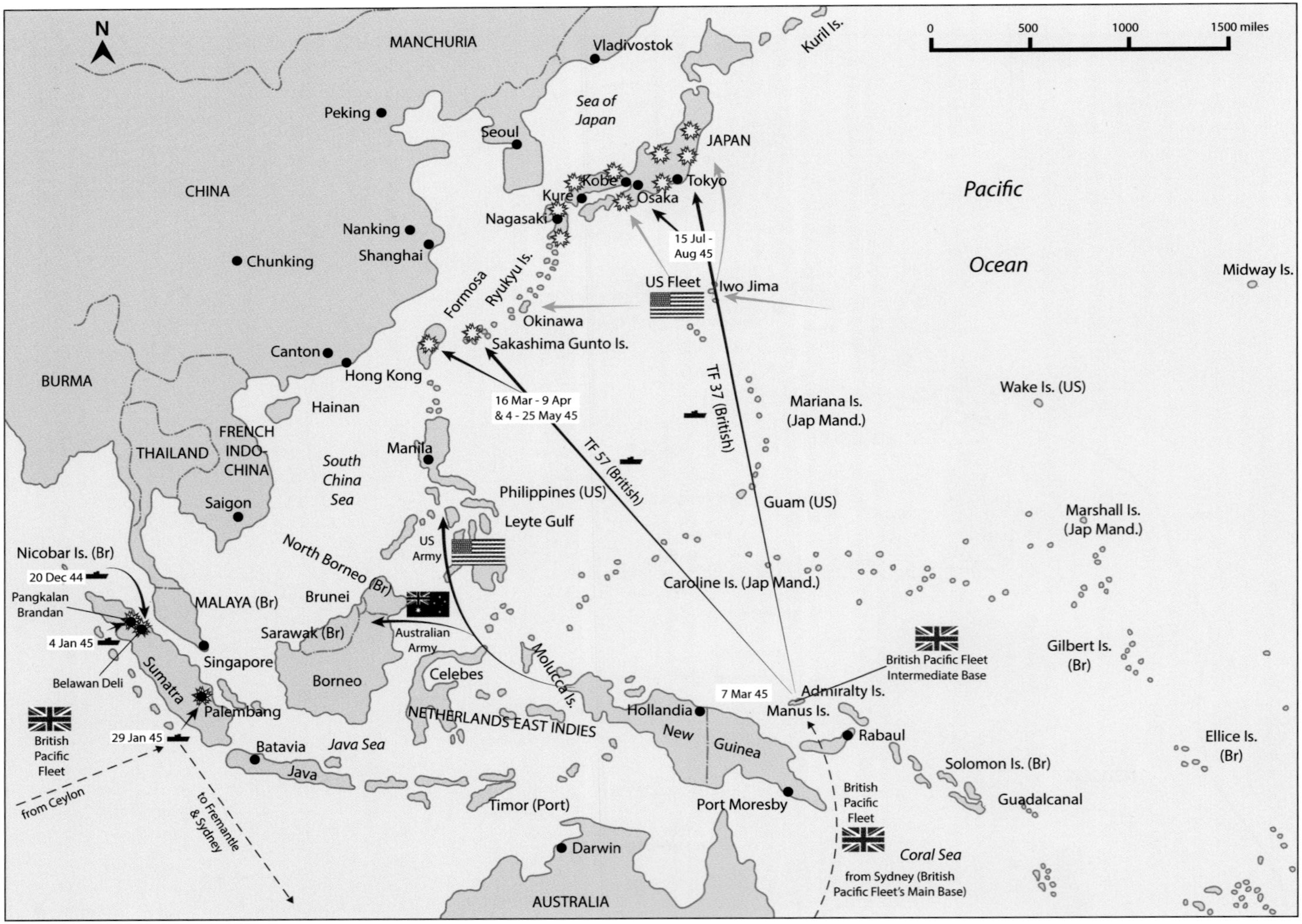

Map 14 The Pacific Theatre.

I liked it very much. H2S gave you a bearing and a direction but the special radar maps that were prepared for us showed the outline of the various towns and the coastlines that we could expect to see. On the coastline, it did not differentiate between high and low tide which meant that, at low tide, the shape of a headland could be completely changed. As far as the shape of towns was concerned, it did not really help at all. All that really mattered was the relative size of the town. What you had to do was associate the bigger blobs with the smaller ones and try and fix up a pattern as you saw it on the radar screen, you could often get a fix short of the Ruhr on towns 10 or 15 miles away and by means of triangulation you could establish pretty exactly where you were.[18]

Navigation of the aircraft, though primarily the responsibility of the navigator was nonetheless an activity that involved the whole crew. Eric Cropper describes the navigator's duties on a typical mission and also how he depended on others for important information:

As the airfield fell away below us there would be many aircraft visible in the air above and around us. Using the Gee lattice we would navigate around a small triangular pattern close to Elsham until the precisely prescribed time came to set course. Climbing steadily as the light failed, we would cross the coast near Cromer or Orford Ness if we were bound for Germany, and soon everybody would be on oxygen, with the masks clamped tight to our faces. There would be little conversation on the intercom – alterations of course or height, perhaps a short warning from a gunner if another aircraft came close, and the occasional check from Al [the pilot] to see that everybody was functioning and alert.

Soon we would run out of the navigational cover of Gee as the enemy jamming took effect, reducing the ratio of signal to noise until the transmitter pulses on the cathode-ray tube gradually became lost in the 'grass'. Mickey would be taking H2S fixes, and we usually got an accurate one as we crossed the Dutch or French coast. The navigation compartment was a little world on its own, with my attention wholly concentrated on plotting symbols on the chart, logging the multiplicity of readings and working out wind velocities for the next course, while constantly checking our progress against the briefed time.

As we crossed the enemy coast, those who could see out increased their alertness, and the gunners would keep their turrets slowly moving to cover their full range of vision. As we came closer to the target, Mickey would relinquish the H2S to me and struggle down under Ken's legs to the bomb aimers position in the nose, setting up the Mark XIV bombsight and check-ing on his bombing controls.

Occasionally Willy would pass me a list of wind velocities he had received in a Group broadcast. More experienced members of the bomber force, flying at the head of the main stream, would send their found winds by W/T back to Group, who would re-transmit them, adjusted by Met officer if necessary for the benefit of the force as a whole. If my navigation was going well I tended to ignore them, but sometimes – if we had had no fix for some time – they would come in useful.

Al, Ken and Mickey up front would now be looking out for target markers, and if I had done my job properly they would be dead ahead at the appointed time (not invariably the case) ... I had to record airspeed, course, height and precise time at 'bombs gone', to take a fix if possible, and be ready to give Al the new course out of the target area, much to everyone's relief.[19]

18   IWM Sound Archives, Catalogue No. 10743: Thomas Tredwell interview.
19   Eric Cropper, *Back Bearings – A Navigator's Tale 1942 to 1974* (Barnsley: Pen and Sword, 2010), p. 30.

Flying Officer R.W. Stewart, a wireless operator on board an Avro Lancaster B.I of 57 Squadron based at Scampton, Lincolnshire, speaking to the pilot from his position in front of the Marconi TR 1154/55 transmitter/receiver set. (Crown Copyright – Air Historical Branch)

The pilot would be flying the Lancaster at an operational ceiling of up to 20,000 feet. No attempt was made at formation flying, instead the bombers flew in a gaggle up to three miles wide and five miles long, converging at the aiming point where the risk of collision inevitably increased. In the later daylight raids over France, after D-Day, there was sometimes a sense of embarrassment about how untidy the British bomber formations looked, certainly when compared to the highly disciplined American formations. However, the Americans had spent much time in perfecting formation flying designed for mutual supporting daylight defence and it was rightly decided as unnecessary for the British to devote any time to the practise, now that daylight air superiority had been achieved.

Pathfinder Leader Donald Bennett dismissed the pilots unfairly as mere chauffeurs for the navigators and bomb aimers.[20] That is an over-statement, for the pilot would be critical in avoiding collisions, night-fighters and if his aircraft were to be damaged, in ensuring it returned to base safely. The latter would require the highest standards of airmanship. The pilot was always the captain, more usually called 'Skipper', of the aircraft, even if he was just a junior sergeant and outranked by the navigator, flight engineer, bomb aimer or any other crew member. The pilot would check frequently over the intercom that all members of the crew were attending to their duties and it would be up to him to decide whether a fault with the aircraft, or any damage sustained, was sufficient to cause them to abandon the mission and be catergorised as an 'early return'. Although

---

20 Leo McKinstry, *Lancaster*, p. 157.

The pilot of an Avro Lancaster of 103 Squadron based at Elsham Wolds, Lincolnshire, wearing his oxygen mask while flying the aircraft at high altitude. (Crown Copyright – Air Historical Branch)

he might ask others in the crew for advice, some might even have offered it unsolicited, it was the pilot who was answerable to the squadron commander on return to base.

The captain's responsibility for the crew extended to being the last man to bail out of a damaged aircraft, often having to hold it steady as the other six members of the crew extracted themselves as fast as they could. Many pilots would go down with their machines to save their crew members' lives. This was a lot to ask of pilots who would often arrive at their bomber squadrons with little more than 200 hours flying experience. Efforts were made to ensure pilots would at least get to fly as a passenger with an experienced crew, once or twice, before they took their own aircraft on actual operations (a practice usually referred to as being a 'second dickey'). Despite these efforts, it was still the case that the most likely period for a bomber crew to be shot down was in their first five missions.[21]

Sergeant Russell Margerison was one of many Lancaster crew members who owed their lives to their pilot's devotion and skill. He recalls his aircraft being hit during a raid on Duisburg on 21 May 1944:

> We had turned early onto the target and this put us ahead of the bomber stream and we were on our return home at 23,000 feet. We had gone through a lot of heavy flak, then it was quiet.

---

21   Kevin Wilson, *Men of Air* (London: Wiedenfeld and Nicholson, 2007), p. 97.

The pilot had just been told by the navigator it was half an hour to the coast when a stream of tracer came from our port side up. I heard the sound of heavy cannon and it was pouring straight through. It was a pitch-black night and it was obvious a fighter had been vectored onto us. He must have seen us at the last second, nearly crashing into us and had opened fire and broken away. The two port engines were on fire and we were in a tremendous dive, the centrifugal force meant you couldn't move. Someone was shouting, 'Pull the bugger out.'

From my mid-upper turret I could see strips of metal peeling off the tailplane and careering away exposing the framework. The pilot and engineer did manage to level the aircraft out enough for five of us to bale out. When I climbed down from my turret and leaned against the side of the fuselage it was like a blow torch inside. I couldn't see through the flames to the front at all. I never put my chute in its stowage. I used to drop it on the floor below my turret and after a trip it was somewhere at the back of the aircraft. On this occasion it was exactly where I left it and as I picked it up, flames were licking around it. The rear gunner had opened the back door and gone, but I couldn't clip my chute on. I leaned against the fuselage and thought, 'You've had it, this is it'; but then I roused myself and had one last go and found the clips. I got to the back door, knelt down and was sucked out by the slipstream. I pulled the ripcord, then as I hung beneath the chute I heard the German fighter coming closer and I thought he was going to hit me, but he flew away. I think he was just having a look at the Lancaster. I must have been suffering from lack of oxygen because I was convinced I was going up instead of down. I watched the aircraft curl round as it went down and crashed.

Neither the pilot nor the engineer got out. The wireless operator, who was one of the three to go through the front hatch, told me later he had seen the two of them with their arms around the control column pulling as hard as they could to keep the Lanc reasonably straight to enable everybody else to get out.[22]

Though the Lancaster was less likely to get shot down than the Halifax, the chances of survival were much worse in a Lancaster, partly because of its huge bombload but also as a result of its badly located and smaller escape hatches. Only 19.2 percent of Lancaster aircrew survived being shot down during the Berlin air raids of 1943/44, whereas that figure rose to 35 percent in the Halifax.[23]

The routes the pilots flew were planned by the Pathfinder Force and were designed to avoid concentrations of flak near the big cities, as well as the night-fighter airfields and the beacons they orbited around. The routes selected would try and deceive the Germans as to the actual target of the attack, though this was hard to achieve if the object was to saturate a city like Berlin with a close sequence of raids. The Pathfinders' Light Night Strike Force Mosquitoes were often used to deceive the enemy by attacking an alternative target and the main bomber force routes would need to be coordinated with them.[24] Long, predictable and straight routes were never a good idea and there was usually an attempt to turn once or twice to keep the enemy off the bomber stream's track. The planners had to be careful in this regard, for sharp dog-legs risked the chance of collision, Arthur Doubleday describes the dangers:

There was a case, I think this was on Leipzig where we had to climb, had to go out low across the North Sea then turn north and climb quickly, which I didn't think was a very good operational tactic. It had a 90 degree bend in it and that meant that some of the aircraft still

22   Kevin Wilson, *Men of Air*, pp. 269-70.
23   Martin Middlebrook, *The Berlin Raids* (London: Penguin, 1980), p. 377.
24   Donald Bennett, *Pathfinder*, p. 172.

going on would cut across the path of the others turning north, and my gunners reported seven flashes over that area of the sea before we crossed in at Texel and I think seven flashes was 14 aircraft.

Providing you didn't have an abrupt angle in the course, your risk [of collision] wasn't very high except when compressing into the target itself. But my tactic was to search the sky in a figure eight and if the exhaust stacks and there's four on a Lancaster, if that line of exhaust stacks pointed below the horizontal to me, I just gently moved up, went above it. If they pointed above, I just pressed the stick down a little bit and went underneath them. I went through this sort of manoeuvre all the time and had the gunners keeping their eyes out to say, Lanc or Halli or something, just above, or just on the side.[25]

Gunners were key to keeping a lookout as Ron Smith also remembers:

The weather had deteriorated – dense cloud without any sign of a break. I constantly rotated the turret ever searching for that darker patch that might show up against the blackness around to indicate an enemy fighter. It was a relief when the aircraft entered cloud for a short time, its protecting folds hiding us from prying eyes. As we came clear, I had a paralysing sensation that we were not alone. Looking around frantically, I could not see anything until I glanced upward through the Perspex top of the turret and there, almost on top of us, was the massive outline of another Lancaster completely overshadowing us. As I stared hypnotised, tiny rivulets of moisture formed moving patterns on the curve of the Perspex as the slip-stream compressed the droplets picked up in the cloud. I could see flames from the exhausts streaming back under the colossus above, as with a dry throat I switched on my microphone and croaked a warning to the skipper. His reaction was instantaneous: we dived steeply lifting me almost to a standing position although I was held by my flying boots firmly entrenched below the gun mountings. The huge shadow appeared to shoot upwards and away.[26]

Though the aircraft might hope to pass around some of the German defences, they learned not to expect a clean passage, certainly by the spring of 1943 the Germans had developed a well-structured defensive system. The first line of which was the signals intercept operation run by the *Luftwaffe's Nachrichtentruppe* or Signal Service. This would be listening for any relevant transmission and emphasised the necessity for bombers to maintain radio silence, even when taxiing. The Germans might gain an indication that a raid was likely through this source, but not much more and certainly not the actual target. The next layer of warning was the *Freya* long range radars, these could pick the bombers up as they climbed to altitude, sometimes while the aircraft were still over England. The two German radar stations at Texel and Ostend were most effective. The *Freya* would give early warning of direction and height which would be useful for those manning the next line of German defence, the *Kammhuber* Line, named after the German general in charge of the night-fighter force Josef Kammhuber. Kammhuber had set up a series of boxes (known as *Raum*) which would contain both night fighters and two narrow-beam high definition *Würzburg* radars. These were set up in a double line of boxes along the coast, with a further group of boxes around Berlin, all of which were given animal or marine code names such as Viper, Whale, Lobster, Toad etc.

The *Würzburg* radars were able to pick up a bomber 30 or so miles away, at which point the German night-fighter, under the control of a *Jagerleitoffizier* (JLO) or fighter control officer, would then be vectored towards its target. The JLOs were mainly signals officers, with a few searchlight

---

25   AWM SO0546: Sound archive interview with Arthur Doubleday.
26   Ron Smith, *Rear Gunner Pathfinders*, p. 24.

Handley Page Halifax B.II Series 1A, LW235/EY-E, of 78 Squadron based at Breighton, Yorkshire, in flight on 25 September 1943. The aircraft is fitted with the rectangular tail fins which were introduced to cure rudder-stalling experienced under certain conditions with the original triangular fin. Five days after this photograph was taken, LW263 was lost while returning from a raid on Bochum, when the crew were unable to locate their position over Lincolnshire. The aircraft stalled when the pilot was forced to pull up sharply to avoid colliding with a factory chimney and crashed into a wooded area on the Foxhill Road near Scunthorpe. None of the crew survived. (Crown Copyright – Air Historical Branch)

commanders and pilots amongst them. They were critical in guiding the night-fighter sufficiently close to the bomber for its own *Lichtenstein* AI radar set to pick up the target.

During a typical raid, the JLO would have about 30-40 bombers on his radar screen at any one time, as the bomber stream passed through. He would also have the position of the German night-fighter in his box. Having selected a particular bomber as a target he would concentrate one radar on that aircraft and the second on his own night-fighter. The two plots were projected onto a glass table called the Seeburg, the bomber as a red dot and the German fighter as a blue one. The JLO would then broadcast frequent directions to the fighter, which would try to close-in and destroy the bomber, before it flew out of the box and out of range. While the Germans had developed the process into a slick drill, this form of night-fighting was extraordinarily inefficient for two reasons. First, the bomber-stream would pass through only 3 or 4 boxes in the *Kammhuber* Line, the rest would remain inactive which included all the night-fighters orbiting within them. Secondly, the system could only vector one night-fighter at a time against an individual bomber, meanwhile all the other night-fighters in the box were dormant, despite many bombers flying through the box on their way to German cities. It was a little more effective on the return journey, when the bomber stream was wider and contained more stragglers, but still hardly efficient. This system of defence was abruptly changed when the Germans encountered 'Window' for the first time, during the RAF's raid on Hamburg in July 1943.[27]

---

27   Martin Middlebrook, *The Battle of Hamburg* (London: Penguin, 1984), pp. 57-9.

Window was a simple technology that consisted of paper strips, 27cm long by 2cm wide and covered with a thin aluminium foil coat, these were gathered together in bundles of 2,200. The aluminium strips had been designed to simulate a precise wavelength and confuse all the German radars with a mass of false signatures, from which it would be impossible to discern individual bombers. As well as masking aircraft within the bomber stream, it could also be dropped by a few aircraft and used to fake a large bomber formation as part of a deception plan. Window was first used during a raid on Hamburg in the summer of 1943, a decision that was taken at the highest level, based on fears that the Germans might copy it and use it in their own bomber raids against Britain. Harris had been pressing for its use for some time, but it was only the decline of the German bomber fleet to negligible proportions that convinced British leaders it could be used. Ironically the Germans had understood the technology for some time, indeed they had developed their own version of Window, called *Duppel*. So alarmed was Goering when he discovered its capabilities that he forbade any talk of *Duppel* and even the development of any countermeasure against it.

When first used, Window was often dropped out of the flare chute, sometimes coating the mid-upper gunner's turret with black ink from the underside of the strips. As its use became more established, a special chute was developed next to the bomb aimer, though this still remained an unpopular and tiring task. The result the first time Window was used was severe confusion amongst the German night-fighters. Yet over the coming weeks and months the Germans quickly adapted to this latest technological innovation by the British. They learnt how to discern the faster moving bombers within the slower clutter of Window, as well as adapting their overall operational technique to a more fluid and flexible model. By March 1944, this had become so effective, that the RAF's night-time bomber offensive against targets deep within Germany would begin to become almost prohibitively expensive.

As the British bombers began to approach their aiming point in the German city, the flak inevitably became more intense. They might have encountered earlier belts along the Dutch or German coast, or if they had inadvertently strayed off course and overflown a city by accident. The flak over Berlin was perhaps the most dangerous that the British bomber pilots faced, stretching over an area 40 miles wide. It originally consisted of an inner and outer-belt, but this was later adapted to meet the bomber stream tactics and had all guns firing in co-ordinated box-barrages, though both early and late bombers, as well as those caught in searchlights, would also be engaged individually. The centrepieces of the Berlin flak were the eight large flak towers that contained twenty-four 128mm guns. These could fire a salvo every 90 seconds to 48,000 feet and the eight shells, when detonated in its pre-planned pattern, had a lethal radius of 250 yards. Similar flak towers were constructed in Hamburg and Vienna.[28] The flak was often used in conjunction with radar-guided searchlights, these Master-Lights were 200cm in diameter and had a distinctive blue light. Flak guns of many different calibres would be co-located with this searchlight and when it identified an aircraft many other searchlights would also swing around and concentrate on it. The flak and searchlight defences over Berlin, the Ruhr and Munich were particularly notorious. Australian pilot Lionel Rackley was unfortunate enough to be picked up by a searchlight and recounts his experience:

> I was in the first wave and I knew I was less than a half a minute early and I tried to wash some of that speed off, I could have dog-legged out but I was worried about getting out and getting back into the stream and collision and so forth as everybody would be fairly well on track … so I pressed on … but must have been one of the earliest ones because all of a sudden

---

28   Martin Middlebrook, *The Berlin Raids* (London: Penguin, 1988), p. 26.

we hit the outer defences of Munich. Now Munich after the Ruhr and Berlin was the most heavily defended target there was and the searchlight belt was a fair way out and so without any warning, boom! A big blue searchlight got me and as soon as the blue searchlight got me I was coned in and just handed on across the city. I was handed on cone to cone to cone and of course all they do is just sit there and fire at the middle of the cone.

We were coned for 12 minutes across Munich and we had anti-aircraft fired at us all the time and no matter what I did to the aircraft I could not get out of the cone; I just could not escape the cone until I got out the other side of the city. After 12 minutes of that sort of flying you are rather weary and on the way through we lost the intercom at one stage. The wireless operator took off his parachute harness and crawled in underneath his set and did the repair that was necessary, both turrets were put out of action, the engineer's instrument panel was shattered, and he had no petrol gauges or anything else. The only engine instruments we had were on the pilot's cockpit display. At one stage I saw petrol pouring out of one of the starboard wing tanks, so I knew we had lost petrol. We lost the port outer engine on the way through and we were down to 10,000 feet, we'd lost 6,000 feet on the way through, we dropped our bombs … we did not aim them, but we were in the middle of the city, so we just let them go and got out …

By then the force had gone through and they were to have turned west and gone round the northern side of the city and gone home. But I knew that if I were to follow them with one engine gone and another about to go I would have no chance of catching them and I would just lose time all the way back. so I would be further and further behind them and I knew then that the German fighters would pick me off as a straggler.[29]

Rackley and his crew took the unusual decision to turn south and crossed the Alps, heading across Italy and landing at recently-liberated Sardinia on just two engines. An impressive achievement in both airmanship and engineering terms, for by the time they landed the two surviving Merlin engines had been on maximum revolutions, for well over the recommended time.

---

29   AWM 016231: Lionel Rackley, Sound Archives.

13

'The King's Thunderbolts are Righteous'[1]
A Bomber Command Mission – The Strike and Return Leg

Once over the target city, the Lancaster's bomb aimer would try to identify the exact aiming point. By 1943 he was helped by the Pathfinder crews who had recently come into possession of Oboe. This system was based on two ground stations. The first (occasionally referred to as the 'mouse') directed a radio pulse over the centre of the target. Along this the aircraft travelled hearing a continuous Oboe-sounding note in his headphones. If he deviated off the course, to either port or starboard a series of dots and dashes would inform him of his error, concurrently the set in his aircraft would re-broadcast the Oboe signal back to the second ground station (known as the 'cat') which, by measuring the time taken to receive this, could make periodic calculations of the aircraft's progress. When the aircraft approached the centre of the target, the 'cat' ground station would broadcast the letters ABCD, then a series of dashes, followed by a series of dots. When the dots ceased, the bomb-aimer released the target markers. The accuracy of the equipment was very high, normally placing the aircraft's markers within a couple of hundred yards of the target in all weathers. Oboe was an excellent system, but its range was limited to no further than the Ruhr and the system could only track two aircraft at a time over the immediate confines of the target.[2] The improvements in equipment like Oboe and H2S were complemented by dramatic changes in the Target Indicator (TI) pyrotechnics available to the Pathfinders. This had been a particular focus for Bennett as he explains.

> I was in contact with the various pyrotechnic experts made available to me by the Armament Branch, and we got all sorts of fireworks underway. Flares were made available in bigger numbers, and development was immediately begun on hooded flares, which had a device in the form of an umbrella above them which helped prevent the glareback in the eyes of the bomb aimer who was trying to see the ground. The advent of the barometer fuse for opening these and other devices was speeded up, particularly at the request of the Pathfinders. Some high-powered candles were produced, which we named Target Indicators. These were my special requirements and we used them extensively for the rest of the war. They were made in all colours and varieties, plain, red, green, yellow, white and each of these colours as a basic colour with ejecting stars of the same or different colours. Many combinations were,

---

1   The 44th Squadron Motto. This bombing squadron was initially equipped with Hampdens before being the first unit to convert to Lancasters on 3 March 1942.

2   Denis Richards and Hilary Saunders, *Royal Air Force 1939-45, Volume II*, p. 155.

therefore, available for us to use as and when we chose, and the enemy could not copy them until he discovered what the colour of the night might be …

These British TIs were far brighter than anything produced by the enemy, which was helpful as the Germans went to great lengths to produce dummy towns, fires and searchlights, all of which could look pretty convincing. They even went so far as putting false radar signatures on the lakes near big cities such as Berlin, to confuse the bombers' H2S. But the German dummy TIs consistently lacked the intensity of the British originals and were relatively easy for experienced crews to spot and discount. Bennett continues on the development of sky-marking TIs:

> In addition to these target indicators for ground use, we prepared something which was ridiculed and laughed at by a good many people. These were sky markers and consisted of parachute flares of various colours throwing out stars (or not as the case may be) so that we could mark a spot in the sky for a limited period, usually three to five minutes. I had done a few calculations on the use of such a method for blind bombing through thick cloud when it was impossible to see the glow of Target Indicators because of the density and/or depth of the cloud. These rough calculations seemed to me to indicate that the results to be achieved by such an apparently difficult method would probably prove just as effective as the slap-dash visual bombing that I had so often seen in the past. Roughly speaking, the idea was that the sky markers would be put down by a marker aircraft using Oboe or H2S, in a position so that after it had burned half its time it had drifted, in accordance with the wind found by the navigator to the correct point through the line of sight of a bomber on to the aiming point.[3]

The Target Indicators allowed the Pathfinders to develop highly sophisticated methods of target marking, the first and arguably simplest of which, was the visual method. This would involve groups of 'finders' with some 'supporters'. The finders were drawn from the best crews amongst the Pathfinders and would fly in over the targets at about zero minus five minutes, dropping illuminating flares. Once the correct aiming point had been identified, further flares would be dropped on it. As soon as this had happened the 'supporters' would come in consisting of first 'Illuminators', who would put a whole stick of illuminating parachute flares across the aiming point as identified by the 'finders'. Next would come the 'primary markers', these were highly-skilled bomb aimers who, having identified the aiming point visually in the excellent light of the flares, dropped a mass of TIs on that spot. As the main bomber force arrived, the 'backer-ups' would put further TIs on the aiming point, ensuring that the main bomber force had a mark at which to aim throughout the duration of the attack.[4]

Cloud cover often meant that the aiming point could not be identified visually. In that instance Oboe/H2S would have to be used to identify the target/aiming point and TIs dropped 'blind' on to the ground which would shine through the cloud. The final method of 'sky marking' was used when the cloud was very thick and the TIs on the ground would not be visible, it involved TIs set to go off between 3,000 and 10,000 feet which would drift under parachutes on the wind.

Separate code names were given to these different types of marking methods; visual ground marking was known as 'Newhaven', ground marking using H2S was known as 'Parramatta' and sky marking as 'Wanganui'.[5] These names originated from Bennett's staff's hometowns, including

3   Donald Bennett, *Pathfinder*, pp. 160, 166.
4   Donald Bennett, *Pathfinder*, p. 173.
5   Donald Bennett, *Pathfinder*, p. 173.

A Lancaster B.III of 619 Squadron from RAF Coningsby, 14 February 1944. (Crown Copyright – Air Historical Branch)

his WAAF clerk, Corporal Ralph who came from Newhaven. They could all be preceded by the term 'Musical' if aircraft using Oboe were part of the plan.

British target marking methods would continue to improve throughout the war. Some as a result of the Pathfinder Force, but others from the innovations and exploits of 5 Group's 617 Squadron. These included the idea of a Master Bomber, first employed by Wing Commander Guy Gibson VC on Operation CHASTISE, the Dams Raid, as well as offset and low-level target marking. Walter Thompson was a Pathfinder pilot in 83 Squadron, a unit that was moved back to 5 Group after the Battle of Berlin in 1943/44. He describes some of the innovations introduced into Bomber Command operations:

> 5 Group lost no time in perfecting independent methods of attack. Instead of the Lancaster illuminators, or blind markers, of 83 and 97 Squadrons dropping flares while all flying on the same heading, they were split into two forces. Flare Force One, for example, at 11 minutes before zero hour might drop their 5,000 candlepower illuminator flares while flying on, say, a southerly heading. Flare Force Two might then approach the target at nine minutes before zero hour on a heading at right angles to that of Flare Force One, say on an easterly heading. In this way the risk of overshooting or undershooting the target was minimised because the visual markers, who were coming in behind the flare forces, could see the intersection of the two lines of illuminators. With the target area thus illuminated the Mosquito visual markers could search the area and when one of them thought he had found the aiming point he would yell 'Tally Ho' and drop a red or a green flare on it. The target having been visually marked at four or five minutes before zero hour the marker leader could assess the marker accuracy and, if satisfied, call in the main force to bomb on the red or green. 5 Group also, when the weather permitted applied the techniques of offset bombing in cases where the aiming point had been obscured by smoke, cloud or smokescreens. This method, pioneered by the Americans, of selecting a point which could be seen a short distance from the aiming point, allowed for this distance and thus the attackers were able to strike the obscured aiming point.[6]

---

6   Walter Thompson, *Lancaster to Berlin*, p. 196.

A Handley Page Halifax is silhouetted against target indicators descending over the target during the bombing of a flying-bomb storage dump at Biennais, France, at 3:38 a.m. on 6 July 1944. (Crown Copyright – Air Historical Branch)

These technical and operational improvements all helped Bomber Command to transform itself into a more precise and effective instrument that could find its targets and concentrate the bombs onto it for maximum destructive impact.

The role of Master Bomber was an undoubted improvement in not only directing aircrew on to the right target, but also in ensuring the bomber stream passed swiftly over the target, which was of course a vital aspect of their survivability. As part of the preparatory support to Operation OVERLORD Bomber Command targeted Mailly-le-Camp, a German armoured garrison east of Paris, on the night of 3/4 May 1944. During the raid precious time was wasted in marking aiming points, the Master Bomber halting the bombers' arrival by placing them in an orbit north of the target. This delay allowed German night-fighters to enter the bomber stream, causing a loss of 42 out of 362 bombers or 11.6 percent of the force committed. Prior to the raid on Mailly-le-Camp Bomber Command had been considering recategorising the apparently short and easy trips to France so that they counted as just 1/3 a mission. The punitive losses at Mailly-le-Camp quickly caused them to revise such a plan.[7]

---

7   Jack Currie, *Battle Under the Moon* (Trowbridge: Airdata, 1995), p. 53.

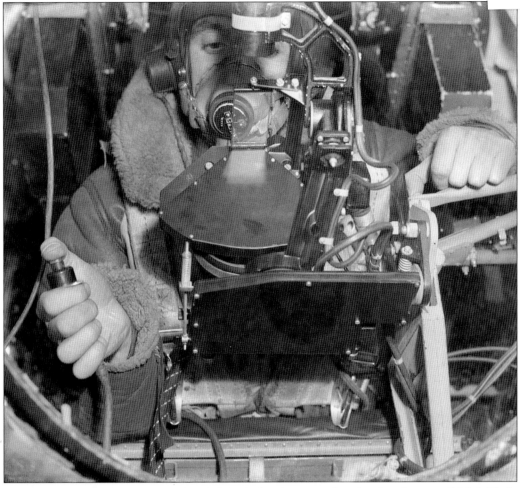

Flight Lieutenant P. Walmsley of Hull, Yorkshire, the bomb-aimer on board an Avro Lancaster B Mark III of No. 619 Squadron RAF, operating a Mark XIV Stabilised Vector Bombsight at his position in the nose of the aircraft, at Coningsby, Lincolnshire. (Crown Copyright – Air Historical Branch)

Once the target was marked by the Pathfinders, the success of the operation lay with the bomb aimer. Earlier in the flight, he might have been helping the navigator on the H2S set, or bundling strips of Window out of the aircraft, but as the target approached he would move past the pilot and engineer into his position at the very front of the aircraft, there he would have his Mark XIV bombsight, F24 camera and, on his right-hand side, a box. On the top of this box were 16 selector switches and a selector arm, which controlled the timing and the order of release of the bombs. This was important in ensuring the aircraft did not suddenly become too nose or tail heavy. Above and to the right of the bomb aimer, was the control for a thermostat to heat the 4,000lb Cookie hook and prevent a hang up, there was another panel below that which controlled the photo flash. The actual bomb release button was on a long lead that the bomb aimer held in his hand whilst lying down and looking through the bomb sight.[8] The bombsight on the Lancaster was a dramatic improvement on its predecessor as Tom Tredwell explained:

---

8   Ron Mayhill, *Bombs on Target*, p. 20.

The original Mark IX bomb sight was frankly a very rudimentary affair, which gave little accuracy and took no account of the different variabilities that were met in bombing. The Mark XIV was a jump into a completely new age. We suddenly, for the first time, had a device which enabled us to look at both the bombsight and ground at the same time. One of the problems with the old bombsight was that if you were looking at the bombsight itself, then you had to adjust when you wanted to look at the ground, which was over 20,000 feet below. With the new type of bombsight this was completely overcome. You actually looked into a solid block of glass, and by means of a light source from over the top of your head, you saw reflected there what appeared to be a sword of red light. The idea was to guide the aircraft onto the target and get the target to slide down, in effect, the shaft of the sword until it met the cross section. And at the cross section you pressed the bomb release and away the bombs went.[9]

Lancaster bomb aimer, Ron Mayhill, describes how the process actually worked during a mission:

The horrifying brightness of the fires and searchlights took my breath away more than the squeeze under the seat without oxygen. A final check of my panels and switches to ensure nothing could go wrong and I leaned over the bombsight to stare through the optically flat and slanting nose panel. I judged I had something over five minutes to concentrate on the awesome spectacle …

Red TIs (Target Indicators) began cascading down into the orange flames. Explosion after explosion rent the orange docks and warehouses, momentarily wiping gaps in the thick smoke. Curving stars soared skywards to burst in black puffs while clusters of searchlights wavered and held some of the sleek, black Lancasters and Halifaxes clearly visible in the smoky glow, yet somehow they all seemed to fly straight through unharmed.

We banked slightly to starboard onto our final bombing run, Dunc calling two minutes to H-Hour, winds unchanged. As the eyes in the nose I undoubtedly had the best view of the target, and it was far more vivid and horrifying than I had expected. Night had become a diffused ruddy day and I could smell the ugly patches of boiling smoke as we rocked through, bomb doors open. A piercing needle of light blinded a plane ahead. More searchlights crossing over to form a cone as the victim dived and squirmed to escape. To port a necklace of red jabs took my attention and I had to force myself to concentrate on the TIs.

'Left, left steady,' and the target moved onto the end of my sights, but the severe buffeting caused the markers to leap alarmingly back and forth as slipstreams from other planes tore us away from our line.

'Right, steady,' I adjusted then re-corrected, 'Left, left, steady.'

'Watch the markers, they're drifting,' warned the Master Bomber who had the unenviable task of circling the inferno, thousands of feet below.

'Wireless Operator to skipper, there's smoke coming from the rear of the fuselage, I'll go back and have a look!'

'No, you go Taffy. Wireless Operator, stay in the dome and keep watching for aircraft coming too close. Mid-upper, do you see smoke?'

'Mid-upper to skipper, there's smoke coming from the rear.'

'Left, left steady.' I was still trying desperately to line up the rocking plane knowing Jake was trying to hold it straight and level and he had a lot on his mind. Somehow in the last few seconds I had to average the surges up and back, side to side and guess the split second

9   IWM Sound Archives, Catalogue Number 10743, Tom Tredwell interview.

the TIs should reach the cross line. The drills flashed through my mind, aware that I mustn't undershoot and that some bomb aimers released too soon causing 'creep-back'.

'Engineer to skipper, the fire's out now. It was mainly smoke from the rear fuse box, I'm on my way back.'

There was too much happening at once too fast. I wished I could call a dummy run and go around again to gain more time for a better approach but made a quick decision against it. For one thing it was hazardous to turn against the bomber stream in the crowded airspace, and it exposed a crew to double the time over the target area.

'Engineer to skipper … '

'Get off the intercom,' I snapped, 'Right, steady.'

We were almost there. The nose bumped up, the target shot off the bombsight, the nose thumped down and the target was through the sights. I was uncertain, hoping the aircraft would settle quickly, knowing we must be there, and I jammed my thumb down on the bomb tit.

'Bombs going,' I called, and I could tell they were going to overshoot, each release causing an upward lurch as the selector arm unwound.

'Jettison bars across,' in case of hang-ups and I double checked through the bomb bay window behind me.

'All gone, skipper, bomb doors closed.'[10]

Ron Mayhill mentions he considered the possibility of doing a dummy run in the above account, though these were an incredibly unpopular option over dangerous targets. Lancaster pilot Jack Currie recalled being guided by a new bomb aimer over Berlin:

'Right … steady, Right … steady. Right … right … dummy run!'

I sensed rather than saw the flight engineer stiffen in horror beside me. I spoke as calmly as I could.

'You don't do dummy runs on Berlin. Let em go.'

'But … '

'Let 'em go.'

I felt Charlie Two lift as the high explosive tumbled out of the bomb bay and my heart lifted with her.'[11]

Once the bombs had been released the pilot would have to hold the aircraft steady, for up to 36 seconds, whilst the mission's photograph was taken. This process started when a 4.5-inch photo-flash, consisting of 20lbs of aluminium powder was released simultaneously with the Lancaster's bombload, this flashed at 200 million candle-power lighting up the target. At the same time a camera in the aircraft automatically took a sequence of photographs. The crews unsurprisingly hated this process, which exposed them to further danger as they flew across the flak-ridden target area, unable to take any form of evasive action. Once the bomb aimer called 'photo taken', the navigator would pass across a new course to the pilot and begin the journey home. Of course, throughout this period there were many other bombers dropping their high explosive and incendiary cargoes over the same area. Accidents were frequent as Flight Sergeant Edgar Ray who flew with 61 Squadron testified:

---

10   Ron Mayhill, *Bombs on Target*, pp. 31-32.
11   Leo McKinstry, *Lancaster*, p. 189.

At 19:55 hours we, in QR-O, commenced our run up to the target aiming point through a barrage of moderate flak. From my position in the nose of the aircraft I could see many Lancasters flying close by releasing their deadly cargo. Moments later I had the target in my bomb sight and pressed the tit to release our load of 11,450 lb HEs. Within seconds disaster struck as I felt our aircraft shudder and then fall away to starboard in an uncontrolled dive. The skipper hauled back on the control column and managed to regain control before calling over the aircraft's intercom for a damage report from all crew positions.

Ken Johnson our mid-upper gunner reported that we had been bombed from above and that a large section of the starboard wing tip was missing. Further investigation revealed that a second bomb had broken off the starboard tail-fin and rudder, while a third, had removed the whole of the rear turret carrying away Jack Foy, our rear gunner.[12]

The falling British bombs would now encounter the final line of German defence, the German civil defence system. In his book *The Battle of Hamburg* Martin Middlebrook makes the astute point that the critical contest was never between the *Luftwaffe*'s active defence either, flak, searchlights, or night-fighters. He argues, that since 90 out of every 100 bombers successfully passed through these defences, the really decisive fight was therefore between each city's civil defence network and the high explosive and incendiary devices that rained upon them. By 1943, when Britain's bomber offensive was properly established, the Germans had established a thorough civil defence system, consisting of the professional fire and police services, backed up by auxiliaries such as those too old for military service and the Hitler Youth. In addition, every significant industrial firm had to provide workers to man mobile pumps either for service in their own factories, or elsewhere and every office, shop and apartment block also had its fire-watchers armed with buckets of sand and water, ready to deal with incendiaries.[13] The Germans made extensive use of their basements for protection as air raid shelters and there were also numerous communal public shelters.

The architectural character of the town itself played an important part in its survival. Medieval Lübeck we have already seen was very combustible, whereas Berlin's wide streets meant that many incendiary bombs burnt themselves out in open ground and that routes for fire-fighters and their engines were rarely blocked by rubble. Berlin was also acknowledged to have had higher quality flats and buildings, which could withstand the bombing better than industrial Hamburg. A German city's civil defences would also ensure that gangs of workers were always on hand to quickly patch up the roofs, windows and doors after a raid. Roof repairs were necessary, so that the small 4lb incendiaries did not lodge in them, but instead clattered down to the streets below. Windows and doors needed repairing to prevent air being sucked in by any fire started within a building, further fuelling the flames. Within blocks of flats, the partitions between attic spaces were also removed, so that any incendiary bombs that had broken through the roof tiles could be more easily accessed and extinguished.[14]

On many occasions, the best efforts of the German civil defence system were overcome by Bomber Command's onslaught, which was scientific in its approach to destruction. The 4,000lb high explosive cookies blasted buildings, providing an environment for the 4lb incendiaries to lodge in roofs and potential fuel for their fire. The larger 30lb incendiaries were also able to smash their way down to the ground floor, so that the building would be burnt bottom up as well as top down. One of the most destructive nights Bomber Command inflicted was the 31 July 1943 raid on Hamburg, known as Operation GOMORRAH. This created the infamous firestorm, a

---

12   Derek Brammer, *Thundering Through the Clear Air*, pp. 86-7.
13   Martin Middlebrook, *The Battle of Hamburg*, p. 86.
14   Martin Middlebrook, *The Berlin Raids* (London: Penguin, 1988), p. 24, Band 143.

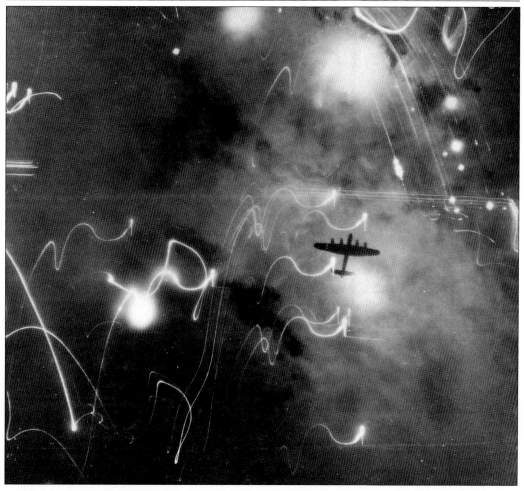

An Avro Lancaster of 1 Group, silhouetted against flares, smoke and explosions during an attack on Hamburg on the night of 30/31 January 1943. (Crown Copyright – Air Historical Branch)

phenomenon previously unknown to mankind. The raid was so destructive, partly because of a long spell of hot, dry July weather, but also because of the impact of the previous raids on the city that had damaged the buildings and overstretched fire fighters. Additionally, not all the fires from previous raids had been extinguished, partly because of the householders' practise of storing coal in their basements, which ultimately fed the fire and made it hard to extinguish.

A total of 787 aircraft were sent to attack Hamburg that night. Their bombing was particularly concentrated, partly because of good work by the Pathfinders, but also by the tactical initiative obtained through the first use of Window.[15] Within 15 minutes of the first bombs dropping, the fires were raging out of control, the flames bursting through the roofs, to turn the buildings into blazing torches. As the fires burned, they sucked in cold, fresh air from the streets outside and this, combined with the heated air from other burning buildings, carried brands, embers and sparks on the wind, spreading the fire further. As the fires joined up the area became one large conflagration, greedily sucking in air, the centre of which is estimated to have reached 800 degrees centigrade.

---

15   Middlebrook, *The Battle of Hamburg*, p. 259.

The surrounding winds also increased, to hurricane strength. The final extent of the firestorm area was approximately one and a half miles, from north to south, and nearly three miles east to west. A total of approximately 45,400 Germans died in what became known as the Battle of Hamburg, 40,000 alone in the firestorm of 31 July 1943.

Few RAF raids caused the same level of destruction as at Hamburg. An example, at the other end of the scale, occurred during a Berlin raid on 31 August 1943. On this night 613 aircraft dropped 1,396 tons of bombs and killed 87 Germans. When that damage is compared to 46 aircraft lost and 225 aircrew casualties the heavy British cost of this raid, for little gain, is apparent.

The deployment of Window over Hamburg had given the British a temporary advantage in their battle with night-fighters, but the Germans adapted quickly. Recognising that their highly structured system of boxes in the *Kammhuber* Line was now redundant, they committed single-engine fighters directly over the target. These aircraft had no ground control or radar on their aircraft, but instead relied on the ambient light of the fires, the glow of searchlights and British Pathfinder Force flares to pick out the silhouettes of British bombers. The *Luftwaffe* initially gave free rein to these fighters and little support, but as the system evolved, they provided a central running commentary on where the bomber stream was and appeared to be heading to, as well as employing Ju 88s to drop powerful flares over the bomber stream, silhouetting the British bombers further. The Germans referred to these fighter aircraft as *Wilde Sau* (Wild Boar) fighters, the British often called them 'cat's-eye fighters', the same term reserved for non-radar equipped British night-fighters. Sgt Wilkie Wanless of 76 Squadron describes these on a raid over Berlin:

> There were fighters dropping these bright flares way above us and it was like flying down Main Street. The fighters would fly right by you and take a shot at you as they went. One bang and they were gone. I couldn't see anything through the Perspex because the light was reflected on it.[16]

For the system to work effectively, the *Luftwaffe* controllers would need to predict the target city accurately, for if they failed the *Wilde Sau* could miss the stream entirely. When successful this technique could be devastatingly effective. P/O Alan Bryett was a bomb aimer on Halifaxes and recalls the *Wilde Sau* attacking his aircraft:

> We had just bombed on the markers and as we turned away, we were caught by one search-light and in a matter of four, five or six seconds about 10 searchlights had come on us. We were in this 400 or 500 feet band of light. All of us were immediately blinded; it was quite terrifying. The German fighters above us at 23,000 feet or so were just waiting for planes to be coned. There were a handful of us lit up and they swept down. You couldn't see them coming until they were right on top of you. They fired incendiary bullets into the plane which set our aircraft on fire in six or eight different places in the fuselage and on the wings. The rear gunner and mid-upper yelled 'Corkscrew!'
>
> As we became a flaming beacon more fighters came round and made a beeline for the rear gunner and mid-upper gunner and killed them both. The pilot said: 'Don't bale out' as he was corkscrewing, but the navigator, engineer and wireless op only heard the 'bale out' as the plane was obviously doomed and went out. I went up and sat with the pilot. It was quite obvious we weren't going to make it, but then the terrifying thing was that as the plane twisted and turned we couldn't get to the escape hatch. We were being tossed around in the nose of the plane. Eventually Kevin did manage to get to the escape hatch, pulled it open, got

---

16   IWM Sound Archives, Catalogue Number 28428, Wilkie Wanless interview.

German Me 110 night-figher fitted with AI Radar. (Bundesarchiv)

hold of me and pushed me out with his feet, shouting: 'I'm coming.' We knew we were very low. I pulled my ripcord and was only coming down for seconds before I felt what I thought were bushes. In fact I was in a forest of fir trees about 80 feet up. The pilot was all ready to follow me, but as I was up in the trees I saw the aircraft crash in a bit of open ground. It was burning furiously, and he didn't get out.[17]

Alan Bryett was lucky, not only to have successfully bailed out, but perhaps also to have been captured by German troops so quickly. Those that were caught by recently bombed German civilians, who routinely called the RAF bomber crews *Terrorflieger,* were usually given a very hostile reception, sometimes being beaten. There are 367 reported cases of aircrew being lynched by furious German civilians throughout the war.

The *Wilde Sau* fighters were usually only effective in the bright lights over the city, further out the *Zahme Sau* or Tame Boar fighters would be used. These were the same types of aircraft as had been used in the *Kammhuber* Line, mainly Me 110s or Ju 88s – the latter aircraft being more effective at getting to the bomber stream because of its greater endurance and speed. They were fitted with either *Lichtenstein* radar, or the newer SN2, which could not be jammed by Window. Under the new system the fighters would orbit radio beacons and be guided into the bomber stream by ground controllers, who would issue their usual running commentary on the bomber stream's progress. The fighters would normally recognise they had joined the stream by the turbulence caused by the slip-streams of large numbers of British aircraft. A shadowing method was also sometimes used, where a German aircraft picked up the active transmissions of the British H2S sets and guided other aircraft in.

When the *Zahme Sau* was sufficiently close it would be able to pick up the bomber through its own integral AI radar set, moving into a position slightly below the aircraft. The Germans identified that this was a blind spot in all British aircraft, including the Lancaster, where the originally-planned ventral turret was omitted from the final design. To mitigate this vulnerability some British pilots would try banking or 'weaving' gently from side to side, so that their rear and mid-upper gunners could see what was underneath the aircraft. A small number of British commanders discouraged this practise, advocating a straight and level flight in order to assist the

---

17   Kevin Wilson, *Bomber Boys* (London: Wiedenfeld and Nicholson, 2005), p. 322.

British gunners, though as Flying Officer Harry Bentley of 467 Squadron comments, it was often not easy to engage a German night-fighter even if it was spotted:

> I recall that night very vividly. Fighter flares had been released ahead of our track. The first indication of the night-fighter's presence was a stream of tracer from below our aircraft, port quarter. The target was a Lancaster flying some 100 feet higher, on the same heading as our aircraft and located approximately 50 yards on the port bow. In less than two seconds, both wing tanks of the Lancaster were ablaze. The night-fighter was still not seen by our rear gunner. A second attack almost simultaneously by the night-fighter was directed at a Lancaster also some 100 feet above our altitude on the same heading, but on our starboard bow at a distance of also approximately 50 yards. The fate of the second Lancaster was exactly the same – both wings ablaze. The sky was now like day. This attack had also originated below and astern of our aircraft. The fighter was still not seen by our rear gunner and myself in the mid-upper position.
>
> I was about to instruct the captain to commence corkscrewing when the night-fighter, a silver Messerschmitt, appeared immediately below altitude. It was actually formatting on us. I immediately took action to engage him with my own guns sufficiently to bring his aircraft into my range of fire. The German pilot was aware of his safe position. He wore a black helmet and black goggles. He immediately made a smart salute to me. I had already requested the skipper to lower the starboard wing in an endeavour to be able to bring the fighter into my line of fire. At that instant, he, the German, dived away to our port side and was gone in a flash, I felt great anger and frustration. Two Lancasters had been destroyed in less than five seconds.[18]

Once the German night-fighter acquired visual contact of its target bomber it would descend and accelerate underneath the aircraft until it was almost in front of it, then the *Zahme Sau* would slowly drop back observing the bomber's exhausts and engines silhouetted above it. The Germans adapted their night-fighter aircraft to exploit this '*von unten hintern*' (from under and behind) approach and from the middle of 1943 the German night-fighters began to be fitted with fixed 40mm or 20mm cannon, angled upwards at about 40 degrees, the pilot also had a special sight fitted in the roof of his cockpit to aim them. Hitting the Lancaster's bomb bay ran the risk of detonating the 4,000lb Cookie immediately, so the preferred technique was to fire at the fuel tanks between the two port engines. This invariably started a fire but gave enough time for the night-fighter to peel away before the Cookie detonated. This fixed-cannon arrangement was known as *Shrage Musik* (jazz music), it was widely fitted to German night-fighters and became the deadliest killer of British bombers flying both to and from the target. The night-fighters did not use tracer rounds in these later cannons, so the attacks were often not seen, as rear gunner Jim Chapman explains:

> There was nothing happening in our vicinity to suggest we were likely to be under attack, then suddenly I'm gazing out the back, operating my turret and I hear a noise at the back of the Lancaster. I can only describe it as like somebody rattling a dustbin lid. That was followed by a glow from underneath the rear end of the aircraft. It wasn't until then that I realized we were under attack. I realized this noise was his cannon fire. The mid-upper gunner had picked him up as well and within seconds the captain was ordering, 'Bail out!' Those were the words I never wanted to hear.[19]

---

18   Martin Middlebrook, *The Berlin Raids*, pp. 205-6.
19   James Taylor and Martin Davidson, *Bomber Crew* (London: Hodder, 2004), p. 334.

The crew of Chapman's Lancaster all successfully bailed out and survived, with the exception of the 18-year-old flight engineer who, in his panic, jumped from the Lancaster without his parachute. On some occasions the rear gunner was able to engage the night-fighter, but the German pilots were usually canny enough to stay unobserved, or out of range of the Browning .303-inch machine guns. If the night-fighter was spotted, then the bomber pilot would put the aircraft into a violent 'corkscrew', descending in a rapid dive to starboard and then a lurching climb to port. Rear gunner Ron Smith provided an account of a German attack:

> I saw a Junkers 88 banking at an incredible angle, to come in again slightly below, clearly discernible against the floodlit target area. I had no time to wonder at his folly as I gave him a long burst that appeared to pass right through him, with some rounds deflecting off in all directions, before down we went into a violent corkscrew.
>
> For a few minutes I watched the enemy, now on our port quarter up, flying along with us yet out of range. The crew were silent while I gave a constant running commentary to keep the skipper informed.
>
> The Junker's pilot's tactics made me wonder if he had a partner with him, who might attack from starboard. Dougie was watching this area from his vantage position, as I kept my eyes glued on the persistent enemy …
>
> My problem, therefore, was if I gave evasive action too soon, he could adjust and follow, so I prepared the skipper for a corkscrew and gave the approaching menace a long burst, even though at maximum range for my Brownings. As he opened fire the tracer seemed to come straight at me. I gave the instruction to 'Go', and as we went down on the first part of the manoeuvre his tracer passed overhead well away, not as I supposed directly at me. I immediately lost sight of him. We came up, to dive again on the second leg of the corkscrew, my skipper's action precise but violent enough to pin me to my seat by the centrifugal force.
>
> Dougie had opened fire when I did, and he said that the Junkers had broken away to our port below but, as the skipper weaved from side to side, nothing could be seen, no outline against the blackness, no patch darker than the surrounding void.
>
> As I turned restlessly to starboard, the whole sky lit up in an instant behind me, and our aircraft banked away at our pilot's reaction. I turned the turret to port against the pressure, in time to see a Lancaster falling to the ground below, other bombers here and there, flying steadily on, as if awaiting their execution passively.[20]

As the mounting toll from night-fighter attacks increased, Bomber Command looked for solutions and created 100 (Bomber Support) Group. Headquartered at Bylaugh Hall, Norfolk, it had a mixed fleet of 260 aircraft including B-17s, Lancasters and 140 Mosquitoes. The Mosquitoes conducted intruder missions against the night-fighter bases and hunted German night-fighters near the RAF bomber stream heading towards its target. They were equipped with AI radar but also sometimes carried 'Perfectos', for picking up the German IFF transmissions, or 'Serrate', which could home in on the German aircraft's radar transmissions, occasionally infra-red detection equipment were in the machines too. The British had been able to develop these counter-measures through the very occasional landing by German aircraft at United Kingdom airfields, usually as a result of a clumsy navigational mistake, or outright desertion by the German aircrew. These rare and lucky breaks allowed the British to reverse-engineer German technology and develop equipment that could detect the German emissions. In the AI-equipped Mosquito missions over Germany the pilot did most of the navigating and the radar operator would focus on his AI set, only becoming

---

Handley Page Halifaxes of 10 Squadron based at Melbourne, Yorkshire, gain height in the failing evening light while outward bound on a raid to Turin, Italy. (Crown Copyright – Air Historical Branch)

involved in the navigation to confirm to the pilot he was on track or to work out a new course on the Dalton Navigation Computer.

Graham White was a pilot on 100 Group Mosquitoes spending the majority of his time 'Beacon Bashing', so called because it involved circling known German night-fighter assembly points waiting for something to turn up. On other occasions, the Mosquitoes would conduct bomber escort duty and patrol under, above and alongside the unseen bomber stream at 15 minute intervals. They acted like sheepdogs circling a flock and protecting them from wolves.[21] White describes one mission to Bremen:

> We are over the northern edge of the Ruhr, near Munster, and without provocation the sky suddenly erupts in orange splashes of anti-aircraft fire. We hear only the nearest shells, bursting with a soft crump sound. Instinct screams out to duck and weave, to try to dodge the bursts, but they are too evenly spread, it is a box barrage. Like players in a giant game of Battleships, the enemy don't take aim, they blindly fill the aerial space with as many shells as they can in the shortest time. The longer you hang around the more chance there is that they'll hit the jackpot, so you fly straight and level at top speed, and soon leave it behind.
>
> An hour after Ostend we suddenly get a contact. Dagwood is brooding quietly over his electronic box and I am mentally calculating the fuel consumption, when he gives a shout.

---

21   Graham White, *Night Fighter Over Germany* (Barnsley: Pen and Sword, 2006), p. 97.

'Contact!' Twelve thousand feet, 10 degrees at three o' clock.'

I turn slightly starboard so that the blip of light slides to the centre of the radar tube.

'Steady! Dead ahead, coming down fast … looks like a head-on, prepare to turn 30 degrees starboard.'

It's the Whiting manoeuvre, the only thing to do in a head-on, when you have a maximum range of no more than 16,000 feet and a combined closing speed of around 600 miles an hour. The little blob of green light charges down the screen like a Formula One glow-worm. Four thousand feet! Turn starboard now.' And as we complete it, 'Turn hard port 210 degrees.'

The green hands on the blind-flying panel clocks lurch to one side and we are pushed deep into our seats. There is no up, no down, no horizon; we rotate slowly in a world of black velvet, the only things in the universe. There is nothing out there any more – the radar echoes are blanked out by the turn – only the slowly spinning gyro compass seems to be moving. One ninety, 200, and we start to come out of the turn. We should be right behind him.

Dagwood sings out in triumph. 'Got him! Two thousand feet and closing. Climb 500, turn 10 degrees port.'

I see nothing, but totally trusting, I follow the directions blindly. We creep slowly in to 1,200 feet. Where the hell is he?

'He's diving – turn port – hard port.'

Damn! He must have picked us up on his *Naxos* rear warning device, and he's running for the electronic shelter of the ground returns. The little green numbers whirl again as I ram the stick forward and a great unseen hand tries to prise us from our seats.

'He's pulling away – increase speed – keep turning hard port.'

Increase! What speed are we doing, anyway? The altimeter seems to be racing round faster than the propellers. Then suddenly it's over.

'We've lost him.'[22]

On that occasion Graham White had lost the German night-fighter, who had disappeared into a glare of electronic interference that flooded the radar tube as both aircraft dived towards the ground. In an attempt to increase the bomber stream's protection further other electronic counter-measures were also introduced, these included 'Boozer' a passive radar detector, that would warn the pilot if a *Lichtenstein*-equipped night-fighter was approaching through a red-light in the cockpit. There was also 'Monica', an active radar in the tail of the bomber, which would detect an approaching aircraft and give a series of bleeps in the rear gunner's headphones. Sadly the system could not differentiate between friend and foe and because it was an active system the radar energy it transmitted could also be detected by a German system called *Flensberg*, which used the Monica's emissions to guide their night-fighters onto a target.[23] The British recognised the vulner-abilities their electronic signatures generated and tried to reduce their electronic emissions, as one example they sometimes restricted the use of H2S for critical phases of the operation, rather than leaving it on for the entire duration of the flight, when it could be picked up and tracked by the German *Naxos* radar warning system.

100 (Bomber Support) Group also contained electronic warfare aircraft that could intercept, jam or disrupt enemy radar and radio transmissions. These utilised equipment like 'Airborne Cigar', a spectrum analyser that could be used to detect the German radio frequencies being used to co-ordinate the night-fighters. They also carried a German-speaking operator as an extra crew man who, having identified the German night-fighter controller's frequency, would attempt to jam

---

22   Graham White, *Night Fighter Over Germany*, pp. 101-2.
23   Leo McKinstry, *Lancaster*, p. 253.

or spoof it. These aircraft still carried a bomb-load and apart from a few extra aerials looked like a normal bomber. Nonetheless the Germans did learn to detect EW aircraft from their distinctive electronic signature and deliberately began targeting them. During the first 10 weeks of the Battle of Berlin in 1943, a total of 21 EW aircraft and 168 crew were lost.[24]

Other measures were also taken by Bomber Command to reduce the casualties. Varying the routes helped, as did the diversionary attacks by the Mosquitoes of the Light Night Strike Force, however Window had compelled the Germans to break apart their rigid *Kammhuber* Line system and adopt a more flexible approach to attacking the British bombers. It was this new system, together with the *Zahme Sau* and *Wilde Sau* fighters, that in the latter half of 1943 and early part of 1944, made the cost of the British bomber offensive against targets such as Berlin prohibitive.

Harris had declared to Churchill, in November of 1943, that his bomber offensive alone could bring about the strategic defeat of Germany. He argued that his programme of general and area bombing was already well advanced and that he felt 'certain that Germany must collapse before this programme, which is more than half completed already, has proceeded much further'. He appealed for American support for his renewed focus on Berlin insisting: 'We can wreck Berlin from end to end … if the USAAF will come in on it. It will cost between 400-500 aircraft. It will cost Germany the war.'[25] The Americans however were incapable of flying to Berlin in daylight without being shot out of the sky, the raid against Schweinfurt in Bavaria on 17 August 1943, when 60 out of 376 B-17s were lost, had proved that. Nor were the Americans willing or able to transition to a night bomber force. Harris' ambition was too great and the Battle of Berlin would witness British bomber casualties rise to an unsustainable rate of over five percent per mission. The raid on Nuremburg during the night of 30/31 March 1944 was most shocking, when 11.8 percent of the force (94 aircraft) were lost. This represented a greater number of aircrew casualties in that single night than were lost in the entire Battle of Britain.[26]

The key was that Nuremburg was not an isolated disaster, but the peak of a trend that highlighted the German night-fighter's ascendancy over the RAF bombers in the German night skies. Yet the character of the bomber war was set to turn again in the early part of 1944, as the pendulum swung back in the Allies favour and American long-range Mustangs successfully began to battle and defeat the German day-fighters over German cities. At the same time both Bomber Command and the US Eighth Air Force were refocussed from their strategic bomber offensives, to providing support for Operation OVERLORD. The eventual success of the Allied armies in Europe in 1944 would see them advance right up to the German borders by September 1944, destroying much of Germany's early warning radar system as well as reducing the time British aircraft spent over the progressively shrinking enemy-occupied territory to shorter, more manageable and survivable levels.

Until that moment came, British bomber crews would continue to make the long transit home through threatening skies, sometimes in badly damaged aircraft. Flight Engineer Sergeant Charles Cawthorne of 467 Squadron was on the British raid to Peenemunde when his Lancaster, skippered by Australian pilot Warren Wilson, was attacked by night-fighters.

> The skipper called over the I/C for everyone to be extra vigilant but without warning we felt our aircraft judder as it was riddled with both machine gun and 20mm cannon fire. Standing beside the pilot, I clearly recall seeing tracer bullet trails looping high over our port wing and hearing the terrifying noise of the enemy's ammunition hitting our aircraft. George Oliver, our mid-upper gunner, made an immediate response to the attack and our rugged Australian

24   Leo McKinstry, *Lancaster*, p. 364.
25   N. Frankland and C. Webster, *The Strategic Air Offensive Against Germany 1939-1945, Volume II*, p. 49.
26   N. Frankland and C. Webster, *The Strategic Air Offensive Against Germany 1939-1945, Volume II*, p. 193.

skipper put the aircraft in a violent dive to port in the hope of escaping further attention from the fighter. However, after losing several thousand feet of altitude he announced he was having great difficulty in getting the aircraft out of the dive. Without further ado I leaned over to assist by grasping the control column with both hands and together we pulled it back until the aircraft responded and we were flying straight and level again.

On recovery I checked the engine gauges and fuel control panel and looking aft saw what looked like the whole of the rear fuselage on fire with thick black acrid smoke billowing forward. Out of the smoke climbing over the main spar came George the mid-upper gunner and he was soon joined by David the wireless operator. Both had their chutes clipped on ready to jump out of the front emergency exit. I reported the fire to the skipper and expected him to give the order to abandon aircraft, but to my amazement he coolly said, 'Well go and put the bloody thing out then'. If it had not been for those cool calculated words, we would have all finished our ops tours there and then.

Armed with fire extinguishers, George and I went aft over the main spar to tackle the blaze and there we were quickly joined by David. We found the ammunition lines to the rear turret ablaze with one round setting fire to the next with alarming speed. The fuselage was full of thick smoke which made our progress difficult and soon it was realised the dead man's handle, a device for rotating the rear turret in the event of a hydraulic failure had received a direct hit. The turret's hydraulic oil supply had been sprayed around the floor not only adding fuel to the fire but making it difficult to stand in our rubber flying boots. When all extinguishers had been emptied, we resorted to smothering the blaze with our gloved hands and eventually we succeeded in putting the fire out.

It was then we realised the rear gunner, Paddy Barry, was wounded and trapped in his turret. With the aid of the aircraft axe, George, the mid-upper gunner managed to open the back doors of the rear turret and I assisted in manoeuvring Paddy over the tailplane and up to the rest bed near the main spar. Despite Paddy's precarious state, we had to leave him and return to our crew positions to report on the fire damage sustained from the night-fighter attack and take stock of the battle that was taking place all around us in the bomber stream.

From the flight engineer's panel I calculated that we were losing a considerable amount of fuel and after reporting this to the skipper and navigator it was decided that we would divert to an airfield in neutral Sweden. At this juncture Swill, the bomb aimer, and I were told by the skipper to make Paddy as comfortable as possible. By the light of a masked torch, we realised he had sustained a serious injury to his left foot from an exploding cannon shell. I attempted to inject morphine to ease his pain but could not get through his protective clothing. In desperation, I started to cut away his flying boot which was torn and saturated with blood. In the semi-darkness of the fuselage it was difficult to see any detail and what I thought to be a large piece of boot was in fact a piece of skin which I immediately replaced and bound the wound with a shell bandage. I then returned to my seat in the cockpit and after rechecking the gauges I realised the self-sealing fuel tanks had been effective and the loss of fuel stemmed. Following a hurried crew conference, it was decided we had sufficient fuel to attempt the return journey over the North Sea to England.

The skipper announced he was still having trouble controlling the aircraft which continu-ously wanted to climb, and it was necessary for him to stand on the rudder pedals and wedge his back against the seat with fully extended arms to prevent the aircraft climbing. In an endeavour to relieve the physical effort of the situation the skipper and I removed our Mae Wests and after inflating them jammed them both between the control column and the pilot's seat. We did not realise that the problem was caused by the loss of our elevator trim tabs which had been shot away during the night-fighter attack.

Short Stirling N3751/BU-P of 214 Squadron was one of 144 aircraft involved in the Bremen raids, 27/28 June 1942. It was damaged by flak and night fighter fire but the pilot managed to bring the aircraft back to Stradishall for a crash-landing. (Crown Copyright – Air Historical Branch)

By this time the Lancaster had crossed the enemy coast, but the pilot was completely exhausted, causing Charles Cawthorne to take over flying across the relatively safe area of the North Sea. As they approached the Lincolnshire coast the pilot took over once more:

> David Booth, the wireless operator, called our base for a priority landing due to our seriously wounded gunner and the precarious state of our aircraft. Bottesford responded to our request and the skipper ordered all crew members to their crash positions for an emergency landing. I had to remain in my normal crew position to assist the skipper with the handling of the aircraft. On final approach, I was fully prepared to select full flap which was the normal procedure but the skipper quickly reminded me that only a couple of weeks before an Aussie pilot on the Squadron called Tillotson had suffered a complete fracture of the rear fuselage on his aircraft following full flap selection after suffering serious battle damage to the rear fuselage. His aircraft's tail fell off with disastrous results. I didn't require any further warning and my hand kept a respectful distance away from the flap lever.
>
> In the early morning light after nearly seven hours in the air we glided over the threshold of the runway and touched down at 04:20 hours. With engines spluttering we taxied off the runway and came to a stop on the grass, where we were immediately attended to by the fire and ambulance staff who carefully extricated Paddy, our injured gunner.[27]

For those aircraft that were undamaged the passage across the North Sea was a period when the tension began to lower. Flasks of coffee would be broken out and the rations consumed. As the machine began to descend below 10,000 feet the oxygen masks would be taken off and perhaps an illicit cigarette smoked. The Elsan toilet at the back of the aircraft, might be used, though as it was cumbersome to take off their flying gear, the aircrew usually just urinated in a bottle. In these last stages the crew still had to find their own airfield with its unique beacon, they could then call up

---

27   Derek Brammer, *Thundering through the Clear Air*, pp. 103-5.

Flying Control and ask permission to land or 'pancake'. Unless they had a particular emergency, they would be put in a circuit awaiting permission to land in their turn, Ron Mayhill describes these last tired minutes of a trip:

> Landing was always a tense time, in fact closing in on solid earth at any time was a reminder of the frailty of aircraft and flight itself. We followed the dim wing tip lights of the aircraft ahead, down from the crowded circuit towards the flashing beacon of Mepal airfield [RAF Mepal, east of Ely in Cambridgeshire] calling, 'Hallo Mawkish, this is Sailmaker Uncle,' R/T silence finally broken by the code in use.
>
> 'Mawkish to Uncle, turn eight, orbit at Angels three.'
>
> We were at 3,000 feet already and not surprised at our place in the queue as we had been listening to the other kites reporting. The skipper, tired but keyed up, checked supercharger M ratio, air intake cold, brake pressures OK, as he listened to the circuit chatter. There was no doubt the WAAFs and men in air control were bang on, being quite used to bringing the 25 or so squadron aircraft down in rapid succession with coolness and authority. 'Mawkish to Uncle, turn five, Angel two,' and we followed the aircraft ahead in the sweeping 20-mile orbit down to 2,000 feet.
>
> Suddenly we pricked up our ears; someone was requesting an emergency landing and the plane in the funnel was being ordered to overshoot. We watched as another Lancaster, ignoring the regular orbit, made a long, straight approach from the direction of the neighbouring Witchford circuit, a little fast it seemed, but the faint navigation lights went down the parallel runway yellows, slowed up and turned away safely.
>
> 'Mawkish to Sailmaker Uncle, turn three, Angel One,' and the skipper banked onto the downwind leg, undercarriage down, the hooter and engineer confirming fully locked, flaps 20, the aircraft lifting momentarily, revs 2,900, the sound of the engines being throttled back.
>
> 'Sailmaker Uncle, three plus,' The aircraft ahead sank slowly towards the runway, our turn next.
>
> Jake called, 'Uncle funnels,' control responding, 'Uncle pancake.'
>
> The glide path indicators winked green for a moment as we dropped, green and white, then white, correct angle of approach, aware that reds meant too low and we would be powering on an overshoot, losing our turn to land. We continued down in the friendly white, engines crackling as excess fuel burned and popped in the exhausts, over the fence, throttles right back, 120, 110 mph, the blurred runway between the tapering yellow lights rushing at us.
>
> A skip and squeal of rubber and we were safely down. A touch of brakes, the airframe seeming to compress, another touch and then another and we rolled slowly to the end, a short burst of motor and we turned off, 'Uncle clear'.
>
> Then came the long taxi around the blue-studded perimeter track, past control tower to our dispersal where the loyal and patient ground crew waited, torches guiding us to the correct position, torches crossing, signal for a final burst to clear the plugs and switch off, the props reluctantly milling to a halt. Jake had opened the bomb doors slightly so the ground crew could confirm no malfunction concealed a wayward bomb. The rear exit door was opened from outside, the ladder put in position, the twins leading the procession to clamber out. We were back safely, savouring the sheer joy of having knocked off another op.[28]

The ground crew were always keen to see both the aircrew and their aircraft arrive safely. They took a proprietary interest in the machine, keen to know that it had performed well and also quick on

---

28   Ron Mayhill, *Bombs on Target*, pp. 155-7.

Avro Lancaster B.I, R5729/KM-A, of 44 Squadron runs up its engines in a dispersal at Dunholme Lodge, Lincolnshire, before setting out on a night raid to Berlin in early January 1944. This veteran aircraft had taken part in more than 70 operations with the Squadron since joining it in 1942. It was finally shot down with the loss of its entire crew barely a week after this picture taken during a raid on Brunswick. (Crown Copyright – Air Historical Branch)

occasions to scold a captain for bringing it back damaged. Stephen Rew was an engine fitter with 44 Squadron at RAF Waddington, he describes waiting at dispersal for the end of the mission and the return of the aircraft:

> The scene outside appears to be chaotic. Red, green and white navigation lights and behind them patches of blackness, black even in the darkness revealing the presence of an aircraft, seem to be everywhere, while flashes of blue torchlight reveal the presence of the ground-crew men. The air is full of the sound of engines, some idling and some being given bursts of throttle to swing the aircraft round. The pilot identifies his plane by flashing the navigation lights. The ground man gives the pilot a mental pat for remembering and flashes back on one of his torches. As his plane approaches, he starts to wave both torches in circles, indicating 'straight ahead'. As the aircraft comes closer, he holds his left hand still, waving with his right. The aircraft swings uncertainly to starboard, and then he guides it in with both torches. The aircraft stops with a hiss of brakes. One by one the four engines rustle into silence, and there she stands, noticeably higher off the ground than before she went, looking somehow tired but cheerful, like a man after a game of rugger. The ground crewman drags the heavy chocks into position in front of the wheels. He fetches the access ladder from the tent and waits for the door to be unlocked. It opens after a few minutes and the dim interior lights reveal the figure of one of the gunners, looking huge and unnatural … The gunner scrambles down the ladder, followed at intervals by the others. The nav lights are extinguished, and finally the engineer followed by the skipper make their way down.[29]

Accidents and collisions in the congested air space were not uncommon, the airfields of Lincolnshire, Yorkshire and East Anglia were wedged in together tightly and some airfield circuits for orbiting

---

29   IWM Ref. No. 6384: Stephen Rew private papers.

aircraft would come perilously close to that of its neighbour, or even overlap. On other occasions an unreleased-bomb, known as a 'hang-up', would detonate as the aircraft touched down, or some part of the aircraft would unexpectedly fail from undiscovered damage inflicted during the trip. Some airfields, known as emergency landing grounds, were equipped with larger runways to cope with lame aircraft; the one at RAF Woodbridge in Suffolk had a runway 3,000 yards in length and 250 yards wide.

Like the British, the Germans would sometimes send intruder night-fighters across the Channel to attack aircraft around the airfields, though this was less frequent than feared. It seems as if Hitler preferred to have the German night-fighters operating over home skies where they boosted morale. There were very few German intruder raids in 1943, none in 1944 and only two in 1945, of which one was very successful, destroying 19 Bomber Command aircraft as they crossed the British coast on the night of 3/4 March 1945.[30]

Fog was a significant danger, with some aircraft hitting the ground in poor visibility at the last stages of their trip. If it was very bad, the airfield controller might direct the aircraft to divert to an open runway, the crew would then fly back the following day, usually having spent an uncomfortable night in a transit block or on the mess floor. In dire emergencies the aircraft could be diverted to one of 15 airfields, or emergency landing grounds, equipped with the Fog Investigation Dispersal Operation (FIDO) system. This equipment, invented by the Anglo-Iranian Oil Company (now British Petroleum), pumped high-octane fuel along a pipe pierced with burner holes, which were lit when the fog had descended. The intensity of the flames pushed the fog up and also meant that the runway could be seen from as far away as 60 miles, even in foggy conditions. Landing at a FIDO-equipped airfield was a dramatic experience, the roar of the burning petrol was enough to drown out the engine noise and the turbulence caused by the heat was not for the faint-hearted. Some described it as 'a bit like entering the jaws of hell'.[31] It was an expensive operation too, costing 80,000 gallons of fuel per hour of operation, but it was effective.

Once safely down at their airfield, the aircrew would be collectively de-briefed by the Intelligence Officers, primarily so that any operational problems and evolving enemy techniques could be understood, as well as establishing the level of destruction achieved over the target. This last assessment would be reviewed and updated by subsequent photographic reconnaissance and other intelligence, the level of destruction from Bomber Command's raids was always hard to establish precisely: though the roof of a factory may be blown in, the machine tools might well be undamaged. It was also impossibly hard to measure how far German morale had been damaged, or even how many days production had been lost. The detailed answers to these questions were only truly understood at the conclusion of the war, even then the answers were not clear cut as, in contrast to Britain, the German economy was not fully mobilised until later in the war. There was therefore both resilience and spare capacity in the German war machine that the British bomber offensive found difficult to overcome. (Annex T gives a comparison of actual output of particular classes of armaments in Germany and the United Kingdom).

In the last year of the European war, the requirement to support OVERLORD transformed Bomber Command's efforts and operations, turning it temporarily and partially into a support force for land operations in France. Once the Allied armies broke out of Normandy there was a focus on specific targets in the form of attacks on oil production and distribution. These produced important results and significantly hampered the weakening German war machine. Harris however remained unconvinced that such attacks would prove superior to his own focus on area bombings. His preferred approach was to continue these right up until the attack on Dresden in

30   Hilary Saunders, *Royal Air Force 1939-45, Volume III*, p. 3.
31   Leo McKinstry, *Lancaster*, p. 197.

Flying Officer A.E. Manning and his crew gather by their aircraft, Avro Lancaster I, W4964/WS-J, of 9 Squadron shortly after their return to Bardney, Lincolnshire, in the early hours of 6 January 1944, after raiding Stettin, Germany. (Crown Copyright – Air Historical Branch)

March 1945, an attack prompted by Churchill to bolster his strategic influence with Stalin at the Tehran Conference. The subsequent firestorm has become a 'cause celebre' for those who wish to attack the moral foundations of the bomber offensive and prompted Churchill, one of its primary authors, to begin to distance himself from the bomber campaign.

Questions of morality are important, but it should always be remembered that at the time few had such qualms. Bomber crews were regarded as popular heroes in Britain throughout the war and being spontaneously and publicly thanked in London, by complete strangers, was a common experience for those off duty. Few in wider society would have had any illusions about what the impact their bombing missions may have had on the German civilian population, even if the Air Ministry and senior politicians would avoid saying so explicitly. That the senior leadership were aware of the level of destruction and necessity of the operations is best illustrated by the visit of Smuts, to the Bomb Damage Assessment Section at the Allied Central Interpretation Unit at RAF Medmenham, in the summer of 1943. Flight Lieutenant Ronald Gillanders was showing Smuts a mosaic of air photographs of Hamburg after the July bombings. Gillanders pointed out the extent of the devastation, sweeping his hand right across the city with a dramatic gesture. He glanced up to see what sort of impression he was making on Smuts and was rendered surprised, deflated and speechless to see the tall old South African statesmen with tears in his eyes shaking his head from side to side. 'Hamburg was a beautiful city,' he said, 'a beautiful city'.[32]

---

32   Constance Babington-Smith, *Evidence in Camera* (London: David and Charles, 1957), p. 177.

Tiredness etched on the face of a young Halifax pilot of 405 (Vancouver) Squadron RCAF after returning from an operation over Germany, July/August 1942. (Crown Copyright – Air Historical Branch)

For a bomber crew the end of a trip would simply be a chance to sleep, with the knowledge that they may have to do it all again tomorrow. Between 3 September 1939 and 14 August 1945, 47,268 officers, non-commissioned officers and airmen lost their lives or disappeared on operations carried out by Bomber Command (Annex U and V provide details of Bomber Command casualties and Bomber Command aircraft destroyed and damaged between 3 September 1939 and 8 May 1945). Questions of morality or strategy were largely academic for the bomber crews, who were far more concerned with what progress they were making through their 30-mission operational tour. As Harry Yates later observed:

A tour was a construct of three aspects, each distinct, each characterised by a potentially lethal weakness. In the beginning, of course, was naivety. A few hours flying together at OTU and [Lancaster] Finishing School barely qualified as preparation for the real thing. From the moment a sprog crew arrived on station it had to learn – before the lesson was driven home by the enemy. There was plenty of help at hand. The path to survival was well-trodden even though not everyone reached its end.

The dozen or so ops in the middle of a tour tended to coincide with the assumption that this learning period was over. The logbook was filling up. The enemy and Lady Luck had done their worst. One was not blasé about being shot at but had reached a certain, internal accommodation with it. Instead of operating at maximum vigilance throughout, there might … perhaps … occasionally be a tendency to cut corners or relax a little. But might and occasionally were enough. Even that was complacency and it invited the Reaper along for the ride.

Towards journey's end aircrew had survived and surmounted these hazards. They were secure in the knowledge of their own expertise. But then came the still more insidious danger of staleness. It was all too easy to be weary of the sheer repetition in operational life. The months of Battle Orders and Briefings were bound to pall, along with the pills to keep you wide-eyed or knock you out; the ops scrubbed on the tarmac and others re-ordered because of scattered bombing; and always, the losses, the pals known but briefly and who, in the relentless drive to mount the next op, somehow went unmourned.

Naivety, complacency, staleness: these were the killers in their own right. The cruellest was naivety, but the most undeserved was this business of going stale, like old bread.[33]

---

33   Harry Luck, *Luck and a Lancaster*, p. 226.

14

'Through to The End'[1]
The Development of a Precision Bombing Capability

It would be wrong to give the impression that British strike operations in the Second World War were exclusively restricted to saturation area bombing by night. Though Harris' ideas may have dominated Bomber Command's operational approach, there were many occasions when a specific target required a level of precision that necessitated a completely different method. Sometimes this was best achieved by adapting the methods used by Bomber Command. The Pathfinder target marking techniques, together with new technology such as H2S often helped provide sufficient accuracy, particularly when combined with intensive training in low-level flying and navigation.

One of the earliest examples of precision bombing by Lancasters was the April 1942 raid on the Augsburg AG (MAN) factory which produced diesel engines for U-boats. Following the catastrophically high losses earlier on in the war, Bomber Command had deliberately avoided using heavy bombers in daylight. However, the arrival of the new, fast Lancasters earlier that year may have been a factor in tempting Harris to try once more. The raid would involve just 12 aircraft drawn from two squadrons of Lancasters (44 and 97 squadrons), they would fly in two separate waves, ultra-low-level (approximately 50 feet) across France, skirting south of Paris and then turning at Lake Constance towards Augsburg, which they would each hit with 4 x 1,000lb bombs on 11 seconds delay. It was hoped that a diversionary raid by 2 Group's Boston medium bombers in the Pas de Calais area would draw off German fighters as the Augsburg-bound Lancasters crossed the coast. To say the plan was audacious would be an understatement. When the curtain was drawn back, to reveal the location of the target at a briefing in Woodhall Spa, 97 Squadron's location, the aircrew burst out laughing thinking it was a practical joke.

It was no laughing matter – the raid was launched on 17 April. As the aircraft crossed France six Lancasters, all from 44 Squadron, were intercepted by Me 109s and four shot down. The surviving eight aircraft did get through and successfully bombed the factory setting it ablaze, but another three Lancasters were shot down over the target and only five Lancasters successfully made it back across Europe under the cover of dusk. The raid on Augsburg was another salutary lesson in the hazards of daylight operations, even with an aircraft as good as the Lancaster. Bomber Command would very rarely undertake daylight raids by heavy bombers until well into 1944, when air superiority over European skies had been achieved by the Allied air forces, even then missions would focus on coastal or French targets rather than deep penetration raids. The Augsburg raid also highlighted the independence of Bomber Command's selection of targets. The Ministry of Economic Warfare was angry that Harris had selected the Augsburg target, without any reference to themselves, arguing that it was not an important factory and that there were higher priority targets, at

---

1   The 487 Squadron RNZAF motto. The squadron was initially equipped with Lockheed Venturas and then Mosquitoes. It took part on a number of precision raids with 2 Group RAF.

Film still showing Avro Lancaster B Mark Is of No. 5 Group, flying at low level over the
French countryside on the evening of 17 October 1942, while en route to attack the Schneider
engineering factory at Le Creusot, France. The nearest aircraft, R5497 'OF-Z', of No. 97
Squadron RAF, is being flown by Flying Officer J.R. Brunt and crew, who were shot down and
killed on an operation in the same aircraft exactly two months later. The film was shot by the
navigator of the Lancaster flown by the Commanding Officer of No. 106 Squadron RAF, Wing
Commander G.P. Gibson, who was to command No. 617 Squadron RAF the following year.
(Crown Copyright – Air Historical Branch)

either Schweinfurt or Stuttgart.[2] The Chief of the Air Staff backed Harris who argued, probably
correctly, that only Augsburg could be found and accessed by low-flying Lancasters.

Bomber Command's greatest attempts at precision bombing were through the establishment of
617 Squadron. This Squadron was initially formed to execute Operation CHASTISE, the 'Dams
Raid'; against the Mohne, Sorpe and Eder dams. No. 617 Squadron would drop the Barnes Wallis
'bouncing bomb', which was designed to skip across the water, strike the dam wall, sink to the

---

2   N. Frankland and C. Webster, *The Strategic Air Offensive Against Germany, Volume I* (London: HMSO,
     1961), p. 46.

bottom of the reservoir and then detonate. The night-time flying by the Lancasters on this mission would have to be at ultra-low-level, all the way to the target. Once there they would need to fly straight and level, at precisely 60 feet and at a speed of 220 mph during their run-ups, dropping their bombs between 425 and 475 yards out. Bomber Command recognised that such a mission required a squadron with significant training in night-time, low-level flying and consequently directed 5 Group to set up a new Squadron. Cochrane, the commander of 5 Group, selected Wing Commander Guy Gibson, who was just coming to the end of his third tour in bombers and had been awarded a bar to his DSO. The operation involved 19 aircraft, which were split into three formations departing from RAF Scampton on 16 May 1943. The mission was always going to be dangerous.

Sergeant Tony Burcher was the rear gunner on Flight Lieutenant 'Hoppy' Hopgood's Lancaster (AJ-M), one of the nine aircraft heading for the Mohne dam, he recalls how the low-flying approach did not entirely reduce the risk of flak.

> We were actually hit before we got to the target. I think we were about 20 minutes from the target. I can't remember the name of the place, but it was about that time when I shot the searchlights out that we got hit. Hoppy was wounded; he got a shell burst in the cockpit. The front gunner I think was either killed or wounded because we never heard anything from him from then on because Hoppy called up [the whole crew] after this happened. I got some pieces of shrapnel in my stomach and lower leg, but they were only scratches really; they just drew blood. But the wireless operator, I don't know, he might have been hit then … He might have been hit later on when we actually made the bombing run. But I know the front gunner [George Gregory] was not answering. You see, Hoppy, after this happened, Hoppy checked around the crew to see how we all were, and he didn't reply.
>
> Hoppy then decided, he said, 'Right, well, what do you think? Do you think we should go on? I intend to go on because we've only got a few minutes to go. We've come this far. There's no good taking this thing back with us. The aircraft is completely handleable. I can handle it okay. So any objection?' We wouldn't have actually said okay, just go on. The engineer [Charles Brennan] said, 'Well, what about your face? – it's bleeding … ' He said 'Just hold a handkerchief over it.' So the engineer got out of his position … He was sitting on a jump seat right beside him, just to the right of him, and he held a handkerchief against his face or head or whatever it was. Just to stem the bleeding … I don't know how bad he was hurt but I would think pretty badly hurt from what the engineer was saying … I think it was terrific tenacity. But that was Hoppy, that was the type of man he was.

Hopgood's aircraft would bomb second, after Gibson's Lancaster. As the rear gunner on the Lancaster, Burcher did not have a great view, but he recalled the risks and the activities of that final bombing run:

> It was discussed that whoever went in first might get them by surprise, but the second bloke they would certainly be waiting for and we knew that. We knew that when Gibson went through, we knew, that they knew, where we were coming from, what direction, what height. So, we knew that we were in a pretty dicey situation. I can't remember exactly but it seemed an eternity to me … we had to get down to the height … the actual bombing height which was between 60 and 80 feet, and that was done by coordinating the two lights. The bomb aimer had to set his sights up and, of course before then we had to start the motor up which started revolving the bomb. The engineer operated that on a little APU [Auxiliary Power Unit], a little two-stroke engine. And, of course, all that coordination was going on upfront, so it was a matter of all the crew working together from that point.

I knew that we were taking a certain amount of risk, but my main worry was being found out that I was scared.

When the bomb was released, Burcher felt a terrific shuddering in the aircraft. With light AA guns set up on two towers on the top of the Mohne dam wall, the Germans simply set up two interlocking arcs of fire, through which each Lancaster had to fly. Burcher describes the final stages of Hopgood's attack:

> I could see this flak shooting past us, so I had the turret on the beam waiting till it came within my range because I could only go to 90 degrees of the axis of the aircraft. He hadn't come into my view then, and then suddenly with all the flak going around and all these flames, suddenly my turret stopped, and it was one of the port engines that actually drove the hydraulics on my turret, so that it became inoperative. This all happened and next minute I heard, 'Christ, the engine's on fire.' Hoppy said, 'Feather it, press the extinguisher,' and the flames got even worse, so he said, 'Right, prepare to abandon aircraft.'
>
> And then soon he said, 'Right, everybody get out.' So I cranked the turret back. Normally that would take a time, but you could imagine I got that back very quickly; that was the fastest wound turret you ever saw and got out – had to get back into the aircraft, put my parachute on … We were about to go. And then I saw Minchin coming along and dragging his leg and he was on hands and knees, he was terrible, he was in a hell of a state. I didn't know what to do but he was dragging his parachute with him; it was a detachable parachute and I took it from him and put it on. I was on a rear step with the door open – I'd opened the door – and he wasn't moving so I thought, there's only one thing to do and throw him out. I grabbed his D-ring on his parachute and threw him and hung onto it, breaking his parachute [open] but I don't know to this day whether I did the right thing or not. I still do agonise about it. But what does one do?
>
> Hoppy, I don't know whether he realised or not, but he was in a steep climbing turn to starboard, going to the west of the target, the dam, but of course by this time we only had two engines, don't forget, and you can't climb a 'Lanc' on two engines … The two starboard we had. The two port ones were shot out. So he was actually turning into the two good engines we had but we were light, we only had a very light fuel load on because we were only going to the Ruhr, normally a 'Lanc' would have about 2,000 gallons on; I think we had about 1,200 and, of course, we'd got rid of our four and a half ton bomb, so we were pretty light, and he just couldn't get any more height and the other crews reckoned it was about 300 feet when the aircraft blew up. And, of course, at that time when Minchin went I was squatting on the step, which is a step just by the door, and it was that time suddenly there was a great rush of air and the next thing I felt was a belt across my back … and I hit the fin apparently, the top of the fin. Normally you would go out underneath the tailfin but I actually hit it so I was going up in the air. This is one of the things that saved me because my parachute must have been dragged out after me.[3]

Burcher followed Minchin out of the door and miraculously landed with a broken back and kneecap. He was captured by the Germans almost immediately and spent the remainder of the war in a German POW Camp. Only two others managed to get out of the aircraft, the remainder, including Hopgood, were killed as the Lancaster crashed.

---

3   AWM S01656: Sound Archive interview with Tony Burcher.

Of the 19 aircraft dispatched, eight were shot down and 53 aircrew killed, with three taken prisoner. In return Operation CHASTISE had breached two dams, the Mohne and Eder, as well as lightly damaging the Sorpe. In addition two hydro-electric power stations were also destroyed and several more damaged. The success of the Dams Raid should not be exaggerated, the long-term effect on German industrial production was minimal and the Germans soon found alternative methods of providing electrical power to the areas of the Ruhr that were disrupted.

Rather than disband the unit after CHASTISE, Harris maintained the continued existence of 617 Squadron, aiming to use it on missions where precision bombing was required.[4] Initially the Squadron tried to emulate its sucessful low-flying technique. However, a costly mission to destroy a section of the Dortmund-Ems Canal caused the squadron to change this method to precision from altitude. The arrival of the new Stabilising Automatic Bomb Sight (SABS), in November 1943, also meant such a high-altitude technique was now a feasible proposition. The SABS sight consisted of a gyroscopically-stabilised telescopic sight, mounted in the nose of the Lancaster. The bomb-aimer would keep the sight over the target and feed in a number of variables including height, airspeed and external air temperature, the SABS would then generate aiming corrections and release the bomb automatically at precisely the right moment. Although a step forward technologically the SABS required the 617 Squadron Lancasters to fly a long, steady and accurate run up to the target of between five to seven minutes duration, with no deviation in either height or course. By 1944 the highly accurate, radar-predicted German 'flak' meant that this was a risky matter. Robert Knights describes the difficulties in using SABS:

> This bombsight was quite uncanny, provided you flew the aeroplane well. I remember we had to do a bombing test and learn how to use the bomb sight, we had a man called Squadron Leader Dickie Richardson, he was an expert on this bomb-sight and he would fly with new crews and tell the bomb aimer and pilot how it worked and how to get the best out of it. I can remember when we first flew with practice bombs and he said that we had to get within so many yards … 20 yards anyway a very small limit. I said no way can we ever get near that we have tried so hard and we never get near a target like that. He said, 'You can with this bomb sight', and I remember the first few bombs we dropped were extremely close and I was absolutely thrilled with this …
>
> We had to fly, for those days, extremely accurately in fact we had to fly absolutely spot on the height, and we could fly the aeroplane to half a degree in each direction because we had a little indicator on the pilots combing, and when the bomb aimer moved his drift it moved this indicator over and this would be marked in half degrees and it was extremely accurate. Once you had been told how to do this, it was merely a question of practice really. It was a very challenging thing in fact, because I remember one time asking my rear-gunner to stop moving his turret, because the movement of the turret at the back was waving the back of the aeroplane about and put me off so I could not fly the plane accurately.[5]

The accuracy that 617 Squadron was able to attain with the SABS was remarkable. Bombs were generally dropped several miles back from the target, between 12,000 and 15,000 feet, while flying at a speed of 200 miles per hour. From that height and distance even the white square on the bombing range looked like the size of a pin-head. On occasions however the Squadron's concentrated accuracy could work against it, as was the case on 16/17 November 1943 when the squadron was attacking a V1 site at Abbeville and dropped its nine 12,000lb bombs within a

---

4   Paul Brickhill, *The Dam Busters* (London: Macmillan, 1954), p. 157.

5   IWM Sound Archives, Catalogue Number 9208, Richard Edgar Knight interview.

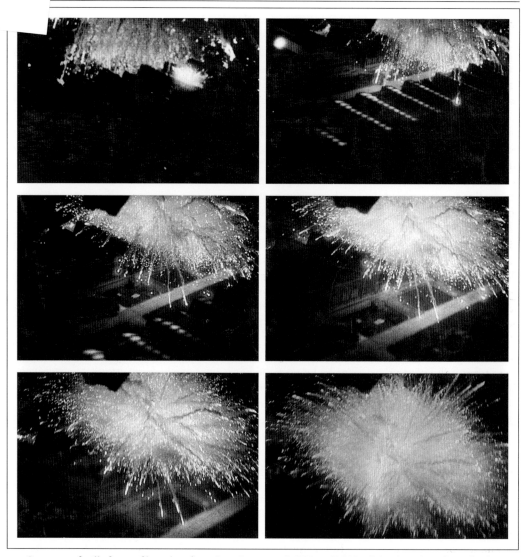

Sequence of stills from a film taken from Avro Lancaster I, DV380/AJ-N, of 617 Squadron flown by the Squadron commander, Wing Commander G.L. Cheshire, during the low-level marking of the Gnome-Rhone aero-engine factory at Limoges, France, on the night of 8/9 February 1944. Cheshire was given official permission to try his low-level marking techniques on this raid, leading 12 Avro Lancasters of the Squadron to the target. He made three runs over the factory at rooftop height to ensure correct identification and to warn French workers of the impending attack. This sequence shows 30lb incendiary bombs exploding over the centre of the factory during Cheshire's fourth pass. Each of the following Lancasters then dropped a 12,000 HC bomb on the markers with great accuracy. (Crown Copyright – Air Historical Branch)

100-yard radius of the target marker. As this had been dropped by Pathfinders 350 yards from the target, the site was therefore undamaged – a larger spread of bombing would ironically have been more destructive.

The new CO of 617 Squadron, Wing Commander Leonard Cheshire, believed the answer to this dilemma lay in better target marking, using one of their own aircraft to conduct low-level marking of the targets with incendiary flares. This was initially tried out during a raid on Limoge's Gnome et Rhone aircraft engine factory on 8/9 February 1944, where the requirement to avoid nearby French civilian housing was important. In this instance the low-level marking technique was a success and Cheshire adopted it as standard practise, utilising Mosquitoes and Mustangs for the actual marking.

The final innovation that helped 617 Squadron become a precise and destructive bombing capability, were the 'Tallboy' series of bombs produced by Barnes Wallis. Barnes Wallis had first expounded on the idea of such weapons in his 1941 paper: 'A note on a method of attacking the Axis Powers'. This new generation of bomb was designed to penetrate deep underground, before detonating and generating a 'camouflet effect'; essentially an explosion which created a large void that undermines the foundations of otherwise very difficult targets, such as hardened concrete bunkers or submarine pens. These earthquake bombs were all given the generic term 'Tallboy' and by the summer of 1944 two types had been satisfactorily developed, a 4,000lb Tallboy S and a 12,000lb Tallboy M. The bomb was not just simply larger than existing bombs, its slender and streamlined casing meant the bomb attained near supersonic speeds before impact and could bury itself to depths of 100 feet. The bomb's steel shell was also heat-treated to harden it and had a specially thickened nose to avoid shattering when it struck the surface. Additionally, an enhanced explosive called TORPEX (40 percent TNT, 42 percent RDX) was poured under pressure into the casing, for a greater explosive effect. Tallboy M measured 21 feet in length and had a three-foot diameter, the tail of the bomb was fitted with four fins that were offset five degrees, to cause the bomb to spin at 500 rpm when dropped. This meant that unlike conventional munitions, which wobbled and tumbled when dropped, Tallboy bombs were ballistically stable in flight and could be dropped consistently and predictably. Good target marking combined with the use of the SABS sight meant that 617 Squadron's bomb aimers could exploit Tallboy's predictable and consistent ballistic flight and deliver highly accurate bombing.

In time Tallboy would be dropped by regular Lancaster squadrons, but its first use was by 617 Squadron on 8/9 June 1944 against the Saumur railway tunnel. The aim of this mission was to cut this important German Army line of communication to the Normandy bridgehead. Twenty-three Tallboys were dropped, most falling near the markers at the mouth of the tunnel causing great damage. It was however the Tallboy dropped by Flight Lieutenant Joe McCarthy which highlighted the unique 'earthquake' characteristics of Barnes Wallis' bomb. His Tallboy struck the side of the mountain, penetrated some 90 feet and detonated above the roof of the tunnel. The earthquake bomb worked as intended and completely collapsed the tunnel so that the Germans were still digging it out three months later when the Americans overran the area.

A further illustration of the effect of Tallboy and 617 Squadron was the mission against the Normandy port of Le Havre on the night of 14 June 1944 where, following the German Naval evacuation of Cherbourg on 12 June, there was an unusually large concentration of E-boats in the harbour. The mission was designed not only to use Tallboy against the hardened E-boat pens where many of the craft were sheltering, but also to generate a sufficiently large 'tidal wave' that would damage many of the craft moored in the basin and outer harbour.

Three special marking Mosquitoes led by Cheshire would lead the attack and mark the targets, followed by 22 Lancasters from 617 Squadron, each equipped with one 12,000lb Tallboy M and a further 199 normal Lancasters carrying 1,000lb and 500lb bombs. There were two aiming points for the Tallboys, the first was the roof of the E-boat pen itself, the second was where intelligence had indicated the heaviest concentrations of E-boats were: the area of the tidal basin alongside the *Gare Maritime* (harbour railway station). As a result of the raid the 12 boats inside the E-boat pen were all sunk, in addition the tidal wave effect in the basin smashed many boats against each other and the harbour walls and in some cases the craft were beached. British intelligence estimated that the Germans had lost 38 vessels sunk outright with another 31 to 34 damaged.

Tallboy also proved it could tackle even the most heavily armoured warships. On 12 November 1944, a force of 32 Lancasters from 9 and 617 Squadrons scored two direct hits on the *Tirpitz*, while it was harboured near Tromsø in Norway. The ship capsized rapidly, and a deck fire spread to the ammunition magazine for one of the main turrets, which caused a large explosion. It was this precision raid which neutralised the major German surface threat to the North Atlantic and Arctic Oceans, a threat that had necessitated tying down a large element of the Royal Navy in Scapa Flow for much of the war.

Though the 12,000-pound Tallboy was the first of Barnes Wallis' weapons to enter service, his original idea had always been to build a much larger weapon configured along the same lines. After five years of design work this new bomb, known as 'Grand Slam', was brought into service in March 1945. Grand Slam was much larger and heavier than Tallboy with a weight of 22,400 pounds and a length of twenty-five feet, indeed such was the scale of Grand Slam that the British needed to build thirty-two 'B1 Special' Lancasters just to carry it. These new aircraft were fitted with powerful Rolls-Royce Merlin 24 engines and had the bomb doors removed to accommodate the bomb. Weight was also an issue so the airframe was lightened by removing H2S as well as the mid-upper and forward gun turrets and other internal equipment. For safety reasons it was unusual for Lancasters to land with their bombloads and munitions were normally jettisoned if a mission had to be aborted, but in Grand Slam's case the bomb was too precious to lose, and crews were instructed to land with them if the aircraft was still safe to fly. To cope with this extra weight on landing the undercarriage of the B1 Lancaster had to be strengthened considerably.

Like the Tallboy the Grand Slam was also fitted with fins in order to generate a stabilizing spin that meant it was ballistically predictable. It also had the thick case and hardened exterior necessary to penetrate the reinforced concrete roofs of large bunkers, or bury itself deep into the ground before detonating and producing its 'earthquake' effect. The new TORPEX explosive was again used as the explosive filling, though because Grand Slam was so large it took a month for the warm liquid explosive to cool and set after it was poured in. Barnes Wallis had anticipated that Grand Slam would need to be dropped from an altitude of 40,000 feet to reach its terminal velocity, but the modified Lancasters struggled to carry the bomb higher than 20,000 feet, though even at this height the munition was found to be adequate. Grand Slam was a potent new weapon and its introduction into service meant that Bomber Command could attack a new range of difficult targets. Grand Slam also utilised SABS and the sight was critical in obtaining the accuracy required to strike small targets, such as bunkers or railway viaducts, from high altitude. Athough other Lancaster Squadrons were now carrying and dropping Tallboy, 617 Squadron was the only squadron with the B1 Lancasters that could deliver Grand Slam and the first Bomb was delivered to Woodhall Spa on 20 January 1945. There they waited in the bomb dump until the Squadron began to receive the B1 Lancaster from 5 March 1945.

Wing Commander Johnny Fauquier, the Canadian CO of 617 Squadron in early 1945, was keen to fly the B1 on its first flight with a Grand Slam on board:

> The first one (Grand Slam) arrived and was put in the bomb dump with no instructions from Bomber Command whatsoever. Everybody, I think, realized that the war was drawing to a close and I thought what a pity that this should never be dropped. So, without authority from Bomber Command, I ordered the bomb hoisted onto my own aircraft and cleared the personnel out of the station and started to takeoff. At one point, I didn't think we would make it because usually we got airborne with a full load at around 110 miles an hour and I was at 145. The wing tips of the airplane started to bend up and I was wondering whether the wings would come off or what would happen, but finally she did takeoff. So, I flew it around for about 20 minutes and brought it back and landed and then called up Bomber Command and said it was quite safe.[6]

---

6   *Bomber Command Museum of Canada* <https://www.bombercommandmuseum.ca/chronicles/grand-slam/>.

Avro Lancaster B.I (Special), PB996/YZ-C, of 617 Squadron, flown by Flying Officer P. Martin, releasing a 22,000lb medium capacity deep penetration bomb (Bomber Command codeword 'Grand Slam') over the viaduct at Arnsberg, Germany, during a raid on 19 March 1945. (Crown Copyright – Air Historical Branch)

On 14 March, the weapon was used to bomb the Bielefeld railway viaduct, a key part of the German railway communication network and a target that had been unsuccessfully attacked by the British many times during the war. Fauquier was to lead the mission of 15 aircraft, only two of which, his and his second in command, Jock Calder's Lancaster, were carrying Grand Slams. Immediately prior to take-off Fauquier's aircraft began to leak oil and his starboard-inner engine seized up. Fauquier ran towards Calder's aircraft and tried to get his attention so that he could 'commandeer' his Lancaster. Calder claimed that he was unable to make sense of Johnny's frantic waving and sign language, opened the throttles and took off for Bielefeld, leaving a very angry Fauquier behind. Over Bielefeld Calder released the Grand Slam at 11,965 feet, and judged it landed only 30 yards short of the viaduct. The Tallboys dropped by the remainder of 617 were also judged to have been on target. Eleven seconds after penetrating the ground, the Grand Slam exploded, and 260 feet of the span was destroyed. Harris was briefed on the first use of the Grand Slam the following day and sent a note to 617 Squadron that read as follows:

> I have just seen a stereo-pair of the Bielefeld Viaduct taken after your visit yesterday afternoon, my congratulations on your accurate bombing. You have certainly made a proper mess of it this time and incidentally added another page to your history by being the first squadron to drop the biggest bomb on Germany so far, good work. Keep up the training. We can't afford to put these new little pets in the wrong place.[7]

617 Squadron dropped a total of 41 Grand Slams during the closing weeks of the war, targets included the submarine pen near Bremen, where it penetrated 23 feet of concrete, as well as other viaducts and railway bridges. Fauquier personally dropped six, which may have appeased his anger towards Calder.

Elsewhere, 2 Group, the only RAF medium bomber formation in the UK, were developing more precise methods to strike targets. By the summer of 1942 the Group was beginning to receive Boston, Mosquito and Mitchell aircraft. These were faster, more potent and less vulnerable than the

---

7   *Bomber Command Museum of Canada* <https://www.bombercommandmuseum.ca/chronicles/grand-slam/>.

Douglas Boston Mark III of No. 88 Squadron RAF, flying from Ford, Sussex, heads inland over France after bombing the German gun batteries defending Dieppe. (Crown Copyright – Air Historical Branch)

Blenheims, with which the Group had started the war. The Lockheed Ventura bomber, in effect a converted Hudson, was also part of the Group though it lacked speed, defensive armament and manoeuvrability, consequently being phased out of service relatively quickly. It was a shame that the Group had to have such a hotchpotch of aircraft, as this caused both operational and maintenance complications, but the increasingly modern machines were nonetheless a step in the right direction.[8]

For the first part of the war 2 Group had been employed either in direct support of the British Army, or on shipping strikes, both of which had proved costly. They had also acted as 'bait' for the various Circuses that had been conducted by Fighter Command from 1941 onwards. These involved bombing from medium level, but they had not penetrated far into France and target selection was a matter of secondary importance, when compared to drawing the *Luftwaffe* fighters into battle.[9]

The arrival of the new aircraft, especially the Mosquito, meant that low-level strikes against targets deep in enemy territory, now became a realistic possibility. The attack on the Philips Radio works at Eindhoven, on 6 December 1942, was 2 Group's first large scale attempt to attack a target with precision bombing at low-level. Ninety-three bombers were involved (47 Venturas, 36 Bostons and 10 Mosquitoes) and were despatched from a series of bases in East Anglia, the Bostons and Mosquitoes went via a northerly route, the Venturas via the south. The approach was below 100 feet, which meant the German radar operators failed to detect them, though there were still hazards as the aircraft streams crossed the coast, both from sea bird strikes on the aircraft and German AA Gunners. The Venturas, in particular, were hit badly by flak as they drifted off

8   Michael Bowyer, *2 Group RAF* (London: Faber and Faber, 1974), p. 223.
9   Basil Embry, *Mission Accomplished* (London: Purnell and Sons, 1956), p. 240.

track and over the German fortified island of Walcheren, in the Scheldt estuary. The first wave of Bostons were led by Squadron Leader James Pelly-Fry, who had to pick up and follow a railway track that would help the bomber force navigate the final leg to their target in Eindhoven:

As the seconds ticked away and the ground rushed past underneath in a blur of fields, minor roads, streams, and farm buildings, we were getting even closer to the target and Zero-hour; 12.30 precisely. We were now only about eight miles away from Eindhoven; and at 250 mph that meant two minutes to go. Jock and I with our hearts pounding stared ahead; no railway! If we were late in spotting it [the railway], and so had no option but to cross it, then the whole damn business would collapse within spitting distance of the target. And then it happened. I saw a thin plume of white smoke, ahead and slightly to left of our track. It could only be a providential locomotive, very nicely placed to give me the message to begin the turn. I said to Jock 'Moving loco with smoke at 10 o'clock; turning left'. He confirmed the sighting (which was a great relief, I have to say) and as we turned we began to fly alongside the single-track line, now comfortably on our right-hand side. That fellow who was driving, (or perhaps it was his mate refuelling the boiler) will never know the vital contribution that he made to our cause; a cause that it is fair to say had hung by the proverbial thread a few moments before. Now all was well. All was very well indeed. The job was in the bag.

The Armada was now correctly positioned for the final run up, and with Jock Campbell still chasing my tail I gave a wing waggle to give him the signal for the 'Bomb doors open' where-upon the rest of the Bostons successively zoomed up to 800 feet, the reason being that apart from Jock and I who had 11-second delay 500 lb bombs, the rest carried instantaneous fuses. Jock was now acting as bomb aimer, and as the main building in the factory lay dead ahead broadside on – the specific planned target for 88 Squadron – all I had to do was to aim the Boston at it, lift up to clear the flat roof, and leave the rest to Jock. Almost at once he called 'Bombs gone' and as I moved the bomb door lever to 'close' I could see the two anti-aircraft gun positions on the roof blazing away furiously.

One of them must have hit us because the Boston had barely reached the target when without warning it shuddered violently and then began to slow-roll to starboard. It was only when the wings were almost vertical that I was able to begin recovery, but it was necessary to employ maximum correction and the response was painfully slow. As we staggered away from the big building, the Boston was not behaving at all well, I could not but smile briefly when we passed over a game of football in progress – some of the players beginning to run very briskly off the pitch to take what cover was available. This fleeting cameo illustrated as nothing else could do that our arrival had been a complete surprise to them; but not, unfortunately, to the vigilant German gunners who must have had the advantage of the excellent view from the roof-top. They must have been shooting DOWN at us!

The new problem, now that I had succeeded in getting the aeroplane the right-way up, was that I could not make the planned turn onto a westerly heading to begin the dash back to the coast. The best that I could persuade the Boston to do was to inch its way to the left very slowly, painfully slowly. The next thing I saw after about 60 miles of difficult flying was the big dock area of Rotterdam with all the cranes sticking up like tall fingers. This was certainly no place to be in broad daylight, as earlier Blenheim crews had discovered to their cost. In the meantime the other Boston pilots were still following and probably wondering why I had wandered so much off track. I called them on my radio to tell them to press on as I had problems, and one after the other they overtook me with their superior speed.[10]

---

10   James Pelly-Fry, *Heavenly Days* (Manchester: Crecy, 1994), p. 222.

Pelly-Fry managed to stagger over the Dutch coast where he was set upon by two Fw 190s. Unable to corkscrew as they attacked, all he could do was bob up and down as the fighters closed in, surprisingly this worked, and they gave up over the North Sea. The Boston crew reached England, Pelly-Fry offered his crew members the option to bale out, but they both elected to stay with him and the aircraft. Pelly-Fry describes what happened next:

> I called the control tower and said that the Boston was flying on one engine after a fashion and that I had no hydraulics for undercarriage and flaps, the aircraft was badly damaged, and I would have to make a fast belly landing to maintain adequate control. Fire and ambulance services were put on instant readiness. I was given immediate clearance to land – if land was the correct word – and without further ado the Boston was brought in over the threshold fence at something approaching 190 mph, levelled off, and after throttling back, switching off magnetoes and fuel, made a bumpy arrival and slid across the damp grass. I jettisoned the long pilot's canopy and after freeing the harness and my flying helmet jumped onto the ground. Buster was just as quick to escape but we had to lend Jock a hand as he seemed a bit winded; after all, he got the worst of the thump when the Boston flipped onto its belly. As all this was happening the fire truck arrived and stood by but mercifully there was no fire. The three of us gazed at the tired old Boston, full of holes and with bent propellors and important bits missing, and for the first time in my recollection in the abrupt silence I heard Buster mutter 'Dicey do; Very dicey do indeed!' We then elected to leave 'G' – George, the remarkable Boston that had done us so proud, to the salvage people.[11]

Operation OYSTER was one of 2 Group's most celebrated raids; 83 percent of the formation succeeded in dropping their bombs on target and both factories at Eindhoven were significantly damaged. This was at the cost of 15 aircraft: an unsustainable loss rate of 16 percent, casualties mainly falling amongst the Venturas which were hastened out of service.[12] The raid was deliberately timed for Sunday morning when it was hoped few Dutch workers would be present – in fact Dutch loss of life amounted to just 25 people.

The raid further demonstrated the excellence of the new Mosquito aircraft, which by the nature of its speed, range and payload could routinely conduct long range penetration raids at low-level, with reasonable chances of survival. At the end of May 1943, Air Vice-Marshal Basil Embry took over command of 2 Group and gave the precision raids of his Mosquitoes, Bostons and Mitchells further impetus. He stated that he was disappointed at the general accuracy of the Group's bombing (an average error of 1,200 yards) and set about reducing it to just 200 yards. As Embry later observed:

> I foresaw that the future of the Group lay in its ability to operate by day and night and being able to find and hit any target down to a single building. It would have to make up for lack of numbers by a high standard of accuracy, and I argued that if the bombing error could be reduced from 1,200 yards to 300, it would be tantamount to increasing its strength by four times; but I saw no reason why the error should not be lowered to 200 yards for medium-altitude bombing, and to no error for low bombing. I anticipated that future targets for the Group would be small in area for tactical bombing, so I decided that in future our targets should, as far as possible, be isolated factories, power stations, bridges, headquarters or indeed any small target within our power to destroy if we placed our bombs accurately. I felt sure that

11   James Pelly-Fry, *Heavenly Days*, pp. 222-25.
12   Kees Rijken, Paul Schepers, and Arthur Thorning, *Operation Oyster* (Barnsley: Pen and Sword, 2014), p. 164.

Operation OYSTER, the daylight attack on the Philips radio and valve works at Eindhoven, Holland, by No. 2 Group. Douglas Bostons fly over the burning Emmasingel lamp and valve factory at the height of the raid. The works were so severely hit that full production was not resumed for six months. (Crown Copyright – Air Historical Branch)

once we proved our ability to find and hit small targets of this kind, the work of the Group would steadily increase in volume and importance, which would greatly benefit our training and morale. By concentrating on these targets, it would help to prepare the Group for its tactical role. Once 'Overlord' was launched I anticipated that the kind of objectives we would be required to attack would be fuel and ammunition dumps, bridges, radar stations, heavy gun positions and headquarters.[13]

Embry set about producing a programme of intensive training, not just on bombing accuracy, but on navigation too. He was particularly insistent that the navigators of those who would lead the missions must be up to the highest standards and if they were not, then he replaced them. He also requested that the Royal Aeronautical Establishment, at Farnborough, check the accuracy of the Group's bombsights, subsequently finding that nearly all of them were out of alignment and needed re-calibrating. Effort was also put into bombing by radar, where Embry found that he could achieve accuracy to within 300-400 yards bombing through cloud at medium altitude

13   Basil Embry, *Mission Accomplished*, p. 248.

using H2S. Finally, 2 Group also explored the naturalist Peter Scott's understanding of waterfowl, to reduce the chances of encounters with sea birds as they crossed the coast, still a frequent hazard to 2 Group's low-flying sorties. A series of low-level operations, including one against electricity transformer stations in France, highlighted that the Group was still learning as Embry continues:

> This operation was very useful so far as the Mosquitoes were concerned, teaching us several valuable lessons in the planning and execution of low attacks which benefited us in the future. In particular it brought out the necessity for a study of the problem of low altitude navigation, the need for positive and speedy identification of the target early in the final approach, and the importance of selecting well-defined landmarks as a lead on to the target. Because we had not studied the final approach with sufficient care, several leaders had made too rapid changes of course at the last moment, making station keeping difficult. In certain cases the leader had approached at too high a speed, so that pilots at the rear of the formation had found it impossible to keep position, and one or two had been unable to cross the target before the bombs of the leaders exploded.
>
> For low altitude bombing, bombs were fused so that there was a delay of about nine seconds between the time the bombs hit the target and their explosion. In that space of time an aircraft flying at 300 miles an hour covered a little over 1,300 yards. We ruled that the last aircraft across the target must be a minimum distance of 300 yards outside the target area by the time the leader's bombs exploded. That meant that the distance between the leading aircraft and the last one must not exceed 1,000 yards. In practice by accurate station keeping we could fly three sub-formations of six aircraft each across the target with safety, but on this occasion some had become strung out as described.[14]

The need for pilots to find the target in built up areas took particular care. Embry produced his own model section within 2 Group, who could construct models of any target and its surrounding area. The model would accurately depict tall vertical structures that would not only be hazards but could also be used as important visual markers for the crews on their approach to the target. Initially the structures selected as visual markers might be as far as two miles apart, but the space between them would be gradually narrowed in distance as they neared the target, until it was almost as if the aircraft was flying down a funnel, or visual beam approach. Considerable care was also taken to plot the anti-aircraft positions and adjust the approach route accordingly, 2 Group paid particular attention to all intelligence reports of anti-aircraft positions, even setting up an anti-flak section within Group HQ, which factored these enemy dispositions into the planning of their operations. The Group's operational judgement was that if at any point there were more than 12 guns that could be brought to bear at any particular section of the approach route, then losses would simply be too high. Approaches to neutralise these positions were taken, though Embry candidly admitted after the war that they could have paid more attention to this.[15] Embry explained his philosophy to flak was quite simple, commenting 'To attack a target it was first necessary to reach it, and anyone who thinks that remark is as absurd as it sounds should consider the story of the United States 9th Air Force attack with B-26 Marauders on Ijmuiden late in 1943, from which not a single aircraft returned. Had the No.2 Group operational planning staff been consulted as to the advisability of attacking such a target with Marauders at low altitude, they would have replied. 'We do not think you will reach it'.[16] The Americans lost ten twin-engine B-26 Marauder medium bombers in that mission to Ijmuiden, through a combination of flak and Fw 190s.

---

14   Basil Embry, *Mission Accomplished*, p. 249.
15   Basil Embry, *Mission Accomplished*, pp. 251-4
16   Basil Embry, *Mission Accomplished*, p. 259.

Air Vice Marshal Basil Embry, Air Officer Commanding 2 Group, and his staff study a a scale model of a prospective target at the Group Headquarters in Brussels. They are (left to right): Air Commodore D.F.W. Atcherley (Senior Air Staff Officer), Group Captain P.G. Wykeham-Barnes (Group Captain Operations), Wing Commander H.P. Shallard (Group Intelligence Officer) and Air Vice-Marshal Embry. Photo dated May 1945. (Crown Copyright – Air Historical Branch)

By 1943, the fast and unarmed Mosquito bomber was rapidly proving it could penetrate deep into German airspace. On 30 January 1943, during the celebrations for the tenth anniversary of Hitler's rise to power, a small force of Mosquitoes, under Squadron Leader Reggie Reynolds, led the first daylight raids over Berlin. The first sortie that day interrupted Goering at 1100hrs, just as he was due to speak at the headquarters of the *Gross Deutsche Rundfunk*, the German state broadcasting company. The second raid took place at 1600 and also disrupted Goebbels' address to the German crowds.

Later in April 1943, a small force of 139 Squadron conducted the longest penetration raid of the war by Mosquitoes, flying the 1,000-mile round trip to strike the adjoining Schott glass and Carl Zeiss optical works at Jena, near Leipzig. These factories produced important military optics, including periscopes for German U-boats. Reynolds was again the leader of that mission and was aided once more by his navigator, Flight Lieutenant Edward Sismore, judged to be one of the best navigators in the RAF. Reynolds described the raid in a letter to Major Geoffrey de Havilland, whose visionary company had of course designed and built the Mosquito. It was published in *Flight Magazine* the following month.

I was leading in 'B' for 'Beer' No. D.Z.601, a particularly fine Mossie, and I was airborne with the rest of the formation at a certain hour in the early evening.

The North Sea was crossed at wave-top height and, on approaching the enemy coast, always the most-tense moment, speed was increased, and the formation closed up for the quick dash across. Once over, the trip becomes more interesting. One sees such things as cyclists jump off their cycles to have a look round to see what is coming, children look up at us, then put their heads down and run as hard as they can. Mechanical vehicles are almost non-existent—everyone cycles. Startled horses, sheep and cows scatter in every direction.

There were no further incidents until we ran over one of Germany's reservoirs, when the Hun pushed up some accurate flak at us; fortunately, no one was hit, but shortly afterwards two of the formation collided and crashed. It was another 50 miles or so farther on when bad weather was encountered. First thick industrial haze, and then heavy low clouds covering the tops of the hills over which we had to fly. Of course, we had to enter cloud and climb high enough to clear the hills with a margin of safety. As soon as we estimated that we should have cleared the high hills we descended into the gloom beneath the clouds.

To enable the other aircraft to keep track in the murky weather, Reynolds took the unusual decision to switch on his navigation lights for a short while, so that the other crews could locate him. This was also done by the leader of the second section, Squadron Leader Blessing. The other members of the raid afterwards stated that this was a great help for them to regain formation. Reynolds relates that they were now nearing their mission's objective:

At this stage we had arrived at a point approximately 20 miles from the target and we turned on to our run up, increasing speed and then opening bomb doors. We picked up various landmarks which we were looking for and knew from these that we were dead on track. The visibility was now down to about 1,500 yards—not much when one is travelling at such high speed. The target was now only two miles away but not yet in sight. At 1,000 yards I picked up the tall chimneys and opened up to full throttle. My observer pointed out the balloons and immediately the flak came up at us in bright red streams and unhealthily close. Now it was every man for himself; I picked out a tall building and went for it, releasing my bombs at point-blank range. I yanked the stick back to climb over the building, and as I topped it the airscrew received a direct hit. There was a violent explosion in front of my eyes, and I felt something tug at my hand and leg but took no notice for the time being—things were too hot! Now we were in a veritable hail of tracer shells, dodging and twisting for dear life. More balloons ahead, which we missed by the grace of God, and now, apart from a few inaccurate bursts, we were clear, and I was able to survey the damage.

My left hand was bleeding freely, as was my left leg. The kite was vibrating considerably, and I could see holes in the fairing immediately in front of the radiator. Flak had pierced a hole just aft of the port radiator and close to one of the main tanks. There were two large holes in the fuselage close to the throttle box where some fitting had been blown away. My intercom had packed up and I discovered later that a splinter had severed the lead just below my starboard ear. The collar of my battledress was torn also; this wasn't noticed until I arrived back at base; when Flt. Lt. Sismore, my navigator, asked me what I had done to get that! However, to continue; after that one violent explosion it seemed a miracle that the aircraft could keep in the air. I was especially anxious about my port radiator with that hole so near, and constantly checked the temps, to watch for any rise. Fortunately it remained constant at 98 deg. C, and the vibration got no worse, so the need to feather the damaged propeller never arose.

We were now returning individually and so I nipped into the low cloud for safety—to clear hills and avoid any flak that may have been put up. My observer bound up my hand and then we settled down to the long journey home with frequent apprehensive glances at the engine instruments and fuel. I, personally, felt satisfied that I got the target with my bombs, and later one of the boys said he saw them go in followed by a sheet of flame 100 feet high—and it would be some time before they actually exploded.

105 Squadron Mosquito B.IVs pictured on 13 May 1943 prior to an operation over Berlin by aircraft of 2 Group. DZ483/GB-R is about to be loaded with four 500lb medium capacity bombs. Two weeks later, DZ483 crashed at Marham while attempting to land on one engine killing its pilot, Flying Officer J. Rae, and navigator Flying Officer K.S. Bush. (Crown Copyright – Air Historical Branch)

On the way back we ran into more trouble by entering two more defended areas. The second one was very, hot, and it was with luck that we escaped by means of violent evasive action combined with full throttle and fine pitch. Even though 'B—Beer' was badly damaged, she behaved magnificently throughout and is now being repaired, which will take a few days. One of the port engine bearers had a large hole through the middle of it, but the vital parts of the engine were sound.[17]

During the closing years of the war 2 Group's Mosquitoes perfected their precision bombing techniques to a fine art and produced some of the most spectacular raids of the war. These included the destruction of the Gestapo headquarters' in both Copenhagen and Aarhus in Denmark, as well as the aptly named Operation JERICHO. This last famous raid breached the walls of the prison at Amiens on 15 February 1944 and allowed a number of French resistance fighters to escape, many of whom had been condemned to execution and were due to be shot on 19 February. All highlighted the precision 2 Group were able to achieve, particularly important where the target was surrounded by a friendly civilian population.

A similar mission was the bombing of the population registry in a government building in the Hague. It acted as a central repository of data and statistics on the entire Dutch population and prevented the Dutch resistance from creating forged papers, that could assist both their own efforts as well as Jews avoiding persecution. A request was made to the Dutch underground for the RAF to bomb the building and a mission was flown on 11 April 1944 by six Mosquito fighter-bombers. Wing Commander Bateson led the mission and produced a short report that was subsequently edited in the *Vliegende Hollander*, a small newspaper which was dropped by Allied Air Forces as part of the propaganda effort.

17 Letter from Wg Cdr Reynolds to Major De Havilland quoted in *Flight Magazine*, July 1943.

We flew very low. The inundation of certain parts of the country [the Germans had flooded the polder area], looking like marshes, did not help to make it easier to find our way. At first we thought to be over the wrong coastal area, but when we finally managed to find our way all went smooth. On the mock up we had paid special attention to a number of chimneys, but when we arrived at the spot we saw so many chimneys that we didn't trust too much on those marks. I ascended to approximately 700 metres, took a good look around and noticed at a distance of approximately six kilometres, the tower of the Peace Palace, which was situated really close to the target. I descended again and started the nose dive towards the target.

The building counted five stories and was estimated to be 25 metres high. We bombed from an altitude of approximately 18 metres, so lower than the roof. A sentry was posted outside, but he threw his rifle away and ran. I myself could not see what happened but my number 2 told me later, that he had been able to follow my bombs exactly, that one hit the middle of the front door and that the two others entered two large windows.

All bombs landed on the target and the incendiaries functioned as intended. When number 5 and 6 had had their turn nothing very much remained of the whole building.[18]

Throughout this period 2 Group were also heavily committed to the NO-BALL operations against the V1 sites in France and the low countries. In the period from November 1943 to the middle of May 1944 they succeeded in destroying 32 sites in both low-level and medium-altitude attacks. These attacks, were complemented by fighter-bomber attacks, as well as American B-17 and B-26 Marauder attacks, illustrating how a blend of different capabilities is often more effective than just one particular approach. There were undoubtedly some targets that only a Mosquito could attack and others that were best suited to medium bombers such, as Mitchells, Bostons and Marauders. [19]

On 1 June 1943, the Group was transferred to 2nd Tactical Air Force and from mid-May 1944 onwards the Group was committed to the support of land forces, as part of Operation OVERLORD. As Embry had predicted, the targets now given to 2 Group were important operational targets for the Army, some of which were mobile and fleeting requiring precise missions to be generated quickly. We will examine air support to the British Army's ground campaigns in Volume 2, but it is worth highlighting now the 2 Group strike on the *Panzergruppe West* headquarters.

The Headquarters of this large German armoured striking force, clumsily signalled their location 'Battle Headquarters Panzer Gruppe West evening ninth at La Caine'. The signal was intercepted by Bletchley Park and it prompted a daylight attack on the Chateau de la Caine, 12 miles south west of Caen, on 10 June. A large force of 2 Group Mitchells would bomb from medium height with their full bomb load of 4,000lbs, made up of eight 500 pounders, Typhoon fighter bombers would also attack at low levels. Initially the morning briefing scheduled for 1030 had to be deferred because of heavily overcast sky and thick cloud, however, as the day progressed Squadron Leader Scott recalled the weather slightly improved and the aircraft took off:

The bombers climbed steadily, circling over base as they formed up, before setting course at 2022. Over Selsey Bill they were joined by another 18 aircraft of 226 Squadron led by their Commanding Officer, Wg Cdr Mitchell. Soon after, 33 Spitfires took up their escort positions, close escort being provided by Mark Vs from an Air Defence Great Britain Squadron while three Mark IX Squadrons of 84 Group flew high and low cover to the Mitchells. One 226 Squadron aircraft had to abort with mechanical trouble. Two others from 180 Squadron

18   Wing Commander Bateson, *Vliegende Hollander*, 4 May 1944. See *Traces of War* <www.tracesofwar.com>.
19   Basil Embry, *Mission Accomplished*, pp. 258-9.

Low-level oblique aerial photograph taken by one of two De Havilland Mosquitoes of 21 Squadron during a daylight attack on Gael airfield near St Malo. (Crown Copyright – Air Historical Branch)

turned back before bombing; one with an oil pressure problem and the other with an instrument fault. Yet another suffered bomb release failure and brought its bombs back.

Two of the four Typhoon Squadrons flew their 'spare' aircraft also and of the 42 Typhoons taking part in the operation, two from each squadron were 'fighters' with no rockets but fully–loaded cannon, the remaining 34 were all rocket-firing 'Tiffies' [Typhoons]. The plan was for the Typhoons to attack in two waves with 30 minutes between them, the first wave's attack on the parked vehicles and tanks to coincide with the assault by the bombers, the second wave's task was to 'clear up'.

The Chief of Staff of *Panzergruppe West*, General Von Dawans, was reportedly dining with his staff officers in the Chateau's large dining room. On hearing the air raid sirens the headquarters staff exited the building to view the aircraft, never imagining that they were the target. At the moment the raid began General Geyr Von Schweppenburg, the commander of *Panzergruppe West*, arrived at the chateau in his staff car. The timing of his arrival would nearly cost him his life as Squadron Leader Scott continues:

> Seventeen 'Tiffies from 181 and 247 Squadrons loosed off 136 rockets from 2,000 feet with devastating effect.
>
> Above at 12,000 feet, the three squadrons of 139 Wing spread in a 'vic', with the Mitchells of 226 Squadron flying tight up behind 180 Squadron in the No. 4 position, converged on the target in boxes of six aircraft. At 2115 the Mitchells released 536 x 500 lb bombs with great accuracy and saturated the chateau and the whole target area. Great clouds of dust and debris, flame and smoke rose into the air. Geyr Von Schweppenburg and another officer were wounded, but von Dawans and the remainder of his staff perished in the attack.
>
> Four 'fighter' Typhoons meanwhile swept into the nearby village of Montigny, shooting up the place with their cannon.
>
> As the Mitchells swung onto a north-westerly course after dropping their bombs some Flak was experienced from Caen, but no real damage was suffered. By the time the second wave of

North American Mitchell IIs of 98 Squadron RAF taxiing along the perimeter track at Dunsfold, Surrey, for a morning raid on targets in northern France. (Crown Copyright – Air Historical Branch)

RP [Rocket Projectile] Typhoons arrived on the scene, the chateau was a charred and smoking ruin and the radio trucks and other vehicles were scattered and scorched wrecks. The 'Tiffies' fired their rockets and cannon into any outbuildings that remained standing. All the bombers were down by 2225 (2025 GMT) and there was an immediate call for a 'turn round' for night operations. At de-briefing the elated aircrews of each squadron reported on the complete success of the operation. Almost everyone claimed to have seen their bombs fall on the target or close to it; Flak had been light, there was no enemy fighter opposition and the raid appeared to have taken the enemy defences completely by surprise.'[20]

This rapidly-arranged daylight attack, prompted by an Ultra intercept, illustrates how important timely intelligence is to air operations generally and precision strike operations in particular. Today we take such precision operations for granted, enabled by some of the most advanced technologies the West can produce. It therefore remains remarkable how the Allies were able to achieve the levels of bombing precision they did, with such rudimentary technology in many instances. In the war at sea, technology would also help underpin the British approach to the anti-boat campaign. It was another example of where air support would prove a decisive advantage. Yet that opportunity was almost squandered and the campaign only narrowly avoided disaster, partly because of the RAF's overwhelming obsession with its own bomber offensive and a refusal to meet Coastal Command's modest requirements.

---

20   Christopher Shores and Chris Thomas, *Second Tactical Air Force* (Surrey: Ian Allen, 2005), p. 148.

Part IV
The Air War at Sea

15

'They Shall Not Pass Unseen'[1] Coastal Command's Hunt for U-Boats

There were few parts of the RAF that began the war as ill-prepared as Coastal Command, perhaps that is unsurprising given the flawed conceptual approach the Command initially laboured under.

Immediately prior to the war, the RAF had identified four main roles for Coastal Command, first to assist the Royal Navy's Home Fleet in preventing enemy vessels from escaping from the North Sea to the Atlantic. Secondly, to provide air patrols to support Royal Navy anti-submarine forces and convoys. Thirdly, to conduct air searches in home waters and finally to provide an anti-shipping strike force for duty mainly on the East coast.[2]

These next two chapters will cover the second, anti-submarine role, a major task upon which Allied victory in the Second World War would depend. It was a role that was initially vastly under-rated by both the Royal Navy and the RAF who were both misled into thinking that the First World War experience of U-boat warfare would not be repeated in a future conflict with Germany.

The Royal Navy's emotional attachment to traditional surface fleet actions was one factor in this mistaken attitude, but so too was an over-estimation of the capability of ASDIC.[3] Developed in the First World War, ASDIC had improved considerably from the rudimentary directional hydrophones of 1918, so that the Royal Navy were now able to operate it from fast moving ships and could detect submarines at much longer ranges. By 1935 more than half the destroyers in the fleet carried ASDIC, with a programme in hand to equip the remainder and plans for all future destroyers and anti-submarine vessels under construction to have it on completion. As a result of these improvements, a dangerous and widespread belief arose in the Royal Navy that they had found 'the answer' to the submarine.[4]

One should not criticise these Royal Navy pre-war assumptions too harshly, the Germans also rated ASDIC's capabilities highly and instead of concentrating on building submarines, focused their pre-war efforts on constructing a large surface fleet capable of major combat in the Atlantic. Known as the Z-Plan, this German programme of construction further encouraged the Admiralty to concentrate on the threat of German surface raiders spilling out of the North Sea, into the Atlantic and attacking Allied merchant convoys.

---

1   The motto of 461 Squadron RAAF. This squadron was formed at RAF Mount Batten on 25 April and flew Sunderlands throughout the war with RAF Coastal Command. It is credited with the destruction of six U-boats.

2   TNA AIR 15/4: Employment of Coastal Command in a Continental War, 13 June 1939.

3   ASDIC – The Admiralty term for Sonar, the underwater sound echo-ranging technology for detecting underwater objects. It comes from initial letters of the Allied Submarine Detection Investigation Committee set up in 1917.

4   Alfred Price, *Aircraft Versus Submarine* (London: Janes, 1980), p. 33.

In contrast to its surface ship programme, the German outlay in U-boat construction was more modest. There were only 52 boats available at the beginning of the war, of which a mere 22 were suitable for use in the Atlantic. One of the more compelling 'What ifs?' in history, must include the scenario where the German Navy prioritised U-boat construction earlier and before the Allies had begun to master anti-submarine operations.

The new German U-boats were much more advanced than their First World War forbears, with improvements in under-water handling, silent running, torpedo effectiveness, endurance and the ability to dive deeply. Taken overall, they offered a step-change in lethality.[5] Once the war started, the British were quickly forced to revise their opinion of the effectiveness of the U-boat, recognising that their pre-war faith in ASDIC was wildly over-optimistic, particularly in detecting U-boats attacking on the surface of the sea at night. They also noted that U-boat lethality had been enhanced by improved German naval radio communications, which now permitted U-boats to coordinate their operations as 'Wolf Packs'. These tactics allowed up to 20 U-boats at a time to concentrate on specific convoys, regularly overwhelming the Allied escorts and the convoy defences. Although German surface raiders had achieved some success early in the war, a re-appreciation of Coastal Command priorities in the light of the potent threat by U-boats was undertaken. By 1942 anti-submarine warfare was well-established as the Command's highest priority, with reconnaissance and anti-shipping strikes, against both enemy naval and merchant shipping a secondary priority.[6]

The Coastal Command and Royal Navy view that the Battle of the Atlantic was the most immediate priority for the Allies, was endorsed by the Combined American and British Chiefs of staff, at the Casablanca Conference in 1942.[7] Belatedly and grudgingly the Air Staff, who were fixated with building their strategic bomber offensive, would begin to equip Coastal Command with the necessary quality and quantity of equipment it required to combat the U-boats. The Air Staff's inability to recognise the battle against the U-boats as one of the most decisive campaigns in the war, upon which its own bomber offensive and the invasion of western Europe depended, must rank as one of their greatest oversights.

A combination of pre-war parsimony and the underestimation of the U-boat, meant that Coastal Command was initially equipped with either unsuitable or outdated aircraft, weapons and equipment. This was compounded by both the lower level of priority Coastal Command was afforded in comparison to Fighter and Bomber Command and two significant procurement failures – the Blackburn Botha torpedo bomber and the Saro Lerwick flying-boat. The latter was expected to have replaced the Short Sunderland Flying Boat and allow Shorts to focus on construction of the Stirling Bomber. When the Saro project failed Coastal Command found that, in anticipation of transferring production to Stirlings, Shorts had prematurely dismantled the jigs used to manufacture the Sunderland. It would take many months for them to renew large-scale production of the vital Sunderlands at what was a critical time.[8] The initial lack of suitable aircraft was also combined with anti-submarine weaponry that was woefully inadequate. Not for nothing did Coastal Command refer to itself as the 'Cinderella Service'.

More positively, Coastal Command's progress in the Second World War was characterised by considerable efforts within the Command to develop new equipment and the right blend of tactics. These operational improvements were achieved through strong inter-service understanding and

---

5   Alfred Price, *Aircraft Versus Submarine*, p. 42.
6   TNA AIR 15/46: Coastal Command's Aircraft Requirements. File S/7012/Tactics to ACAS c. Feb 1942.
7   John Slessor, *The Central Blue* (London: Cassell and Co., 1956), p. 464.
8   John Terraine, *The Right of The Line*, p. 228.

Airmen of 10 Squadron RAAF attend to an overhaul of a Bristol Pegasus XXII engine.
(Crown Copyright – Air Historical Branch)

cooperation, an efficient lessons-learnt process and the integration of operationally focussed scientists within the Command.

HQ Coastal Command worked particularly hard to develop close relations with the Royal Navy generally and C-in-C Western Approaches in particular. War often allows talented individuals to come to the fore and make a profound strategic contribution, the assignment of the energetic and experienced ex-submariner, Captain D.V. Peyton-Ward RN, as the Royal Navy's liaison officer to Coastal Command is such an example. He was by all accounts a particularly 'air-minded' individual and remained part of the Coastal Command inner-circle throughout the war (to the extent that he was trusted to write the RAF's Second World War Coastal Command narrative, '*The Royal Air Force in the Maritime War*'). It was on Peyton-Ward's initiative that every individual sighting and attack on U-boats by Coastal Command crews was forensically recorded, with the probable results carefully analysed. Peyton-Ward invited the aircrews whenever possible to come to Coastal Command's headquarters at Northwood and discuss the event in detail, sharing their practical experiences whilst events were still fresh in their minds.[9] This helped develop a common understanding of the best way to sink submarines.

In 1941 Coastal Command also created an Operational Research Section under Professor Patrick Blackett, who went on to become the Command's Scientific Adviser. Professor E.J. Williams was one of the first to be assigned to Coastal Command's Operational Research Section and highlights

---

9   Air Historical Branch Narrative/II/117/3 (C), *The Royal Air Force in The Maritime War*, p. 43.

the role of the scientists, which was not just limited to identifying new technological requirements, but also included evolving the right tactics:

'New Weapons for old' is apt to become a very popular cry. The success of some new devices has led to a new form of escapism which runs somewhat thus: 'Our present equipment doesn't work very well; training is bad, supply is poor, spare parts non-existent. Let's have an entirely new gadget!' Then comes the vision of the new gadget, springing like Aphrodite from the Ministry of Aircraft Production, complete with spare parts, and attended by a chorus of trained crews. One of the tasks of an Operational Research Section is to make possible at least an approach to a numerical estimate of the merits of a change-over from one device to another, by continual investigation of the actual performance of existing new weapons, and by objective analysis of the likely performance of new ones ...

In general, one might conclude that relatively too much scientific effort has been expended hitherto in the production of new devices and too little in the proper use of what we have got. Thus, there is a strong general case for moving many of the best scientists from the technical establishments to the operational Commands, at any rate for a time. If, and when, they return to technical work, they will be often much more useful by reason of their knowledge of real operational needs.'[10]

The blending of tactical and technological innovation was particularly apparent when the commanders, aircrew and scientists would come together, in what were known as the 'Sunday Soviets', at the Telecommunications Research Establishment at Swanage. Here the frankest exchanges would take place between the scientists who designed the equipment and the men who had to operate it in action. These meetings fulfilled three important purposes. They first ensured scientists faced 'reality' and did not become solely fixated with the technical brilliance of their inventions. Secondly, they ensured commanders understood how new equipment was performing and being used in action. This often took the form of a senior officer having his 'ears pinned back' by animated junior aircrew. Perhaps most importantly the 'Sunday Soviets' helped the aircrew operate the equipment to maximum effect and get the most out of any new device. Interestingly, the German Navy had no equivalent process and the resulting gap in trust and mutual understanding between scientists and U-boat personnel, would cause them significant problems during important periods of the campaign.[11]

The conclusions from Captain Peyton-Ward, the Operational Research Section and the 'Sunday Soviets' fed Coastal Command's tactical instructions, as well as the *Coastal Command Review* instituted by Air Chief Marshal Sir Philip Joubert in January 1942. Official military publications are frequently dull, superficial and largely ignored, but the *Coastal Command Review* was an exception to this rule and widely recognised as an important factor in developing Coastal Command's tactical understanding and excellence. Joubert's successor as AOC Coastal Command, Air Chief Marshal Sir John Slessor commented:

It was a serious professional review of the previous month's work and was a valuable medium for keeping the squadrons informed of what was going on throughout the Command and how the air/sea war was going, making generally known the tactical lessons that were constantly being learnt in the course of operations, and dealing with the whole range of professional activities of the Command in a way that would be interesting as well as instructive for the

10   Alfred Price, *Aircraft Versus Submarine*, p. 67.
11   Alfred Price, *Aircraft Versus Submarine*, p. 77.

crews … Its regular features included surveys of the previous month's operations against the U-boats, in which a number of individual attacks were carefully analysed and criticized.[12]

It was in this manner that those lessons, experienced and identified by a few, could be cascaded across the whole Command and the enemy's weaknesses systematically exploited. Coastal Command's prowess was continually improved upon during the war, in a virtuous cycle of introducing new measures, observing changes in the enemy's tactics and then developing further measures, or even counter-measures to retain the initiative. This process had reached a mature stage by the decisive year of the Battle of the Atlantic 1943.

There were compelling reasons why the Allied Combined Chiefs of Staff had afforded first priority to the war against the U-boat at the Casablanca Conference. During 1942, the British had reached the lowest point in the delivery of seaborne supplies required to sustain its war effort. Imports of food, munitions, materials and fuel had dropped from 61 million short tons in 1940, to just 39 million. Prioritising the Battle of Atlantic in 1942 was also important because in the following year Operation BOLERO, the great movement of American forces into Britain, would begin. Without BOLERO subsequent operations on the continent of Europe, as well as in the Mediterranean and North Africa, would be impossible. The U-boat destruction of shipping was not just about a temporary lack of material and supplies, it inflicted strategic damage on the Allies ability to make full use of the sea and prosecute the war effectively. The commander of the German U-boat arm, Admiral Doenitz, concisely observed: 'The enemy's shipping constitutes one single, great entity. It is therefore immaterial where a ship is sunk. Once it has been destroyed it has to be replaced by a new ship; and that's that'.[13]

In 1942 the Allied shipping losses, of 650,000 tons a month, massively exceeded their rate of new ship construction. Quite simply these losses meant that without a victory against the U-boats, the Allies, ability to defeat Germany through a large, strategic bomber campaign or a land invasion of continental Europe, could not be achieved. It was these stark facts, that make the Air Staff's intransigence in not supplying Coastal Command with the necessary aircraft, so harmful.

Slessor took over command of Coastal Command in February 1943. His predecessors had not only raised the efficiency of the Command, but also dramatically increased its size from a modest 19 squadrons to a total of 60 squadrons, with a strength of some 850 aircraft. The Command included squadrons manned by Canadians, Australians, New Zealanders, Norwegians, Poles, Czechs and Dutch, as well as three US Navy Squadrons under operational command.

The anti-submarine squadrons made up the bulk of the Coastal Command force, by 1943 these consisted of 34 squadrons, with approximately 430 aircraft. Twelve of these squadrons were flying boat squadrons, four of which were equipped with the comparatively slow and vulnerable US-built PBY-17 Catalina. Whilst it would take a brave Catalina crew to tackle U-boat AA fire, this stately aircraft did have the advantage of tremendous endurance and dependable reliability. Eight of Coastal's squadrons were equipped with the large, imposing British-built Sunderland flying-boat and it is this aircraft that is perhaps the most evocative of Coastal Command and the Battle of the Atlantic. Much loved by its crews, it remained in service with the RAF until 1958 and the RNZAF until 1967.

The Sunderland should be thought of as a boat as well as an aircraft, and many of the first impressions RAF aircrew received in encountering the machine at its mooring, might have led them to believe they had joined a different service altogether. Flight Lieutenant Les Baveystock

---

12   Sir John Slessor, *The Central Blue*, p. 471.
13   Admiral Karl Doenitz, *Memoirs: Ten Years and Twenty Days* (London: Wiedenfeld and Nicholson, 1958), p. 228.

Sunderland I, L2163/ DA-G, of 210 Squadron based at Oban, Argyll, banking over the Atlantic while
escorting Canadian Troop Convoy 6 (TC.6), inbound for Greenock on 31 July 1940.
(Crown Copyright – Air Historical Branch)

was posted to 10 Squadron RAAF at Mount Batten in Plymouth, an experienced squadron that
was the first Empire unit into action and would serve with Coastal Command until VE Day. He
recalls his first encounter with a 10 Squadron RAAF Sunderland at Mount Batten in Plymouth:

> A motorboat some 18 feet long with a motor amidships took us out to a Sunderland moored
> in the Cattewater. There were already two crew members on board. At that time Sunderlands
> were never left unattended, and two members of the crew always remained on board as boat
> guards, doing watches of 24 hours. However, officers did not do these duties, which was hard
> luck on the crew that had few NCOs. Perhaps that is why I was popular among the fellows,
> for I was to find that I was the only sergeant pilot on the squadron and later the only RAF
> pilot.
>   Although I enjoyed this first ride, later I was to hate the sight of a dinghy as did all flying-
> boat crews. We seemed to spend most of our time either waiting for one to take us out to an
> aircraft or waiting for one to take us ashore. On a wet and choppy night we often got soaked
> through before we ever reached our Sunderland. Of course I did not realise this as I waited my
> turn to board. A tradition on 'boats' that I was soon to learn was that the skipper always went
> on board first and after a flight came off last. It must have been some sort of archaic custom
> handed down from HMS *Victory* via the Royal Naval Air Service.'[14]

The Sunderland was an enormous aircraft for its day, possessing a wingspan of over 112 feet and a
length of almost 86 feet. Most of the Sunderlands were equipped with four Bristol Pegasus Engines
that gave a cruising speed of between 105 and 120 knots, an endurance of nine hours, and a range

---

14   Leslie Baveystock, *Wavetops at My Wingtips* (Shrewsbury: Airlife Publishing), 2001, p. 137.

A peaceful scene at Lough Erne in Northern Ireland on 20 May 1943, as a seaplane tender passes a
Sunderland of 201 Squadron. The censor has removed all trace of the aircraft's fuselage-mounted ASV aerials.
(Crown Copyright – Air Historical Branch)

of approximately 2,980 miles. In 1943, Coastal Command's Sunderlands were based primarily at
Lough Erne, Oban and Bowmore (15 Group RAF), or at Mount Batten (Plymouth), Pembroke
and Hamworthy (Poole) (19 Group RAF).[15] There were of course other Squadrons throughout the
world, as part of Middle East and Far East Commands for instance, which also carried out anti-
submarine warfare operations as well as reconnaissance and transportation duties.

The manner in which Sunderlands operated was different to land-based aircraft. Flying boats
required both seamanship skills, as well as flying abilities in their day to day operations. As one
example, when a Sunderland was taxiing from its alighting area to its moorings the pilot often
needed to carefully apply extra power for engines on the windward side, to prevent it from weather-
cocking into the breeze. Flying Boat operations also required special considerations for take-off
and landings, particularly in selecting suitable stretches of water and determining whether the
conditions and sea state were safe. The widely differing moods of the sea could create unusual
hazards, even in relatively sheltered areas of water. Freshwater bases, such as Lough Erne, could
also cause problems as the aircraft would be less buoyant than in salt water and therefore took
longer to get 'on the plane' during takeoff, greater distances were therefore required. Sunderland
crews always needed a marine section as support. This section would ferry them to and from the
Sunderland, help refuel the aircraft, set-up, light and manage the floating flare path at night,
assist in beaching the Sunderland for longer-term maintenance and sweep the alighting area for
floating debris before landing and take-off. Most routine maintenance on Sunderlands was done
at mooring, which required platforms to be slung under each engine and patient mechanics, who

---

15   Andrew Hendrie, *The Cinderella Service – RAF Coastal Command 1939-1945* (Barnsley: Pen and Sword,
2006), p. 215.

frequently had to operate on the engines or airframe in an unrelenting swell. Many engineers record how frustratingly easy it was to drop a spanner into the sea under such circumstances.[16]

Sergeant Ken Robinson, undertook his flying training in Pensacola, Florida and had learnt to operate on Catalinas in that exotic location. So his first view of an RAF Sunderland was on his return to the United Kingdom in May 1943 at the rather less glamorous Pembroke Dock, he remembers boarding the Sunderland through the forward hatch on the front turret.

The Front Turret had been withdrawn into the bow compartment to enable the crewmen to moor and unmoor the boat. There was a bollard hinged at the bottom, which was normally horizontal when the aircraft was in flight but was now fixed in an upright position adjacent to the bomb aimer's hatch. Strapped to the hull on the port side were a mooring ladder and an anchor for use when there was no suitable fixed mooring facilities.

On the starboard side, there was a J-type inflatable dinghy and alongside a companionway leading to the flight deck was the toilet compartment, complete with lavatory and wash basin, both small but unexpectedly comfortable. Just aft of the forward hatch through which we'd boarded the aircraft was the entrance to the wardroom and a through route to the tail.

The skipper referred to the men in the bows as riggers. I was unfamiliar with the term as applied to aircrew and he explained that they were Straight Air Gunners who, in addition to looking after the guns, ammunition and bomb equipment, were also responsible for the airframe. Their varied tasks included mooring and unmooring, carrying out galley duties and deploying the drogues for slowing the boat down in the water when approaching the buoy. It was not unusual, however, for other crew members to assist with these jobs.

Moving towards the rear of the aircraft, we passed through the wardroom which contained two bunks doubling as seats on either side of a table with hinged flaps. Further aft was the galley where food and drinks were prepared. The equipment included two primus stoves separated by a small oven. Another companionway ascended to the rear end of the flight deck and on either side of the galley was a square hatch used, amongst other things, for deployment of the drogues, which were stowed in semi-circular receptacles just below the hatches.

Beyond the galley was the bomb bay in which eight 250lb Torpex-filled depth charges were normally suspended from racks. These racks would be run out along the underside of the wings when the depth charges were made ready for an attack. Under the port bomb door was a removable wedge-shaped panel which enabled a spare engine or other sizable cargo to be loaded.

The next compartment had two more bunks in it and then there was a very spacious area leading up to the tail of the aircraft and the rear turret. The equipment in this space included a fitter's bench and there was a rear hatch on the starboard side providing an exit at a higher level above the water line than the forward hatch.

Attached to one of the bulkheads was the IFF (Identification Friend or Foe) transmitter, provided to enable our forces to identify us as friendly. It could be switched to a distress frequency in an emergency. The control box in the pilot's cabin included a detonating device so that the equipment could be destroyed should there be any risk of it falling into enemy hands.

The forward companionway came up between the two pilot's seats on the flight deck. Immediately aft of the starboard seat was a small darkened cubby-hole housing the ASV (Air to Surface Vessel) radar equipment … Adjacent to the radar position was the navigator's chart table, equipped with instruments used for dead reckoning navigation.

---

16   Ken Robinson, *Dice on Regardless*, p. 10.

On the port side was a wireless operator's position dominated by its R1155 receiver and transmitter. The latter was conspicuous by its enormous brilliantly coloured control knobs. The main spar, the strongest part of the aircraft, crossed the fuselage from wing to wing behind this and the navigator's table. Beyond it on the starboard side the flight engineer had his station. There was one other compartment on the flight deck, where the mid-upper, or dorsal, turret was normally located. This turret replaced the two waist hatches in the Mark I. A second J-Type dinghy was stowed here.

I was suitably impressed. Although I had yet to get airborne in the flying boat, I certainly appreciated how much more comfortable it must be than fighters or bombers, or even Catalinas, where space was so restricted. I was slightly over six feet in height, yet I was able to stand erect in most of the compartments. It was much like being on a ship. I decided that it wasn't going to be so bad flying in these things after all.[17]

A Sunderland's patrol would be planned and directed by their relevant Group Headquarters. 15 Group, based at Liverpool, had primary responsibility for providing air cover for the Atlantic convoys and 19 Group, at Plymouth, for air cover over the Bay of Biscay, including convoys from Gibraltar, or West Africa (see Map 11). The Group Commanders would have received their directives at the morning Naval Combined Staff Conference, this brought together over secure telephone, the Admiralty submarine tracking room at Whitehall, Coastal Command's operations room at Northwood and the four Combined Area Headquarters (such as Western Approaches). The Admiralty submarine tracking room would begin with a report on the positions of U-boats and their expected movements, as well as the sightings and attacks made during the previous 24 hours. This was followed by the Admiralty briefing relevant convoys, either under-way or planned, as well as the large, fast, independently–routed troopships such as the *Queen Mary* or *Queen Elizabeth*.[18] Known as 'Monsters', these could travel at speeds up to 28 knots, out-pacing the U-boats as well as Allied escorts. It therefore made sense for them to sail alone, rather than attach them to either a slow (typically around 7 knots), or fast convoy (10 knots plus).[19] It would be these latter convoys which received the priority for air cover from the Admiralty.

A succession of commanders at Coastal Command would periodically argue that the U-boats were most vulnerable as they transited from their French bases, across the Bay of Biscay, to the open Atlantic. In 1943 for instance Slessor directed his Command to focus once more on this operational area and prioritised support to 19 Group operations, in the hope that it may pay better dividends. He explains his rationale:

> The obvious course, if it were possible, was to fell the tree by cutting through its trunk – the little patch of water about 300 by 120 miles in the Bay of Biscay through which five out of six U-boats operating in the Atlantic had to pass within range of aircraft based in England and Gibraltar. That was one place where we could be absolutely certain there would be U-boats to be found and killed ... There was the decisive point on which we should concentrate; our tactics should be offensive, to find and kill him along the trunk before he could get into the branches, not defensive cover and escorts except where necessary.[20]

---

17 Ken Robinson, *Dice on Regardless*, p. 40.
18 Alfred Price, *Aircraft Versus Submarine*, p. 122.
19 Martin Middlebrook, *Convoy – The Greatest U-boat Battle of the War* (London: Cassell, 1976), p. 91.
20 Sir John Slessor, *The Central Blue*, p. 512.

Though the argument to attack the U-boats in transit sounded convincing, the reality was that aircraft were more profitably employed in direct support of convoys, or in their close vicinity. German U-boat operations always suffered the most under these types of operations. Not only was there greater chance of sighting and killing a U-boat, but the mere presence of an aircraft would force a U-boat to submerge, switch from diesel to its electric engines and travel at a much slower speed. This frequently caused U-boats to lose track of a convoy, disrupting the concentrated wolf pack attacks that had proved so effective. Admiral Doenitz constantly worried that it would be the provision of air cover over his intended victims in the open Atlantic that would have the most impact on his operations. As the war progressed the range of Allied aircraft would increase and their ability to cover convoys far out in to the mid-Atlantic improved. Admiral Doenitz noted one such extension of range on 2 September 1942, when air cover was able to be provided for the first time for a convoy 800 miles out from the UK and 400 miles from Iceland. He noted the consequences in his war diary:

> By systematically forcing the boats under water it made them lose contact at evening twilight, thus spoiling the best prospects for attack of all boats in the first four moonless hours of the night. The enemy made clever use of the boats' loss of contact to make a sharp leg so that contact was not regained until [later on] and it was no longer possible to get the boats of the Group (except 2) near to the convoy. The convoy operation had to be broken off in the morning of 2 September as it no longer seemed possible for boats to haul ahead in the face of the expected heavy air activity.[21]

The first element of any patrol undertaken by the crews of the Sunderlands, or other Coastal Command aircraft, would be the pre-flight preparations. A typical patrol in a Sunderland might take-off at 0100, the crew would therefore try to sleep in the early afternoon and evening, waking up at 2200 to struggle into flying clothes and head for the aircrew mess to consume a last dinner. At 2300, they would assemble for a briefing in the Operations Room, where they would be instructed on the details of their task. Their patrol line would be marked by a ribbon on a huge map, that detailed other patrols, as well as the positions of Allied and neutral shipping. Bombing restriction areas such as Allied submarine safe lanes were marked, as well as enemy aircraft and U-boat sightings and the briefing would capture a host of further details, including key timings, code-words and radio frequencies. The aircrew would then stumble out into the dark and head towards the pier, laden with equipment and rations for 13 hours in the air. A pinnace would take the crew to a larger seaplane tender, on to which they would transfer and roar out to the Sunderland. As the boat approached the Sunderland, the aircraft lights would come on in the wardroom and the duty hand would welcome the crew aboard. Flight Lieutenant Les Baveystock recalls the frenzy of activity that a Sunderland crew undertook before take-off:

> The aircraft rigger and one other member of the crew were up front, with the gun turret wound back from its usual position, grappling with the complicated set of strops that kept us attached to to our mooring buoy. Gunners were fitting guns into the turrets, while the flight engineers were up on the main wing, turning over each of the four Bristol Pegasus engines with the aid of handles inserted through holes in the side panels. This was to make sure that oil or fuel was not trapped in the cylinder heads of the lower cylinders, which might cause

---

21   Corelli Barnett, *Engage the Enemy More Closely – The Royal Navy in The Second World War* (London: Hodder and Stoughton, 1991), p. 478.

Close-up of the nose of a Sunderland of 210 Squadron at Oban, August 1940. A mooring compartment was situated in the nose of the Sunderland, containing anchor, winch, boat-hook and ladder. The front turret was designed to slide back, enabling the crew to secure the aircraft to a buoy, as demonstrated here. The circle painted on the fuselage just below the cockpit is a gas-detection patch. (Crown Copyright – Air Historical Branch)

hydraulic locking when the engines started. The second pilot was also outside the aircraft looking over the control surfaces, including the rudder and elevators.

What intrigued me most was the little twin-cylinder engine (known as the auxiliary power unit) that was situated in the inboard leading edge of the starboard wing. An access section was let down when the engine was required. It was buzzing away merrily while one member went to each watertight compartment and operated a valve to pump out any water that might have leaked into the bilges under the floor. It also ran a generator to charge the 24-volt battery system supplying the aircraft's electrical power … Soon, each member of the crew came on the intercom to report to the skipper that his particular job was done and that the aircraft was ready to leave the mooring. The final report was,

'All hatches and bulkheads closed, Skipper.'

'Skipper to moorings; you fellows all ready up front?'

'Okay Skipper; ready to slip moorings.'

'Starting port outer engine, engineer.'

'Okay Skipper, ready to prime outer.'

The engine sprang to life and the same procedure was followed to start the starboard outer engine. When both were running, the skipper called the rigger to slip moorings. This was done, and from my position behind the pilot's seat I watched the front turret being wound forward over the mooring compartment.

The aircraft was then taxied out to the take-off area in Plymouth Sound. As soon as we were clear of other aircraft, the inner engines were started. Leaving the sheltered water of the Cattewater, we ran into quite a chop, but this did not disturb the Sunderland, now moving

comfortably at a speed of about 10 knots. When the engines reached their correct temperature, each one was run up to 1,200 revs and the separate ignitions systems (magnetos) were
checked. Then with the wind coming in from the west, we were all ready for take-off. The
skipper did his final check, which first entailed checking with the flight engineer that engine
temperatures and pressures were normal. This was followed by running out one-third flap;
ensuring that the propellers were in fully fine pitch; setting the Direction Indicator to 'zero';
turning the aircraft into wind; uncaging the gyro; and finally warning the crew to stand-by
for take-off.

   The skipper opened up the outer engines first, at the same time hauling the control column
back into his stomach. This allowed the nose of the aircraft to rise as high as possible before
opening the throttles of the inner engines. The purpose of this was to cut down the amount
of spray from the bow wave that would strike the propellers when the inner engines were
opened up. In heavy seas especially, spray would cause 'pitting' of the propeller tips. With the
nose at its maximum height, the inner engines were gradually opened up until the props were
finally clear of the spray. Full throttle was then given to all four engines. With the aircraft now
coming up 'onto the step' (in other words 'planing'), the control column was centralised with
the speed reaching about 50 knots. At about 85-90 knots the skipper eased back on the stick
and the aircraft rose gracefully into the air. Once airborne, the aircraft was held straight and
level until normal climbing speed was reached at 105 knots.[22]

Having taken off successfully the Sunderland would fly out to its patrol location; this could be
many hundreds of miles out over the ocean and posed considerable navigational challenges for
crews. Navigation was largely by 'dead reckoning' and depended on sufficient visibility for the
aircraft to measure the the angle between the course being steered and the actual track of the
aircraft over the water – or 'drift'. As over land, the speed and direction of the wind accounted
for any difference between course and track. Measuring the drift was done in several ways as Ken
Robinson discusses:

   The drift recorder in the navigator's position gave a view of a section of the surface immediately below the aircraft. A calibrated ring with a grid of parallel lines was rotated until the
   features on the ground or water appeared to be moving along these lines. The drift could then
   be read off directly from the scale. The rear turret was calibrated for the purpose of reporting
   bearings of targets or landmarks, but it could also be used for drift readings. An object on
   the ground or water could be followed with the guns and the reading taken from the scale.
   This method was particularly useful when flying over a calm sea, when the drift recorder was
   unusable. It was then necessary to throw out a smoke puff or flare on which the guns could be
   trained when it was floating in the water. The aircraft's bomb sight, located in the bows, could
   be used in a similar way to the drift recorder.[23]

Navigation by dead reckoning would also be supplemented by astro-navigation, using a sextant
to measure the vertical angle above the true horizon of stars or planets. Any such astronomical
body could be used, but as the aircraft was in constant motion a number of sights would be taken
and averaged. Calculations would then be made using a series of tables and the resulting position
plotted on the chart.[24] Radio navigation could also be used, but only if the aircraft could pick up

---

22   Baveystock, Leslie, *Wavetops at My Wingtips*, p. 140.
23   Ken Robinson, *Dice on Regardless*, p. 60.
24   Dundas Bednall, *Sun on my Wings* (Pembroke: Paterchurch Publications, 1989), p. 56.

Short Sunderland I, P9604/RB-J, of 10 Squadron RAAF Detachment based at Oban, Argyll, about to take off from Oban Bay, August 1940. (Crown Copyright – Air Historical Branch)

transmissions from land-based radio stations and bearings obtained from the D/F loop antenna. Two different stations some distance apart could also provide a fix, though sadly this was rarely possible in the mid-Atlantic. Finally, when close to land, sightings could be taken of the coastline and its distinctive landmarks, either visually, or through the ground clutter detected by the ASV radar. The navigator on a Sunderland was often the crew member under the most pressure. Weighed down with the responsibility of trying to find convoys deep in mid-Atlantic on radio silence, then having to calculate the last safe point of return before navigating the aircraft, often through inclement weather, back to base.

Having found the convoy, the aircraft would have one of two roles, either close escort of the convoy itself, usually by circling around it for two to three hours at low speed and altitude, which was always demanding for the pilot. Or, alternatively, conducting sweeps along the convoy's route, which would disrupt the submarine's ability to shadow the convoy. On occasions sweeps could be done in conjunction with other aircraft on parallel tracks, this had the advantage that if a submarine was sighted by an aircraft, it could gain rapid support from at least one other aircraft on a parallel sweep. Ken Robinson describes meeting up with a convoy in the Atlantic.

One of our WOPs was stationed in the radar position, assiduously scanning the ASV screen for blips which would indicate shipping in the area. His target was the convoy itself, but he had to be equally aware of the possibility of other ships, in particular U-boats. Eventually he reported that something was coming up on his screen. It was a fairly healthy response at about twenty miles, but at this range it was impossible to say whether it was from one target or several. A number of ships could produce blips which were merged together on the screen to make one.

We couldn't guarantee that this response was from our convoy, so the skipper alerted the crew to the possibilities and told them to keep a sharp lookout and report anything they saw immediately. He asked the navigator how the position of the contact tied up with his own calculations. He'd expected the convoy to be five miles closer to us, but on the same bearing. The pilot decided to stay on course until more information was available.

The visibility was hazy, and we had to strain our eyes to scan the horizon. When the radar op reported that the blip had broken up into several and that they were now about 12 miles away, I picked up something ahead through the binoculars. The skipper confirmed that there was certainly a ship ahead, but he couldn't make any accurate identification yet. He continued to explore the horizon and then announced that he could now see more than one vessel. The nearest one appeared to be a British sloop.

He told me to get the Very cartridges ready and asked the navigator for a course to point about 10 miles ahead of the convoy, so that we would avoid approaching it up sun. Since enemy aircraft had a habit of attacking out of the sun, we did not want to be mistaken for one. Before long, we were able to see all eight ships which met the descriptions given at our briefing that morning.

When making the first contact with a convoy, it was vitally necessary to get our identification right, otherwise we could be giving ourselves a great deal of trouble. We had to be certain that we'd identified our vessels correctly before having any direct communication with them. We then approached them cautiously, firing Very cartridges of the appropriate colour of the day. It was forbidden to break radio silence in the vicinity of a convoy except for emergencies. The reasons for this were clear. The air needed to be kept open for us to receive any reports concerning the disposition of enemy forces and of course we had to deny them the opportunity of determining our own or the convoy's position …

There was then an exchange of brief coded messages by Aldis lamp between Robinson's aircraft and the convoy, until the Navy were quite satisfied as to the aircraft's identity. They then agreed the area of the Sunderland's first patrol …

The ships, steaming slowly but purposefully northwards at about 10 knots, were spaced at least 400 yards apart. Their wakes added the only bright relief to a blue-green expanse of ocean punctuated by small grey shapes. From our viewpoint, the wakes were a giveaway, visible from some miles distant. From sea level they would be less evident and the ships' camouflage more effective. This was a small convoy by any standards, but it was my first experience of escort work and I felt that at long last I was doing something useful. I had not really known what this work entailed and in the months to come I was astounded at the size of some of the convoys we escorted and also the apparent inconsistency of the escort/MV ratio.

Sitting above these eight ships with ocean spreading to infinity all around them, it was difficult to believe that they were in any kind of danger. Indeed, I felt that, but for technology, there'd be little chance of their being detected at all except by pure accidental encounter. The reality was, of course, very different. As long as they were at sea, they were at risk. We were there to protect these vessels, their crews and their cargoes from what were likely to be sudden attacks from an enemy who would do everything to ensure that he gave no warning of his presence. It was clear from the reception we got that the escort ships valued the support that we were giving them. We wanted their confidence in us to be justified …

The most commonly used and indeed most effective method of sweeping an area of ocean in search of the enemy, or any other target, was the creeping-line-ahead, or CLA, search. This entailed deciding the boundaries of the square or rectangular area that you wished to search and then covering the whole area with parallel sweeps from one side to the other. Successive

A Short Sunderland I flying boat – L2163/DA-G – of 210 Squadron based at Oban in Scotland, pictured on shipping escort duties, 31 July 1940. This aircraft was later sunk in a gale at Stranraer on 15 January 1941. (Crown Copyright – Air Historical Branch)

sweeps would be spaced at twice the visibility by day or twice the workable ASV range by night ...

As many pairs of eyes as possible were brought to bear on scouring the area. The five main lookout posts in the aircraft were manned for the duration of the search. Occasionally this was supplemented by other crew members who were engaged on their normal duties but were also in a position to look out of conveniently placed hatches, such as those in the galley. The ASV was continuously manned and was expected to give us first warning of any ships within its range. Keyed up throughout the search, I anticipated some dramatic development on my very first operation, but much to my disappointment we covered the area without seeing anything.

Several hours later we were back with the convoy, reporting on our search and agreeing another sector with the leading escort vessel. The new CLA proved equally unexciting and we returned to the convoy a second time with a negative report. Our relief aircraft was due at any moment and our fuel supply was according to the engineer, just enough to get us back to base 'with a teaspoonful to spare'. It was time to take our leave and the escort thanked us for our help as we set course for base.[25]

The majority of patrols undertaken by RAF Coastal Command would be very similar to the account above, yet even these apparently uneventful aircraft patrols might force a U-boat to submerge and therefore prevent it from shadowing a convoy, or closing in to an attacking

25   Ken Robinson, *Dice on Regardless*, p. 65.

position.[26] It was only on the rarest of occasions that an aircraft would spot a U-boat, when there was then a race for the aircraft to get in to a position to attack, before the submarine dived to a safe depth. The odds, however, were normally stacked against the aircraft, unless the visibility was poor or the German lookouts careless. Coastal Command's Operational Research Section had studied whether changing the aircraft's camouflage might improve things. Aircraft are normally seen as dark objects against a sky and many of the Whitleys and Wellingtons, that had been transferred from Bomber Command, still retained black undersides for night operations. Trials were undertaken with a Wellington whose undersides were painted white and the Operational Research Section was able to prove, that the average range at which the Wellington was detected by observers was 20 percent lower than a Wellington in standard camouflage. In the final months of 1941, all Coastal Command aircraft were repainted with white under-surfaces. These aircraft became known as the 'White Crows' of the Atlantic War and as cynics commented was perhaps overdue 'recognition of the advantages of a colour scheme gulls and other sea birds had adopted some millions of years ago'.[27]

Flight Lieutenant D.M. Gall of 201 Squadron was flying his Sunderland in 19 Group's area of operations and detected a U-boat by visual means. Normally a U-boat would be expected to dive, but in the Spring of 1943, Doenitz had increased the AA weaponry on a U-boat and for a while insisted that they fight it out on the surface when attacked by aircraft:

> We were on a routine anti-submarine patrol to the south-west; for once the weather was beautiful, and we were able to fly at our optimum height of 5,000 feet. (We had radar, but it was very rudimentary, and we preferred to fly below cloud and use our eyes. On this day, however, there was no cloud).
>
> I should say here that we dislike A/S patrols, as compared with convoy escort work. With the latter at least we had something to look at, but on the patrols we had to suffer the extreme boredom of flying mile after mile with nothing to see but sea for something like 15 hours at a time. We got to the stage of thinking there were no U-boats to be sighted. It therefore came as a tremendous surprise to us when the submarine was sighted visually in the distance. It was some way away – I wouldn't like to trust my memory to say how far (eight miles) – but we headed straight towards it, making our best speed which was something in the region of 150 knots – downhill!! And, of course we were going downhill, as we wanted to get to our depth-charge dropping height of 50 feet as quickly as possible. I'm afraid I didn't even think about refinements such as coming out of the sun. I just wanted to get there before he dived, because of course that's what he was going to do – any second. And in any case, this was our first sighting.
>
> Now I am not sure how early this was in the period of 'fighting back'; all I know is that if there were previous incidents, I was not aware of them, and we all expected him to dive. Indeed, when he did not, I asked the navigator to check whether we were near one of the 'free lanes' for our own submarines. I was pretty sure we were not near one, but I had to be absolutely certain.
>
> As we approached, I still had this haunting fear that it might be one of ours, and when he began to flash us, I had the navigator check the recognition of the day. I do not remember what it was, but it was certainly not an 'H' or 'S', which was what he was flashing.
>
> It was my Scottish rear-gunner who eventually put my mind at rest by calling on the intercom, 'He's no' flashin' skipper; he's firin'.' There was a bit of a swell running, and the U-boat's

---

26   Alfred Price, *Aircraft versus Submarine*, p. 140.
27   Alfred Price, *Aircraft versus Submarine*, p. 70.

gunners may have been inexperienced, for we did not feel a tremor. Here I must pause to say that we were fortunate enough that day to have the squadron gunnery officer as a 'guest' crew member, a Pilot Officer Martin. Luckily, too, he was manning the front turret at the time, using the 'pea-shooter' as we called the one forward-firing Browning. And he used it to great effect, as witnessed by the dead bodies I saw in the conning tower as we passed over.

We dropped our stick of four depth charges from about 50 feet above the water. The dropping in those days was done visually by the pilot, and I must admit that I missed by yards! But it was to be my lucky day, for the U-boat captain decided to turn at the last minute. I was amazed at the speed with which he turned through 90 degrees, but delighted to see that he made the turn the 'wrong way' right into the middle of the stick.

As we turned round we saw a shimmering explosion over the surface of the sea, the bows came out of the water to a vertical position, and then slid down. There was much jubilation and cheering on board R of 201 but even in the excitement then, I couldn't help feeling, as I have felt so often since – the poor devils.'[28]

Detection of U-boats was not solely accomplished by visual means. The British had begun to develop airborne ASV radar as early as July 1937, carrying out trials using Anson aircraft to see if they could detect warships in conditions of bad visibility at night (submarines were omitted from the trials as a potential target, probably reflecting continued misplaced faith in ASDIC). Technical difficulties, including the large wavelengths and the size of the transmitter involved, were gradually overcome by the British scientists and these early trials proved successful at identifying ships at some distance. Despite this positive progress the priority for radar development, not unreasonably, was on the early warning radar for the defence of Britain from air attack, therefore progress in ASV remained frustratingly slow.

By 1939 however an aerial system had been produced and the first ASV Mk I production sets went into trial against a Royal Navy submarine in November of that year. During the War British home waters were not the safest of areas to undertake trials and this unfortunate 'target' submarine was attacked first by a German aircraft and then by a British fighter, forcing it to submerge on both occasions. However, the Coastal Command Hudson that was conducting the experiment, eventually made contact and proved that the submarine could be detected at ranges up to 5 ½ miles. The sets were issued to Hudson Squadrons and though still unreliable at detecting submarines, they did help aircraft rendezvous with convoys and assist in general navigation. The British continued to work on improving their radar and eventually introduced the ASV MK II, this equipment contained both a powerful transmitter and a more sensitive receiver which gave improved location ranges against submarines. Furthermore, the set had been deliberately engineered for mass production, so was therefore more robust and reliable than its predecessors. Positive though all this progress undoubtedly was, the priority in 1940 was for Airborne Interception (AI) radars for British night-fighters which again slowed the ASV programme down once more. By October 1940 only 45 out of an order of 4,000 ASV radars had been issued to Coastal Command.

The ASV Mk II came with a new aerial system which gave a separate, sideways looking aerial array as well as retaining the forward-looking aerials that already existed on the ASV Mk I. Although there were variations in the way the ASV Mk II was fitted in aircraft, it typically comprised eight radiating elements on either side of the aircraft's rear fuselage or eight reflectors mounted above the fuselage. The radar operator could use either sideways or forward looking aerials, but not both simultaneously, therefore the normal method of search was to initially use the sideways looking aerial radar to cover a 24-mile wide strip of water and when a contact was established turn the

---

28   Norman Franks, *Conflict over the Bay* (London: William Kimber, 1986), p. 7.

aircraft 90 degrees and home in on it using the forward looking aerials.[29] For the wireless operators using the sets on the early ASV took some getting used to, Pilot Officer Tony Spooner flew on
Wellingtons equipped with ASV and describes the equipment:

> Modern radar now has a circular screen which virtually draws plan view pictures of all objects
> ahead. All we had was a tiny screen on the centre of which a green vertical line would appear.
> If the set picked up anything at all the object so detected appeared as a small "tick" across the
> vertical line. Unless the object was dead ahead this tick would be longer on one side of the
> centre line than the other. By turning the aircraft towards the longer side of the tick until the
> two sides were of equal length, and noting the compass reading, the direction of the object
> could be determined. The theoretical maximum range was 100 miles, and there were three
> range-scales, enabling an accurate assessment of range to be made when running towards an
> unknown 'blip', as the tick or echoing return came to be called.
>
> The viewing end of the set was housed between the radio and navigational compartments,
> and since no additional crew member was supplied to operate it and since it required continu-
> ous manning, we all handled it in turn.[30]

Initially Spooner, like others, found the ASV set not much use for anything other than detecting
an approaching shore line. However, with experience and tuition aircrew were able to use the
device effectively and discern, within the interference and clutter, the blips that designated actual
targets. Effective though British ASV radar was becoming it was still not sufficiently accurate for
aircraft to actually drop bombs or depth charges at night, indeed the 'blip', depending upon the
height of the aircraft, would tantalisingly disappear in the last mile or so of the approach to the
target as the U-boat became lost in sea clutter. What was therefore needed in the final stages of
a night attack to supplement ASV radar was a method of turning night into day, ensuring that
surprise could still be achieved and the aircraft's weapons brought to bear accurately. Flares were
used with some success, but it was the development of the Leigh Light which would have the
most impact.

Squadron Leader Humphrey de Verde Leigh had flown as a pilot in the First World War, but
in 1940 he was working as an administrative officer in HQ Coastal Command where, through
an indiscreet colleague, he had become aware of the closely guarded ASV capability and its
night-time limitations. The current AOC of Coastal Command at the time, Air Chief Marshal
Bowhill requested those in his command to submit any 'bright ideas' they might have to combat
the submarine menace – particularly at night. On his own initiative Leigh submitted a paper
in October 1940 which suggested that a 90cm searchlight should be fitted into the nose of a
Wellington bomber. Leigh went into some detail in his paper suggesting that the electrical generating equipment used in the Directional Wireless Installation (DWI) Wellingtons employed by
the command earlier in the year (to detonate magnetic mines) would give ample power for the
searchlight. There were of course obstacles to be overcome, including the initial opposition of
the Royal Aircraft Establishment at Farnborough, but by March 1941 a prototype was ready that
used a Naval 24-inch (61cm) searchlight in a retractable turret under the nose of the Wellington.[31]
The complexities of this technological achievement by the British should not be underestimated.
The turret had to have a very precise hydraulic system, (designed by Fraser Nash) that allowed the
beam of light to be accurately controlled for angle and elevation. The light needed careful siting

29   Alfred Price, *Aircraft versus Submarine*, pp. 54-60.
30   Tony Spooner, *In Full Flight* (Canterbury: Wingham Press, 1991), p. 153.
31   Alfred Price, *Aircraft versus Submarine*, pp. 60-66.

under the nose, so that the pilot was sufficiently above the top of the beam and not blinded by the glare. Finally, this was the first occasion that a large searchlight had been placed in an aircraft and significant ventilation and fume extraction problems needed to be overcome. The first time the Leigh Light was used in action with ASV was in June 1942 when a Wellington of 172 Squadron, flown by Squadron Leader Jeff Gresswell, picked up the Italian Submarine *Luigi Torelli*[32] in the Bay of Biscay.

> We made contact with the *Torelli* on the return leg of our patrol having fixed our position by radar and a lighthouse on the Spanish coast. My radar operator, using the forward aerials, reported a contact 5½ miles to port. Using the standard attack procedure, the Leigh Light was lit at ¾ mile range at 250 feet but failed to pick up the target dead ahead in the beam as we hoped. However, both Pilot Officer Alan Triggs and myself spotted a large U-boat disappearing under our port wing, but which at that moment was impossible to attack.
>
> I quickly realised what had happened. The barometric pressure set on the altimeter some 400 miles away at Chivenor was such that, when indicating 250 feet, we were actually flying nearer 400 feet when the Light was switched on, so the beam had overshot the target. Cursing our misfortune, I re-set the altimeter reading and climbed away. We had reached a height of about 500 feet, turning, when I was amazed to see the U-boat start firing coloured flares into the sky, giving me a perfect reference point for a second approach. This time the procedure worked perfectly. The Leigh Light illuminated the U-boat and I attacked from the starboard beam, straddling the vessel with four depth charges. The submarine was severely damaged. After the attack we shadowed the damaged boat and carried out two runs over it to enable the rear gunner to strafe it. I reached the PLE (Prudent Limit of Endurance) about 30 minutes later and set course for home. On the return leg of our patrol, I successfully carried out a perfect homing and Leigh Light attack on an East-bound U-boat (with rear turret machine-gun fire, having no depth charges left).[33]

Onboard the *Luigi Torelli* Girolamo Fantoni, served as Navigation Officer and recalls the Wellington's initial pass:

> On the bridge of the *Torelli* [the watch] tried to analyse the situation. The low-level fly past, without an attack, led to the thought that it might have been a German aircraft; in any event the Commander manned the two machine guns, cleared the bridge of personnel, and prepared to crash dive. Being unaware of the existence of radio location, and in particular, airborne radar, it was thought that the sighting by the aircraft was made by chance, due to the phosphorescence from our broad wake; consequently the Commander limited his actions to reducing speed to lessen the visibility of the wake, thus making it impossible for the aircraft to repeat the chance night sighting. Whilst the few men on the bridge were going down into the conning tower, the aircraft turned again into the attack, but this time without mistake. At a range of a mile, at 250 feet, the Light was switched on and lit up the submarine. Fire was opened up by the gunners, and the aircraft released its four depth charges which exploded on each side of the boat under the hull. The submarine started to shake in an incredible way. The Commander, last

---

32   We tend to think of the Battle of the Atlantic submarines as being exclusively German. In fact, 32 Italian submarines were dispatched in June of 1940 and based out of Bordeaux. The Italian submarines operating in the Atlantic were to sink 109 Allied ships totalling 593,864 tons.

33   Norman Franks, *Dark Sky, Deep Water – First Hand Reflections on the Anti-U-boat War in WWII* (London: Grub Street, 1999), pp. 5-7.

Coastal Command Liberator GR.V BZ877/2-Q, of 86 Squadron based at Ballykelly, County Londonderry, in flight. (Crown Copyright – Air Historical Branch)

but one to leave the bridge, began to descend into the tower to give the order to dive, when the violent jolts sheared off the closing hook from the small door to the bridge, which as a result, closed itself, and the Bosun, the last to descend was trapped on the bridge, In a few seconds, the diesel engines, still running, sucked all the air from the cabins, creating a strong depression, which impeded the ability to hear. The engines then stopped by themselves due to lack of air. An unaccustomed silence and the pitch darkness dominated the scene inside the submarine which floated motionless and bow heavy – no noise, no voices, no light.

When finally air was restored in the boat, and the depression relieved, immediate action was taken to attend to the serious damage. To improve buoyancy, the Commander pumped air into the ballast tanks containing fuel, dumping the fuel overboard into the sea. A fire in the vicinity of the forward batteries, which was emitting smoke and chlorine gas, had to be isolated by closing the watertight doors to all forward compartments, including the radio station. Many of the ship's stations were damaged, and because there was no electrical power, the rudder and the steering compass were not working. The ammunition store, which was close to the fire, had to be flooded, after having withdrawn some ammunition for the gun. The Bosun, who had been left on the bridge, stated that the aircraft had carried out two more runs, firing machine guns haphazardly. Having got the boat moving again, the Commander decided to head for the Spanish coast, navigating by the stars on a southerly course and steering by hand-controlled rudder. In the distance more lights from the searchlight could be seen, but from time to time banks of fog gave some relief to the crew.[34]

---

34   Norman Franks, *Dark Sky, Deep Water*, pp. 5-7.

The account above demonstrates Coastal Command's increasing ability to detect and attack U-boats at night, a period when U-boats had previously felt immune from attack. Even attempts to shoot out the searchlight bearing down on them proved fruitless as the German sailors were unable to acquire the target properly in the dazzling glare. Not for nothing did they come to call the Leigh Light: '*das verdammte licht*' – that damned light.[35] Disappointingly for the British this success was to be short-lived, for the Germans had captured an ASV set in 1941, fitted it into a *Focke Wulf Kondor* aircraft and conducted trials with it to understand its technical capabilities. By September of 1942 the Germans had created a counter-measure, a simple receiver that, through a buzzing noise in his earphones, alerted an operator in the submarine's radio room to an ASV transmission from a patrolling aircraft. This equipment was called *Metox*, after the name of one of the French firms who manufactured it. The Germans found that with *Metox* they could pick up the transmissions from an aircraft more than 30 miles away, ample time in which to unclip the wooden-framed *Metox* aerial from the conning tower and submerge to a safe depth. Initially, only a few submarines were fitted with this device and they acted as escorts to other submarines transitting the Bay of Biscay or other dangerous areas. By the end of year however, all German submarines carried *Metox* and the submariners came to affectionally call it the *Biskayakreuz* or Biscay Cross, based on its wooden cross-shaped frame.[36] With the advent of *Metox* many Coastal Command aircraft had to be temporarily satisfied with simply causing German submarines to submerge, but there were still occasional lucky breaks:

> Our luck changed on the night of 22/23 December 1942 – an early Christmas present. At this stage let me emphasise that I had a very competent crew who flew some 500 operational hours on Leigh Light Wellingtons with me, in particular, Sergeant (later commissioned on our crew) Eddie Goodman was an 'ace' on both ASV II and III and this could make all the difference between picking up, particularly on a cluttered screen, an ASV contact on a U-boat or not, especially if the U-boat was not fully surfaced. Anyway, at just after 0315 hours we got an ASV II contact at six miles; we switched on the Leigh Light at one mile and, at the end of the beam, there was a fully surfaced U-boat heading west at good speed. It is, and was, difficult to describe one's immediate feelings on seeing an enemy submarine for the first time, especially after many long sorties without a sighting, and particularly at night – a very sinister sight, I recall.
>
> In brief, I felt a combination of surprise, excitement, elation, intense satisfaction, etc. but all subordinated to carrying out immediately the correct attack procedure in the ensuing seconds – we might never sight another U-boat. The U-boat started to dive as soon as it was illuminated but its conning tower was still visible when I dropped a 'stick' of four depth charges (DCs) at an angle of about 60 degrees (because of the stick spacing and because the lethal range of our DC was only six yards) just ahead of the U-boat. The rear-gunner reported that the DCs had exploded across the centre of the conning tower swirl. Flame floats had been dropped with the DCs and we homed back over the position but saw nothing of the U-boat.[37]

The *Metox* receivers gave the Germans only a temporary advantage, for the British were able to exploit one of the most important technological breakthroughs of the war by developing the ASV Mk III. Both the ASV Mk I and Mk II radars transmitted on frequencies around 200 megacycles, this was simply because the valves available in 1939 could not generate sufficient power at

---

35 Alfred Price, *Aircraft versus Submarine*, 1980, p. 92.
36 Alfred Price, *Aircraft versus Submarine*, p. 95.
37 Norman Franks, *Conflict Over the Bay* (London: Kimber, 1986), p. 20.

a higher frequency. But if a higher frequency (centimetric wave radar) could be used, then many advantages would be gained, not least aerial systems small enough to rotate mechanically in a full circle – allowing 360-degree coverage. In February 1940 British Scientists at Nuffield Research Laboratory in Oxford built a high-power 'magnetron' oscillator that generated a power of 500 watts at 3000 megacycles.[38] This was a remarkable technological breakthrough, unmatched by any other Allied or enemy scientists. The technology looked highly promising and was developed both by the British Telecommunications Research Establishment (TRE) and by the Massachusetts Institute of Technology's radiation lab. By the end of 1940 the improved TRE centimetric radar could detect surface submarines over 7 miles away,[39] and by 1942 this had increased to 12 miles.

As the metric-wavelength ASV Mk II advantage had been neutralised by the *Metox* receiver the requirement for a new centimetric radar (which *Metox* would be unable to detect) for Coastal Command became even more pressing. If the new radar could be kept secret, then a tactical and technological surprise over the German U-boats could be achieved in 1943.

Disappointingly for Coastal Command, they were not the only ones interested in centimetric wave radar. We have already seen how Fighter Command incorporated it into their night-fighter AI radar to give 360 cover and track low-level targets, this was not necessarily an issue as their missions against German bombers were generally over Britain and the risk of the new capability being compromised was minimal. However, Bomber Command had also latched on to the advantages of centimetric wave radar. Its navigational aid, H2S, used similar technology and despite strong arguments not to fly this sensitive equipment over Germany, Bomber Command began to fit it in to Pathfinder Force aircraft. Inevitably a Stirling fitted with H2S came down in Holland in February 1943 and the Germans were able to recover the H2S set intact, which they called 'Rotterdam'. In March 1943, 172 Squadron, a Leigh Light-equipped Wellington unit became the first to patrol the Bay of Biscay with ASV Mk III. The Germans immediately noted a step-change in U-boat detections by Coastal Command aircraft that *Metox* was not picking up. Doenitz immediately grasped the significance commenting in his war diary:

> The Enemy is making use of radar on frequencies outside the coverage of the present search receiver [i.e. *Metox*]. Until now the only confirmation of this is from an enemy aircraft shot down over Holland which apparently carried a device with a wave-length of 9.7 cm.

Coastal Command naturally feared that the Germans would have a new centimetric radar warning receiver in place to pick up ASV Mk III within months, making their technological leap forward redundant. Yet the Germans were surprisingly slow to adapt. In fact, the German company manufacturing the all-important crystal detectors for the receiver, to be known as *Naxos-U*, ran into difficulties early on. Even when *Naxos-U* began to be fielded in May 1943, it often failed to pick up the the British ASV Mk III radar at all and if it did, only at a reduced range of five miles out. This stemmed from a lack of sensitivity in the system, as well as frequent damage to the fragile aerial sets and their co-axial cables as they were dismantled from the conning tower each time the submarine dived. Internal damage within the cables in particular was not easy to spot by the U-boat crews.

Had the Germans possessed better relations between scientists and the fighting men, in the way Coastal Command had achieved through its Operational Research Section and 'Sunday Soviets', these issues might have been resolved. Instead the Germans became more bewildered and

---

38   A frequency of 3,000 megacycles equates to a wavelength of 10 centimetres. Magnetron radar sets including the new ASV Mk III were therefore to be called 'centimetric' radars. The Mk I and Mk II radars operating around 200 megacycles, or 1.5 metre wavelength, were known as 'metric' radars.

39   Alfred Price, *Aircraft versus Submarine*, p. 59.

Anti-Submarine Weapons: Leigh Light used for spotting U-boats on the surface at night fitted to a Liberator aircraft of Coastal Command. (Crown Copyright – Air Historical Branch)

questioned their original and correct assumption that centimetric radar was responsible. They also began to consider that these increases in detection might be for other reasons, including emissions from the *Metox*. This is not quite as daft as it sounds. Although a receiver, the *Metox* did radiate a small amount of energy and the Germans were still reeling in shock from the technological capabilities of the British centimetric-wavelength radar. Who was to say that the British, now known to be technically more advanced in electronics, could not have produced a detector able to pick up the small amount of emissions being radiated by *Metox*? Doenitz at least was convinced and ordered the submarine crews to desist from using the *Metox* as well as directing German scientists to set about creating a metric-wavelength receiver that did not emit at all. To Coastal Command's considerable advantage *Naxos-U* was put on a back burner and was only to enter service in the spring of 1944, long after the decisive stage of the campaign had passed.[40] Doenitz also ordered his submarines to submerge at night whilst transitting 'the Bay' and surface only in daylight when lookouts would be more likely to spot Coastal Command aircraft. Coastal Command were fortuitous: with greater chances of detecting the U-boats, they would be in a much better position to attack the German submarine fleet.

---

40   Alfred Price, *Aircraft versus Submarine*, pp. 180, 188.

16

'We Ambush the Ambusher'[1] Coastal Command's Battles to Sink the U-boats

The technological advantage the British had achieved in 1943, in finding and accurately locating German U-boats, by day and by night, also came at a time when the weapons Coastal Command needed to destroy German submarines had also been improved. The primary British anti-submarine weapon of the war was the Depth Charge. At the outbreak of the war only the 450lb Naval Depth Charge was available to the British and this was modified with nose and tail fairings, to enable it to be safely dropped from an aircraft. The 450lb weight of this Depth Charge was too heavy for many aircraft, so the Admiralty developed a 250lb Depth Charge which could be dropped from heights up to 250 feet. This Depth Charge was improved further, by replacing the earlier Amatol explosive with a more powerful Torpex filling, giving it a lethal range of about 19ft.

Anti-submarine bombs of 100 and 250lbs had also been used by Coastal Command earlier in the war, but they lacked destructive power and their fuses were more complex and less reliable than the hydro-static pistols fitted to Depth Charges.[2] Hydrostatic pistols were very important in ensuring the main charge was only detonated at the depth previously set, so there was little danger to the aircraft. The anti-submarine bomb's forward momentum on the other hand meant that they were liable to 'skip' off the water and detonate in the air, a considerable hazard to the aircraft. In addition, a number of inadvertent mis-drops on Royal Navy submarines early in the war, had shown that even a direct hit by the underpowered 100lb bomb was too small to cause anything other than minor damage.[3] On 3 December 1939, the British submarine *Snapper* was mistakenly attacked and received a direct hit at the base of her conning tower, the resulting damage was limited to four broken electric light bulbs.[4]

Though it was recognised that Depth Charges would be more effective against submarines than anti-submarine bombs, there was concern at the beginning of the war that they were still failing to sink submarines in expected numbers. Coastal Command's Operational Research Section investigated this problem and concluded that the depth settings on the depth charge were set too deep at 100-150 feet. The logic of this depth setting had centred on the average depth a submarine could dive to, this in turn was based upon the average distance at which an aircraft was spotted by U-boats. Logical enough, but the majority of the U-boats encountered would be alert and dive very quickly, which because of the uncertainty of where exactly a submarine was once it had been

---

1 The motto of 172 Squadron. This squadron was formed at Chivenor on 4 April 1942 and equipped with Wellington bombers fitted with Leigh Lights and from March 1943 Mark III ASV radar. The combination soon brought results, U-665 being sunk on 20 March 1943.

2 Andrew Hendrie, *The Cinderella Service*, p. 49.

3 TNA AIR 15/57: Coastal Command's Naval Staff Anti-U-boat file, Sep 1939-Dec 1944, para 8.

4 Denis Richards, *The Royal Air Force – Volume 1* (London: HMSO, 1954), p. 61.

Armourers on board a bomb scow attach two 450lb Depth Charges to the starboard-side mobile bomb rack of a Short Sunderland of 95 Squadron, moored in Fourah Bay, Freetown, Sierra Leone. The outer bomb has been fitted with a detachable nose fairing and tail fin, which improved the weapon's ballistics and reduced drag while being carried externally. (Crown Copyright – Air Historical Branch)

submerged for even a short period of time, made them very difficult targets to hit. The Operational Research Section argued that the Depth Charges should be set to 20 feet below the surface, based not on the average distance an aircraft was spotted at, but on the much smaller set of U-boat targets that were caught napping and surprised. The Section's judgement was that although smaller in number the location of these targets was much more certain, as they would either be in the process of diving or still surfaced. A setting of 100-150 feet would be too deep in these instances and the Depth Charge would simply detonate harmlessly under the U-boat. The new depth charge required a new hydrostatic pistol to be developed, but in the interim the existing minimum setting of 50 feet was utilised.

Flight Lieutenant Leslie Baveystock describes one such attack at night using a combination of ASV Mk III, 250lb Depth Charges and flares. His Sunderland crew had already encountered a U-boat on the surface that had dived when attacked, they now 'baited' it by remaining in the vicinity knowing that it would soon need to come up for air. The Sunderland had also been fitted with additional machine-guns in both the forward turret and wings in order to suppress increased U-boat AA weaponry. A new radio altimeter was also fitted replacing the older barometric altimeter, the disadvantages of which we have already seen. This was much more accurate in measuring the distance between the sea and the aircraft, allowing the pilot to undertake risky manoeuvres at low level:

> Suddenly at 0244 hours, when we had just turned at the end of one of our 12-mile legs, Currie broke the silence of the intercom to report a contact at 11 miles … Once again we carried out the pre-attack drill, exactly as before, and started our run in. Every one of the crew (especially

me) was keyed up as never before; since we all felt certain that the U-boat commander would elect to stay on the surface and fight back; he must now charge his batteries or perish.

From the bearings that Currie gave me, I found that the aircraft was drifting slightly to starboard. So, I offset our course a few degrees to port to compensate. About three degrees port was sufficient to keep the target on a constant bearing, and this was exactly what was required. Another signal had already been sent to base, and the flare chute was manned and ready. With Colin in the second pilot's seat, Andy under the Astro dome and two gunners in their turrets, four pairs of eyes searched the darkness ahead. My own never left the blind-flying panel, watching airspeed, course and altimeter, while listening to Currie's constant repetition of the bearing of the enemy ahead.

Then suddenly, without warning, when we were about three-quarters of a mile away, gunfire opened up ahead and below us. Two long streams of coloured tracer bullets that at first seemed to be travelling quite slowly, swung towards us and accelerated rapidly past us. Although we were flying only 300 feet above the surface of the sea, I instinctively dived below and turned to starboard. At the same time Anderson shouted 'There's the U-boat', and Colin switched on the flare chute. At once, Sharland began dropping the flares, immediately the whole area lit up like day, and there was our U-boat, fully surfaced about half a mile away and a little to our left.

The U-boat commander was no fool, for on the first occasion he steered straight towards us and presented the smallest area for our radar to detect. With the wind now drifting us to the north, he turned sharply south, compounding our difficulty in getting him lined up. It was essential for us to pass forward of his conning tower if our Depth Charges were not to explode astern of him. As he turned broadside on to us, his quadruple-mounted cannon opened fire, surrounding us with streams of tracer shells. The intensive training of the last few weeks now came to my aid. I banked the aircraft around and aimed the nose amidships at the U-boat. Our front gunner had already opened fire, and, lining up the target, I fired the four fixed Brownings. Our mid-upper gunner also opened fire; although he could not depress his guns low enough with the astro-dome in front of him. Andy must have had quite a shock as the streams of tracer flew over him.

A maze of criss-crossing tracer filled the air with literally hundreds of of bullets hitting the U-boat and surrounding sea, many of them ricocheting high into the night sky. I held my gun button down for six or seven seconds, then had to stop firing in order to bank slightly to port for my final run. Fortunately, our combined fire-power had been enough to knock out his gun-crews, and our final few seconds of attack were unopposed. At just the right moment, I pressed the 'bomb tit' and our stick of six depth-charges fell clean across his hull, just forward of the conning tower. Immediately I pulled hard back on the control column to avoid diving into the sea. As the aircraft's nose started to lift, a tremendous shock wave hit the underside of the hull. Usually, the aircraft does not feel exploding depth charges as their concave noses are designed to make them go 25 feet below the surface with 36 feet of forward travel. Thus, the explosion was underwater and the column of water that rose from the sea was well behind our tailplane by that time. My first thought was that a lucky shot from the U-boat's deck gun might have hit us. With deep relief, I found that the aircraft was still responding normally to the controls.

As we climbed away, Currie reported that the blip on his screen, which he had held quite firmly for the previous 11 miles, had vanished. As there was no sign of the U-boat attempting to crash dive only seconds earlier, we felt certain that it had been well and truly sunk. Anderson in the astro-dome and our rear gunner had both seen plumes rising high into the air around the U-boat.[5]

5   Leslie Baveystock, *Wavetops at My Wingtips*, p. 22.

The attack above could give a false impression that it was easy to sink a submarine with depth charges. In fact, it took great skill and without a bombsight much depended on the pilot's judgement and sportsman's eye on when to release – clearly regular training helped in this regard. The Operational Research Section also recommended that the depth charges were set to release in a manner which generated 100-foot spacings between them. This was less concentrated than some aircrews preferred, but analysis had shown that most attacking aircraft either under or overshot the U-boat and the new method meant it was more likely that the target would be straddled, with at least one depth charge within lethal distance.[6]

The other important weapon available for Coastal Command to use were the rockets fitted to some aircraft, these were either the 25lb armour-piercing rocket or the 60lb high explosive variety. They were used for both anti-submarine and anti-shipping missions and would be fired at 400 feet in a 20-degree dive. Pilots formed the habit of making violent climbing turns after firing because the rockets were unpredictable underwater and sometimes after a shallow entry would emerge from the water in front of the aircraft. Rockets were generally fitted to the smaller Coastal Command aircraft such as Beaufighters or Mosquitoes.

Frequently a U-boat was not actually sunk in one attack but might be damaged and unable to submerge. If the aircraft was out of depth charges it could act as a command and control platform and if near a convoy, direct escort vessels to the scene. By 1943 this could include one of the Royal Navy's increasingly effective Support Groups, whose remit was to search and destroy gathering wolf packs and single U-boats beyond the immediate confines of a convoy. Captain Frederic 'Johnnie' Walker RN was regarded as one of the greatest U-Boat hunters, his Support Group usually consisted of the sloops *Starling, Wren, Woodpecker, Kite* and *Wild Goose*.[7] For a six-week period in June and July 1943 these ships, together with aircraft from Coastal Command, wrought havoc among the U-boats. The Royal Air Force Liaison Officer on board *Woodpecker* described the events of 30 July, when between them, Walker's Support Group and aircraft from 502 Squadron and 461 Squadron sank every one of a group of three U-boats.

> About 8.30 [he records] the fun really started. What a terrific day! A Sunderland and a Catalina were around, and they signalled that no less than three U-boats were on the surface about 10 miles away ahead. The Senior Naval Officer in *Kite* made the signal 'General Chase'. Off we went at full speed, line abreast – a grand sight, smooth blue sea and blue sky – all ratings and officers at action stations. Soon we saw the aircraft circling low and diving to drop depth charges. Two of the U-boats were visible by this time and the Sunderland dropped a couple of depth charges plumb on either side of the conning tower of one of them. That broke the U-boat's back and he disappeared pretty quickly, leaving some survivors and a raft in the water. Simultaneously, all our ships had opened fire with 4-inch [gun] on the second U-boat.[8]
>
> He, too, left survivors who had to wait until U-boat No. 3 had been located and dealt with. Not unnaturally, No. 3 dived in some haste and we were now set the task of finding him beneath the surface. It was like great cats stalking an oversized mouse. *Kite* found him first and dropped a pattern of depth charges. Then *Woodpecker* set about him and dropped depth charges. *Kite* got a 'fix' and with his direction we proceeded to lay a 'plaster', which

---

6 John Herrington, *Air War Against Germany and Italy in 1939-45* (Canberra: Australian War Memorial, 1954), p. 426.

7 Walker suffered a cerebral thrombosis on 7 July 1944 at the age of 48 and was buried at sea. His death was attributed to overwork and exhaustion. During the Second World War he sank more submarines than any other Allied commander, a statue was unveiled of him in Liverpool in 1998.

8 This vessel was already sinking as the result of a Halifax attack.

Photograph taken from Short Sunderland III, W4030/H, of 10 Squadron RAAF, while attacking German type VIIC submarine U-243, west of St Nazaire in the Bay of Biscay on 8 July 1944. Depth charges dropped by W4030, one of which crippled the U-boat, explode by its stern. Splashes from machine gun fire from the Sunderland's rear turret, which put both the submarine's 37mm and twin 20mm guns out of action, can be seen leading across the water below the depth charge explosion. After further attacks by another Sunderland of 10 Squadron RAAF and a Consolidated Liberator of the US Navy, U-243 was abandoned by its crew and sank (11 men died and there were 38 survivors). (Crown Copyright – Air Historical Branch)

is rather what the name denotes. *Wild Goose* repeated the dose, but while she was doing so the first patches of oil were observed and soon it was coming up in great quantities – the sea stank of it. Wood and other wreckage came up too. This was about 3.30 p.m. We recovered various things. *Wren* found some German clothing. The evidence was decisive and the ships (which had been shielding one another during the action) reformed and made off to pick up survivors. We picked up 17, including the captain and 1st officer. The other ships picked up a further 50 or so altogether. Ours were in, or clinging to, a rubber float, shaped like a big rubber ring. Some were injured. One had a bullet in his stomach and a broken ankle. They were mostly shaking with cold, and/or reaction from their experience. Several of them were truculent.[9]

Often the Royal Navy Support Groups were far away and it was frequently another aircraft that was the first to arrive at the scene and take instructions, this was not as easy as it might seem as Wing Commander Oulton, Commanding Officer of 58 Squadron, found out when he took off in his Halifax from St Eval, Cornwall on 30 May 1943:

9   Hilary Saunders, *Royal Air Force 1939-45, Volume III*, p. 54.

We were on a planned offensive patrol, running north-south roughly parallel with the Biscay coast of France and creeping westward. My squadron practise was to use the H2S (ASV Mk III) only intermittently, because of the effective U-boat receivers, and to make the maximum use of any cloud cover below about 5,000 feet. So we were lolloping along just in and out of the cloud base, when we spotted an irregularity in the pattern of waves and 'white horses' about 10 miles ahead, as far as I can remember. So back into the cloud, up to 2600 rpm and maximum boost, dipping out of the cloud about once a minute, and about three minutes later we identified the U-boat, proceeding about 12-14 knots on the surface, and we went into the attack. We had been trying out a technique to get some help from the mid-upper turret, i.e. approaching quite high, then at about 1000 yards diving quite steeply down to the surface, which allowed the mid-upper gunner to spray the target to put the U-boat gunners off their job a little, and flattening out at the last moment at about 50 feet for the final run in. This seemed to work out all right and we laid a stick of six Depth Charges across the boat from her starboard quarter to her port bow, just ahead of the conning tower.

As we came round in a tight turn and the explosions sank away, the U-boat had lost way and was turning slowly to starboard. With only three Depth Charges left, we made another attack, coming under some flak but suffering no damage. My rear gunner reckoned we had bracketed the stern, and the U-boat was obviously in bad shape, but still turning to starboard.

We reported the action and state of play to 19 Group, asked for reinforcements and set up the standard W/T homing procedure, uncomfortably aware that we might have visitors other than the RAF. The first to arrive after about 20 minutes was another Halifax of my own Squadron J/58 who had found us but didn't see the U-boat; so we formated on J and led him down into the attack, then pulling off about 200 yards on his starboard beam and giving him covering fire to keep the flak-gunners' heads down a bit. Alas, he was a young pilot and over-anxious and dropped his stick of Depth Charges about 100 yards short. He did the same again on the second attack, which one could understand and sympathise with. It must have been a bit unnerving.

So back on the homing procedure and presently a Sunderland, E/10 of the Australian Squadron based at Mount Batten, turned up, obviously not knowing what was going on and not knowing what we wanted him to do. I couldn't raise him on voice radio, and we flew in circles for several minutes on close formation, while I made signals with my hands and my wireless operator tried to pass a message by Aldis lamp. Eventually I shepherded him down to the crippled U-boat, and as soon as the Australian saw it no more time was wasted. Once again, we formated and gave covering fire during the run in, but his Depth Charges weren't close enough to administer the coup de grace.

A few minutes later, another Sunderland arrived, X/228 who evidently understood the situation. He went straight into the attack and laid his first stick across the U-boat midships. Before gouts of water from the Depth Charge explosions had half fallen away, there was a great sheet of blue and orange coloured flame with a great deal of white and some black smoke. When this cleared, the U-boat was gone but the sea was littered with wreckage and bodies, some of whom were still alive. Meanwhile 19 Group had warned us of considerable Ju 88 traffic in our area, so we thought it prudent not to linger. At that point, I felt sorry for those poor devils in the water. They had only been doing their duty as they saw it and were as brave as any other combatant. So we flew down over the mess and dropped our two rubber dinghies and a couple of Mae-Wests in the hope that some of them might survive and be picked up by one of the RN hunter-killer groups operating in the area. Then we climbed into the nearest cloud and beat it for St Eval.[10]

---

10   Norman Franks, *Conflict over the Bay* (London: Kimber, 1986), pp. 78-80.

U-426, a Type VIIC submarine, down by the stern and sinking, after attacks by a Sunderland of 10 Squadron RAAF on 8 January 1944. Fifty-one men went down with the U-boat, there were no survivors. (Crown Copyright – Air Historical Branch)

The dangers to Coastal Command aircraft in these sorts of missions was significant. Not only could they quite easily be shot down by the U-boat's AA defences, but in 1943 the *Luftwaffe* strengthened their forces in France, including the heavy fighters of *KampfGeschwader 6*, which were under the command of *Fliegerfuhrer Atlantik*. Increasing numbers of British aircraft began to be destroyed over the Bay of Biscay and both Coastal Command, as well as Fighter Command, began to fly long-range fighter patrols over the Bay known as 'Instep' patrols. These were undertaken by aircraft such as Beaufighters and Mosquitoes and challenged German air superiority off the coast of France and in the Bay. Even when Coastal Command aircraft were attacked it was not entirely one-sided, most German aircraft encountered were longer range machines, such as the Ju 88 or Me 110, so even an ungainly machine like the Sunderland might be able to throw them off long enough to duck into a useful piece of cloud.[11] Additionally, many crews began to supplement the existing machine guns on the Sunderland to the extent that they began being christened the 'flying porcupines' by the Germans.

The story of Sunderland 'N' from 461 Squadron RAAF at Pembroke Dock remains one of the more incredible stories of the war. N/461 was the same as any other Sunderland – a typical aircraft with an ordinary crew of 11, nine Australians and two Englishmen. It did have an interesting unauthorised modification – two extra Vickers K guns, one at each lower galley hatch. The crew had fitted these after N/461 had been shot up quite badly by Ju 88s and Fw 190s in February 1943. Although the crew was unhurt, the airframe had suffered from bullet-holes and cannon blasts all round and had to be patched up before resuming operations. Like many Sunderland crews, the men of N/461 were wary of the aircraft's naked and unprotected underside and had devised the galley guns in their own workshops, fitting them without asking permission. That meant the aircraft had one gun up front, two on top, one in the mid-upper turret, four in the tail, as well

---

11   Hilary Saunders, *Royal Air Force 1939-45, Volume III*, p. 54.

as the two new galley guns, all of which were Vickers .303 machine guns, effective, but still very small weapons when compared to the 20mm cannons fitted to German aircraft like the Ju 88.

The captain of N/461 was Flight Lieutenant Colin Walker, who was coming to the end of his first tour of operations and this was to be his last mission with 461 Squadron. Flying Officer Bill Dowling and Pilot Officer Jim Amiss were the other pilots, Flight Lieutenant Kenneth Simpson was the navigator, Flight Sergeants Miles and Turner the engineers and Fuller, Miller, Lane, Watson and Goode were the wireless operators and air gunners.

N/461 took off from its base at Pembroke Dock at 1331 on 2 June 1943, on what was supposed to be a typical anti-submarine patrol. At the operations briefing the crew had been told of the *Luftwaffe* shooting down a civilian airliner flying from Lisbon to Britain which crashed in the Bay of Biscay; its crew and 12 passengers, including the actor Leslie Howard, were missing. N/461 was asked to look out for dinghies along their route.

The weather at Pembroke was gloomy as N/461 took off and after a short period into the flight a dull, drizzling rain began to enclose them over a dreary looking sea. The cloud forced them down low, but the further south they flew the more the sun began to break through the clouds until eventually the sky was full of sunshine and the cloud had vanished. Walker took the Sunderland up to its cruising altitude of 2,000 feet and continued south, N/461 began to behave a little temperamentally. The port-inner engine was fluctuating and every now and then it would emit little explosions of flame and smoke. Walker put up with it in an uncomfortable and worrying silence for an hour or two, it was a common enough occurrence, sometimes these engines would get better on their own accord. Like all good captains he was reluctant to return to base unnecessarily but was well aware that on the Sunderland he had no way of feathering the propeller if the engine was to pack up. It would just spin slowly until it sheared off completely potentially ripping into the cockpit or port outer engine. After an hour or two he called Miles, his engineer, on the intercom. They agreed that they would give it another 30 minutes and if it hadn't cleared by then they would think about turning back.

It was now 1835 hrs and the crew changed watch, as they did every hour. The pilots changed over, Walker into the flying seat and Amiss out of it, Dowling into the right-hand seat. Another wireless operator took over the set and plugged himself in; the engineers changed over and the relief gunners moved into the turrets; Goode into the tail, Fuller into the mid-upper and Watson into the nose. Once the gunners were in position the reports came over the intercom in the correct sequence, tail, mid-ships and nose. At 1835 Simpson, the navigator, left his charts to go into the astrodome and stared out into the sky and sea, he reminded the crew that they were now in hostile territory and the area where the airliner was believed to have been shot down. At 1845 hours the boost gauge and rev counter for the port-inner engine was still fluctuating, the sea calm and a slight haze softened the tones of the water and blurred the sky. At 1900 Goode swinging his tail turret to the right, suddenly stopped and his eyes widening barked 'Tail to Control, eight aircraft. Thirty degrees on the port quarter. Six miles. Up 1,000 feet!'

Simpson jumped back to the astrodome. Walker rammed the throttles wide open and sounded the alarm. Dowling hauled on the pitch levers as the engines screamed at 2,600 rpm. The aircraft, which were quickly identified as Ju 88s, began to sweep in at high speed. Walker sent an immediate report to 19 Group that he was being attacked by Ju 88s. He quickly ascertained from the engineer that the port inner-engine had neither improved nor deteriorated. In the galley the gunners rolled out the bomb racks onto the underneath of the wing and Walker jettisoned the Depth Charges quickly, before instructing the air gunners to close the doors and man the galley guns. Miles was on the starboard gun and Lane on the port.

Simpson, the navigator who had been tracking the eight Ju 88s from his astrodome, announced that they had now spread all around N/461, three on the starboard beam, three on the port beam, one on each quarter. The range was 1,500 yards and they were 1,500 feet up. Simpson was ideally

The pilot of a Short Sunderland of 201 Squadron scans the sea through binoculars while on patrol over the Atlantic from its base at Castle Archdale, County Fermanagh. (Crown Copyright – Air Historical Branch)

The captain of a Sunderland aircraft gives directions to his air gunners from the bridge, better known as the fire control position. (Crown Copyright – Air Historical Branch)

placed in the astrodome to control the battle, directing the gunners to hold their fire until the Ju 88s were within the 600-yard range of the Sunderland's Vickers .303 machine guns. There was a pause and then the enemy aircraft made their move, Simpson called out that one Ju 88 had peeled off from each beam and then counted down the range to 800 yards, directing Walker to pitch the Sunderland into a corkscrew to starboard. The Sunderland lurched steeply as it was hit by both cannon shell and tracer from the attacking aircraft. Walker then flung the Sunderland into a cork-screw to port, N/461 shuddering with the effort as it climbed giddily to the left. The port-outer engine burst into flames and smoke and fire spread over the wing, incendiary bullets from the Ju 88 smashed into the cockpit and the aircraft's compass in front of Walker blew up, the alcohol inside it ignited covering Walker with liquid fire.

Simpson urged Walker to straighten up, as two more Ju 88s began to close in. Walker yelled at Dowling to take over the aircraft whilst Amiss wrenched the fire extinguisher from its bracket and turned it full onto the burning Walker. Simpson counted down the ranges of this second attack to 800 yards and then yelled at Dowling to again throw the Sunderland into a corkscrew to port, N/461 plunged to the left and whilst Amiss held onto the fire-extinguisher bracket, Walker oper-ated the Graviner switch to extinguish the blazing engine. The fire petered out into clouds of white smoke which trailed behind the aircraft. The port outer-engine ground to a halt and the propellers windmilled uselessly, suddenly making N/461 even harder to fly. At Walker's instruction the wire-less operator sent a new message to 19 Group, stating the Sunderland was now on fire. The Ju 88s attacked for a second and third time, each time Dowling threw the Sunderland into a corkscrew turn, whilst winding the trimming tabs as fast as he could to take up the pressure, his full weight was jammed against the rudder pedal just to hold N/461 in control.

Simpson announced that the Ju 88s were re-forming once more into their familiar positions off the starboard and port beams, as well as both the quarters. The crew of N/461 knew they were in serious trouble by this stage, Simpson again counted the ranges down as the Ju 88s closed in and he instructed Dowling to throw N/461 once more into a starboard corkscrew. The shells and bullets from this Ju 88 crashed into the Sunderland again but this time the tail gunner was able to engage, as was Fuller the mid-upper gunner who, despite the bullets spattering around him, held his fire until the Ju 88 was within 200 yards before hitting the German aircraft with several hundred rounds, which caused it to dive vertically into the sea in a cloud of flame and black smoke. N/461 straightened up, gained a little height and then prepared to dive to port once more as two Ju 88s in line astern came at the Sunderland from the port quarter. Dowling threw N/461 into a tight dizzying dive to the left. The Ju 88s fired into N/461 shooting away the elevator, rudder trim-ming wires and tail hydraulics, the latter slamming the tail turret violently against its stops and knocking Goode, the gunner, unconscious. As the enemy came in closer the nose and mid-ships guns engaged the second Ju 88, which then emitted a thin stream of smoke from its starboard engine. This quickly turned to flames and this aircraft also fell towards the water striking the surface, bouncing vertically and then plunging into the sea leaving a small column of oily smoke. N/461's wireless operator transmitted a message to 19 Group that they had just destroyed two enemy aircraft.

The Ju 88s attacked again, this time from below. Simpson instructed the galley gunners, Miles and Lane, as well as Goode in the tail turret to engage. The galley gunners scared the Ju 88 off, but Simpson not hearing from Goode over the intercom or seeing any fire from the tail turret assumed him to be dead. Walker detailed another galley gunner to take Goode's place and Amiss set off to do so. It was then that the most damaging attack occurred. Two Ju 88s came in from starboard in line astern. A cannon shell burst inside the aircraft, against the radio bulkhead. The bridge was filled with smoke, flying shrapnel and broken glass, every petrol gauge and many instruments were shattered and the wireless wrecked. Miller, the wireless operator and Dowling were both injured and Simpson fell down from the astrodome in a heap, a lump of steel embedded in his leg. Miles

A German Ju 88, based in France 1943. (Bundesarchiv)

down on the starboard gun, clasped his stomach and collapsed. Simpson raised himself back up to the astrodome once more, to find the intercom was now dead, Walker looked out of the window to see the port outer-engine's propellors and their reduction gear fall off the engine and into the sea.

Simpson warned of another attack, using Miller the wounded wireless operator, to pass on hand-signals to Walker and direct his next manoeuvre. Amiss struggled to the tail turret to relieve Goode and on the way encountered Miles, collapsed over his gun and dying fast. Turner, the engineer, came down and after helping Amiss to lay Miles on the bomb-room floor, took his place on the starboard gun. The last attack had been so destructive that N/461's airframe was now badly warped to the extent that all the doors were jammed open or shut. Amiss managed to struggle through on all fours and was shocked to see the rear of the aircraft was shot to ribbons with large rents, tears and holes. The turret was jammed over hard to port but when Amiss thumped on the door, Goode opened it and grinned. Amiss tried to get him out, but Goode had recovered consciousness and was having none of it, even though the hydraulics in his turret had gone, he was still able to elevate his guns and use his bodily weight to shift the turret about. Amiss made his way back to the cockpit.

The six remaining Ju 88s withdrew to their previous positions on the beams and quarters for what they must have felt was the final kill. On the next attack, Fuller engaged the fighter attacking from the starboard side which broke off and Goode in the tail fired his four .303 machine guns into the engines, the Ju 88 carved a flaming arc into the sea. There were a number of further attacks on N/461, but all seemed to be beaten back by the collective fire of the Sunderland's gunners. Yet another Ju 88 came at the Sunderland from the starboard bow, but Watson, in the nose, engaged it with his Vickers and the enemy aircraft was seen trailing smoke, never to be seen again.

It came as a surprise to see that the Ju 88s now only numbered two aircraft, after one last, half-hearted approach they turned away at 800 yards and headed east for France. The attack was over but N/461 was now down to 1,000 feet. Walker inmmediately started to re-organise his crew. Simpson had his wound dressed and after a cigarette went up into the astro-dome, took a few sightings and passed on a more accurate course for home. Amiss moved into the right-hand cockpit seat and helped Dowling fly the plane. This largely consisted of forcing his weight onto the starboard rudder-bar to keep the Sunderland straight. When that grew too tiring he pulled on the port rudder bar as hard as he could. With no operable petrol gauges to tell them how much petrol they had, Turner went in to the starboard wing and inspected the tanks for leaks, all seemed well and despite much damage the petrol tanks were intact, Walker pulled up the floorboards in the hull and inspected the damage. He directed his crew to plug the holes below the fuselage with wooden leak-stoppers and smash down the jammed doors, Walker concluded that he would have to beach the aircraft for, with all the holes in her hull, she would not be able to float.

The engineers took axes and stripped the aircraft of all the surplus gear and furniture, before throwing it overboard to lighten the load. Only the guns and ammunition were retained. At 2235hrs, in the summer twilight, they sighted land: Cornwall. Walker realised he would never make Pembroke and therefore flew half an hour up the coast looking for a good place to land. N/461 ditched near the village of Marazion in Cornwall, off a likely looking stretch of beach known as Prah Sands, the starboard inner-engine failing just before Walker landed the Sunderland 300 yards offshore in a seven-foot sea. N/461 wallowed in the troughs, and Walker's initial thought was for his crew to paddle ashore in the dinghy, but he detected the seas were not coming in as rapidly as he thought and recalled the crew from the wings where they had begun to inflate the dinghy. He powered N/461 ashore at full bore until she shuddered in the shallows within walking depth of the shore. Walker cut the engine switches and turned to his crew saying, 'Lets go, I think we've had enough for one day.'

The local Cornish villagers came running up to help the crew and showered them with tea, eggs and fried sausages, Walker telephoned Pembroke Dock to let them know they had arrived and it was agreed that they would stay the night at Prah Sands, making their way back in the morning. As the crew woke up the next day, they saw that N/461 had been pounded by the Atlantic surf into lumps of wreckage, pieces of which were strewn across 100 yards of beach.

Walker was posted from the Squadron soon after, having finally completed his tour. Amiss, too, moved on to another crew and would become first pilot in his own right. Dowling took over command of most of the surviving N/461 crew and two months later, on 13 August, together with Simpson, Turner, Watson, Miller, Lane, Fuller and Goode he set off on another patrol from which their aircraft failed to return.[12] It is believed that the aircraft was shot down by a Ju 88 of *Kampfgeschwader* 40. Their names are commemorated on both the RAF Memorial at Runnymede and the Australian War Memorial at Canberra.

The operations by Sunderlands, Wellingtons, Halifaxes and Whitleys were to have a profound impact on the U-boat campaign, whether it was in the Atlantic or over the Bay of Biscay, but no matter how good these aircraft were, they still did not have the range to fly right out into the middle of the Atlantic. It was to be the eventual closure of this gap which would turn the course of the Battle of The Atlantic. The mid-Atlantic gap was 600 miles north to south, from the southern tip of Greenland to the Azores, stretching 300 miles across from west to east (see Maps 12a and 12b). It was in this part of the ocean, that in 1942 and early 1943, Doenitz focussed the bulk of his U-boat operations to almost catastrophic effect and posed the greatest challenge to the Allies in how to ensure continuous coverage of convoys across the principal trade routes. The Allies only achieved this in 1943 by a combination of Fleet Air Arm aircraft flying from escort carriers and merchant aircraft carriers, (whose operations we will cover in a subsequent chapter), together with Coastal Command's Very Long Range (VLR) Liberators. Obtaining VLR Liberators had not been a simple task for Coastal Command. The years 1941 and 1942 had witnessed a series of bitter disputes between the Air Staff and the Royal Navy and Coastal Command for possession of them. The Air Staff took the view that any diversion of VLR aircraft to Coastal Command was a purely defensive action and could only ever be at the expense of its offensive bomber campaign, an attitude summed up by the Air Staff on 8 March 1942:

---

12   Ivan Southall, *They Shall Not Pass Unseen* (London: Angus and Robertson, 1956), pp. 83-9.

A Coastal Command Sunderland and its Spitfire escort passing the Eddystone Lighthouse, 14 miles south of Plymouth, during a sweep of the Channel in June/July 1944. (Crown Copyright – Air Historical Branch)

It remains the opinion of the Air Staff that squadrons of Bomber Command could best contribute to the weakening of the U-boat offensive by offensive action against the principal industrial areas of Germany within our range, including the main naval industries and dockyards. To divert them to an uneconomical defensive role would be unsound at any time. It would be doubly so now when we are about to launch a bombing offensive of which we have high expectations, and which will enable us to deliver a heavy and concentrated blow against Germany when German morale is low and when the Russians are in great need of our assistance.[13]

Bomber Command Chief Harris was even more blunt about the waste in sending good bomber aircraft to Coastal Command:

The purely defensive use of air power is grossly wasteful. The naval employment of aircraft consists of picking at the fringes of enemy power, of waiting for opportunities that may never occur, and indeed probably will never occur, of looking for needles in a haystack. They [i.e. Coastal Command] attempt to sever each capillary vein, one by one, when they could, with much less effort, cut the artery. Bomber Command attacks the source of all [German] Naval Power rather than the fringes of one type of enemy naval operations which obviously menace us – the submarine.[14]

The view of the Royal Navy was in total accord with Coastal Command; together they presented the starkly accurate view that the war at sea would be lost if the Allies could no longer maintain the communications essential to a maritime alliance, or to put it more bluntly if the Allies lost

---

13   TNA CAB 69/4: DO (42) 24, 8 March 1942.
14   Arthur Harris, *Bomber Offensive* (New York: Macmillan, 1947), p. 25.

the war at sea, they would lose the war. This was the essence of the Battle of the Atlantic and well understood by Joubert, who as one of Coastal Command's first commanders, played an important role in the argument:

> While fully aware of the importance of the sustained bomber offensive, it appeared to him that, if England was to survive this year, in which we were already losing shipping at a rate considerably in excess of American and British building output, some part of the bomber offensive would have to be sacrificed and a long-range type such as the Lancaster diverted to the immediate threat on our Sea communications.[15]

It is ironic that Germany, essentially a continental landpower, having failed to overcome Britain through a seaborne invasion was attempting to subdue her indirectly through a stranglehold on her sea communications by U-boats. Simultaneously Britain, essentially a maritime power, having withdrawn from France unceremoniously in 1940, was now attempting to subdue Germany's military power indirectly by the destruction of her industrial capacity through a bomber offensive. The outcome would depend on which side was most effective at waging their particular campaign,[16] in 1942 an objective bystander would probably have concluded that the U-boat offensive showed much more promise. Yet the Air Staff, backed by Churchill, was still reluctant to prioritise air support to the Battle of the Atlantic, including the transfer of even modest numbers of Lancasters or American Flying Fortresses[17] which could help to close the mid-Atlantic gap. Even the recommendations of a joint RAF/Royal Navy report, commissioned by the Chiefs of Staff Committee in July 1942 and calling for a substantial increase in long range aircraft for Coastal Command failed to elicit the right response. In addition, Bomber Command flew few missions against the operational bases of the U-boats. In five of these bases – Lorient, Brest, St Nazaire, Bordeaux and La Pallice substantial concrete protective pens were being built for the submarines. 1941 offered an excellent chance to disrupt the building programme when deep foundations were being laid behind caissons that could be breached and flooded. By early 1942 the opportunity had passed and shelters were in place providing U-boats with bomb-proof sanctuaries at each location.[18]

The bomber offensive continued to have over-riding priority in Britain's strategic approach to war. This was until the First Sea Lord finally managed to convince both Churchill, as well as the Chief of the Air Staff, that simply in aviation fuel terms alone, their ambitions for an increased bomber offensive were impractical given the level of shipping losses, particularly tankers that the Allies had suffered in 1942.[19] Furthermore the loss of shipping was impacting both BOLERO and the minimum level of imports required to sustain Britain. It was to be these blunt arguments, accepted only at the eleventh hour, that finally prompted Britain's leaders to make the correct strategic decision.

The first VLR Liberators arrived with 120 Squadron in Iceland in the summer of 1941. These VLR Liberators were in effect Bomber Command cast-offs, unwanted for night bombing because their exhaust flames were easily detectable at night. The original VLR Liberator was actually the MK 1 with a range of 2,400 miles which meant it could patrol 1,100 miles from its base. No other aircraft within Coastal Command came close to this distance or had the operational range to

---

15   AHB II/117/3 (C) p. 10 and John Terraine, *The Right of The Line*, p. 418.
16   Corelli Barnett, *Engage the Enemy More Closely*, 1991, p. 463.
17   Though in the Air Staff's defence, they worried over potential American criticism in moving B-17s from the strategic bomber offensive to Coastal Command.
18   Denis Richards, *The Royal Air Force – Volume 1*, p. 350.
19   Corelli Barnett, *Engage the Enemy More Closely*, p. 474.

close the mid-Atlantic air gap. This handful of Liberators were barely maintained with reinforcing aircraft, until they had been reduced to only five by the end of 1942. Joubert had maintained that 40 was the minimum number required and Churchill, shocked by October 1942's shipping losses, accepted a shift in priority and directed that Coastal Command was reinforced in 1943 by MK 2 and MK 3 Liberators.

These newer Liberators needed considerable modification to undertake a VLR, low altitude, anti-submarine role. This included removing the self-sealing liners to the fuel tanks, the armour-plating, the turbo-superchargers on the engines, the upper turret, the tunnel gun, the mid-side gun as well as ammunition, all of this in order to carry the extra two 335 gallon fuel tanks and eight depth charges.[20] Thankfully some of the American aircraft, delivered by a grudging Bomber Command in January 1943, also came equipped with the SCR 517, the American 10-centimetric ASV radar that had been developed by the Massachusetts Institute of Technology, others would be fitted with ASV Mk III.

Two squadrons of Liberators were created, a total of 34 machines of which 20 were operational by the end of March. These numbers were still too small to tip the balance decisively or perma-nently in the Allies' favour who only narrowly avoided defeat in the Atlantic in the early spring of 1943. Had the Allies suffered such a defeat, history would have judged that the main cause would have been for the lack of two more squadrons of VLR aircraft for convoy escort work.[21]

It was only the direct and personal intervention by President Roosevelt that led to a further increase in VLR aircraft numbers. Troubled by March's shipping losses and the impact it would have on BOLERO, he allocated more American shipping to British routes and enquired about the level of VLR aircraft that would support the convoys. His surprise at the low numbers and that no sorties were being flown from the western Atlantic – compelled him to place more pressure on the USAAF to release Liberators from their heavy bomber force. As one reads these manoeuvrings it may lead to a false impression that very few Liberators were produced, in fact approximately 18,500 of these aircraft were manufactured by the Americans, making it not only one of the most numerous bombers of the Second World War, but in American history itself. Another way of putting the Coastal Command requests in some sort of proportion would be to compare the 40 aircraft Joubert stated he required to close the gap, with the 53 Liberators lost, during just one raid on the Ploesti oilfields on 1 August 1943, to no great strategic effect.[22]

The optimum use of VLR Liberators took them far out into the mid-Atlantic, but here the weather was at its most unpredictable and tested the crews' flying and navigation skills to the limit. Each aircraft would try to provide cover up to its maximum Prudent Limit of Endurance (PLE), but that could still present huge problems on its return. Ernest E. Allen was a Canadian pilot on 59 Squadron, he had flown medium-range Liberators across the Bay of Biscay in 1942 and then converted to VLR Liberators in the spring of 1943. One of his earlier missions was on 7 May escorting the *Queen Mary* on a trip to the United States. Medium range aircraft such as Wellingtons and Halifaxes had provided cover for the initial stages, but Allen's VLR Liberator, along with two others from 59 Squadron, would do so for the mid-Atlantic section. Sadly, all was not well with the weather and Allen's account graphically captures the hazards Coastal Command crews faced as they flew out into the depths of the Atlantic:

20 TNA Air 20/3094: Air Ministry to Coastal Command, 30 November 1942; AIR 8/1400 D.O. R. Memorandum, 'Modification work carried out on Liberator aircraft on arrival in the UK', 9 March 1943.
21 Stephen Roskill, *The War at Sea, Volume* II (London: HMSO, 1961), p. 371.
22 Jay A. Stout. *Fortress Ploesti: The Campaign to Destroy Hitler's Oil Supply* (London: Casemate Publishing, 2003), p. 318.

Daily inspection for a Liberator III of 224 Squadron at Beaulieu in Hampshire, December 1942. (Crown Copyright – Air Historical Branch)

By the time we were one hour out we knew it was going to be a rough trip weather-wise. There was low cloud with moderate to – at times – severe turbulence. We had to fly below 500 feet to keep below the cloud. As we progressed it was the normal thing to transfer fuel from the wing tip tanks to the inner tanks. This was our first trip with a flight engineer as an eighth man in the crew. One of his duties was this fuel transfer. This clod was transferring from one wing tip at a time, which created severe control problems for the pilots. We finally realized what the problem was and Tommy went back and balanced up the fuel, thus easing up the aileron work. We invited the engineer to find a comfortable spot in the airplane, stay out of the way and not touch anything, otherwise we'd turn Al Henry loose on him.

The turbulence continued and got worse – not the nicest thing for a crew that was hung over. La Forme did a wind calculation and it was over 100 knots – mostly on the nose. He then did a calculation of our E.T.A. on the *Queen Mary* and announced we would arrive there two hours after dark. The *Queen* was moving away from us at 24 knots, we had a headwind component of 90 knots, and in the reduced airspeed of 150 knots because of the turbulence, this meant we were gaining on the *Queen* at about 35 nautical miles per hour. About this time we got a wireless signal from the Group Control that 'the winds are backing and increasing!' I guess they were trying to convey something to us we didn't know. We came to the conclusion that we should be heading for either Aldergrove or, a better bet, to Gibraltar. While we were still discussing it, a signal came through giving us an immediate diversion to Gibraltar.

Now, 'Gib' as it was called in the vernacular, was a place you did not approach casually. They were trigger-happy and if an aircraft, any aircraft, failed to give the proper identification, they opened up with the ack ack and shot the aircraft down. Anticipating we might possibly want to go to Gibraltar, we had been issued the usual sealed envelope with Gibraltar codes. We opened the sealed envelope and it was empty – no codes. This obviously was not our day and we could not go to Gibraltar.

Ernest Allen and his crew held a short council of war and decided to climb above cloud, into smooth air, before heading for Land's End and then, depending on the weather, deciding on which airfield to land at:

We were on top of all cloud at 10,500 feet. George worked out an E.T.A. for Land's End based on a 100-knot tailwind. To cover the possibility of there being stronger tail winds, I decided to descend one hour before the E.T.A. Henry had picked up diversions of other aircraft to Aldergrove, Northern Ireland, so we felt that the weather must be expected to be above landing limits there. On descent, at about 1,000 feet, we broke out of cloud and identified an island near Land's End. This meant that we had had a ground speed of over 300 mph, which meant we were in an area of hurricane force winds. We contacted St. Eval – the field was closed – weather. Visibility was good under the cloud over the Irish Sea and we decided to go up to Chivenor, North Devon, where we had operated from with the B-17s. We were in touch with Chivenor by radio and he was reporting acceptable weather. Then, when we were out only about 25 miles, Chivenor called to say that a fog had just rolled in and they were zero-zero in fog. We circled while making another decision. Henry intercepted messages that Aldergrove aircraft were being diverted to Gibraltar. Henry contacted Group on the alternate. They suggested Beaulieu, just west of Portsmouth. We knew Beaulieu; it was almost completely surrounded by balloons and to try to approach through the balloons, in the dark, was something we'd rather not do ... However, Thorney Island was in the same direction as Beaulieu, so we decided to climb to 5,000 feet and try for Thorney. At 5,000 feet we were icing pretty badly, and it cut off our radio reception as well, so we climbed and finally got on top of cloud and out of it at 12,500 feet.

I should mention that in the modifications to the Liberators they had removed the nose and top turrets, among other things, to reduce weight to carry more fuel and bomb-load and had removed the entire oxygen system. Now, flying at anything over 10,000 feet, it was accepted that crew members might do unusual things, we could pass out, get overly aggressive and other unknowns. We discussed this as a crew and that we should watch one another for signs of trouble. I told Tommy that if he saw signs that I was in trouble, he was to take over and get the aircraft down to at least 8000 feet, and I mentioned that if I saw signs of him getting aggressive, I would take the removable hydraulic hand pump which was between the two pilots and thump him on the head. Al Henry was on the radio set just behind the pilots and he told us later that Tommy and I sat there, head to head, eyeballing each other.

We were navigating blind but hoped to get radio bearings to Thorney when we got closer in. One of the pieces of emergency radio equipment we had was called a DARKIE set. This had a very low-powered transmitter and the procedure recommended that when a crew were uncertain of their position (lost), they could call out 'DARKIE, DARKIE, PLEASE RESPOND'. Thus the station that responded, and was heard by us, had to be within 25 miles of our position. We discussed whether we should declare an emergency.

We called Darkie and R.A.F. Boscombe Down responded. We knew we were within 25 miles of Boscombe Down – La Forme gave me a course alteration and we proceeded easterly. The cloud tops continued to rise, and we got up to 16,500 feet – still no oxygen. Eventually, while we were trying to get a radio bearing from Thorney, through a hole in the cloud we could see a set of runway lights. This was good enough for me. I pulled off all power and steep turned in a rapid descent through this hole, got below the cloud about 1,000 feet above the ground, found the identifier beacon for this aerodrome and found it was a fighter base called Ford.

From there it was only about 50 miles to Thorney Island and, when in range, I called the Thorney Island tower for permission to land. The tower said that the field was closed on

Consolidated Liberator GR.VI, KG869/ZZ-K, of 220 Squadron based at Lagens, Azores, in flight off Terceira. (Crown Copyright – Air Historical Branch)

account of high winds. I informed him that we had declared an emergency a half hour previously, so he gave us an OK to land at our own discretion and turned the runway lights on. He was reporting winds of 90 knots with gusts on our approach. We touched down, used almost no runway and parked the airplane on a dispersal point. I think a prayer of thanks went out from all the heathens on board … Of the four aircraft that set out to escort the *Queen Mary* in the middle of the Atlantic (a completely unnecessary escort with the *Queen* doing 24 knots) we lost three aircraft and eight experienced crewmen. It wasn't a good start for the 59 Squadron VLR Liberators.[23]

The new Liberators also came equipped with a new weapon in the war against the U-boat; the acoustic torpedo. This American designed weapon could be dropped over a submerged submarine and would home in on the noise of U-boat propellers. The technology was so sensitive that Liberator crews were banned from dropping the torpedo if a U-boat was on the surface, less this new weapon was compromised.

The increase in coverage in 1943 by VLR Liberators made a marked difference, Coastal Command's capability was also supplemented by further reinforcements of medium to long range aircraft, such as Halifaxes and Wellingtons, which increased the frequency of patrols in the outer Bay of Biscay and the approaches to the United Kingdom. This land-based air power working in concert with escort carriers, surface vessels and improved intelligence (including Bletchley Park's decryption of U-boat communications) was able to make the cost of U-boat attacks on convoys punitive. By May 1943 convoys such as SC 130 (a 37 ship slow convoy sailing from Sydney, Cape Breton, to Liverpool) were protected throughout their transit by air cover including VLR aircraft for three days and two nights. During this period, these aircraft made 28 sightings of U-boats, launched 10 attacks on them and succeeded in sinking two. Doenitz was to lose a catastrophically high total of 41 U-boats in the month of May[24] which prompted him to reduce his campaign and write:

---

23   Ernest Allen, *An RCAF Pilot's Story* <http://doralholdings.com/eallen/part3.html>.
24   Corelli Barnett, *Engage the Enemy More Closely*, p. 611.

The enemy Air Force therefore played a decisive part. This can be attributed to the increased use of land-based aircraft and aircraft carriers combined with the advantages of radar location ... To a very great extent, the enemy aircraft brought about the failure of our U-boats against convoys SC 130 as well as HX 239. In the former they prevented the U-boats from manoeuvring into an attacking position ahead of the enemy. In the case of HX 239, the enemy precluded all contact.[25]

It was not just the physical destruction of U-boats that was so pronounced. German U-boat morale and stress were constantly attacked by the presence and threat of attacking Coastal Command aircraft. The interrogation of captured U-boat crews brought regular evidence of this. The telegraphist of the U-523 reported 'The Commanding Officer was continually on my tail telling me to report immediately the slightest contact. His nerves communicated themselves to the entire crew.' Another prisoner from U-202 observed 'You've no idea how unnerving is the effect of repeated alarms. The loudspeaker begins to sound like the voice of doom.'[26]

The U-Boat peril would not disappear entirely, but through technological and tactical innovation Coastal Command developed a sophisticated air instrument, that allowed the Allies to retain the upper hand from 1943 onwards. German developments of new types of submarine, including snorkel equipped U-boats and the impressive Type XXI, which had an unprecedented submerged speed and endurance, were fortunately too little and too late. They were also heavily disrupted by the mining of the Baltic ports by Bomber Command in the last year and a half of the war.[27] Like so many endeavours in war, victory passed to the side that was best able to comprehend the unique character of the conflict it was experiencing and use that understanding tactically and technologically to improve its fighting effectiveness. Coastal Command's combination of scientists, intelligence officers, sailors and airmen, working in harmony, was much more successful than its German counterparts in developing a fertile environment for innovation and adaptation to occur. By the end of the war Coastal Command had accounted for 188 U-boats, out of a total of 783 lost through various causes (Annex W provides further analysis of submarines destroyed by Aircraft 1939-45).

Commendable though this was, victory might have occurred much more swiftly had senior Allied leadership, particularly the Air Staff, shown greater strategic insight in matching resources to the right ends. Their error nearly cost the Allies the war.

25   Corelli Barnett, *Engage the Enemy More Closely*, p. 611.
26   Hilary Saunders, *Royal Air Force 1939-45, Volume III*, p. 57.
27   W.J.R. Gardner, 'Smart Mining without Smart Mines – Second World War British Operations in the Baltic', *International Journal of Naval History*, August 2007, Volume 6, No.2.

17

'Woe to the Unwary'[1] The RAF's Early Anti-Shipping Operations

The U-boat's threat to Allied strategic lines of communication had brought Britain's maritime-based alliance close to defeat. Disappointingly for the Allies however, the risks to Germany's shipping were never quite so severe. Germany's great strength was as a continental land power, which from 1940 occupied almost the entire European mainland. In contrast to the Allies her strategic lines of communication were primarily ground based and internal and it was largely through these that she was able to maintain her industrial capacity and sustain her military operations. Blockading Germany would be an important element of the British strategy, though it was always recognised as unlikely to yield outright victory. There were a few vulnerable areas where RAF attacks on enemy merchant shipping could frustrate and weaken the Axis. In the North Sea, between Narvik and Rotterdam in particular, the interdiction of coastal shipping carrying Swedish iron ore, one of Germany's most vital raw materials, would potentially disrupt German war production. In the Mediterranean, anti-shipping operations could be launched against the Axis lines of communication to North Africa hampering Rommel's plans and ambitions for his Afrika Korps. Finally, Further away, in the Far East, Japan was undoubtedly a maritime power and her ability to sustain its forces in Burma, Indonesia and the Philippines through sea and coastal supply lines could also easily be disrupted.

The German dependence on Swedish Iron Ore had been identified by the Ministry of Economic Warfare (MEW) soon after war broke out. From commercial information the MEW had concluded that to maintain her industrial output, Germany needed to import nine million tons of Swedish iron ore per annum. German pre-war stockpiles were also reportedly low and some 43-50 percent of German steel industries, including most armament and munition industries, utilised the Bessemer smelting process which was particularly dependent on the unusually phosphorous rich Swedish iron ore.[2] Germany also required other critical raw materials from Scandinavia, including nickel for the production of armour piercing shells and armour plate, and molybdenum for hardening steel.[3] A cursory study of a map of Europe might lead one to assume that much of this war material could be safely transported from Sweden, across the Baltic, to German ports such as Lübeck or Rostock, or alternatively across the North Sea to ports such as Hamburg or

---

1 The motto of 217 Squadron, this squadron began to receive Beaufort torpedo bombers in May 1940 and was based out of St Eval in Cornwall for the first few years of the war. It later served in the Mediterranean, spending two months in Malta in the summer of 1942, before subsequently deploying to Ceylon.

2 Christina Goulter, *A Forgotten Offensive – Royal Air Force Coastal Command's anti-shipping campaign 1940-1945* (London: Frank Cass, 1995), p. 116.

3 Christina Goulter, *A Forgotten Offensive*, p. 118

Bremerhaven (see Map 13). In fact, the capacity of many of those ports was limited, as were the railway connections to the Ruhr valley where much of the steel production occurred.

Instead Rotterdam had been developed over many years as the quickest and most practical gateway into Germany's industrial centre. It was at Rotterdam that large quantities of cargo, including iron ore, were transhipped onto barges and then sailed up the Rhine directly to the steel plants in the Ruhr. German and Swedish merchant ships also preferred the sea journey across the North Sea, as the majority of the iron-ore mines were located in the far north of Sweden. The severe nature of the weather in that region meant that the most practical way for the ore to be moved was not via a long overland journey to Sweden's Baltic ports, but a much shorter railway route to Norway's permanently ice-free port at Narvik. The vessels would then hug the Norwegian coast, passing through the inner-leads, a network of islands just off Norway's distinctive coastline, before crossing the North Sea and hugging the German and Dutch coasts to Rotterdam. It was this traffic that would dominate much of Britain's anti-shipping focus in the European War.

Despite these potential opportunities the RAF had not seriously considered striking merchant shipping at the beginning of the war at all, but were more focussed on spotting enemy warships in support of Royal Navy surface fleet actions. Coastal Command aircraft were initially tasked to identify German surface vessels breaking out in to the Atlantic and therefore patrolled between the Kattegat and Skagerrak (the two channels that separate Denmark from Norway and connect the Baltic to the North Sea). Although patrols started in August 1939, they still missed the *Deutschland* and *Graf Spee* transiting into the Atlantic immediately prior to the outbreak of the war in September. Some of these early patrols were flown by aircrew in the newly delivered Hudson aircraft, a conversion of the Lockheed 14 Airliner. The Hudson had been procured early in 1938 by a direct purchasing commission, led by the then Air Commodore Arthur Harris. His team had travelled to America with the intention of buying a reconnaissance aircraft to replace the ageing and operationally limited Avro Ansons (which simply did not have the range to patrol all the way to the Norwegian coast and back). The purchasing commission were impressed not just with the sleek, modern lines of the aircraft but also the competence and professionalism of the Lockheed Company. Their positive view was further strengthened when having expressed some misgivings over the layout in the nose of the aircraft, Lockheed executives quickly re-designed two alternatives overnight, fitting them on hinges onto the full-size plywood mock up. The commission were impressed not just with the new design, but by a company that was so receptive to their ideas and keen to satisfy their demands.[4]

The first batch of Hudson aircraft were shipped across the Atlantic from the Lockheed factory in Burbank, California in 1939. They were fitted with a Boulton-Paul dorsal gun-turret which had an excellent field of fire. Inside, the aircraft was well-heated, spacious and furnished with unusually comfy seating for the period. These were important advantages given the long distances these aircraft would be required to fly. The new aircraft's Wright Cyclone engines were reliable and gave three times the horsepower available to the Anson, twice the range and a maximum speed of 246 mph. When this was combined with increased firepower and a 1,000lb bombload, the Lockheed was a dramatic improvement on its predecessor.[5] The one negative feature of the Hudson were its fuel tanks, rather than self-contained cells in the wing, these were directly built into the wing itself and the slightest rupture of the wing would cause many gallons of petrol to spill. If the fuel came into contact with the engine's hot exhaust the aircraft would usually catch fire immediately. Belly landings or crashes sufficient to cause the undercarriage to pierce the wing were often enough to create considerable fire hazards.

---

4   Geoffrey Jones, *Attacker – The Hudson and its Flyers* (London: Kimber, 1980), p. 15.
5   Gron Edwards, *Norwegian Patrol* (Shrewsbury: Airlife publishing, 1985), p. 5.

Hudsons would be flown in many different roles throughout the war, but the first to arrive in the UK in May 1939 were sent to 224 Squadron at RAF Leuchars. This Coastal Command squadron was tasked to patrol across the North Sea to Norway. Gron 'Dopey' Edwards flew Hudsons throughout that period, so that by May of 1940 he could consider himself a highly experienced pilot. He describes one of the typical patrols across the North Sea that the Hudsons frequently carried out, on this occasion it included coaching a young pilot called Paton – whom he had initially placed in the pilot's seat. During the initial 'Phoney War' period of the conflict these patrols had been long tedious affairs searching for German naval and merchant shipping, but by May 1940 Norway had been occupied and the Germans had begun to operate Me 109s from airfields in the country. This made the Hudson's anti-shipping reconnaissances more hazardous missions.

As soon as we'd settled down on course I went down the stairs into the navigator's compartment in the nose, slid my seat forward on its runners and lay down to take a drift with the bombsight through the transparent floor panel, using one of the larger white horses of spray on the sea's surface as a mark, By general size of these white horses the wind speed was a bit over what the met forecast had given and our drift was 4 degrees more to starboard than I'd reckoned. Uncorrected, that would have given us an error of 25 miles in our landfall. I switched on my intercom.

'Alter course 4 degrees port on 042 degrees magnetic', I told Paton.

'Oh four two magnetic it is, Dopey. Testing Guns.'

There were two clunks from the Browning guns mounted two feet above my head as Paton pulled the gun loading handles. As I looked up at the right-hand gun the cocking handle vanished into a blur as both guns banged and rattled into action at 20 shots a second apiece. Spent cases and links tinkled down into the empties bags and cordite fumes leaked and swirled round my compartment. The aircraft yawed; that would be Morgan swinging his turret on to the beam to do a test firing of his guns. Faintly above the engine noise, a muted rat-tat-tat confirmed this.

I settled down to 10 minutes of forward planning. Using the amended groundspeed derived from my drift checks I marked off along our track line my estimated position at 10 minute intervals so that if anything turned up suddenly I would have a fair idea of its position immediately and could leave the accurate estimation until an opportunity to work it out presented itself. It could save precious seconds in one's preliminary sighting report. The Hudson settled down on its patrol, Paton would be sweeping the horizon forward from wing tip to wing tip and Morgan in the turret would be doing the same astern, their sideways sweeps overlapping each beam. Paton would probably be the first to spot anything, and he had a pair of binoculars available for confirming any suspicious sighting. As navigator I would be reinforcing his search forward through the transparent nose, when I wasn't occupied on my own chores, though navigators often came up the stairs and stood or sat on alongside the pilot in companionable silence, or to pass the time of day. There was a better view up top as the engines blanketed a lot of the lateral vision from the navigator's seat.

'How's the petrol consumption?' I asked on one of my trips upstairs and gave Paton full marks for his answer.

'About 75 gallons in the first hour,' he replied. 'Just about right. We should be cruising at 67 gallons an hour and probably used that 8 gallons extra in takeoff and climb-away. The cylinder-head temperatures are in the green and I can lean out the mixture a bit more, if you like.'

'67 gallons an hour will do. Don't want to run the engines too hot; it shouldn't be all that long a trip, so I don't think we need to conserve fuel at the expense of engine wear.'

We saw nothing on the way over so ran into the mouth of Boknafiord and started our hunt for hiding ships.

'Now keep below the level of the tops of the mountains as much as you can,' I told Paton. 'They will have got us on their radar on our approach over the sea, so they know we're here, but there's no point in making it easy for them. Stick below mountain level and their radar's useless. It'll be luck if their fighters find us as it'll be all eyeball stuff for them. If we have to go over a mountain range to get into the next fiord do a daisy-cutter across the top of it but be prepared for a good bump in a fresh wind like this one. There'll be a lot of turbulence around the tops, and a good number of downdraughts which you must be prepared for. If you get into a dodgy downdraught use every bit of throttle you have – right up to the gate, yank the levers sideways and shove them through to the stops. And you'll need all your physical strength occasionally, too; really haul on the controls if you have to. Just don't hit those mountains on the side of the fiord, they're damned hard.' We flitted up and down the tortuous waterways and I told Paton to nip over into the next fiord. 'Now are you strapped in really tight? No, leave it to me, I'll do it. You just fly.'

I yanked at the safety harness straps until they'd move no more and got a good hold of the bulkhead.

'We're going just about down-wind so there's bound to be a down current the other side of the ridge, so not too low, mind you,' I shouted to Paton. 'Not below 150 feet off the top.' The Hudson shook and buffeted in the turbulence as it went over and I felt my stomach rise as we sank rapidly into the expected downdraught on the other side. Paton anticipated adequately and we slid down the mountain into the next branch fiord.

'Nicely done, old boy' I told him. 'But don't forget, in really turbulent conditions you've got to watch things like a hawk. And never go so far up a fiord that you can't do a 180 with plenty of spare room to get out in. If you go right to the top of some of these beauties you'd find yourself unable to climb out through the down draughts and unable to turn around, you'd just take your crew right into the rock.'

Gron Edwards had found no ships in any sections of the fjord and the time limit for the end of the patrol was beginning to approach. After climbing to mountain top height, for one final observation of the surrounding area, they dived back down to sea level and headed for the departure point which would take them back across the North Sea to Scotland. Gron Edwards continues with his account once more.

'O.K., Paton', I said, 'Do a complete instrument and fuel check and set her up for cruising.'

He'd just started on his chore when the intercom came to life as LAC Morgan cried 'Gunner to Captain. Four 109s five miles astern.'

I heard the rattle as he test-fired his guns and I shouted 'Out of it Paton. Quickly please.'

As Paton flung off his straps and scrambled out of the pilot's seat I slid in behind him. It took me about 10 seconds to strap in, set the mixtures to rich, airscrew fully fine pitch and throttles to the gate.

'O.K. Morgan, got that. It'll be a minute or two before they catch up with us. Have a good look round to see if there are any more of them. I hope not or you might never sing Sospan Fach at Cardiff Arms Park again.'

'Paton, get on the Lewis. Stick it out of the starboard window.'

Paton dashed off to the cabin and I felt the drafts rushing round the cockpit as he removed the two side windows through which we stuck our Lewis gun. As I pressed my gun button to test my own Brownings Paton opened up with the slower-firing Lewis gun, two short check bursts. We were as ready now as we ever would be.

'Captain to crew. They may not, of course, have seen us yet as we are fairly low. I am going down on the deck now and turning out to sea. Paton. I'm turning on to our reciprocal six minutes early. We'll correct the navigation later.' I dived down to sea level, turned south-westwards and made a swift note on my knee pad of the time and compass course.

'How are the 109s Morgan?' I asked the gunner.

'I think they're carrying on southwards, sir, They haven't turned out to sea yet.' I blessed the freshness of the wind that had given us that bumpy ride over the mountain tops. That same strong wind that had churned the surface of the sea into a mass of white horses, the best camouflage there was. It would take a very keen eye to spot us 50 feet off the surface from three or four miles away. And the radar couldn't help the 109s at this height either.

As we rushed towards our home 350 nautical miles away, an air of suspense pervaded the silent aircraft, silent because, as far as our alerted main senses went, the roar of the 2,000 horsepower and hiss of the slipstream were of no account. What we were waiting for was the gunner's next announcement, which seemed an age in coming. I nearly broke the silence as the tension mounted, because we hadn't a hope of surviving against four 109s, even if the pilots were inexperienced, which they probably weren't. Too many of them for comfort had fought in the Spanish Civil War. I was about to get Tubby Davies off the wireless set and send him down to Paton in the cabin to see if he knew what was happening when the intercom clicked again.

'Gunner. The 109s have passed astern of us at about three miles range still on a southerly course!'

'Fine! Paton, get the Lewis over to the port side, just in case they do have a go at us. Keep a good eye on them.'

Within a few seconds Paton came on.

'O.K. Dopey. Lewis on the port side. I can just about see the sods now, still going south. They can't have seen us.'

I ran on for five minutes, during which the fighters and, eventually, the mountain tops of Norway disappeared, throttled back to climbing revs and took her up to 2000 feet. Paton put the Lewis gun back in its stowage, replaced the two side windows and joined me in the cockpit.[6]

Gron Edwards successfully landed back at RAF Leuchars with his crew later that day.

Coastal Command's initial operational priority of finding enemy warships was also accompanied by a reticence from the RAF to attack enemy merchant shipping. This caution reflected British concerns that unrestricted air attacks on merchant shipping would invite hostility from neutral countries, most noticeably the United States. It was only following the invasion of Norway on 9 April 1940 that this restriction was lifted, even then the RAF were still initially limited to only attacking vessels underway in the Skagerrak.[7] Though the Hudsons and Sunderlands employed in the brief Norwegian campaign had some anti-shipping successes, it was the loss of France and the Low Countries in 1940, together with the subsequent heightened threat of invasion that led to a dramatic increase in prioritisation of the anti-shipping role by Coastal Command. However, the German occupation of Europe meant that Coastal Command's new anti-shipping task would now have to encompass a much larger area with operations spanning from the Norwegian North Cape to the Spanish border.

This area would be divided between three of the Command's Groups: 18 Group for the Norwegian Sector, 16 Group for the Netherlands and 19 Group for the French Coastline (see Map 13 for detail on the Coastal Command Group Areas of operation). Once the threat

---

6   Gron Edwards, *Norwegian Patrol*, pp. 107-110.
7   Andrew Hendrie, *Cinderella Service*, pp. 132-5.

A crew of a Bristol Blenheim IV of 404 Squadron RCAF prepare to take off from Dyce, Aberdeen, in the evening of 17 May 1942, to take part in the attack on the German heavy cruiser *Prinz Eugen* off Norway. Six Blenheims were detailed to accompany the strike force of Bristol Beauforts in order to make dummy torpedo attacks on the cruiser so as to confuse the enemy anti-aircraft defences, and to provide fighter cover.
(Crown Copyright – Air Historical Branch)

of invasion had passed in late 1940, the Command's emphasis changed, from the twice daily anti-invasion reconnaissance of enemy ports, to anti-shipping strike operations. Within Coastal Command's overall operational area, the shipping off the Dutch and Norwegian coasts would remain the priority throughout the war, it was here after all that German imports of iron ore and other critical Scandinavian raw materials could best be intercepted. Initially such operations were conducted with Hudson and Blenheim aircraft which attacked shipping with bombs at very low level. Though effective, the casualties were often catastrophically large. Ron Gillman recalls this early period in the anti-shipping war, when he was posted to fly Blenheims at 114 Squadron. He remembers his first glimpse of a MK 1 Blenheim aircraft.

> I made my way towards the perimeter track and there I came upon my first Blenheim. Even in its drab camouflage pattern of Khaki and Green there was a sleek look about it. The engines were Bristol Mercurys large radial engines driving three-bladed propellers. They seemed altogether too big for the aircraft, but therein lay the power. From the domed turret half-way along the machine's back, two Browning machine-guns pointed skywards ... The type had an odd background, for it was designed initially as a civil transport under the sponsorship of Lord Rothermere way back in 1934. Being of all-metal construction and having a retractable under-carriage, it was well ahead of its time, and its range of 1,000 miles and cruising speed of 240 mph attracted the military authorities – which was obviously the sponsor's intention. The design was adopted by the Air Ministry, modified for its fighter-bomber role and put into production.
>
> In its original form, the aircraft had been a low-wing monoplane, its narrow tube-like fuselage accommodating eight people; but in the military version the wing had been raised so that the mainspars came through the body behind the cockpit, forming what was known as the

bomb well. It was necessary to clamber over these to get through to the back of the aircraft, the only other access being a hatch in the top of the fuselage forward of the gun turret.[8]

The Blenheim may have looked good, but it was, in fact, a poor tactical daylight bomber, its cruising speed was just 180 mph when fully loaded, significantly slower than the German fighters, it also had only half the rate of climb of a German fighter, which again made it a very easy target. Moreover, it was very lightly built and not able to withstand punishment from a German fighter's cannons and its own firepower was limited to just three single .303 machine guns.[9]

The Blenheim was able to bomb at high (around 10,000 feet), medium (1,000–5,000 feet), and low-level altitudes. Though for anti-shipping strikes medium- and low-level attacks were mainly employed. At medium level the navigator, in the nose of the aircraft, would use a course setting bombsight to drop the bombs accurately. This consisted of a magnetic compass as a base with two long metal bars, about a foot long sticking out ahead of it, to which were attached 'drift' wires. As the aircraft was running into the target the navigator would set the aircraft's speed, height and assumed drift. Once the target appeared through the Perspex bomb aiming panel, the navigator would give the pilot directions to change course so that it appeared to travel between the drift wires from the navigator's point of view. When the target reached the ring sight, he pressed the button and the bomb was released. The sight was not stabilised, so a smooth approach was necessary to prevent the target swinging either side of the drift wires, which was hard to achieve in turbulence and it took a particularly cool individual to remain stoically straight and level when illuminated by searchlights or under AA fire.

Low-level bombing was in theory much more accurate. It simply required the pilot to fly at the ship straight and level a few feet above the sea, and as the target loomed up ahead the pilot would press a button on his control column to release the bombs. The pilot would not use any sight, the idea simply being to get so close to the ship that the bombs could not miss. The anti-shipping bombs used were the standard 250lb general purpose (GP) bomb, fitted with an 11-second delay fuse to allow the aircraft to be well clear of the vessel before the bomb exploded. The trajectory of the aircraft at low level was sufficient for the bomb to hit the side of the ship and pass into its hull before detonating. Whilst this approach was effective against merchant shipping, it would not work against the armoured hull or deck of a warship. In this instance the bomb would need to have a much harder, armour-piercing case and be dropped from high level altitudes, so that terminal velocity could be achieved and the deck penetrated. That may sound like a practical proposition, but hitting a moving target like a ship from such high levels was very difficult, particularly with the crude sights available to the British early on in the war – though as we have seen SABs would eventually make this a practical proposition and was devastating when used in conjunction with Tallboy.

In early 1941, the anti-shipping effort was stepped up and Coastal Command was reinforced to include 2 Group's light bombers, who would concentrate on attacking shipping off the German held coast from Brittany to Norway. The plan for 2 Group was to create a series of free bombing areas which were divided into six 'beats.' The Blenheim formation would fly extremely low at the start of the beat, with their aircraft at specified distances apart in line abreast. On arrival at the start line of the beat, usually some 30 miles from the British coast, the aircraft would cross the sea at right angles to the coast and then when 3 miles from the enemy shore turn to port. The orders were to sink any ship sighted and withdraw rapidly before German aircraft appeared. Given the

---

8   R.E. Gillman, *The Shiphunters* (London: Murray, 1976), p. 40.
9   Max Hastings, *Bomber Command*, p. 62.

high likelihood of a strong German reaction, fighter escorts were usually provided on a number of beats.[10]

Considerable low-level flying training and bombing was undertaken by 2.Group prior to their anti-shipping operations and the Blenheims recamouflaged from brown and green upper surfaces with black underneath, to dark grey and green with duck-egg blue under-surfaces. This was a much more effective toning for low-level maritime operations over the sea,[11] an escorting Spitfire pilot remarking that in some cases the Blenheims could only be identified during their low-level strikes by the wake on the sea left by the aircraft's slipstream. The anti-shipping strikes were sobering missions for 2 Group, who found the casualty rate worse than any comparable missions they had previously undertaken, either in France in 1940, or during the Battle of Britain. The attendant risks of anti-shipping operations reportedly made the Circuses, that they were also undertaking at that period, seem like a picnic. On 18 April Wing Commander L.V.E. Atkinson set off on a low-level attack against German shipping off Heligoland. Atkinson was one of the more experienced practitioners of anti-shipping attacks and had become increasingly dissatisfied with the standard tactical approach directed by 2 Group:

> I disagreed with Stevenson and those at Group over the method of attack they ordered which was broadside on. I wouldn't make beam attacks because (a) the enemy could easily see you coming, and (b) you faced all the fire power from the ships. I reckoned that with a Blenheim and its almost total lack of fire power the whole chance of success depended upon surprise. How could it be achieved? In my opinion the only way was low level, really low level right down to the wave tops and to attack from astern. I worked on the theory, laugh as one may, that a seaman always looks where he is going and not where he's been. If the Blenheim made broadside attacks they would be under maximum fire both before and after the attack.
>
> There was today this big convoy of 12-14 ships in three lines. I took the middle one of the back three. We could see them when some way off. I was right on them before they saw us, as the sailors manning the tripod gun were leaning over the side and forward. This method therefore successfully achieved more surprise. At the last moment we altered position for a quarter attack. We normally flew into an attack in a vic and final orders were flashed by lamp. We made our escape between the lines of ships very low indeed, so that if they fired they would hit each other. It was most important to maintain strict discipline. You had to plan for two or three forms of precise attack as you were not always told the strength or pattern of the convoy.
>
> We aimed our bombs at just below the waterline. On this attack the flak was still very intense and by the time the third ship was being attacked the gunners had woken. Plt. Off. Marshall's aircraft was soon ablaze, and Sgt. Dunning was shot into the sea.[12]

The enemy would often try and sail at night to avoid 2 Group's strikes and therefore a number of attacks were also undertaken on moonlit nights when the ships could still be seen. However, daylight raids were always seen as more effective and were undertaken more frequently, despite the increased casualties. Ron Gillman describes exactly what these hazardous operations were like during not only his first ever anti-shipping attack, but also his first ever operational sortie. On this occasion his MK IV Blenheim was crewed by his air gunner, Ron Weeks, and navigator, Benny Howlett. Gillman's squadron had taken off in three vics, of three aircraft each, to attack a convoy

---

10   Michael Bowyer, *2 Group – A complete History, 1936-1945* (London: Faber and Faber, 1974), p. 140.

11   Michael Bowyer, *2 Group*, p. 143.

12   Michael Bowyer, *2 Group*, p. 145.

53°41'N. 06°42'E.

Low-level oblique aerial photograph taken during an attack on an enemy radio-equipped trawler off Borkum Island by three Bristol Blenheim IVs of 21 Squadron. Sergeant Leaver's aircraft, V6034/YH-D, can be seen (left) spinning out of control after hitting the ship's mast during his attack. The 21-year-old pilot and his crew, Sergeant I. Overheu and Sergeant J. Phelps, were all killed, although the 'squealer' (a vessel equipped with radio to warn enemy shipping of impending aerial attack) was sunk. (Crown Copyright – Air Historical Branch)

comprising of four merchantmen, escorted by three flak ships off the coast of Heligoland. As the most junior crew in the attack, Gillman's aircraft had the unenviable tail-end Charlie position:

Both Weeky and I saw them together, dull grey shapes, to our left, probably two miles away, but things were beginning to happen. Orange and scarlet flashes burst intermittently along the superstructure of the nearest ship.

'They've bloody seen us too!' shouted Weeky.

The formations in front were now in some disarray, the leader pulling into an even tighter turn while others were widening out and starting to take evasive action. Having seen the ships so late, we were coming in awkwardly. The leader was trying to get on a course parallel to the line of ships before turning to attack. Ideally, attacks should be made at right angles and in the middle of a ship so that if not sunk it will be immobilized by damage to the engine room.

[This approach as we have already seen was not universally recognised as the most effective, many preferred an attack from a quarter rather than from a beam].

The whole formation was swinging wide, and being tail-end Charlie, I found myself desperately trying to hang on, like the victim at the end of a line of skaters. I couldn't get round any tighter, as the section leader inside me was beginning to cavort so violently that I had to sheer away. This was taking me onto the bows of the first ship at an acute angle. It would be fatal to run the length of the ship. I had to get out and turn in again. I rolled the port wing hard down and pulled her round in a steep turn just above the water. I had lost sight of the quarry now and my belly was exposed, but I was desperate to get round.

A hail of scarlet tracer was shooting past the nose and we were flying into it. I cranked the ailerons hard over the other way and as we rolled round, I realised with a shock that we were almost alongside the massive shape and level with the superstructure. The technique should be to come in at sea-level and at right angles, letting the bombs go like torpedoes and then climbing over the ship.

Cannon fire from the boat deck and fo'c'sle was coning in on us with vicious intensity. Both Benny's and Weeky's guns racketed as if they fired indiscriminately. We were too close in, but I had to attack it would be fatal to turn away. In desperation, I wound on full bank and dived. The grey sea rushed up at a crazy rate. I heaved back on the control column and felt the aircraft shudder with the strain. The ship's side was a blank wall ahead of me.

I stabbed the bomb-release button and pulled the aircraft in a steep climb to clear the ship's side. But we weren't going to make it! She'd stall! The mast and derricks were coming towards us. Of course – the ship was moving at right angles! With frantic strength, I twisted the control-column yoke hard over. The aircraft started to roll, but the boom of the derrick was dead in front of us. I pulled the turn tighter still and the boom with its huge block and tackle whipped under the nose. I ducked instinctively, but we were now over the sea again, miraculously, and I dived for it twisting and turning on the way down. Weeky was still firing back at the ship with a murderous racket.

Quite suddenly, the following tracer stopped. To the left I could see the sleek grey shapes of the other aircraft floating swiftly through the murk like a school of fish. I put the aircraft in a turn towards them.

'Christ! That was close,' said Benny.

'I'd thought we'd got that bloody crane,' said Weeky. 'It went under my turret.'

'You and me both,' I said fervently. My heart was still pounding.

'What's up?' demanded Benny. 'There's a hell of a lot of vibration.'

'I can't see any damage', called Weeky. 'Oh! Hang on – er yeh, there's some holes right over your bloody head, Ron, and some in the port wing just behind the cowling. Nothing serious though.'

Then I realised that the engines were still in boost override and I pulled the lever down so sharply that the engine note dropping, and consequent deceleration brought cries of alarm from the crew.

'Sorry about that,' I said, 'but if I had left the plus-nine tit in, we wouldn't have made Great Yarmouth.'

'Glad you remembered,' said Weeky with a touch of irony.

Back in the briefing-room we learned that of the 12 aircraft two had been lost. I overheard the Wing Commander's navigator describing the anti-aircraft fire to the Intelligence Officer as 'Just moderate.'[13]

---

13   R.E. Gillman, *The Shiphunters*, p. 46.

In late April 1941, the British introduced the infamous 'Channel Stop' operation, designed to prevent the enemy using the Straits of Dover in daylight, whilst leaving it to the Royal Navy's Motor Torpedo Boats to continue the task of attacking enemy ships at night. Increased fighter protection was provided for these new operations, the escort often including six cannon-armed Hurricane IICs and six 12-gun Hurricane IIBs. When the Blenheims were about 20 miles from the target the cannon-armed Hurricanes would draw ahead and climb to 1,000 feet to engage the enemy flak ships. This might lose the element of surprise for the ensuing attack, but it was also hoped this new tactic would degrade the effectiveness of the German's withering AA fire. Wing Commander Atkinson explains the new methods:

> Channel Stop had started in April. The basis of it was that we had a squadron of Blenheims at Manston and by the time I was there a squadron of Hurricanes to act as front gun attack, with a wing of Spitfires as escort. The Hurricane and Blenheim crews lived at Manston. Average life of a Blenheim squadron there was about two weeks by which time it was depleted to such an extent that it had to be withdrawn and replaced. A similar thing happened, to a lesser degree, to the Hurricane squadrons. The first of these involved was 242 Squadron commanded by Squadron Leader Whitney Straight. These chaps lived together and fought together. The Directive was 'No ship is to pass between Cherbourg and Ostend' without us attacking it in daylight – there was no point in night attacks and in any case the Navy was busy then. We used as our eyes, 91 Squadron based at Hawkinge. We used to call them Jim Crows. They went out in Spitfires flying up and down the route to see if anyone was coming out of the ports. The ships used to do the port run at night, and the object of the exercise was to catch ships leaving port a bit early or not having made it in time. Consequently attacks were nearly always at dawn or dusk, and very seldom in the middle of the day.
>
> Three Blenheims would go out with about a dozen Hurricanes and a Wing of Spitfires, a wonderful sight over Manston. You'd see the boys taking off and as they came back over the airfield the Hurricanes would be to either side of the bombers, and outside this the squadron of Spitfires. They used to come over Manston at nought feet and, with a 'whoosh', they'd soon be down over the sea. Thirty or 40 minutes later they'd be back – one Blenheim and 10 or so Hurricanes.
>
> As the Blenheims went in the Hurricanes pulled away and climbed over the top, diving and making front gun attacks to keep the enemy heads down. The most they had to face was, I think, 19 Flak ships. There was also the shore guns and the fighters. You hadn't a hope in Hell as you tossed your bombs at the ships.
>
> I well remember Sqn. Ldr. Harris, the Canadian commanding 88 Squadron, coming home his hat shot to ribbons. He crash landed at Manston, the only one in formation to get back. Although the casualty rate was tremendous, the morale was never higher … I was at this time Bomber Controller at 11 Group, the person responsible for despatching these squadrons. On occasions when one attended the squadron briefs of these crews you were looking at two crews out of three who would not get back. How did you feel? It is impossible to express it, but then this was true of all the raids 2 Group was doing. On Channel Stop you knew that you were going to get it – no 'ifs' and 'buts'; and there was nothing you could do about it. Did it stop the passage of ships? It certainly made life difficult for them, but for their forces this was their life blood and they were always going to try and run the gauntlet.[14]

---

14   Michael Bowyer, *2 Group, 1936-1945*, pp. 157-8.

Between March and September 1941, the Admiralty recorded that 101 German ships (328,000 tons) were either sunk, or seriously damaged and another 70 slightly damaged. The German records examined after the war showed only the loss of 29 ships (29,836 tons) with just 21 (43,715 tons) seriously damaged. For these results the losses being sustained by 2 Group were appalling. In August alone of 77 aircraft which attacked ships, 23 were lost; at 30 percent this was an unsustainable rate and was described by the Group as 'a terrifying period, a very demanding and expensive war'.[15] The AOC of 2 Group, Air Vice-Marshal Stevenson was however unsympathetic to the losses within his group, or the appalling odds. Described as arrogant and ruthless, he was widely disliked and seems to have put his own career interests above the fate of his crews.[16] Questions began to be asked in high places, Churchill querying the loss of seven out of 17 Blenheims on 29 August, arguing that had it been against ships like *Scharnhorst, Gneisenau* or the *Tirpitz* it might have been justified – but merchant shipping?[17] The Minister of Aircraft Production, John Moore-Brabazon, also wrote to the Chief of the Air Staff in December of 1941.

> I think it is much the best to let you know sometimes the general chat which goes on with regard to the Air Force, and I have run into a singular unpleasant piece of feeling with regard to Bomber Command, which I think it is my duty to pass on to you. It concerns the bombings of ships by Blenheims at low altitude. These are looked upon as purely suicide trips if the ships are surrounded by 'flak' ships which is usually the case. I don't know whether this is true or not, but I understand the pilots doing this work look upon it as pure suicide, and I was wondering whether that particular form of attack is worth the expenditure of life and material which it entails.[18]

The 2 Group aircrews were well aware of these stark and sobering odds. Gillman capturing the thoughts of his Blenheim crew after only their first anti-shipping operation:

> The trip had a chastening effect. To us, our first taste of action had been dramatic. But the experienced boys had voted it a relatively quiet one. The normal tour of operations was 30 such trips, if one survived. Our lives, up till now, had always involved planning for the future. Suddenly we couldn't see it any more. Reality had taken its place, a reality which said, 'I'm awfully sorry, but from here on in there is an element of doubt. I shouldn't make any plans if I were you. There's an awful lot to be done.'[19]

The prohibitive cost of such operations thankfully meant they were reduced in frequency in the latter part of 1941, equally gratifying to many was the relief of Stevenson, as AOC 2 Group, in December of that same year.[20]

Another less risky method employed by Coastal and Bomber Command to disrupt German shipping operations included dropping bombs at night on enemy ports, as well as 'gardening' operations where influence mines were laid in approaches to ports, estuaries or coastal waters. These mines differed in appearance from the typical sphere with steel horns one might imagine from the movies, being instead cylindrical in shape and about nine feet long with a diameter of

15   Michael Bowyer, *2 Group*, p. 163.
16   Max Hastings, *Bomber Command*, p. 76.
17   Max Hastings, *Bomber Command*, p. 77.
18   Portal Papers, Letter to Portal from Lord Moore-Brabazon MP, 8 Dec 1941, Box C, File 4, Item 7.
19   R.E. Gillman, *The Shiphunters*, p. 47.
20   Max Hastings, *Bomber Command*, p .77.

seven inches. A small parachute was attached at one end of the aerial mine to slow its descent and a nose fairing was fitted at the other to stabilise it through its initial fall. There were several types of aerial sea mines, each typically weighed about 1,500lbs, half of which was the Amatol explosive.

The mines were all non-contact or influence mines. Some were set off by acoustic signatures, on these the microphone on the mine was sophisticated enough to determine engine and propeller noise, and it could also be tuned to detonate only when the unique audio-signature of a vessel over a certain tonnage had passed. The magnetic mine was also used extensively, detonating when the magnetic field of a passing ship was detected. This mine could be countered by de-gaussing the ship, a process where electrical cables were strung around the perimeter of the ship's hull to neutralise the magnetic field's charge. The air-dropped mines could also be fitted with a period-delay mechanism where the mine did not detonate on its first detection but on subsequent ones, this hampered the German minesweeping operations by targeting the following merchantmen rather than the escorting minesweeper itself. When a mine was successfully detonated it generated a violent gas bubble with a powerful pressure wave travelling through the water at the speed of sound, the harder the sea bed, the greater this energy was focussed upwards towards the vessel. The forces exerted by this pressure wave were often enough to buckle and rip apart the ship's hull plates, as well as damaging internal structures in the vessel.

Gardening operations were undertaken almost exclusively at night and the aircraft had to drop the mine in a very precise location, usually in a swept channel between existing minefields. This operation typically took place between 1,000-1,500 feet and the aircrew needed to consider a number of factors, including prevailing currents, high and low tides as well as the depths of water. Before being dropped the mine would be armed by removing a steel fork, with a secondary arming switch activating once the mine had descended to five fathoms (or 30 feet). The dropping aircraft would usually fly at 180 mph and was guided on some occasions by Pathfinder aircraft, which would have laid coloured markers that the aircraft could then take bearings upon. After dropping its mine the aircraft would continue to fly straight and level, in order to confuse the enemy as to the precise location in which the mine had been dropped.

Gardening operations were conducted against many German or occupied ports with each geographic area given a codename, the Weser estuary was 'Yams', Boulogne was 'Dewberry' and Lorient was 'Artichoke'.[21] Additionally from April 1944, Liberators and Wellingtons of No. 205 Group conducted Gardening operations against enemy vessels on the River Danube. This river was a vital communications link for the Germans and connected them not just to the Eastern Front and the grain lands of Hungary, but most importantly to the Rumanian oil fields. During this six month campaign a total of 1,382 mines were laid in 18 separate attacks. The Germans found these mines hard to clear and barge traffic was suspended for a while, the broad result was that the volume of traffic on the Danube was reduced by 60-70 percent.[22]

Mines were also used against Japanese held ports including Rangoon and Singapore, some of these missions were flown by Liberators operating at extreme range from newly constructed airfields in the Cocos (Keeling) Islands in the Indian Ocean. One Liberator from 160 Squadron, based in Ceylon, flew to Singapore on a successful gardening mission, a 21-hour round-trip of 3,350 miles, an extraordinarily long sortie for the period.

Gardening missions were highly effective and carried out by Bomber Command, as well as Coastal Command. From 1941 some missions were flown by the new Bristol Beaufort aircraft, which was beginning to be delivered to Coastal Command's frontline Torpedo, Bomber and

---

21 W.E. Jones, *Bomber Intelligence, 103, 150, 166, 170 Squadrons Operations and Techniques 1942-1945* (Leicester: Midland Counties Publishing, 1983), Chapter 5.
22 Hilary Saunders, *Royal Air Force 1939-45 Volume III*, p. 147.

Three Bristol Beaufort Is of the 86 Squadron detachment based at St Eval, Cornwall, flying in formation over the sea. (Crown Copyright – Air Historical Branch)

Reconnaissance (TBR) squadrons. This aircraft was built at Filton and part of the same family as the Blenheim, but had a larger 58-foot wing span and was 44-foot in length. Earlier versions of the Beaufort were powered by two Taurus engines of 1,130 hp, which gave the aircraft a cruising speed of 165 mph and maximum speed of 270 mph, the aircraft's endurance was about six hours. The Beaufort could carry either one torpedo, 2,000lb of bombs, or land mines and sea mines of a similar weight. These new aircraft were considered difficult to handle and had a reputation for being both mechanically unsound and sinking like a stone if ditched. Crews were also particularly concerned that the aircraft was unable to fly on just one engine – entirely understandable given the long distances they would have to travel over the sea. Roy Conyers Nesbit served in Beaufort Mk Is with 217 Squadron at St Eval, Cornwall and describes this aircraft:

The Beaufort carried a crew of four. The pilot sat in the left-hand front seat looking over the nose. The navigator sat beside him on takeoff or landing, but his office was in the Perspex nose, from which he had an excellent view. Our aircraft had one forward-firing Browning .303 mounted in the port wing and operated by the pilot, whilst the navigator was equipped with a similar machine-gun mounted in a 'blister' perspex turret under his seat; this was a backward firing gun intended to protect the aircraft from a belly attack and was fired from a prone position looking through the mirror, but the cartridge belt constantly fouled in its chute and later this gun was removed.

The navigator sat on a revolving seat so that he could work on his chart table on the left, whilst from a slightly different position he could look through his bombsight in the nose. He also had various instruments such as an automatic bomb distributor, nicknamed 'Mickey Mouse', an Aldis Lamp for signalling, and a bearing compass. Behind the pilot was an armour-plated bulwark, then the radio equipment and the wireless operator's seat. The wireless operator was also an air gunner and carried a Vickers K machine gun which he could mount in the hatch during an attack. Lastly, there was the air gunner, who sat in his power operated turret with its two drum fed Vickers K guns. Originally the Beaufort's turret was equipped with only one drum fed Vickers K gun, but some of our aircraft were fitted with two, and later in 1941 were equipped with two belt-fed Brownings.[23]

Although the Beaufort carried bombs in a similar manner to the Blenheim and other light bombers, it was really designed to be a torpedo bomber and its introduction into Coastal Command provided commanders with a new method of attacking enemy shipping. Air-dropping torpedoes against shipping had been a technique that had been developed as far back as the First World War, but though this method of warfare was not new, sinking a vessel with a torpedo remained a tricky proposition. The Mark XII or 18-inch torpedo that was supplied to Coastal Command and the Fleet Air Arm in 1941 was less powerful than the standard 21-inch naval torpedo fired by ships and submarines. Consequently, it often took two or three air dropped torpedoes to sink a large ship, particularly those with many compartmentalised tanks or holds, such as tankers. Additionally, torpedoes were expensive in comparison to bombs, which meant that they were uneconomic if used against low-tonnage vessels, for this reason targets needed to be carefully selected. Delivery of the torpedo, often called the 'fish' by aircrew, was also difficult because it would need to be dropped at the relatively slow speed of 90 knots and no higher than 80 feet. Failure to conform to these limits and the torpedo risked breaking up. In addition, the trajectory of the torpedo and its entry into the sea needed to be controlled so that it hit the water nose first and at a shallow angle. There were a number of ways to achieve this, one way was connecting the torpedo to a drum in the bomb bay of the Beaufort by two cables, one at the nose and one at the tail. On releasing the torpedo, the tail cable would remain connected a fraction longer than the nose cable, which meant that the torpedo would descend and enter the water nose first, ideally at an angle of 17 degrees.

Dropping distances from the ship also needed to be carefully controlled. The forward impetus of the aircraft and the torpedo's smooth 16-foot long aerodynamic profile, meant that it would normally fly through the air for 250 yards before it entered the water. As the torpedo hit the sea, a small bar attached to the tail of the torpedo would be ripped off and the torpedo would begin to swim under its own power, stabilised by four wooden fins. Fan blades at the nose of the torpedo would then arm the 176 kg TNT warhead once the torpedo had travelled a certain distance, usually 350 yards, which, when combined with the flying distance of 250 yards, meant that any torpedo dropped closer than 600 yards would not function correctly. Normally, 800 yards was considered an optimum dropping distance, as it allowed the torpedo time to function, stood a good chance of hitting the target and gave the pilot sufficient time to manoeuvre away from enemy flak. With an overall speed of 37 knots, torpedoes were relatively slow-moving projectiles and both the torpedo aircraft, as well as the torpedo tracks, could be spotted by an alert crew. This frequently allowed the ship's captain to turn towards the attack and 'comb' the approaching torpedoes, an easier tactic for a faster, more manoeuvrable naval vessel to perform than a merchant ship, but both could theoretically do it. As a result of this, air-launched torpedo operations usually involved several aircraft both to overwhelm the ship, but also in the hope that a mass of aircraft would cause the enemy's AA fire to be more dispersed, increasing the aircrew's chances of survival.[24]

By late 1941, anti-shipping tactics as well as technology had begun to alter. Beaufort squadrons sent aircraft out at night on what were termed 'Moonlight Rovers'. These would occur when a combination of clear skies and a moonlit night made it possible to pick out ships silhouetted in the moon path, during these sorties both torpedoes and bombs were used. Not solely satisfied with night attacks, the squadrons also began to undertake 'Daylight Rovers'. These took advantage of periods when there was both a relatively low cloud base, certainly no higher than 1,000 feet, and

23   Roy Conyers Nesbit, *Woe to the Unwary* (London: William Kimber, 1981), p. 36.
24   Arthur Aldridge and Mark Ryan, *The Last Torpedo Flyers* (London: Simon and Schuster, 2013), p. 66.

Bristol Beauforts of 22 Squadron wait to be loaded with torpedoes ahead of an anti-shipping patrol from Thorney Island, Hampshire. (Crown Copyright – Air Historical Branch)

poor visibility, up to three or four miles typically. This allowed the Beauforts to not only sneak up on a convoy, but also to duck into cloud cover if German fighter aircraft were encountered. As the German ships sailed within 10 miles of the coast, the provision of fighter protection by the Germans was easy to achieve and a Beaufort in open skies would be almost defenceless. Higher cloud than 1,000 feet was never sufficient for Daylight Rovers, as the Beaufort would never be able to reach this cover in time. As one can imagine the closest liaison with the RAF's own meteorological officers was maintained, with the decision to fly or not delegated right down to squadron level.[25]

Flight Lieutenant Pat Gibbs was based out of North Coates on the Lincolnshire coast in 1941, an airbase regularly used by the anti-shipping squadrons throughout the war. Not only was it convenient for attacking German coastal shipping, but its low altitude and flat approach from the sea made it the ideal aerodrome for aircrew who might have to find it in conditions of low visibility. On his second 'Daylight Rover', Gibbs was accompanied by a Sergeant Pilot, Norman Hearn-Phillips. This was to be Gibbs' first sortie as a leader, but as they neared the Dutch coast he found not the expected cloud and low visibility that might provide vital cover, but instead a threateningly clear blue sky:

> I confess to then taking a foolish risk, which experience would now forbid me, for I continued for some 20 minutes roving in these dangerous conditions within sight of the enemy coast-line. Poor H-P, who knew the danger so much better than I, must have been seething with something less mild than disproval, but he kept following all the same when he could have been justified in leaving me and turning for home.

25   Patrick Gibbs, *Not Peace but a Sword* (London: Grub Street, 1993), p. 91.

All this time not only were we flying in sight of observers on the coast but passed several suspicious-looking small vessels which would, in all probability, report our presence to the shore if it were not already known. But this was my first Rover, as a leader, and although I knew that to remain near the coast under a clear sky was playing with fire, I was determined to find some target to attack, and kept persuading myself to stay a little longer when all the time I knew I should turn back.

Just as I was reaching a decision to abandon this foolish pursuit and return to our base, two ships appeared steaming in line ahead and not very close inshore. Without wasting time, for the blue sky was worrying me, I signalled to H-P to attack, only to find he had anticipated the signal by breaking formation, and we both went in to attack low over the water, dropping our torpedoes simultaneously. The lesson which I had learnt from my last attack on the dangers of lagging behind the leader had not been lost on H-P, who was well up with me as I dropped, and we turned away together. Afterwards we circled out of range for a few minutes, waiting to see the result of our attack, but the leading ship, which had been our target, had turned sharply towards us as we were attacking and we now saw the tracks of our torpedoes pass harmlessly ahead of the vessel. During the attack there had been little opposition, and it was not until we were turning away that first one and then several guns had started firing. Although the water around us had been dotted with the splashes of exploding shells, nothing had come very near us, and for the first time I realized the benefits to be obtained by taking a target by surprise. We had not dallied over the attack and so had enjoyed an approach free from flak, during which we had been able to take steady aim.

As we flew back empty handed, I felt dissatisfied with the day's work, knowing that I should not really have remained out roving in these weather conditions, and also feeling a little guilty at having wasted two valuable torpedoes on a ship which was really too small a target. For a torpedo to have a reasonable chance of a hit, the target should not be less than 200 feet long, a length achieved by ships of about 5,000 tons, while I estimated our little target at 2,000 tons, and even then made a generous allowance to cover my poor choice of target. Nevertheless, the flight and the attack did constitute added experience; if I was making mistakes, at the same time I was learning, and if the mistakes were not fatal ones, I had to thank good fortune for her generosity.[26]

The British anti-shipping squadrons were not the only ones that were gaining in experience and learning lessons. The Germans were not blind to the successes that were being achieved and how the British would take advantage of poor weather. The Germans began to sail ships in convoy more frequently and these were often accompanied by small flak ships, mounting multiple quick-firing AA guns, usually 20 and 40mm in calibre. These flak ships were carefully positioned in the areas where the Beauforts would ideally have wished to drop their torpedoes. A Heinkel 115 floatplane was often provided as an air escort, flying above the ships at a height where it could spot approaching Beauforts more easily. The aircraft itself was too slow to be a menace to the attacking British aircraft, but it could warn the convoy and summon help from nearby aerodromes quickly. The threat to Beaufort aircraft was always high as Gibbs, encountered when conducting another patrol, this time further down the Channel, off the Normandy coast:

I had been keeping a watchful eye on the cloud during the run down the coast, since Met had warned me that it would become less dependable as we flew westward. I knew equally well that our presence on the coast could not be hidden any longer, and if the enemy thought

Beaufort I W6537/OA-F of 22 Squadron starting up at St Eval, December 1941. The accumulator trolley in the foreground supplied the necessary electrical power to the aircraft and was disconnected once the engines were running. Unlike other Beaufort squadrons, No 22 fitted a Vickers K gun in the nose compartment of its aircraft, to be used for flak-suppression during low-level attacks. (Crown Copyright – Air Historical Branch)

it possible to catch us in the open sky he would not hesitate to send out a fighter force, for there was no shortage of convenient fighter aerodromes in this area. In fact, I had reluctantly reached a decision to turn for home, considering the cover insufficient, when a small ship appeared straight ahead, and, thinking to photograph it or investigate, I carried on.

Almost immediately Bill sang down the intercom that there were fighters coming out from the land; they were a pair of Me 109s, he said, coming up behind and closing rapidly. A pilot is completely dependent on his rear-gunner for information during fighter attack, for he is the only member of the crew who is facing backwards and can see exactly what is happening, so a pilot will normally manoeuvre his aircraft according to the gunner's instructions. Bill now kept up an admirable running commentary from his turret, letting me know where the fighters were and when they were turning in to attack; he even had time to describe our opponents as being painted red with yellow noses! The climb to cover seemed endless; I twisted and turned, but not violently as there was a Beaufort trying to keep formation on either side, while all the time Bill's voice in my ear told me that two unseen fighters were spraying first the right-hand aircraft, then my own, and across to the left of the formation. His steady voice continued over the roar of the engines at full throttle and the din of the guns firing, poetry to the accompaniment of a brass band. Normally we only tested our guns by firing a short burst into the sea at the start of every flight, but now this was firing in earnest. As the interior of the Beaufort filled with burnt gunpowder smoke I could hear the clatter of spent cartridge cases above the bark of the machine guns, and all the time Bill's unvarying commentary, calm as ever but becoming more pointed as the fight went on. With tracer pouring over my port wing, I looked backwards for an instant to see one of these enemy fighters for myself, just turning away from the attack, while tracer from the other streamed between me and the right-hand Beaufort, whose gunner was sending a steady flow of lead back at his assailant. The pair must have made five attacks before we made cloud at just over 1000 feet above water; not a moment too soon, I thought, with some relief.[27]

---

27   Patrick Gibbs, *Not Peace but a Sword*, pp. 236-7.

As well as hunting for German ships in the Channel and North Sea, the Blenheims and Beauforts of Coastal Command would also spend much of 1941 striking German warships in Brest harbour. The *Scharnhorst*, and *Gneisenau* had both managed to evade Royal Navy ships in the Atlantic and had holed up in the French dock. Coastal and Bomber Command regularly attacked the vessels in the harbour including sowing mines to trap the ships in port. After one mission an unexploded 250lb bomb on the *Gneisenau* meant she was towed from the dry dock to the outer harbour, there it was captured by one of the photographic reconnaissance Spitfires that regularly overflew the port. On 6 April four Beaufort torpedo bomber from 22 Squadron were sent to Brest to strike the *Gneisenau*. Only one, piloted by the Canadian Flying Officer Kenneth Campbell, succeeded in penetrating the haze and locating the *Gneisenau* lying in the inner harbour alongside one of the quays. Campbell's Beaufort swept down, flew through the flak ships at mast height, climbed over the mole and released his torpedo at 500 yards. His aircraft was struck by German anti-aircraft fire and crashed, the entire crew perishing. However, Campbell's torpedo ran true and struck the *Gneisenau* in the stern, piercing her below the water-line and causing damage to her starboard propeller shaft which would take eight months to repair. Campbell was awarded a posthumous Victoria Cross as a result of his heroic deed. This together with delays to *Scharnhorst*'s refitting, because of damage to the dry docks, prevented these two ships from joining *Bismarck* and *Prinz Eugen* on their foray into the Atlantic in May 1941. When the *Bismarck* was sunk *Prinz Eugen* would escape into Brest and join her sister ships in their dash up the Channel from 11-13 February 1942.

Terence O'Brien was a Coastal Command pilot, who had joined the RAF from Australia. After training he had been posted to 53 Squadron flying Blenheims from St Eval and he and his crew would regularly strike the ships and harbour at Brest. He remembered his first raid on Brest, in March 1941 well:

'Alter course o-seven-five.'

There was no need to look at the re-set gyro to watch the numbers roll past. You knew his figure would come up when we were pointing directly into the middle of all that venomous activity. Sure enough, we were exactly on his course when the chaos of splintering, streaking, exploding light was centred in the front perspex. As we approached it the light flak became visible below the heavy AA explosions, first as thin pale lines, then developing colour as we drew nearer, flame-red, orange, and a silvery white. And then John switched to bombsight to ensure there was no averting the maelstrom:

'Left, left. Steady. Steady. Hold it there.'

Perhaps I had edged away subconsciously, slight pressure on the right rudder to divert from the centre of the fury. It was too much, just a flit through the edge was all I wanted, just a spice of danger, not a plunge into the middle. Inexorably, however, he forced me with a deadly precision back into line for the centre. It was like a hellish forest, a tangle of fiery trunks below a canopy of stabbing explosions, with great shafts of searchlights swaying about in the turmoil. The heavy AA explosions formed a rough rectangle from about 8-12,000 feet, we were heading towards the base where it merged into the top curves of varicoloured light flak …

I was trying to pick out the harbour entrance when suddenly we seemed to be caught up in a current that swirled us swiftly into the maelstrom. A shell burst close to our left, the flash so savagely bright I was blinded for a moment, the aircraft juddered from the explosion, and as vision returned I glimpsed the small black cloud fleeting past the port wing. What surprised me was that I had heard the explosion. I thought at first we must have been hit; it never occurred to me, nor had anyone ever told me, that you could actually hear above the roar of your engines the sound of an AA shell exploding nearby. In the next minute or so I had learned that lesson for ever. Also that there was a smell to an AA barrage – the smell you associate with a smoking gun barrel, acrid cordite … Three searchlights were groping about near us like tentacles of a monstrous squid, I tried to focus on them alone, to ignore all other threats, but then a stream of the red light flak came shooting up like hosed fire directly in front of us and instinctively I swung away to avoid it. John commanded me back instantly into line: 'Right. Right. Steady.' The flaming stream came straight up at us, lazily down below but then speeding up rapidly to zip past like a flash – in front, across, from behind. The coloured light flak seemed to be closing in on us, like a crowd converging on a gateway, some of the lines with a swerve in the middle when the gunner must have been swinging the barrel. Suddenly the aircraft shook, just a quick sharp shiver that caused me to grip the wheel more tightly, and again John called me back into steady line. This time I came back at him:

'Can't you see the bloody docks?'

'Difficult to pick them out.'

I would have thought impossible. Down below I could see nothing but streams of coloured lines shooting up out of a flickering cloud of smoke. The searchlights could penetrate it, one swung across the cockpit in a painful blinding flash, and I ducked below the perspex with eyes clenched tight to reclaim night-sight. When I dared look up again another searchlight came slanted up to stand still directly in front of us, one with a markedly different bluish light, looking so sinister that impulsively I banked away to the right to pass clear of it. The awful result was that John lost whatever sight he had glimpsed of the target area, and called out, 'No good. We'll have to try again.'

'For Christ sake!'

But the release from his terrible discipline was something of a relief. I opened the throttles wide, pulled the 9-boost and put the nose down in a dive that sent us searing through the coloured streaks, both hands pumping the stick ever forward until sudden concern about balloons made me jerk it back to level flight. By then we were through, ahead was only safe blackness.[28]

Terence O'Brien and his crew took another run over Brest, coming in at 12,000 feet in a shallow dive that would have them over the barrage at 8,000 feet where they successfully released their bombs, before heading back to St Eval landing safely that night. In the latter half of 1941 over 1,000 sorties were sent against the three German warships at Brest.

---

28   Terence O'Brien, *Chasing After Danger* (London: Collins, 1990), p. 82.

18

'Strike and Strike Again'[1]
Anti-Shipping Operations Mature

The British anti-shipping squadrons also had to meet commitments in other theatres and from the end of 1941 this included the Far East, where the threat of Japanese amphibious and maritime operations compelled the dispatch of squadrons. Nearer to home there was also a pressing demand for squadrons to operate in the Mediterranean, for it was here that a climactic battle over the German and Italian lines of communication had developed, centred on the island of Malta.

By early 1941, it had become clear that Malta's position was vital in the war against Axis shipping and Rommel's line of communications. The convoys that plied across the central Mediterranean were critical to supplying the war effort of the German and Italian Armies in North Africa. These regular transits all fitted into a broad pattern that is worth some explanation. Some of the Axis convoys originated from the main Italian ports of Naples and Genoa and sailed to the west of Sicily or sometimes through the straits of Messina. From here a western route was preferred and the convoys would cross from Sicily to the Tunisian coast near to Pantelleria. They would then hug the Tunisian shore before striking out to the main axis port of Tripoli (see Map 6, The Mediterranean Theatre).

Axis convoys that took this route would be carefully scheduled so that they minimised the risk of air attack, usually steaming through the area closest to Malta during the hours of darkness. Given these tactics the best options the British had in interdicting western convoys was either when they approached the Sicilian straits in daylight, during the night when they were passing through them, or at any time the following day. The second night was usually difficult for the British anti-shipping night capability, (typically the Fleet Air Arm's Swordfish) which would have to operate at maximum range. The day after that was also much harder, as axis air cover could be provided over the convoys from the airfields on the Tripolitania coast.

The second route taken by axis convoys was through the Straits of Messina, around the toe of Italy and then an easterly voyage, hugging the coast to the Gulf of Taranto on Italy's heel. Here they would pick up further escorts, a tanker or other merchant ship and sometimes combine with a convoy from the Adriatic ports of Brindisi or Fiume before passing through the Ionian Sea. There the ships would start the long passage southwards, along 300 miles of Greek coastline, passing the Greek islands of Corfu and Zante, before a further 300 mile transit across the Mediterranean, to reach either Tobruk, Benghazi or Tripoli.[2] Whilst the routes were well known, the exact timings and dispositions of the convoys were harder to predict. Intelligence undoubtedly helped, the pivotal

---

1   The Motto of 455 Squadron, Royal Australian Air Force, this squadron was equipped with Hampdens and Beaufighters and took part in many anti-shipping strike operations mainly against German shipping in the North Sea.

2   Hugh Lloyd, *Briefed to Attack: Malta's Part in Africa's Victory* (London: Hodder and Stoughton, 1949), pp. 50-4.

moment being the breaking of the Italian C38M cypher in June 1941, which gave the British not only advance notice of the departure of Italian ships, but also the planned routes of the convoys.[3]

The British at Malta also benefitted considerably from a highly efficient and effective air reconnaissance capability, which provided almost constant coverage of the key Italian ports. The air photographs brought back by the Martin Maryland reconnaissance aircraft, allowed the intelligence staff at Malta to understand the regular routine at these Italian ports, from which it was possible to predict, to within 24 hours, when a convoy would be ready to sail. Typically, a group of four to six ships bound for North Africa would assemble in the area of the port of Naples known by the British as 'Rommel's Quay' or 'African Quay'. The loading here would be monitored until the cargo hatches had been closed on the last ship, at this point there might be a further delay before sailing, as deck cargo was added onto the ship's decks. At Taranto, the patterns were less discernible and the loading a little harder to track. For instance, four tankers could be filled at the harbour's jetty simultaneously, some might then loiter for a week. Others would depart on the day they were filled, and a further group might move out into the outer harbour and rest there for an indeterminate period.

Not only were the Axis ports constantly monitored by the British intelligence staff, but all relevant Axis merchant ships in the Mediterranean were also tracked, logged and their details recorded. These included its size, shape, where it was, what it had been doing, which ports had it visited and finally what state it was in: unloaded, loaded or preparing to sail. All ships using Taranto, Brindisi, Naples, Trapani, Palermo, Messina, Tripoli and many other ports were all categorized and catalogued.[4] From 1942 photographic reconnaissance missions were supplemented by ASV radar in Wellington bombers, which ensured that the convoys could also be tracked through the night. The benefit of having increasingly good signals intelligence and photographic reconnaissance meant that the British were able to directly target convoys and ships known to be at sea, rather than conduct generalised shipping sweeps for potential targets. Given the scarcity of fuel on the besieged island of Malta, this was a critical advantage and intelligence was the start point for many British anti-shipping operations. As a result of excellent naval cooperation with Royal Navy surface vessels and submarines, the British were able to hunt Axis shipping in a coherent manner. As Air Vice-Marshal Hugh Lloyd recounted, the task for the British on Malta was very clear, 'to sink ships as often and as fast as we could: no supplies – no Rommel: no Rommel – no campaign in Africa. The victory in Africa hinged on sinking ships.'[5]

The initial British approach to sinking ships in the Mediterranean was similar to that used by the RAF in the Channel and North Sea; low-level bombing by Blenheims armed with four 250lb bombs in a closely placed stick from 50-100 feet. However, just like the Germans in the North Sea, the Axis merchant ships began to arm themselves with AA guns and surface vessels were increasingly provided as escorts. The low-flying Blenheim became an easy target in the run in to these enemy ships, moreover, the clear skies of the Mediterranean made covered approaches and surprise almost impossible to achieve. Ron Gillman travelled to Malta from the UK in his Blenheim in 1941 and was tasked with attacking a convoy of one tanker, five flak ships and two corvettes on the Axis' eastern route. The ships were 250 miles from Malta, almost at the limit of the Blenheim's range and were to be attacked by two vics each of three Blenheims.

As Ron Gillman's aircraft left Malta, Robbie, the leader of the mission, levelled off at a height below 50 feet and the 'vic' spread out to about two wing spans distance between aircraft, speeding

3   Richard Hammond, British Anti-Shipping Campaign in the Mediterranean, *Air Power Review*, 16, 2013, p. 55.
4   Hugh Lloyd, *Briefed to Attack*, 1949, pp. 50-55.
5   Hugh Lloyd, *Briefed to Attack*, p. 55.

Low-level oblique photograph taken from one of a force of Bristol Blenheim Mark IVs attacking an Italian motor vessel in the Mediterranean, showing the first bomb exploding on the stern. (Crown Copyright – Air Historical Branch)

across the sea at 210 mph. This looser formation was less demanding on the pilots and allowed them to relax slightly on the hour-long approach to the target. After one hour the formation began to tighten up once more and the aircraft dropped even lower to avoid radar detection, the slip-stream of the aircraft causing a wake in what was reportedly a very calm sea. Shortly afterwards a smudge of smoke was seen on the horizon and the aircraft turned to starboard and banked towards it. Ron Gillman continues his account:

Robbie's aircraft began to pull away as he accelerated for the run-in. I opened up the throttles but had difficulty in closing the gap. He must have been using nearly full throttle himself, leaving me very little in hand. Number three had fallen even farther behind, but we were tucked in laterally. In such perfect visibility, the ships' superstructures began to appear over the horizon even though they were some 15 miles away, then we would see the bulk of their hulls as we raced towards them. Conversely of course, they would also see us!

Weeky began to count from his turret 'One, two, three, four, yes seven of the buggers!' I stole another quick glance ahead. They were still hull down on the horizon, but the big tanker stood out clearly. There were three smaller ships aft, and three in front. They appeared to be stationary waiting for us. Had they seen us yet? Could they, with us as close to the sea as we were? Foolish hopes of a surprise arrival were suddenly shattered. A fountain of water shot up in our path directly ahead. They had seen us all right! That was the first of the big bricks; the 12-pounders. Another spout erupted just to our starboard, the spray glistening in the sun. We were running into their range now, but Robbie kept straight. Three more columns shot up in quick succession, one so close that I thought it must get number three, but he was still flying.

The ships were looming large now. It was time we were taking some sort of avoiding action. Immediately ahead, the sea began to break into little holes. We were running into the anti-aircraft stuff. In a second it was all around us, the sea boiling viciously. I pulled away from the leader, kicking the rudder-bar to put the aircraft in a series of violent skids. Scarlet lines of tracer arced gracefully towards us, then gathering speed, whipped by in a deadly dotted line. I realised with a shock that the ships were not line astern. They were deployed in a V-formation with the tanker at the bottom, and we were flying into it.

I began to corkscrew with such force that I could hear the ammunition belts slamming about in the turret. Weeky opened up his guns with the microphone switched on. The deafening roar gave urgency to my actions. I could smell the reek of cordite. It seemed very personal. I was ill-treating the aircraft, diving it to within an ace of the sea, then pulling it up in a skidding climbing turn only to push it down so violently that my harness tugged at the shoulders. We were in the crossfire now and it was murderous. The sea was being chopped to pieces by the hail of metal. Above it, the way ahead was criss-crossed by a lattice of cannon fire. Anti-aircraft shells were injecting their dirty puffs in the sky around us … Then I glimpsed Robbie's aircraft, well ahead, low down, and going dead straight. In that moment tracer was flying gracefully all around him, but the aircraft appeared to fly on unperturbed.

I now dived below deck level as we passed the first of the two flak ships so that they couldn't fire at me without hitting each other. I could see from the stuff leaving them that it was aimed at the aircraft following behind, but I was running into a hail of head-on fire from the tanker. It now looked huge. It sat massively in front and barred the way. Countless flashes sparkled along the superstructure as the guns spat out a defence. I was now at the same height as Robbie. He was still flying dead straight. I nearly lost control of a skidding turn to port and slid behind his tail. He was attracting a cascade of Bofors fire from the tanker but miraculously it didn't seem to be hitting him.

I threw my aircraft down to sea-level now for the final bombing run. The tanker loomed above me like a great black cliff. Smoke was pouring from its funnel. It certainly wasn't stationary. I winced as a stream of tracer from amidships raked my flight path from left to right. Unbelieving, I saw Robbie's aircraft above me still flying straight and level. A second later, I jabbed the release button and let my bombs go as a salvo into the ship's side. I pulled up in a skidding climbing turn to try and clear the ship. I glimpsed Robbie's aircraft as it flew straight into the middle of the bridge deck. The explosion was immediate. A great ball of flame that spewed out debris. I ducked instinctively as we shot through it.

One only needs about 150ft to clear a ship, but the climb seems to take all the steam out of the aircraft's performance. It hangs there above the masts and derricks and the lifeboats, and in one intimate glimpse you see a gun-crew swing round frantically. Then the dive over the far side, pushing down so violently that both engines fade momentarily due to fuel starvation. The punitive fire is coming from behind now; tracer streaming by on either side lends urgency if any more were needed. Then the cry from Weeky, 'We've got it! We've got the bloody thing! But someone else has gone in on this side!'

Gradually the sky clears of missiles. 'Are we out of trouble, Weeky?'

He looks back from his mid-turret position, 'I reckon so.'

'Can you see any others?'

'Not a sod!'

'I don't see how anything could have got through that lot,' Benny said. 'I don't know how we did'.[6]

Darkness had traditionally been a time when the Axis shipping could feel comparatively safe. The arrival of three Wellingtons equipped with ASV MK II radar changed that. Their strange array of aerials had prompted the name 'Sticklebacks' in the United Kingdom. In Malta they were called the Special Duties Flight or more colloquially 'Goofingtons'. Pilot Officer Tony Spooner describes one of the early SDF flights:

We were nosing about the Maritimo Islands off the west tip of Sicily, still seeking the convoy, which was supposed to have been heading out of Palermo, when young Haynes, on the ASV set, said that he thought we might have a 'blip'. With so many small islands in the area I didn't see how it was possible to interpret the overcrowded patterns on the screen with any certainty, and I asked 'Chiefy', who was behind him, to have a look too. The whole crew had developed an uncanny sense at picking up objects on the ASV. I spent about five minutes above thin, scattered cloud, turning this way and that as the two of them tried again and again to re-tune the set so as to give optimum results.

'Yes, Skipper, we think there is a ship or two between the islands. If you could approach from the mainland it might become clearer.'

This suited me as it meant that I would also be running towards the setting moon ... We opened the bomb doors, manned both turrets, dropped down to a few hundred feet, and began a cautious run-in as directed by Haynes, who had decided to remain on the ASV set. Evans was in the rear turret. Terrington took over the nose turret. Haynes curbed his excitement and went through the drill like a veteran.

'ASV to Skipper.'

'Answering.'

'They are definitely ships, sir, and they are at least two-five miles almost dead ahead.'

At three miles I could see a large hull shape crossing the broad, silvery moonlight path. I had prepared for such an event for the best part of a year. I knew the obvious error to avoid.

---

6   R.E. Gillman, *The Shiphunters*, p. 126.

The pilot (left), and navigator (right), of a Bristol Beaufort of 22 Squadron sitting at their respective positions in the aircraft before take-off from North Coates, Lincolnshire, on 19 July 1940. (Crown Copyright – Air Historical Branch)

At all cost I must never drop my bombs at the middle or towards the rear of the ship as the forward movement of the ship could easily result in a miss astern. I shifted the aircraft to aim at or ahead of the bows. 'Must drop early', I was muttering to myself. This would give us a double chance over the calm sea, since, provided the aircraft was very low and on a level keel, bombs so dropped would skip or bounce along the flat surface of the sea. Also the fatal underwater hits can only be achieved by an early bomb release.

We flashed over an accompanying destroyer at less than 100 feet. Still not a shot had been fired at us, and as my finger trembled on the bomb-release button, I realised with horror that I was going to pass too far in front. I kicked furiously on the rudder and flung the aircraft at the ship which I could now see was of large proportions. But this banked the plane so steeply that my bombs could only fall outwards and away from the ship's bows. With our bomb load still on board and the aircraft standing on one wing, we swept over the ship's bow. Still in this banked and turning attitude I passed over another destroyer on the far side of the target – after which all Hell came up to meet us. The gunners of the three vessels were blasting away, furious at having been caught napping, and now it was I and not they who was silhouetted against the bright Mediterranean moon.

Lowery, the squadron-leader, was saying something. Evans was firing back from the tail. Everyone was shouting at once on the intercom. A wild fury gripped me. By my stupidity I had fouled up a near perfect surprise attack. All I now wanted to do was to get back quickly before I lost sight of my target. With throttles wide open I hauled the aircraft round in a violent rate 4-plus turn, and sped back towards the target, being guided to it by the wild firing from all three ships. Only one gunner, in the bows of the big vessel itself, was at all near the mark, the tracer bullets of the rest were merely illuminating the scene for me. This time I never let the big bows out of my sight.

I was a bare 50 feet above the calm sea and was almost staring upwards at the vessel's high bows when I pressed the bomb-release and heard 'Chiefy's' matter-of-fact voice report, 'All bombs gone, sir.'

I kept low and flashed below and ahead of the deck of the target before turning and twisting my way out of the area. The smell and smoke of cordite from my own front turret filled the plane. But we didn't seem to have been hurt. Nor, alas, did the enemy. I was yelling at Evans.

'Skipper to tail. Do you see anything? Did we hit her? Did you see anything? Did you see anything? Can you hear me? Did we hit her?'

The horrible dull certainty of failure was beginning to overwhelm me when suddenly Evans erupted into a garrulous garble of 'Yippee, wow, oh boy, oh boy!' I could get little sense from these ecstatic rantings, but it was the noise I most wanted to hear, and it instantly calmed me.[7]

Spooner's aircraft had struck the ship with at least two of the eight bombs, on climbing to 2,000 feet Tony Spooner found that the ship had stopped, was billowing smoke and had begun to list.

The SDF Wellingtons were also used to guide other aircraft to the attack, particularly Swordfish and Albacore Torpedo bombers of the Fleet Air Arm based at the Maltese airfield of Hal Far. Alternatively targets were identified for the conventional medium Wellington bombers, in both cases the SDF Wellington would often drop a line or two of flares to illuminate the target for attacking aircraft. At the instigation of Lloyd, the SDF Wellingtons began to develop a very close working relationship with Force K, A Royal Navy unit of cruisers and destroyers based at Malta and commanded by Captain Agnew RN. Whilst it was considered too dangerous for Force K to sail from Malta in daylight, there was just enough time for the vessels to safely steam towards the enemy convoy routes, so long as they departed one hour before dusk and then returned back one hour after dawn. The SDF flight and Force K rapidly worked out a set of drills that would allow the ASV equipped Wellingtons to guide the Royal Navy ships to the target. These included fitting an ASV beacon on the mast of Captain Agnew's Force K flagship the *Aurora*, which identified the *Aurora* and Force K as a special blip on the SDF Wellington's radar, as well as a special code that helped guide Force K on to the enemy convoy. Tony Spooner described a typical sortie:

> It would start when the Navy received an intelligence report or was passed one of Warburton's famous low-level photographs that a supply convoy was due to pass through the straits of Messina or was to leave Naples or Palermo on a certain tide. Naval navigators would then work out where the enemy was most likely to be at various times during the passage to North Africa. These calculations indicated where Force K was most likely to be able to attack at night. One hour before dusk Force K would leave Grand Harbour, Valetta, and, in their line astern formation, would head towards where they hoped the enemy would be. At much the same time we, too would head towards the area of probable interception. Our ASV Wellington would be loaded with fuel and flares. Sometimes as night fell, we would pass over Force K. It was a thrilling sight to see our ships in a long straight line of foaming wake heading at speed away from the island.
>
> We were 'their aircraft'. They were 'our ships'. Captain Agnew had this kind of effect on us all.

---

7   Tony Spooner, *In Full Flight* (Canterbury: Wingham Press, 1991), p. 166.

We would hasten to the 'most likely interception' area, and there commence the long drawn out ASV search for our probable foe. Sometimes the ASV was first rate; at other times, in poor weather, the best ranges we could obtain would be less than 15 miles. With winter approaching, air-frame and engine ice menaced us whenever weather conditions forced us to fly in cloud. Usually the search area would be 150-200 miles or so from Malta.

Sometimes the enemy wasn't there at all, but if they were we usually found them in the end, even if it required several hours of search. We would just make one run over the ships to get a better idea of their numbers and size. If we suspected that the convoy escorts included battle-ships or heavy cruisers we knew that Captain Agnew would wish to be informed at once. At all times he wanted to know the enemy's approximate number (SAIR WILLIAM 7), approximate course and speed (SAIR EDWARD 190 degrees – 12) and the approximate number of their naval escorts (SAIR CHARLES 3), We would endeavour to get this information during one straight run over or alongside the enemy.

Thereafter we would shadow by ASV, keeping at least 12 miles away out of sight and beyond earshot in order to lull them into a false sense of security. I am told that aboard Force K ships' companies would cheer when told that their 'Goofington' had located a prey. Next, we would turn back towards Malta carefully plotting our time, course and speed until, at about 90 miles the big special blip reflected off the ASV beacon we had affixed to *Aurora* would make its welcome appearance on our tiny screen. And when Evans, Terrington or Haynes would shout, 'I've got them, Skipper!' it was our turn to cheer. Some quick plotting then had to be done on the Bigsworth board I still carried for this purpose, and in a few minutes I was able to pass to Captain Agnew his direction and distance relative to the enemy. This was our key SAIR message – SAIR HENRY 128-140 i.e., 'You are 128 miles away and the enemy bears 140 degrees from your present position.'

Back we would now turn to relocate the enemy and, as soon as we had positively done so by ASV, we again reversed course in Captain Agnew's direction. SAIR HENRY 104-160: 'You are now 104 miles and he bears 160 degrees from you.' As the night wore on and as I shuttled between the two groups I would eventually get to the position where I could get both blips on my ASV screen simply by turning my aircraft through 180 degrees. At this point I would have undoubtedly got myself into the classic 'night fighting muddle' had not the *Aurora* blip been of such distinctive size and character. As it was, friend and foe were readily recognisable. In the final stages Captain Agnew would begin to work Force K into a position from which he would be able to launch his attack into the bright Mediterranean moon. Using his superior speed he could manoeuvre his fighting ships so that they would not only be sure to intercept and engage but that they could do so on his own terms; he could silhouette them against the moonlight whilst remaining hidden in the darker segment of sky opposite.

And if there wasn't a moon, we would make one! 'SAIR GEORGE 5' sent to me meant that I was to drop parachute flares (on the opposite side of the convoy to where Force K lay) in five minutes time. I would drop these so that they drifted slowly down about two or three miles from the enemy again with the intention of keeping Force K hidden in the dark.[8]

The arrival of the Beauforts at Malta, in the early summer of 1942, also began to make a big differ-ence, bringing a new capability in the form of longer-range torpedo strikes. Some of these aircraft were not officially posted to Malta but were due to be dispatched to Ceylon to help repel the threat of a Japanese seaborne invasion of that island. However, the Malta-based Beaufort squadrons had been so depleted of aircraft and crew, that it was the only way the RAF at Malta could maintain

---

8   Tony Spooner, *In Full Flight*, p. 177.

Enemy cargo vessels under attack by cannon fire from Bristol Beaufighters of 201 Group in the eastern Mediterranean. (Crown Copyright – Air Historical Branch)

the required numbers for continued torpedo operations. Lloyd turned a blind eye to the hijacking activities of his team and a deaf ear to the protests from the Air Ministry, who struggled to keep track of individual squadrons, aircraft and crews.

The casualties to the Beauforts were once more severe, but tactics and techniques were steadily improved. One lengthy memorandum had been issued in May of 1942 by HQ Middle East and captured the key lessons. This document, together with the surviving aircrew returning to the United Kingdom, would help inform the development of the new Coastal Command strike wings.[9] There were many key recommendations in the memorandum; first, that the aircraft must fly all the way to the target at no more than 50 feet, they should do so in 'Vic' formation, for that provided the best defence against enemy fighters (which seems unlikely!) and attacks should be made at either dawn or dusk. It was acknowledged that the former was harder to achieve with large numbers of aircraft, given the difficulties of forming up and flying in close formation at night. Secondly, when the Vic formation was about three miles from the target it should break up into attacking formations, if the enemy ships were being approached from ahead then the sections should adopt a line astern formation, with aircraft 150-200 yards apart. The attack should ideally be preceded by fighter and bomber attacks, these were there to distract and suppress the vessel's AA fire, the ideal time between these attacks and those of the torpedo aircraft should be about 20 seconds. Thirdly, as the torpedo aircraft neared the target the aircraft would turn, so that they were in line-abreast and attack the target. The ideal dropping range was said to be 800-1,000 yards, though it was acknowledged that the short-range AA was very effective out to 2-3,000 yards.

9   TNA AIR 15/633: Middle East Tactical Memorandum, No. 15, 'Torpedo Operations', May 1945.

Finally it was recommended that F.26 torpedo aiming cameras were carried, to provide feedback to the pilot on his torpedo release and aim, the idea being to improve future attacks.[10]

Arthur Aldridge had arrived in Malta in early 1942 and had already flown on a number of sorties. The sighting of a convoy on 21 June, including two key merchant ships, prompted a new mission for his squadron of Beauforts:

We took off at 11.15 hrs; three vics, a total of nine aircraft. I was leading a vic on the port side of Squadron Leader Lynn, who was spearheading our formation. To starboard was the vic led by Stevens. Our chances had been slightly improved by the fact that one of the escorting destroyers, the *Strale*, had run aground near Cape Bon.

But the *Reichenfels* and the *Rosolino Pilo* were still escorted by the destroyer *Da Recco,* and they were all hugging the Tunisian coast on their way to Libya. They were watched over by three twin-engine Junkers JU-88 A-1s, which could be fighters or bombers, depending on any given situation. On this day they'd be fighters. The ships were also protected by a Sparrowhawk or *Sparviero*, a three-engine bomber, and a Cant Z.501 – an old fashioned flying boat. These aircraft were less likely to hurt us.

We flew west for the Kerkennah Islands and the Gulf of Gabes, and Vince noted the island of Lampedusa on our right. We stayed low at 50 feet, while the fighters above us looked for opponents coming in from the south.

I spotted the killer specks on the horizon, hoping to sail unnoticed against the hazy Tunisian coast. When we were close enough to attack, Lynn waggled his wings and tried to lead in the first vic and that's when all hell broke loose.

Poor Robert Lynn took a shell right through him, and from that moment on the entire first vic was doomed. His plane lurched violently as his navigator Dick Dickinson tried in vain to shift his body and wrestle with the controls. Their aircraft struck the sea, but not before their torpedo had separated from the plane and rebounded off the water. Lynn's death had already forced another Beaufort in his vic, piloted by Sergeant Smyth, to veer sharply and fly only a few feet beneath us. I climbed for my life to avoid that collision after hearing Bill's warning. But poor Smyth, having narrowly avoided my Beaufort, flew straight into the path of the rogue torpedo from Lynn's plane. Though there was no explosion, the torpedo did enough damage to send Smyth crashing into the waves. Flying Officer Phillips was taken down by flak at about the same time.

So the entire first vic had been wiped out in seconds. And we could so easily have joined them in the drink. In all the chaos, it was a wonder we were still in the air … We'd avoided a friendly collision, but there was still the enemy to deal with. And when I saw the greeting they'd arranged for us in the form of that dreadful, seemingly impenetrable wall of flak, that's when I felt it. The empty, queasy feeling in the bottom of my stomach, the unwelcome stranger – fear. All I could do was fly on, knowing the next few seconds were going to be deeply unpleasant.

I flew into the flak at a speed of 140 knots. There were puffs of smoke everywhere and I realised I was now inside it. Locked inside a wall of flak, which surrounded us, darkening everything. I knew a more final oblivion could come at any moment. I couldn't hear anything, not even the shell bursts, because I had my headphones on. The explosions didn't rock the plane or invade it with the smell of cordite. The puffs of smoke, black and grey and all around us, rendered us almost senseless. Yet I could see enough to know why I was afraid. They couldn't come any closer, those bursts, or we would die … And then we came straight through. None

10   TNA AIR 15/633: Middle East Tactical Memorandum, No. 15, 'Torpedo Operations', May 1945.

of us in that plane will ever know how we managed it. Somehow we were clear, momentarily and nearing the perfect torpedo range. The supply ship was taking evasive action; it was turning away to starboard, thus presenting no deflection shot. This meant I wouldn't have to aim ahead of the ship to anticipate its path at all, not even slightly. Aim straight for the ship and you'll normally miss because you haven't allowed for its movement. But not this time. This one was slow, and after what we'd been through, I was determined to get it.

I rose to between 60 and 80 feet and aimed at the bow. With no deflection necessary, I could go for the jugular, the point of maximum damage. This was going to be perfect. 'Time it right, Arthur. How's your distance? Eight hundred yards … gone! I'd pressed the button on my control column and dropped the torpedo at a distance of 750 yards from the ship. For the second time in a week, this felt just right; but there was no time to wait and see what would happen. The flak was still horrendous. It was all about trying to stay alive now. But I was rattled, and I wasn't thinking straight.

I just wanted to get out of there. I wanted to get the hell out as fast as I could. I was so rattled that I did a stupid thing. When you take evasive action you normally snake from side to side. That's what I should have done; take the usual evasive action, skim low over the water, skid as you go. But like an idiot, I panicked and banked to starboard. I banked so steeply that I presented some very angry Germans with a better target. They couldn't miss now, and they didn't … An explosion! Another, a third and a fourth! We'd been hit by four cannon shells; I saw sparks fly and felt my plane go out of control. One shell had struck the starboard tail plane, another the port wing-tip; and a third had hit the leading edge of the starboard wing, putting one of the ailerons out of action.

The starboard aileron control wires had been severed, that's probably what had caused my loss of control. The shell that had done the most damage to the crew had struck one of the ammunition pans that Aspinall had taken off its peg and put on the floor.

The shell's argument with the ammunition pan had created shrapnel from the exploded casing, and now a piece had hit me. It might have been worse if the pan hadn't been there to absorb some of the shell's impact.

A splinter had entered my right forearm. It wasn't very painful, but the blood worried me for a fraction of a second, until I realised there was no time to worry, because it looked like we were about to slap into the sea. We were less than 80 feet from the waves by now. We were going in …

The starboard wing was edging ever –closer to the sea, almost touching it. When it hit, that'd be it. Instinctively, I opened both throttles wide. For a moment I felt I was managing to get the Beaufort under control again. How could this be? My port aileron was out of action. But, by sheer luck, that act of opening the throttles had given me the slipstream over the undamaged aileron to allow me to regain control. I'd only been out of control for a few seconds, but it had felt like so much longer.

A bit of extra slipstream. That was the difference between getting shot down or not. Having been given a second chance, I didn't hang around. I did all I could to gain enough height to fly us out of there. I still had only one aileron functioning; but that didn't seem to be causing a major problem. Good old Beaufort.[11]

Arthur Aldridge had succeeded in sinking the 7,744-ton *Reichenfels,* which had been carrying 4,000 tons of munitions and 600 tons of fuel to Tripoli. A total of 246 seamen on board the Axis ship survived.

---

11   Arthur Aldridge and Mark Ryan, *The Last Torpedo Flyers,* pp. 215-21.

Aircrews of 39 Squadron gather round Flying Officer AOS Jepson in front of his Bristol Beaufort II as he recounts his part in the Squadron's attack on the Italian Battle Fleet on 15 June 1942, for the benefit of the press cameras at Fayid, Egypt. A force of 12 Beauforts set out from LG 05 near Sidi Barrani to attack the Fleet but was soon reduced to five following an attack off Derna by German fighters. The remainder attacked two battleships, and a further three aircraft were badly damaged in the process before the survivors flew on to Malta. Although strikes on the warships were claimed, the Italian Fleet was undamaged, except for one hit on the battleship *Littorio* with a 500lb bomb dropped by aircraft of the USAAF 'Halpro' Detachment which also participated in the attacks. (Crown Copyright – Air Historical Branch)

The impact of these anti-shipping missions seems clear. Rommel's obvious problems with logistics hampered his campaign at critical junctures and though a long land route between Tripoli and the front line undoubtedly exacerbated his logistical problem, the impact of the anti-shipping campaign was still decisive. Between 1 June and 31 October 1941 some 220,000 tons of axis shipping was sunk on the convoy routes to Libya, the RAF and Fleet Air Arm accounted for 115,000 tons of this amount, with the Malta based squadrons about three-quarters of this. In August 1941, 35 percent of Rommel's supplies were lost before they reached him; in October, just before Operation CRUSADER was launched by the British, the figure was 63 percent.[12] A significant element of this was down to Malta's anti-shipping operations, and whilst the island's offensive potential would wax and wane, it was never permanently neutralised by the Germans. This allowed it to recover once *Luftwaffe* attention was diverted elsewhere and ensure that Rommel's

---

12   John Terraine, *The Right of the Line*, pp. 354, 365.

Afrika Korps would always be 'a starveling, short of supplies, short of men, short of equipment.'[13] Count Galeazzo Ciano, Italy's Foreign Minister, also highlighted the crisis in shipping at the end of September 1942: 'In all, we have little more than a million tons [of merchant shipping] left, at this rate the African problem will automatically end in six months, since we shall have no more ships with which to supply Libya.'[14]

Shipping strikes were not just limited to Europe and the Mediterranean. In the Far East the Japanese operational-level offensives were characterised by a series of well executed amphibious assaults, where the integrated use of air and maritime forces proved highly effective in over-running or out-flanking Allied defences. The Allied anti-shipping capability was too weak to do much to prevent these assaults initially, but it steadily improved over time.

The first Japanese amphibious assault on Malaya took place in the Kota Bharu and Singora areas of Malaya and Siam, though the mixed RAF and RAAF force of Hudsons and Vildebeest torpedo bombers could do little to prevent them. The first into action were the Hudsons of 1 Squadron RAAF who were the first Allied unit to sink a Japanese ship in the war – the *Awagisan Maru*. They were joined later on by 8 Squadron RAAF (Hudsons) and 60 Squadron RAF (Blenheims) who flew sorties against the invasion barges and ground reinforcements but could not stem the tide.

Hudsons were not particularly suited to the formidable task of attacking a heavily defended convoy of assault ships, but the Vickers Vildebeest Mk IV was even more vulnerable. An obsolete aerial antique, first flown in 1928, it was typical of the third-rate aircraft maintained in the Far East by the British, in the mistaken hope they would never have to be used in anger. This open-topped biplane had a maximum speed of just 156 mph and was fitted with just two machine guns, a Vickers gun firing forward and a Lewis gun facing to the rear. The crew of three could carry a torpedo or 1,100lb of bombs. The Vildebeest-equipped 100 Squadron and 36 Squadron were both based at Seletar, on Singapore Island. Richard Allanson was a pilot with 36 Squadron which had moved to Gong Kedah airfield, further north up the Malayan peninsula, where they would be well positioned to launch an attack. Allanson explains what happened next:

> About 3 or 4 o'clock we were called up by telephone and told to go and look for an invasion fleet, but again it was awful weather with one violent rain storm after another all about a mile apart. We went round and round, to and fro, before in the end we located a Cruiser, a 12,000 tonne Cruiser. I can't remember the class of the Cruiser but it was very easy to recognise as it was the only one to have truncated funnels that came through the deck to make one wider funnel that was raked ... two of us had a go at that with torpedoes but owing to the bad weather we were not able to synchronise the attack. Flight Lieutenant Witney was leading the other horn of the crescent, as it was called, he had two aircraft formatting on him, but they had lost sight of him in the rain storms, so he did an attack by himself.
>
> A minute, or a minute and half later, I also did an attack by myself which was rather alarm-ing, because the Japanese had seen us some time before and were shooting at us as we were popping in and out of the bottom of the clouds. They threw everything at me, I was very lucky to get away with it ... I don't think I even got a hole in the fabric ... I could see tracer going past underneath the aircraft ... well I am damn sure I even saw a vapour trail from a four-inch shell that went underneath me nicely clear of my starboard wing leaving something akin to a vapour trail. I was only flying 20 feet off the water going up and down and throwing

13   R. Lewin, *Life and Death of the Afrika Korps* (London: Batsford, 1977), p. 39.
14   Denis Richards and Hilary Saunders, *Royal Air Force 1939-45, Volume II*, p. 231.

Vickers Vildebeest III K4176/B, of 36 Squadron in flight over Singapore, 22 September 1936.
(Crown Copyright – Air Historical Branch)

it about as much as I dared which is difficult because at sea level you cannot do much diving to get speed, very obviously![15]

The British launched further attacks on future Japanese amphibious assaults, including that at Endau on 26 January, where Japanese fighters decimated the attacking forces of Vildebeest, Hudsons and Buffaloes. In the Dutch East Indies on 15 February, the same day Singapore capitulated, a force of Hurricanes and Hudsons did find a gap in the Japanese air defences and were able to get direct hits on the transports landing assault forces at the mouth of the Palembang river in Sumatra. The RAF and RAAF sank an estimated 20 landing craft and killed hundreds of assaulting Japanese troops. It showed what could be done with modern aircraft and even temporary local air superiority, some have said it represented the greatest success in the war against the Japanese at that point.[16]

The need to replace the obsolete Vildebeest aircraft in the Far East, had prompted Britain and Australia to reach an agreement that Australia would produce the Beaufort bomber, for both the

15   IWM Sound Archives, Catalogue Number 11372, Richard Allanson interview.
16   Denis Richards and Hilary Saunders, *Royal Air Force 1938-45, Volume 2*, p. 44.

RAF and RAAF. At the time, the Beaufort was the fastest medium bomber, as well as a recognised torpedo dropping aircraft and it therefore seemed a natural choice. The Australian Department for Aircraft Production (DAP) established assembly and testing plants at Mascot, Sydney and Fishermen's Bend, Melbourne and the first aircraft were assembled and flown at Laverton on 5 May 1941.[17] It took a while for these aircraft to become operational and though a squadron was flown to Malaya in December 1941, in the hope they could be used against the Japanese, only one was found to be operationally ready. The remainder all possessed significant defects (including inefficient fuel systems, airscrew problems, inadequate brakes and a lack of armament) that required them to be returned back to Australia. The one Beaufort that remained did important work, including spotting the Japanese invasion fleet 30 miles off shore. In this the first operational sortie by an Australian-manufactured aircraft, the Beaufort was hit by Japanese Zeros but managed to make it back to Kota Bharu. It was then subject to a later strafing attack by the Japanese and burnt out on the ground.[18]

Australia was to create 10 Beaufort squadrons in total. They were categorised as a reconnaissance-bomber-torpedo aircraft and their speed and range were invaluable given the great distances to be covered in the South West Pacific. The American successes at Coral Sea and later Midway regained the initiative from the Japanese and though the threat of their long-distance amphibious assaults had passed, the Japanese remained dependant on maritime lines of communication within their Pacific empire. The Beauforts were therefore regularly used to bomb Japanese positions in New Guinea, as well as launch occasional shipping strikes when opportunities presented themselves. One of the most memorable was a combined strike by six Beauforts on a Japanese invasion force that had struck at Milne Bay, close to the airstrips and Port Moresby itself. The Beauforts and accompanying Beaufighters arrived at Port Moresby on 5 September 1942, two days later an attack was launched involving Hudsons bombing from 10,000 feet, Kittyhawks and Beaufighters providing covering fire and the six Beauforts coming in low to drop their torpedoes. The Japanese directed the lighter 20mm anti-aircraft fire at the fighters and their naval guns at the torpedo bombers which caused huge waterspouts. Kim Bonython was a pilot in one of the Beauforts and recalls the attack:

> It was the kind of day you dream about for a holiday. Visibility was good. The air was dead still. The sea was an oily mirror. For a torpedo attack it was a nightmare. The enemy began shooting at us when we were still 10 miles away. By the time we were three miles away, barely skimming the surface, we were dodging through great fountains of water thrown up by everything the cruiser and destroyer could fling at us. When we reached dropping range, which was supposed to be 1000 yards, we seemed to be flying through a solid mass of bursting shell, incendiary bullets, cannon shells and foaming explosions. We dropped the torpedo on course, only a few hundred yards from the target and made frantic left-hand turns, almost over the enemy's bows.[19]

Max Mahoney was a turret gunner with 'Smoky' Douglas' aircraft and recalls the weight of fire too.

17 Colin King, *Song of the Beauforts – 100 Squadron RAAF and Beaufort Bomber Operations* (Tuggeranong: Australia Air Power Development Centre, 2008), p. 5.
18 Colin King, *Song of the Beauforts*, p. 8.
19 Colin King, *Song of the Beauforts*, p. 55.

Rounds from the Jap pom-pom guns were hitting the water on either side of our Beaufort and made it look like we were flying along a roadway. Then their shells were coming more accurately at us. We were flying in two flights of three, in right echelon formation. The Kittyhawks on their strafing runs would come pretty close to the cruiser's masts. They pulled out and the two Beaufighters looked as if they were on fire, as they fired their four cannons. The recoil action made the aircraft appear to move slightly backwards during each burst.[20]

Though no torpedoes struck their targets, it was found that the Japanese ships were reluctant to approach Milne Bay after this attack. This first torpedo strike was followed up by more ambitious raids, such as that on 3 October 1942, on a convoy of Japanese ships off the Shortland Islands that lie at the southernmost tip of Bougainville Island. The round trip in this case was 950 nautical miles – which posed a considerable navigational challenge. The Australian Beaufort navigators had learnt not to trust their magnetic compasses, in part because of the magnetic influence from the retracted undercarriage and instead relied on the astro compass, though the cloud cover in the tropics could make star sightings problematic. Tropical storms were also a regular feature in the South West Pacific and the anvil-headed cumuli clouds, that towered from 50 to tens of thousands of feet, were avoided wherever possible. The fierce currents inside them could toss a Beaufort around like a leaf and electrical discharges were thought to carry great risk, particularly after one report that a trailing aerial had been burnt off at the fuselage following a lightning strike. Avoiding these storms further complicated a navigator's task. Ralph Wiley was in Beaufort A9-29 and recalls the nightime raid:

> It was 0100 local time when we took off with our torp, after stripping the plane of all surplus gear. Wing Commander Balmer, OBE, led the way for the Beauforts, while Warrant Officer Greenhill, once with 100 Squadron in the early days and now on loan from 30 Squadron Beaufighters, was the flight navigator. Balmer was later to congratulate Greenhill for his 'spot-on' navigation to the target area.
>
> On the way, we encountered a storm, which forced us to open up formation and we lost sight of two of the planes. We arrived in the Shortland Islands area and found the Japanese ships nearer Buin on Bougainville Island. It was a long harbour backed by a mountain range. The moon was obscured by cloud and visibility was poor, but I could see three cruisers and another 20, or perhaps more, vessels in the harbour. We made a low-level attack and released our torpedo on one of the cruisers. The Japanese were taken completely by surprise and, as we swept across the stern of the cruiser, the ack-ack came too late to worry us. By getting in close to drop the torpedo it is unlikely that we missed our target. However, we did not see any explosion.[21]

Ron Munro was also on the raid and attacked the Japanese ships after Riley's aircraft. His account highlights that the Japanese defences were now fully alert.

> We reached Buin-Faisi, which was shaded by the mountains and cloud cover, and the place was in darkness. As we flew to the head of the bay at about 500 feet, we could see a long line of about 30 ships and they all seemed to start firing at once. Then ack-ack guns on the hillsides began firing. 'Smoky' dived to sea level and weaved the aircraft between two of the warships, which reduced their firing to avoid hitting each other. I saw this shell coming towards us and

20   Colin King, *Song of the Beauforts,* p. 56.
21   Colin King, *Song of the Beauforts,* p. 60.

Australian Beaufort takes off. (Royal Australian Air Force Museum)

I was sure it was going to hit me. I folded up my radio cable and put my arms over my face. There was a deafening thud and smoke came up through the floor but that was all. A cruiser loomed up directly ahead and we dropped our torpedo. As we flew through a hail of fire from the cruiser, Max in the turret reported that he had seen an explosion.

The return trip was uneventful until we had to climb above dense black rain clouds. On nearing our estimated time of arrival (ETA), 'Smoky' asked the navigator where we were, and Doug Shetiffe said that he thought we were over the sea outside Milne Bay. 'Smoky' said he had only 10 minutes of fuel left, so he'd better be right, and with that, we dived almost vertically through the cloud, to pull out a few hundred feet above the water. Full marks to Doug as he had not been able to get a star shot and there was no radio beacon at Milne Bay to get a bearing. On landing, we inspected the aircraft and found a dent where a shell had hit us but had not exploded.[22]

During this raid eight aircraft had entered the target area and seven had sighted ships and launched their torpedoes. Frustratingly it seemed that the American manufactured torpedoes with which the Australians were supplied, were faulty. American submarines were also missing a string of targets with the US Mark 13 and Mark 14 torpedoes and tests at Fremantle showed that the American torpedoes were running at depths of 25 feet, rather than the 10 feet which they were supposed to. The United States Navy admitted that the torpedo's depth control mechanism was at fault, as a result instructions were then issued for modifying the torpedo so that it ran within a few feet of its intended setting.[23] Some also believed that the tactics of the Beaufort crews needed improvement, there was a belief that the pilots might be releasing their torpedoes too close to

---

22   Colin King, *Song of the Beauforts.* p. 61.
23   Colin King, *Song of the Beauforts*, p. 56.

the target. Consequently, a new torpedo sight was introduced which consisted of a long, narrow curved mirror calibrated in degrees and mounted in front of the pilot. Further training on dive-bombing and torpedo dropping was undertaken on a wreck near Townsville. These additional measures meant the Australian crews had the satisfaction of seeing their targets well and truly struck on future operations.

On Saturday 9 January 1943 a Flight from 100 Squadron, under the command of Flight Lieutenant Mercer set off to find a Japanese convoy sailing from Lae to Rabaul. The Flight hoped to find the convoy shortly after dark, when the likelihood of Japanese fighters being around was reduced. Mercer's aircraft had ASV radar fitted and it was his wireless air gunner who detected the Japanese convoy near Gasmata. Pilot Officer Ivan Morris was a navigator for pilot Bill Hamblin's Beaufort aircraft, he recalls the successful attack:

> The five Beauforts swung away to the east of the target and descended to wave top height before turning in to carry out a torpedo attack on the ship, which was now silhouetted by the afterglow of the setting sun. There were some dark clouds about, but not enough to prevent a clear sighting of the vessel, which appeared to be a heavy destroyer or light cruiser. It was heading north-east towards Rabaul and was apparently unaware of us.
>
> The torpedo attack was not properly coordinated, as we were strung out, and we actually attacked individually. John Mercer in A9-183 went in first, lifting the aircraft to 200 feet to drop his torpedo, but no result was seen, and we followed one minute later. As we approached the target, which had been alerted by John Mercer's attack, it was running at full speed across our path and began firing with everything it had in our direction. Shells from its main armament set up a splash barrage in front of us, while its ack-ack guns were firing with virulent accuracy.
>
> When flying directly into gunfire, the tracers show up as slowly moving blobs or streams of light until they reach you, then hopefully they whiz past. It was quite spectacular, and I moved back out of the nose of the aircraft to stand alongside the pilot, and operate the torpedo release mechanism, so I had a good view of the action. Bill Hamblin had his hands full controlling the aircraft and positioning it ready for the drop point. When straight and level at the right spot, I released the torpedo.
>
> It fell truly from the aircraft, and Laurie Webb in the turret, reported that it, had entered the water cleanly, and did not offset sideways as so many of them did. Meanwhile Bill Hamblin was jinking the Beaufort violently all over the sky to avoid the flak. I returned to the front, to use the nose guns, as we broke away over the stern of the ship at an altitude of about 100 feet, with engines that were at full boost. Shortly afterwards Laurie Webb in the turret excitedly reported a huge flash amidships on the target, and we knew that the torpedo had run true. A series of red flares or rockets went up from the ship immediately following the torpedo hit, and their guns stopped firing.[24]

Australian Beaufort Torpedo aircraft were to continue to do important work in Pacific waters, though their role would increasingly branch out to include air support to ground forces, as the Australian Army regained the initiative and began its own offensives in New Guinea and Borneo. The success the Australians had against shipping were not simply limited tactical actions, whose impact was confined to just the South West Pacific campaign. Japan had begun the war with six million tons of shipping, of which she had lost one million tons in the first year of the war. If this was reduced to four million tons then she would find it difficult to maintain her garrisons running

---

24   Colin King, *Song of the Beauforts*, p. 78.

in a great half circle from Burma to New Guinea. The Australian anti-shipping operations there-fore served a wider important strategic purpose too.[25]

Back in the United Kingdom, Coastal Command's anti-shipping operations had also developed. They had been particularly informed by lessons from the Mediterranean and the humiliating passage, through the Straits of Dover, of the Battleships *Scharnhorst* and *Gneisenau* in February 1942.

The British attempt to track and strike the *Scharnhost* and *Gneisenau*'s Channel dash had been characterised by a series of poorly co-ordinated operations, by Fighter, Coastal and Bomber Command. The subsequent official inquiry, known as the Bucknill Report, began to address deficiencies in Coastal Command's material, command and control as well as maintenance. Intelligence support to anti-shipping operations was also improved, this included better photo-graphic reconnaissance which now provided good coverage of ports from France to Germany and had worked out how to accurately measure the speed of a vessel from the bow wave patterns it generated. Understanding a vessel or convoy's speed was important, not just in terms of the accurate release of the torpedo,[26] but also so that the strike wings could intercept the convoy at a fixed point of their choosing.[26] Signals intelligence support had also improved and a notable break-through had been achieved, in early 1941, when the enemy's signals traffic between dockyards was cracked. This provided ship and convoy departure and arrival times between one port and another, again allowing Coastal Command to calculate times when the vessels might pass a particular point.[27] In addition the value of the convoy and its cargo could also be determined by the level of German air support the convoy might receive, these *Luftwaffe* operations were known as 'Citrone' and the intercepted signals allowed Coastal Command to correctly prioritise their strikes against the most valuable targets.

It was also agreed, in September 1942, that the Beaufighter was to become Coastal Command's principal strike aircraft. Joubert, the commander of Coastal Command at the time, was impressed by the aircraft's remarkable combination of adaptability, speed, strength and endurance and suggested that these admirable aircraft could be modified to carry torpedoes and concentrated in special 'strike wings'. A total of 10 Beaufighter anti-shipping squadrons were to be initially estab-lished, in three self-supporting wings of both torpedo and anti-flak squadrons, based out of North Coates, Leuchars and Wick. The North Coates Wing was the first to reach maturity with three squadrons of Beaufighters. One of these, 254 Squadron, would operate as a torpedo squadron with 31 'Torbeau' Beaufighters, meanwhile 236 and 143 Squadrons would use their 38 Beaufighters as an anti-flak section.[28] A wing comprising 455 Squadron RAAF and 489 RNZAF Squadron was also generated and based out of Leuchars and Langham, unsurprisingly it became known as the ANZAC Wing. A Canadian Squadron, 404 Squadron, was also based with the strike wing at Wick. The Beaufighters not only had their standard armament of four 20mm cannons, but also began to use rockets. These three-inch rockets were fitted with a 60lb head filled with HE, good for suppressing flak, or a solid armour piercing 25lb head for penetrating a ship hull and sinking her. The Beaufighter could carry eight rockets, four under each wing, which could be fired in pairs or launched as a salvo of eight, the Beaufighter aircrew usually synchronising the cannon fire with that of the rockets.[29] Wing Commander Jack Davenport was an Australian who commanded

25   Denis Richards and Hilary Saunders, *Royal Air Force 1939-45, Volume II*, p. 275.
26   Christina Goulter, *A Forgotten Offensive*, p. 205.
27   Christina Goulter, *A Forgotten Offensive*, p. 151.
28   Christina Goulter, *A Forgotten Offensive*, p. 199.
29   Roy Conyers Nesbit, *The Strike Wings: Special Anti-Shipping Squadrons 1942-45* (London: William Kimber, 1984), pp. 54-6.

Beaufighter TF.X, LZ293/ MB-T, of 236 Squadron based at North Coates, Lincolnshire, in flight, armed with eight 60lb rocket projectiles on rails under the wings. (Crown Copyright – Air Historical Branch)

455 Squadron, during some of the most intense periods in the unit's anti-shipping war. He was a clear fan of the 25lb armour piercing rocket in strike operations and gave his own account of the weapon's use:

> To fire the rockets, one had to be within 1,100-600 yards from the target and in a dive, and you had to be flying at a speed of about 200 or 220 knots and you fired eight rockets and they went in pairs one after the other when you fired them. You had to be in a dive and the technique we would use was to fire the cannons and they would hit the water short of the target and you would keep firing the cannons until you hit the ship at the waterline and then you would press the rocket button and that meant that two would hit the waterline and the other six would go underneath the water and through the hull and out the other side. They were an amazing weapon … the thing about them was that they were so accurate, they travelled at 1,100-odd miles per hour from the time they left your aeroplane. The trouble was the escort vessels were out to just beyond where you would have to fire your cannon.[30]

The solid shot 25lb rocket could not only penetrate a merchant vessel's hull easily, they also had the added advantage of being much cheaper than a torpedo and the aircraft needed less distance in the approach to a target. This was a particularly important advantage in the close confines of a harbour, or a Norwegian fiord, which was becoming an increasingly important operational area for Coastal Command. The 60lb HE-rocket was also particularly effective as an anti-flak weapon, an attribute of increasing importance, as by 1943 the German convoys were extremely well protected.

Not only were the merchant ships heavily armed and now usually flying a barrage balloon to complicate matters, but the convoys were normally escorted by three distinctive types of escort

---

30   AWM Sound Archives SO1651: Interview with Jack Napier Davenport.

Oblique aerial photograph taken from a Bristol Beaufighter during an attack on shipping lying at anchor off Marsdiep, between Den Helder and Texel, Holland, on 25 September 1944 by the combined North Coates and Langham strike wings. The main target, the hull of an uncompleted merchant ship of 3,000 tons, can be seen at upper right, surrounded by minesweepers and auxiliary vessels which, with the shore batteries, are putting up a intense barrage of anti-aircraft fire. Three Beaufighters failed to return and 17 others were damaged, although 11 vessels were sunk or damaged. (Crown Copyright – Air Historical Branch)

vessels. The first of these were *Sperrbrechers*, literally barrier breakers, these 8,000-ton former merchant vessels were festooned with both 20mm and sometimes 40mm AA guns usually on two raised platforms at the bow and stern, they also had reinforced hulls to withstand mine detonations. Secondly there were *Minensuchboote*, or M-Class minesweepers, who would sweep a channel in front as well as provide AA support. Finally, there were larger numbers of 800-ton *Vorpostenboote*, normally called flak ships by the aircrew, these were armed with 105mm, 88mm, 40mm and 20mm AA artillery and would position themselves to the flanks of the convoy in likely torpedo dropping areas. These also had raised platforms on the bow, stern and either side of the bridge for their AA guns. Finally, the Germans began to fit parachute and cable rocket launchers, or *Drahtseilgerat*, to their ships. These would rise to 400–1,000 metres where the parachute would deploy and hopefully entangle an aircraft in its dangling 100 metre metal cable usually supplemented with a mine on the end.[31]

Dangerous though these defences were the Beaufighter operations were becoming both increasingly successful and large in scale, with sometimes multi-wing operations being conducted involving 100 or so aircraft. Squadron Leader Colin Milson was an Australian in 455 Squadron and took part in an operation off Heligoland in July 1944:

31   Roy Conyers Nesbit, *The Strike Wings: Special Anti-Shipping Squadrons 1942-45*, p. 64.

Bristol Beaufighters from 144 and 254 Squadrons, 455 Squadron RAAF and 489 Squadron RNZAF attacking German M-Class minesweepers escorting a convoy off the Dutch coast, north-west of Borkum, with rocket-projectiles on 25 August 1944. Thirteen aircraft can be seen in the photograph, which was taken over the tail of an aircraft from 455 Squadron after delivering its attack. 'In an attack of this sort avoiding collision with other aircraft was one of our problems – and pilots needed to keep a very sharp look-out', Wing Commander Tony Gadd, Commanding Officer of 144 Squadron. (Crown Copyright – Air Historical Branch)

They were a hell of a long way off when we first saw them, it must have been 15 miles away and although it was only three minutes until we were onto them it seemed an interminable time. They looked rather like a small invasion fleet and there were actually 40 ships altogether, only nine of them were merchantmen, but these had 31 escort ships to look after them. They must have been expecting trouble. Our strike force immediately got ready to attack, each crew knew exactly what he was to do, I gave the signal to attack and all of us who were flak busting dived down into the convoy shooting at everything we got into our sights. The Aussies were in the centre with the New Zealanders on our port and the Canadians on our Starboard side. The RAF squadron flew in at deck level with their tin fish.

The Jerries must have seen us at the same time as we saw them, and they also knew exactly what to do for things began to happen fast and furious. I saw two torpedo hits and it was not very long afterwards that both ships were well on their way to the bottom. One of the Aussies attacked a merchantmen that must have carried barrels of oil on deck for after a few bursts from his cannons the oil got going and went up in a big blaze. I went in at one of the escort vessels and got in a burst at the depth charges that were on the deck. One of them went off with a terrific explosion that appeared to blow the stern right off the ship. In 10 minutes a pall of black smoke covered the convoy and practically every single one of the 40 ships was either sinking or on fire. We returned to base without losing any aircraft though Flight Lieutenant Pilcher, a Queenslander, returned with only one good engine after what he called an uneventful trip across the North Sea. One of our New Zealanders even brought back a souvenir, the Germans had been using rockets trailing steel cables which they fired into us hoping the cables would foul our airscrews. They didn't, but he came back with 40 feet of cable wrapped around his wing.[32]

The improvement in weapons and tactics, as well as the greater number of aircraft which helped swamp the enemy's defences, all contributed to a reduction in RAF losses. The Germans did hit many aircraft but often claimed more than they shot down, in fairness they may have been genuinely misled by the Beaufighter's engines, which often produced a stream of black smoke as it powered away after an attack, something that must have looked a little like engine trouble. Though the German defences had undoubtedly improved, the volume of fire now being directed at the German ships was immense. It was undoubtedly a harrowing experience to be at the end of a Beaufighter rocket attack, where each aircraft was able to deliver the equivalent in fire power to a salvo from a cruiser.

Hans Joachim Meyer, a gunner on a flak ship experienced such an attack in September 1943:

We were escorting four cargo ships along the Dutch coast, heading for Emden, when our look-out warned of some approaching enemy aircraft. Every crew man dropped whatever he was doing and leapt to his appointed battle place; in my case to a twin 20mm cannon mounting in the forward part of the deck. Within minutes a wave of two-engine fighters came at us with cannons and machine guns blazing at mast height. I commenced firing but immediately found myself in the midst of a hail of shells exploding and ricocheting on and off the deck and superstructure. The noise was ear-splitting, with smoke and fumes everywhere – a frightening experience.

I stuck to my guns during the first onslaught – more by automatic obedience to my duty than common sense – but when this was immediately followed by another wave of Tommies firing rockets, I let go my guns and fell flat on the deck with my hands over my ears – and praying … An awful bang only inches away from me must have been a rocket missile direct hit on my gun emplacement because when I dared to open my eyes I saw the gun mounting was wrecked, while my No 2 gunner was lying yards away, dead, with an awful stomach wound.

The whole attack could only have lasted a few minutes – then all was quiet again. My head was throbbing with the after effects of the noise and sheer fear, but I was lucky to still be alive. The deck was a shambles of twisted metal shattered wood and glass, with the bodies of eight of my comrades lying among the debris. The most frightening part of such attacks was the suddenness – we never really had time to steel ourselves for defence before the Tommies were upon us, strafing and slaughtering; experiences I can never forget.[33]

At last Coastal Command's strike wings were beginning to get in to their stride, but there was still a sense that the anti-shipping results were not worth the effort expended, particularly given the pressing demand for Beaufighters elsewhere. Slessor, when AOC Coastal Command, questioned the whole rationale in August 1943, drawing a comparison between the 79 ships sunk through Bomber Command's Gardening operations between May 1942 and May 1943, versus the 21 ships the anti-shipping squadrons had sunk during the same period. Arguments were made that aside

32   AWM Sound Archives SOO197: 'Beaufighters attack convoy off Heligoland' by Squadron Leader Colin Milsom, 455 Squadron RAAF, 22 July 1944.
33   Chaz Bowyer, *Beaufighter* (London: William Kimber, 1987), p. 79.

Oblique aerial photograph taken during a low-level attack on two German trawler-type auxiliaries south of Heligoland, by Bristol Beaufighters of the North Coates strike wing. Two Beaufighters are seen clearing one of the vessels after raking it with rocket projectiles and cannon fire. This trawler was left burning fiercely while the other was torpedoed and blew up. (Crown Copyright – Air Historical Branch)

from shipping losses the anti-shipping squadrons had also served to reduce the level of shipping off the Dutch coast and forced the convoys to travel at night, when Royal Navy torpedo boats could better attack them. The Ministry of Economic Warfare again highlighted the importance of Rotterdam in the iron ore trade and was able to prove, through photographic reconnaissance, that there had been a decline in port activity associated with iron ore at that Dutch port. They were also able to highlight that Swedish insurance companies were no longer willing to issue policies for vessels that wished to travel as far as Rotterdam. Slessor relented and despite continued concerns that he was losing Beaufighters to the Mediterranean theatre and that he also needed them for protecting RAF aircraft operating in the Bay of Biscay, he allowed the strike wings to continue.[34]

The reprieve allowed further developments in anti-shipping tactics. Outriders began to be used by the strike wings, these would be detached from the main attacking force to scout ahead and radio back, helping guide the attack wing to its optimum attacking point. In addition, the use of 'Drem' or floating flares was adopted, these would be dropped some distance from the convoy, to help a force to cross the sea in darkness and formate on the flares allowing them to attack just as dawn was rising. It was used by the North Coates wing in August 1943, in conjunction with Wellington bombers, but became particularly useful against axis ships in Norwegian waters which

34   Christina Goulter, *A Forgotten Offensive*, pp. 200-203.

would often turn into a fjord as dawn broke. German merchant shipping along the Norwegian coasts had always been an important target for Coastal Command and increased in priority following the invasion of Normandy and the clearance of the French, Belgian and Dutch coasts.

By 1944 Beaufighters were increasingly being replaced by Mosquitoes as strike aircraft and the torpedo was being phased out as less useful in the close confines of the fjords. Rockets were used far more frequently, including a new J-class solid-shot, streamlined rocket which not only had a greater range but could travel 180 feet under water. This was very important if the aircraft was going to be able to climb over the mountains at the head of the fjord, where the ships were usually moored right up against the cliffs. One Beaufighter pilot described the difficulties in hitting these targets:

> One needed to approach any ship moored alongside a cliff ideally from the land side and pass out over the mouth of the fiord towards the open sea if surprise was to be maintained. This method often meant skipping over a bloody steep mini-mountain first, instantly dive into the fiord, line up and fire within seconds, then bank like hell to avoid spreading oneself all over the cliff sides. We usually made such attacks – when possible in very close single file, which often meant having to fly through a hail of rock splinters and ricocheting cannon shells and bullets fired by the Beau immediately in front. I had two windscreens smashed by 'friendly' cannon shells bouncing off the cliffs as I passed over my target. Another danger was from the fire of the Beau behind you during any attack. If its skipper was a sprog on operations of this kind he was liable to start firing too soon – which gave me very loose bowels on occasion.[35]

As 1944 progressed more and more Mosquitoes became available to the strike wings, who were also issued with the TseTse Mosquito which was equipped with a 6-pounder gun. This was an enormous gun, weighing nearly a ton, but it was highly accurate, and the Tse Tse Mosquito could also be equipped with eight rockets as well. The recoil of the 6-pounder gun was immense and always dramatic when fired:

> At about 1,200 yards or thereabouts, slight pressure on the gun button resulted in a simultaneous blast and flash visible from the cockpit. My navigator, sitting on my right and slightly to the rear, looked stunned. Dust and debris from the floor mixed with blue-grey fumes, sprang into the sunlight. The spring mounted flight instrumental panel danced against its stops. The instruments were unreadable. The aircraft seemed to pause in the air and I was thrown forward against the safety harness. The mayhem was multiplied many times as the feed mechanism shovelled in the shells at a rate of one every 1.5 seconds. I thought the wooden wonder would never stay glued together.[36]

Though fast and well equipped the Mosquitoes were not indestructible. The 15 January 1945 would become known as Black Monday for the strike wings and witnessed the second largest air battle over Norway. A Mosquito pilot, who wished to remain anonymous, recorded in his diary the following account of the Banff wing's attack on the little harbour of Leirvik and the clutch of merchant ships and escorts in its fjord:

---

35   Chaz Bowyer, *Beaufighter*, p. 90.
36   Andrew D. Bird, *A Separate Little War – The Banff Coastal Command Strike Wing versus the Kriegsmarine and Luftwaffe 1944-45* (London: Grubb Street, 1993), p. 28.

Picturesque Norwegian fjords hitherto untouched by the war became a battleground as the strike wings sought out enemy vessels lurking in them during the last months of hostilities. Three beaufighters from the Dallachy Wing are seen here attacking enemy vessels sheltering beneath the 3,000ft cliffs of Sognefjord on 23 April 1945. The freighter D/S Ingerseks was sunk and a couple of flak ships strafed with cannon fire. (Crown Copyright – Air Historical Branch)

We made the approach from the north-west. There was lots of snow and everything looked bleak. I watched Maurice go down to attack and Freddie [Lt Alexandre] kept our section well to the left, leaving me to have a clear run in on a TTA [Trawler Type Auxiliary]. The leading sections had fixed the main target well. I saw Tony Hawkey's rockets go and there was a considerable explosion on the TTA as the boiler room blew up. I released my rockets too early and would score only underwater hits …

Then I turned my cannons onto a horrible 'M' Class that was pumping all forms of flak at us. I remember one red lump bursting just a few yards in front and above of us. There was no way out except to go between an island and the shore, both were firing at us. Consequently, we passed over the 'M' Class at mast height. I just kept pressing the gun firing button all the time; we could see our rounds knocking pieces off his bridge and superstructure; anyway, it made them keep their heads down! Clear of the ship, I broke to port and lost the remaining few feet down onto the water, weaving as hard as I could. Maurice's order after his 'Attack, Attack, Attack' was to break to port. This I did and found myself all alone flying up a fjord in a northerly direction, with high mountains on either side. I saw a gap between two of the mountains on the left, and realised if we continued up the fjord, we would find ourselves in Bergen. I climbed at full throttle just managing to go through the gap and dived down the other side.

While climbing through the mountains I heard a 235 Squadron aircraft call up and say he was on one motor, and this was followed by Freddie saying 'Alright, I will keep with you.' We crossed out over the coast just south of Marsten Light, and went straight into a huge snow cloud, groping our way through the maze of flakes. As I cleared the snowstorm and continued westwards the voice of Maurice came up: 'Bandits, get together everyone.' Just ahead I saw another Mosquito; he formed up as my No.2 and then another one joined us making a section. I decided that this dogfight would develop just about where we had crossed out, (i.e. on the northern side of the snowstorm). Hence, I took my section back to the coast looking for trouble. On the way Maurice's voice came over very cool, calm and deep: 'Help, help, help, I am being heavily attacked.'

We again found the coast and I circled with the section formatting on me but saw no signs of any other aircraft. We were truly mystified. Then over the air came Fitch's voice, 'I'm badly hit and need escort and assistance. Please protect my tail somebody,' My navigator Tom suggested a south-westerly course from the coast where we had been waiting, which skirted us around the snow and in the rough direction of home. On the way out, we saw a large fishing fleet, and my No. 3 'Wally' Woodcock went over and photographed it to check for 'squealers' [radio masts]. After 15 minutes or so away from the coast I called up Fitch and said, 'Now you are clear, fire a cartridge to see if we can locate you.' This he did, and at about 2,000 feet and a couple of miles ahead I saw him and the starburst. We climbed up and formated, then reassured him he had an escort of four other Mosquitoes. A Norwegian then joined us, one of the outriders. I then chatted to Fitch about his damaged ailerons and tails telling him what course to steer … We all got home all right landing in 2,500-yard visibility.[37]

The Banff wing was to lose five Mosquitoes on Black Monday and whilst the harbour of Leirvik was bristling with AA fire it was the arrival of *9 Staffel* and its Fw 190 A and F aircraft at the nearby airfield at Herdla that was to cause the majority of the Wing's casualties. Although the Mosquito was fast, well-armed and manoeuvrable, it was particularly vulnerable whilst concentrating on its anti-shipping strike and needed a top cover of fighter escorts to protect it. By 1944, RAF Mustang aircraft had the range to get to Norway when fitted with drop tanks, usually refuelling at the Shetland Island airbase of Sumburgh to top up the aircraft's tanks on the way. Kaz Kijak served with 315 (Polish) Squadron on Mustang Mk IIIs, he had flown bomber escorts, as well as strike missions in the run up to the Normandy invasion, as well as on D-Day itself. In November his squadron was moved to Peterhead to support Mosquito and Beaufighter anti-shipping strikes over Norway:

> I found escorting Mosquitoes a bit more pleasant than escorting the Beaufighters simply because the Mosquito flew faster, around 240 mph instead of the Beau's 180, making the Mustang's controls much firmer. Secondly, that blasted awful trip took less time, although I am surprised when looking at my log-book on 13 December 1944, to find that a trip to Molde with the Mosquitoes took only 10 minutes less. I have an idea that we loitered in the target areas with the Mosquitoes who were looking for additional things to hit. The Dallachy crews were just in and out on the one pass. If the weather was good, which was rare, we used to like to hang around a bit and make sure the Beaufighters got away safely and we would try to find something German to shoot at. We could just about double their speed and so could afford to let them get away from us. With the Mosquitoes, we did not have such a great speed advantage and so we couldn't let them get too far away. At the target we tended to sit high over the coast and watch for fighters while they did their business on the flakships and merchantmen. More usually, the weather was pretty poor and so we just stuck like glue to either the Banff or Dallachy aircraft so we wouldn't get lost.

---

37   Andrew D. Bird, *A Separate Little War*, p. 95.

We were all on the deck under the radar and we headed to our primary target via Sumburgh Island. We always hung behind and out to the sides of our charges, just out of their prop washes. These were long, stressful yet boring and usually quite cold flights. I was quite thankful that the manufacturers of the Mustangs had included heaters, which I put to good use. Even more useful was the ashtray, which the Americans had so thoughtfully provided although you had to supply your own lighters and cigars. At the beginning of every flight we were issued with 10 Woodbines which came in very handy. Flying along at around 200mph was like walking for us, so a smoke was a nice diversion. We were also given a small packet of sardine sandwiches for every flight. On the long flights, those sandwiches kept the wolves in our stomachs at bay and gave us something to do. Unfortunately, the Germans never invited us down for a drink to cap off the afternoon.

I only once had need to use the piss funnel also fitted by those thoughtful North American designers but that was on a Beau raid. Using it in flight was quite a feat in its own right. I remember bursting and couldn't hold on any longer, so I pulled away to port, still at 50 feet and unbuckled all my harnesses. Then with the stick between my knees, undid my fly and with one hand dug around inside my pants until I found my own little hose and exposed it to the passing seagulls. I pulled the funnel over into my lap and let loose. What a blessed relief! Being that low there was plenty of moisture around, so the side of the plane got a wash before our mechanics had to work on it. Then it was the whole process in reverse with the trickiest bit being buckling my harness back on. That was a two-handed job with the stick back between my knees ...

Once they found the target we'd pop up a few thousand feet, weather permitting, and keep our eyes peeled for trouble coming out from land ... On one of these trips we were just tootling along when my engine coughed and died. At 50 feet and 180 mph in a Mustang, that's a dire situation. I glanced at my wing tanks and noted one had just dropped off. With some consternation I flicked the fuel switch over to the main tank and hit the booster pump. With prayers to the god of ground crews, I thanked them all sincerely as the motor responded and I could pull away from the cold sea. Afterwards my friends told me that they saw the wash from my prop on the sea as I recovered. I count myself as fortunate that ever since I had been flying I had rehearsed such a situation in my head and was subconsciously ready for it. Only a couple of weeks later, the same thing happened to a Flight Lieutenant, but he went in and was killed.[38]

Whether it was 2 Group's original anti-shipping strikes in 1941, or the Mosquitoes of the Banff wing in 1945, the anti-shipping strikes conducted by the British were hazardous right up until the end of the War. Though tactics, techniques and weaponry were constantly improved, as was the supporting intelligence, there are still questions to be answered about how effective these operations really were. In the Mediterranean the issue seems relatively clear cut and Rommel's obvious supply problems are well documented. In the Far East too the anti-shipping capability was important in both blunting the Japanese offensive edge and then subsequently increasing their difficulties in holding their defensive ring of islands.

In Northern Europe the issue over anti-shipping success is more controversial. Immediately after the war the British Bombing Survey Unit's sea communications panel, established that minelaying was the most cost-effective way of destroying a ship. From April 1940 to May 1945 Gardening operations accounted for 638 enemy vessels, with the loss of 450 RAF aircraft in the process, in contrast direct attacks on shipping resulted in the loss of 857 aircraft but only 366 vessels were

---

38   Andrew D. Bird, *A Separate Little War*, p. 70.

Oblique aerial photograph showing Bristol Beaufighters of the Dallachy strike wing diving into the steep-sided Risnesfjord to attack a merchant vessel, smoke and spray from rocket projectiles fired by the photographing aircraft, and cannon fire from the other Beaufighters, have almost obscured the target, which was left listing and on fire. (Crown Copyright – Air Historical Branch)

sunk[39](Annex X also provides further details of enemy surface vessels destroyed in the Atlantic and North West European waters by RAF Aircraft 1939-45). However, that long time period ignores the improvements that the strike wings were able to make from 1943 onwards, as well as the wider impact and disruption on German shipping patterns caused by direct strikes, such as forcing enemy convoys to travel only at night. The two approaches should probably best be seen as complementary, rather than competing alternatives. Perhaps more interestingly the Bombing

---

39   Christina Goulter, *A Forgotten Offensive*, p. 297.

Survey Unit compared the man hour months lost when an average sized German vessel was sunk (3,000-man months for the vessel and 400-man months for its cargo) to the man hours expended by the Coastal Command aircraft to sink it (2,500-man months on average although each type of strike varied).[40]

Whilst this might point to an attritional success, the Survey Unit was still circumspect on whether the strategic advantage gained through the interdiction of iron ore had been achieved. Post-War analysis highlighted that the Ministry of Economic Warfare's proposition that cutting off Swedish iron ore imports would create a decisive impact on Germany's war machine was flawed, as it rested on two false premises. First, that the German war machine was fully mobilised and on a war footing, which it would not be until the end of 1942 and secondly that Coastal Command had the necessary resources and techniques to carry out the role properly in the face of strong German resistance. This was not to occur until the strike wings were properly set up in 1943. When the anti-shipping campaign did begin to get into its stride the effect on German shipping was marked but 1943 was too late to make a fundamental strategic difference to the war.[41] The anti-shipping strikes highlight the challenge military leaders always face in determining whether the intended results from a proposed operation or campaign are worth the risk and cost that may have to be paid. Canadian Ernest Raymond Davey was a Beaufighter pilot, with 404 RCAF Squadron of the Banff wing, his aircraft was downed in a mid-air collision in 1944. After his death his comrades found the poem below amongst his effects and it was initially pinned to the operations room door. It is also on the memorial stone to 'Black Friday' in Fordefjord in which nine Beaufighters and a Mustang were shot down on 9 February 1945:

Almighty and all present power,
Short is the prayer I make to thee;
I do not ask in battle hour
For any shield to cover me.

The vast unalterable way,
From which the stars do not depart,
May not be turned aside to stay
The bullet flying through my heart.

I ask no help to strike my foe;
I seek no petty victory here;
The enemy I hate, I know
To thee is dear.

But this I pray, be at my side,
When death is drawing through the sky;
Almighty Lord, who also died
Teach me the way that I should die

---

40   Christina Goulter, *A Forgotten Offensive*, p. 299.
41   Christina Goulter, *A Forgotten Offensive*, pp. 302-303.

19

'I Seek Higher Things'[1]
The Fleet Air Arm's War –
Ships and Aircraft

Parsimony appeared to characterise all aspects of British maritime air operations during the Second World War, but whilst Coastal Command might consider themselves the 'Cinderella Service' they could at least take comfort from the fact that even Cinderella had a fairy godmother. The Fleet Air Arm seems to have had no such luck, certainly not between the wars where Naval aviation had been an un-wanted arm within the Royal Air Force, retained not for any belief in maritime air power, but rather a Trenchardian insistence that the RAF must control everything that flew. The attitude in the Air Ministry between the wars was that maritime aviation came a distant third in priority of effort, after both the land fighter and the strategic bomber.[2] This may have stemmed from the lack of Royal Naval Air Service officers in the senior ranks of the RAF. The few that existed, Bowhill, D'Albaic and Peirse for instance, were vastly outnumbered by their former Royal Flying Corps colleagues, which may have prevented maritime aviation issues being given the prominence they deserved.

The Royal Navy succeeded in wrenching back administration of the Fleet Air Arm in 1937 with full control granted in the Inskip Award of 1939. This decision also kept Coastal Command, as part of the RAF, a situation that split key elements of maritime aviation apart. It stands in contrast to the Japanese and American practise where land based maritime patrol aircraft were part of their naval air components. Prior to the Inskip Award, inter-service rivalry over possession of the Fleet Air Arm had hindered development of aircraft, weapons, training, expansion and overall organisational design. In the lean years between the wars there was not only an absence of powerful voices in the RAF to speak on behalf of the Fleet Air Arm, there were also no serious advocates within the Royal Navy, including no senior officer naval pilots either afloat or ashore and no Admiral with a flying background.[3] This was a grave weakness given that the specifications for naval aircraft originated from the Admiralty. The general lack of knowledge of maritime aviation amongst Royal Navy officers was often combined with scepticism and downright hostility about the potential of air power in a coming war. Views that the power of maritime aviation was over-stated were not uncommon, as one Commander-in-Chief, writing in 1936, put it:

> My general impression is that we are heading for a very ambitious carrier programme and we may be rating the carrier's value in War too high, in view of the fact that its power of

---

1   The motto of HMS *Hermes*, the world's first ship to be designed as an aircraft carrier. Launched in 1919 she served in the Mediterranean and China station as well as home waters. She was sunk by the Japanese off Ceylon on 8 April – 307 men were lost during the sinking.

2   Corelli Barnett, *Engage the Enemy More Closely*, p. 39.

3   John Winton, *Find, Fix and Strike! The Fleet Air Arm at War 1939-45* (London: Batsford Books, 1980), p. 1.

hitting and destroying the enemy is not in measuring distance of the power possessed by other vessels.[4]

This was all in striking contrast to the view, held by many during the First World War including the First Sea Lord, Lord Fisher, that it would be the aeroplane and the submarine that would dominate future maritime wars. As all its First World War aviation talent later transferred to the RAF, or left altogether, the Royal Navy view that prevailed between the wars was that maritime aviation and carriers were there solely for air defence of the fleet or distant reconnaissance.[5] The concept of the carrier aircraft as a strike weapon in its own right was not widely accepted, the dominating thought was that their chief tactical use was to damage and slow down enemy ships so that the main battle fleet could then overhaul and dispatch them.[6] Underestimating the power of maritime aviation also led the Royal Navy to overrate the effectiveness of their own defences, the gunnery branch in particular believed that the power of the fleet's own guns would not allow a hostile aircraft to approach close enough to do them real damage. Such optimism was certainly not borne out by the standard of Royal Navy AA gunnery directed at towed drogues. During one trial in 1937 a Queen Bee radio-controlled drone circled the fleet for two and a half hours, totally unscathed by the Fleet's fire. The Fleet's AA armament might look impressive on paper, but its High Angled Control System for directing fire was hopeless and certainly no match for equivalent American systems.[7]

Royal Navy ships were to pay a heavy price for such optimism, the battering from the air that the Mediterranean fleet received off Crete in May 1941 is illustrative. In what was perfect shooting weather well over 200,000 tons of merchant shipping was sunk, two Battleships and one carrier (HMS *Formidable*), were severely damaged, three cruisers and six destroyers sunk and six cruisers and seven destroyers more or less severely damaged. The sinking of the *Repulse* and the *Prince of Wales* also sent shock waves around the Royal Navy. For some, these events proved their pre-war predictions over air power's potency were correct, a substantial number of this group included members of the Fleet Air Arm and their differing operational views regularly put them at odds with their Lordships at the Admiralty, or even senior officers afloat.[8] For these reasons, Fleet Air Arm officers would often view themselves as outsiders within their own service, not an enviable position to be in, but it forced a close-knit sense of identity, that saw them through some of the most dangerous phases of the War.

Given this background it is not surprising that the development of British aircraft carriers prior to the war was haphazard. This was partly because of a confused British view of the potentials of carrier aviation, but also because of the economies of the 1920s and the limits of the Washington Naval Treaty of 1922, which was specifically designed to scale back defence spending and avoid a naval arms race. The Washington Treaty imposed strict tonnage limits on aircraft carriers; Britain and America were permitted a total of 135,000 tons each, the Japanese 81,000 tons and the French and Italian navies 60,000 tons apiece. Signatory countries were limited to no more than two carriers with a displacement of more than 27,000 tons and no individual ship could exceed 32,000 tons. Britain had developed carriers during the First World War, most notably *Argus,* a converted Italian liner, which would be used largely as a training ship in the Second World War and *Vindictive* which was based on a Hawkins Class cruiser and only taken out of service in 1928.

Immediately after the First World War *Eagle* was launched, based on the hull of an incomplete Chilean battleship, the *Almirante Cochrane.* In September 1919, *Hermes* too was launched and

---

4   John Winton, *Find, Fix and Strike!*, p. 1.
5   Corelli Barnett, *Engage the Enemy More Closely*, p. 39.
6   John Winton, *Find, Fix and Strike!*, p. 1.
7   Corelli Barnett, *Engage the Enemy More Closely*, p. 39.
8   John Hoare, *Tumult in the Clouds – A Story of The Fleet Air Arm* (London: Michael Joseph, 1976), p. 17.

HMS *Indomitable*, two Sea Hurricanes can be seen on the outriggers on the starboard side of the ship.
(Crown Copyright – Air Historical Branch)

was one of the first ships to be laid down as an aircraft carrier, including having an island on the starboard side of the hull. Most, but not all, carriers had islands fitted on the starboard side, the gyroscopic effect of early rotary powered aircraft made them much easier to turn left, rather than right, so a starboard island therefore facilitated a left-hand approach to landing and was safer.

Britain also converted two *Courageous* Class battlecruisers into carriers. These aircraft carriers were ideal, the superstructure was cut down at Rosyth and built up again in Devonport dock-yard. Everything above the main deck was removed and two large hangers added, the top hanger leading onto a flying off deck through two lifts which pierced the deck. The 550-foot flight deck did not run the entire length of the ship, instead there was a small quarter deck at the stern and also a forecastle overlooked by the flight deck, which sloped upwards at the bow to assist take-off. *Courageous* was brought into service in 1928 and *Glorious* in 1930. Modifications were added over the next decade, including arrester gear for increasingly heavy aircraft, as well as improved AA armaments. The two carriers were fast and carried 48 aircraft, though this was still less than their American and Japanese counterparts.[9] *Courageous* was sunk off Ireland by a U-boat within the first two weeks of the war, *Glorious* was also destroyed by the *Scharnhorst* in 1940, whilst steaming back from Norway.

---

9   Angus Kostam, *British Aircraft Carriers 1939-45* (Oxford: Osprey, 2010), pp. 9-10.

Good though *Glorious* and *Courageous* were, it was HMS *Ark Royal*, commissioned in 1938, which became the first modern Royal Navy purpose-built aircraft carrier. It was, at the time, the most expensive ship ever constructed for the Navy (close to £3 million). The carrier set the benchmark for future British carrier design and included a number of unique features. For a start the flight deck was to be the main structural deck of the ship, on previous ships the strength deck for aircraft carriers had existed below the hangars and flight deck on the original warship's deck. In *Ark Royal* the strength deck, hangars and flight deck would form one integrated whole. The ship's AA fire was also properly integrated into the design, with the guns mounted high up at the level of the flight deck, so that they had a good field of fire. The armament consisted of eight twin-mounted 4.5-inch guns and six eight-barrelled 2-pdr pom-poms. The carrier had two hangar levels, giving her space for 60 aircraft and the 800 ft long and 94 ft wide flight deck was equipped with three small lifts, all set slightly off the deck's centreline to avoid compromising its strength. The carrier had a number of arrestor wires that ran across the deck, landing lights for receiving aircraft in poor visibility, or at night, as well as a radio homing beacon mounted on the mast to guide returning aircraft. Two accelerators, or catapults as we would call them now, were fitted to the bow of the ship and enabled heavily loaded aircraft to take-off in conditions of light wind. The ship could manage a relatively high speed of 32 knots and had a double skinned hull to suppos-edly protect her against torpedo attack – it did not. Indeed the three parallel rooms containing the boilers and engines were vulnerable to flooding, which would ultimately prove the carrier's undoing in November 1941 when she was sunk by U-81 near Gibraltar.[10]

By 1936 the Royal Navy began to wake up to the threat that land-based aircraft might pose to the fleet. Two more carriers were laid down, but given growing Admiralty fears, a greater level of protection was thought necessary and the new *Illustrious* Class carriers were to have armoured flight decks able to withstand a direct hit by a 500lb bomb. In order not to make the carrier too top heavy the vessels would only have one hangar level as opposed to two, which drastically reduced the amount of aircraft that could be carried to only 36. This is in stark contrast to both the *Ark Royal*'s 60 and the wooden-decked American carriers such as the *Lexington* and *Saratoga* (commissioned 1938-39), which were able to carry up to 90 aircraft. Even the Japanese *Hiryu* and *Soryu* were able to carry 60 aircraft. These larger complements perhaps reflected those nation's view that the ability of carrier borne air-power in establishing favourable air superiority and striking opposing fleets was the main purpose of the aircraft carrier, therefore they should be designed to carry and fly the maximum number of aircraft.[11] In contrast the Royal Navy were placing greater emphasis on the *Illustrious* Class as a ship able to preserve itself from attack, partly by means of its well armoured hull (4 1/2 inches thick) and flight deck (3 inches thick). Royal Navy doctrine was that the carrier's defence under close attack should be to stow all aircraft below and turn the ship into an armoured shelter. Though the decks were able to shrug off attacks on many occasions, the penalty that had to be paid was in reduced air power for either achieving air superiority, fleet protection or for maritime strike operations. The arguments are finely balanced – certainly the ability of the British armoured fleet carriers to stand up to kamikaze attacks in the Pacific stands in contrast to the American carriers' vulnerability. As some have argued it may well be impressive to carry more aircraft, but is the advantage that great if there is no ship to land them on at the end of the mission?

The *Illustrious* Class ships were to include *Victorious*, *Formidable*, *Indomitable* as well as *Illustrious* herself. The ships were well equipped with both AA weapons and a variety of radars for warning as well as height finding. Arrestor wires and hydraulic catapults were also fitted, together with a

---

10   Angus Kostam, *British Aircraft Carriers 1939-45*, pp. 13-14.
11   Corelli Barnett, *Engage the Enemy More Closely*, p. 40.

A photograph taken during Operation PEDESTAL 3 – 12 August 1942, showing the deck of HMS *Victorious* with Sea Hurricanes and Albacores and HMS *Indomitable* and *Eagle* in the background. (Crown Copyright – Air Historical Branch)

barrier landing system which would bring to a stop any aircraft that missed the arrestor wires. The barrier was essentially a wire net and hitting it usually resulted in minor damage to the aircraft and sometimes pilot, though this was still preferable to running into parked aircraft. It also provided an important degree of safety for the flight deck ground crew working forward of the barrier. During their wartime service outriggers were developed for the carriers, which allowed more aircraft to be carried on deck by extending the deck space through rails for tail wheels that jutted out from the edge of the flight deck. This increased the aircraft capacity from 36 to 52 and was essential for aircraft such as the Seafire, initial variants of which did not have folding wings and were therefore too big for the lifts that would take them down to the hangers. The last of the armoured carriers to be built (*Implacable* and *Indefatigable*) were derivatives of the *Illustrious* class but had reduced side armour and incorporated a second hangar which brought their capacity up to a more respectable 81 aircraft apiece. These two later ships were commissioned in the summer of 1944 and saw service in the Home and Pacific Fleets.[12] Fleet Air Arm pilot, Hugh Popham recollects the layout of *Indomitable*:

> The essence of the ship, her brain and nerves, are housed in the island. Tucked away on the starboard side, streamlined, threaded with narrow passages and steep metal ladders, it contains the Compass Platform from which the Captain handles the ship; Commander Flying's position, a narrow gallery with an uninterrupted view of the flight deck; the Admiral's bridge, the Fighter Direction Office, the Air Operations Room and the Signal Bridge. It embraces the

---

12   Angus Kostam, *British Aircraft Carriers 1939-45*, p. 22.

funnel and supports the radar aerials, and contains, besides all these, the Pilots Ready Room, the hot little box with one scuttle which is our refuge when waiting to fly.

The armoured table-top of the flight deck runs away for'ard and aft. It is bare but for the arrestor wires and the barriers that traverse it, and the innumerable ring-bolts for lashing down aircraft. Surrounding it for the greater part of its length are the nets, narrow walkways below the level of the deck-coaming where the flight deck party crouch out of the wind and where all manner of equipment from fire-extinguishers to chocks lives or is slung. Here, on the port side, the Batsman has his perch and screen, and the Flight Deck Engineer his controls for raising and lowering the wires and barriers. The nets terminate fore and aft with the twin turrets of the twin 4.5's the ship's main anti-aircraft armament. The tops of the turrets project a foot or two above the level of the deck.

There are two lifts. The for'ard is the only one big enough to take a Hurricane – and then only athwartships – and communicates with the upper hangar, which we share with the Fulmar Squadron and one of the two Albacore squadrons. The after-lift serves both upper and lower hangars. The upper hangar runs the length of the ship from lift to lift, a hollow echoing steel box which is the headquarters of the squadrons' non-flying activities. It is garage work-shop with points for petrol, oil, compressed air and power for the tools; and about it, through innumerable watertight doors and lobbies, are grouped the endless cubby-holes that ships, and squadrons need for their well-being: squadron stores, battery charging rooms, black-smith's shop, paint store, dope-store, bosun's stores, engineering and electrical workshops and the squadron offices. It is two full decks high, and among the arrestor gear machinery in the deckhead are sprays that can flood it from end to end in case of fire. Spare mainplanes and propellers are clamped to the bulkhead like trophies.

The aircraft are parked almost touching; the Hurricanes in echelon up the starboard side, the Fulmars up the port side, and the Albacores with the whole of the after end to themselves. To prevent them getting adrift, they are chocked fore and aft and lashed down with wire lash-ings. These are so arranged that it is almost impossible to take more than three steps without tripping over one. The air has a dead, flat taste, and stinks of oil and petrol; and this smell a sickly, cloying smell, seems to condense on to the metal surfaces of the deck and the aircraft and the tools in a tacky, black film.

This is where the maintenance ratings, fitters, riggers, electricians and radio mechanics spend most of their time.

Amidships, one of the watertight doors leads out through a lobby and a second door to a ladder up to the island; and another aft; down to the cabin flats and the wardroom. Others give access to the weather decks where the ship's boats are stowed, and where there is fresh air and the sea sluicing past and the paintwork carries a bloom of salt.

The hangar and the flight deck and their appurtenances are the domain of the Air Department; they take their shape and situation from the ship, but their function and charac-ter from the aircraft. Only on the Compass Platform, or among the capstans and cables on the enclosed foc'c'sle under the for'ard round down, on the narrow, cluttered weather decks or on the quarter deck with its bell and brightwork and gratings, right aft and far below the flight deck, where at 26 knots the vibration makes one's teeth chatter is the ship's other essence expressed. It is there, nevertheless. For before she is a floating aerodrome, she is a ship, with the beauty of a ship, and a ship's particular, apprehensible character.[13]

---

13   Hugh Popham, *Sea Flight*, p. 61.

A Grumman Martlet of 888 Squadron, Fleet Air Arm with its wings folded being brought up in the lift for ranging on board HMS *Formidable*. (Crown Copyright – Air Historical Branch)

Wartime conditions on aircraft carriers varied, though the accommodation was frequently cramped and the segregation between officers and ratings strictly enforced. The officers would usually have a cabin shared with a few others, but for ratings the accommodation frequently meant a hammock in a large mess deck. Whilst an RAF air station would revolve entirely round the needs of the aircraft and aircrew, the prejudice on some ships against the Fleet Air Arm made life very difficult for the aircrew. Furthermore, though the sea crew of a ship like *Illustrious* would always remain on board, the Fleet Air Arm Squadrons were more transient and would be moved on and off different ships as operational demands dictated. Rather than take the approach that the aircraft carrier's sole reason for existence was to support these squadrons and their aircraft, the permanent crew instead took the view that, as temporary members of the ship, the Fleet Air Arm should put up with the poorer accommodation.[14] The ratings in particular suffered unduly from this lack of hospitality. As one example meal times were usually rigidly enforced and if the rating was away on a patrol, he might miss out altogether. Fresh water availability was frequently a problem on some of the older ships, though salt water showers and salt water soap were available. There were of course some comforts, the officers did enjoy the wardroom, where duty free alcohol and tobacco made the young pilot's money stretch a little further and gin was the ubiquitous drink. For those

---

14   Hank Adlam, *On and off the Flight Deck – Recollections of A Naval Fighter Pilot in World War II* (Barnsley: Pen and Sword, 2007), p. 71.

interested in such things, Plymouth Gin was the most popular brand, though after its distillery was badly bombed, the drink apparently had a peculiar taste of methylated spirits and some ships switched to Gordons.[15]

The six aircraft carriers constructed in the 1936-39 building programme were an impressive investment by the Royal Navy and further ships would be constructed during the war. Even after the loss of *Courageous, Eagle, Glorious, Hermes* and *Ark Royal,* the Royal Navy were still able to generate a powerful carrier fleet for action in the Pacific at the end of the War (a full list of British Carriers in Service with the Royal Navy throughout the Second World War is contained at Annex Y). Disappointingly, this investment in ships was not matched by similar efforts on aircraft, consequently the Fleet Air Arm started the war with a collection of machines that were pitifully obsolete. This stemmed not just from a lack of investment, but also doubts that high-speed, high performance aircraft could land safely on a carrier's flight deck, together with a belief that it was possible for naval aircraft to have a poorer performance than land-based aircraft, or that existing land-based aircraft could be easily modified to land on carriers. Bespoke naval designs were few and those that were produced by the British aviation industry throughout the war did not reflect well on the designers, manufacturers or those who commissioned them. This was in stark contrast to the American carrier aviation programme, which produced excellent aircraft of all types, many of which were subsequently operated by a grateful Fleet Air Arm in the war.

A typical example of the poor quality of British-designed aircraft, with which the Fleet Air Arm would initially have to fight, was the Fairey Fulmar. This obsolescent aircraft was brought into service in September 1940, to fulfil the Fleet Air Arm's role of air defence of the fleet, it was therefore intended to battle with German, Italian and Japanese land-based aircraft who easily out-matched it in speed, manoeuvrability, firepower and often range. John Hoare, an Observer on Fulmars during 1941, served on *Victorious* and was frank on his opinion of the aircraft:

> The Fulmars in which we flew were of the Mark I variety with a maximum speed of 250 mph at 10,000 feet using a Merlin VIII engine. It was like so many of our aircraft adapted from an RAF design. The original specification at Fairey's had been as a high-speed light bomber to supplement the obsolete Battle from the same firm. It would have been adequate for purely naval functions but was at every disadvantage when engaged with land-based fighters. It was heavy, its loaded weight being about five long tons and not very manoeuvrable. It had a slow rate of climb, 15 minutes to 12,000 feet, and it had no guns in the rear cockpit, which cost the squadrons very dear. The aircrews did not think too highly of them, but they did make 112 kills in two years which was a tribute to the pilots.[16]

The contempt with which Fleet Air Arm pilots held the Fairey Fulmar was subsequently expressed in a piece of doggerel verse:

> *Any old iron, any old iron*
> *Any, any, any old iron*
> *Talk about a treat*
> *Chasing round the Fleet,*
> *Any old Eyetie or Hun you meet!*
> *Weighs six ton*
> *No rear gun*

---

15   John Hoare, *Tumult in the Clouds – A Story of The Fleet Air Arm* (London: Michael Joseph, 1976), p. 141.
16   John Hoare, *Tumult in the Clouds*, p. 87.

Damn all to rely on!
You know what you can do
With your Fulmar Two
Old iron, old iron![17]

The Fulmar would gradually be replaced by a number of aircraft in the air superiority role, including the Grumman F4F Wildcat, an excellent machine and one of the most outstanding Navy fighters of the war. The British initially renamed it the Martlet – this confusing Royal Navy tendency to give already named US aircraft a British identity, would cease as the war progressed, from January 1944 the name Martlet was dropped and replaced with Wildcat. The Fulmar would also be replaced by the less successful Sea Hurricane and Seafire, which were simply adaptations of existing RAF aircraft. The idea of taking a superb fighter like the Spitfire and converting it for carrier use might seem a perfectly practical proposition, but the Seafire story was not a happy experience for the Fleet Air Arm.

The Seafire, was entirely unsuitable for carrier operations. In essence it was a normal Spitfire with a hook for deck-landing, but the narrow track of its undercarriage, as well as the aircraft's overall fragility made the Seafire unable to cope with the constant stresses of carrier landings. The large wooden propeller constantly shattered from striking the deck, it had a very limited range, small bomb load and its speed was reduced with the extra weight of the hook, making it not much faster than a Wildcat, but with less fire power. The in-line engine, with scoop-type coolers under the wings, also made a successful 'ditching' difficult. Furthermore, although a beautiful aircraft to fly, it tended to 'float' over the wires when the engine was cut, making it a difficult machine to land on a small space.[18] In the opinion of many pilots, the Seafire's overall unsuitability seriously injured, or killed, many pilots during the course of the war.[19]

As the war progressed, the Fleet Air Arm became equipped with another large, fast American fighter, the Chance Vought F4U Corsair. This was a truly fearsome looking machine. With its distinctive 'gull wings' and large radial engine, it radiated power and had a speed of over 400 mph and range of 1,100 miles, far in excess of the performance of existing Fleet Air Arm fighters. It possessed four 0.5-inch machine guns and an advanced hydraulic system that did useful things at the touch of a button, such as automatically folding the wings as well as lowering the under-carriage and hook. It was initially not an easy aircraft to fly off carriers, for its under-carriage had a built in oleo 'bounce' which was only rectified after many US Navy accidents. Its exceptionally long engine cowling also dramatically restricted visibility to the pilot on landing, which meant his approach had to be in a controlled but steep port hand turn, so that the pilot could see the batsman over the port side engine cowling.[20]

As well as fighters, the Fleet Air Arm also possessed Torpedo Strike Reconnaissance (TSR) or Torpedo Bomber Reconnaissance Aircraft (TBR). These included the Fairey Swordfish, a biplane aircraft that looked so ungainly and Heath Robinson, it almost defies belief that it was a serious weapon of the Second World War. The Swordfish was an attempt by Fairey's to satisfy every naval requirement for an aircraft, save that of air defence of the fleet. The aircraft was designed to be capable of landing on small, pitching decks and robust and sturdy enough to shrug off carrier life. Its duties included reconnaissance at sea and over land, shadowing by day and night, 'spotting' the

17   John Hoare, *Tumult in the Clouds*, p. 87.
18   An excellent wartime video of Fleet Air Arm Seafires can be viewed at <https://www.youtube.com/watch?v=06kldAC7nus>.
19   Hank Adlam, *On and Off the Flight Deck*), p. 74.
20   John Winton, *Find, Fix and Strike!*, p. 117.

A Chance Vought Corsair fighter returning to land on board HMS *Trumpeter* with flaps and arrestor hook down. The arm and hand of the batman can be seen in the foreground. (Crown Copyright – Air Historical Branch)

fall of shot from ship's guns, convoy escort duties (including anti-submarine searches and attack), torpedo and dive-bombing attacks against shipping, minelaying – and the carrying of other heavy loads which could include rockets, depth charges and flares. The Swordfish had the exceptionally slow cruising speed of 90 knots and a top speed of just 180 knots (often described by pilots as only achievable downhill). It was basic, with none of the modern refinements such as a covered cockpit, flaps or a variable pitch airscrew. Incredibly, it was quite effective, and its slow speed and flight characteristics became strengths in their own right. Much loved by the aircrew that flew it, it became nicknamed the 'stringbag' because of the variety of items it was expected to carry.

Charles Lamb was an undoubted fan and flew Swordfish on the Taranto raid from *Illustrious*. He describes the virtues of this extraordinary aircraft that was still in operational use in 1945:

Of its many weapons the most devastating was the aerial torpedo. This weighed 1,610 lb and was capable of sinking a 10,000-ton ship within minutes of the moment of impact. To deliver this weapon in the face of intense opposition in daylight, pilots were taught to attack from a steep dive, at speeds of 180 knots and more. They have been known to reach 200 knots in that dive – in extremis – but there was then a real danger of the wings folding back or tearing off. In that headlong rush to sea level, the pilot had the impression that he was standing on the rudder bar, looking over the top of the centre-section of the upper mainplane. His face was only partially screened so that a helmet and goggles were a 'must' for all normal individuals. Those dives had to be very nearly vertical. Any modern clean-surfaced aircraft needs many thousands of feet to pull out of a dive, but the Swordfish could be eased out, with a pull-out of less than 500 feet. After straightening out and throttling back, the forward speed came right down to 90 knots very quickly, because of the drag provided by the fixed undercarriage

Fairey Swordfish on the deck of the HMS *Striker*. (Crown Copyright – Air Historical Branch)

and all the struts and wires between the mainplanes. This violent alteration in speed made the aircraft a difficult target for the gun-aimer on the ground, or in the ship being attacked, and the sudden deceleration helped the pilot to deliver his weapon very accurately.

There was a well-worn jest amongst Swordfish pilots that the enemy had no speed settings on their gunsights as low as the Stringbag's cruising speed of 90 knots, and therefore a Swordfish could only be hit by shells aimed at a flight astern. This was an exaggeration, of course, yet there was an element of uneasy truth in the statement. But the lumbering old ladies were an easy prey for a capable fighter pilot, providing he appreciated the remarkable manoeuvrability of the old biplane he was attacking.

Its defence armament was a pathetic hangover from the First World War; the Vickers gun in the front cockpit was fired by the pilot through the propeller and was all of one stage more advanced than a bow and arrow. The Lewis gun, in the rear cockpit, fired by either the air gunner or observer, had been very successfully used in the First World War but was quite useless in the Second. The sensible Swordfish pilot ignored these weapons and put his faith in his own ability to out manoeuvre the other man. Given enough height and space in which to throw the aircraft about, the Stringbag could outfly almost every other aircraft – with the possible exception of the Gladiator.

The Stringbag could be very roughly handled in incredible attitudes without stalling, providing the pilot knew what he was doing. To stall a Swordfish by mistake was almost an impossibility. Marcel Lobelle [the designer] had given the aircraft a stalling speed of 55 knots, and no pilot, however ham-fisted, could allow his speed to drop to that extent without noticing … It could be very cold in these open cockpits, strapped to one's parachute, but I always felt the deepest respect for the observer and air gunner, exposed in the rear cockpit, sitting with their heads lowered away from the slipstream, concentrating on their exacting but less exciting task of navigating or tuning the radio. They were entirely in the hands of the man in the front seat and had to rely on him to get them safely there and back. He had the excitement of delivering the weapon and avoiding the flak, while they sat helplessly in the rear cockpit, praying that he would not make a mistake. They were brave men indeed, and I would not have changed places with them for all the inducements on earth.[21]

The Swordfish was supposed to be replaced as a TBR aircraft by the Albacore, still a biplane and only 5 knots faster than the Swordfish but lacking its agility. The Albacore offered no step change in improvement but at least had a covered cockpit. Less impressive still was Fairey's later answer for a TBR machine – the Barracuda; Hugh Popham describes this abomination:

> The two TBR squadrons were equipped with Barracudas: it was our first glimpse of this extraordinary aeroplane at close quarters. It was of immense size and of truly formidable aspect, for the solution of each problem with which the designers had been faced had generated fresh problems involving fresh and elaborate solutions. Thus it had a high wing in order to give the observer and air-gunner maximum downward visibility. But to produce an undercarriage that would retract into it meant a vast structure which looked as if it had been built from components robbed from the Forth Bridge. And in order to enable the flight-deck party to handle the wings for folding – they were out of the reach of the tallest – special handles had to be provided, with tackles to give a proper purchase.
> The same massive clumsiness obtained in the design of the dive-brakes and the high set tailplane with its supporting struts; and, as if to complete the resemblance to an umbrella blown inside-out, the mainplanes were decorated with numbers of highly complicated aerials. But worst of all, the Barracuda had idiosyncrasies which were never sorted out; and soon after we joined *Illustrious* I heard with bitter sorrow that Jock, flying one straight and level at 1500 feet, had for no accountable reason got out of control and gone straight in. For all his wild ways, he was an impeccable pilot, and this accident was difficult to explain nor was his, an isolated case.[22]

There was a frequent saying amongst pilots; 'that if it looks right, it flies right' the Barracuda is strong evidence that the converse is also true, and it was deeply unpopular. In a similar manner to fighters, salvation was to come from the efficient American maritime aviation industry and by the end of the war the Fleet Air Arm was equipped with the Grumman TBF Avenger. John Wellham had spent much of his war on Fairey Swordfish, his first experience with an Avenger was in stark contrast to that aircraft:

> It was very large for a single engine aircraft and had a solid appearance. The fuselage was all metal and the wings folded hydraulically. It could carry bombs and torpedoes in a bomb bay closed by doors; there were none of the external brackets and wires that festooned the old Stringbag. Both cockpits were covered by Perspex canopies and the air gunner had a proper turret with twin machine-guns. The undercarriage was fully retractable with sturdy and well spaced wheels. The engine was a Wright R-2600-8 with variable pitch propeller, which I was told gave her a top speed of 250kts, she was comfortable when dived at well over 300kts.

Welham found the pilot's cockpit very roomy, but as in all American aircraft there were far too many dials, switches, levers and wheels. Overall, he noted the marked contrast to the dreadful British aircraft, commenting that 'it was in a different league to misfits like the Barracuda.'[23]

---

21 Charles Lamb, *War in a Stringbag* (London: Cassell, 1977), pp. 41-3.
22 Hugh Popham, *Sea Flight*, pp. 162-3.
23 John Wellham, *With Naval Wings – The Autobiography of a Fleet Air Arm Pilot in World War II* (Staplehurst: Spellmount, 2003), p. 173.

This sorry tale of poor British aircraft being gradually replaced by excellent American designs, highlights the 20-year penalty inflicted upon the Fleet Air Arm, through its reliance on the RAF for the development of its aircraft. As the war started the Fleet Air Arm could at least console itself that though it possessed a mixed bag of aircraft, it had some good ships, with more coming on line and now independence from the Royal Air Force. The Fleet Air Arm was still relatively small, having some 500 operational aircrew, some were career naval officers who had chosen the air branch in the same manner as others had chosen gunnery or signals, others were transferred from the RNR and a good many had served in the RAF. Even in 1940 there were still some 2,000 officers and men of the RAF serving in the Royal Navy, many as ground crew. As the Fleet Air Arm's wartime expansion began to kick in so too would the Fleet Air Arm bases at Donibristle, Gosport, Lee-on-Solent, Worthy Down, Ford, Yeovilton and Arbroath develop. By 1945 the Fleet Air Arm would possess 45 naval air stations world-wide, as well as 2,790 aircraft. However, there was still much for this junior branch, as well as the wider Royal Navy, to absorb about air power at sea, as the list of aircraft carriers sunk or severly damaged in the first two years of the war illustrates.[24]

British aircraft carriers and their crews had developed a highly professional method of operating aircraft from ships that was well drilled and practised. Most air sorties were pre-planned and whilst the air crew were being briefed in the crew room the mechanics and riggers would wheel the aircraft to the lift and take it up to the flight deck. There under the auspices of the Flight Deck Officer (FDO or 'Fido') the machine would be placed in its take-off position, along with the other aircraft. This was known as 'ranging' and on occasions, such as massed air strikes, the carrier would often have its entire complement of aircraft on the deck ready for take off, one after the other in the shortest space of time. The aircraft would be handed over to the pinning party, who would un-fold the wings and chock the aircraft until it was its turn to fly. The aircrew would then join the aircraft and once the FDO was content all aircraft were ready to take-off he would signal to Commander Flying in the island. At that point the ship's captain would need to turn the vessel into wind, this was to generate sufficient wind across the flight deck to assist the aircraft in taking off in a short distance. If for instance the carrier was steaming 30 knots into a 10-knot wind then a 40-knot headwind would be achieved. The Swordfish had a take-off speed of 60 miles per hour, so it would only need to accelerate to about 20 miles per hour for it to take-off. A steam jet was fitted on the flight deck at the bow of the aircraft carrier, so that the direction of wind across the Flight Deck was accurately gauged.

The carrier was an important asset and to protect the ship from U-boat attacks or other threats, it would normally be accompanied by a small escort which would protect the carrier as it deviated from the main body of the fleet. Additionally, when flying on and off there would be a destroyer or frigate, sometimes known as the 'sheepdog' in particularly close attendance. This was mainly there to rescue any aircrew that had to ditch on take-off and landings. Taking off was not without its risks, so pilots would have the cockpit hood open to help extract themselves quickly if need be. Even then, those aircraft that ditched on take-off still ran the risk of being run down by their own ship, if they were carrying depth charges (as many would on anti-submarine patrols) there was also the risk that they would be killed as these detonated at their pre-set depth. Once the aircraft were flown off they would circle the carrier until they were all present and then set off on their mission in formation.

Donald Judd was the pilot of a Grumman Avenger and recalls the take-off from *Illustrious* during the attack on Surabaya in May 1944:

---

24   John Winton, *Find, Fix and Strike!*, p. 4.

The aircraft were ranged overnight with wings folded. Fighters in front as they needed a shorter run than the bombed up Avengers. Shaken at 0500. Dressed in flying overalls and soft shoes, making sure not to carry any private papers. Butterflies in the tummy and half asleep but with a fearful realisation that this was it. God can't they cancel it? I wish I wasn't here. To the wardroom for a good breakfast of bacon and eggs, toast and coffee. Don't feel like it. Feel more like a condemned man being given the obligatory breakfast before facing the noose. No talking except for one or two who had to vent their nerves with cheap jokes – wish they would shut up.

Action Stations blaring throughout the ship. Noise and pandemonium let loose. Collect Mae West and helmet and make way to the ready room in the island. Someone says it's a fine morning. Wish it would rain. The silence of aircrews sitting emotionally and with their own thoughts is broken by the order 'Man your aircraft'.

We jump to it and race across the dawn-lit and windy flight deck to our aircraft. Up on the wings and into the cockpit. The fear is still there but it begins to take a back seat as there are now many things to do. Two groundcrew follow up the wings and help with fixing parachute harness and safety strap. Check around the cockpit, look around at the parked aircraft. Hope the engine starts, will look a proper Charlie if it doesn't as that will hold up the takeoff. There is a strange hush on deck as the fleet turns quickly into wind.

No sooner straight and Commander (Flying) from the bridge calls through the loudspeaker, 'Corsairs start up.' The silence is broken into a deafening din of 16 engines. Then 'Avengers start up' and the din is appalling.

The deck officer takes over and waves the fighters, first to the centre of the deck, wings are extended and then the first one roars along the flight deck, followed in quick succession by everyone else. God, what the hell am I doing here, is everything OK, fine pitch, wings locked – it's me now. Oh! My God, it's me. Scared stiff and shaking as I open the throttle to full but keep the brakes on. At full revs, take the toes off the brakes and start rolling. The wind over the deck makes it feel as if the aircraft is hardly moving. Pass the island and the end of the flight deck looks ominously near. I won't make it. But it's too late. I can't stop now. The heavily laden Avenger falls off the end of the deck and sinks to sea level. But she is flying. Will I clear the sea? Up wheels quickly and a jinx to starboard to clear the slipstream and gradually but ever so gradually the plane becomes stable and starts climbing. The only obviously good thing is the feeling that you're on your own away from the panic and hubbub reigning on deck. That is a relief. But now to chase the others in front to 2,000 feet for the big form up.[25]

After the aircraft and squadron had completed its appointed mission, it would need to think about returning to the carrier and much of this would depend on the observer or pilot's navigational skill. Carriers had a good radar that could detect aircraft 100 miles out, but they would rarely break radio silence and endanger their own safety to guide one wayward aircraft back. Some fleet carriers were fitted with radio beacons that helped guide pilots back, though they were temperamental and notoriously tricky to acquire. The beacon system was a little like a radio lighthouse, the ship transmitting a narrow, high frequency radio beam which rotated every 60 seconds and started its 360-degree sweep at a due north heading. This beam was displayed on a master beam chronometer in the carrier operations room, from which an observer would set his own chronometer. When in the aircraft the observer could pick up the brief signal and note the heading on his chronometer when he heard the signal. The carrier would be on a reciprocal bearing which would allow him to home in on the carrier. It sounds easy, but the radios were very hard to tune, and the process was

---

25   Donald Judd, *Avenger from the Sky* (London: William Kimber, 1985), pp. 133-134.

Ranging Corsair fighter bombers on HMS *Formidable*, July 1944. (Crown Copyright – Air Historical Branch)

more of an art than a science. At night the carrier might on occasions light a searchlight to guide aircraft back, this was clearly at some risk to herself. Unsurprisingly there were many aircraft, that as a result of poor visibility or navigational errors, never made it back to their ships and were lost to the sea. These hazards all added to the particular stress of maritime flying.

The process for landing back on was also highly organised. The aircraft would approach the carrier and adopt a circuit around it, awaiting their turn to land. The carrier would again turn to wind, sometimes just a little to starboard so that the funnel smoke and hot air was not passing across the flight deck and causing turbulence at the touchdown zone. Normally when an aircraft lands the pilot would try and maintain a significant margin above its stalling speed, but on carrier landings this was reduced to a minimum. The aircraft would also need to adopt a descent that allowed it to achieve a precise three-point landing and allow the tail hook to catch the arrestor wire, the aircraft attitude adopted to achieve this was sometimes described as forcing the aircraft to 'hang by its prop'. The final approach of the aircraft would entail the landing aircraft turning in from the port side of the carrier and controlling the machine's descent through use of his throttle, keeping his speed as slow as possible. Assisting him in this process was a Deck Landing Control Officer (DLCO) or 'batsman'. He was usually an experienced pilot himself and would advise the pilot on his approach, using his bats to indicate whether the aircraft was too high, too low, too fast or off the centre line. If the DLCO was dissatisfied with the approach, then he would wave them off and require them to re-attempt a landing, the pilot too could decide this on his own accord too. Donald Judd describes the batsman's role well:

> It may sound strange to say that landing on the deck of a carrier was easier than landing on a runway but in ideal conditions a deck landing certainly had some advantages. In the first place the landing was assisted by a deck landing officer or batsman. He stood on a platform on the after end of the flight deck on the port side. He had a safety net round his platform so that he could throw himself into it if a plane careered towards him. He had two bats like large table tennis bats which he held at arms' length and facing the approaching aircraft. When he had the bats parallel to the ground, it indicated to the pilot that he should continue as he was. Both lowered towards the ground meant, 'Descend quicker', (or you are too high). A frantic lowering of the bats meant: 'For Christ's sake get down lower and quick'. To get higher (or you are too low) was indicated by the bats held in a 'V' shape. A frantic action upwards meant, 'Bloody hell, you're going to hit the stern of the ship or worse still, go into the drink.' The batsman crossed the bats below his head to indicate 'Cut engine' or if the approach was hope-less one bat was waved round the head meaning 'Go around again and make another pass at the deck'. It was essential that the pilot obeyed the batsman's signals instantly and to the letter and if he got the 'Come on as you are' signal the aircraft would pick up Nos 1, 2 and 3 wires on the deck with his arrestor hook which trailed out behind the aircraft's tail.[26]

Not every landing was a smooth one and on smaller carriers, with narrower decks, this opera-tion was trickier for both batsman and pilot. Furthermore, if the carrier was pitching in rough seas the batsman would position himself further back along the deck and try to land the aircraft more amidships where the pitching motion of the ship was less extreme. Hugh Popham acted as a batsman and explains:

> For the pilots, a landing eight or 10 feet off the centre line meant putting a wheel in the nets; for me it meant a hasty dive into my safety net; and while off-centre landings are not

---

26   Donald Judd, *Avenger from the Sky*, p. 113.

uncommon during the day, they are rather more common in all the confusing and variable factors of darkness. The climax to a series of mishaps came when Flossie Howell, the most senior of the three, and the most experienced, rejected my signals to get up a bit and hitting the round-down, was bounced back into the air in a shower of sparks and landed with an impressive screeching of torn metal at my feet, while I was busy making up my mind which way to run.[27]

Waving off a pilot was not taken lightly as heavy under-powered aircraft, like the Fulmar, could only drunkenly stagger in the air as power was re-applied. Aircraft were not just allowed to land when they felt like it. A series of screens on the carrier would indicate whether fighters or TBR aircraft were expected to land, or whether the carrier was taking any comers in whatever order. On occasions the screens would show that no aircraft were allowed to land, usually because of a mechanical snag that needed resolving. As on take-off the carrier would need to land aircraft as quickly as possible, given that she would not wish to be heading into wind for longer than necessary. It was therefore important that a number of aircraft would be 'stacked up' behind each other in the circuit, waiting to approach about once every 30 seconds. A squadron or carrier's effectiveness was often judged on the speed with which it could receive and land on aircraft.

Once the aircraft landed, the arrester hook would catch on one of up to eight wires, depending on the size of the carrier. These wires would normally lie flat on the deck, but during landing operations would be raised 10 or so inches off the deck by hydraulic risers, which would allow the hook to engage the wire more cleanly. When engaged, the wire would play out and hydraulic resisters would slow the aircraft down. Once the machine had been stopped properly the pilot would release the brakes, and members of the pinning party would run out to un-snag his hook. The aircraft would then taxi forward over the lowered barrier and the arrestor wire would automatically retract to its original position for the next aircraft to land.[28] The whole process, undertaken by an efficient crew, could take as little as 30 seconds for an individual aircraft and allowed a squadron of 12 machines less than five minutes to land.[29] The use of the barrier was a marked improvement in allowing work to take place on deck, whilst aircraft were still landing. This would include folding the aircraft's wings, to then take it down the lift into the hangar or ranging it on deck for another sortie.

Landing on carriers when the sea was calm was difficult enough, but the sea can be one of the most hostile environments in the world, making flying over land seem tame by comparison. John Wellham had joined the Fleet Air Arm prior to the war and had flown Swordfish in the Mediterranean Fleet. In due course, he was appointed 'Wings' or Commander (Flying) in the escort carriers *Biter* and *Empress*. All those officers appointed as Commander (Flying) on ships were experienced airmen, as only they would be able to understand the conditions required to operate off a carrier. In the midst of a winter storm in the Atlantic the conditions could rapidly turn horrendous, so there was often a fine balance to be struck between ensuring the security of a convoy or needlessly sacrificing the safety of a crew. In his third trip across the Atlantic the ships Met Officer reported that a violent storm was raging over the eastern side of the United States and was due to pass to the south of their convoy. Everything had been initially quiet when Wellham had flown off two Swordfish for A/S patrol and landed-on their predecessors, but just two hours later the swell had increased, the flight deck was pitching violently and the rain had thickened, reducing visibility further. Wellham was understandably concerned:

---

27   Hugh Popham, *Sea Flight*, p. 178.
28   Admiralty Instructional Film, *Deck Landing*, Produced for the Admiralty by G.B. Screen Services, 1942
29   Charles Lamb, *War in a Stringbag*, p. 76.

I decided to cancel further flying and recall the A/S patrol. At that point one aircraft appeared with his navigation lights burning and signalling with an Aldis lamp; his message read that the cloud base was down to less than 600 feet and the sea returns on the radar was making it impossible to differentiate between them and anything else. I replied that they were to circle the ship while we recalled the other aircraft, then switched on the flight deck lighting to help them.

We could not contact the other aircraft so, as no U-Boat or shadowing aircraft could be operating in that weather, I ordered a search-light to be aimed at the base of the clouds. This worked, and soon both of them were circling. My wind indicator was showing gusts over 45 kts, so I asked for the ship's speed to be reduced to the lowest possible to retain steerage way. Each made two attempts before the DLCO was happy enough to give a 'Cut' signal. They both landed safely but it took the whole aircraft handling party to hold them down while the wings were folded, and they were struck down.

I went through the hanger myself to be satisfied that all aircraft were firmly secured with double lashings, and that no other equipment was loose. After a quick visit to my cabin to collect oilskins and more sweaters I dragged myself up ladders to the inside of the island, intending to check that the flight deck gear was properly tied down, because heavy transport like 'Jumbo' the mobile crane, fork lift trucks and tractors could do a great deal of damage; we could even lose them over the side. In the passageway I met the Flight Deck Officer and his Petty Officer who assured me that they had moved everything to the relatively sheltered area abaft the island and secured it with wire strops and bottle screws. They strongly advised me not to attempt to go on to the flight deck as it was no longer possible to keep one's feet, so I hauled myself up to the compass platform. It was now well into the middle watch and as I reached the open bridge the full force of the storm struck us; the ship shuddered and seemed to gasp; it was a world of noise and blackness. The Captain was jammed in his chair on the port side of the platform, the Navigator on the other and the Officer of the Watch had his arms round the gyro repeater; I heard him calling for more engine revolutions.

The wind was howling out of the east as though in personal hate. It screamed through the rigging and slammed against the island structure. Although protected by armoured glass screens and shields, a man's breath was pushed back down his throat if he attempted to speak. Hail and sleet were blasting down like icy needles. As the bows dipped, stinging salt spray hurled over us. The screw rose clear of the water to scream in protest as it over-revved. As our prow plunged into the troughs, tons of black water crashed on to the foredeck.[30]

If the North Atlantic and Arctic convoys provided one form of environmental challenge, the heat of the tropics were just as problematic. In these latitutdes many of the crew cursed that the ships had not been 'tropicalised' and there was no air conditioning, or few compartments with any access to the open air. In busier parts of the ship, such as the Aircraft Direction Room for example, the offices would become densely packed with men, in a sweltering atmosphere of hot air circulated by the ship's fans. The engine room was often an inferno and the cabins of those immediately under the flight deck, including the Captain, Commander (Ops) and Commander (Flying) would usually become ovens as the sun scorched the deck. Conditions were very bad in harbour when there was no movement of the ship. At sea, operations permitting, some officers always kept the lifts slightly down to allow some air to flow through. At night the lifts were often kept fully down to allow most of the crew to sleep on them or on the hangar deck. During the daytime uniform

---

30   John Wellham, *With Naval Wings – The Autobiography of a Fleet Air Arm Pilot in World War II* (Staplehurst: Spellmount, 2003), p. 162.

regulations were largely ignored and everyone worked in the lightest and smallest pair of shorts that they could find. Despite these measures, 'prickly heat' and other heat induced illnesses were rife.[31]

In these testing environments the Fleet Air Arm had to fulfil a number of important roles for the Royal Navy. These included scouting for an enemy fleet, convoy and fleet protection against both submarines and aircraft, strike operations against an enemy fleet or land targets and the one the pre-war Royal Navy seemed to value most; directing the guns of the Royal Navy. Despite the considerable amount of training of observers to accurately spot and direct the fall of shot, this skill was only used rarely. Once for *Warspite* in the second Battle of Narvik where the battleships guns were firing blind at eight German destroyers in the Rombaks and Herjangs Fjords (all eight were destroyed). Again, during the battle of the River Plate where *Ajax's* guns were directed onto the *Graf Spee,* at the Battles of Cape Spartivento for *Newcastle, Sheffield*, and *Manchester* and at the Battle of Gavdo for *Gloucester*. Finally, on 22 November 1941 the German sea raider *Atlantis* was also destroyed by gun fire from *Devonshire,* that was directed by a Fleet Air Arm aircraft. Interestingly, none of these aircraft were launched from carriers, instead they had all been catapulted from a cruiser or battleship.

There were a number of different catapult aircraft used within the fleet, one of the most common was the Supermarine Walrus, affectionately known as the 'Shagbat'. It was as ungainly as both its official and nickname suggest. The Walrus was a flying boat with a large cockpit and undercarriage that could be lowered, to enable it to land on a runway or even a carrier deck. It was a biplane and had a crew of three and a 'pusher' airscrew behind the cockpit and was incredibly stable and robust, some saying that at 56 knots the craft would almost land itself. A cruiser would normally have two Walruses embarked, whereas a battleship had just one. In both types of ship the Walrus was launched from a catapult, that used a cordite charge rather than the gentle steam or hydraulics present on aircraft carriers. John Hoare was the observer on the battleship *Rodney's* Walrus, which was mounted on a catapult that rested on 'X' turret. *Rodney* had not been equipped with a Walrus for a few years, so the first launch was loaded with tension:

> We were catapulted for the first time, to do an A/S search ahead of the squadron and then fly in to our usual berth in harbour, at the RAF seaplane base [at Gibraltar]. Walker had been a catapult pilot before, but neither Geare nor I had experienced it yet. I should think that every single officer and rating not on watch came up on deck to watch the fun. Nick Travers in his white overalls, very much the racing driver, gloved too, had put the charge of cordite into what we hoped was the right place, X turret was turned 90 degrees, broadside on, and the catapult was extended, giving us what looked like rather a short length of railway line off which we were to be shot. The engine was revved up, Walker and I braced ourselves against our head rests, a flag was dropped, and with a tremendous bang we were shot off into the air. We dropped only a few feet and then were away and airborne. The acceleration was so formidable that in my belly and balls it felt like a minor orgasm. Indeed we were shifted from zero to 60 knots in a very limited distance. In a much later naval incarnation I was to experience the steam catapult, which was really tame by comparison. I imagine that a few brows were mopped in relief aboard *Rodney* when we were seen to be safely off. I knew Geare and I mopped ours, but Walker affected a lordly indifference and began to pick his teeth. We were suitably humbled.[32]

---

31   John Wellham, *With Naval Wings*, p. 178.
32   John Hoare, *Tumult in The Clouds*, p. 116.

A Supermarine Walrus being catapulted. (Crown Copyright – Air Historical Branch)

Recovering the Walrus also took a certain amount of skill. Usually the battleship, or cruiser, would turn broadside to the wind and form a protective lee for the aircraft. A ship the size of the 40,000-ton *Rodney* was certainly large enough to produce calmish waters, even a cruiser would make a big difference, but in extreme cases oil would be discharged to dampen things down. The Walrus would land heading into wind and then motor as quickly as possible to the lee side of the ship, whilst maintaining the same speed as the ship the air gunner climbed on to the upper mainplane and grasped the hook from the ship's crane, slipping it through a ring which locked it on to the aircraft. The crane would then hoist the aircraft back onto its turret, the aircraft's engine turning all the while to give some sort of lateral control. It won't be surprising to know that it took a lot of practise for the operation to be described as anything approaching smooth.[33]

33   John Hoare, *Tumult in the Clouds*, p. 121.

20

'Safeguard and Avenger'[1]
The Operational Roles of the
Fleet Air Arm

As well as spotting for guns, the Fleet Air Arm was also tasked to strike the enemy's surface fleet, a capability that, at the beginning of the war, was vested in the Swordfish. The Fleet Air Arm are rightly proud of their battle honour Taranto, where they launched the world's first significant maritime air strike against an enemy fleet on the night of 11/12 November 1940. The seeds of this operation had actually stemmed from the Abyssinian Crisis in 1938, HMS *Glorious* had been an aircraft carrier in the Mediterranean at the time and it was one of her officers who had drawn up the plan to strike the Italian Fleet in its home base. The 1940 plan was an adaptation of that idea and the strike was originally to be from both *Illustrious* and *Eagle*. The Italian fleet at Taranto consisted of six battleships, two of the new *Littorio* class and four of the recently constructed *Cavour* and *Duilio* class. There were also about five cruisers and 20 destroyers in the port. So far Italian ships had proved to be timid and every attempt by the Royal Navy's Mediterranean Fleet to encourage them out to fight had been ignored by the Italians, who had consistently steamed for the security of their base whenever they became aware of the Royal Navy's presence. A strike on their home port therefore seemed a sensible approach. The first strike, due to take place on 21 October 1940, was cancelled as *Illustrious* experienced a severe hangar fire which, though only damaging two aircraft, had resulted in the remainder being doused with sea water, which required their total stripping. The new date was set for November, but then *Eagle* was put out of action by Italian aircraft which had damaged her aviation fuel system and required her to return to Alexandria. At this point the decision was made to carry on and the aircraft from *Eagle*'s 813 and 824 Squadrons flew on to *Illustrious,* joining the already embarked 815 and 819 Squadrons.

Twenty-four Swordfish aircraft were to be involved in the attack, some carrying bombs and others torpedoes. Air photographic reconnaissance gave the pilots a good indication of where the Italian warships were lying, but the harbour would also be lit up by flares dropped by one Swordfish circling above.[2] Darkness would protect the Swordfish from Italian fighter aircraft, but naval bases are obvious targets and usually well protected by AA defences and barrage balloons. Bad luck seemed to be trailing the British and immediately prior to the attack a case of contaminated fuel reduced the aircraft available from 24 to just 21. In retrospect, it seems amazing that this tiny number of antique-looking Swordfish were to pull off one of the most successful maritime strikes in naval history.[3]

---

1   The motto of 820 Naval Air Squadron, which was equipped with Swordfish, Albacores and Avengers and served in the Mediterranean, Atlantic and Far East.
2   David Wragg, *Fleet Air Arm Handbook 1939-45* (Stroud: Sutton Publishing, 2003), pp. 16-18.
3   Ministry of Information, *Fleet Air Arm* (London: HMSO, 1943), pp. 55-7.

A torpedo being wheeled into positon under a Fairey Swordfish torpedo-bomber.
(Crown Copyright – Air Historical Branch)

At 1800 the main Mediterranean Fleet had reached a position west of the island of Zante, *Illustrious'* striking force was then detached and steamed a further three hours closer to Taranto, before launching her first wave of 12 aircraft. These formed up some eight miles from the *Illustrious* and at 2057 hrs set course for Taranto reaching the port at about 2300. John Wellham was a Swordfish pilot from *Eagle* and had landed on *Illustrious* prior to the raid, then taking off with the second wave of torpedo aircraft at 2130. The distance to Taranto meant a soberingly long flight and had necessitated the gunner being replaced with an additional fuel tank. This was perched almost on top of the Observer, much to their physical discomfort and, one would imagine, mental disquiet. John Wellham describes his attack on Taranto, which by now was very much alert after the first wave's attack:

> Ahead there seemed to be a partial hole in the flak, just where I wanted to be – I aimed for it calling to Pat: 'Hang on I'm going down.' 'OK. Do your worst. Good luck.'
>
> I pushed the nose down, easing back the throttle to avoid over revving the engine. The speed built up – 140kts, 150kts, 155kts, – I wanted to dive as steeply as possible, knowing that a gentle angle would give me more time in the barrage. We were in it – the familiar red, green and yellow lines of tracer were crawling up towards us then hurtling past; ahead they appeared as a tangle of colour. The slip-stream was screaming through the struts and bracing wires, and past my ears; my nose was filled with the stench of cordite; there was tracer above us, tracer below us and tracer seemingly passing between the wings. The dive was steepening and the speed building up – 160kts, 170kts, – we met a barrage balloon! No self-respecting

balloon should have been at that height; its cable must have been shot away. I hauled the stick over to the left – I missed it. There was a tremendous jar, the whole aircraft juddered, and the stick flew out of my hand. 'Christ! I've hit the balloon cable' but the wings were still there. I grabbed the stick – it wouldn't move we were completely out of control.

It was no time for finesse. I applied brute force and ignorance. It moved most of its travel to the right but only partially to the left – was it working the ailerons? – No idea! I looked ahead. 'Bloody Hell!' We were diving almost vertically into the centre of the City of Taranto! I hauled the stick back into my stomach – were the elevators working? They were; an elephant seemed to be sitting in my lap but slowly we began to level out, but still curving round to the right. Were we going to make it? Buildings, cranes and factory chimneys were streaking past below us then we shot over the eastern shore of the harbour and were level over a black mirror speckled with the reflection of flames and bursting shells. I stirred the stick around and found that I had, at least, some sloppy lateral control. Air speed? Far too fast to ditch if we had to and too fast to drop a torpedo. I was determined to aim it at something after carrying the bloody thing all that way and having a rather hairy dive – I'd be damned if I didn't do something with it.

A quick glance around: to my right and slightly behind me was a massive black object covering most of the horizon and having a vast castle towering above it – a battleship. I heaved the stick over to the right putting us into a near vertical turn towards the target. I thought: 'That was a damned stupid thing to do; she might not go back.' She did. I levelled out after turning 180° and pointing towards the great hulk of the ship. Height OK, judging from the level of her deck – air speed dropping nicely – angle of attack not ideal but the best that I could do – aircraft attitude for dropping a torpedo rotten. The only way I could achieve a straight line was skidding with some left rudder and the right wing slightly down. Torpedoes don't like being dropped when not perfectly level. There was surprisingly little flak around us. I was forced to revise this opinion. She was awake and had seen us. Strings of lights prickled along her decks and multiple bridges and grew into long, coloured pencil lines drawn across the dark sky above us. She was giving us everything except her 15-inch guns but, thankfully, she seemed unable to depress her other guns low enough to hit us. Closer and closer we came her decks ablaze with muzzle flashes, the superstructure towering above us. 'Look out! Don't get too close, these things have a safety range.' I pressed the button on my throttle lever, felt the torpedo release, held straight for a couple of seconds then threw the stick over into a vertical turn to starboard.

Inevitably, after dropping a nearly 2,000lb load, an aircraft rises and Welham's aircraft was no exception, rising right into the ship's gunfire. Though his aircraft was hit twice more, he fought the increasingly sloppy controls to force her down, and scraping the surface of the sea, Welham shot out of Taranto harbour and into the security of darkened skies.[4]

The Taranto attack was astonishingly successful. Three Battleships were sunk (*Littorio*, *Conte di Cavour* and *Caio Duilio*) and the cruiser *Trento* severely damaged. The oil storage depot was a blazing hulk too and all except two aircraft made it safely back to *Illustrious*.[5] The Swordfish casualties were very light, many attributing the high rate of survival to the aircraft's confusingly slow speed and spidery silhouette which made it hard to spot and track at night. Even when damaged the aircraft had proved incredibly robust. John Wellham's observer found *Illustrious* after an over 100-mile transit across a darkened Mediterranean, no mean feat in itself, Wellham successfully

4   John Wellham, *With Naval Wings*, pp. 88-9.
5   Ministry of Information, *Fleet Air Arm* (London: HMSO, 1943), p. 57.

landed on the carrier and only in the hangar did he realise the damage to his aircraft. Both aileron rods were smashed with the result that one was slightly up and one slightly down, and there was a hole in the mainplane about a yard long and half a yard wide. Not many other aircraft were able to survive such punishment.

The action at Taranto tipped the balance of naval power in the Mediterranean firmly towards the British, Admiral Cunningham was phlegmatic in his signal to *Illustrious,* limiting himself to a simple 'Manoeuvre well executed'. Yet, in contrast to big gun surface actions – such as the Battle of Cape Matapan, the decorations awarded were paltry, causing *Illustrious'* sailors to tear down the notices on the ship's notice boards in disgust. It reinforced opinions in the Fleet Air Arm that they remained an unwanted Royal Navy step-child and that maritime aviation was still not fully appreciated.[6] Taranto was closely observed by the Japanese, who modelled the Pearl Harbor attack on it, launching 353 planes in daylight from six carriers.[7] The difference in scale of attack is illustrative of the differing levels of ambition and capability between the Japanese and Royal Navy carrier forces, though interestingly the Pearl Harbor attack, against an unprepared enemy, was only marginally more destructive, emphasising still further the remarkable achievements of the 21 Taranto Swordfish.

Attacking a stationary fleet, at a known anchorage, is one matter; it is very much harder to *find* and strike a fleet or naval vessel *underway* at sea. This too was one of the conceived roles of the Fleet Air Arm, but on many occasions the distances involved, and endurance required in finding the fleet and guiding either surface, or other air assets to it, would fall to the long-range, land-based maritime reconnaissance units. We have already seen how Coastal Command's Hudsons were fulfilling this role in the North Sea, it was RAF Sunderlands too that spotted and tracked the Italian fleet in the Ionian sea, prior to the Battle of Matapan.[8] Finding a vessel or fleet in European waters was relatively easy, detecting and identifying one in the vast swathes of the Pacific and Indian Ocean was a different proposition.

In April 1942, the requirement to find a Japanese fleet, in what Churchill described as one of the most dangerous moments of the war, was pressing. Following the defeat of the British in Malaya and Burma the Japanese intentions were to press westwards and, by destroying the British Eastern Fleet and the naval base at Colombo in Ceylon, dominate the Indian Ocean. There was even talk in Japanese circles of securing the Vichy-held island of Madagascar. Such an action would have had the gravest consequences for British sea lines of communication, including that required to reinforce the Middle East and Far East. To defend the Indian Ocean, Admiral Somerville's Eastern Fleet was composed of decrepit, old battleships. There was also a small air base at Colombo holding Hurricanes, Blenheims, Wildcats, Fulmars and Swordfish together with eight, long-range, Catalina flying boats. Somerville hoped that the Catalinas would obtain early warning of the Japanese Fleet, alerting the defences at Ceylon and giving him time to manoeuvre his outmatched fleet either away from the danger, or to a position from which it could launch a night attack using torpedoes. The Japanese fleet, commanded by Admiral Nagumo, consisted of modern well worked up battleships as well as five of the six carriers used at Pearl Harbor. Nagumo had 377 aircraft at his disposal.

It was a Catalina of 413 RCAF Squadron, commanded by Flight Lieutenant Leonard Birchall, that spotted the fleet. His Catalina had only arrived at Ceylon on 2 April 1942, when he was tasked to patrol South-South-East on 3 April as part of a longer, wider patrol plan involving

6   John Winton, *Find, Fix and Strike!*, p. 32.
7   Gordon Prange, *December 7, 1941 – The Day the Japanese Attacked Pearl Harbor* (New York: Wings Books 1987), pp. 86-90.
8   Dundas Bednall, *Sun on my Wings*, pp. 68-72.

A Consolidated Catalina taking off from Koggala flying boat base, Ceylon, for an evening patrol over the Indian Ocean. (Crown Copyright – Air Historical Branch)

other Catalinas. The aircraft was flying at 2,000 feet and had just about reached the point when they were due to turn back, when Sgt Colarossi, a gunner in one of the blisters on the side of the Catalina, spotted specks on the south horizon. Sergeant Brian Catlin was the Flight Engineer:

> As we got closer there were more specks and then they started to take form. Obviously they were warships and so there was nothing to do but to go in and identify them. We had just obtained a good position fix and so it was easy to tell their position, course and speed. As we got into range where we could identify by binoculars we ran into the outer air screen of fighters [the scouting aircraft from the carriers].
>
> What we saw were 4 battleships, 5 aircraft carriers, with cruisers and destroyers. We still could not see enough of the fleet to justify an assumption of nationality as the number we saw still was less than the number of ships given to us in the Allied naval section. Just as we started our transmission five flights of 3 zeros each peeled off over the top of us and we were into it.[9]

Initially the Japanese Zeros thought the aircraft was a captured Catalina that had been sent to guide them to Ceylon. However, they swiftly recognised their mistake and peeled off to attack. Fred Phillips was the Catalina's radio operator and picks up the story …

> I had been on radio watch doing my four hours when the action began. When the first cannon shells blasted in they knocked out my receivers but left the transmitters luckily. I'd got two

9   Arthur Banks, *Wings of the Dawning* (London: Images (Booksellers and Distributors), 1996), p. 53.

transmitters, but I had to use the generator of one to support the other. And I'd got a smashed Morse key, so I had to bang the parts together hopefully. People say I got two messages out and had stopped during the third.

How many went out I don't know, I just kept on. There was no time for encoding but I used the priority code known as O-Break-O which implied an enemy air attack. I had a vague hope that if anyone heard it they'd realise there was an aircraft out there in trouble. I was also sending the ordinary observation reports like 4 BS meaning four battleships or 2 AC for two aircraft carriers and so on.

O-Break-O also meant that all other radio traffic was to keep off the air, to allow an urgent message to be passed. Fred Phillip's signal was picked up both in Ceylon and also in Attu Atoll, the secret base of the Eastern Fleet in the Maldives, but whilst this signal was being passed the Zeros had continued to attack, setting fire to the Catalina's fuel and wounding a number of the crew, including Fred Phillips. Sergeant Brian Catlin describes the impact of these attack:

It got to the state where the aircraft was taking a lot of punishment. We got into a little cloud and I thought 'Oh, we've made it!' Then we came out of it. Kenny told me later the only cloud he saw was the hot air coming off the decks of the carriers which had risen and condensed into a cloud, when we were right over the carriers. I took over Colarossi's guns again and aimed. I had a go at each as it dived but there was always another behind it.

I changed the pans of ammunition and so it went on. I got hit once or twice myself and then the guns finally jammed so that I couldn't clear them. So I went up to Onyette and said, 'You'd better tell the boss the aircraft has taken as much as it will take. Tell him to get out of it and go home.'

Shortly after that the Zeros burst the tanks externally and the whole wing span was a mass of flame from end to end. Clearly the end was near and burning petrol started to come down the tower again. I thought 'This is it!' so left the guns, went and got the Mae Wests, tossed a couple out and put one on myself.

I could only do the bottom tie up because my left arm had gone. I wasn't conscious of being hit [Catlin was found later to have 74 separate wounds, as well as burns], only that I couldn't use my hand except the little and fourth fingers. I knew I'd been hit in the chest because I felt that one. Then I passed out the parachutes, but Davidson waved them off and pointed downwards. I had a look and we were only about 50 feet up. Colarossi had his harness on and I'm almost sure he had a Mae West but apart from his eyes being open there was no other sign of life.[10]

Birchall managed to get the aircraft down after a couple of skips. The aircraft began to sink very fast and the burning gasoline fanned out on the surface of the sea, making it necessary for the crew to swim away quickly. They had no dinghies as they began to exit the aircraft. Catlin continues his story.

Now I hadn't blown my Mae West up and I'd only got the bottom tied, and that helped. I stayed under water as long as possible – I was past swimming. When I came up I was clear of the fire. Davidson was floating about 20 yards away. His Mae West was blown up, but I did not use my gas bottle. When the bullets started splashing I sank myself doing a reverse

---

10   Arthur Banks, *Wings of the Dawning*, p. 53.

dog-paddle. There was one very big burst round Davidson and I never saw him after that. I kept going unconscious and I guess I prayed plenty.

I had little regret of dying – there never was much future to wartime flying – but I did regret I had lived 22 years and done nothing to be proud of. I regretted I had struggled, worked hard, got over serious illness, and recovered from motorcycle accidents just to go and die in the middle of the Indian Ocean on 4 of April 1942. Each time I came round I spat to see if there was any blood in my spit because in cowboy films before the cowboy dies he always spits blood. There was this round hole in my chest, bullet-sized, and I think the bullet's still there actually. When I eventually got back to England they said it was too near my heart – so leave it there.

I saw nothing of the others at this time [One member (Colarossi) had died in the aircraft and two members (Henzell and Davidson) in the water, leaving six surviving members]. The next thing I remember was this massive ship. Then about three waves away from me, there was a whaler-type boat being rowed, with a soldier in the front with a rifle.

They pulled me over the gunwale of the boat and put me in the bottom and the first words they said were 'Your frequency? Your frequency?' so I said 'Engineer' and they said 'Ah so! Engineer.' I passed out again and the next thing I remember was other people being dragged in over my feet.[11]

The Japanese were now determined to confirm whether the Catalina had in fact been able to send out a transmission prior to its destruction. Flight Lieutenant Birchall, aware of the predicament the radio operator would find himself in, instructed Phillips to claim he was an air gunner and nothing else. The crew were taken on to the destroyer *Isokaze*. Birchall was beaten several times and claimed that no message was sent, sadly this was seen to be a lie when the Japanese heard Colombo asking for a repeat of the message. The rest of the crew, including the wounded, were locked in the ship's tiny paint locker for three days, before being transferred to Admiral Nagumo's flagship, the *Akagi,* here they were given medical treatment, but the three least wounded were still regularly taken out for beatings and interrogation. The crew of the Catalina eventually reached Japan, though their relatives were not informed they were alive until a full year later. Thankfully, all six survived the war.

The Catalina's information came at a critical time. Colombo was prepared for the Japanese raid on 5 April 1942, Easter Sunday. The merchant shipping had been dispersed and the RAF and Fleet Air Arm were able to put up a spirited defence. The Japanese foray into the Indian Ocean was to cost the British fleet two cruisers (*Dorsetshire* and *Cornwall*) as well as the old aircraft carrier *Hermes*. But the Japanese did not succeed in their mission to capture Ceylon or destroy the Eastern Fleet. As the pendulum began to swing in Britain's favour, Somerville's surviving ships would become the nucleus around which a powerful striking force – the British Pacific Fleet would eventually be built.

Once an enemy fleet had been located, there would then begin a game of cat and mouse, as the aircraft carrier manoeuvred into a position from which it could fly off its aircraft. The Hunt for the *Bismarck* illustrates just such a dilemma. *Bismarck's* foray into the Atlantic is well known, as is her sinking of HMS *Hood* on 23 May 1941 in the Denmark straits. After this *Bismarck* continued further out into the Atlantic (see Map 11) and was spotted by a Catalina of 209 Squadron on 26 May. Whilst its surface ships shadowed the battleship from a distance, the Royal Navy began to plan a daylight strike by Swordfish. This attack was to be made by aircraft from *Victorious,* led by Lieutenant Commander Esmonde of 825 Squadron. The nine aircraft had taken off at about

---

11   Arthur Banks, *Wings of the Dawning*, p. 59.

1630 and were to rendezvous with *Sheffield,* which was trailing *Bismarck,* before attacking in three sub-flights of three aircraft each. Leslie 'Bill' Bailey was one of the observers in an 825 Squadron Swordfish, piloted by Jack Thompson who described the airstrike in detail:

The only scene in the operations room that I recall is of Captain Bovell standing in a gloomy light, part-way down a ladder from the bridge, wishing us well and re-assuring us that 'few casualties were to be expected in this kind of operation'. Shortly afterwards, in my aircraft, which was due to leave second after Esmonde's, I saw the third aircraft of the sub-flight lurch towards us and stop with its propeller within a whisker of our tail unit. The pilot caught my startled look and gave a wry grimace. What had happened, I never knew, but assumed he had fumbled his brakes, or perhaps more likely, his aircraft had slid with a roll of the deck, which was running wet with rain. Anyway we very nearly had an early night after all.

Then we were away, to give me my first sight of a carrier deck and island slipping away astern. Still moist, at least behind the ears from observer training, and obsessed with trying not to do anything stupid, my main anxiety was to keep an accurate plot soon after we formed up, but I soon found my compasses and ASI (Air Speed Indicator) swinging and lurching like a trio of drunks. This, I eventually decided, was due to our constant jinking to keep formation, a form of flying which I had experienced only once or twice and then had no need to keep a plot. So I settled for the course and speed arranged before we left; but then it nagged at me that Colin Ennever (Senior Observer) might have made changes on viewing the sea surface and thinking better of the 'Met' wind. (No orthodox wind-finding was done, presumably because of the difficulties of breaking formation and possibly losing touch in rain squalls). But wouldn't he have 'zogged' (hand-signalled) any changes to us? Should I ask? He seemed permanently head down in the 'office', probably peering down the tube of one of the two radar (ASV) sets in the squadron; and his TAG never seemed to look my way.

Anyway he had got it right. After something over the hour we encountered the *Norfolk* in company with the now somewhat disabled *Prince of Wales* and I was reading the message being flashed to us from the flagship: 'Enemy bearing [I forget] 15 miles [I think]'. The reality of the day sank into my mind as I read the first word.

Away we all went, just beneath the overcast, and after a few minutes I saw the *Bismarck.* She seemed alone. The *Prinz Eugen* had slipped away, unbeknown to us, under cover of rain squalls some four hours earlier. Of the US coast-guard vessel, *Modoc,* which features in various post-war accounts, I saw nothing and heard nothing subsequently. For all I know, she may have been detected by Ennever's ASV on our way, and he, among others, may have seen her, but *Bismarck* was all that Jack Thompson, my pilot, and I saw. Soon Jack said, in a rather offended tone, 'She's pooping at us!' as I saw salvoes begin flashing over her. The gunnery was impressive, with shell's bursting at exactly our height, but mainly ahead. Esmonde, whose aircraft suffered slight damage, promptly rose into the cloud just above with the rest of us following, whereupon I lost sight of everything. We bumbled along for maybe less than a minute when one Swordfish suddenly emerged, heading towards us but crossing our track from right to left, in a shallow dive, missing us it seemed by less than a span and then vanishing back into cloud. Being in cloud was becoming more dangerous than being shot at, so after another very short while we broke out and found ourselves alone, with the *Bismarck* below, slightly to our starboard and heading the opposite way. Another brief hesitation and then Jack said, 'I'm going in', pushing over into a steep dive. As we began to level out I heard loud fire-crackers about my ears and saw white streaks of tracer passing by. At first I thought the crackers were strikes on the aircraft, but they must have been sounds of near misses: we suffered no damage.

As we turned away, after what seemed an interminable run in, I had a full view of the starboard side of the ship, which now seemed to have gone surprisingly quiet. I called to Jack, who was now waltzing about, 'She has stopped firing – we seem to be all right now' or some such inanity, and he replied, 'She's chucking big stuff at us ahead'. Looking forward, I saw water spouts rising, around which Jack had begun his slaloms. At that moment I received two great blows on on my back. 'This is it!' I thought, but it was only Don Bunce tactfully drawing my attention back astern to see a high water spout rising from the water-line of the ship, about midships. Otherwise she still seemed strangely quiet. There was no sign of other aircraft nearby, but we saw a gaggle against the grey sky, some way off.

As we reached the others and formed up again on the left of Esmonde, Colin Ennever immediately zogged me for information and I signalled back that we had seen one hit on the starboard side. Our clocks now showed about midnight, although it was still daylight. However we had about an hour to go, provided we intercepted well, and then it would be after sunset in gloomy weather. After about an hour, I seem to recall some large changes in our headings before sighting the wash of *Victorious*, now in near darkness sometime before 0200. We must have been searching around for her, perhaps for half an hour or so. One post-war account tells of us over-flying the ship in the rain squalls and gloom, which may well be true. Others speak of searchlights switched on by *Victorious*, where Captain Bovell was becoming anxious (there was no radio beacon throughout the operation), but we saw nothing of them. Esmonde first saw red signalling lamps of our cruiser escort. Anyway we were soon down with no mishaps.[12]

The Swordfish from *Victorious* were to hit the *Bismarck* once only. The damage was not sufficient to sink a ship like the *Bismarck*, but it exacerbated the previous problems inflicted in the German ship's encounter with the *Prince of Wales*. Specifically, *Bismarck* could not access her forward fuel tanks and was leaking oil badly, she had to reduce her speed now to 21 knots making her increasingly vulnerable to further attacks. The attack had also significantly alarmed the German Commander of the *Bismarck* task force Admiral Lutjens.[13] The following day a further Swordfish attack by 15 aircraft from *Ark Royal* were to strike the *Bismarck* once more. On this occasion two torpedoes struck near the rudder of the ship and caused the vessel to turn in one continuous circle, she was finally dispatched the next day by the combined gun fire of the battleships *Rodney* and *King George V*.

The casualties to the Swordfish crews were light in these operations, probably because the *Bismarck* was isolated from protective escorts and out of range of German land-based aircraft. Sadly, for the crews of 825 Squadron, it was to be an altogether different story when they encountered the *Scharnhost* and *Gneisenau* in their so called 'Channel Dash' from Brest to Germany on 12 February 1942. 825 Squadron was still led by Esmonde, who was old and wise enough to know the suicidal risk that was being asked of his squadron and its antique aircraft. The attack was launched at 12:45 p.m. with a poor fighter escort from the RAF, Esmonde's six aircraft were attacked by Me 109s and shot at by heavy AA fire. All six Swordfish were shot down and there were no strikes from torpedoes. Only five men were to survive the raid having been picked up by Royal Navy Motor Torpedo Boats. Sadly, Esmonde was killed and received the VC posthumously, the first ever VC for the Fleet Air Arm. Bill Bailey had by that stage been transferred from 825 Squadron to the Mediterranean, but his pilot during the strike on the *Bismarck*, Jack Thompson, was killed, their Air Gunner, Don Bunce, also took part on the raid and survived, the only rating to do so.

---

12   Frank Ott, *Air Power at Sea in the Second World War* (Yeovil: Fleet Air Arm Museum, 2005), pp. 48-50.

13   David Bercuson and Holger Herwig, *The Destruction of the Bismarck* (New York: Overlook Press, 2001), p. 192.

HMS *Victorious* as she waits for her squadrons of planes (Fairey Fulmars and Fairey Albacore) to return after they have patrolled over the North Atlantic. (Crown Copyright – Air Historical Branch)

HMS *Indomitable* with a flight deck of Sea Hurricanes. (Crown Copyright – Air Historical Branch)

The Swordfish attacks on *Bismarck* and at Taranto were all part of the Fleet Air Arm's task to conduct maritime strikes against the enemy's main fleet or major units. The Fleet Air Arm also had to protect Royal Navy vessels and wider merchant shipping from enemy air attack. This role was most severely tested in the Mediterranean, where Axis fighters based in Sicily, Italy and North Africa were able to utilise land-based aircraft to attack Allied shipping. It was here that the obsolescence of the Fleet Air Arm fighters was highlighted. Fulmars were certainly no match for German fighter aircraft, even Ju 88s were too fast for the under-powered Fleet Air Arm fighter to intercept in a speedy manner.

As well as operations against the Italian Fleet, the Royal Navy used carriers to provide air protection for Royal Navy operations in the Mediterranean including the evacuation of Crete, where *Formidable* had been damaged and put out of action. There was also a frequent requirement to provide air cover for the Malta convoys and Royal Navy carriers had been regularly used for this purpose (e.g. *Ark Royal* for the HALBERD convoy in September 1941 and *Eagle* and *Argus* for the HARPOON convoy in June 1942).[14] By 1942 the Royal Navy had managed to equip the Fleet Air Arm with better aircraft such as the Wildcat and Sea Hurricane, so it was now able to defend the fleet more successfully.

It is hard to overestimate the importance of the PEDESTAL relief convoy in August 1942, an operation that the War Cabinet had determined was to be given priority over every other Allied naval commitment, anywhere in the world. This convoy was to arrest the deterioration of the Malta supply situation and was probably the most critical relief convoy to be sent to besieged Malta during the war. It consisted of 14 fast merchant ships, including the prized tanker *Ohio,* carrying the 11,500 tons of oil, without which Malta would not be able to retain its offensive edge. Had it not been for PEDESTAL the island would undoubtedly have fallen, with dire consequences for the British position in North Africa. Given the importance of the convoy the Royal Navy and Fleet Air Arm produced its strongest force to date, including the carriers, *Indomitable, Victorious* and *Eagle.* The veteran carrier *Furious* was also to take part as an aircraft ferry, she had 38 Spitfires on board that would be flown off to Malta, as soon as the island was within range. The force would contain 74 fighters – TBR aircraft such as Albacores in many cases being off-loaded for extra Fulmars, Sea Hurricanes and Wildcats. This impressive figure was still much less than the 600 German and Italian fighters, known to be in range of the convoy's route, and who had been warned of the convoy's presence on the night of 9/10 August 1942, as it passed through the straits of Gibraltar.

The PEDESTAL convoy began dramatically with the destruction of *Eagle,* on 11 August, after it was hit with four torpedoes fired by U-73. Two hundred and fifty men were lost as well as 25 percent of the convoy's fighters, four hurricanes were airborne at the time and able to land on *Victorious* and *Indomitable. Furious* was able to fly off her reinforcing Spitfires later that afternoon and having completed her task she returned to Gibraltar with a small escort. Elsewhere in the convoy, the Fleet Air Arm fighter aircraft awaited news from the carrier's radar that enemy aircraft were coming. Typically, each carrier would have two machines in the air above the convoy, two on deck with pilots strapped in their cockpits and engines warmed up, as well as a further four aircraft at immediate notice with their pilots in the ready room.[15] The scene aboard *Victorious* was vividly described by one of the officers on board at the time:

> The standby squadron was all set on deck, with the aircraft armed, fuelled and waiting and the pilots in their cockpits gazing upwards and perhaps munching on a biscuit. Men stood by the lanyards which secured the wingtips of the aircraft – others lay by their chocks and

---

14   John Winton, *Find, Fix and Strike!,* p. 73.
15   John Winton, *Find, Fix and Strike!,* p. 74.

A Hawker Sea Hurricane fighter on board HMS *Indomitable* is armed during the PEDESTAL convoy. (Crown Copyright – Air Historical Branch)

yet more men sat astride their starter motors. The flight deck officers fiddled with their flags and Commander Flying nursed his flight deck microphone. There was a tenseness in the air, expectancy and waiting, all waiting for those vital 17 seconds which would follow the Boatswain's Mate's call 'Fighters Stand-to'. The mad scramble to get the aircraft off and then the 18th second should see the ship returning to her station with her fighters safely airborne over the sea.[16]

The 11 August looked like it might pass without an attack by the Germans. But then at 20:45 a force of 36 Ju 88s and He 111s attacked from the East. Hugh Popham was a member of the standby Sea Hurricane crew on *Indomitable*.

The Tannoy crackled. 'Scramble the Hurricanes! Scramble the Hurricanes!'
The fitters in the cockpits pressed the starter buttons, and the four Merlins opened up with a blast of sound and a gust of blue smoke. As we scrambled up the wings, the crews hopped out the other side, fixing our straps with urgent fingers. Connect R.T.; switch on. Ten degrees of flap. Trim, Quick cockpit check. The ship was under full helm, racing up into wind – and – we were off and climbing at full boost on a northerly vector up to 20,000 feet, heads swivelling. Down to 12,000; alter course; climb to 20,000 feet again. And there they were, a big

---

16   Michael Apps, *Send Her Victorious* (London: William Kimber, 1971), p. 92.

formation of 88's below us. One after another we peeled off and went down after them. They broke formation as they saw us coming, and Brian and I picked one and went down after him. He turned and dived away, and we stuffed the nose down, full bore, willing our aircraft to make up on him. At extreme range we gave him a long burst; bits came off and smoke poured out of one engine, and then he vanished into the thickening twilight. We hadn't a hope of catching him and making sure; already he had led us away from the convoy; and so, cursing our lack of speed we re-formed, joined up with Steve and Paddy, the other members of the flight, and started to climb back to base.

The sight we saw took our breath away. The light was slowly dying, and the ships were no more than a pattern on the grey steel plate of the sea; but where we had left them sailing peaceably through the sunset, now they were enclosed in a sparkling net of tracer and bursting shells, a mesh of fire. Every gun in the fleet and convoy was firing, and the darkling air was laced with threads and beads of flame.

For a time we hunted round the fringes of it, hoping to catch somebody coming out; but the light was going, and we were running out of petrol. We had already been in the air for an hour, most of it with the throttle wide open. There was no sign of the 88's which had started it all; and it was not clear at first what the ships were still firing at. Then we saw the tracer coming morsing up towards us, and one or two black puffs of smoke burst uncomfortably close. We moved round the fleet, and the bursts followed us; and the truth could no longer be disregarded. They were firing at anything that flew.[17]

A very rattled convoy and poor AA discipline caused considerable confusion and chaos as the returning fighters struggled to land. Hugh Popham eventually managing to land on *Victorious* almost out of fuel. His 880 Squadron Commander, Lieutenant Commander Judd, was so furious with the *Indomitable*'s AA gunner's actions that he leapt from his cockpit and ran across to some of the offending AA guns, grabbing the officer in charge by the neck and roaring: 'You bloody useless bastard! You brainless oaf! Don't you know a Hurricane when you see one!'[18]

The next day the attacks again began in earnest. These were complex attacks that involved Italian Cant Z 1007s, Ju 87 and Ju 88s undertaking medium and high-level bombing, as well as He 111s laying mines in the convoy's path. The convoy's fighters had a difficult task throughout these days, their primary duty was always to defend and protect the ships beneath them and this was more important than shooting down enemy aircraft. They would instead try to break up the formations before they could attack and then having done so, get into a position from where they could intercept the next wave. Although always tempting to rack up their personal number of 'kills', the pilots needed to be careful about being drawn too far away from the convoy, as this would leave it unprotected. The Germans and Italians were said to have lost somewhere between 30-40 aircraft during the convoy battle, the majority to the guns of the fleet's fighters.

The PEDESTAL convoy was also being attacked by enemy submarines and MTBs as it neared the North African coast, necessitating 48 emergency turns during the two-day period up to the 12 August. Such a high surface and sub-surface threat required carrier operations to be slick in landing aircraft on and off. Efficiency was also required from those who kept the aircraft in the sky including the flight deck crew who un-hooked, stowed and ranged the aircraft as required and the engineering staff who ensured the machines were serviced, maintained, fuelled and armed.

---

17   Hugh Popham, *Sea Flight*, pp. 123-4.
18   John Winton, *Find, Fix and Strike!*, p. 74.

The Royal Navy aircraft carrier HMS *Indomitable* on fire after being bombed on 12 August 1942. A Dido Class cruiser, HMS *Charybdis*, is attempting to screen the carrier. *Indomitable* was hit by three bombs which put her flight deck out of action and started severe fires. By 9:15 p.m. the fires were put out and she was able to return to port under her own steam at a a reduced speed. (Crown Copyright – Air Historical Branch)

Although the German's primary targets were the merchantmen, the Royal Navy's aircraft carriers were also frequently struck by air attack. In the late afternoon of 12 August the two surviving carriers, *Victorious* and *Indomitable* were operating about a mile apart as separate units. Gordon Wallace was normally an observer on Albacores but was being temporarily employed as a duty officer in *Indomitable*'s operations room throughout the attack:

> I caught sight of a closely bunched formation of 12 Stukas at about 10,000 feet almost directly above us with not a shot being fired at them. I got up and ran onto the flight deck shouting and waving my arms wildly but to no avail. The first Stuka peeled off and I had my first head-on view of its sinister cranked wing heading straight towards us with others following behind. I felt disembodied and without fear, unable to move – not that there was anywhere to move to.
>
> Looking like beer barrels the 1000lb bombs seemed to float down towards us as though in some dimly remembered dream. The ship shuddered and the dream expanded into a huge sheet of flame which rose up ahead of the island and engulfed it. There was an enormous explosion just ahead of me and then several behind me which seemed to lift the ship several feet. A wall of water rose alongside to some 100 feet then cascaded down on top of me, washing me into the catwalk. For a moment there was a strange silence such as occurs at the end of a great orchestral performance, it could have been the final moments of Gotterdammerung, as flames and smoke billowed near the for'd lift and behind the aft lift.
>
> The ship began listing to port and was moving in a slow circle to starboard. I am told that the list never exceeded 10 degrees but it seemed more at the time and I felt the first knot of fear in my stomach, thinking we were doomed and expecting at any minute another enemy

attack as we were now a sitting target, unable to operate aircraft, or even land-on all those we still had in the air. The flight deck was a confusion of people and a snakepit of hoses. Tom Troubridge [*Indomitable*'s captain] appeared up on the flying bridge, like Zeus, bellowing at the human ants below. I helped to haul hoses along the slanting deck towards the fire at the stern, passing groups of wounded being helped along the deck. I avoided a direct look at them, but a glance told me most had been burnt.[19]

Indomitable had been struck on the starboard side ahead of the for'd lift. The 1,000lb bomb had pierced three inches of the armour-plated flight deck and detonated at the base of one of the 4.5 inch gun turrets, blowing the massive lift out of its mountings and causing it to project 2 feet above the level of the deck. It was here that most of the ship's 44 killed and 59 wounded casualties had occurred. A second bomb had pierced the armoured deck right aft, damaging the after lift and some officer's cabins. The third bomb had hit the hull just above the water line (and as well as cascading water onto Wallace) also caused damage; a hole 30-40 feet wide had been opened up beneath the waterline and it says much that the ship's damage control parties were able to correct the list in little under 20 minutes. This last bomb had wrecked the wardroom ante-room and killed a number of officers, including six aircrew one of whom was Gordon Wallace's cabin mate 'Willy' Protheroe. In true Royal Navy tradition the bodies were buried at sea on the passage back to Gibraltar, the service taking place on the port side for'd of the island. Wallace continued:

> By the end of the Service and with the playing of the 'Last Post' I could hardly swallow for the lump in my throat. The words 'Burial at Sea' were just words until this moment, the reality was harrowing. I was only a few feet away from the incongruous wooden chute down over the side. The first few white canvas covered parcels, Willy's no bigger than a small case, slid down the bleached wood to disappear with a distant splash. On and on until I could no longer see for tears. All that was left of shy, gentle Willy was a pipe and a few photographs in my album.[20]

Operation PEDESTAL was one of the most critical operations of the war and kept Malta operational at a period when the Allied position in North Africa was stark. The Fleet Air Arm's role was profound, only one merchantman was lost whilst under carrier protection, but when these ships had to turn back on the evening of 12 August the convoy's casualties mounted. Proximity to the German and Italian airfields led to an intensification of attacks and although Maltese-based aircraft helped to a degree, they had problems locating the convoy, as well as operating effectively without radar control and fighter direction. This, it had been hoped, would be provided by the specially equipped anti-aircraft cruiser *Nigeria*, but she was struck by a torpedo on the evening of 12 August and also had to turn back to Gibraltar. Only five of the 14 merchantmen were able to make it to Malta. The last to arrive was the tanker *Ohio* who, her engines stopped, was lashed between two naval escorts *Braham* and *Penn*. She had been struck by bombs three times and was low in the water with a crashed Ju 87 on her poop deck and a Ju 88 on her Forecastle. There are some moments in the war which stand out as deeply symbolic and moving; the arrival of the crippled *Ohio* in the Grand Harbour, Valletta, Malta at 09:30 on 15 August 1942 is undoubtedly one of them.[21] The Maltese referred to it as the 'Santa Maria' convoy and watched in stunned silence as the life-saving ship entered their historic harbour. It remains carved into their national consciousness.

---

19   Gordon Wallace, *Carrier Observer* (Shrewsbury: Airlife, 1993), p. 122.
20   Gordon Wallace, *Carrier Observer*, p. 124.
21   Michael Apps, *Send Her Victorious*, p. 99.

The maritime air defence of convoys was equally important in the depths of the Atlantic. There, the convoys were being tracked by long-range, four-engine, Focke Wulf 200C-3 Condor aircraft (sometimes known by their German sobriquet 'Kurier'). These could either bomb the unprotected convoy or radio the position to the German U-boats, allowing them to concentrate a wolf pack against them. The range of the aircraft allowed them to fly 700 miles out into the Atlantic, beyond the range of even twin-engine fighter aircraft. What was needed was air defence within the convoy. Fleet carriers were too rare to spare, so the Lordships in the Admiralty did what Britain always does well – they improvised. This was initially attempted using Catapult Aircraft equipped Merchantmen, or CAM ships for short. The ships carried one aircraft, a Hurricane, which would be launched when the German aircraft was sighted. Having shot the intruder down, the pilot was faced with a stark choice of either ditching near a ship or parachuting into the sea. One can imagine the strength of character required for such a role. Fifty ships were converted, though only eight operational launches were ever made, the aircraft involved shooting down six enemy aircraft and damaging three. CAM ships were used not only in the Atlantic, but also on Arctic convoys to Russia and on the run to Gibraltar.[22]

Whilst CAM ships were a useful short-term expedient, what was really needed was something more akin to a traditional carrier, able to fly aircraft on and off, but a little more modest and economical. The first attempt was the escort carrier *Audacity,* a converted ex-German liner and banana carrier captured by the Royal Navy off Puerto Rico in February 1940. To convert her into an escort carrier, the *Audacity*'s masts, derricks, funnel, upper bridge work and other superstructure were cut down to deck level and a small steel flight deck, 112 metres long and 18 metres wide was added. There were four hydraulically retarded arrestor wires and a fifth 'Jesus Christ' wire used as a last-ditch mechanism that would stop the aircraft with a jolt.

The *Audacity* carried only six Wildcat fighters. As there was no hangar or lift, these were all ranged on deck which reduced the overall length to only 90 metres. It also meant that the engineering crews had to service the aircraft on the flight deck and in the open. Not only was this uncomfortable work in the cold Atlantic air, but the extra exposure to the damp sea air was notorious for seizing up guns, earthing firing circuits, as well as corroding gun wells, breech-blocks, barrels, IFF switches, spark plugs and contact breakers. In order to maintain the blackout, no lights could be used at night and the mechanics would have to operate by dimly lit torches. On a more positive note the *Audacity*'s luxurious staterooms had been kept, and these were allocated to the aircrew, who no doubt appreciated the comparison between *Audacity*'s cabins with their double beds and en-suite bathrooms, to the accommodation on a fleet carrier.[23] *Audacity* was first employed on the Gibraltar run in August 1941 and quickly made her presence felt both against U-boats, who typically dived when the Wildcats attacked, even though their 0.5 inch guns were harmless, as well as their chief targets: the German Condors. Eric 'Winkle' Brown would become one of the country's most famous test pilots and aviators, but in November 1941 he was one of the six Wildcat fighter pilots on *Audacity,* sailing in a convoy from England to Gibraltar. He described a Wildcat pilot's carrier duties as follows:

> We did two things, we did anti-submarine patrol which isn't really a fighter's job, but we had no choice because these were the only type of aircraft we had. We did a dawn patrol, around the convoy first thing, just to see that the area was clear of U-boats and we did one last thing at night, the dusk patrol ... Then during the day we were at immediate readiness for take-off against the Focke-Wulfe *Kurier* aircraft which were raiders against convoys of course, but in

---

22   John Winton, *Find, Fix and Strike!*, p. 74.
23   Kenneth Poolman, *Allied Escort Carriers of World War Two* (London: Blandford Press, 1988), pp. 13-16.

the main they were providing information to the U-boat wolf packs which were frequenting the Atlantic. So they were very, very dangerous aircraft from our point of view. They were also heavily armed, extremely heavily armed so they were not an easy target to fire against.

We spotted two of these, my section leader was the one that caught sight of them first and he called and assigned one to me and he went off to chase the other. I chased mine and we knew the main weakness on the *Kurier* was that it had a rather weak tail unit, that is to say that on landing for example you could easily snap the tail on a heavy landing, so this was a weak point which we knew about from intelligence reports. We already had one success with a section firing at the tail unit and breaking it off, so this was the point we tended to aim for at first. But I found this difficult when I was against this particular *Kurier*.

He was flying against a particular cloud base, just below it and therefore you had to come in very flat and you had no real chance to break away above him, you had to break away below, which of course is the more desirable way to go. With visibility etc. I was only getting in a one or two second burst at a time, but on one of these bursts I did set one of his inner engines on fire and he popped up into the cloud. I thought I had lost him completely. It was a fairly thin cloud layer, possibly about 400 feet, so I went above it, hopefully so I might see him if he popped through it, but he didn't. I was just milling around, generally hoping that something might happen, when I saw a wing tip come out of the cloud, he was obviously turning. So on that basis I reversed course with him, but did not get it quite right, for eventually when he did emerge, I found I was head on to him. This was the only chance I was going to get so I came down fairly flat, because I had realised that the top dorsal gun, it was a cannon in fact, could not be depressed below a certain elevation. If you kept very flat, he probably would not be able to fire at you. So I came in and the main risk was that you have a very high closing speed with a great risk of collision, so you have a very, very short firing time, but after all we had four .5 inch machine guns, which is quite a heavy armament and I just blasted away as I went in for two or three seconds, I could see the cockpit glass and nose of the aircraft shattering, before I pulled away and then it just spiralled down into the sea.[24]

Brown noticed the port wing broke off on impact and as he circled over the crash, to his surprise, he saw two men crawl out of an escape hatch at the top of the fuselage. The aircraft filled with water and sank, though these two clung to the broken wing, which still floated.[25]

Audacity was sadly sunk on the night of 21 November 1941. She had just landed on her Wildcats and was zig-zagging to starboard of the convoy. She would normally have expected to have had an escort, but these were staging a mock battle with depth charges and flares far to the rear of the convoy, in an attempt to lure U-boats away as the convoy sharply altered course. The only ones fooled were the Allied merchantmen who fired snowflake flares, highlighting the convoy once more. *Audacity* was struck by a torpedo aft, destroying her rudder and flooding her engine room and she was soon settling down with her stern awash. Her hold was full of empty barrels which kept her afloat as the convoy's escort vessels rushed towards her. Eric Brown takes up the story:

Suddenly we could see on the port side a U-boat surfacing, you could see it because though it was dark it was covered in phosphorescence, a tremendous glow as this thing rose up, quite eerie. We could actually also see the U-boat commander on the conning tower, we could see his hat, they were as close as that when they came up. It was the U-751, commanded, as we later found out, by Leutnant Bigalk and there was this tremendous hiatus as we stood looking

---

24   IWM Sound Archives, Catalogue Number 12279, Melrose Brown interview.
25   Eric Brown, *Wings on My Sleeve* (London: Orion Books, 2006), pp. 29-30.

A Martlet naval fighter warming up on the flight deck of HMS *Formidable*.
(Crown Copyright – Air Historical Branch)

at each other. Then somebody's nerve cracked, and they opened fire with a 20mm cannon [from HMS *Audacity*] which was like using a pea shooter against this thing, it was the catalyst for what happened afterwards, for within seconds we had four torpedoes rushing towards us. You could see them quite clearly; they left a noticeable trace in the water. All four struck us and the complete bows of the ship fell off, they literally just vanished, about a third of the ship seemed to just disappear.

As they did the real chaos started because the Captain had quite sensibly assembled the entire crew, apart from those who were at specific stations such as the engine room, on the flight deck. So we were all up there on the flight deck, all wearing our Mae Wests or the equivalent which the seaman had. There were about 400 people up on the flight deck and when the bows fell off some of them went with that, but the worst thing that happened was that immediately the bows went the ship tilted very, very steeply nose down and the Martlets at the back … they all broke their moorings. They were all tied down by steel hawsers, but they all broke and the entire number of aircraft just rushed down the flight deck and with all that number of people on the deck just scattered them right left and centre. A number were hit by the machines or just swept over the side. I saw them coming and I just jumped over the side, you are talking about 50 feet or more, but it was that or get wiped off. I think many people were killed in the jump or people jumping on top of people in the water already, that is always a nasty thing and usually means both get killed. That is how I finished in the water by just jumping off the flight deck … I think we lost well over a third of the crew.[26]

After six hours in the water Brown was eventually picked up by the crew of a corvette. He was so exhausted and weak from his time in the water, that he could not stand upright on the deck of the ship. The captain of the *Audacity*, Commander McKendrick, sadly went down with his ship,

26 IWM Sound Archives, Catalogue Number 12279, Eric Melrose Brown interview.

but in the short period under his charge, the *Audacity* had proved the operational utility of escort carriers, driving off the Condors, spotting U-boats and directing the surface ships onto them.[27] Admiral Doenitz himself commented on the importance of *Audacity's* role in what was to be the escort carrier's final convoy: 'In HG 76, the worst feature from our point of view was the presence of the aircraft carrier *Audacity*. The year 1941 came to an end in an atmosphere of worry and anxiety for U-boat Command.'[28]

Promising though *Audacity's* performance had been, it was many more months before escort carriers began to appear in sufficient numbers to make a difference to the Battle of the Atlantic. This may seem strange, but it is sadly symptomatic of those bureaucratic and procurement messes that always seem to plague the armed forces. A total of 11 escort carriers were initially ordered by the British, five to be built in British shipyards and six in American. The British vessels were all planned to be conversions from a series of existing passenger liners. Sadly, this was opposed and blocked by the Ministry of War Transport who refused to give up these valuable ships without a fight. Only one was eventually released (*Pretoria Castle*) and that was not fully converted until mid-1943. The delay of the six American-built escort carriers into service was a rare instance of American ingenuity and lend-lease failing to live up to expectations. The six escort carriers (*Archer, Avenger, Biter, Dasher, Tracker* and *Charger*), known officially as Bogue Class or Carrier Vessel Escorts (CVEs), were nicknamed 'Woolworth' carriers by the British, reflecting their cheap nature. They were constructed in San Francisco, not from conversions of existing ships but rather adaptations of new pre-fabricated all welded hulls. The ships would have a large hangar designed to accommodate 18 aircraft, two lifts and proper AA defences – all impressive improvements on *Audacity*. The CVEs were also fitted out with wonderful galleys (utilising steam cooking), launderettes, barbers and more importantly workshops for wood and metal work, as well as a generously equipped sick bay. They were also furnished with an impressive Fighter Direction Control centre.[29]

More disappointingly they were described from the outset as 'lively' vessels, gaining a reputation as ships which would 'roll on wet grass'. The CVEs were also plagued with mechanical faults. They needed conversion in British shipyards to rectify the supposedly unsafe American petrol system, fix the temperamental engines and improve the poor construction of the plating joints which reflected the fact that these all-welded ships were built at considerable speed. The British also wanted to add extra ballast to the ships to prevent the excessive rolling. This could total somewhere between 2,000 and 12,000 tons of extra weight, as the British were not prepared to copy the US Navy practice of pumping sea water into empty fuel tanks. The British also lengthened the flight decks, partly because the British aircraft could not utilise the American catapults, but also because the British wished to use the carriers for full fighter operations. This caused some disagreement with the Americans, who had intended the CVE ships to be used primarily for anti-submarine work in the Battle of the Atlantic. None of the new CVEs would appear on Atlantic convoys until the middle of 1943, a shockingly lengthy delay given the criticality of anti-U-boat operations. The excuses for each ship varied, one CVE was being retained by the US Navy for deck landing training (*Charger*), but others (*Avenger, Biter* and *Dasher*) were diverted to the Mediterranean, where there was a pressing need to provide air defence for a series of amphibious operations.

As the tide of the war turned in the Mediterranean in 1942 and 1943, the Allies began to execute a number of amphibious operations which, to varying degrees, needed carriers to provide air defence until the land forces established themselves ashore. Once sufficient airfields had been captured and occupied by the RAF, then air defence responsibilities would be handed over to

27   Kenneth Poolman, *Allied Escort Carriers of World War Two*, pp. 13-16.
28   Carl Doenitz, *Memoirs: Ten Years and Twenty Days* (London: Wiedenfeld and Nicholson, 1959), p. 18.
29   Kenneth Poolman, *Allied Escort Carriers of World War Two*, pp. 63-64.

The escort carrier HMS *Avenger* with Sea Hurricane aircraft ranged on the flight deck. (Crown Copyright – Air Historical Branch)

land-based aircraft. This was a perfectly sensible approach, but it was reliant on skilful planning and execution of carrier operations, as well as good aircraft able to maintain a high sortie rate. Carriers had supplemented the amphibious landings in North Africa (Operation TORCH) and were used again during the landings in Sicily (Operation HUSKY – during which *Indomitable* was struck by a torpedo dropped by a Ju 88 – especially disappointing as she had only just returned to service following repairs to her after Operation PEDESTAL and would be out for yet another year). It was nevertheless the amphibious landings at Salerno (Operation AVALANCHE, 3-16 September 1943), which showed the Royal Navy still had much to learn about carrier operations. The Royal Navy's carriers were divided into a group of five escort carriers under Admiral Vian (*Attacker, Battler, Hunter, Stalker* and *Unicorn*) known as 'Force V' and a force of two fleet carriers (*Illustrious* and *Formidable*) which remained with 'Force H'.[30] The Allies' plan was that the escort carriers would fly Seafires close in shore and provide air defence over the beach head, controlled by the Fighter Direction Ship *Palomares*. The fleet carriers concurrently provided Combat Air Patrols (CAP) with Wildcats and anti-submarine support using TBR aircraft for both the fleet and Force V's escort carriers.

Admiral Vian's plan was flawed and he has been criticised for failing to understand the constraints the escort carriers would be operating under so close inshore. Many have argued that as a non-aviator he had little understanding of such matters. First, he did not appreciate that

30   John Winton, *Find, Fix and Strike!*, p. 83.

A Seafire takes off from HMS *Hunter* during Operation AVALANCHE the amphibious landing at Salerno.
(Crown Copyright – Air Historical Branch)

carriers operating together must have more sea room. The five carriers were working in circuits that were almost over-lapping and far too close inshore, which resulted in nervous and hasty landing-on operations, often with no wind over the deck. Initially all appeared to be going well, Force V launched 20 of its 107 Seafires at a time over the beachhead and fresh fighters were launched every hour, the average sortie rate being 85 minutes in length for Seafires. On the first day Force V generated an impressive 265 sorties. On the second day 232 sorties were generated and on the third; 165. The aircraft were simply being written off by accidents. Some were caused by pilots inexperienced in landing on the short escort carrier deck, others by sun dazzle off a very calm sea. Yet more accidents were caused by the very light winds, the carriers often only being able to generate 18 knots headwind over the deck, rather than the 28 or so knots able to be generated by the faster fleet carriers, even when there was no wind.

The conditions and pilot's inexperience were compounded by the unsuitability of Seafires for carrier operations. Pilots struggled to see round the long Seafire nose that obscured their vision, the Seafire's long propeller 'pecked' the deck of the carrier and during heavy landings the fragile landing gear broke, frequently writing off the aircraft and pilot as it slithered across the deck, shedding its airscrew, airscoop, tail wheel and ailerons.[31] Alternatively the pilot might be going too fast or catch an unexpected wind and after the cut from 'Bats' the Seafire's aerodynamics would cause it to float over the wires, into the barrier or over the side.

It had been expected that Montecorvino airfield would be in Allied hands at the end of the first day. But unexpectedly fierce German resistance at Salerno had prevented the Allies from securing this quickly. Once it was captured it was found to be so badly damaged by shell fire that a new airfield had to be built at Paestum, which only became operable on the fourth day.

---

31   Kenneth Poolman, *Allied Escort Carriers of World War Two*, pp. 70-73.

The lack of serviceable fighters caused the Royal Navy to transfer first Seafires and then Wildcats from the fleet carriers to Force V. The Wildcats were much more suitable, first because they were more robust and secondly, because their two-hour range meant the escort carriers needed to turn into wind only half as frequently as when flying off Seafires. It was a salutary lesson for the Fleet Air Arm in the complexity of multi-carrier operations, as well as a further demonstration of the unsuitability of the Seafire. It is also a reminder to us that carrier aviation carries particular risks and high attrition rates. Hank Adlam was a Wildcat pilot on *Illustrious* and after the first two days was sent with his squadron to reinforce the Force V component. At the conclusion of his patrol he noted a hiccup from his engine, which then began to run roughly. A glance at his instruments showed the temperature gauge at red and his oil pressure at nil:

> Down below one of the carriers was already turning into wind preparing to take our flight on-board anyway and, when I saw this, I made up my mind definitely to go for a landing on it.
>
> Meantime, I was getting very little power out of the engine and by now was down to about 3,000 feet. I was ahead of the ship and more or less on the downwind leg calculating that I had sufficient height to circle round to position myself reasonably well for the final approach. I glanced quickly round; no other aircraft near me or in the circuit they were all keeping clear. I decided to assume that there would be no power at all from the engine should I need it, so I closed the throttle completely to concentrate on an engineless landing. I would have to come in very high on the final approach and might have to do an old-fashioned side slip to get down. Also I must remember how very little wind speed there would be over the flight deck, 16 knots no more and therefore the deck would appear to be rushing at me twice as fast on my final approach.
>
> All this had gone through my mind but now, at some 2,000 feet, I selected wheels down, half flap, hook out, straps very tight and hood locked open. I had already put the prop into fine pitch as soon as the engine had started running rough. There was no going back now; the decision to attempt a deck landing instead of ditching was made. If I missed the deck, it would not be possible to ditch safely as the wheels would catapult the Wildcat on to its back as soon as they touched the sea and, whether I could swim or not, I would be drowned. Meantime, over the R/T from the Carrier, which was now into wind, I had received the affirmative to land.
>
> I was turning on to the final approach, prop still rotating, speed at 85 knots, selecting full-flap now, very high up astern of the Carrier with the batsman frantically signalling me to 'Come down'. Everything was happening very fast. Yes, I was too high; would fly straight over the crash barrier at this rate; side slip down to port, red Very light from the DLCO platform, meaning 'Abort landing, go round again.' A second red light with the batsman waving me off furiously. Straightening up from the side-slip speed 80 knots. Oh dear Lord, I had overdone it, I was now slightly lower than I should be, and I might not quite make it to the deck. I opened the throttle for the first time but only a brief response from the engine for a second before it expired, then I was over the deck to stall and thump down catching the first arrestor wire. Somehow I was down and safe.[32]

Hank Adlam's propeller ground to a halt the moment his aircraft landed, and he lay back in the cockpit gasping in relief. The furious batsman jumped onto his wing and shouted abuse at him for not following his instructions when waved off. Adlam, passed caring, simply waved two fingers at him.

---

32   Hank Adlam *On and Off the Flight Deck*, pp. 104-105.

With the small number of CVEs focussed on providing air defence support to operations in the Mediterranean, the burden on providing air cover to Atlantic convoys was to fall on another type of carrier, the Merchant Aircraft Carrier or MAC ship. Both Fleet and CVE carriers saw anti-submarine duties as one of the functions they would carry out on behalf of the fleet, but the MAC ships were different in that, now the Condor menace had been resolved, they would be configured to exclusively support merchant convoys in the anti-U-boat role, primarily on the Atlantic run. As air defence was not a role for which they were required, this meant that they could continue to use the slow-moving Swordfish whose endurance, reliability and adaptability in carrying a variety of loads was still operationally useful.

MAC ships came from an Admiralty requirement to fit the simplest possible flight deck to an existing merchantman. Much simpler than CVEs they took only a few months to convert and importantly retained their ability to carry cargo. The ships were usually either petrol tankers, or grain ships, as both cargoes were more easily loaded and unloaded despite the presence of a flight deck. The grain ships had a small hangar and lift and a flight deck about 130 metres long and 11.5 metres wide, the petrol tankers had a slightly longer flight deck but no hangar.[33] These decks were truly miniscule, and the MACs could only therefore carry four Swordfish aircraft. The MAC ship design was much admired, the bulk of the merchant ship was left intact, the funnel being turned horizontally; and an island constructed on the starboard side amidships in which the Air Staff Officer (ASO) would control the Air Party of aircrew and engineers as well as the small Navy party of gunners, signalmen and medics. Unlike CVEs or even the *Audacity,* the MAC ships would remain Merchant Navy vessels under the orders of the ship's Master. It would be he who would handle the ship turning it into wind for landing on and off as required. The Senior Officer Escorts (SOE) was the senior Royal Navy officer in charge of the convoy's escorts and he would determine the actual programme of flying. This was an inspired and pragmatic decision, though it necessitated the Royal Navy personnel signing the MAC ship's articles (for which they received a shilling a month and a bottle of beer a day). The result was that Royal Navy and Merchant Navy relations were generally harmonious and the Swordfish crews took great pride in their role, to the extent of painting MERCHANT NAVY on the side of their aircraft.

The aircrew all came from 836 Squadron, based in Maydown, Northern Ireland. Each MAC ship would have 3-4 Swordfish[34] as its Air Party, with a complement of four fitters and riggers to care for the engines and air frames respectively. Three electricians and two ordnance mechanics would also be embarked upon the MAC ship, to look after the Swordfish's weapons. The Swordfish had been steadily improved upon throughout the war and were now much better equipped. They now had an ASV radar set, as well as Rocket Assistance Take-Off Gear (RATOG) so that they could launch carrying heavy loads, including up to six Depth Charges and armour-piercing Rocket Projectiles (RPs). These RPs were the same as those used in the anti-shipping campaign and the Swordfish was found to be a particularly stable firing platform, with good crews able to achieve high levels of accuracy. The rockets were highly destructive when used against a U-boat.[35]

The Swordfish would land on the MAC ship as it left port and await instructions from the SOE. On occasions he would simply require them to maintain a constant patrol around the limits of visibility of the convoy (known as a VIPER), or patrol back and forth (an ADDER). On other occasions the aircraft might be tasked to do a search of a position up to 100 miles from the convoy (known as a LIZARD, PYTHON or MAMBA). These searches of suspected U-boat positions might be triggered by either an intercept from Bletchley or an HF/DF fix of the U-boat by other

33   Poolman, Kenneth, *Allied Escort Carriers of World War Two*, pp. 62-63.
34   Petrol Tanker MAC vessels had only three.
35   Lord Kilbracken, *Bring Back My Stringbag*, p. 10.

vessels in the convoy. On other occasions the SOE simply wished for the Swordfish to be on cockpit standby. John Godley (later Lord Kilbracken) was a Swordfish pilot on the MAC ship *Accavus* and describes a typical patrol, where HF/DF had located the presence of a U-boat some 60 miles south of the convoy:

> Ten-tenths cloud at under 1000 feet so six depth charges are loaded under my mainplanes in place of the customary RPs. The convoy already dead into wind, so no need to leave our station for me to scramble. *Acavus* pitching quite badly but this doesn't affect take-off: with almost 40 knots over the deck, my groundspeed is little more than a walk as we shudder skywards. Jake gives me a course to steer and I hold it just below the clouds. Visibility five miles. The convoy soon disappears astern of us.
>
> It was the first time, though it became a frequent experience, that I had flown out of sight of any vessel and far out of range of land. This brings a special sense of loneliness, especially when in a relatively small, single engine aircraft with radio silence in force except in emergency or on sighting the enemy. On such flights, the monotony and vastness of that unending expanse beneath us becomes so intense that any break is welcome – a slick of oil, a flight of sea-birds, a large patch of seaweed, a whale perhaps or an iceberg – and we would swoop down to examine it. Well over an hour to reach the U-boat's reported position. All eyes skinned but nothing to be seen. And we start our square search, which will take another hour, of the area surrounding it.
>
> The inherent dangers of flying in these conditions, amazing as this now seems, really worried us not at all. We carried four inflatable dinghies – a big one in the upper mainplane, large enough for all of us, equipped with all necessary equipment, and a small one for each of us, which formed part and parcel of our parachutes – and had total confidence (as we had to have) that our May-Day signal would be heard if our engine stopped turning, that our well-equipped dinghies would operate efficiently and that an escort vessel would be sent for us and find us …
>
> We completed our search and headed homewards. *Acavus* still pitching badly, her stern rising and falling some 15-20 feet as she rode the long Atlantic swell. But my groundspeed would again be so low that instead of landing the Stringbag on the deck I should practically be able to wait for the deck to rise up and catch the Stringbag. I approached with a fair bit of motor and was given the signal to cut, whereupon the deck rose so violently that the impact neatly snapped off my tail wheel. I had no problem catching a wire and damage was minimal – it was repaired within the hour – but I must say it was a pity.[36]

During their two years of service, from May 1943 until 8 May 1945, the MAC ships undertook 323 Atlantic crossings and their aircraft flew 4,177 patrols, on only one occasion was a convoy which included a MAC ship, successfully attacked. Though successful attacks on U-boats were rare, the Swordfish undoubtedly played their part in keeping the U-boats submerged and making it much harder for them to track a convoy successfully, let alone get in to a good attacking position as a wolf pack. A total of 19 vessels were converted to MAC ships and, together with CVEs, operated in the Arctic as well as Atlantic convoys, countering very dangerous and highly effective submarine and air attacks from German bases in Norway.

By 1944, the Fleet Air Arm was almost unrecognisable from its 1939 forbears and undoubtedly becoming more and more sophisticated in its operations. Not a moment too soon for as the war concluded in Europe, the Royal Navy's focus began to shift to the Indian and Pacific

---

36 Lord Kilbracken, *Bring Back My Stringbag*, p. 117.

A Fairey Swordfish comes in to land on the escort carrier HMS *Smiter*.
(Crown Copyright – Air Historical Branch)

A Corsair awaits the signal to take off. Behind it a formation of Avengers is forming up.
(Crown Copyright – Air Historical Branch)

Oceans. In these waters the full suite of Fleet Air Arm capabilities was required in a large coordinated maritime campaign against a determined and highly effective Japanese enemy. Initial views, including Churchill's, were that the Royal Navy should concentrate on the Indian Ocean and ejecting the Japanese from Burma and Malaya. This was more logistically practical and would restore the elements of the Empire lost in 1942. A campaign here would also make this theatre an almost exclusively British affair and allow Britain to win its own peripheral victory against Japan. However, the Chiefs of Staff argued that a British Pacific Fleet should be formed, which would join forces with the United States Navy participating in the main direct attack on Japan itself. A fleet in the Pacific would also help cement Australia and New Zealand back into the commonwealth fold.[37] Churchill correctly argued that the ever-increasing power and might of the United States Navy, would make a British contribution both unwanted and redundant. In many ways he was right and though the Pacific campaign would highlight the high level of seamanship and fighting power within the Royal Navy and Fleet Air Arm, it would also demonstrate that Britain was at the end of her financial tether and the technological dynamism that Britain possessed in her ship building and maritime aviation industry had been eclipsed.[38]

Nonetheless the Admiralty were successful in establishing a Main Fleet Base at Sydney, Australia as well as an advanced base in the Pacific (constructed by the Americans for the British at Manus – in the aptly named Admiralty Islands (see Map 14). The Royal Navy also assembled and equipped a fleet train so that the Pacific Fleet was logistically self-sufficient. On its way to the Pacific, the British Fleet conducted a series of raids against Japanese oil refineries in the Dutch East Indies code-named Operation ROBSON and LENTIL. These took place against Pangkalan Brandan and Belawan Deli. Although these affairs were limited to 'tip and run' type raids against negligible opposition, they nonetheless gave the aircrews valuable experience in strike operations. This was useful practice for a further attack at the request of the US Navy commander, Admiral Nimitz, on the major Japanese oil refinery at Palembang.

Palembang contained both the largest and second largest oil production facilities in the Far East (Royal Dutch Shell's facility at Pladjoe and Standard Oil's at Soengi Goreng respectively). Together they produced nearly two-thirds of Japanese aviation fuel and therefore any disruption to this supply would be a major blow to the enemy. A strike on Palembang (Operation MERIDIAN 1) was a hazardous proposition, not just because of the target's importance, but also because the refinery was a significant way in-land and was expected to be well defended.

There were to be three strikes, one initially at Pladjoe, a second at Soenie Goreng and a third to exploit the strikes at both. Both strikes involved a strong force of Avengers armed with four 500lb bombs each (the fleet had sensibly offloaded its Barracuda TBRs and was now entirely equipped with the Avenger TBRs). These would be escorted by Corsair and Hellcat fighters, which would be stacked at three separate levels giving high, middle and close cover. *Indefatigable*'s Fairey Fireflies[39] would also strike specific targets with their 60lb rockets and two Corsair groups would suppress the Japanese airfields through offensive sweeps. The remaining fighters, which comprised Corsairs, Hellcats and Seafires would provide a Combat Air Patrol (CAP) over the Fleet during the operation. Two Walrus amphibians, known as 'Darby' and 'Joan', would provide air sea rescue in conjunction with a well-positioned submarine on the aircraft's route back.[40] This largely forgotten raid, involving 45 Avengers as well as some 80 fighters, was to be the largest Fleet Air Arm strike

---

37 Corelli Barnett, *Engage the Enemy More Closely*, p. 876.
38 Corelli Barnett, *Engage the Enemy More Closely*, p. 88.
39 The Fairey Firefly was single-engine two-seater fighter and reconnaissance aircraft that entered service in 1944.
40 John Winton, *Find, Fix and Strike!*, pp. 120-4.

A Seafire hits the barrier on HMS *Indefatigable* after returning from the strike on a Japanese oil refinery at Pangkalan Brandan, Sumatra. (Crown Copyright – Air Historical Branch)

undertaken during the war, its complexity and sophistication demonstrate how far the service had come in the war. Eric Rickman was an Avenger pilot with 854 Squadron on *Illustrious,* his Squadron was asked to return to Palembang on 30 January and strike Soenie Goreng:

> At dawn the next day, in JZ240, and in tight formation, we approached Soenie Gerong at 12,000 ft. The CO called, 'Line astern … go!' and we dropped back to 100-yard intervals. I heard my gunner's Browning start chattering, then stop. 'There's an Oscar on our tail!' Vick said, 'But my guns jammed.' 'Never mind,' I replied, 'I'm going down now.' And as I put the Avenger into a vertical dive, I could see three Avengers ahead of me, then the balloons, and below them, yes there it was the pump house!
>
> But between us and our target I could see a balloon cable, and I thought Charlie [Lieutenant Commander Charles Mainprice] would go round it, but he didn't. To my horror he hit it, shearing off most of his port wing, like a hot knife through butter, then going into a vicious one-wing spin, and blowing up on impact, seconds later. The second Avenger rounded the cable and made its attack, then next, just ahead of me, was Roland Armstrong. I couldn't believe my eyes when he hit the same cable as the CO, with exactly the same result. I felt sick and angry, why the hell didn't they see that cable?
>
> I jerked myself back to reality, time to bomb! I jinked round the damn cable, pressed the bomb-button, and at about 300 mph started to pull out, only to find myself facing a huge rising smoke cloud, black with jagged gouts of flame billowing up right ahead. Realising that I couldn't do anything else, I went straight into it. It seemed a good idea at the time, might avoid flak, but the turbulence was so violent that the stick was whipped out of my hand and the 7-ton Avenger was tossed around like a cork. All my navigator's equipment was sent flying around, a wet accumulator had fallen over and its acid had nearly reached the aircraft's self-destruct device.

A Grumman Avenger of 846 Squadron, Fleet Air Arm lands on HMS *Trumpeter*.
(Crown Copyright – Air Historical Branch)

When we emerged from the smoke, on our side at 500 ft, I grabbed the stick, went down to tree-top height, and headed for the coast, blasting away with my front guns at anything worth firing at. I had just started to climb, when I spotted another Avenger, away down to Starboard, it seemed O.K., wasn't trailing smoke, but I realised it was in a shallow dive, and it blew up as it hit the sea.[41]

Sixteen aircraft were lost on the strikes at Palembang, but the results were worth it for by May 1945 Palembang's production had still only risen to half its normal capacity, and it would not attain full-flow until the end of the War. An estimated total of 35 aircrew were captured by the Japanese, who carried out their brutal practice of beheading them over the coming months, both in Sumatra and in Singapore.[42] It is always surprising that given the success, sophistication and scale of this operation, that the raid on Palembang is not better known.

Buoyed by the success at Palembang, the British Pacific Fleet sailed to Manus, joining Admiral Spruance's American 5th Fleet in March 1945 as Task Force 57. The Fleet by this stage consisted of four armoured fleet carriers (*Formidable, Victorious, Indefatigable* and *Implacable*), two battle-ships, six cruisers and 11 destroyers as well as its rather ramshackle fleet train of supply ships. From 25 March, the British Pacific Fleet was used to neutralise the Japanese airfields on the Sakishima Gunto group of islands, whilst the Americans assaulted Okinawa. This was then switched to Japanese airfields on Formosa, where the *Kamikaze* attacks were thought to be originating from. The British had encountered *Kamikaze*'s before in the Indian Ocean, but the intensity of *Kamikaze* attacks in the Pacific war was much higher. The *Kamikaze* pilots were briefed to attack the flight

41   Frank Ott, *Air Power at Sea in the Second World War*, p. 123.
42   John Winton, *Find, Fix and Strike!*, pp. 130-134.

deck lifts or the funnel, as a result false lifts had been painted on the deck of some British ships to deceive the Japanese aircrew. Whilst many Japanese aircraft were destroyed by the combat air patrol over the fleet, some inevitably got through. Ivor Morgan was a pilot on 894 Squadron and was grounded on 1 April because of an ear infection. He was instead being employed as the Duty Pilot on *Indefatigable,* where he witnessed the first strike by a *Kamikaze* on the carrier:

The first inkling I had of trouble was the sound of aerial firing and, looking upwards, saw two aircraft in the tail chase about 2,000 feet above the ship. At first I thought they were two of ours and it had only just registered that the leading machine had a radial engine, whereas our Seafires had in-lines, when it turned on its back and I distinctly saw the 'Rising Sun' roundels on its wings as the pilot commenced a power dive directly at the spot where I was standing.

By this time all hell had broken. All of our guns, from 5.25s to pom-poms and additions, had opened fire, people were yelling. The Captain gave a helm order, I rushed to the main bridge, closed the armoured door behind me – and flung myself down the full length on the deck, together with everyone else.

We waited as the engine roar got louder and louder. There was no escape. This was it, this was how it was going to end. Pity, I thought, life is so enjoyable on the whole. I felt no fear, only a vague disappointment that the curtains were about to be drawn … Then came the crash, followed immediately by flame and a searing heat. I choked. I could not draw breath. I believe I lost consciousness. I next remember opening my eyes to see all the recumbent forms near me. All immobile. All dead, I thought I must be dead too. I tried to raise my shoulders and found that I was able to move although no one else had followed suit. Oh well, if this was being dead it wasn't so bad after all. Interesting to find that there was indeed a life hereafter, a fact in which I never had much faith.

'Port Fifteen'.

The Captain's voice brought us to our senses, and we shambled rather sheepishly to our feet. He above all, in his 'ice cream' suit, had remained erect and in command. This was the moment for which he had trained since joining, the navy as a 13-year-old cadet in 1914. And he did not fail.

From then on things moved fast. With certain communication lines out of action I was ordered below to assess damage and casualties, for we could now see that the *Kamikaze* had crashed into the bottom of the island at flight deck level. Flames engulfed both forward and after bridge ladders, so I swarmed down the thick knotted Manila rope which had been rigged for just such an emergency.

As I made my descent I saw Lt Cdr Pat Chambers, RN, Lt Cdr (Flying) staggering aft, his back covered with blood. Someone ran forward and guided him to safety. An Avenger, in the process of being taxied forward, had collided with the superstructure, engine and cockpit blown to smithereens. Of the pilot there was no sign.

The Damage Control Party was already hosing the flames and I could now see a gaping hole where the island sick bay had been. Being of small stature I was able to crawl through the wreckage and there they were, my comrades Al Vaughan and Bill Gibson, showing no sign of injury but both killed by the blast, which had removed most of their clothing. In the passage between the sick bay and the Fighter Ready Room lay Lt Leonard Teff, RNVR, Air Engineer Officer, also killed by the blast which, miraculously had left untouched the man either side of him. Looking upwards I realized that the bridge mess was no more. Oh Lord, what has happened to 'Wings'?

On regaining the bridge I was relieved to see Pat Humphries on the flight deck. A last minute dash to his cabin for some forgotten article had undoubtedly saved his life … Lt Cdr 'Sandy' Sanderson RN, Flight Deck Engineer, and his party were already rigging a replacement for

A Japanese suicide plane crashes on the flight deck of HMS *Formidable*, whilst operating off the Sakishima Gunto Islands in support of the Okinawa landings. A Corsair can be seen next to the island whilst wreckage burns at the far end of the flight deck. (Crown Copyright – Air Historical Branch)

No. 3 barrier which had been destroyed. Twenty minutes later we were landing on, S/Lt (A) Dick Reynolds RNVR (894 Sqdn) holding aloft a gloved hand to indicate two victories.

As soon as I was relieved, I went below to the hangar where maintenance crews were working with every sign of normality. They had thought their last moment had come when, unable to see what was happening, a terrific explosion occurred right above their heads. Flaming petrol ran down the hangar bulkhead, presumably through a fissure in the flight deck, threatening to engulf men and machines alike. Under the leadership of CPO 'Jimmy' Green, Senior Air Artificer, the fire was brought under control without having to resort to sprinklers.[43]

Fortunately for the British the armoured flight decks proved their worth, *Indefatigable* was operational within an hour of the attack described above. *Indomitable* and *Formidable* were also both struck on 1 May 1945, *Formidable* suffering a large dent that was resolved by pouring concrete into the hole to make a level surface once more. On 9 May 1945 there were more hits on *Victorious* and *Formidable,* but though aircraft were destroyed the ships remained operational. This survivability is in contrast to the wooden-decked American carriers who were to have seven carriers made unfit for action by Kamikazes over the same period.[44]

The British Pacific Fleet continued to operate alongside the Americans throughout the summer. Task Force 37 was formed from the British Pacific Fleet, based around the carriers *Formidable*,

43   Stuart Eadon, *Kamikaze – The Story of The British Pacific Fleet* (Worcester: Square One, 1991), pp. 236-238.
44   Frank Ott, *Air Power at Sea in the Second World War*, p. 123.

Victorious, *Implacable* and *Indefatigable* and took part in a series of raids on the Japanese main-land, as well strikes on shipping off the Japanese coast. Disappointingly the Americans behaved in a churlish manner to the Royal Navy, excluding them from the final action against the immo-bile Japanese fleet at Kure. To the American's shame, this seems to be simply so that the British would not be able to claim a major part in the final destruction of the enemy's fleet.[45] The British Pacific Fleet's operations, which were undoubtedly characterised by the effective use of maritime air power, were only brought to a halt by the Japanese surrender on 15 August.

It had been a long, hard war for the Fleet Air Arm. They had been originally poorly served in aircraft, but that had been put right, they were also sometimes ignored or treated resentfully by a Navy that hankered after surface ship action and instinctively begrudged the aviation upstarts and their new weapons. The combination of these produced a unique culture, observed by many members and described well by Hugh Popham:

> The Branch lived under the assumption that the odds in any action would be unfavourable, but I don't think this daunted anyone particularly. High odds and indifferent weapons, if attended with occasional successes, breed a perverse pride in those who suffer from them, or at worst, a useful fatalism. And, of course, as a service it was still small, and had the intense, compact loyalty of an arm in which the majority of members know each other. Loyalty, pride and fatalism provide a sound emotional basis for first-line squadrons operating under difficult conditions, and the Branch had all three.[46]

There had been precious few of them at the start, a mixture of straight ringed regular aircrew and peace-time amateur enthusiasts who had joined on the outbreak of war. Few of the former were left and whole training courses of the latter had been wiped out. The risks of flying at sea had killed many, of the others, the odds of surviving encounters with an enemy in superior aircraft were sometimes too great. There were however sufficient of them that did survive to hold the ring, while the large inject of RNVR crews arrived. Unlike other areas of aviation, the Fleet Air Arm pilot's operational tempo rarely relented. There were few operational breaks, or even a concept of what a tour length should be, the unique demands of carrier flying over a hostile sea being barely appreciated. An arguably unsympathetic Royal Navy was unaware of the stresses being imposed on its flyers. Some men were undoubtedly pushed too far and over time began to develop what was known as 'The Twitch'. This manifested itself, ultimately, in a fear of flying, a fatal weakness in a pilot. John Godley recognised the early signs after he had taken over command of a training squadron. After an accident, where the ether in the leaking hydraulics of the deservedly unpopular Barracuda had very nearly sent him unconscious, his fear of flying had become severe. The close of war finally gave him the impetus to see the doctor:

> He was so very sympathetic. As though he'd been expecting me. So I hadn't flown at all since that very unpleasant incident two months ago? Well, you know, it isn't really surprising. And only seven hours since April. We're always getting cases like this, it's nothing out of the ordinary. Tell me more about flying. Well, over three years in front-line squadrons, Doc. Yes goddammit and 67 operations. And 132 deck landings. And flying more than 1000 hours in every kind of God-awful weather. And four total engine failures and being hauled frozen from the Atlantic and flying through the Newcastle balloons and *Bluebell* disappearing. And the Albacore sinking under me and the Chesapeake overturning and the bloody flak coming

45   Corelli Barnett, *Engage the Enemy More Closely*, p. 894.
46   Hugh Popham, *Sea Flight*, p. 48.

up at me time and time again and the ship pitching like crazy for Arctic landings. But worst of all, Doc these fucking Barras. I was a Stringbag boy, Doc, bring back my Stringbag and I'll fly it, but not these gremlin-filled Barracudas which will spin as soon as look at you, their wings folding in mid-air, and now they fucking anaesthetize you for God's sake. And if I don't kill myself I'll kill someone else, Doc. Maybe one of these kids, and Jesus, I can't take it anymore, I'm just twitched to hell, I've had it.

Sitting there with my DSC ribbon and the ribbons of all the campaign gongs that had just been dished out to everyone and my two-and-a-half stripes and yet still not 25. And this torrent of fears, which pride, or self-deceit had so long kept damned inside me, pouring forth once the first crack had been opened in the gates to this silent concerned hearer.[47]

John Godley's fear of flying prevented him from getting in an aircraft for decades to come, but it is fair to say he would count himself as one of the lucky ones who survived the war. Most pilots in the Fleet Air Arm were well aware that the odds were heavily stacked against them. Olivia Fitzroy was an officer in the WRNS and served in Ceylon in 1942, where she met a Fleet Air Arm pilot. He was sadly killed during the war and her poem about a lost boyfriend seems the most appropriate way to close this chapter:

'Good show!' he said, leaned his head back and laughed
'They're wizard types!' he said, and held his beer
Steadily, looked at it and gulped it down
Out of its jam jar, took a cigarette
And blew a neat smoke-ring into the air
'After this morning's prang I've got the twitch;
'I thought I'd had it in that teased out kite.'
His eyes were blue and older than his face,
His single stripe had known a lonely war,
But all his talk and movements showed his age.
His jargon was of aircraft and of beer.
'And what will you do afterwards?' I said.
Then saw his puzzled face and caught my breath.
There was no afterwards for him but death.[48]

47   Lord Kilbracken, *Bring Back My Stringbag*, p. 214.
48   Olivia Fitzroy, *Fleet Fighter Pilot* (Oxford: Salamander Oasis Trust, 2012).

Concluding Thoughts

The preceding chapters have touched on a number of elements in the British Commonwealth's air war. Of primary importance were the battles for air superiority, either over Britain itself, or other parts of the Commonwealth including Australia and India. These included battles to safeguard manufacturing areas, seats of government and centres of population, but also a number of front-line battles, to neutralise the enemy's offensive potential, such as at Malta or New Guinea. The failures at Crete, Singapore and Java highlight that winning air superiority is only ever possible if there is a functioning air defence system and the right quality and quantity of aircraft and aircrew.

The air superiority the Allies attained, meant they could secure and protect their own lines of communication – which at a strategic level were maritime in nature. This is essentially what Coastal Command did during the Battle of the Atlantic, using the speed, reach and flexibility of airpower to constrain the U-boats and strike them when they were encountered. It was one of the decisive battles of the war and Coastal Command's part in it was profound. In a different manner the Fleet Air Arm too contributed to the same end of protecting the sea lanes, striking enemy surface raiders or fleets, battling enemy aircraft over convoys or even hunting U-boats from escort carriers or MAC ships. It is hard to under-estimate the importance of this aspect of the air war. In Europe it allowed Britain to survive and the Allies to build up a large land capability that would eventually invade the continent, initially through the Mediterranean and subsequently through Normandy. In the Far East it helped supply India, Australia and New Zealand, as well as support an amphibious island-hopping campaign that ultimately took the Allies to Japan.

Over continental Europe the British could not achieve 'air superiority and recognising that daylight raids for heavy bombers were impractical, adapted their approach to an area night bombing offensive. It was a major element of the war and whilst it did not knock Germany out of the war, it is reasonable to state that it supressed and disrupted German industrial capacity and helped create the conditions for a decisive ground campaign. It was only the entry of Russia and America into the war alongside the British Empire that made a land campaign in Europe a practicable and preferred option for Britain and her Allies, up to that point and for a good while afterwards the only method the British had of directly bringing the war to Germany itself was by air attack.

We have already partially seen how Commonwealth air forces were able to contribute to the ground campaigns in profound ways. The actions of the anti-shipping squadrons in Malta weakened the Axis lines of communications across the Mediterranean and the role of the Australian squadrons in New Guinea played a similar role in disrupting Japanese maritime support to its garrisons in the South West Pacific. Volume 2 – *Undaunted* will expand further and show how the British Commonwealth utilised air power to deliver a decisive advantage to its Armies, innovating a new approach to air-land integration. It included air intelligence in the form of air photographic reconnaissance, close air support of frontline troops, as well as battlefield air interdiction of the enemy's supplies and reinforcements just beyond the front. Volume 2 will also cover usage of air transport for glider and parachute operations in Europe, as well as in the Far East where it allowed the armies deployed there to conduct tactical and operational manoeuvre in some of the harshest environments in the world.

The themes of innovation, flexibility, cooperation, leadership, courage and determination were key to the operational success recounted in this first Volume – *Through Adversity*. They remain equally important in Volume 2.

Annexes

Annex A

Personnel Strength of Royal Air Force 3 September 1939 to 1 September 1945[1]

DATE	RAF		WAAF		TOTAL		GRAND TOTAL
	Officers	Other Ranks	Officers	Other Ranks	Officers	Other Ranks	
3 Sep 1939	11,519	162,439	234	1,500	11,753	163,939	175,692
1 Oct 1940	23,636	396,473	1,170	16,194	24,806	412,667	437,473
1 Oct 1941	37,880	734,727	3,012	61,297	40,892	796,024	836,916
1 Oct 1942	54,483	846,065	5,379	136,088	59,862	982,153	1,042,015
1 Oct 1943	74,034	914,362	5,880	174,459	79,914	1,088,821	1,168,735
1 Oct 1944	92,577	907,600	6,276	164,968	98,853	1,072,568	1,171,421
1 Sep 1945	100,107	840,760	5,638	135,891	105,745	971,013	1,076,758

---

1   TNA AHB/II/116/14: Manning Plans and Policy, Appendix 3.

Annex B

First Line Aircraft Strength of the RAF and German and Italian Air Forces, 30 September 1938 to 1 January 1945[1]

Date	RAF[2]	German[3]	Italian
30 September 1938	1,982	3,307	-
3 September 1939	1,911	4,161	-
1 August 1940	2,913[4]	4,549	1,529 (June)
1 December 1941	4,287	5,178	2,212 (Nov)
1 March 1943	6,026	6,107	1,947
1 June 1944	8,339	6,967	-
1 January 1945	8,395	6,638	-

1   Hilary Saunders and Denis Richards, *Royal Air Force 1939-45, Volumes I-III* (London: HMSO, 1954), drawn from Appendices IV or V in each volume.

2   These figures are based on the official 'establishment' for the initial equipment (I.E.) of squadron, home and overseas, Moreover, there was an immediate reserve (I.R.) varying from four to five aircraft per squadron. After June 1944 this initial equipment and immediate reserve were grouped together in what became Unit Equipment (U.E.).

3   The German figures extracted from *Luftwaffe* records are for actual strength. They include in each case a powerful transport force.

4   Aircraft of Dominion or Allied air forces under RAF control inclusive.

Annex C

Flying Training Schools in Operation on 3 September 1943[1]

Schools	United Kingdom	Canada	Australia	New Zealand	South Africa	Southern Rhodesia	Middle East	USA and Bahamas	India	Total
Initial Training Wing	23	7	5	1	1	1	-	-	1	39
Elementary Flying Training	17	21	6	3	7	4	-	-	2	60
Service Flying Training	2	29	5	2	7	4	-	-	1	50
Bombing and Gunnery	-	11	3	-	-	-	-	-	-	14
Air Observer Navigation and Bombing and Gunnery	-	-	-	-	7	1	-	-	-	8
General Reconnaissance and Air Navigation	-	-	-	-	-	-	-	-	1	1
General Reconnaissance	-	1	-	-	1	-	-	-	-	2
Air Observers	-	11	4	-	-	-	-	-	1	16
Air Gunners	10	-	-	-	-	-	-	-	-	10
Wireless schools	7	3	-	-	-	-	-	-	-	10
Wireless Operator (Air Gunner)	-	-	3	-	-	-	-	-	-	3
Advanced Flying Unit (pilot)	10	-	-	-	-	-	-	-	-	10
Advanced Flying Unit (Observer)	9	-	-	-	-	-	-	-	-	9
Operational Training Units	57	7	-	-	2	-	6	1	2	75
Heavy Conversion Units	17	-	-	-	-	-	-	-	1	18
Technical Training Schools	1	2	-	-	-	-	-	-	-	3
British Flying Training schools	-	-	-	-	-	-	-	5	-	5
Total	153	92	26	6	25	10	6	6	9	333

---

1   Air Historical Branch, Air Publication 3233, *Flying Training* (London: HMSO, 1952), Appendix 3, p. 285.

Annex D

Analysis, by Air Forces, of the Total Output of Qualified Aircrew 1939-45[1]

Location of Output	Nationality	Pilots	Observers and Navigators	Air Bombers	Wireless Operators (Air Gunners)	Air Gunners	Flight Engineers	Total
United Kingdom	RAF	15,287	9,869	728	27,190	28,243	17,885	99,202
	RIAF	15	4	1	6	2	----	28
	Total	15,302	9,873	729	27,196	28,245	17,885	99,230
Canada	RAF	22,068	15,778	7,581	755	2,096	--	48,278
	RCAF	25,918	12,855	6,659	12,744	12,917	1,913	73.006
	RAAF	4,045	1,643	799	2,875	244	--	9,606
	RNZAF	2,220	1,583	634	2,122	443	--	7,002
	RIAF	18	--	--	--	--	--	18
	Total	54,269	31,859	15,673	18,496	15,700	1,913	137,910
Australia	RAAF	10,998	5,929	159	7,158	3,286	369	27,899
New Zealand	RNZAF	6,118	165	--	--	208	--	6,491
South Africa	RAF	4,227	10,170	2,404	--	445	--	17,246
	SAAF	4,123	2,072	56	1,909	622	79	8,861
	Total	8,350	12,242	2,460	1,909	1,067	79	26,107
Southern Rhodesia	RAF	7,216	717	--	--	1,591	--	9,524
	RAAF	514	61	--	--	8	--	583
	Total	7,730	778	--	--	1,599	--	10,107
India	RAF	165	21	--	--	--	14	200
	RIAF	791	93	--	185	17	--	1,086
	Total	956	114	--	185	17	14	1,286
Middle East	RAF	272	38	--	--	1,116	--	1,472
USA	RAF	13,673	1,715	--	662	--	--	16,050
Grand Total	RAF	62,909	38,308	10,713	28,607	33,536	17,899	191,972
	RCAF	25,918	12,855	6,659	12,744	12,917	1,913	73,006
	RAAF	15,557	7,633	958	10,033	3,538	369	38,088
	RNZAF	8,338	1,748	634	2,122	651	--	13,493
	SAAF	4,123	2,072	56	1,909	622	79	8,861
	RIAF	824	97	1	191	19	--	1,132
	Total	117,669	62,713	19,021	55,606	51,283	20,260	326,552

1   Air Publication 3233, *Flying Training* (London: HMSO, 1952), Appendix 3, p. 279.

Explanatory Notes

1. The figures for RAF personnel include the following approximate numbers of foreign aircrew personnel trained for Allied Air Forces serving with the RAF:-

Belgium	550
Czechoslovakia	950
Denmark	25
Netherlands	575
French	2,000
Greece	50
Poland	4,400
Yugoslavia	200
Total	8,750

2. The figures for the RAF personnel trained in Canada include 3,792 Fleet Air Arm personnel.
3. The figures for the USA include 598 American volunteers who were trained in refresher schools in the USA and served in the RAF.
4. The figures for Wireless Operator (Air Gunner) trained in the United Kingdom include 2,109 who were awarded their wireless operator brevets in the United Kingdom and subsequently received gunnery training in the Middle East.

Annex E
Organisational Diagrams

See diagrams following.

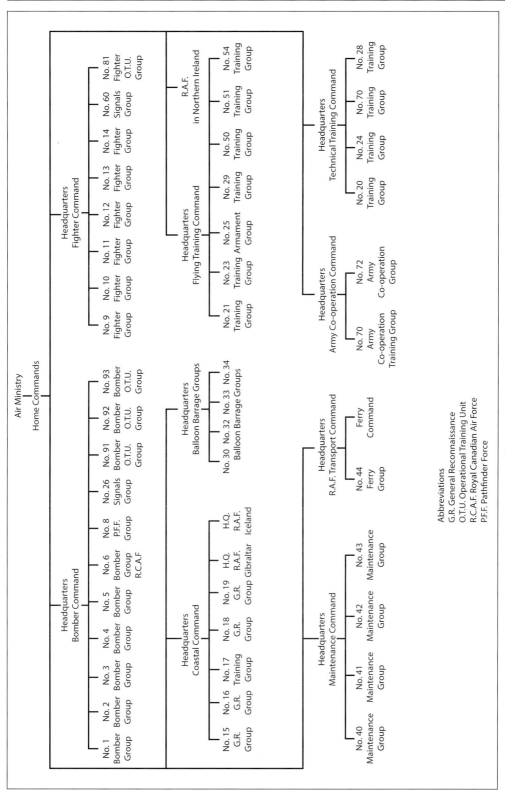

Diagram 1 Home Command as at March 1943.

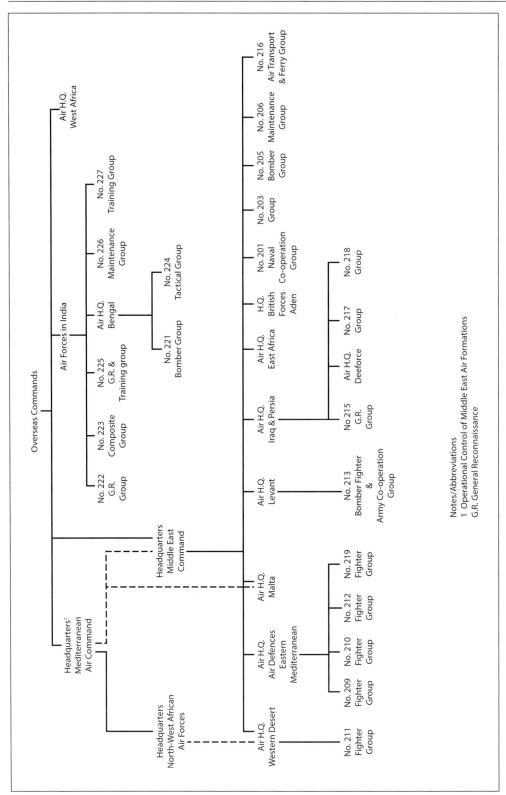

Diagram 2 Overseas Command as at March 1943.

Notes/Abbreviations
1 Operational Control of Middle East Air Formations
G.R. General Reconnaissance

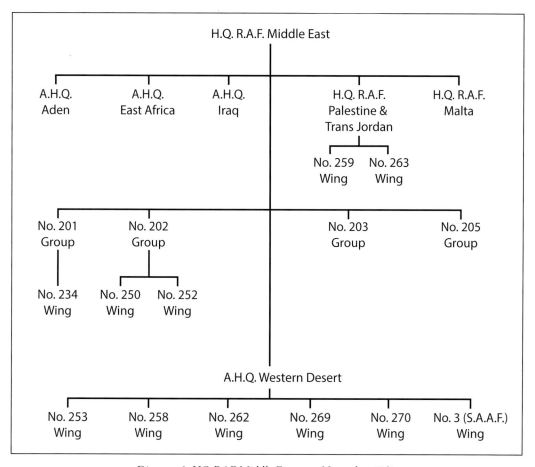

Diagram 3 HQ RAF Middle East as at November 1941.

Annex F

Order of Battle Fighter Command, 8 August 1940[1]

Sector	Squadron	Aircraft	Station
No. 10 Group, Rudloe, Nr Bath			
(Air Vice-Marshal Brand)			
Pembrey	92	Spitfire	Pembrey
Exeter	87	Hurricane	Exeter
	213	Hurricane	Exeter
St Eval	234	Spitfire	St Eval
	247	Gladiator	Roborough
Middle Wallop	238	Hurricane	Middle Wallop
	609 (West Riding)	Spitfire	Middle Wallop
	604 (County of Middlesex)	Blenheim	Middle Wallop
	152	Spitfire	Warmwell
No. 11 Group, Uxbridge			
(Air Vice-Marshal Park)			
Tangmere	43	Hurricane	Tangmere
	601 (County of London)	Hurricane	Tangmere
	145	Hurricane	Westhampnett
Kenley	615 (Auxiliary)	Hurricane	Kenley
	64	Spitfire	Kenley
	111	Hurricane	Croydon
Biggin Hill	32	Hurricane	Biggin Hill
	610 (County of Chester)	Spitfire	Biggin Hill
	501 (County of Gloucester)	Hurricane	Gravesend
	600 (City of London)	Blenheim	Manston
Hornchurch	54	Spitfire	Hornchurch
	65	Spitfire	Hornchurch
	74	Spitfire	Hornchurch
	41	Spitfire	Hornchurch
Northolt	1	Hurricane	Northolt
	257	Hurricane	Northolt
North Weald	151	Hurricane	North Weald
	56	Hurricane	Rochford
	25	Blenheim	Martlesham
Debden	17	Hurricane	Debden
	85	Hurricane	Martlesham

---

1   Basil Collier, *The Defence of the United Kingdom* (London: HMSO, 1957, Appendix XII).

Sector	Squadron	Aircraft	Station
No. 12 Group, Uxbridge **(Air Vice-Marshal Leigh-Mallory)**			
Duxford	19	Spitfire	Duxford
Coltishall	242	Hurricane	Coltishall
	66	Spitfire	Coltishall
Wittering	229	Hurricane	Wittering
	266	Spitfire	Wittering
	23	Benheim	Colly Weston
Digby	46	Hurricane	Digby
	611 (West Lancashire)	Spitfire	Digby
	29	Blenheim	Digby
Kirton-in-Lindsey	222	Spitfire	Kirton-in-Lindsey
	264	Defiant	Kirton-in-Lindsey & Ringway
Church Fenton	73	Hurricane	Church Fenton
	249	Hurricane	Church Fenton
	616 (South Yorkshire)	Spitfire	Leconfield
No. 13 Group, Newcastle-on-Tyne **(Air Vice-Marshal Saul)**			
Catterick	219	Blenheim	Catterick
Usworth	607 (Auxiliary)	Hurricane	Usworth
	72	Spitfire	Acklington
	79	Spitfire	Acklington
Turnhouse	232 (one flight only)	Hurricane	Turnhouse
	253	Hurricane	Turnhouse
	605 (County of Warwick)	Hurricane	Drem
	141	Defiant	Prestwick
Dyce	603 (City of Edinburgh)	Spitfire	Dyce and Montrose
Wick	3	Hurricane	Wick
	504 (County of Nottingham)	Hurricane	Castletown
	232 (one flight only)	Hurricane	Sumburgh
Aldergrove	245	Hurricane	Aldergrove

Annex G
Order of Battle Middle East Command, 11 November, 1941[1]

Headquarters, Royal Air Force Middle East

267 Squadron   Lodestar, Audax, Proctor
2 Photographic Reconnaissance Unit   Hurricane, Beaufighter

Air Headquarters Aden

8 Squadron   Various

Air Headquarters East Africa

3 (SAAF) Squadron   Mohawk
15 (SAAF) Squadron   Battle
16 (SAAF) Squadron   Junkers 86, Maryland
41 (SAAF) Squadron   Hartebeeste
34 (SAAF) Flight   Anson
35 (SAAF) Flight   Junkers 86
51 (SAAF) Flight   Junkers 52

Air Headquarters East Africa

52 Squadron   Audax
244 Squadron   Vincent
261 Squadron   Hurricane

Headquarters, Royal Air Force, Palestine and Trans-Jordan

259 Wing
213 Squadron   Hurricane
815 (FAA) Squadron   Albacore, Swordfish
263 Wing
335 Squadron   Hurricane
Free French Fighter Squadron   Morane
Free French Flight   Blenheim

Headquarters, Royal Air Force, Malta

18, 104, 107 Squadrons   Blenheim
40 (Det) Squadron   Wellington
69 Squadron   Maryland
126, 185, 249 Squadron   Hurricane
828 (FAA), 830 (FAA) Squadrons   Albacore, Swordfish

---

1   Denis Richards, *Royal Air Force 1939-45, Volume II* (London: HMSO), 1954, Appendix X, p. 382.

201 Group

2 (Yugoslav) Squadron	Dornier 21, Sim 14
13 (Hellenic) Squadron	Anson
Sea Rescue Flight	Wellington
RN Fulmar Flight	Fulmar
234 Wing	
39 Squadron	Boston, Maryland
203 Squadron	Blenheim, Beaufort
230 Squadron	Sunderland

202 Group

117 Squadron	Various
216 Squadron	Bombay
223 (Acting as Operational Training Unit)	Maryland
250 Wing	
73 Squadron	Hurricane
1 General Reconnaissance Unit	Wellington
252 Wing	
73 (Det), 213 (Det) Squadrons	Hurricane

203 Group

6 Squadron	Hurricane, Lysander
47 Squadron	Wellesley

205 Group

37, 38, 70, 108, 148 Squadrons	Wellington

Air Headquarters, Western Desert

31 (Det), 117 (Det) Squadrons	DC 2
33 Squadron	Hurricane
39 (Det), 60 (SAAF) Squadron	Maryland
113 Squadron	Blenheim (Fighter)
203 (Det) Squadron	Beaufort
216 (Det) Squadron	Bombay
272 (Det) Squadron	Beaufighter
826 (FAA) Squadron	Albacore, Swordfish
Strategic Reconnaissance Flight	Maryland
No.1 RAAF Ambulance Unit	DH 86
253 Wing	
208, 237, 451 (RAAF) Squadrons	Hurricane
258 Wing	
1 (SAAF), 94, 238, 274 Squadrons	Hurricane
2 (SAAF), 3 (RAAF) Squadrons	Tomahawk
262 Wing	
4 (SAAF), 112 and 250	Tomahawk
80 Squadron	Hurrican
229 and 260 Squadrons	Hurrican
269 Wing	
30 RN (Fighter) Squadron	Hurricane
270 Wing	
8 (Det), 14, 45, 55, 84, Lorraine Squadrons	Blenheim
3 (SAAF) Wing	
11 Squadron	Blenheim
12 (SAAF), 21 (SAAF) Squadron	Maryland

Annex H

Order of Battle, Coastal Command, 15 February, 1943[1]

Headquarter Coastal Command

15 Group

201,228, 246, 330, 422 (RCAF), 423 (RCAF) Squadrons	Sunderland
206, 220 Squadron	Fortress
120 Squadron	Liberator
280 (Det) Squadron	Anson (Air Sea Rescue)
1402 (Meteorological Calibration) Flight	Spitfire, Hudson, Gladiator

16 Group

143, 236, 254 Squadrons	Various
53, 320, 407 (RCAF) Squadrons	Hudson
86 Squadron	Liberator
415 (RCAF) Squadron	Hampden
521 (Meteorological Calibration) Flight	Spitfire, Hudson, Gladiator, Mosquito
279 Squadron	Hudson (Air Sea Rescue)
280 Squadron	Anson (Air Sea Rescue)
833 (FAA), 836 (FAA)	Swordfish
540, 541, 542, 543, 544	Mosquito, Spitfire, Wellington (PR)

18 Group

144, 235 Squadron	Beaufighter
455 (RAAF), 489 (RNZAF) Squadrons	Hampden
190 Squadron	Catalina
612 Squadron	Whitley
540 (Det) Squadron	Mosquito (PR)
1477 Flight	Catalina
1406 (Meteorological Calibration) Flight	Spitfire, Hudson

19 Group

172, 179 (Det), 304, 311, 547 Squadrons	Wellington
224, 1st and 2nd Antisubmarine (USAAF) Squadrons	Liberator
10 (RAAF), 119, 461 (RAAF) Squadrons	Sunderland
248, 404 (RCAF)	Beaufighter
502 Squadron	Whitley
58 Squadron	Whitley, Halifax
59 Squadron	Fortress
210 Squadron	Catalina
405 (RCAF) Squadron	Halifax
543 (Det) Squadron	Spitfire (PR)
1404 (Meteorological Calibration) Flight	Hudson, Ventura, Albermale
10 OTU (Det) Squadron	Whitley

---

1   Denis Richards, *Royal Air Force 1939-45, Volume II* (London: HMSO), 1954, Appendix VIII p. 378.

Headquarters, Royal Air Force, Iceland

269 Squadrons	Hudson
84th (US Navy) Squadron	Catalina
330 (Det) Squadron	Northrop
120 (Det) Squadron	Liberator
1407 (Meteorological Calibration) Flight	Hudson

Headquarters, Royal Air Force, Gibraltar

48, 233 Squadrons	Hudson
202, 210 Squadrons	Catalina
179 Squadron	Wellington
544 (Det) Squadron	Spitfire (PR)

Annex I

Order of Battle, Bomber Command, 4 March 1943[1]

Headquarter Bomber Command

1 Group

166, 199, 300, 301, 305 Squadrons	Wellington
12, 100, 101, 103, 460 (RAAF)	Lancaster

2 Group

21,464 (RAAF), 487 (RNZAF)	Ventura
88, 107, 226 Squadrons	Boston
98, 180 Squadrons	Mitchell
105, 139 Squadrons	Mosquito

3 Group

15, 75, 90, 149, 214, 218 Squadrons	Stirling
115 Squadron	Lancaster, Wellington
138 (Special Duties) Squadron	Halifax
161 (Special Duties) Squadron	Lysander, Halifax, Hudson, Havoc, Albermale
192 (Special Duties) Squadron	Halifax, Wellington, Mosquito

4 Group

10, 51, 76, 77, 78, 102, 158 Squadrons	Halifax
196, 429 (RCAF), 431 (RCAF), 466 (RAAF)	Wellington

5 Group

9, 44, 49, 50, 57, 61, 97, 106, 207, 467 (RAAF) Squadrons	Lancaster

6 Group

405 (RCAF), 408 (RCAF), 419 (RCAF) Squadrons	Halifax
420 (RCAF), 424 (RCAF), 425 (RCAF), 426 (RCAF), 427 (RCAF), 428 (RCAF) Squadrons	Wellington

8 Group

7 Squadron	Stirling
35 Squadron	Halifax
83, 156 Squadrons	Lancaster
109 Squadrons	Mosquito

---

1   Denis Richards, *Royal Air Force 1939-45, Volume II* (London: HMSO), 1954, Appendix IX, p. 380.

Annex J

Operational Aircraft of the Royal Air Force and Fleet Air Arm, 1939-1945[1]

British Bomber Aircraft
1939-1941

Aircraft Name/Mark	Maximum Speed (i)		Service Ceiling (ii)	Range plus Bombs (iii)		Armament
	mph	at feet	feet	miles	lbs	
Battle I	241	13,000	23,500	1,050	1,000	2 x .303 inch
Blenheim IV	266	11,800	22,000	1,460	1,000	5 x .303 inch
Halifax I	273	17,750	18,200	1,840	6,750	8 x .303 inch
				Or 850	13,000	
Hampden I	254	13,800	19,000	1,885	2,000	8 x .303 inch
				Or 1,200	4,000	
Manchester I	265	17,000	19,200	1,630	8,100	12 x .303 inch
				Or 1,200	10,350	
Maryland I	278	11,800	26,000	1,210	1,500	8 x.303 inch
				Or 1,080	2,000	
Stirling I	260	10,500	17,200	2,050	3,500	8 x .303 inch
				Or 750	14,000	
Wellington IC	235	15,500	18,000	2,550	1,000	6 x .303 inch
				Or 1,200	4,500	
Wellington II	247	17,000	20,000	2,450	1,250	6 x .303 inch
				Or 1,400	4,500	
Wellington IV	229	13,000	20,000	2,180	500	6 x .303 inch
				Or 980	4,000	
Whitley V	222	17,000	17,600	1,650	3,000	5 x .303 inch
				Or 470	7,000	

---

1   Hilary Saunders and Denis Richards, *Royal Air Force 1939-45, Volumes I-III* (London: HMSO, 1954), Appendices.

**British Bomber Aircraft
1942-1943**

Aircraft Name/Mark	Maximum Speed		Service Ceiling	Range plus Bombs		Armament
	mph	at feet	feet	miles	lbs	
Halifax II	260	18,500	21,800	1,900	3,000	8 x .303 inch
				500	13,000	
Halifax II-IA	260	19,000	21,000	1,900	4,000	9 x .303 inch
				600	13,000	
Halifax V	260	18,500	21,000	1,900	4,500	9 x.303 inch
				650	13,000	
Lancaster I and III	270	19,000	22,200	2,350	5,500	9 x .303 inch
				1,000	14,000	
Stirling III	270	14,500	17,000	2,010	3,500	8 x .303 inch
				590	14,000	
Wellington III	255	12,500	19,500	2,200	1,500	8 x .303 inch
				1,540	4,500	
Wellington X	255	14,500	19,600	2,085	1,500	6 x .303 inch
				1,470	4,500	
Mosquito IV	380	14,000	33,000	1,620	2,000	Nil
				1,450	4,000	
Mosquito IX	408	26,000	36,000	1,870	1,000	Nil
				1,370	5,000	
Baltimore III	302	11,000	22,000	950	2,000	10 x.30 inch
						4 x .303 inch
Boston III	304	13,000	24,250	1,020	2,000	8 x .303 inch
Mitchell II	292	15,000	20,000	1,635	4,000	6 x .50 inch
				950	6,000	

**British Bomber Aircraft
1944-45**

Aircraft Name/Mark	Maximum Speed		Service Ceiling	Range plus Bombs		Armament
	mph	at feet	feet	miles	lbs	
Halifax III	280	13,500	20,000	1,985	7,000	9 x .303 inch
				1,030	13,000	
Halifax VI	290	10,500	20,000	2,160	7,400	9 x .303 inch
				1,260	13,000	
Halifax VII	280	13,500	20,000	2,215	5,250	9 x .303 inch
				985	13,000	
Lancaster I, III and X	280	11,000	20,000	2,250	10,000	8 x .303 inch
				1,660	14,000	
Liberator VI	270	20,000	27,000	2,290	4,000	10 x .50 inch
				990	12,800	
Stirling III	270	14,500	17,000	2,010	3,500	8 x .303 inch
				590	14,000	
Wellington X	255	14,500	18,250	1,885	1,500	6 x .303 inch
				1,325	4,500	
Mosquito XVI	408	26,000	36,000	1,795	2,000	Nil
				1,370	5,000	
Mosquito XX	380	14,000	33,000	1,870	2,000	Nil
				1,620	3,000	
Baltimore V	300	13,000	19,000	1,000	2,000	8 x .50 inch
						4 x .30 inch
Boston IV	320	11,000	24,500	1,570	2,000	5 x .50 inch
				710	4,000	
Marauder III	305	15,000	28,000	1,200	4,000	11 x .50 inch

**British Fighter and Fighter-Bomber Aircraft
1939-1941**

Aircraft Name and Mark	Maximum Speed		Service ceiling	Climb Time to Height		Armament
	mph	at feet	feet	minutes	feet	
Beaufighter I F	324	11,750	27,000	9.4	15,000	6 x .303 inch 4 x 20 mm
Blenheim IV F	266	11,800	26,500	10	15,000	7 x .303 inch
Gladiator	245	15,000	32,500	7	15,000	4 x .303 inch
Hurricane I	316	17,500	33,200	6.3	15,000	8 x .303 inch
Hurricane II A	342	22,000	37,000	8.2	20,000	8 x .303 inch
Hurricane II B	342	22,000	36,500	8.4	20,000	12 x .303 inch
Hurricane II C	339	22,000	35,600	9.1	20,000	4 x 20 mm
Spitfire I	355	19,000	34,000	6.2	15,000	8 x .303 inch
Spitfire V	375	20,250	38,000	7	20,000	2 x 20 mm 4 x .303 inch
Tomahawk I	338	16,000	30,500	7.8	15,000	2 x .5 inch 4 x .303 inch

**British Fighter and Fighter-Bomber Aircraft
1942-1943**

Aircraft Name and Mark	Maximum Speed		Service ceiling	Climb Time to Height		Armament
	mph	at feet	feet	minutes	feet	
Beaufighter VI-F	333	15,600	26,500	7.8	15,000	4 x 20mm 6 x .303 inch
Hurricane II-C	339	22,000	35,600	9.1	20,000	4 x 20mm
Hurricane II-D	316	19,000	33,500	.75	2,000	2 x 40mm 2 x .303 inch
Kittyhawk I	350	15,000	29,000	8.7	15,000	4 or 6 x .50 inch
Mosquito II	370	14,000	35,000	7	15,000	4 x 20mm 4 x .303 inch
Mosquito VI	378	14,000	32,000	9.5	15,000	4 x 20mm 4 x .303inch (4 x 500lb)
Mosquito XII (N/F)	370	14,000	35,000	7	15,000	4 x 20mm
Mustang I	390	8,000	32,000	8.1	15,000	4 x .50 inch 4 x .303 inch
Spitfire V-B (L/F)	357	6,000	35,500	1.6	5,000	2 x 20mm 4 x .303 inch (1 x 500lb)
Spitfire IX	408	25,000	43,000	6.7	20,000	2 x 20mm 4 x .303 inch (1 x 500/2 x 250lb bombs)
Typhoon I-B	405	18,000	33,000	6.2	15,000	4 x 20 mm (2 x 1,000lbs or 8 x 60lb R.Ps)

**British Fighter and Fighter-Bomber Aircraft
1943-1945**

Aircraft Name and Mark	Maximum Speed		Service ceiling	Climb Time to Height		Armament
	mph	at feet	feet	mph	feet	
Meteor I	445	30,000	42,000	15	30,000	4 x 20mm
Meteor III	476	30,000	44,000	14	30,000	4 x 20mm
Mosquito XIII (N/F)	370	14,000	33,500	6.75	15,000	4 x 20mm
Mosquito XXX (N/F)	400	26,000	37,000	7.5	15,000	4 x 20mm
Mustang III	442	24,500	41,500	10.5	20,000	4 x .50 inch (2 x 500lb bombs)
Spitfire IX (H/F)	416	27,500	44,000	6.4	20,000	2 x 20mm and 4 x .303inch or 2 x 20mm and 2 x .50inch (1 x 500lb and 2 x 250lb bombs)
Spitfire IX (L/F)	404	21,000	41,500	6.4	20,000	2 x 20mm and 4 x .303inch or 2 x 20mm and 2 x .50inch (1 x 500lb and 2 x 250lb bombs)
Spitfire XIV	448	26,000	43,500	7	20,000	2 x 20mm and 4 x .303inch or 2 x 20mm and 2 x .50inch (1 x 500lb and 2 x 250lb bombs)
Spitfire XVI	405	22,500	41,500	6.4	20,000	2 x 20mm and 4 x .303inch or 2 x 20mm and 2 x .50inch (1 x 500lb and 2 x 250lb bombs)
Spitfire XXI and XXII	454	26,000	43,000	8	20,000	4 x 20mm (1 x 500lb and 2 x 250lb bombs)
Tempest V	435	19,000	36,000	7.5	20,000	4 x 20mm
Thunderbolt I	420	26,000	35,000	10.5	20,000	8 x .50inch (2 x 1,000lb)
Typhoon IB	405	18,000	33,000	6.2	15,000	4 x 20mm (2 x 1,000lb or 8 x 60lb R.Ps)

**British Coastal Command Aircraft
1939-41**

Aircraft Name and Mark	Cruising Speed and Endurance (iv)		Associated Bomb (or Depth Charge) load	Armament
	knots	hours	lbs	
Anson I	103	5½	200lb	6 x .303 inch
Beaufighter I C	180	5	-	4 x .303 inch 4 x 20 mm
Beaufort I	150	6	1,500 lb/1x 18-inch Torpedo	4 x .303
Blenheim IV F	150	6	-	6 x .303 inch
Hudson I	125	6	750 lb	7 x .303 inch
Sunderland I	115	12	2,000 lb	7 x .303 inch
Vildebeest IV	82	4.3	1,000lb/1 x 18-inch Torpedo	2 x .303 inch
Wellington I C	125	10.6	1,500lb	6 x .303 inch
Whitley V	110	9	1,500lb	5 x .303 inch

British Coastal Command Aircraft
1942-43

Aircraft Name and Mark	Cruising Speed and Endurance (iv)		Associated Bomb (or Depth Charge) load lbs	Armament
	knots	hours		
Catalina I	100	17.6	2,000	6 x .303 inch
	Or	25	Nil	
Catalina III	100	14.5	2,000	5 x .303 inch
Fortress II	140	10.7	1,750	9 x .50 inch
	Or	12.9	Nil	
Halifax II	135	10.4	2,250	9 x .303 inch
	Or	13.3	Nil	
Hampden (T/B)	120	7.25	1 x 18-inch torpedo	6 x .303 inch
Hudson VI	140	6.9	1,000	7 x .303 inch
Liberator I (VLR)	150	16.1	2,000	4 x 20mm 6 x .303 inch
Liberator III	145	11.6	3,000	6 x .50 inch
Liberator V	150	15.3	1,500	6 x .50 inch
Wellington I-C	120	9.3	2,000	6 x .303 inch
Whitley VII	105	10.3	2,000	5 x.303 inch
Wellington VIII	120	8.8	1,000	6 x .303 inch
Wellington XII	140	8.3	2,400	7 x .303 inch
Sunderland II	110	11.6	2,000	7 x .303 inch
Sunderland III	110	11.9	2,000	7 x.303 inch

British Coastal Command Aircraft
1944 – 45

Aircraft Name and Mark	Cruising Speed and Endurance (iv)		Associated Bomb (or Depth Charge) load llbs	Armament
	knots	hours		
Catalina IV	106	15.5	1, 500	2 x .50inch
Liberator III and V (VLR)	150	16.1	2,000	3 x .50inch
Liberator VI	138	10.5	3,500	6 x .50inch, 4x.303 inch
	Or	12.5	2,000	
Liberator VIII	138	10.5	3,500	6 x .50inch, 4 x.303inch
Sunderland III and V	110	13.5	2,000	7 x .303inch
	Or	15	1,000	
Warwick V	164	11	2,000	3 x .50inch, 4 x .303inch
Wellington XIV	140	10	1,500	7 x 303inch

Coastal Command Fighter and Strike Aircraft
1943-1945

Aircraft Name and Mark	Crusing Speed and Endurance		Associated Bomb (or RP) load	Armament
	knots	hours		
Beaufighter X (T/B)	180	4.5	1 torpedo	4 x 20mm
Beaufighter X (RP)	180	4.5	8 x 25lb or 8 x 60lb RPs	4 x 20mm
Beaufigher X (F/B)	180	4	1 x 2,000lb or 2 x 500lb and 2 x 250lb	4 x 20mm
Mosquito VI (F/B)	210	3.5	4 x 250lb	4 x 20mm, 4 x .303inch
Mosquito VI (F/RP)	210	5	8 x 25lb or 8 x 60lb RPs	4 x 20mm, 4 x .303inch
Halifax III	145	10	5,500lb	9 x .303inch
Wellington XIV	140	9.5	1,700lb	7 x .303inch

British Transport Aircraft
1939-1945

Aircraft Name and Mark	Still Air Range with Associated load		Most Economical Cruising Speed in miles per hour	Maximum Speed in miles per hour	Armament
	miles	load			
Bombay	1,500	10 troops	120 at 10,000 feet	159 at 10,000 feet	2 x .303inch
	330	24 troops			
Dakota C-47	1,910	26 troops with full equipment or 6,000lb freight	160 at 10,000 feet	220 at 10,000 feet	None
			183 at 14,000 feet	267 at 15,000 feet	None
Commando C-46	1,600	35 troops with full equipment or 10,000lb freight	157 at 15,000 feet		
			123 at 10,000 feet	212 at 4,500 feet	4 x .303inch
Lysander	1,410	500lb			

British Fleet Air Arm Aircraft
1939-1941

Aircraft Name and Mark	Fuel and Still Air Range at Most Economical Cruising Speed		Most Economical Cruising Speed mph	Maximum Speed in mph	Armament
	galls	miles			
Fulmar	155	820	170 at 10,000 feet	253 at 10,000 feet	8 x .303inch
Martlet III (Wildcat)	136	1,150	166 at 15,000 feet	330 at 19,500 feet	4 or 6 x
Corsair	192	673	251 at 20,000 feet	374 at 23,000 feet	.50inch
					6 x .50 inch

Aircraft Name and Mark	Still Air Range with Associated Bombload		Most Economical		
	miles	bombload	Cruising Speed mph	Maximum Speed in mph	Armament
Albacore	521	1 Torpedo or 1,500lb	105 at 6,000 feet	163 at 4,800 feet	2 x .303inch
Barracuda	1,010	1 Torpedo Or 1,600lb	138 at 6,000 feet	249 at 9,000 feet	1 x .303inch
Skua	980	500lb	157 at 15,000 feet	212 at 15,000 feet	5 x .303inch
Swordfish	528	1 Torpedo or 1,500lb	103 at 5,000 feet	139 at 5,000 feet	2 x .303inch
Walrus	600	500lb or 2 x Depth Charges	95 at 3,500 feet	135 at 4,750 feet	1 x .303inch

i.   **MAXIMUM SPEED** was only possible for an extremely limited period. Apart from tactical manoeuvring, bomber and fighter aircraft in the main flew at speeds between 'most economical cruising' and 'maximum continuous cruising'. Varying with the different aircraft, these speeds were respectively between 55-80 percent and 80-90 percent of the maximum speed.

ii. **SERVICE CEILING** The height at which the rate of climb has a certain defined low value (British practice 100 feet per minute). Ceilings quoted are for aircraft with full load.

iii. **RANGE AND ASSOCIATED BOMB LOAD** The main purpose of this table is to give some idea of the relative performances of various aircraft. The figures quoted relate to aircraft flying at 'most economical cruising' speed at the specified height (i.e the speed and height at which the greatest range could be obtained). Allowance is made for take-off but not for landing, the range quoted being the maximum distance the aircraft could cover in still air 'flying to dry tanks'. Furthermore in the planning of operations a reduction range of about 25 percent had to be made for navigational errors, tactical manoeuvring, weather conditions and other factors.

iv. **ENDURANCE** The time an aircraft can continue flying under given conditions without refuelling. This being a vital factor of Coastal Command operations an economical cruising speed, consistent with maximum safe endurance as determined under normal operational conditions is quoted.

v.   **ABBREVIATIONS** (F/B) Fighter Bomber; (F/RP) Fighter Rocket Projectile; (H/F) High Flying; (L/F) Low Flying; (N/F) Night-Fighter; (R/P) Rocket Projectiles; (T/B) Torpedo Bomber; (VLR) Very Long Range.

Annex K

Operational Aircraft of the German Air Force, 1939-45[1]

German Bomber and Reconnaissance Aircraft 1939-41

Aircraft Name/Mark	Maximum Speed		Service Ceiling	Range plus Bombs		Armament
	mph	at feet	feet	miles	lbs	
Junkers Ju 87B[2]	245	15,000	23,500	360	1,100	3 x 7.9mm
Henschel Hs 126	230	13,000	25,000	530	620	5 x 7.9mm
Dornier Do 17	255	15,000	21,000	1,440	1,100	7 x 7.9mm
				Or 890	2,200	1 x 20mm
Heinkel He 111	240	14,000	26,000	1,510	2,200	7 x 7.9mm
				Or 1,200	4,000	2 x 20mm
Junkers Ju 88	287	14,000	22,700	1,280	4,400	7 x 7.9mm
						1 x 20mm
Dornier Do 215	275	15,000	28,000	1,450	1,100	7 x 7.9mm
				Or 900	2,200	1 x 20mm
Focke-Wulf Fw 200[3]	240	13,600	20,500	2,150	3,600	3 x 13mm
				2700	(Recce)	3 x 15/20mm

German Bomber and Reconnaissance Aircraft 1942-43

Aircraft Name/Mark	Maximum Speed		Service Ceiling	Range plus Bombs		Armament
	mph	at feet	feet	miles	lbs	
Junkers Ju 87D	255	13,500	18,500	720	2,200	4 x 7.9mm
Junkers Ju 88B3	333	20,000	25,000	1,280	2,200	2 x 13mm
						2 x 7.9mm
Junkers Ju 188	325	20,000	33,500	1,200	4,400	1 x 20mm
						2 x 13mm
						2 x 7.9mm
Heinkel He 111	240	14,000	26,000	1,510	2,200	7 x 7.9mm
						2 x 20mm
Heinkel He 177	305	20,000	21,000	2,650	2,200	5 x 13mm
				1,150	12,320	4 x 13/20mm
Focke-Wulf Fw 200	240	13,600	20,500	2,150	3600	3 x 13mm
				2700	(Recce)	3 x 15/20mm

---

1   Hilary Saunders and Denis Richards, *Royal Air Force 1939-45, Volumes I-III* (London: HMSO, 1954), Appendices.

2   Stuka dive-bomber.

3   Known as the Condor or Kurier.

German Bomber and Reconnaissance Aircraft
1943-45

Aircraft Name/Mark	Maximum Speed mph at feet		Service Ceiling feet	Range plus Bombs miles lbs		Armament
	mph	at feet	feet	miles	lbs	
Junkers Ju 88S	370	26,000	35,000	700	1,980	1 x 13mm 1 x 7.9mm
Junkers Ju 188	325	20,000	33,500	1,200	4,400	1 x 20mm 2 x 13mm 2 x 7.9mm
Heinkel He 111	240	14,000	26,000	1,510	2,200	7 x 7.9mm 2 x 20mm
Heinkel He 177	305	20,000	21,000	2,650 1,150	2,200 12,320	5 x 13mm 4 x 13/20mm
Dornier Do 217E	305	18,000	21,500	1,170	4,000	4 x 7.9mm

German Fighter Aircraft
1939-1941

Aircraft Name and Mark	Maximum Speed		Service ceiling	Climb Time to Height		Armament
	mph	at feet	feet	minutes	feet	
Messerschmitt Me 109 E	355	18,000	35,000	6.2	16,500	2 x 7.9mm 2 x 20mm
Messerschmitt Me 109 F	395	22,000	36,500	5.75	17,000	2 x 7.9mm 3 x 20mm
Messerschmitt Me 109 G	400	22,000	38,500	6	19,000	2 x 7.9mm 3 x 20mm
Messerschmitt Me 110 D[4] A	360	20,000	34,000	8.5	18,000	6 x 7.9mm 4 x 20mm
Focke-Wulf Fw 190	385	19,000	36,000	6.5	18,000	2 x 7.9mm 2 x 20mm
Junkers Ju 88 C6	295	14,000	24,200	13.8	16,500	7 x 7.9mm 3 x 20mm

---

4   Marks E and F were of similar performance.

German Fighter Aircraft
1942-1943

Aircraft Name and Mark	Maximum Speed		Service ceiling	Climb Time to Height		Armament
	mph	at feet	feet	mins	height	
Junkers Ju 88C5	347	20,000	30,200	10.3	18,500	6 x 7.9mm 3 x 20mm
Messerschmitt 109G	400	22,000	38,500	6	19,000	2 x 7.9mm/13mm 3 x 20mm
Messerschmitt 110G	368	19,000	34,800	7.3	18,000	6 x 7.9mm 4 x 20mm 1 x 37mm
Messerschmitt 210	370	21,000	29,000	11.8	19,000	2 x 20mm 2 x 13mm
Messeschmitt 410	395	22,000	30,000	11.5	19,000	2 x 20mm 2 x 13mm 2 x 7.9mm
Focke-Wolfe Fw 190A3	385	19,000	36,000	6.5	18,000	4 x 20mm 2 x 7.9mm

German Fighter Aircraft
1944-1945

Aircraft Name and Mark	Maximum Speed		Service ceiling	Climb Time to Height		Armament
	mph	at feet	feet	mins	feet	
Junkers Ju 88C5	347	20,000	30,200	10.3	18,500	6 x 7.9mm 3 x 20mm
Messerschmitt 109G	400	22,000	38,500	6	19,000	2 x 7.9mm/13mm 3 x 20mm
Messerschmitt 110G	368	19,000	34,800	7.3	18,000	6 x 7.9mm 4 x 20mm 1 x 37mm
Messerschmitt 210	370	21,000	29,000	11.8	19,000	2 x 20mm 2 x 13mm
Messeschmitt 410	395	22,000	30,000	11.5	19,000	2 x 20mm 2 x 13mm 2 x 7.9mm
Focke-Wolfe Fw 190D	435	25,000	39,000	6.5	20,000	1 x 30mm 2 x 20mm 2 x 13mm
Messerschmitt Me 262	500	29,000	39,500	5	32,800	4 x 30mm/ 3 x 20mm or 6 x 30mm
Messerscmitt Me 163[5]	560	-	40,000	-	-	2 x 30mm
Arado	490	25,000	38,000	8	20,000	4 or 5 x 20mm

5   Liquid rocket propulsion: Range 70 miles/endurance of 8.5 minutes.

Annex L

Operational Aircraft of the Italian Air Force, 1939-45[1]

Italian Bomber and Reconnaissance Aircraft
1939-43

Aircraft Name/Mark	Maximum Speed		Service Ceiling	Range plus Bombs		Armament
	mph	at feet	feet	miles	lbs	
Savoia Marchetti Sm 79	255	13,000	21,500	1,570	1,100	3 x 12.7mm
				1,190	2,750	2 x 7.7mm
Savoia Marchetti Sm 81	210	15,000	24,500	1,030	2,200	6 x 7.7mm
				895	4,400	
Savoia Marchetti Sm 82	205	7,000	17,000	2,200	3,200	1 x 12.7mm
						4 x 7.7mm
Cantieri Riuniti Cant Z.506	230	13,000	19,000	1,685	1,750	1 x 12.7mm
				1,465	2,640	3 x 7.7mm
Cantieri Riuniti Cant Z.1007b	280	13,000	27,500	1,650	1,100	2 x 7.7mm
						2 x 12.7mm
Fiat B R 20	255	13,500	25,000	1,350	2,200	12 x 7.7mm
						1 x 12.7 mm

Italian Fighter Aircraft
1939-43

Aircraft Name and Mark	Maximum Speed		Service ceiling	Climb Time to Height		Armament
	mph	at feet	feet	minutes	feet	
Fiat C R 32	233	10,000	28,000	5.3	10,000	2 x 12.7mm
Fiat C R 42	270	13,100	32,000	5.5	13,000	2 x 12.7mm
Fiat G 50	300	14,500	32,000	6.4	15,000	2 x 12.7mm
Fiat G 55	380	20,000	38,000	5.8	20,000	2 x 12.7mm
						3 x 20mm
Aer Macchi C 200	310	15,000	32,000	6.25	15,000	2 x 12.7mm
Aer Macchi C 202	345	18,000	32,000	8.2	18,000	2 x 12.7mm

---

1   Hilary Saunders and Denis Richards, *Royal Air Force 1939-45, Volumes I-III* (London: HMSO), 1954) various Appendices.

Operational Aircraft of the Japanese Air Forces, 1942-45[1]

**Japanese Bomber and Reconnaissance Aircraft
1942-1943**

Aircraft Name/Mark	Maximum Speed		Service Ceiling	Range plus Bombs		Armament
	mph	at feet	feet	miles	lbs	
Nakajima – Navy 96 'Nell 23'	270	19,600	34,250	2,125	1,100	4 x 7.7mm 1 x 20mm
Mitsubishi – Army 97 'Sally 2'	294	15,500	30,500	1,635	2,200	4 x 7.7mm 1 x 12.7mm 1 x 20mm
Nakajima – Army 100 'Helen 2'	312	16,900	30,900	1,600	2,200	3 x 7.9mm 2 x 12.7mm 1 x 20mm
Nakajima – Navy 1 'Betty 22'	283	13,800	30,500	3,075	2,200	4 x 7.7mm 4 x20mm
Nakajima – Navy 2 'Liz 11'	270	16,100	29,100	2,990	7,240	No data
Kawasaki – Army 99 'Lily 2'	228	19,900	34,300	1,500	880	1 x 12.7mm 1 x 12.7mm 3 x 7.9mm
Nakajima Navy Tenzan 'Jill 12'	327	15,100	35,400	1,740	1 x Torpedo	2 x 7.7mm
Mitsubishi Navy-97 'Kate 12'	225	8,000	27,500	645	1 x Torpedo	4 x 7.7mm
Aichi Navy 99 'Val 22'	281	20,300	33,600	965	550	3 x 7.7mm

---

1   Hilary Saunders and Denis Richards, *Royal Air Force 1939-45, Volumes I-III* (London: HMSO, 1954), Appendices.

Japanese Bomber and Reconnaissance Aircraft
1944-1945

Aircraft Name/Mark	Maximum Speed		Service Ceiling	Range plus Bombs		Armament
	mph	at feet	feet	miles	lbs	
Mitsubishi Army 97 'Sally 2'	294	15,500	30,500	1,635	2,200	4 x 7.7mm 1 x 12.7mm 1 x 20mm
Nakajima Army 100 'Helen 2'	312	16,900	30,900	1,600	2,200	3 x 7.9mm 2 x 12.7mm 1 x 20mm
Nakajima Navy-1 'Betty 22'	283	13,800	30,500	3,075	2,200	4 x 7.7mm 4 x 20mm
Nakajima Navy- 'Frances 11'	367	17,200	35,500	2,430	1,875	2 x 20mm
Mitsubishi Army-4 'Peggy 1'	346	18,700	30,100	1,840	1,875	4 x 12.7mm 1 x 20mm
Mitsubishi Army 100 'Dinah 3'	420	10,700	40,600	1,730	(Recce)	1 x 7.7mm
Nakajima Navy Tenzan 'Jill 12'	327	15,100	35,400	1,740	1 x 1,765 Torpedo	3 x 7.7mm
Aichi Navy Ryusei 'Grace 11'	350	19,700	-	1,242	1 x 1,765 Torpedo	3 x 7.7mm
Aichi Navy Susei 'Judy 12'	377	19,300	36,400	2,445	550	3 x 7.7mm
Aichi Navy Susei 'Judy 33	376	18,500	38,300	2,505	550	3 x 7.7mm

Japanese Fighter Aircraft
1942-1943

Aircraft Name and Mark	Maximum Speed		Service ceiling	Climb Time to Height		Armament
	mph	at feet	feet	minutes	feet	
Nakajima Army 1 'Oscar 3'	358	21,900	37,400	7.4	20,000	2 x 12.7mm
Kawasaki Army 3 'Tony 1'	361	15,800	35,100	8.5	20,000	2 x 7.7mm
Nakajima Navy O 'Zeke 52' Or 'Zero'	358	22,000	35,100	7.8	20,000	2 x 13.2mm 2 x 7.7/13.2mm
Kawasaki Army 2 'Nick 1'	346	21,100	35,000	8	20,000	2 x 12.7mm 1 x 7.9mm 1 x 20mm

Japanese Fighter Aircraft
1944-1945

Mitsubishi Navy Raiden 'Jack 21'	417	16,600	38,800	5.1	20,000	4 x 20mm
Nakajima Army-4 'Frank 1'	427	20,000	38,800	5.8	20,000	2 x 12.7mm 2 x 20mm
Nakajima Navy Gekko 'Irving 11'	333	19,700	32,740	12.1	20,000	5 x 20mm
Kawanishi Navy Shiden 'George 11'	416	19,000	39,100	6.1	20,000	2 x 7.7mm 4 x 20mm
Nakajima Army-2 'Tojo 2'	383	17,400	36,350	6	20,000	6 x 12.7mm 4 x 20mm

Annex N

Spitfire MK II Cockpit Check[1]

Entering the Cockpit

Put on brakes. Check that ignitions switches are OFF, undercarriage selector level in DOWN gate, indicator showing IDLE. Switch on light indicator and note that green lights come on. Note that flaps and landing lamps are UP. Check contents of fuel tanks. Test flying controls.

Starting Up

Open radiator flap. Set mixture control to NORMAL and pitch controls fully FORWARD. Raise both fuel cocks levels to ON. Unscrew priming pump and give five effective shots of fuel. Screw down. See airscrew area is clear. Indicate readiness to erk at battery. Start Up.

Preliminaries to Testing

Wait until oil temperature is 15°C min and radiator temperature reaches about 70°C. Note fuel pressure is 2 and a half to three pounds and brake reservoir pressure at least 120 lbs p.s.i. Put flaps down and up again. Set altimeter and directional gyro. See hood is locked open and set emergency exit door at half cock position. Set harness release in 'fixed' position. Proceed to run up.

Engine Testing

In fine pitch, open up to rated gate, check that boost is + 9 lbs p.s.i., R.P.M. 2,750 to 2,850 and oil pressure is 60 lbs p.s.i. at NORMAL temperature. With pitch control fully forward check that magneto drop does not exceed 80 r.p.m. Keep throttle fully open and draw back airscrew control until r.p.m. drop to 2,400 (no further). Throttle down a little and notice that r.p.m. do not drop in spite of throttle movements. Return to fine pitch and close throttle. Wave away chocks.

Taxiing Out

Check brake pressure. Before starting, release parking brake and see radiator Taxiing shutters are open. Taxi out and get into position for take-off.

---

1   Bob Spurdle, *The Blue Arena* (Manchester: Crecy, 1986), p. 209.

Final Preparations for Taking off

Check rudder setting. Set elevator about one division nose down from neutral. Note that mixture control is back in NORMAL. Place pitch control FULLY FORWARD. FLAPS. Check they are UP.

Take-off and Climb

Become airborne. Gather speed and raise undercarriage. Note that red light comes ON. Wait for speed to become 140 m.p.h. A.S.I and then start a gradual climb. Reduce boost to + 9 lbs p.s.i. and reduce pitch to give 2,850 r.p.m. Accelerate to 185 m.p.h. A.S.I at 9 lbs p.s.i. boost and maintain this speed. Note that oil pressure is 60 lbs p.s.i. Fully shut emergency exit door and then cockpit hood. Do systematic cockpit check.

Cruising

Plus 7 lbs p.s.i. boost and 2,650 r.p.m. in NORMAL mixture, are the maximum (normal) continuous cruising settings. the greatest cruising range can be obtained at 200 m.p.h. A.S.I. with airscrew pitch set to give 1,700 r.p.m.

Approach and Landing

Stow maps. Open hood. Check radiator shutter setting: lower undercarriage and see that green light comes on. Ensure that mixture control is back to NORMAL. Place pitch lever in fully FINE. FLAPS: Lower after turning in to land. Glide at about 120 m.p.h. A.S.I. without engine. Land.

Annex O
Common RAF Codenames

Angels – height in thousands of feet.

Bandit – identified enemy aircraft.

Bogey – unidentified (possibly unfriendly) aircraft.

Buster – radio-telephony code phrase for ‹maximum throttle› or full power climb.

Channel Stop – air operations intended to stop enemy shipping passing through the Strait of Dover.

Circus – daytime bomber attacks with fighter escorts against short range targets, to occupy enemy fighters and keep them in the area concerned.

Diver – radio-telephony code word for a sighted V-1 flying bomb.

Flower – counter-air patrols in the area of enemy airfields to preventing aircraft from taking off and attacking those aircraft that succeeded.

Gardening – mine-laying operations.

Instep – missions to restrict attacks on Coastal Command aircraft by maintaining a presence over the Western Approaches.

Intruder – offensive patrols to destroy enemy aircraft over their own territory, usually carried out at night.

Jim Crow – coastal patrols to intercept enemy aircraft crossing the British coastline; originally intended to warn of invasion in 1940.

Kipper – patrols to protect fishing boats in the North Sea against air attack.

Mahmoud – sorties flown by de Havilland Mosquitoes equipped with rear-facing radar; when an enemy aircraft was detected a 180° turn enabled an attack.

Mandolin – attacks on enemy railway transport and other ground targets.

Noball – attacks on V-weapons launch sites and related targets.

Ramrod – short range bomber attacks to destroy ground targets, similar to Circus attacks.

Ranger – freelance flights over enemy territory by units of any size, to occupy and tire enemy fighters.

Rhubarb – fighter or fighter-bomber sections, at times of low cloud and poor visibility, crossing the English Channel and then dropping below cloud level to search for opportunity targets such as railway locomotives and rolling stock, aircraft on the ground, enemy troops, and vehicles on roads.

Roadstead – dive bombing and low level attacks on enemy ships at sea or in harbour.

Rodeo – fighter sweeps over enemy territory.

Rover – armed reconnaissance flights with attacks on opportunity targets.

Scramble – fast take-off and climb to intercept enemy aircraft.

Tally-ho – radio-telephony code word for ‹enemy in sight›.

Annex P

Civilian Casualties Caused in the United Kingdom by various Forms of Long-Range Bombardment 1939-45[1]

	Killed	Seriously Injured	Total
Bombing	51,509	61,423	112,932
Flying Bombs (V1)	6,184	17,981	24,165
Rockets (V2)	2,754	6,523	9,277
Cross-Channel Guns	148	255	403
Totals	60,595	86,182	146,777

---

1   Basil Collier, *Defence of the United Kingdom* (London: HMSO), 1957, p. 528.

Annex Q

Analysis of British Night-fighter Effort January to May 1941[1]

Month	Sorties		Detections		Combats	
	Single Engine	Twin Engine	A.I. Radar	Visual	A.I. Radar	Visual
January	402	84	44	34	2	9
February	421	147	25	33	4	9
March	735	270	95	54	21	35
April	842	342	117	55	50	44
May	1,345	643	204	167	74	122

---

1   Basil Collier, *Defence of the United Kingdom* (London: HMSO, 1957), p. 510.

Annex R
Flying Bomb Offensive[1]

Numbers of Bombs	Main Offensive		Phase 2	Phase 3	Whole Campaign
	12/6/44 – 15/7/44	16/7/44 – 5/9/44	16/9/44 – 14/1/45	3/3/45 – 29/3/45	12/6/44 – 29/3/45
Launched:					
from ramps	4,271	4,346	-	275	8,892
from aircraft	90	310	1,200	-	1,600
Total	4,361	4,656	1,200	275	10,492
Observed by defences	2,934	3,791	638	125	7,488
Destroyed					
by fighters	924 1/3	847	71 ½	4	1,847
by guns	261 1/3	1,198 ½	331 ½	87	1,878
by balloons	55 1/3	176 ½	-	-	231
Total all arms	1,241	2,222	403	91	3,956
Eluded defences	1,693	1,569	235	34	3,531
Reached London Civil Defence Region	1,270	1,070	66	13	2,419

---

1   Basil Collier, *Defence of the United Kingdom* (London: HMSO, 1957), p. 523.

Annex S

Yearly Tonnage Dropped by Bomber Command and the United States Eighth Air Force[1]

Year	Tons Dropped by Bomber Command	Tons Dropped by US Eighth Air Force
1939	31	-
1940	13,033	-
1941	31,704	-
1942	45,561	1,561
1943	157,457	44,185
1944	525,518	389,119
1945	181,740	188,573
Total	955,044	623,438

---

1   G. Webster and N. Frankland, *The Strategic Air Offensive Against Germany, Volume IV – Annexes and Appendices* (London: HMSO, 1961), p. 454.

Annex T

Comparison of Actual Output of Particular Classes of Armaments in Germany and the United Kingdom[1]

Category	1940		1941		1942		1943		1944	
	Ge	UK	Ge	UK	Ge	UK	Ge	UK	Ge	UK
Military Aircraft (total numbers)	10,200	15,000	11,000	20,100	14,200	23,600	25,200	26,200	39,600	26,500
Bombs (filled wt in 1,000 tons)	Not known	48	245	143	262	241	273	309	231	370
Tanks	1,600	1,400	3,800	4,800	6,300	8,600	12,100	7,500	19,900	4,600
Other AFVs	500	6,000	1,300	10,500	3,100	19,300	7,800	24,200	9,900	22,600
Heavy Wheeled Vehicles (1,000s)	Not known	112	62	110	81	109	109	104	89	91
Heavy Guns (75 mm and over)	6,300	1,900	7,800	5,300	13,600	6,600	38,000	12,200	62,300	12,400
Light Guns (under 75 mm; excluding 20mm)	Not known	2,800	3,400	11,400	9,600	36,400	8,100	25,800	8,400	3,600
Small Arms Infantry Rifles (1,000s)	1,350	81	1,358	78	1,370	594	2,244	910	2,585	547
Infantry Machine Guns (1,000s)	170	30	320	46	320	1,510	440	1,650	790	730
Ammunition (million rounds) Small Arms (20mm and under)	2,950	540	1,340	1,120	1,340	2,190	3,170	3,010	5,370	2,460
Naval war vessels over 1,000 tons standard displacement (including submarines)	Not known	222	162	346	193	300	221	292	234	270

---

1   G. Webster and N. Frankland, *The Strategic Air Offensive Against Germany, Volume IV – Annexes and Appendices* (London: HMSO, 1961), p. 469.

Annex U

Bomber Command Casualties
3 September 1939 to 8 May 1945[1]

	3 Sep 1939 to 2 Sep 1940	3 Sep 1940 to 2 Sep 1941	3 Sep 1941 to 2 Sep 1942	3 Sep 1942 to 2 Sep 1943	3 Sep 1943 to 2 Sep 1944	3 Sep 1944 to 8 May 1945	Total
Aircrew Operational Casualties							
Killed	216	659	727	820	1,550	1,610	5,582
Presumed dead	1,159	2,786	5,819	11,302	14,933	5,549	41,548
Died POW	6	15	31	31	43	12	138
Missing now safe	43	38	186	496	1,178	927	2,868
POW now safe	419	906	1,437	2,466	3,596	960	9,784
Wounded	269	600	786	871	1,030	644	4,200
Aircrew Non-Operational Casualties							
Killed	383	774	1,382	1,933	2,413	1,205	8,090
Wounded	217	535	786	1,112	1,070	483	4,203
Died other causes	15	26	39	36	58	41	215
Missing now safe	8	12	14	21	19	9	83
POW now safe	4	20	12	8	6	4	54

---

1   G. Webster and N. Frankland, *The Strategic Air Offensive Against Germany, Volume IV – Annexes and Appendices* (London, HMSO, 1961), p. 441.

Annex V

Bomber Command Aircraft Destroyed and Damaged[1]

	Total Despatched		Total Missing	
	By Night	**By Day**	**By Night**	**By Day**
1939	170	163	4	29
1940	17,493	3,316	342	152
1941	27,101	3,507	701	213
1942	32,737	2,313	1,291	109
1943	62,736	1,792	2,255	59
1944	113,352	35,096	2,349	224
1945	44,074	20,664	507	90

Bomber Command Grand Total of Sorties and Aircraft Destroyed and Damaged[2]

Total Despatched 1939-1945	Night: 297,663 Day: 66851
Total Missing 1939-1945	Night: 7,449 Day: 876
Total Damaged February 1942 – May 1945	Night: 13,778
Estimated Cause of Loss, July 1942 to May 1945	Night: 2,278 by fighters 1,345 by flak 112 not by enemy action (mainly collisions) 2,072 from unknown causes
Estimated cause of Damage, February 1942 to May 1945	Night, 1,728 fighters (163 wrecked, 1,565 repairable) 8,848 by flak (151 wrecked, 8,697 repairable) 3,159 not by enemy action (876 wrecked, 2,283 repairable) 43 from unknown causes (37 wrecked, 6 repairable)

---

1   G. Webster and N. Frankland, *The Strategic Air Offensive Against Germany, Volume IV – Annexes and Appendices* (London: HMSO, 1961), p. 437.

2   Webster and Frankland, *The Strategic Air Offensive Against Germany, Volume IV – Annexes and Appendices*, p. 439.

Annex W
Analysis of Submarines Destroyed by Aircraft[1]

German Submarines Destroyed by Allied Shore-Based Aircraft

Region	1939	1940	1941	1942	1943	1944	1945	Total
Atlantic, Arctic and Home Waters	-	1	3	33	113	71	81	302
Mediterranean	-	-	-	5	4	11	-	20
Indian Ocean	-	-	-	-	2	2	-	4
Grand Total destroyed by Shore Based Aircraft	-	1	3	38	119	84	81	326

Italian Submarines Destroyed by Allied Shore-Based Aircraft

Region	1939	1940	1941	1942	1943	1944	1945	Total
Atlantic, Arctic and Home Waters	-	-	1	-	2	-	-	3
Mediterranean	-	2	-	4	4	-	-	10
Grand Total destroyed by Shore Based Aircraft	-	2	1	4	6	-	-	13

Analysis of German and Italian Submarines Destroyed 1939-45

Region	Allied Shore-Based Aircraft		Joint Action Shore-Based Aircraft/Naval Forces		Allied Naval Forces Including Ship-Borne Aircraft		Accident, Soviet Action, Scuttling, Unknown Causes		Total	
	Ge	It	Ge	It	Ge	It	Ge	It	Ge	It
Atlantic, Arctic and Home Waters	302	3	27	1	302	10	74	3	705	17
Mediterranean, Red Sea and Black Sea	20	10	9	4	26	47	13	7	68	68
Indian Ocean	4	-	-	-	6	-	1	-	11	-
Total	326	13	36	5	334	57	88	10	784	85

---

1   Hilary Saunders, *Royal Air Force 1939-45, Volume III* (London: HMSO, 1954), p. 404.

Annex X

Enemy Surface Vessels Destroyed in the Atlantic and NW European Waters by RAF Aircraft 1939-45[1]

Sunk at Sea

Coastal Command Results			No.	Tonnage
Sorties	39,305	Surface Warships	150	86,303
Aircraft Lost	797	Cargo and other Vessels	193	427,501
Bomber Command				
Sorties	2, 671	Surface Warships	4	1,651
Aircraft Lost	126	Cargo and other Vessels	21	29,503
Fighter Command				
Sorties	22,621	Surface Warships	32	12,928
Aircraft Lost	239	Cargo and other Vessels	37	44,613
Total Sunk at Sea			437	602,499

Destroyed in Port			
Bomber Command	Surface Warships	152	166,576
Air Raids	Cargo and other Vessels	127	163,618
Total Destroyed in Port		279	330,194

Sunk by Air-Laid Mines

		No.	Tonnage
Coastal Command	Surface Warships	215	145,743
936 mines laid in 1,158 sorties for loss of 42 aircraft	Cargo and other Vessels	544	576,234
Bomber Command			
47,278 mines laid in 18,431 sorties for the loss of 468 aircraft			
Total Sunk by Air Laid Mines		759	721,977

Total Enemy Losses of Surface Vessels in The Atlantic and North-West European Waters

Cause	No	Tonnage
Sunk by Western Allies	2,340	3,439,270
Captured, confiscated, scuttled etc.	545	1,254,566
Grand Total	2,885	4,693,836

---

1   Hilary Saunders, *Royal Air Force 1939-45, Volume III* (London, HMSO, 1954), p. 405.

Annex Y

British Carriers in Service with the Royal Navy[1]

Aircraft Carrier Type	Aircraft Carrier Class	Ships in Class	Aircraft carried	Tonnage Standard
Assault Carrier	*Attacker*	*Attacker, Battler, Chaser, Fencer, Hunter, Pursuer, Stalker, Striker, Tracker*	20 operational, 90 as a ferry	10,200 tons
Escort Carrier	*Activity*	*Activity*	15	11,800 tons
Escort Carrier	*Archer*	*Archer*	12-15	12,860 tons
Escort Carrier	*Audacity*	*Audacity*	8	10,200 tons
Escort Carrier	*Avenger*	*Avenger, Biter, Dasher*	15	12,150 tons
Escort Carrier	*Campania*	*Campania*	20	13,000 tons
Escort Carrier	*Nairana*	*Nairana*	20	13,825 tons
Escort Carrier	*Ruler*	*Ameer, Arbiter, Atheling, Begum, Emperor, Empress, Khedive, Nabob, Patroller, Premier, Puncher, Queen, Rajah, Ranee, Ravager, Reaper, Searcher, Shah, Slinger, Thane, Trouncer, Trumpeter*	30 operational 90 as a ferry	15,390 tons
Escort Carrier	*Vindex*	*Vindex*	20	14,500 tons
Merchant Aircraft Carrier	Modified Tanker	*Acavus, Alexia, Adula, Amastra, Ancylus, Empire MacCabe, Empire MacColl, Empire MacKay, Empire MacMahon, Gadila, Macoma, Miralda, Rapana*	3	-
Merchant Aircraft Carrier	Modified Grain Ship	*Empire MacAlpine, Empire MacAndrew, Empire MacCallum, Empire MacDermott, Empire MacKendrick, Empire MacRae*		
Light Fleet Carrier	Colossus	*Glory, Ocean, Pioneer, Venerable, Vengeance*	42	13,190 tons
Fleet Carrier	*Argus*	*Argus*	15 in 1941	16,500 tons
Fleet Carrier	*Ark Royal*	*Ark Royal*	54 in 1941	22,000 tons
Fleet Carrier	*Courageous*	*Glorious*	48	27,650 tons
Fleet Carrier	*Eagle*	*Eagle*	22	22,600 tons
Fleet Carrier	*Furious*	*Furious*	33 in 1939	22,450 tons
Fleet Carrier	*Hermes*	*Hermes*	12 in 1939	10,850 tons
Fleet Carrier	*Illustrious*	*Illustrious, Formidable, Victorious, Indefatigable, Implacable*	54 81 for *Implacable*	23, 207 tons
	Indomitable	*Indomitable*	56	23,207

---

1   Wragg, David, *The Fleet Air Arm Handbook 1939-45* (Stroud: Sutton Publishing, 2001), p. 213.

Bibliography & Sources

Air Historical Branch Monographs

Air Publication AP 3396 *Escape from Germany,* issued by the Air Ministry 1951
Air Publication AP 3368 *The Origins and Development of Operational Research in the Royal Air Force,* issued by the Air Ministry 1963
Air Publication 3231 *Airborne Forces,* issued by the Air Ministry 1951
Air Publication 3232 *Air Sea Rescue,* issued by the Air Ministry 1952
Air Publication 3235 *Air Support,* issued by the Air Ministry 1955
Air Publication SD719 *Armament Volume 1 Bombs and Bombing Equipment,* issued by the Air Ministry 1952
Air Publication SD737 *Armament Volume 2 Guns, Gunsights, Turrets, Ammunition and Pyrotechnics, Bombs and Bombing Equipment,* issued by the Air Ministry 1954
Air Publication 3368 *Operational Research in the RAF,* issued by the Air Ministry 1954
AHB/II/116/16 Photographic Reconnaissance

Air Historical Branch Narratives

AHB/II/117/1 The Bombing Offensive Against Germany
AHB/II/117/2 Air Defence of Great Britain
AHB/II/117/3 The Royal Air Force in the Maritime War
AHB/II/117/4 The Campaign in Norway
AHB/II/117/5 The Campaign in France and the Low Countries
AHB/II/117/8 Middle East Campaigns
AHB/II/117/10 The Sicilian Campaign
AHB/II/117/11 The Italian Campaign

Imperial War Museum Documents

Allanson, Richard, Interview with Imperial War Museum, Sound Archives 11372
Brown, Eric Melrose, Interview with Imperial War Museum Sound Archives 12279
Knight, Richard Edgar, Interview with Imperial War Museum, Sound Archives 9208
Rew, Stephen, Private Papers Imperial War Museum documents collections, Catalogue Number, 6384
Thomas Tredwell, Interview with Imperial War Museum, Sound Archives 10743
Wanless, Wilkie, Interview with Imperial War Museum, Sound Archives 28428

Australian War Memorial Documents

Burcher, Tony Interview with Australian War Memorial, Sound Archives S01656

Chester-Master, Robert, Interview with Australian War Memorial, Sound Archives S01664

Davenport, Jack Napier, Interview with Australian War Memorial, Sound Archives SO1651

Doubleday, Arthur, Interview with Australian War Memorial, Sound Archives S00546

Milsom, Colin, 'Beaufighters attack convoy off Heligoland' by Squadron Leader Colin Milsom, 455 Squadron RAAF, 22 July 1944, Australian War Memorial. Sound Archives SOO197

Murphy, Robert Basil Gray, Interview with Australian War Memorial, Sound Archives S00523

Piper, John, Interview with Australian War Memorial, Sound Archives S00577

Rackley, Lionel, Interview with, Australian War Memorial, Sound Archives O16231

Tucker, Arthur, Interview with Australian War Memorial, Sound Archives S00701

The National Archives (Kew)

AIR 8/226: Aide Memoire on Air Policy by Sir Thomas Inskip, 9 Dec 1937

ADM 234/381: Submarines vol II – Operations in the Mediterranean

AIR 23/1200: Letters and ciphers relating to the number of aircraft flown to Malta and copies of Parks 'Forward Interception Plan

AM/WIS 75: 5 February 1941

WO 252/125: Bombers Baedeker

AIR 15/4: Employment of Coastal Command in a Continental War, memo 13 June 1939

AIR 15/46: Coastal Command's Aircraft Requirements. File S/7012/Tactics to ACAS c. Feb 1942

AIR 15/57: Coastal Command's Naval Staff Anti-U-boat file, Sep 1939-Dec 1944

CAB 69/4: DO (42) 24, 8 March 1942

AIR 20/3094. Air Ministry to Coastal Command, 30 November 1942

AIR 8/1400: D.O. R. Memorandum, 'Modification work carried out on Liberator aircraft on arrival in the UK', 9 March 1943.

AIR 15/633: Middle East Tactical Memorandum, No. 15, 'Torpedo Operations', May 1945

RAF Historical Society Papers

Wood Derek (ed.), Seek and Sink – A symposium on the Battle of the Atlantic, Royal Air Force Historical Society, 1995

Wood, Derek (ed.), The RAF and the Far East War 1941-45 – Bracknell Paper, Royal Air Force Historical Society, 1995

Wood, Derek (ed.), Reaping the Whirlwind – A symposium on the Strategic Bomber Offensive 1939-45 Royal Air Force Historical Society, 1993

Wood, Derek (Editor), OVERLORD – 1944, A symposium on the Normandy landings, Royal Air Force Historical Society, 1994

Probert, Henry and Cox Sebastian (ed.), The Battle Re-thought – A symposium on the Battle of Britain, Royal Air Force Historical Society, 1990

Academic Publications

Weston, Brian, *A Coming of Age for Australia and its Air Force – The Air Campaign over Northern Australia 1943*, (Canberra, Australia, Air Power Development Centre), 2013

Hammond, Richard, *British Anti-Shipping Campaign in the Mediterranean*, (Air Power Review 16), 2013,

W.J.R. Gardner, *Smart Mining without Smart Mines – Second World War British Operations in the Baltic,* (International Journal of Naval History) August 2007, Volume 6, No.2

Books

Adlam, Henry, *On and Off the Flight Deck – Reflections of A Naval Fighter Pilot in World War II* (Barnsley: Pen and Sword, 2007).

Atkinson, Tom, *Spectacles, Testicles, Fags and Matches – The Untold Story of The RAF Servicing Commandos,* (Edinburgh: Luath Press, 2004).

Alcock, Allan, *Hey Don't You Remember* (Privately Published).

Aldridge, Arthur and Ryan, Mark, *The Last Torpedo Flyers* (London: Simon and Schuster, 2013)

Allen, Dizzy, *Fighter Squadron 1940-1942* (St Albans: Granada, 1982).

Allen, H.R., *The Legacy of Lord Trenchard* (London: Cassell, 1972)

Allen, Louis, *Burma, The Longest War 1941-45* (London: Phoenix Press, 1984).

Alford, Bob, *Darwin 1942 – The Japanese attack on Australia* (Oxford: Osprey, 2017).

Anon., *Tattered Battlements – A Malta Diary by A Fighter Pilot* (London: Peter Davies, 1943).

Anderson, Bruce, *Ploughshares and Propellers,* (Victoria: Heritage Collection RAAF Museum Point Cook, 2009).

Apps, Michael, *Send Her Victorious* (London: William Kimber, 1971).

Arnett, Roger, *Drop Zone Burma – Adventures in Allied Air Supply 1943-45* (Barnsley: Pen and Sword, 2008).

Babbington-Smith, Constance, *Evidence in Camera – Photographic Intelligence in World War Two* (London: David Charles, 1974).

Banks, Arthur, *Wings of The Dawning – The Battle for The Indian Ocean* (Malvern: HMR, 1993).

Barker, Ralph, *The Thousand Plan – The Story of The First Thousand Bomber Raid on Cologne,* (Shrewsbury: Airlife, 1992).

—— *Strike Hard, Strike Sure* (Barnsley: Pen and Sword, 2003).

Barnett, Corelli, *Engage the Enemy More Closely – The Royal Navy in The Second World War* (London: Hodder and Stoughton, 1991).

Barnham, Denis, *Malta Spitfire Pilot* (London: Grub Street, 2010).

Bartz, Karl, *Swastika in The Air,* (London: William Kimber, 1956).

Baveystock, Leslie, *Wavetops At My Wingtips* (Shrewsbury: Airlife Publishing, 2001).

Beaumann, Katherine Bentley, *Partners in Blue: The Story of The Women's Service with the Royal Air Force* (London: Hutchinson, 1971).

Beck, Pip, *Keeping Watch – A WAAF In Bomber Command* (Manchester: Crecy Publishing, 2004).

Bednall, Dundas, *Sun on My Wings* (Pembroke: Paterchurch Publications, 1989).

Bennett, Donald, *Pathfinder* (Manchester: Crecy Publishing, 1998).

Bennett, Tom, *617 Squadron – The Dambusters at War* (Wellingborough: Patrick Stephens, 1986).

Bird, Andrew, *A Separate Little War – The Banff Coastal Command Strike Wing Versus the Kriegsmarine and Luftwaffe: 1944-1945* (London: Grub Street, 2008).

Bishop, Patrick, *Air Force Blue – The RAF in World War Two* (London: William Collins, 2017).

Bishop, Patrick, *Fighter Boys* (London: Harper Perennial, 2004).

Bowman, Martin, *The Reich Intruders: Dramatic RAF medium bomber raids over Europe in World War 2,* (Yeovil: Patrick Stephens, 1997).

Bowyer, Chaz, *Wellington at War,* (London: Ian Allan Ltd, 1982).

——*History of the RAF,* (London: Hamlyn, 1978).

——*Beaufighter,* (London: William Kimber, 1987).

——*Guns in The Sky – The Air Gunners of World War Two* (London: J.M. Dent, 1979).

——*Coastal Command in War* (London: Ian Allan, 1979).

——*Men of The Desert Air Force* (London: William Kimber, 1984).

Bowyer, Michael, *2 Group – A Complete History, 1936-1945* (London: Faber and Faber, 1974).

Bowyer, Michael and Martin Sharp, *Mosquito* (London: Faber and Faber, 1967).

Brown, Eric, *Wings on My Sleeve* (London: Phoenix, 2006).

Braham, Bob, *Scramble* (London: William Kimber, 1985).

Braithwaite, Denys A, *Target for Tonight – Flying Long Range Reconnaissance and PFF Missions in World War Two,* (Barnsley: Pen and Sword, 2010).

Brammer, Derek, *Thundering Through Clear Air – No. 61 (Lincoln Imp.) Squadron at War* (Lincoln: Tucann Books, 1997).

Brickhill, Paul, *Escape or Die* (London: Evans Brothers, 1952).

——*The Dam Busters* (London: Evans Brothers, 1952).

——*Reach for The Sky,* (London: The Companion Book Club, 1955).

Campbell, Arthur, *The Siege – A Story from Kohima* (London: George Allen and Unwin, 1956).

Campbell, Christy, *Target London – Under Attack from The V Weapons* (London: Little, Brown Book Group, 2012).

Caygill, Peter, *Spitfire Mark V in Action* (Shrewsbury: Airlife Ltd, 2001).

Caygill, Peter, *The Biggin Hill Wing 1941, From Defence to Attack* (Barnsley: Pen and Sword, 2008).

Chappell, F.R., *Wellington Wings – An RAF Intelligence Officer in The Western Desert* (Bodmin: Crecy Books, 1992).

Charlwood, Don, *No Moon Tonight* (Manchester: Crecy, 2012).

Cheshire, Leonard, *Bomber Pilot* (St Albans: Mayflower, 1975).

Clark, David, *Angels Eight Normandy Air War Diary* (Bloomington: Privately Published, 2003).

Clark, Ronald, *Rise of the Boffins* (London: Phoenix House, 1962).

Clayton, Tim and Craig, Phil, *The End of The Beginning* (London: Hodder and Stoughton, 2002).

Clostermann, Pierre, *The Big Show* (London: Chatto Windus 1953).

Clutton-Brock, Oliver, *RAF Evaders* (London: Grub Street, 2009).

Collier, Richard, *Eagle Day – The Battle of Britain* (London: J.M. Dent, 1980).

Collier, Basil, *Defence of the United Kingdom* (London: HMSO, 1957).

Cooling, Benjamin Franklin, *Air Superiority* (Washington, DC: Air Force History and Museums Program, 1994).

——*Close Air Support* (Washington, DC: Office of Air Force History, 1990).

Conyers Nesbit, Roy, *Eyes of The RAF – A History of Photo Reconnaissance* (Godalming: Bramley Books, 1996).

——*Coastal Command in Action 1939-45* (Stroud: Sutton Publishing, 1997).

——*The Battle Of The Atlantic* (Stroud: Sutton Publishing, 2002).

——*Woe To The Unwary – A memoir of low level bombing operations in 1941* (London: William Kimber, 1981).

Corbin, Jimmy, *Last of The Ten Fighter Boys* (Stroud: History Press, 2007).

Cotton, M.C., *Hurricanes Over Burma* (London: Grub Street, 1995).

Cropper, Eric, *Back Bearings – A Navigator's Tale 1942 to 1974* (Barnsley: Pen and Sword, 2010).

Cross, Kenneth, *Straight and Level* (London: Grub Street, 1993).

Cull, Brian, Lander, Bruce and Weiss, Heinrich, *Twelve Days in May* (London: Grub Street, 1995).

Cull, Brian and Sortehaug, Paul, *Hurricanes Over Singapore* (London: Grub Street, 2004).

Cull, Brian, Lander, Bruce and Galea, Frederick, *Hurricanes over Malta* (London: Grub Street, 2001).

Cull, Brian, Lander, Bruce and Galea, Frederick, *Spitfires over Malta* (London: Grub Street, 2005).

Currie, Jack, *Mosquito Victory,* (London: Goodall, 1983).

——*The Augsburg Raid* (St Albans: Goodall, 1987).

Currie, Jack, *Battle Under the Moon: The Documented Account of Mailly-le-camp* (Manchester: Airdata publications Ltd, 1992)

Darby, Phil, *Press on Regardless* (Privately Published, 1997)

Davies, Norman, *Rising 44 – The Battle for Warsaw* (London: Viking, 2004).

Delve, Ken, *Nighfighter* (London: Cassell, 1995).

Demoulin, Charles, *Firebirds- Flying the Typhoons in Action* (Shrewsbury, Airlife, 1987).

Deere, Alan, *Nine Lives* (Manchester: Crecy, 2005).

De Guingand, Freddie, *Operation Victory* (London: Hodder and Stoughton, 1947).

Devlin, Gerard M., *Silent Wings* (Chatham: Mackays, 1985).

Douglas-Hamilton, James, *The Air Battle for Malta* (Barnsley: Pen and Sword, 2006).

Downing, Taylor, *Spies in the Sky – The Secret Battle for Aerial Intelligence During World War Two* (London: Little, Brown, 2011).

Duncan Smith, W.G.G., *Spitfire into Battle* (London: John Murray, 2002).

Dudgeon, Tony, *Wings Over North Africa* (Shrewsbury: Airlife, 1987).

Dundas, Hugh, *Flying Start – A Fighter Pilots War Years* (New York: St Martin's Press, 1989).

Eadon, Stuart, *Kamikaze – The Story of the British Pacific Fleet* (Worcester, Square One Publishing, 1991).

Edwards, Gron, *Norwegian Patrol,* (Shrewsbury: Airlife Publishing Ltd, 1985).

Edwards, Gron, *Flying to Norway Grounded in Burma – A Hudson Pilot in World War II* (Barnsley: Pen and Sword, 2008).

Embry, Basil, *Mission Completed,* (London: Quality Book Club, 1956).

Ehlers, Robert, *The Mediterranean Air War,* (Lawrence: University Press Kansas, 2015).

——*Targeting the Third Reich – Air Intelligence and The Allied Bombing Campaign* (Lawrence, University Press Kansas, 2009)

Escott, Beryl, *Our Wartime Days – The WAAF in World War II* (Stroud: Alan Sutton Publishing, 1995).

——*Women In Air Force Blue – The Story Of Women in the Royal Air Force from 1918 to the present day,* (Yeovil: Patrick Stephens Ltd, 1989).

Evans, Bryn, *The Decisive Campaigns Of The Desert Air Force 1942-45* (Barnsley: Pen and Sword, 2014).

——*Air Battle For Burma – Allied Pilots' Fight For Supremacy,* (Barnsley: Pen and Sword, 2016).

Eyton-Jones, Arthur, *Day Bomber* (Stroud, Sutton Publishing, 1998).

Forrester, Larry, *Fly For Your Life – The Story of R R Stanford Tuck* (Guildford: Biddles, 1973).

Foster, Ronald, *Focus On Europe, A Photo-Reconnaissance Mosquito Pilot At War, 1943-45* (Ramsbury: Crowood Press, 2004).

Franks, Norman, *Dark Sky, Deep Water – First Hand Reflections On The Anti-U-Boat War In WW II,* (London:Grub Street, 1997).

——*Another Kind Of Courage* (Yeovil: Patrick Stephens, 1994).

——*Beyond Courage* (London: Grub Street, 2003).

——*Conflict Over The Bay* (London: William Kimber, 1986).

——*The Greatest Air Battle, Dieppe 19th August 1942* (London: Grub Street, 1992).

——*Typhoon Attack* (London: William Kimber, 1984).

——*The Air Battle Of Imphal* (London: William Kimber, 1985).

——*Spitfires Over The Arakan* (London: William Kimber, 1988).

——*Hurricanes over the Arakan* (Yeovil: Patrick Stephens, 1989).

Freeman, Roger, *The British Airman* (London: Arms and Armour Press, 1989).

Garbett, Mike and Goulding, Brian *Lancaster at War* (London: Guild Publishing, 1984).

Gardiner, Juliet, *The Blitz: The British Under Attack* (London: Harper Press, 2010).

Gibbs, Patrick, *Not Peace But A Sword* (London: Grub Street, 1993).

——*Torpedo Leader* (London: Grub Street, 1992).

Gibson, Guy, *Enemy Coast Ahead* (London: Pan Books, 1955).

Gibson, T.M. and Harrison, M.H., *Into Thin Air – A History of Aviation Medicine* (London: Robert Hale, 1984).

Gillman, R.E., *The Shiphunters* (London: John Murray, 1976)

Gillison, Douglas, *Royal Australian Air Force 1939-42* (Canberra: Australian War Memorial, 1962)

Gladman, Brad, *Intelligence and Anglo-American Air Support in World War Two – The Western Desert* (London: Palgrave Macmillan, 2009)

Golley, John, *The Day Of The Typhoon – Flying With The RAF Tankbusters in Normandy* (Bury St Edmunds: Wrens Park, 1986).

Gooderson, Ian, *Air Power At The Battlefront – Allied Close Air Support In Europe 1943-45* (London: Frank Cass, 1998)

Goulter, C.J.M., *A Forgotten Offensive – Royal Air Force Coastal Command's Anti-Shipping Campaign, 1940-45* (London: Frank Cass, 1995).

Green, William, *Famous Fighters of The Second World War,* (Abingdon: Purnell, 1975).

——*Famous Bombers of The Second World War* (London: Book Club Associates, 1975).

Greenhous, Brereton, *Crucible Of War: The Official History of the Royal Canadian Air Force 1939-45,* (Toronto: University of Toronto, 1994).

Haarer, A.E., *A Cold-Blooded Business,* (London, Staples Ltd, 1958).

Hall, Roger, *Clouds Of Fear* (London: Hodder and Stoughton, 1975).

Halley, James J., *Squadrons of The Royal Air Force* (Tonbridge: Air-Britain (Historians), 1988).

Hallion, Richard P., *The History of Battlefield Air Attack, 1941-45* (Shrewsbury: Airlife, 1989).

Hamilton, Nigel, *Monty: The Making of a General 1887-1942* (New York: McGraw Hill, 1981).

Harris, Arthur, *Bomber Offensive* (London: Collins, 1947).

Harrison, W.A., *Swordfish Special* (London: Ian Allan, 1998).

Hastings, Max, *Bomber Command* (London: Michael Joseph, 1980).

Hayward, Greg, *D-Day to VE-Day with the Second Tactical Air Force* (Bloomington: Author House, 2009).

Heinemann, William, *Winged Words – Our Airmen Speak For Themselves* (Surrey: Windmill, 1941).

Hendrie, Andrew, *The Cinderella Service – RAF Coastal Command 1939-45,* (Barnsley, Pen and Sword Aviation, 2006).

Hemingway, Kenneth, *Wings Over Burma* (London: Quality Press Publishers, 1945).

Herrman, Hajo, *Eagle's Wings – The Autobiography of a Luftwaffe Pilot* (Shrewsbury: Airlife, 1991).

Herington, John, *Air War Against Germany and Italy, 1939-43* (Canberra: Australian War Memorial, 1954).

Herington, John, *Air Power Over Europe, 1944-1945* (Canberra: Australian War Memorial, 1963).

Hewitt, J.E., *Adversity In Success* (South Yarra: Langate Publishing, 1980).

Hinsley, F.H. and Stripp, Alan, *Code Breakers – The Inside Story Of Bletchley Park* (Oxford: Oxford University Press, 1993).

Hoare, John, *Tumult in the Clouds – A Story of the Fleet Air Arm* (London: Michael Joseph, 1976).

Holland, James, *The Battle Of Britain* (London: Bantam Press, 2015).

Holmes, Ray, *Sky Spy* (Shrewsbury: Airlife Publishing, 1989).

Horden, Dennis, *Shark Squadron Pilot* (Bromley: Independent Books, 2002).

Houghton, G W, *They Flew Through Sand* (Molton: P&M Typesetting, 1991).

Howard-Williams, Jeremy, *Night Intruder – A Personal Account of the Radar War Between the Luftwaffe and RAF Night Fighter Forces* (London: David and Charles, 1976).

Hunter, Jim, *From Coastal Command to Captivity – The Memoir Of A Second World War Airman* (Barnsley: Leo Cooper, 2003).

Ince, David, *Brotherhood Of The Skies – Wartime Experiences Of A Gunner Officer and Typhoon Pilot* (London, Grub Street, 2010).

Jackson, Robert, *The Secret Squadrons – Special Duty Units of The RAF and USAAF in the Second World War* (London: Robson Books, 1983).

James, T.C.G., *The Battle of Britain* (London: Frank Cass, 2000).

Jones, Geoffrey, *Attacker – The Hudson and its Flyers* (London: William Kimber, 1980).

Johnson, J.E., *Wing Leader* (London: Reprint Society, 1956).

—— *The Story Of Air Fighting* (London: Hutchinson, 1985).

Jones, R.V., *Most Secret War – British Scientific Intelligence 1939-45* (London: Hamish Hamilton, 1978).

Joubert de la Ferte, Philip, *Birds and Fishes – The Story of Coastal Command* (London: Hutchinson, 1960).

—— *The Forgotten Ones – The Story of the Ground Crews* (London: Hutchinson, 1961)

Judd, Donald, *Avenger From the Sky* (London: William Kimber, 1985).

Kelly, Terence, *Hurricane Over the Jungle* (London: Arrow, 1990).

Kent, A, *One of the Few* (London: William Kimber, 1971).

Kilbracken, Lord, *Bring Back My Stringbag* (London: Peter Davies, 1979).

King, Colin M., *Song of the Beauforts,* (Tuggeranong: Australian Air Power Development Centre, 2008).

Kingcome, Brian, *A Willingness To Die – Memories Of Fighter Command* (Stroud: History Press, 2008).

Kippenberger, Howard, *Infantry Brigadier* (London: Oxford University Press, 1961).

Kirkness, B. and Poole, M., *RAF Liberators Over Burma – Flying With 159 Squadron* (Croydon: Fonthill Media, 2017).

Konstam, Angus, *British Aircraft Carriers 1939-45* (Oxford: Osprey, 2010).

Lacey-Johnson, *Lionel, Point Blank and Beyond* (Shrewsbury: Airlife, 1991).

Lamb, Charles, *War In A Stringbag* (London: Cassell, 1987).

Leicester, L. Anthony, *Flights Into The Night,* (Manchester: Crecy, 2010).

Levine, Alan, *The War Against Rommel's Supply Lines 1942-1943* (Wesport, Connecticut: Praeger, 1999).

Levy, H., *Aerodynamics Of The Aeroplane* (Nelson: London, 1943).

Lewin, Ronald, *Ultra Goes To War,* (London, Grafton, 1988).

Lloyd, H., *Briefed To Attack – Malta's Part in African Victory* (London: Hodder and Stoughton, 1949).

MacArthur, Brian *Surviving The Sword – Prisoners of the Japanese 1942-45* (London: Abacus, 2005).

Mackenzie, K W, *Hurricane Combat* (London: Grenville Publishing, 1987).

Mackie, Mary, *Wards In The Sky – The RAF's Remarkable Nursing Service* (Stroud: History Press, 2014).

Marshall, Ken *The Pendulum and the Scythe* (Walton on Thames: Air Research Publications, 1996).

Marshall, Bruce, *The White Rabbit: A British Agents Adventures in France* (London: Pan Books, 1955).

Maslen- Jones, *Fire By Order – Recollections of Service with 656 Air Observation Post Squadron* (London: Leo Cooper, 1997)

Mayhew, E.R. *The Guinea Pig Cub* (London: Greenhill Books, 2010).

Mayhill, Ron, *Bombs On Target – A Compelling Eye-witness Account of Bomber Command Operations,* (Yeovil: Patrick Stephens Ltd, 1991).

McIntosh, Dave, *High Blue Battle* (London: Stoddard, 1990).

McInstry, Leo, *Hurricane – Victor Of The Battle of Britain* (London: John Murray, 2010).

——*Lancaster – The Second World War's Greatest Bomber* (London: John Murray, 2009).

——*Spitfire – Portrait of a Legend: The Second World War's Greatest Bomber* (London: John Murray, 2007)

McGregor, Alan Peart, *From North Africa To The Arakan* (London: Grub Street, 2008).

McIntosh, Dave, *Mosquito Intruder* (London: John Murray, 1980).

McKay, Sinclair, *The Secret Life Of Fighter Command* (London: Aurum Press, 2016).

Middlebrook, Martin, *Convoy – The Greatest U-boat Battle of the War* (London, Cassell, 1976).

Middlebrook, Martin, *The Berlin Raids – RAF Bomber Command Winter 1943-44* (London: Viking, 1988).

Middlebrook, Martin, *The Schweinfurt-Regensburg Mission – American Raids on 17 August 1943* (London: Cassell, 2000).

Millar, Andrew, *The Flying Hours* (Hitchin: Fighting High Publications, 2015).

Miller, Russell, *Behind The Lines: The Oral History of Special Operations in World War II* (London: Random House, 2002).

Millington, G., *The Unseen Eye* (London: Anthony Gibbs & Phillips, 1961).

Milton, Brian, *Hurricane: The Last Witness* (London: Carlton Publishing Group, 2011).

Moore, John, *Escort Carrier* (London: Hutchinson, 1944).

——*The Fleet Air Arm* (London: Chapman and Hall, 1943).

Moore, Stephen, *The Battle for Hell's Island* (New York: Caliber, 2015).

Morrison, Will, *Horsa Squadron* (London: William Kimber, 1988).

Muirhead, Campbell, *The Diary of a Bomb Aimer* (Tumbridge Wells: Spellmount Publishing, 1987).

Naydler, Merton, *Young Man You'll Never Die* (Barnsley: Pen and Sword, 2005).

Neave, Airey, *Little Cyclone* (London: Biteback Publishing, 2013).

Neil, T F, *Onward to Malta* (Shrewsbury: Airlife, 1992).

Neil, Tom, *Gun Button To Fire* (Stroud: Amberley, 2010)

Nelson, Hank, *Chased by the Sun – The Australians in Bomber Command in World War II* (Crow's Nest, Australia: Allen and Unwin, 2006).

Nesbit, Roy, *The Strike Wings – Special Anti-Shipping Squadrons 1942-45,* (London: William Kimber, 1984).

—— *The Armed Rovers – Beauforts and Beaufighters over the Mediterranean* (Shrewsbury: Airlife Publishing, 1995).

——*Woe to the Unwary – A Memoir of Low Level Bombing Operations in 1941,* (London: William Kimber, 1981).

Nichol, John and Rennell, Tony, *The Last Escape – The Untold Story of Allied Prisoners of War in Germany* (London: Penguin, 2003).

O'Brien, Terence, *Out of the Blue – A Pilot With The Chindits* (London: Arrow, 1988).

——*Chasing after Danger,* (London: Harper Collins, 1980)

——*The Moonlight War,* (London: Arrow Books, 1989)

Odgers, George, *Air War Against Japan, 1943-45* (Canberra: Australian War Memorial, 1957).

Ogley, Bob, *Doodlebugs and Rockets,* (Westerham: Froglets, 1992).

Oliver, David, *Fighter Command,* (London, Harper Collins, 2000).

Olson, Lynne, and Cloud, Stanley, *For Your Freedom And Ours* (London: Arrow Books, 2003).

Orange, Vincent, *Coningham – The Biography of Air Marshal Sir Arthur Coningham* (Washington, DC: Center For Air Force History, 1992).

Orange, Vincent, *Park – The Biography of Air Chief Marshal Sir Keith Park* (London: Grub Street, 2001).

——*Dowding Of Fighter Command – Victor Of The Battle Of Britain* (London: Grub Street, 2008).

Ott, Frank, *Air Power At Sea in the Second World War* (Yeovil: Fleet Air Arm Museum, 2005).

Overill, Tony, *Crash Boats of Gorleston* (Bognor Regis: Woodfield Publishing, 2005).

Overy, Richard, *The Battle of Britain – Myth and Reality* (London: Penguin, 2010).

——*The Bombing War, Europe 1939-45,* (London: Allen Lane, 2013).

——*The Air War 1939-45,* (London: Europa Publications, 1980).

Owen, Roderic, *The Desert Air Force* (London: Hutchinson, 1948).

Oxspring, Bobby, *Spitfire Command* (London: Grafton Books, 1987).

Page, Geoffrey, *Shot Down In Flames* (London: Grub Street, 1999).

Pape, Richard, *Boldness Be My Friend* (London: Pan Books, 1953).

Pateman, Colin, *B-24 Bridge Busters – RAF Liberators Over Burma* (Croydon: Fonthill, 2016).

——*AF Special Duties* (Croydon: Fonthill, 2015)

Peake, Dame Felicity, *Pure Chance* (Shrewsbury: Airlife, 1993).

Pearce, Frank, *Under The Red Eagle – A Tour Overseas With No. 239 Fighter/Bomber Wing of the Desert Air Force* (Bognor Regis: Woodfield, 2004).

Peden, Murray, *A Thousand Shall Fall – The True Story Of A Canadian Bomber Pilot in World War Two* (Toronto: Stoddart, 1997).

Pelly-Fry, *Heavenly Days – Recollection Of A Contented Airman* (Bodmin: Crecy, 1994).

Pile, Frederick, *Ack-Ack – Britain's Air Defence Against Air Attack During the Second World War* (London: George Harrap, 1949).

Pike, Richard, *Alfie's War* (London: Grub Street, 2012).

Pitchfork, Graham, *Shot Down and in the Drink* (Richmond: National Archives, 2005).

——*Shot Down and On The Run* (Richmond: National Archives, 2003)

Playfair, I S O, *The Mediterranean and the Middle East* (London: HMSO, 1960)

Poolman, Kenneth, *Allied Escort Carriers of World War Two* (London: Blandford Press, 1988)

Poolman, Kenneth, *The Sea Hunters – Escort Carriers vs U-Boats 1941-45* (London: Arms and Armour Press, 1982)

Poolman, Kenneth, *Focke-Wulf Condor – Scourge of The Atlantic* (London: Macdonald and Janes, 1982).

Popham, Hugh, *Sea Flight* (London: Futura, 1974).

Pottinger, Ron, *Soldier In The Cockpit, From Rifles To Typhoons in WWII* (Mechanicsburg, Pennsylvania: Stackpole, 2007).

Powys-Lybbe, Ursua, *The Eye of Intelligence* (London: William Kimber, 1983)

Preston-Hough, Peter, *Commanding Far Eastern Skies – A Critical Analysis Of The Royal Air Force Air Superiority Campaign In India, Burma and Malaya 1941-1945* (Solihull: Helion & Company, 2015).

Price, Alfred, *Aircraft Versus Submarine* (London: Janes, 1980).

——*Battle Of Britain 18 August 1940 – The Hardest Day* (London: Granada, 1979).

Probert, Henry, *The Forgotten Air Force -The Royal Air Force in the War Against Japan 1941-45* (London: Brasseys, 1995).

Rae, Jack, *Kiwi Spitfire Ace* (London: Grub Street, 2001).

Rawnsley, C F and Wright, Robert, *Night Fighter* (Manchester: Crecy, 1998)

Rennison, John, *The Digby Diary – A History of RAF Digby* (Stroud: Aspect Publishing, 2003)

Richards, Denis and Saunders, Hilary St George, *The Royal Air Force 1939-45, Vols. 1-3* (London: HMSO, 1954).

Richardson, Anthony, *Wingless Victory* (London: Pan Books, 1956).

Richey, Paul, *Fighter Pilot* (London: Hutchinson, 1955).

Rijken, Kees, Schepers, Paul and Thorning, Arthur, *Operation Oyster – The Daring Low Level Attack on The Phillips Radio Works,* (Barnsley, Pen and Sword, 2014).

Rivaz, R.C., *Tail Gunner* (Sydney: Endeavour Press, 2017).

Robertson, Terrence, *Channel Dash* (London: Evans Brothers, 1958).

Robinson, Ken, *Dice On Regardless – The Story Of An RAF Sunderland Pilot* (London: R.J. Leach, 1993).

Robson, Martin, *The Hurricane Pocket Manual* (London: Bloomsbury, 2016).

—— *The Spitfire Pocket Manual* (London: Bloomsbury, 2016).

Rogers, Anthony, *185: The Malta Squadron* (Staplehurst: Spellmount, 2005).

Rollings, Charles, *Prisoner Of War – Voices from Behind the Wire in the Second World War* (London: Ebury Press, 2008).

Roskill, Stephen, *The Navy At War 1939-45* (London: Collins, 1960).

Ross, J.M.S., *Royal New Zealand Air Force: New Zealand in the Second World War, 1939-45* (Wellington: War History Branch, 1955).

Rossiter, Mike, *Ark Royal* (London: Corgi, 2006).

Sawyer, Tom, *Only Owls and Bloody Fools Fly at Night* (London: William Kimber, 1982).

Schofield, Ernest, *Artic Airmen – The RAF in Spitsbergen and North Russia, 1942* (London: William Kimber, 2005).

Scott, Desmond, *Typhoon Pilot* (London: Arrow Books, 1982).

—— *One More Hour* (London: Arrow Books, 1989).

Shores, Christopher and Thomas, Chris, *Second Tactical Air Force Vols. 1-4* (Hersham: Midland Publishing, 2008).

Shores, Christopher, *Pictorial History Of The Mediterranean Air War, Volumes I & II* (London: Ian Allan, 1973).

Shores, Christopher, *Air War For Burma* (London: Grub Street, 2005)

Sims, Edward H, *The Fighter Pilots* (London: Cassell, 1967).

Simpson, Andrew, *'Ops' – Victory at all Costs* (Pulborough: Tattered Flag Press, 2012).

Simpson, Bill, *The Way of Recovery* (London: Hamish Hamilton, 1944)

Slessor, John, *The Central Blue – Recollections and Reflections by Marshal of the Royal Air Force Sir John Slessor* (London: Cassel, 1956).

Southall, Ivan, *They Shall Not Pass Unseen* (London: Angus and Robertson, 1956)

Spencer, Dennis, *Looking Backwards Over Burma – Wartime Recollections of a Beaufighter Navigator* (Bognor Regis: Woodfield Publishing, 2009)

Spooner, Tony, *In Full Flight* (Canterbury: Wingham Press, 1991)

—— *Warbuton's War* (Oxford: Isis, 2003).

Spurdle, Bob, *The Blue Arena* (Manchester: Goodall Publishing, 2017).

Smith, David, *Britain's Military Airfields 1939-45* (Wellingborough: Patrick Stephens, 1989).

Smith, Peter C, *Jungle Dive Bombers at War* (London: John Murray, 1987).

Smith, Ron, *Rear Gunner Pathfinders,* (Manchester: Crecy, 1997).

Smithers, Edward, *Backroom Boys,* (London: Cassell, 2002).

Stanley, Peter, *Darwin Spitfires – The Real Battle for Australia* (Sydney: New South Wales Press, 2011).

Stewart, Adrian, *They Flew Hurricanes* (Barnsley: Pen and Sword, 2005).

Stevenson, Derek, *Five Crashes Later – The Story Of A Fighter Pilot* (London: William Kimber, 1988).

Streetly, Martin, *Confound and Destroy: 100 Group* (London: Macdonald and Janes, 1978).

Stubbington, John, *Bletchley Park Air Section Signals Intelligence Support to RAF Bomber Command,* (Alton: Minerva Associates, 2007).

Sutherland Brown, Atholl, *Silently Into the Midst of Things* (Sussex: Book Guild Ltd, 2001).

Sweeting, Dennis, *Wings of Chance* (Singapore: Asian Business Press, 1990).

Taylor, James and Davidson, Martin, *Bomber Crew – Survivors Of Bomber Command Tell Their Story* (London: Hodder and Stoughton, 2004).

Tedder, Lord, *With Prejudice* (London: Cassell, 1966).

Terraine, John, *The Right of the Line – The Royal Air Force In The European War 1939-1945* (London: Hodder and Stoughton, 1985).

Terraine, John, *Business In Great Waters* (London: Leo Cooper, 1989).

Thomas, Andrew, *Royal Navy Aces of World War II* (Oxford: Osprey, 2002).

Thompson, Peter, *Pacific Fury – How Australia and her allies defeated the Japanese* (Sydney: William Heinemann, 2008).

Thompson, Walter, *Lancaster to Berlin* (Manchester: Crecy Publishing, 1997).

Tootal, Stuart, *The Manner Of Men,* (London: John Murray, 2014).

Townshend Bickers, Richard, *Ginger Lacey, Fighter Pilot* (London: Robert Hale, 1962).

Tuker, Francis, *Approach To Battle,* (London: Cassell, 1963).

Van Crefeld, Martin, *Supplying War – Logistics From Wallenstein to Patton* (New York: Cambridge University Press, 1977).

Veitch, Michael, *44 Days – 75 Squadron And The Fight For Australia* (Sydney: Hatchette, 2016).

Verity, Hugh, *We Landed By Moonlight Secret RAF Landings in France 1940-44* (London: Ian Allan, 1978).

Verney, G.L., *The Desert Rats* (Tiptree: Anchor Press, 1957).

Vigors, Tim, *Life's Too Short to Cry* (London: Grub Street, 2008).

Wallace, G., *Biggin Hill* (London: Putnam, 1957).

Wallace, Gordon, *Carrier Observer* (Shrewsbury: Airlife, 1993).

Walley, Brian (ed.), *Silk and Barbed Wire* (Western Australia: Warwick Publishing, 2000).

Warwick, Nigel W.M., *Constant Vigilance, The RAF Regiment in Burma* (Barnsley: Pen and Sword, 2007).

Webster, C. and Frankland, N., *The Strategic Air Offensive Against Germany, 1939-45, Volumes 1-4,* (London: HMSO, 1961).

Weinronk, Jack, *The Vaulted Sky – A Bomber Pilot's Western Desert War Before and After* (Braunton: Merlin Books, 1993).

Wellham, John, *With Naval Wings – The Autobiography of a Fleet Air Arm Pilot In World War II,* (Staplehurst: Spellmount Publishing, 2003).

Wellum, Geoffrey, *First Light* (London: Penguin, 2003).

Wells, Mark K., *Courage and Air Warfare* (London: Frank Cass, 1995).

Wemyess, D.E., *Relentless Pursuit,* (London: William Kimber, 1955).

White, Graham, *Night Fighter Over Germany* (Barnsley: Pen and Sword, 2006).

Winton, John, *Find, Fix and Strike! The Fleet Air Arm at War 1939-45* (London: Batsford, 1985).

Williams, Dennis, *Stirlings in Action With Airborne Forces* (Barnsley: Pen and Sword, 2008).

Wilson, Kevin, *Bomber Boys – The RAF Offensive of 1943* (London: Widenfeld and Nicholson, 2005).

Wilson, Kevin, *Men of Air – The Doomed Youth of Bomber Command* (London: Widenfeld and Nicholson, 2007).

Wilson, Kevin, *Journey's End – Bomber Command's Battle From Arnhem to Dresden and Beyond* (London: Weidenfeld and Nicholson, 2010).

Woodhall, A.B., *Soldier, Sailor & Airman Too* (London: Grub Street, 2008)

Wood, Derek and Dempster, Derek, *The Narrow Margin – The Battle Of Britain 1940* (Washington, DC: Smithsonian, 1990).

Woods, Gerard, *Wings At Sea – A Fleet Air Arm Observer's War 1940-45* (London, Conway Maritime Press, 1985).

Wragg, David, *Carrier Combat,* (Stroud: Sutton Publishing, 1996).

——*Fleet Air Arm Handbook 1939-45* (Stroud: Sutton Publishing, 2003).

——*Swordfish – The Story of the Taranto Raid* (London, Cassell, 2003).

Wynn, Humphrey and Young, Susan, *Prelude to Overlord* (Shrewsbury: Airlife, 1983).

——*Desert Eagles* (Shrewsbury: Airlife, 1993).

Yates, Harry, *Luck and A Lancaster* (Shrewsbury: Airlife, 1999).

Younghusband, Eileen, *One Woman's War* (Cardiff: Candy-Jar books, 2011).

Zuckerman, Solly, *From Apes to Warloads* (London: Hamish Hamilton, 1978).

Index

Index of People

Adlam, Hank 378, 413
Agnew, Captain 348-349
Aldridge, Arthur 336, 351-352
Allanson, Richard 354-355
Allen, Ernest E. 317, 319-320
Allen, Hubert Raymond 61
Amiss, Pilot Officer 310, 312-314
Arnold, General 170-171
Atkinson, Wing Commander L.V.E. 329, 332

Bader, Wing Commander Douglas 63, 68, 79, 92
Bailey, Leslie 'Bill' 399-400
Baldwin, Stanley 19, 198
Bateson, Wing Commander 273-274
Baveystock, Flight Lieutenant Les 283, 288
Beamont, Commander Roland 121
Beaverbrook, Lord 51
Bennett, Air Commodore Donald 209, 222, 224, 226, 228, 233-234
Bentley, Flying Officer Harry 244
Birchall, Flight Lieutenant Leonard 395, 397-398
Bisdee, John 60
Blackett, Professor Patrick 281
Blessing, Squadron Leader 272
Bonython, Kim 356
Bovell, Captain 399-400
Bowhill, Air Chief Marshal 296, 372
Boyd, Sergeant 77-78
Brand, Air Vice-Marshal 47, 83, 379
Brennan, Flight Sergeant 153
Brereton, General 170
Brink, Gunner 35
Brooke-Popham, Air Marshal 161
Brown, Eric 'Winkle' 189, 407-408
Brown, Hilly 58
Bryett, Alan 242-243
Bulloch, Sir Archibald 22
Bunce, Don 400
Burcher, Sergeant Tony 259-260
Burls, Brigadier 124
Butt, Mr David 202

Calder, Jock 265
Caldwell, Wing Commander Clive 191-192
Camm, Sidney 50
Campbell, Flying Officer Kenneth 340
Carey, Wing Commander Frank 186-188
Carroll, Pilot Officer 'Nappy' 188
Catlin, Sergeant Brian 396-397
Cawthorne, Flight Engineer Sergeant Charles 248, 250
Chadwick, Roy 206
Chamberlain, Neville 41
Chapman, Jim 160, 244-245

Chennault, Major 180
Cherwell, Lord 202-203, 224
Cheshire, Group Captain Leonard 36, 200-202, 262-263
Chester-Master, Robert 213, 217-218
Churchill, Winston 19, 21, 38, 84, 102, 124, 131, 138, 142, 151, 169, 189, 202-203, 248, 254, 316-317, 333, 395, 417
Clabaugh, flying instructor 28-29
Cochrane, Air Vice Marshal 208-209, 259, 373
Colarossi, Sergeant 396
Cole, Sergeant Bob 121-122
Collier, Ken 122
Colville, John 'Jock' 84
Conway, Flight Lieutenant A.G. 189
Corbin, Sergeant Jimmy 53-54, 64, 74-75
Coupland, Laurie 35
Cousins, Flying Officer 31
Cropper, Eric 32, 224-225
Crowther, Pilot Officer R.K. 141
Cunningham, Admiral 395
Cunningham, John 110
Curchin, Johnnie 77-78
Currie, Jack 236, 239, 304-305

Darby, Pilot Officer Phil 37
Davenport, Wing Commander Jack 360
Davey, Ernest Raymond 371
Davies, Peter 32, 133
Davis, Flight Sergeant F.W.T. 'Chunky' 185
Dawans, General Von 275
Day, Miss Cecille 127
Deere, Alan 65-67, 73, 81-82
Dickins, Dr Basil 207
Doenitz, Admiral 283, 288, 294, 300, 302, 314, 320, 410
Doolittle, General James H. 98
Doubleday, Arthur 215, 220, 228-229
Douglas, Air Marshal Sir William Sholto 68, 87, 92, 95-97, 107, 144, 161, 168, 170, 172, 177, 182, 266, 269, 356
Douhet, Giulio 197
Dowding, Air Chief Marshal Sir William Sholto 42-44, 47, 50-51, 56, 79, 82-84, 86, 107-108, 177
Dowling, Flying Officer James 310
Duncan Smith, Wilfred 56, 67, 89-90
Dundas, Hugh 'cocky' 53, 65, 72, 76-77, 79

Edwards, Gron 'Dopey' 323-324, 325-326
Eisenhower, General 125
Embry, Air Vice-Marshal Basil 147-149, 266, 268-271, 274
Esmonde, Lieutenant Commander 398-400
Evatt, Dr Herbert 'Doc' 189, 190

Fauquier, Wing Commander Johnny 264-265
Fisher, Lord 373
Ford, Vice-Admiral Wilbraham 147

481

Foxley-Norris, Christopher 85
Freyberg, Major General 141
Fuller, air gunner 310, 312-314

Gandhi, Mahatma 24
Gibbs, Flight Lieutenant Pat 337
Gibson, Wing Commander Guy 235, 259
Gillanders, Flight Lieutenant Ronald 254
Gillman, Ron 327-331, 333, 343, 345-346
Goebbels, Joseph 271
Goering, Reichsmarschall Hermann 56, 70, 80, 231, 271
Goode, air gunner 310, 312-314
Gort, Lord 84
Grant, Squadron Leader 149, 151
Gresswell, Squadron Leader Jeff 297
Gribble, George 67
Grosvenor, Lord 17

Halahan, Squadron Leader Bull 58
Hamblin, Bill 359
Harris, Air Chief Marshal Sir Arthur 97, 129, 206-210,
    214, 231, 248, 253, 257-258, 261, 265, 315, 323, 332
Havilland, Major Geoffrey de 271
Hearn-Phillips, Norman 337
Henderson, Corporal Elspeth 82
Henderson, Sergeant R.B. 185-186
Hill, Air Marshal 125-125
Hill, Flying Officer Jack 81
Hitler, Adolf 19, 86, 102, 128, 142-143, 240, 253, 271, 317
Hoare, John 373, 379-380, 390-391
Hopgood, Flight Lieutenant 'Hoppy' 259-260
Horden, Bert 31
Howard, Leslie 310
Howell, Squadron Leader 138
Howlett, Benny 329
Hughes, Squadron Leader 149

Ince, Pilot Officer David 36
Inskip, Sir Thomas 41-42, 50, 372

Jackson, Squadron Leader John 175, 178, 194
Jeudwine, Wing Commander J.R. 173
Jinnah, Mohammed Ali 24
Johnson, James 'Johnnie' 63, 68, 70, 72, 74, 98, 100
Jones, Len 101
Jones, Dr Reginald V. 104, 128
Joubert, Air Chief Marshal Sir Philip 282, 316-317, 360
Judd, Lieutenant Commander Donald 384-385, 387, 404

Kammhuber, Josef 229
Kelly, Sergeant 169
Kilbracken, Lord 31-32, 414-415, 422-423
Kinninmont, Sergeant 160, 167
Knights, Robert 261
Kops, Benny 101

Lamb, Charles 381, 383, 388
Lane, air gunner 310, 312, 314
Leggett, Dick 126
Leicester, Anthony 30-31, 334
Leigh, Squadron Leader Humphrey de Verde 296
Leigh-Mallory, Air Vice-Marshal Sir Trafford 47, 79, 83, 87
Lerew, Wing commander John 171-172
Liddell-Hart, Basil 19, 197
Linlithgow, Lord 24

Liversidge, Flight Lieutenant 30-31
Lloyd, Air Vice-Marshal Hugh 131-133, 136, 143-145,
    147-149, 151-153, 194, 342-343, 348, 350
Longmore, Air Marshal Arthur 138
Lutjens, Captain 400
Lutyens, Sir Edwin 22

MacArthur, General 174
Mackenzie, Pilot Officer 'Mac' 72-73, 78, 94-95, 107
Mahoney, Max 356
Malan, Group Captain Adolph 'Sailor 62, 75-76
Maltby, Air Vice-Marshal Paul 164
Mann, Sergeant 184
Mann, Squadron Leader 48
Margerison, Sergeant Russell 227
Mayhill, Ron 218-219, 237-239, 251
Maynard, Air Vice-Marshal 136
McAlister, Bruce 169
McCarthy, Flight Lieutenant Joe 263
Mcintosh, Dave 116
Mercer, Flight Lieutenant 359
Meyer, Hans Joachim 364
Micallef, Joe 136
Miles, Flight Sergeant 310, 312-313
Miller, wireless operator 310, 312-314
Milson, Squadron Leader Colin 362
Mitchell, Billy 197
Moore-Brabazon, John 333
Morgan, Ivor 420
Morris, Pilot Officer Ivan 359
Morrison, Herbert 128
Mortimer, Sergeant Joan 82
Munro, Ron 357
Murphy, Robert 222

Nagumo, Admiral 174, 395, 398
Nash, Fraser 213, 296
Nehru, Jawaharlal 24
Neil, Tom 131, 134
Nesbit, Roy Conyers 335-336, 360, 362
Nimitz, Admiral 417
Nuffield, Lord 51

O'Brien, Pat 172
O'Brien, Terence 173, 340-341
Ortmans, pilot 77-78
Oulton, Wing Commander 307

Pain, Pilot Officer John 135, 137
Park, Air Vice-Marshal Sir Keith 46-47, 82-83, 87, 104,
    153-154
Parker, Pilot Officer Jerry 61, 165-166
Parr, flying instructor 32
Paton, Reverend 103
Paxton, Flight Leader George 180
Pearson, Max 65
Peden, Murray 32, 34-36, 204
Pedley, Squadron Leader 28
Peirse, Air Marshal Sir Richard 97, 206, 372
Pelly-Fry, Squadron Leader James 267-268
Perry, Flight Sergeant Bill 221
Pettet, John 176
Peyton-Ward, Captain D.V. 281-282
Phillips, Fred 396-398
Phillips, Admiral Sir Tom 163-164